1984
The Supreme Court Review

1984
The

"Judges as persons, or courts as institutions, are entitled to
no greater immunity from criticism than other persons
or institutions . . . [J]udges must be kept mindful of their limitations and
of their ultimate public responsibility by a vigorous
stream of criticism expressed with candor however blunt."
–*Felix Frankfurter*

". . . while it is proper that people should find fault when
their judges fail, it is only reasonable that they should recognize the
difficulties. . . . Let them be severely brought to book,
when they go wrong, but by those who will take the trouble
to understand them."
–*Learned Hand*

THE LAW SCHOOL

THE UNIVERSITY OF CHICAGO

Supreme Court Review

EDITED BY

PHILIP B. KURLAND

GERHARD CASPER

AND DENNIS J. HUTCHINSON

THE UNIVERSITY OF CHICAGO PRESS

CHICAGO AND LONDON

INTERNATIONAL STANDARD BOOK NUMBER: 0-226-46437-7

LIBRARY OF CONGRESS CATALOG CARD NUMBER: 60-14353

THE UNIVERSITY OF CHICAGO PRESS, CHICAGO 60637

THE UNIVERSITY OF CHICAGO PRESS, LTD., LONDON

© 1985 BY THE UNIVERSITY OF CHICAGO. ALL RIGHTS RESERVED. PUBLISHED 1985

PRINTED IN THE UNITED STATES OF AMERICA

TO
THE UNIVERSITY OF CHICAGO

*On the occasion
of the 25th volume
in this series.*

CONTENTS

RICHARD H. FALLON, JR.

PAUL C. WEILER

FIREFIGHTERS v. STOTTS: CONFLICTING MODELS OF RACIAL JUSTICE

I. Introduction

In *Memphis Firefighters v. Stotts*,[1] the Supreme Court finally addressed the question whether a judge may impose racial quotas as a remedy for employment discrimination. The issue arose in the especially troublesome context of layoffs and demotions, in which the Court was asked to "allocate the burdens of recession and fiscal austerity"[2] between senior white and junior black employees. The Court might have confined its inquiry to this particularly thorny problem. But the majority elected a broader basis—one that re-

Richard H. Fallon, Jr. is Assistant Professor of Law, and Paul C. Weiler is Professor of Law, Harvard Law School.

AUTHORS' NOTE: We are grateful to Charles Fried, Andrew Kaufman, Martha Minow, and Lloyd Weinreb, who read earlier drafts and offered helpful criticisms and suggestions, and to research assistants Florrie Darwin, Glenn Fine, Judith Starr, and David Webbert.

[1] 104 S.Ct. 2576 (1984).

[2] *Id.* at 2591 (O'Connor, J., concurring). During the recession of the early eighties, the unemployment rate leaped from 6 percent at the beginning of 1980 to 11 percent by the end of 1982, the highest point since the Great Depression of the 1930s, while black unemployment rose from 11 percent to 19 percent. ECONOMIC REPORT OF THE PRESIDENT 259 (1984). As a result, the relative economic position of black workers, which had steadily improved from the mid-sixties to the end of the seventies with the help of Title VII of the 1964 Civil Rights Act, not only flattened out but actually dipped in the early eighties. For example, the ratio of black male median wage and salary income to white, which had risen from 59.4 percent in 1966 to 68.4 percent by 1979, receded to 65.8 percent by 1982. See CURRENT POPULATION REPORTS, SERIES P-60, MONEY INCOME OF HOUSEHOLDS, FAMILIES AND PERSONS IN THE UNITED STATES 166 (1982).

quired a stark choice between two antithetical visions of racial justice.

On one side of *Stotts* was a phalanx of civil rights organizations, defending a group-based approach to current racial issues. Their Model of Group Justice argues that discrimination has had harmful effects on blacks as a group, not merely on the victims of particular discriminatory acts, and that group-based remedies—racial quotas[3] —ought therefore to be upheld. Aspiring to economic equality for blacks and minorities, the Model of Group Justice had gained increasing acceptance as a thesis for executive, legislative, and judicial action during the 1970s. But the approach has always been controversial. The Reagan administration was eager to contest it in *Stotts*, and to return to the philosophy of color blindness that had initially inspired the American civil rights movement.[4] The government argued that only proved victims of discrimination should benefit from judicial remedies, and that individually innocent whites could not be "dispreferred"[5] in order to create group preferences for minorities. A majority of the Court[6] opted for this "individual justice" approach, or at least endorsed its prescribed limitations on judicial remedies.[7] For the civil rights movement, *Stotts* represents perhaps its biggest defeat[8] in litigation under Title VII of the 1964

---

[3] In this area, perhaps no choice of vocabulary is entirely neutral. As the NEW YORK TIMES reported recently, "It sometimes seems almost everybody likes 'affirmative action,' nobody likes 'reverse discrimination,' and hardly anybody likes 'quotas.' " July 24, 1984, A16, col. 3. Because the word "quotas" may have negative connotations, we shall more frequently use other terms. See note 10 *infra*.

[4] The position of the Solicitor General was mirrored in the amicus brief of the AFL-CIO, the bitter opponent of Reagan policies on almost every other front, but here seeking to preserve its seniority rights against judicial erosion. Within the Jewish community, the Anti-Defamation League argued that racial preferences could never be ordered under the Title VII, while the brief of the American Jewish Congress defended color-conscious remedies, though only as a last resort.

[5] See Brest, *The Supreme Court 1975 Term—Foreword, In Defense of the Antidiscrimination Principle*, 90 HARV. L. REV. 1, 36 (1976).

[6] Justice White's majority opinion was joined by Chief Justice Burger and by Justices Powell, Rehnquist, and O'Connor. Justice O'Connor also wrote a separate concurring opinion. Justice Stevens concurred in the judgment, but solely on an interpretation of a consent decree entered by the parties. Unlike the majority, he offered no judgment as to permissible judicial remedies for proven statutory violations. Justice Blackmun wrote a dissent, which was joined by Justices Brennan and Marshall.

[7] Seemingly untouched by *Stotts*, and entirely unmentioned by the majority, was the Court's previous holding in United Steel Workers v. Weber, 443 U.S. 193 (1979), that voluntarily adopted racial quotas are permissible under Title VII.

[8] Solicitor General Rex Lee characterized the decision as a "slam dunk," "perhaps one of the greatest decisions of all time!"

Civil Rights Act.[9] It may also signal a judicial attitude of broader import for the future of "affirmative discrimination."[10]

II. THE STOTTS CASE

A. THE FACTS

Firefighters v. Stotts involved a clash between black firefighters, hired by the City of Memphis under a consent decree,[11] and white workers with seniority rights under their labor agreement. The consent decree established racial hiring and promotion goals within the fire department in a class action alleging race discrimination by the City.[12] *Stotts* arose in the spring of 1981, when fiscal difficulties

---

[9] Pub. L. No. 88-352, 78 Stat. 253–66 (current version at 42 U.S.C. 2000e-15–2000C-17 (1982)).

[10] We take the term from GLAZER, AFFIRMATIVE DISCRIMINATION: ETHNIC INEQUALITY AND PUBLIC POLICY (1975). By "affirmative discrimination" we mean to refer to two forms of racial preferences: (i) judicially mandated "quotas" or "race-conscious remedies" prescribed at the end of a lawsuit as a remedy for past unlawful employment practices; and (ii) "voluntarily" adopted racial preferences, often called programs of "affirmative action," undertaken by employers outside the context of a lawsuit. Two reasons make "affirmative discrimination" our most frequent terminological choice in this article. First, the questions of morality and policy are largely the same in cases of voluntary and of judicially mandated racial preferences. "Affirmative discrimination" conveniently encompasses both. Second, this term may carry fewer connotations, either positive or negative, than its alternatives. Many of the questions surrounding affirmative discrimination are extraordinarily difficult, both legally and morally, and we do not wish our choice of terminology to prejudice the weighing of arguments. We assume "affirmative discrimination," as most of the more contentious terms (such as "quota" and "reverse discrimination"), to imply the following: the implementation of racial preferences, not merely to break ties between equally qualified candidates, but at least sometimes to prescribe the selection of a candidate who otherwise appears less qualified than his or her rivals; the conferral of preferences on minority candidates who have not proven that they personally are the victims of illegal conduct by the employer or agency extending the preference; and the use of numerical targets or goals to determine the number of minority candidates to be hired based on the racial preferences.

[11] There were two proceedings resulting in two consent decrees affecting the Memphis Fire Department. The first lawsuit, brought by the Federal government challenging the City's overall employment practices, ended with a 1974 consent decree (with no admission of liability) which, inter alia, established the long-term goal of a racially proportionate work force in the fire department, to be pursued through an interim target of 50 percent new black hirees. The second suit was a class action by the respondent Carl Stotts (later consolidated with an individual suit by Jones) attacking the hiring and promotion practices in the fire department alone. This was settled by a 1980 consent decree, which reiterated the long-term employment goal and the 50 percent annual hiring target and added a 20 percent promotion target. It also contained a directive that eighteen named blacks be given immediate promotions.

[12] Although there had never been any judicial finding of illegal discrimination or any such admission by the City, the district judge was prepared to take judicial notice of discriminatory employment practices within the fire department. The supporting evidence contained in the record strongly indicated purposeful discrimination prior to passage of the 1964 Civil

moved the City to commence a program of layoffs.[13] The City's established personnel policy, detailed in a memorandum of understanding with the firefighters' union, prescribed that lay-offs would occur on a last-hired, first-fired schedule.[14] But when the City proposed to proceed on this basis, the burden threatened to fall primarily on blacks hired under the consent decree.[15] The class represented by Stotts sought an injunction against their discharges. Relying on the consent decree, the district judge forbade the City to apply its seniority policy in a way that would reduce the proportional representation of blacks in the fire department.[16] The City understood this ruling to authorize the dismissal of senior white firefighters, and the fire department acted accordingly in executing its layoffs.

Stotts exhibited many characteristic features of class litigation involving patterns and practices of employment discrimination: the historic exclusion and continuing underrepresentation of blacks

---

Rights Act. (In the period 1950–63, the department hired no blacks in any year except 1955.) Following the enactment of federal antidiscrimination legislation, the City's performance improved somewhat. (From 1964 to 1971, 7 percent of new firefighters were black.) Once the Act was made applicable to public employers such as Memphis, the recruitment of black firefighters jumped sharply. (From March 1972 through November 1974, roughly 10 percent of new firefighters were black in a region where one-third the labor market was black.)

[13] Initially the City projected that it would need to lay off about forty out of approximately 1,500 fire department personnel.

[14] The memorandum was probably not an enforceable contract under Tennessee law. See Fulenwider v. Firefighters Ass'n Local Union 1784, 649 S.W.2d 268 (Tenn. 1982). Regardless of the enforceability of the memorandum, however, the City had adopted and maintained a seniority system reflecting its terms.

[15] Application of a "last-hired, first-fired" policy would have produced a layoff of twenty-five white privates (out of 497) and fifteen blacks (out of eighty-five), all the latter to be drawn from the eighteen new hirees under the 1980 decree, as well as the demotion of fourteen of the eighteen named blacks who had been promoted under that decree. This would have reduced black employment in the fire department from an 11 percent to a 10 percent share.

[16] The district court actually entered three orders: (i) a temporary restraining order on May 4, 1981, barring any layoffs or demotions of blacks at all; (ii) an interim injunction on May 18, 1981, which prohibited the layoff or demotion of blacks if, and to the extent that, this would reduce their existing share of employment in the fire department and its various job classifications; and (iii) an order on June 25, 1981, which apparently approved the City's plan to lay off senior whites to the extent necessary to maintain black representation within the department. There was a sharp disagreement between the parties and within the Supreme Court about the precise import of these judicial directives. Justice White's majority opinion characterized the orders as issuing "an injunction requiring white employees to be laid off, when the otherwise applicable seniority system would have called for the layoff of black employees with less seniority." 104 S.Ct. at 2585 (footnotes omitted). Justice Blackmun interpreted the injunction as doing no more than preventing "the city from conducting layoffs in accordance with its seniority systems insofar as it will decrease the percentage of black," but not requiring "the city to lay off any white employees at all." Id. at 2602.

within the fire department; the institution of multiple suits and the entry of consent decrees, establishing racially defined hiring goals; significant improvements in black employment, though far less than proportionate representation; and, in the context of fiscally mandated layoffs, a collision between the aspirations of the consent decree and the seniority interests of incumbent whites. In other respects, however, *Stotts* was a rather unprepossessing candidate for a momentous legal engagement. Because of changes in the City's layoff schedule, only three additional whites were laid off by the fire department, and these three were recalled less than a month later.[17] Moreover, it was a curiosity of *Stotts* that all six of the firefighters actually affected by the judicial order—the three "senior" whites who were laid off and the three "junior" blacks who were retained—were all hired on the same day, less than two years earlier. The reason the blacks ranked below the whites on the seniority list was that the first letter in their last names came later in the alphabet, and the Memphis seniority system used alphabetical priority as its tie-breaking criterion.[18]

B. A PRELIMINARY ISSUE: MOOTNESS

The peculiar features of *Stotts* furnished plausible arguments that the case was moot.[19] Because the laid-off firefighters had long since

---

[17] They each lost roughly $1,200.00 in back pay, less unemployment insurance benefits. By the spring of 1983, the City's financial position had improved sufficiently that sixty-three new firefighters had been recruited, thus effectively insulating all the white firefighters affected by the 1981 injunction from any future layoffs that might be contemplated.

[18] If the Court had wanted to address the seniority layoffs issue in a situation that did exhibit its true human implications, there was no shortage of candidates. The City of Boston, for example, was confronted in the early eighties with much more serious fiscal problems than Memphis's, resulting in the layoff of 1,300 Boston schoolteachers. A federal judicial order analogous to that in *Stotts* forbade any reduction in the minority share of school employment, with the result that tenured white teachers with up to fifteen years of service were laid off, while the school board continued to hire new black teachers. See Morgan v. O'Bryant, 671 F.2d 23 (1st Cir. 1982). Three years later, there are still over 400 white teachers laid off in Boston, for all intents and purposes having lost their jobs in the cause of racial integration. Yet not once but twice the Supreme Court has refused to accept the Boston Teachers case for review. (We are indebted to Steven Kautner, who is studying the post-layoff experience of the Boston schoolteachers, for providing us with information about the scope and aftermath of the layoff.)

[19] When the Court granted certiorari in June 1983, it already had been apprised by the parties of the facts supporting an argument of mootness. Curiously, in the light of the serious mootness issue, the Court granted certiorari in *Stotts* on the same day that it cited a mootness question in declining to decide an already argued case presenting essentially the same legal issue. In Boston Firefighters v. Boston Chapter, NAACP 103 S.Ct. 2076 (1983), several hundred white firefighters and police officers had been laid off, while junior blacks were

been recalled to work, the controversy had abated.[20] Furthermore, as Justice Blackmun argued in dissent, the judgment under review was only a temporary restraining order, addressed to the layoffs scheduled for June, 1981. It was by no means certain that the order would apply to future layoffs.[21] But the Court dismissed these objections. The majority found that the district court's orders had either effected or reflected a judicial modification in the underlying consent decree that would restrain the City from laying off junior blacks on future occasions.[22] The Court also concluded that white employees, adversely affected by the layoffs, might have rightful claims against the city for lost seniority and back pay, and that the City could be constrained from satisfying these claims so long as the injunction remained unmodified.

Although its analysis was by no means free of difficulty,[23] the majority did not stray indefensibly beyond the bounds of mootness doctrine in finding *Stotts* fit for decision. The contours of justiciabil-

---

retained in order to preserve the level of black employment that had been achieved under an earlier hiring decree. The layoffs were ended unexpectedly by state legislation that provided the City of Boston with additional funds, on condition that the City recall all the laid-off police and firefighters and undertake not to lay them off in the future. Though all these facts were apparent in the record when the Boston case was accepted for review, the Court, after oral argument, decided to return the matter to the First Circuit for a judgment whether the case was moot. Following its mootness decision in *Stotts*, the Supreme Court vacated the Court of Appeals's ruling that the Boston case was moot and remanded the case for further consideration in the light of *Stotts*. 104 S.Ct. 3576 (1984).

[20] 104 S.Ct. at 2596–2600 (Blackmun, J., dissenting).

[21] It was very clear indeed that the order could have no effect on future layoffs if the Supreme Court simply vacated it—the usual practice with temporary injunctions governing specific disputes already concluded. United States v. Munsingwear, Inc., 340 U.S. 36, 39 (1950).

[22] 104 S.Ct. at 2583.

[23] *Id.* at 2584. With respect to back pay, at least, there are two difficulties with the Court's argument. First, the Court assumed that the temporary injunction might have an effect on future negotiations or litigation between the City and the "senior" whites who had been laid off. But the City and the senior whites were aligned on the same side of the suit in the Supreme Court. A hypothetical future controversy between these *Stotts* allies seems a strange basis on which to find that a live dispute existed between either or both of those two parties and a class of black firefighters, the adverse parties in *Stotts*, who presumably would have no role in any future back pay litigation between the union and the City. See *id.* at 2597–2600 (Blackmun, J., dissenting). Second, under principles articulated by the Court in the previous Term, the temporary injunction need not have prevented recovery by the disadvantaged white firefighters. See W. R. Grace & Co. v. Local Union 759, 103 S.Ct. 2177 (1983); see also Note, 97 HARV. L. REV. 70, 269–78 (1983).

ity contain a widely recognized,[24] if often lamented, flexibility,[25] and there was some precedential support for the Court's conclusion that the case remained live for decision.[26] In this context, two facts seem worthy of comment. First, eager to reach the merits, the usual apostles of judicial restraint held the case justiciable, while more "liberal" Justices protested that the case was unfit for the exercise of judicial power.[27] Second, this Term's resolution followed a pattern exhibited before in cases presenting hard issues of racial justice: a dubious decision not to decide one case[28] was followed by an equally doubtful conclusion that a later case, presenting the same but now more "percolated" issue, was fit for judicial resolution.[29] The sequence does not seem coincidental. According to one celebrated argument, justiciability doctrines perform an important

---

[24] See, e.g., Varat, *Variable Justiciability and The Duke Power Case*, 58 TEX. L. REV. 273, 278–79, 319–27 (1980).

[25] The Court itself has occasionally recognized that there is an element of "flexibility" in mootness doctrine, see, e.g., United States Parole Comm'n v. Geraghty, 445 U.S. 388, 400 (1980); Franks v. Bowman Transp. Co., 424 U.S. 747, 752–57 & n.8 (1976). Mootness issues generally arise only in cases in which an issue is framed by facts adequate to inform and delimit a judicial decision. Moreover, in *Stotts* the submissions of the parties and the amici afforded the Court all the benefits of adverse argument as a device to clarify legal issues. When these functional requisites of justiciability are satisfied, it is not improper for the Court to be guided in part by policy considerations as to the desirability of resolving a particular dispute. See Fallon, *Of Justiciability, Remedies and Public Law Litigation: Notes on the Jurisprudence of Lyons*, 59 N.Y.U. L. REV. 1 (1984).

[26] See Super Tire Engineering Co. v. McCorkle 122–25 (1974). Other cases, however, pointed as strongly to an opposite conclusion. See, e.g., University of Texas v. Caminisch, 451 U.S. 390 (1981).

[27] Illustrative of the reversal of characteristic positions is a comparison of *Stotts* with two recent and important standing decisions, City of Los Angeles v. Lyons, 103 S.Ct. 1660 (1983), and Valley Forge Christian College v. Americans United for Separation of Church and State, Inc., 454 U.S. 464 (1982). Holding both the earlier cases nonjusticiable were five-member majorities consisting of Chief Justice Burger and Justices White, Powell, Rehnquist, and O'Connor. In *Stotts*, these same five joined in Justice White's opinion holding *Stotts* not moot and thus fit for judicial decision. By contrast, the three Justices who argued that *Stotts* should be dismissed as moot (Brennan, Marshall, and Blackmun) all would have applied loose tests and upheld justiciability in *Lyons* and *Valley Forge*. Only Justice Stevens prevented the *Stotts* line-up from being an exact reversal of those in *Lyons* and *Valley Forge*: he found all three cases to satisfy the justiciability requirements of Article III.

[28] See note 19 *supra*.

[29] Compare DeFunis v. Odegaard, 416 U.S. 312 (1974), which the Court held moot, with Regents of the Univ. of California v. Bakke, 438 U.S. 265 (1978), in which the Court chose to overlook a difficult standing problem. For a general discussion of the Court's use of "avoidance" techniques in a substantive domain fraught with "ambivalence," see Mishkin, *The Uses of Ambivalence: Reflections on the Supreme Court and the Constitutionality of Affirmative Action*, 131 U. PA. L. REV. 907 (1983).

function in allowing the Supreme Court to pick its time and its case for decision.[30]

C. A SUBSIDIARY ISSUE: CONSENT DECREES

In forbidding the City to engage in seniority-based layoffs, the district judge acted pursuant to a consent decree. As commonly occurs in Title VII litigation, the decree contained no admission of illegal discrimination, and it established guidelines only for the City's hiring and promotion practices, without reference to layoffs. But the decree did authorize the district judge to issue any "further orders . . . necessary or appropriate to effectuate the purposes of this decree."[31] In addition, federal courts ordinarily retain their traditional equitable power to modify consent decrees in adaptation to changed conditions.[32] But the *Stotts* majority denied that the district court's preliminary injunction could be justified on either basis. First, the majority found that the parties had not intended to authorize judicial modification of the City's seniority system.[33] As to the scope of the district court's equitable powers, a question of more general importance was presented, and Justice Stevens's concurring opinion would have put the decision solely on this ground: he would have enforced a strict standard for the identification of "changed circumstances" needed to authorize judicial modification of a consent decree.[34] But the Court did not treat this as an independent question. Linking the district court's equitable powers with the statutory basis for the plaintiffs' cause of action, the majority held that neither a consent decree nor a judicial modification could provide relief that would not have been available had plaintiffs

---

[30] See BICKEL, THE LEAST DANGEROUS BRANCH 205 (1962); cf. Mishkin, note 29 *supra;* but see Gunther, *The Subtle Vices of the "Passive Virtues"—a Comment on Principle and Expediency in Judicial Review,* 64 COLUM. L. REV. 1 (1964).

[31] 104 S.Ct. at 2581 (quoting Stotts v. Memphis Fire Dept., 679 F.2d at 578 (app.).

[32] The Court took the approach that "the 'scope of a consent decree must be discerned within its four corners.' " 104 S.Ct. at 2586 (quoting United States v. Armour & Co., 402 U.S. 673, 681–82 (1971)). It is unclear whether the Court, in citing this familiar maxim, meant to disapprove of the view that the four-corners rule generally should be applied less restrictively in civil rights class actions than in other types of litigation. See Massachusetts Association for Retarded Citizens v. King, 668 F.2d 602, 607–08 (1st Cir. 1981) (noting that consent decrees in public law litigation may require "more flexible interpretation").

[33] 104 S.Ct. at 2586.

[34] See 104 S.Ct. at 2594–95 (Stevens, J., concurring in the judgment).

prevailed at trial.[35] And, the Supreme Court found, the plaintiffs' legal theory, even if proved, would not have justified a judicially mandated interference with bona fide seniority rights.[36]

D. THE LAW OF JUDICIAL REMEDIES

Assuming that relief under a consent decree may not exceed what could be imposed as a judicial remedy for proved discrimination, the Supreme Court easily fit *Stotts* into its existing Title VII jurisprudence. In *Teamsters v. United States*,[37] the Court had held that competitive seniority—seniority giving one employee actual or potential preferences over others—could be awarded only to the individual victims of past discrimination. Relying on § 703(h) of Title VII,[38] which confers express protection on bona fide seniority systems, *Teamsters* found that "mere membership in the disadvantaged class is insufficient to warrant a seniority award."[39] *Stotts* extended the logic of *Teamsters* to consent decrees. By overriding the seniority rights of white employees, the district court had effectively given "competitive seniority" benefits to "junior" blacks. And because the black beneficiaries were not proved victims of past discrimination,[40] the Court found that the district court's *Stotts* decision conflicted with *Teamsters*.[41] This decision will make more

---

[35] Justice Stevens characterized the Court's discussion of Title VII as "wholly advisory." *Id.* at 2594.

[36] 104 S.Ct. at 2587–88.

[37] 431 U.S. 324 (1977).

[38] 42 U.S.C. 200e–2h: "Notwithstanding any other provision of this subchapter, it shall not be an unlawful employment practice for an employer to apply different standards of compensation, or different terms, conditions, or privileges of employment pursuant to a bona fide seniority or merits system . . . provided that such differences are not the result of an intention to discriminate because of race, color, religion, sex, or national origin . . ."

[39] 104 S.Ct. at 2588.

[40] In entering the consent decree, the City had acknowledged no wrongdoing whatsoever.

[41] Even in connection with the seniority issue, while *Teamsters* held that 703(h) precludes any individual right to an award of full constructive seniority for blacks who cannot show that they were the actual victims of their employer's discrimination, Justice Blackmun correctly noted that that case did not address the rather different question of whether it might be appropriate and equitable for a court temporarily to override seniority rights in certain layoff situations in pursuit of the objective of eliminating discrimination against blacks as a group. 104 S.Ct. at 2608 (Blackmun, J., dissenting). Moreover, *Stotts*, unlike *Teamsters*, directly implicated the Title VII policy favoring settlement of disputed issues. See, *e.g.*, Ford Motor Co. v. EEOC, 458 U.S. 219 (1982); Carson v. American Brands, Inc., 450 U.S. 79, 88 n.14 (1981).

difficult the settlement of Title VII seniority issues without resort to trial.

The *Teamsters* rationale was adequate to dispose of the case. The majority apparently decided, however, that it might as well resolve as much legal debate as possible. Consistent with the views urged by the litigants,[42] the Court found a link between the remedial policies governing seniority awards and those applicable to hiring and promotion remedies. It was, said the Court, a general "policy of Title VII" to provide "make-whole relief only to those who have been actual victims of illegal discrimination."[43] The Court thus introduced a broad proposition, unnecessary to resolution of the seniority dispute, that the positive benefit of Title VII remedies could not be afforded to blacks who had not been proved to be personal victims of the employer's discrimination.

Here the majority plainly slid into dictum. But dictum from the Supreme Court is not just so many words, even if it is something less than the law. Among its other effects, the *Stotts* majority's discussion throws into doubt the validity of a large body of law, currently applicable throughout the United States, holding that hiring quotas may be an appropriate remedy for proved violations of Title VII.[44]

III. The Contending Models

The *Stotts* majority adopted the resolutely individualistic approach of what we call the Model of Individual Justice. Writing for three dissenting Justices, Justice Blackmun presented a highly sympathetic statement of the contending group justice position. As we turn to a deeper examination of these alternative views, we concern ourselves less with the legislative history of Title VII than with broader concerns of morality and public policy in civil rights law. We do so for a variety of reasons. First, the surrounding moral

---

[42] Each of the briefs submitted to the Court in *Stotts*, as in *Boston Firefighters* the year before, took the position either that it favored race-conscious remedies, in which case it was ready to override seniority rights so that this kind of remedy could operate in layoffs, or it insisted on the integrity of the seniority rights, in which case it disapproved of racial preferences in any context.

[43] 104 S.Ct. at 2588–89.

[44] The courts of appeals are unanimous on this point. For a collection of cases, see *id.* at 2606 n.10 (Blackmun, J., dissenting).

debate, bifurcated into individual and group approaches, consistently colors judicial readings of Title VII and its legislative history, and also of the Equal Protection Clause of the Fourteenth Amendment. In this area, moral and policy arguments could not be unrelated to jurisprudence. Second, the implications of the moral and policy debate are not confined to judicial orders. Crucially important are the "voluntary" affirmative action programs of private employers, which were upheld as legal by the Supreme Court's 1980 decision in *United Steel Workers v. Weber*,[45] and the incentive to undertake such programs that is provided by Executive Order 11246,[46] which covers a substantial proportion of the national work force.[47] Subject to executive revision, the current Ex-

---

[45] 443 U.S. 193 (1979).

[46] Exec. Order No. 11246, 3 C.F.R. 339 (1964-64 comp.), reprinted in 42 U.S.C. 2000e (1982). Issued by President Johnson in 1965 and still in force as amended, Executive Order 11246 built on an unbroken tradition dating back to 1941 of executive orders imposing nondiscrimination obligations on federal contractors. See generally Contractors Ass'n v. Secretary of Labor, 442 F.2d 159, 168–71 (3rd Cir. 1971) (reviewing progenitors of Order 11246). The current Order applies to all nonexempt federal contracts, subcontracts of federal contracts, and federally assisted construction contracts, Exec. Order No. 11246, supra at § 202(7), 301. The major regulatory exemption from the Order is for contracts and subcontracts not exceeding $10,000. 41 C.F.R. § 60-1.5(a)(1) (1983). The key substantive element of the Executive Order is the requirement that contractors take "affirmative action" to ensure the nondiscriminatory treatment of job applicants and employees. Exec. Order No. 11246, supra at § 202(1). The Regulations specify that nonconstruction contractors with fifty or more employees and a contract of $50,000 or more must develop a "result-oriented" written affirmative action compliance program. 41 C.F.R. § 60-2,1, 2.10. This program includes a sophisticated "utilization analysis" designed to determine whether there are fewer minorities in any job group than would reasonably be expected by their availability. *Id.* § 60-2.11. If "underutilization" is discovered in any job group, the employer must establish and in good faith seek to fulfill goals and timetables "to achieve prompt and full utilization of minorities at all levels and segments of the workplace." *Id.* § 60-2.1, 2.10, 2.12, 2.15. Construction contractors are required to make a good faith effort to meet the goals and timetables for minority employment set for the local region by the governing administrative agency, the Labor Department Office of Federal Contract Compliance Programs. *Id.* § 60-4.6. The present nationwide goal is for immediate minority utilization equal to the percentage of minorities in the local labor force. 45 Fed. Reg. 65979, 65903 (1980). The affirmative action obligations for nonconstruction and construction contractors apply without regard to whether the contractor has discriminated in the past. The Executive Order also provides for a wide range of penalties for noncompliance, including cancellation of the contract and ineligibility for all future federal contracts. Exec. Order No. 11246, *supra*, § 202(2), 209.

[47] As many as two-thirds of the jobs in the national labor market may be in firms affected by the Executive Order. See LEONARD, THE IMPACT OF AFFIRMATIVE ACTION 133 (1983); *cf.* Rousea, *Enforcing a Clear Mandate*, 7 J. INTERGROUP REL. 4 (1979) (one-third). Smith & Welch, *Affirmative Action and Labor Markets*, 2 J. LABOR ECON. 269, 280–83 (1984), report statistics showing that from 1970 to 1980, all the improvement in black employment in private sector firms subject to EEOC reporting requirements under Title VII actually took place in federal contractors subject to Executive Order 11246. LEONARD, *supra*, has demonstrated the causal effect of the incentives generated under the Executive Order. From 1974

ecutive Order establishes a highly controversial set of affirmative action requirements. There are politically powerful forces, capable of forcing the issue into the national political agenda, that would have this powerful vehicle for color-conscious distribution of jobs meet the same fate as did the judicial order in *Stotts*. Third, while *Stotts* dealt with and was constrained by Title VII, there are other statutes that prohibit discrimination by both public and private employers.[48] These statutory provisions forbid only intentional discrimination,[49] a legal condition not established in *Stotts*. But when the issue of remedies for intentional discrimination does arise, the Court will not be able to rely on the special language and legislative history of Title VII. It will need to formulate a judicial definition of the appropriate scope of remedial policy.[50]

A. THE MODEL OF INDIVIDUAL JUSTICE

At the center of the Model of Individual Justice[51] is the antidiscrimination principle—"the general principle disfavoring classifica-

---

through 1980, the fact of being subject to federal contract compliance (rather than Title VII alone) increased the initial black share of employment with contractors by 17% for males and 15% for females. *Id.* at 120. In view of the federal contractors' share of the overall labor market, this implies that the Executive Order increased the total demand for black male workers by 12% and for female blacks by 10%. *Id.* at 120. The broad dicta of *Stotts* conceivably could have legal implications for Executive Order 11246. If Title VII expresses a congressional decision to limit racial remedies to the proved individual victims of employment discrimination, the Executive Order's affirmative action requirements could be vulnerable to judicial invalidation as incompatible with the statute. See *Weber*, 443 U.S. at 209 n.9 (leaving open whether affirmative action efforts to comply with Executive Order 11246 could be incompatible with Title VII).

[48] See 42 U.S.C. 1981 and 42 U.S.C. 1983.

[49] See Washington v. Davis, 426 U.S. 229 (1976); General Building Contractors Assn. v. Pennsylvania, 457 U.S. 375 (1982).

[50] A case presenting this issue, NAACP Detroit Branch v. Detroit Police Officers Ass'n, 35 Fair Empl. Prac. Cas. (BNA) 631 (D. Mich. 1984), has arisen from a factual situation similar to that in Memphis. The Detroit police force recruited large numbers of black police officers in the 1970s to remedy earlier discrimination in hiring. But the City's fiscal problems required major layoffs in 1979 and 1980, and the application of a seniority provision in the City's collective agreement meant that the burden fell disproportionately on black officers. In this context, the district court held that layoffs in order of seniority amounted to intentional discrimination, forbidden under both the Fourteenth Amendment and § 1983. It ordered the recall of all the black police officers who wished to return. *Id.* at 641. Interestingly, the district court also ordered the City not to lay off any senior white police officers pending a further inquiry into the nature and force of their contractual rights.

[51] Judicial opinions reflecting the principles of the Model of Individual Justice, and exhibiting elements that we have used to define it, include Arizona Governing Comm. v. Norris, 103 S.Ct. 3492, 3498 (1983) (opinion of Marshall, J.); Connecticut v. Teal, 457 U.S. 440, 453–54 (1982); Fullilove v. Klutznick, 448 U.S. 448, 522–27 (1980) (Stewart, J., dissenting);

tions and other decisions and practices that depend on the race (or ethnic origin) of the parties affected."[52] Because racial classifications have been used historically to deny the moral worth of human beings, and because race is almost never relevant to any morally permissible purpose, this model holds that race-based decision making ought to be prohibited.[53] But the Model of Individual Justice does not represent simply an ad hoc rejection of racial bias. On the contrary, within this model the antidiscrimination principle derives strength from its location in a cluster of conventional moral values. However vague, these values all reflect a view of individual human beings, each entitled to respect and concern, as the fundamental elements of the moral and legal universe.[54] Within this value scheme, the ideal of human equality represents an important article of moral faith.[55] But equally important are values—reflecting respect for individual autonomy, merit, and achievement—that may foster distributive inequalities.[56] Although welfare statutes may establish the minimal requirements of social justice, above that floor the Model of Individual Justice recognizes the right of individual human beings to reap the benefits of their own hard work and personal talents.

Regents of the Univ. of California v. Bakke, 438 U.S. 265, 289–90, 293, 299, 307, 318 (1979) (opinion of Powell, J., announcing the judgment of the Court); Franks v. Bowman Transp. Co., 424 U.S. 747, 780–81 (1976) (Burger, C.J., concurring in part and dissenting in part); DeFunis v. Odegaard, 416 U.S. 312, 343 (1974) (Douglas, J., dissenting). Among the commentators, see notes 53–65 *infra* and accompanying text.

[52] Brest, note 5 *supra*, at 1.

[53] In Alexander Bickel's frequently quoted words, the Model of Individual Justice affirms that the "lesson of the great decisions of the Supreme Court and the lesson of contemporary history have been the same for at least a generation: discrimination on the basis of race is illegal, immoral, unconstitutional, inherently wrong, and destructive of democratic society." BICKEL, THE MORALITY OF CONSENT 133 (1975).

[54] See, *e.g.*, Regents of the Univ. of California v. Bakke, 438 U.S. 265 (opinion of Powell, J., announcing the judgment of this Court); Reynolds, *Individualism v. Group Rights: The Legacy of Brown*, 93 YALE L.J. 995, 1003 (1984).

[55] See H.R. Rep. No. 914, 88th Cong., 1st Sess. (1963), at 30, reprinted in EEOC, Legislative History of Titles VII and XI of Civil Rights Acts of 1964, at 2151: "Aside from the political and economic considerations, however, we believe in the creation of job equality because it is the right thing to do. We believe in the dignity of man. He is born with certain inalienable rights. His uniqueness is such that we refuse to treat him as if his rights and well-being are bargainable. All vestiges of inequality based solely on race must be removed in order to preserve our democratic society, to maintain our country's leadership and enhance mankind."

[56] See Reynolds, note 54 *supra*, at 1004; Meltzer, *The Weber Case: The Judicial Abrogation of the Antidiscrimination Standard in Employment*, 47 U. CHI. L. REV. 423, 424 (1980); see generally Fallon, *To Each according to His Ability, From None according to His Race: The Concept of Merit in the Law of Antidiscrimination*, 60 B.U. L. REV. 815, 840–43 (1980).

Beyond prohibition of race-based decision making, the Model of Individual Justice assumes that the allocation of people to jobs should be left to the relatively free functioning of the labor market. At least three values—which themselves may stand in an interesting state of tension—commend this approach. First, the market provides an arena for individual liberty in economic action. Liberty is a good in itself. Second, a market based on free exchange serves the economic aim of allocating persons to the jobs in which they will be most productive. There is accordingly a social welfare justification. Third, on the whole the market rewards merit, effort, and productivity. These virtues deserve cultivation, partly as intrinsically valuable, partly as instrumentally useful to the national community.

The Model of Individual Justice recognizes no exception to the antidiscrimination principle for the "benign" quotas of affirmative discrimination. Where a wrong is done, the Model of Individual Justice prescribes that the wrongdoer must correct it. But the model views the aim of legal remedies as the compensation of victims, not the achievement of any particular pattern of distribution across racial classes. For government to prescribe race as a basis for employment decisions would be thoroughly wrong. Racial quotas would interfere unduly with the liberty of the employer to select the best available employee and would undermine the moral and economic values supporting rewards to individual merit.[57] Moreover, racial quotas predictably would visit the burdens of "reverse discrimination" on innocent whites—an independent moral wrong not justifiable for reasons of policy or convenience.[58]

Reflecting in general the views of the early champions of the American civil rights movement,[59] the Model of Individual Justice finds recurrent expression in both the language and the legislative history of Title VII.[60] First, the protections of Title VII are framed

---

[57] See BICKEL, note 53 *supra*, at 133–34.

[58] See Franks v. Bowman Transp. Co., 424 U.S. 747, 780–81 (1976) (Burger, C.J., concurring in part and dissenting in part); Brest, note 5 *supra*, at 39–43.

[59] See, *e.g.*, Reynolds, note 54 *supra*, at 999–1001 (quoting, among others, Jack Greenberg, Hubert Humphrey, Martin Luther King, Jr., and Roy Wilkins). In *Stotts*, the majority relied on quotations from legislative proponents of Title VII, including Senators Humphrey, Clark, and Case. See 104 S.Ct. at 2589–90.

[60] See, *e.g.*, *Developments in the Law—Employment Discrimination and Title VII of the Civil Rights Act of 1964*, 84 HARV. L. REV. 1109, 1166 (1971).

directly and specifically to safeguard the "individual."[61] Though animated by concern for "the plight of the Negro in our economy,"[62] the statute establishes a general right, benefiting non-minority as well as minority, to be free from discrimination on the basis of race, sex, or national origin.[63] Second, beyond the antidiscrimination strictures, Congress seemingly meant Title VII to effect no fundamental change in the operation of the employment market. Title VII gives expression to the traditional value of equality of opportunity, defined formally to bar the exclusion of talented persons based solely on race. With this exception, the market was intended to continue as the principal determinant of employment opportunities and the resulting distributive outcomes.[64] Third, by purifying the market by preventing hiring based on characteristics presumptively unrelated to efficiency, Title VII conforms with the Model of Individual Justice in favoring rewards for merit.[65] Finally, Title VII gives express protection to the benefits that individual work and achievement have attained, again consistently with individual justice. Even where the effect is to perpetuate the effects of past discrimination, § 703(h) ensures the sanctity of seniority systems and thus protects the expectations of incumbent employees, presumably innocent of their employers' discriminatory acts.

---

[61] See, *e.g.*, Arizona Governing Comm. v. Norris, 103 S.Ct. 3492 (1983).

[62] In United Steelworkers v. Weber, 443 U.S. 193, 202 (1979) (quoting 110 Cong. Rec. 6548 (1964) (remarks of Sen. Humphrey)), the Supreme Court termed this "Congress' primary concern in enacting the prohibition against racial discrimination in Title VII of the Civil Rights Act of 1964."

[63] See McDonald v. Santa Fe Trail Transp. Co., 427 U.S. 273, 280 (1976) (holding that Title VII forbids discriminatory treatment of whites). When opponents of the statute protested that it would establish a requirement of quota hiring, supporters of Title VII not only gave repeated assurances that it would not, but also drafted and introduced the amendment that became Section 706(j), 42 U.S.C. 2000e-2j, which provides that "[n]othing contained in (Title VII) shall be interpreted to require any employer . . . to grant preferential treatment to any individual or to any group" because of racial imbalances in the employer's work force.

[64] Title VII imposes no general obligation of fairness in hiring and firing, and the use of aptitude tests as employment criteria was specifically approved. See Chamallas, *Evolving Conceptions of Equality under Title VII: Disparate Impact Theory and the Demise of the Bottom Line Principle*, 31 UCLA L. REV. 305, 379 (1983).

[65] The principal proponents of Title VII argued that a ban on racial hiring would prod employers to make employment decision on the basis of talents, not prejudice or stereotypes, and thus to achieve the economic benefits of a more efficient work force. See Chamallas, note 64 *supra*, at 306. In a particular context it of course is possible that merit traits will correlate sufficiently well with race that a rational, wealth-maximizing employer would find it economically efficient to engage in racial hiring. See Jencks, *Discrimination and Thomas Sowell*, 30 NEW YORK REV. BOOKS, 33, 37–38 (March 3, 1983). Title VII reflects a judgment that racial hiring should not be permitted even in such cases.

Conceived as a framework for interpreting Title VII, the Model of Individual Justice dominated the early jurisprudence under the statute.[66] Where employers made race a basis for employment decisions, as had been the norm in much of the economy, Title VII struck quickly and powerfully at this illegally "disparate treatment." Nor has time shown the Model of Individual Justice to be obsolescent. Today, more than twenty years after the enactment of Title VII, the Model of Individual Justice continues to protect an ideal of individualized treatment that prohibits employers from acting on race- or gender-based animus, or even on true generalizations about classes defined by race or gender.[67]

It was within the Model of Individual Justice that the Supreme Court decided *Stotts*. The district court had forbidden the disproportionate layoff of blacks, and the Supreme Court construed its injunction as either mandating or at least authorizing the dismissal of more senior whites.[68] So interpreted, the order posed a threat to the seniority interests of "innocent" incumbents—a threat offensive to the Model of Individual Justice and, the Court held, to Title VII's § 703(h). Even more expressive of the Model of Individual Justice, however, was the *Stotts* Court's broader pronouncement that the policy of the Title VII was "to provide make-whole relief only to those who have been actual victims of illegal discrimination."[69] On this view of Title VII, only the individually identified victims of discrimination should be entitled to the benefits of a judicial remedy; and no individual white, innocent of personal wrongdoing, should be dispreferred as an incident of race-conscious relief.

The Model of Individual Justice supplies a context in which this view is rooted in morality and economics as well as sources of

---

[66] But *cf.* Blumrosen, *Strangers in Paradise: Griggs v. Duke Power Co. and the Concept of Employment Discrimination*, 71 MICH. L. REV. 59, 70–71 & n.46, 74 (1972).

[67] Even now its implications are occasionally controversial. For example, actuarial tables show that women have a longer life expectancy than men. See City of Los Angeles Dep't of Water and Power v. Manhart, 435 U.S. 702, 704 (1978). Despite strong economic arguments for a contrary result, the Supreme Court has held that Title VII requires individualized treatment and therefore forbids an employer to take account of this difference in fixing either employee contributions, see *id.*, or employee benefits under employee-funded retirement schemes, see Arizona Governing Comm. v. Norris, 103 S.Ct. 3492 (1983). Actuarial tables based on racial differences would warrant a similar condemnation. *Id.* at 3498.

[68] See note 16 *supra*.

[69] 104 S.Ct. at 2589.

positive law. But Justice White's reasoning on the broad issue of permissible remedies—largely composed of excerpts from the 1964 legislative history[70]—is bereft of moral, philosophical, economic, or policy discussion. The paucity of argument is disappointing, not least because it gives no clue as to why the issue of remedial quotas has preoccupied so many judges, lawyers, and scholars, or how it could be that the courts of appeals are unanimous in their approval of quota remedies.

It also fails to reckon with two factors that have changed since the moral consensus of 1964 behind the Model of Individual Justice. First, there has emerged a coherent, powerful, and jurisprudentially plausible alternative. Briefly sketched by Justice Blackmun in dissent, the starting point for the competing position is that the role of civil rights law is not just to compensate individual victims of specific acts of discrimination, but to provide race-conscious relief to undo or prevent the classwide effects of racial injustice.

The second changed factor has been the emergence of powerful critiques, directed to the practical and philosophical merits of the Model of Individual Justice. One criticism is that it misconceives the deep structure of race discrimination, and thus renders the fundamental problem incapable of solution. The Model of Individual Justice imagines, as its paradigmatic wrong, an employer consciously making a racially based employment decision, reflecting either racial animus or a racial stereotype.[71] The standard remedy would involve a prohibitory injunction against the perpetrator, together with compensation to the individual victim for the wrong done to him, with the cost borne directly by the wrongdoer and not, for example, by an innocent employee. It can be argued, however, that the problems of employment discrimination are as often institutional as individual, inhering in "institutionalized societal practices and policies, such as testing procedures, subjective selection standards, race and sex-role stereotypes, and seniority rules"[72]

---

[70] See *id.* at 2588–90.

[71] The framers of Title VII had similar expectations. See S. Rep. No. 415, 92nd Cong., 1st Sess. (1971), at 5, quoted in part with approval in Franks v. Bowman Transp. Co., 424 U.S. 747, 765 n.21 (1976).

[72] Belton, *Discrimination and Affirmative Action: An Analysis of Competing Theories of Equality and Weber*, 59 N.C. L. REV. 531, 545 (1981). See Freeman, *Legitimizing Racial Discrimination through Antidiscrimination Law: a Critical Review of Supreme Court Doctrine*, 62 MINN. L. REV. 1049, 1052–53 (1978).

that have the effect of excluding disproportionate numbers of blacks from desirable jobs. The problem is partly one of costs and incentives: victimized individuals may not seek remedies for the injuries that they suffer; the costs of a lawsuit may be too high, the wrongs too difficult to prove. But also troublesome is the Model of Individual Justice's definition of discrimination: the problem may not be racial animus but racial effect; not intent to exclude individuals but practices that keep out blacks as a group; not willful decisions but continued application of criteria, often unjustified by business needs, that have a racially differential impact. If this diagnosis is correct, race discrimination may not be eliminatable without pervasive systemic reform, unattainable within the conceptual apparatus and remedial limitations that the Model of Individual Justice prescribes.

A related challenge to the Model of Individual Justice addresses its philosophical foundations. The Model of Individual Justice, with its conceptions of equal treatment and equality of opportunity, accepts individuals as it finds them upon their entry into the labor market. Their entitlements, at least in the employment market, are a function of their currently demonstrable aptitudes. But current talents and abilities correlate closely with educational and cultural background; the lone individual does not stand independent of history as he or she confronts the meritocratic world. Moreover, it surely is no coincidence that groups traditionally victimized by discrimination, especially blacks, not only suffer economic disadvantage but are able to demonstrate disproportionately few of the qualities and aptitudes most favored by employers.[73] If current disabilities are traceable to past wrongs, it is possible to argue that historical injustices to disadvantaged groups are not irrelevant to the demands of justice in the current day. More specifically, arguments have emerged for a theory of employment discrimination that makes allowances and prescribes corrections for the unhappy historical legacy.

B. THE MODEL OF GROUP JUSTICE

The Model of Group Justice interprets the leading civil rights laws, including the Fourteenth Amendment, as intended primarily

---

[73] See Griggs v. Duke Power Co., 401 U.S. 424, 430 (1971).

to protect and advance the interests of historically disadvantaged groups, especially blacks.[74] This model emerges less from philosophical abstraction than from perceptions of historical and sociological fact. American blacks were first subjected to slavery, then relegated to segregation and poverty.[75] And, the Model of Group Justice emphasizes, cultures of poverty and ignorance perpetuate themselves through the generations. The deprivations of grandfathers and grandmothers thus are visited on fathers and mothers, sons and daughters.[76]

Consistent with its group orientation, the Model of Group Justice holds that employment practices that have a racially disparate impact should be at least presumptively illegal.[77] Nor would this model limit the scope of the remedy to compensation of direct victims of the legal wrong. Regarding race-based wrongs as harming all members of the stigmatized group, the Model of Group Justice affirms the appropriateness of group-benefiting quota remedies.[78]

Although seldom reflected explicitly in the initial legislative history of Title VII, the Model of Group Justice accords with what was clearly one of Congress's predominant purposes: to open em-

---

[74] Judicial opinions reflecting the principles of the Model of Group Justice, and suggesting the elements we have used to construct it, include *Weber*, 443 U.S. at 202–07 (1979); *Bakke*, 438 U.S. at 363, 369 (1978) (opinion of Brennan, White, Marshall, and Blackmun, J.J., concurring in part and dissenting in part); *id.* at 387–402 (opinion of Marshall, J. concurring in part and dissenting in part); Fullilove v. Klutznick, 448 U.S. 448, 517–28 (1979) (concurring opinion of Marshall, J.) Griggs v. Duke Power Co., 401 U.S. 424 (1971). Among the commentators, see, *e.g.*, Belton, note 72 *supra*; Blumrosen, *The Group Interest Concept, Employment Discrimination, and Legislative Intent: The Fallacy of Connecticut v. Teal*, 20 HARV. J. LEG. 99 (1983); Fiss, *Groups and the Equal Protection Clause*, 5 PHIL. & PUB. AFF. 107 (1976); Freeman, note 72 *supra*.

[75] See *Bakke*, 438 U.S. at 387–94 (Marshall, J., concurring in part and dissenting in part). See generally WOODWARD, THE STRANGE CAREER OF JIM CROW (3d ed. 1974).

[76] Linking current social problems with historical injustices, proponents of affirmative action and race-conscious remedies sometimes have emphasized the relevance of the Thirteenth Amendment, the constitutional provision abolishing slavery and investing Congress with enforcement power. See, *e.g.*, Williams v. City of New Orleans, 34 Fair Empl. Prac. Cas. 1009, 1028–31 (5th Cir. 1984) (*en banc*) (Wisdom, J., dissenting).

[77] See, *e.g.*, Belton, note 72 *supra*, at 538–552; Blumrosen, note 74 *supra*, at 99–103.

[78] A representative discussion of the constitutional limits of group remedies appears in the concurring and dissenting opinion that Justice Brennan, White, Marshall, and Blackmun jointly authored in *Bakke*, 438 U.S. at 356–62 (1978). In the private employment context, Justice Brennan's opinion for the Court in *Weber*, 443 U.S. 193 (1979), which is written from a group justice perspective, would demand a predicate of past discrimination in the affected job categories and would impose some limits on the extent and duration of affirmative action preferences. See *id.* at 208–09.

ployment opportunities that previously had been closed to blacks and other minorities.[79] As a jurisprudential construct, the group justice model rose to prominence in the late 1960s and early 1970s, when impatience mounted with persisting conditions of black economic inequality.[80] Today it is possible to identify at least two types of group-based theory, one weak and one strong, which appear to be supported by divergent rationales. But it is the strong version that lies at the heart of current debate.

The weaker of the group-based approaches attempts to justify only "disparate impact" theory, a theory of Title VII employment discrimination approved specifically by the Supreme Court in *Griggs v. Duke Power Co.*[81] Disparate impact theory does not require a plaintiff to establish that an employer had any intention to discriminate. Instead, the plaintiff need only show that an employment test or practice, neutral on its face, excludes from employment opportunities a disproportionate number of minority applicants. Once a showing of disparate impact has been made, the burden shifts to the employer to demonstrate that its practice is justified by "business necessity."[82]

Champions of disparate impact theory have sometimes portrayed it as supplementing rather than supplanting the Model of Individual Justice. On this interpretation, discriminatory impact has its moral and theoretical force as evidence of intentional, race-based decision making.[83] Because of "the unique difficulties of dealing with discriminatory intent or motive,"[84] concerns of practicality and convenience may justify findings of unlawfulness predicated on group impact alone. But the animating purpose remains that of uprooting intentional discrimination against discrete individuals; the ideal to be advanced is not equality of achievement for blacks as

---

[79] See, *e.g.*, 443 U.S. 193, 204–05 (1979); Belton, note 72 *supra*, at 539 & n.30; Blumrosen, note 74 *supra*, at 122–23.

[80] For a report of this phenomenon and a partial endorsement, see Fiss, *The Fate of an Idea Whose Time Has Come: Antidiscrimination Law in the Second Decade after Brown v. Board of Education*, 41 U. CHI. L. REV. 742, 765–70 (1974).

[81] 401 U.S. 424 (1971).

[82] Dothard v. Rawlinson, 433 U.S. 321, 332 n.14 (1977); Griggs v. Duke Power Co., 401 U.S. 424, 431 (1971).

[83] See, *e.g.*, International Bhd. of Teamsters v. United States, 431 U.S. 324, 339–40 & n.20 (1977); Brest, note 5 *supra*, at 26–31.

[84] *Id.* at 26.

compared with whites, but equality of opportunity for individual blacks who are harmed by discriminatory practices.[85] Disparate impact lawsuits thus may be brought by individual blacks.[86] And the theory seemingly accords with the meritocratic values of the Model of Individual Justice.[87]

Whatever certain proponents may argue, however, two difficulties inhere in this essentially individualistic justification for group-based findings of liability. First, under disparate impact theory, proof of nondiscriminatory intent does not excuse an employer from liability.[88] Accordingly, an irreducible conceptual as well as practical divergence separates the disparate impact theory from the disparate treatment paradigm of the Model of Individual Justice.[89]

Second, disparate impact analysis rejects the principle of color blindness. It puts group concepts and statistics inevitably at the center of litigation.[90] It also gives rise to a racial distinction within the law: although blacks and minorities can sue on disparate impact

---

[85] Cf. Griggs, 401 U.S. at 431.

[86] See Mitchell v. Board of Trustees, 599 F.2d 582, 584, 584–85 (4th Cir. 1979); Spurlock v. United Airlines, Inc., 475 F.2d 216, 218 (10th Cir. 1972).

[87] By requiring that employment tests with racially disparate impact "must measure the person for the job and not the person in the abstract," 401 U.S. at 436, Griggs may have aspired to "transform the theory of meritocracy into reality." Belton, note 72 supra, at 545.

[88] See Griggs, 401 U.S. at 432.

[89] From one perspective this might not appear a significant movement: the employer's liability rests on a close analogue to negligence, which imputes fault based on failure to take reasonable steps to avoid a disparate impact. In fact, the shift to a negligence-type theory entails an enormous departure from the Model of Individual Justice's conception of equality of opportunity and, more importantly, from its principles of autonomy and fairness. The leading disparate impact case, Griggs, is illustrative. Embracing disparate impact theory, the Supreme Court reasoned in Griggs that black applicants for employment had suffered the disadvantages of inferior public education and accordingly that it was unfair to allow the employer to judge blacks on the basis of tests of general knowledge and education. Although the Court did not acknowledge it, this line of analysis essentially abandoned the traditional conception of equal opportunity associated with the Model of Individual Justice, which uses as its starting point the person as he enters the labor market. Further, by precluding the employer's using unvalidated but widely utilized tests, the Court effectively imposed on the employer an obligation to compensate for past societal discrimination, especially in the schools. The individualistic premises of the Model of Individual Justice would regard it as unfair to burden an employer on the basis of past wrongs committed not by him but by third parties.

[90] Not only does the plaintiff establish a prima facie case by showing that an employment test or practice has a disproportionately exclusionary impact on the group, but if an employer then wants to defend a test, it may need to engage in "differential validation"—that is, show that the test is as good a predictor of job performance for blacks, as a group, as it is for whites as a separate group. See Albemarle Paper Co. v. Moody, 422 U.S. 405, 435 (1975).

theories, white males cannot.[91] Finally, and perhaps of greatest
practical significance, the threat of disparate impact liability creates
a powerful incentive for employers to engage in quota hiring.[92] The
group implications of disparate impact theory therefore cannot be
avoided. Yet the weaker version of the Model of Group Justice
offers no adequate rationale for regarding the group as a relevant
entity entitled to a remedial quota or preference.[93]

The stronger, more straightforward version of the group justice
model holds that the group is an independently relevant entity, not
merely a construct invoked to prove individual discrimination. The
nub of the theory is that blacks, and possibly other minorities,
should be regarded for some purposes as an entity, and that the
entity should be conceived as having a moral and legal status of its
own. With the group thus identified as a morally relevant concept,
the wrongs of racial discrimination are regarded as wrongs to the
group, not merely to individuals, and the group (as well as its
individual members) is held entitled to a remedy.[94] The most influential expositor of a group theory, Owen Fiss,[95] has identified
two conditions that must be satisfied for a group to assert morally
compelling claims to group justice. First, there must be a long-
standing practice, whether social or legal, that makes it both possible and commonplace to "talk about the group without reference to
the particular individuals who happen to be its members at any one
moment."[96] Second, Fiss imposes a demand of psychological inter-

---

[91] Whenever the Supreme Court has validated disparate impact analysis the case has
involved either minorities or women. Chamallas, note 64 *supra*, at 366 & n.299. See also U.S.
COMM'N ON CIVIL RIGHTS, AFFIRMATIVE ACTION IN THE 1980s: DISMANTLING THE PRO-
CESS OF DISCRIMINATION 17 n.20 (1981). But see Weisbord v. Michigan State Univ. 495 F.
Supp. 1347 (W.D. Mich. 1980).

[92] See Blumrosen, note 74 *supra*, at 101–02. The incentive arises because the validation of
tests—the alternative to quotas if disparate impact liability is to be avoided—has proved so
difficult. See Meltzer, note 56 *supra*, at 430.

[93] Because judicial remedies for disparate impact violations commonly have taken the form
of racial hiring quotas, it might seem arguable that the weaker group approach cannot justify
its own remedial prescriptions. But while the weaker group theory provides no strong
justification for quota remedies, neither does its logic seem to require them. Quotas—the
central interest of *Stotts* and a large issue in the future of antidiscrimination law—thus seem
inevitably to implicate a second, stronger version of the Model of Group Justice.

[94] See, *e.g.*, *Bakke*, 438 U.S. at 387–402 (opinion of Marshall, J., concurring in part and
dissenting in part); Bayles, *Reparations to Wronged Groups*, 33 ANALYSIS 17 (1973); Taylor,
Reverse Discrimination and Compensatory Justice, 33 ANALYSIS 185 (1973).

[95] See Fiss, note 74 *supra*.

[96] *Id.* at 148.

dependence. The members of the group must so associate with the group—and, as members of the group, with each other—that the "identity and well-being" of individual members is "linked" with their perceptions of the status and well-being of the group as a whole.[97]

Even if the validity of the group concept is conceded, it still might be objected that the most frequently prescribed remedy, a racial quota, cannot be justified. Remedial justice, at least traditionally understood, has typically prescribed compensation from a wrongdoer to a specific victim.[98] Departing from this paradigm, quota remedies frequently result in the disadvantaging of white males, personally innocent of any racial wrongs. And this, arguably, is unfair. To answer this objection, the Model of Group Justice must rely on a concept of "past" or "societal" discrimination.[99] Asserting that past societal discrimination has constituted blacks as a perpetual underclass, the model must contend that racial preferences are necessary to remedy historical wrongs, long antedating the triggering statutory violation, that are taxable less to the guilty employer than to the society as a whole.

This argument appears to create a kind of symmetry within the Model of Group Justice: if widespread acts of racism have created a legacy of poverty and disadvantage, then the remedial obligation—as well as the remedial entitlement—seems to have at least a group dimension. But the appearance is deceiving. Although they constitute a racial class, whites do not satisfy the conditions of historical labeling and psychological interdependence necessary to constitute them as a "group" in the relevant sense.[100] The burdens of affirmative action thus must be recognized to fall less on a group than on discrete individuals, such as the white males who are disadvantaged by employment preferences for minorities.[101] The claims of

---

[97] *Id.* at 148–49.

[98] See, *e.g.*, ARISTOTLE, NICHOMACHEAN ETHICS 405 (McKeon ed. 1947).

[99] See Fiss, note 80 *supra*, at 769–70.

[100] See text accompanying notes 95–96 *supra*.

[101] Not surprisingly, therefore, group justice arguments characteristically blur the concept of remedial and distributive justice. While the argument for racial preferences often is cast in remedial terms, see, *e.g.*, Bayles, note 94 *supra*, quota remedies do not effect specific restitution from wrongdoer to victim. Rather, an employer's conviction of wrongdoing provides the occasion for undertaking an enterprise of redistribution—the according of preferences to blacks or other minorities who otherwise would not receive them. But this redistribution is not justified on the theory that an individual black deserves the preference as a matter of

blacks to group justice simply are conceived as sufficiently compelling to justify the imposition of burdens on individual dispreferred whites.[102]

Despite the generally individualistic tenor of American jurisprudence,[103] by the late 1970s important themes in civil rights law resonated increasingly well with the Model of Group Justice. In *Griggs*,[104] the Supreme Court found that Title VII's general prohibition of race discrimination was broad enough to sustain a disparate impact theory, which is rooted in group-based concepts.[105] Moreover, the general remedial provision of Title VII is entirely open textured in its authorization to the federal courts to order such relief as they may deem appropriate, and the courts of appeals are unanimous in finding there a warrant for remedial quotas.[106] Acting outside of Title VII, the executive branch had strengthened Executive Order 11246 to establish numerical targets and timetables that must be satisfied by employers which have contracts with the federal government.[107] And in a series of cases the Executive Order has received the judicial imprimatur of federal courts of appeals.[108] Too, when Congress adopted the 1972 amendments to Title VII, it appeared to endorse the group-based legal developments proliferating in both the judicial and executive branches.[109] An analysis ac-

---

distributive justice—the term "distributive justice" traditionally has applied to burdens and benefits distributed by political authorities, based on the personal merit, needs, or achievements of the recipient. See, *e.g.*, FEINBERG, SOCIAL PHILOSOPHY 107 (1973). It is supported as made appropriate by past discrimination against blacks as a group.

[102] Rejected are arguments by the dispreferred that to lose a job is to pay more than their fair share of any group-based program of racial preferences.

[103] See, *e.g.*, Horwitz, *The Jurisprudence of Brown and the Dilemmas of Liberalism*, 14 HARV. C.R.-C.L. L. REV. 599, 606–10 (1979).

[104] 401 U.S. 424 (1971).

[105] See text accompanying notes 81–93 *supra*.

[106] For a collection of cases, see *Stotts*, 104 S.Ct. at 2606 n.10 (Blackmun, J., dissenting). Essentially ignoring these cases and their rationales, the *Stotts* majority seemed to suggest that remedial quotas were barred by the plain language of Section 706(g), 42 U.S.C. 20000e-5(g) (1982) (which it quoted in a footnote, 104 S.Ct. 2589 n.12). Compare 104 S.Ct. at 2608 (Blackmun, J., dissenting).

[107] See note 47 *supra*.

[108] See, *e.g.*, Contractors Ass'n v. Schultz, 442 F.2d 159 (3d Cir.), *cert. denied*, 404 U.S. 854 (1971).

[109] Committee reports in both the House and the Senate included language generally supportive of disparate impact theory, see S. Rep. No. 415, 92d Cong., 2d Sess. 5 (1971); H.R. Rep. No. 238, 92d Cong., 2d Sess. 68–69 (1972), and the House report referred to *Griggs* with specific approbation. See *id.* at 5 n.1.

companying the final bill stated that "it was assumed that the present case law as developed by the courts would continue to govern the applicability and construction of Title VII."[110] In addition, both the House and the Senate rejected amendments that would have precluded the use of race-conscious measures under the Executive Order or the 1964 Civil Rights Act.[111]

Finally, at the end of the 1970s, the Supreme Court itself adopted a group-based approach—consistent with and supporting surrounding legal developments—when it addressed the lawfulness of voluntary affirmative action programs. In *United Steel Workers v. Weber*,[112] the Court upheld an affirmative action quota that reserved half the slots in an employee training program for black applicants. Justice Brennan's opinion for the Court stressed the purpose of Title VII to improve "the plight of the Negro in our economy."[113] Despite Title VII's recurrent references to the individual, the majority found the statute's economic aspiration, defined in group terms, to be controlling. While *Weber* presented only a statutory question, *Fullilove v. Klutznick*[114] affirmed the constitutionality of a congressionally mandated quota system reserving fixed percentages of government contracts for minority businesses. Although the direct beneficiaries were not themselves proved victims, the Court apparently found it sufficient that minorities as a group had suffered past discrimination, and that Congress had enacted the quotas to eradicate the continuing legacy of group prejudice.[115]

Justice Blackmun's *Stotts* dissent embodied an appeal to the

---

[110] 118 CONG. REC. 7166 (1972).

[111] Ordinarily the Supreme Court will not place much weight on the views of a later Congress in interpreting the meaning of a provision adopted by an earlier Congress, and in International Bhd. of Teamsters v. United States, 431 U.S. 324, 354 n.39 (1977), the Supreme Court found the 1964 legislative history controlling in reaching a decision about the scope of the seniority provision, § 703(h). But powerful arguments supported a contrary conclusion even in that context. See *id.* at 390–94 (Marshall, J., dissenting). Moreover, it is entirely unclear that the Teamsters holding or logic should extend to an interpretation of § 706(g), the general remedial provision, which was itself rewritten and broadened in 1972 by the 92d Congress.

[112] 443 U.S. 193 (1979).

[113] *Id.* at 202 (quoting 110 CONG. REC. 6548 (1964) (remarks of Sen. Humphrey)).

[114] 448 U.S. 448 (1980).

[115] Although there was no majority opinion in the case, the two opinions that were each joined by three of the Justices composing the six-member majority are in accord on this point. See *id.* at 472–89 (opinion of Burger, C.J., joined by White and Powell, J.J.); *id.* at 517–19 (opinion of Marshall, J., joined by Brennan and Blackmun, J.J.).

Model of Group Justice in the layoff context. Carefully developing a distinction between "individual relief and race-conscious class relief,"[116] Justice Blackmun noted with apparent approbation that "the Courts of Appeals are unanimously of the view that race-conscious affirmative relief can be 'appropriate' " under Title VII.[117] Justice Blackmun did not attempt to justify quotas in the traditional terms of remedial justice, which restores to a specific victim that which a specific wrongdoer has taken from him. Instead, the dissent portrayed race-conscious remedies as attempting a kind of class-based redistribution, noting that "[t]he distinguishing feature of race-conscious relief is that no individual member of the disadvantaged class has a claim to it, and individual beneficiaries need not show that they were themselves victims of the discrimination for which relief was granted."[118] Having argued at length that the *Stotts* case was moot,[119] the dissent appropriately satisfied itself with sketching positions rather than resolving issues. But Justice Blackmun even provided a Model of Group Justice rationale for departing from precedents that had protected seniority systems against restructuring by remedial orders. The earlier cases, Justice Blackmun argued, had dealt with claims to individual relief. Because the issue of classwide relief had not been expressly presented in the Court's leading case on seniority remedies, Justice Blackmun found that the prior decision had "little relevance"[120] for the *Stotts* issue, and he considered the Court free to entertain a group justice approach even to class-based remedies upsetting settled seniority rights.

C. CONFLICT OR COEXISTENCE?

Framed as alternatives, as they were in *Stotts*, the Model of Individual Justice and the Model of Group Justice pose for decision a morally and legally wrenching choice.[121] Group-focused preferences commend themselves as necessary to improve the economic status of minority groups and possibly to eliminate divisive and

---

[116] 104 S.Ct. at 2605 (Blackmun, J., dissenting).

[117] *Id.* at 2606.

[118] *Id.*

[119] See *id.* at 2596–2600.

[120] *Id.* at 2608.

[121] *Cf.* Calabresi, *Bakke as Pseudo-Tragedy*, 28 CATH. U. L. REV. 427 (1979).

debilitating structures of racial caste.[122] To this end the Model of Individual Justice simply seems not merely inadequate in an instrumental sense, but also morally inadequate to the special case of racialism in American history.

On the other hand, there loom two large issues of fairness. First, affirmative discrimination is impossible to defend within the traditional categories of distributive justice or corrective justice.[123] A question therefore arises whether, even in principle, a program of group-based preferences can be justified. Second, "benign" racial preferences are not costless. Preferential employment remedies typically result in the exclusion from employment opportunities of a class of persons, most often white males, who themselves may be innocent of any race-based wrongdoing.[124] Moreover, this excluded class may comprise the relatively least advantaged whites, who may have enjoyed no personal advantages traceable to past racial injustices.

In *Firefighters v. Stotts*, the Supreme Court tipped strongly in the direction of the Model of Individual Justice—a movement entailing important sacrifices, so long as the issue is framed as between the familiarly contending perspectives. But it is as unlikely as it would be undesirable that *Stotts* reflected an ultimate legal choice. Not cited in *Stotts* was the *Weber* case,[125] infused with the Model of Group Justice, in which the Supreme Court found Title VII to authorize voluntary hiring quotas by private employers. *Stotts* made no reference to Executive Order 11246. And the *Stotts* rationale, focused on remedies, leaves untouched the group logic embedded in disparate-impact theories of employment discrimination.

After *Stotts* as before, the Model of Individual Justice and the Model of Group Justice are in a relation of as yet unrationalized conflict. Each of the models possesses substantial normative power and jurisprudential plausibility, and each has at times commended itself to nearly every Justice of the Supreme Court.

---

[122] See, *e.g.*, Fiss, note 74 *supra*, at 151.

[123] See note 101 *supra*. It may be especially problematic that the beneficiaries frequently will be those least likely to have suffered the effects of race-based injustice. See GOLDMAN, JUSTICE AND REVERSE DISCRIMINATION 90–91 (1979).

[124] The burden tends to fall on young white males just entering the job market, rather than on those who may have been parties to past injustices in the employment market. See *id.* at 114–15.

[125] United Steelworkers v. Weber, 443 U.S. 193 (1979).

Debate generally has focused on which of these models ought to be preferred. A more fruitful inquiry may be whether there is some third alternative, which would avoid the need for a tragic election and achieve at least a partial reconciliation at the level of values.

IV. THE MODEL OF SOCIAL JUSTICE

Issues of racial justice can be viewed as subsuming at least two questions. One involves the required affirmative predicates for programs of affirmative action and race-conscious remedies—the conditions that must be satisfied to justify even in principle a program of race-conscious redistribution. Another involves the fairness of cost allocation. Programs of affirmative discrimination entail costs, and many impose those costs directly on particular "dispreferred" individuals.

Although there are two questions,[126] the Models of Individual Justice and of Group Justice each allow but one mode of response. The Model of Individual Justice answers both questions from an individualistic perspective: only those personally harmed by illegal discrimination should be entitled to a remedy, and the costs should not be borne by persons individually innocent of wrongdoing. The Model of Group Justice, viewing discrimination as a wrong against a group, favors group remedies and does not shrink from imposing the costs on "innocent" individual whites.

The law undoubtedly has unfolded less symmetrically. But it does exhibit at least hints of a pattern, traceable along the divide between the two questions that we have distinguished. In cases defining Title VII violations and establishing the necessary predicates for voluntary affirmative action, the Supreme Court very often has reached the results commended by the Model of Group Justice. Group logic underlies the disparate impact theory endorsed in *Griggs*.[127] And while *Griggs* may not logically justify quota remedies, lower courts have regarded them as the natural remedial com-

---

[126] The distinction between the two questions undoubtedly can be blurred or even collapsed; it is possible to frame only the single question whether a particular program of affirmative discrimination, involving its specific benefits and costs, ought to be implemented. For us, however, the relevant issues are exposed more clearly and helpfully when the two questions are separated: attention is focused first on the arguments supporting affirmative action, then on the costs, in a way that systematically develops the relevant concerns.

[127] See text accompanying notes 82–93 *supra*.

plement to a group-based theory of liability.[128] Even more striking are cases in which the Supreme Court has upheld voluntary racial quotas. In both *Weber* and *Fullilove*, past societal discrimination, defined wholly in group terms, established a sufficient predicate for a quota "remedy." Neither individual wrongdoing nor individual victimization was required.

The Supreme Court has tended to respond differently when an issue of cost allocation to innocents has lain on the surface of a lawsuit. In such cases the Supreme Court, often in the language of equity jurisprudence,[129] recurrently has expressed concern about fairness to individuals. Presenting such a burdening-of-innocents question, *Stotts* follows the line of prior seniority holdings: because of potential harm to senior incumbents, *Teamsters v. United States*[130] held that competitive seniority—potentially disadvantageous to incumbent whites—could be awarded only to the proved victims of unlawful discrimination.[131] And the seniority cases by no means sound an anomalous theme. Even when plaintiffs have sought only financial relief, unrelated to any seniority system, two cases arising from discrimination in the management of employee pension plans have weighed the interests of innocents in prescribing that relief should be prospective only.[132] Precisely because retroactive awards might jeopardize the interests of innocent pensioners, the Court found that damage relief would offend the equitable spirit of Title VII. Upholding voluntary affirmative action, *Weber* conditioned its approval on a finding that the plan under review did not "unnecessarily trammel the interests of white employees."[133] And constitutional cases reflect similar sensitivity to the burdens accompanying race conscious remedies and affirmative action. Most notably, Jus-

---

[128] See note 106 *supra*.

[129] See, *e.g.*, International Bhd. of Teamsters v. United States, 431 U.S. 324, 374–75 (1977); Franks v. Bowman Transp. Co., Inc., 424 U.S. 747, 777 (1976).

[130] 431 U.S. 324 (1977).

[131] Even in the case of proved victims entitled to take their "rightful places" in the seniority ladder, the lower courts generally have held that no white incumbent can be directly "bumped" from his job to create a position for the victim. Instead the victims must await the development of future vacancies. See, *e.g.*, Patterson v. American Tobacco Co., 535 F.2d 257, 267 (4th Cir. 1976); Local 189, United Papermakers and Paperworkers v. United States, 416 F.2d 980, 988 (5th Cir. 1969).

[132] See Los Angeles Dep't of Water & Power v. Mahnart, 435 U.S. 702, 722–23 (1978); Arizona Governing Comm. v. Norris, 103 S.Ct. 3492, 3509–10 (1983).

[133] 443 U.S. 193, 208 (1979).

tice Powell's demand for individualized consideration of innocent whites defined the Court's position in the famous *Bakke* case.[134]

Although this pattern can be traced at the level of results, Supreme Court jurisprudence has not expressly distinguished between our two questions—one involving the necessary affirmative predicates for racial preferences, the other defining the permissible limits on cost-allocations. But if the Court's holdings support our distinction, the unfolding law would appear to embody a set of moral beliefs not coherently explicable within either the Model of Group Justice or the Model of Individual Justice. It is our aspiration—independent of arguments about the meaning of Supreme Court decisions—to explain why these questions should be addressed separately, and to develop a theory that locates our intuitions in a moral and legal structure. The gist of our theory, which we term the Model of Social Justice, is this:

Pervasive historical racism has marked blacks as a class that still suffers economic, cultural, and social disadvantages. Against this background, strong arguments frequently support "rectification"—the elimination from economic and social institutions of the presumptive incidents of past discrimination, including racial skewings in the distribution of wealth, jobs, power, and opportunities. Rectification expresses a moral rejection, not only of willful, individual wrongs, but of the pervasive systematic discrimination that has left blacks as a class in a status of economic deprivation. Though this undertaking could be justified in terms of social policy, it also reflects a moral stance opposing racial stratification traceable to past wrongs. Attempting to break the historic connection between race and life prospects in American society, rectification attacks both the psychological and economic bases of minority deprivation. Race-conscious remedies help alleviate the sense of rejection and futility left by a system of racial caste, thus encouraging the development of black talents. Too, affirmative discrimination advances the values associated with a broader and more attractive conception of equality of opportunity, which does not take as given the talents of people as they enter the labor market. Assuming a significant correlation between minority status and current deprivation, rectification extends preferences to the most talented minority applicants. It aspires to locate them close to where they would have

---

[134] Regents of the Univ. of California v. Bakke, 435 U.S. 265, 317, 318 (1978).

been situated but for educational and cultural disadvantages that
may be a legacy of historic racism. Often the triggering incident for
a program of rectification will be the statutory violation of a particular employer. But the deep, underlying wrongs are social and
historical, more than those of a contemporary law violator. In prescribing rectification largely on the basis of past, societal wrongs,
our model views issues of racial justice as ones of social justice.[135]

On the other hand, we do not adopt the justifications for racial
preferences offered by the Model of Group Justice, nor do we
accept its views as to the scope of appropriate remedies. Selecting
the justifiable beneficiaries of affirmative discrimination raises
significant issues, both at the group and individual level. Furthermore, our model acknowledges that questions of cost allocation
raise issues of fairness.[136] The wrongs of racial discrimination often
having been social and legal, we believe that, where feasible, the
costs should be spread broadly across relevant segments of the
economy or the political community.[137] But widespread cost sharing will not always be possible in the labor market, the particular
concern of this article. Where cost spreading would be difficult to
achieve consistently with the ordinary practices of American government, we assume that the costs of affirmative discrimination—
as of any other social policy—may be assigned to identifiable
classes of citizens.[138] The mandatory draft in wartime provides a
relevant if extreme example of socially imposed individual burdens.
We also assume, however, that the moral dubiousness of an assignment of costs will increase with the burden imposed on particular
individuals. In fact, outside the most exigent circumstances, some
individual sacrifices are too large to be demanded. Thus, beyond

---

[135] We use the term "justice" in a loose sense. We do not claim that the particular programs
commended by our model represent the single and perfect solution commended by principles of natural right. Using the term "social justice" somewhat more colloquially, we mean
only to imply that our proposals do not offend anyone's moral rights, and that they are
themselves supported by moral and policy arguments that we find convincing.

[136] We do not understand fairness to require that persons could be taxed only with those
obligations that result from their individually voluntary acts, such as individual wrongdoing.
It is in the nature of national communities that the moral obligations of one historical
generation can be passed on to another, much as the national debt can.

[137] For a classic discussion of the possibilities of cost spreading in another context, see
CALABRESI, THE COSTS OF ACCIDENTS (1970).

[138] See Sedler, *Racial Preferences and the Constitution: The Societal Interest in the Equal Protection Objective*, 26 WAYNE ST. L. REV. 1227, 1240–45 (1980).

the implicit restraints of our positive justification for affirmative discrimination, considerations of fairness in cost assignment will impose limits on the circumstances in which racial preferences ought to be allowed. The arguments for racial preferences therefore need to be stated clearly and, what is more, linked to their specific contexts of application. Only in particular contexts can the costs of racial quotas—the burdens that they impose on nonbeneficiaries—be weighed with precision, and thus only in context can the full range of concerns—encompassing both benefits and costs—be assessed.[139]

A. THE CIRCUMSTANCES OF RACIAL JUSTICE

America's history has given meaning to race.[140] Uprooted from their ancestral homes and transported in chains to American shores, blacks were sold into a condition of slavery endorsed by a Constitution that promised freedom to everyone else.[141] After that "peculiar institution" was abolished, most of the southern states enacted Jim Crow laws—legislation not merely keeping the freedman in "his place" but "constantly pushing the Negro further down."[142] Ultimately many American blacks undertook a second long trek, this time to northern cities, there to be met by a pattern of social and economic exclusion that largely confined them to living in ghettos.[143]

Past racial injustices have left to the present an appalling legacy.

---

[139] By using the language of "costs" and "benefits" we do not mean to imply that our framework is "utilitarian" in the sense of, e.g., BENTHAM, THE PRINCIPLES OF MORALS AND LEGISLATION (1789). Utilitarianism in this sense views a political or moral decision as correct only if that decision maximizes the average level of satisfaction or pleasure within some relevant community. Although not blind to considerations of pain, pleasure, and utility, we assume that moral principles may have a value not reducible to such currency, and that conflicts of values therefore cannot always be resolved by application of a Benthamite calculus.

[140] See, e.g., Wasserstrom, Racism, Sexism, and Preferential Treatment: An Approach to the Topics, 24 UCLA L. REV. 581, 584–87 (1977).

[141] Although the Framers did not explicitly use the words "race" or "slavery," several provisions of the original Constitution implicitly recognize and sanction the legal existence of slavery. E.g., United States Constitution, Art. I, § 9, cl. 1, which forbade Congress to forbid "Importation of such Persons" (before 1808), and Art. IV, § 2, cl. 3, which prevented states from altering the status of any fugitive "held to Service or Labour" in another state, and compelled delivery of fugitives on demand.

[142] See WOODWARD, THE STRANGE CAREER OF JIM CROW 93 (1957).

[143] See, e.g., WILSON, THE DECLINING SIGNIFICANCE OF RACE 62–87 (2d ed. 1980).

The average income of black families is still only slightly more than half that of whites.[144] Black unemployment rates are consistently double those of whites,[145] and while black women have overtaken white women in earnings from work, the black male still earns only two-thirds as much as his white counterpart.[146] These indices of economic deprivation are both cause and effect of a profound dislocation of the black family structure, exhibited in the dramatic growth in single-parent, female-headed households.[147] Nor are the effects of racial injustice measurable solely in poverty statistics. To invoke Wasserstrom's telling comparison:[148]

> Race does not function in our culture as does eye color. Eye color is an irrelevant category; . . . it is not an important cultural fact. . . . It is important to see that race is not like that at all. . . . In our culture to be nonwhite—and especially to be black—is to be treated and seen as a member of a group that is different from and inferior to the group of standard, fully developed white males. . . . That is simply part of the awful truth of our cultural and social history, and a significant feature of the social reality of our culture today.

The impulse to affirmative action and race-conscious remedies has arisen in this economic and social context. In the 1964 Civil Rights Act, Congress expressed the view that racial subordination is morally wrong. At that time the primary engine for correction was the antidiscrimination principle. Within a few years, however,

---

[144] The ratio of median black to white family income, which was 58 percent in 1966, shortly after Title VII came into force, and reached as high as 65 percent in 1975, had dropped all the way back to 55 percent in 1982, in the valley of an economic recession. See CURRENT POPULATION REPORT, note 2 *supra*, at 135.

[145] This ratio of black to white unemployment rates has held from the time Title VII came into force (when it was 8.1 percent black unemployment to 4.1 percent white in 1965) until more recently (13.1 percent vs. 6.3 percent in 1980), in good times (6.4 percent vs. 3.1 percent in 1969) and bad (17.3 percent vs. 8.6 percent in 1982). See ECONOMIC REPORT OF THE PRESIDENT, note 2 *supra*. And these unemployment rates disguise the underlying fact that more and more discouraged blacks have dropped out of the labor market. By mid-1982, the black male nonparticipation rate was up to 28 percent from 17 percent in 1960. As a result, the actual employment rate of black males was only 55 percent, compared with 69 percent for whites. See CENTER FOR THE STUDY OF SOCIAL POLICY, A DREAM DEFERRED: THE ECONOMIC STATUS OF BLACK AMERICANS 19 (1983).

[146] See CURRENT POPULATION REPORT, note 2 *supra*, at 166.

[147] By the early eighties, the number of single-parent, female-headed families was 40 percent for blacks vs. 12 percent for whites. The children of these families accounted for the bulk of black children living in poverty. See Jencks, note 65 *supra*, at 35.

[148] Wasserstrom, note 140 *supra*, at 586–87 (footnote omitted).

there had emerged in judicial,[149] executive,[150] and legislative action[151] an additional policy of affirmative discrimination for blacks,
born out of a desire to achieve tangible economic effects. In contrast
with the antidiscrimination principle, affirmative discrimination aspired not only to forbid future race-based wrongs but to eradicate
the identifiable residues—traceable in racially skewed distributions
of wealth, jobs, and education—of past, legally sanctioned injustices.

Prescribing the award of preferences on group-based racial
grounds, affirmative discrimination reflected from its inception a
departure from the principles more generally prevalent in American law and morality.[152] Nor could this practice be justified within
the traditional categories of justice. Affirmative discrimination is
not corrective in the classic sense. The immediate beneficiaries are
not the actual victims of particular wrongs, and the people on
whom the burden is imposed are usually not the perpetrators of
those wrongs. Similarly, affirmative discrimination is not often
justified as expressing ultimate principles of distributive justice.
Long-term commitment to race-based principles would give race a
moral significance unjustifiably exalted beyond that attached to
other relevant factors, including personal need, effort, achievement, and talent.

If affirmative discrimination is to be supported, the justification
must be extraordinary, linked to the unique features of American

---

[149] The most important developments included Griggs v. Duke Power Co., 401 U.S. 424
(1971), in which the Supreme Court expanded the concept of discrimination, and the early
cases in the courts of appeals approving quota remedies for Title VII violations, see, e.g.,
United States v. Ironworkers Local No. 86, 443 F.2d 544 (9th Cir. 1971).

[150] The Office of Federal Contract Compliance had begun as early as 1965 to establish
special, geographically targeted programs to assure minority representation in firms doing
business with the federal government under Executive Order 11246. The best known of
these, the so-called Philadelphia Plan, required bidders for construction projects to establish
numerical goals for minority utilization. The Philadelphia Plan was upheld against constitutional challenge in Contractors Assn. of Eastern Pennsylvania v. Schultz, 442 F.2d 159 (3d
Cir.), cert. denied. 404 U.S. 854 (1971).

[151] See notes 109–11 supra and accompanying text.

[152] Among other indications, public opinion polls consistently have registered strong majority support for special programs to assist blacks, but also a strong preference for the merit
principle as opposed to racial quotas in hiring. See, e.g., AFFIRMATIVE ACTION AND EQUAL
PROTECTION: HEARINGS BEFORE THE SUBCOMMITTEE ON THE CONSTITUTION OF THE
SENATE JUDICIARY COMMITTEE ON S.J. RES. 41, 97th Cong., 1st Sess. 939, at 939–52,
1050–51 (1981).

racial history. For us, the justification begins with the intuitive judgment that it is appropriate to afford blacks, as a group, strong positive assistance to eradicate the group-based effects of history.[153] From that starting point, we locate the justification for affirmative discrimination in the conjunction of three factors. We cannot, here, prove all the empirical assumptions on which we rely. Our position is only that it has been and remains as morally and intellectually reasonable to act on these assumptions as on any others.[154]

The first material factor is the history of group-based subordination, aided and abetted by government and by law. The injustices were spread over a long span of time.[155] The experience of blacks differs both quantitatively and qualitatively from that of most if not all national groups in the immigrant generation. Moreover, the implication of the law, within an institutional heritage that shapes a na-

---

[153] By terming the judgment intuitive, we mean only to suggest that the decison as to right and wrong with which we are concerned has not yet been located within or rationalized by any coherent legal or moral theory. See HAMPSHIRE, TWO THEORIES OF MORALITY 6 (1977). By beginning the process of moral reasoning with an intuition as to morally correct behavior, we do not suggest that the starting point is infallible, or that it is not subject to correction after argument and reflection. We do assume, however, that a moral intuition is an appropriate starting point in a moral argument. First, if intuitions can be explained by reference to general moral principles, then it becomes possible to engage in a "two-way traffic by which intuitions are modified by reflection on the general principles that explain them, and the general principles are qualified by the particular cases that do not fit under them." *Id.* at 5. Second, the movement from intuitions to explanatory principles brings into view the possibility of a further testing of the principles themselves—an evaluation of their conformity with a general way of life that can be affirmed as desirable or good. This notion of a "way of life" is vague, and probably has to be. We are concerned with a social ideal, but not a social ideal of the utopian society. In evaluating principles, we therefore mean to acknowledge and accommodate many of the habits, values, institutions, and assumptions that give shape to the society in which we live. As much as any critic, we wish that moral theory could offer an Archimedean perspective on moral issues. But when we are prepared to universalize our moral prescriptions as assertions of first-order moral truths, we are aware that we begin our reflections located in time, place, and culture, and acknowledge a second-order awareness of the cultural influences affecting us.

[154] Rationalizing an intuitive judgment, we seek an explanation of how the intuition might be correct, both in terms of the moral principles that explain it and the empirical propositions needed to show that the moral principles in fact apply. In dealing with empirical questions, our method of initially accepting possible explanations is similar to that commended in NOZICK, PHILOSOPHICAL EXPLANATIONS 8–24 (1981). We are open to evidence concerning the truth of the empirical propositions on which we rely, and we must be prepared to abandon positions ultimately shown to depend on false premises. But we are prepared to act initially on empirical assumptions supported by some evidence, or even plausible hypotheses, even in the absence of "proof." Another way of putting it is to say that we reject the argument that the proponents of affirmative discrimination must prove all disputed empirical assumptions before they are justified in going forward.

[155] See generally WOODWARD, note 75 *supra*, at 81–95.

tional community defined by a shared sense of continuity with the American past, establishes a dimension of social responsibility.[156]

Second, historical wrongs against blacks have had an enduring impact, measurable now in economic and social disparities between racial groups. American blacks are more likely than whites to start life, and to enter the employment market, from a background of low family income and single-parent homes, with little cultural or intellectual stimulation in the family or the neighborhood.[157] All of these factors tend to reduce prospects for educational and cultural advancement.

Third, in at least two respects blacks constitute a group, appropriately treated as such in programs of affirmative discrimination. One stems from the social meaning of blackness. In the labor market, employers have tended to appraise blacks through the lens of unfavorable racial stereotypes,[158] thus depressing the economic prospects even of middle-class blacks.[159] In this context, benefits afforded to one black offer a potential spillover benefit to others. Requiring the hiring of blacks in previously all-white jobs or firms, so that they can be seen as performing capably, may be important in opening doors through which others can follow.[160] Moreover, fuller representation of blacks in positions of responsibility pro-

---

[156] For detailed estimates of the dimensions of these relationships, see JENCKS, WHO GETS AHEAD? THE DETERMINANTS OF ECONOMIC SUCCESS IN AMERICA (1979).

[157] See notes 144–48 *supra* and accompanying text.

[158] See text accompanying note 148 *supra*.

[159] Econometric research has documented some of the barriers that racism has raised against black prospects at all levels of American life. Examining data from the 1962 Survey of Occupational Change in Generation for black and white males, Duncan, *Inheritance of Poverty or Inheritance of Race*, in MOYNIHAN (ed.), ON UNDERSTANDING POVERTY 85 (1968), found that if one compared blacks and whites from homes where family heads had the same levels of education and jobs and where each of the individuals had received the same amount of education and scored the same on intelligence tests, the black worker would receive on average one-quarter less income than the white. In effect, this was the price of being black in America. Fifteen years later, Freeman, *Black Economic Progress after 1964: Who Has Gained and Why?* in ROSEN (ed.), STUDIES IN LABOR MARKETS 247 (1981), confirmed these findings in his analysis of the 1966 National Longitudinal Survey of older blacks and whites (ages 45– 59), whose socioeconomic status was largely determined by their experience in the labor market before the Civil Rights Act of 1964 became effective in 1965. Freeman found that differences in region, parental occupation, and personal schooling accounted for only half the black/white disparity in occupational status and earnings. *Id.* at 266–67.

[160] For this purpose, sociological studies suggest that more than a "token" presence of minorities may be needed. Isolated minority workers tend to be the subject of unusually exacting critical scrutiny. When they seek success through exceptionally hard work, they may suffer disabling hostility and resentment from members of the dominant group.

vides some assurance against a reversion to reliance on stereotypes. Second, for many if not most blacks, social and historical experiences have made blackness an important element of self-identity.[161] For this reason, individual perceptions of status, respect, and security may depend on the status and well-being of blacks as a group.[162] As a result, preferences to individual blacks do not constitute mere windfalls to individual beneficiaries. Their aggregate effect—breaking the link between race and economic, cultural, and social status—may advance the aspirations, confidence and self-esteem of other group members.

Implicit in the second and third of these arguments is an acknowledgment of contingency. However true our assumptions may once have been or may be now, the social reality itself could change. In this sense our Model of Social Justice mirrors a familiar belief embedded in the unfolding pattern of civil rights law: that affirmative discrimination is justified by special facts of historical context, to which the historical categories of distributive and remedial justice seem morally inadequate, and that it should be viewed as a short-term response to current exigencies, not as embodying an ultimate vision of the good society.[163]

B. PREFERENCES AND FAIRNESS

The Model of Social Justice assumes that programs of racial preference—even prior to considerations of fairness in cost allocation—are not inherently unjust. Important arguments to the contrary therefore need to be met. These include objections that affirmative discrimination stands on the same moral plane with racial quotas based on bias and that racial preferences abridge the moral rights either of employers or of dispreferred individuals.

1. Quotas and Racial Stigma

The Model of Individual Justice assumes that race is a morally impermissible basis for the assignment of burdens or the award of

---

[161] See, *e.g.*, Wasserstrom, note 140 *supra*, at 585–87 & n.12.

[162] See, *e.g.*, Fiss, note 74 *supra*, at 148–56.

[163] Undoubtedly there is a danger that racial classifications teach the relevance of race, and that they foster race-based hostility and resentment. Although this concern is not to be dismissed, our view is that the balance of considerations support limitations on the scope and duration of affirmative discrimination, not its outright prohibition.

benefits.[164] Stated in strong form, this view holds that people have a moral right to the benefits of color blindness[165] and that affirmative discrimination must therefore be condemned. There is no doubt that this view resonates with widely shared moral sentiments.[166] But it is important, in considering this view, to be clear about its basis.

One version of the argument appeals to universal ideals of justice or to natural law. But this position lacks the surrounding moral structure that would be necessary to support it. Distinctions on the basis of personal characteristics other than race, even immutable ones, generally are not thought to violate moral rights. If the question is pressed why race should be treated differently, the answer seems to be founded not in natural law but in conventional social meanings. As a matter of social fact, racial distinctions have had a clear meaning, involving the assertion of moral inferiority,[167] and that meaning has been deemed singularly wrong and pernicious.

Once the objection is rooted in social meanings and understandings, however, there is a clear distinction between racial quotas based on exclusionary animus and those, motivated by hatred toward none, that undertake not to stigmatize or exclude any group but to compensate for past social injustices.[168] To say that stigmatizing racial classifications are morally impermissible does not entail that noninsulting distinctions must be forbidden also. Indeed, explanation of the difference suggests that the principle applicable to stigmatizing or insulting quotas should not apply to preferences that aspire only to rectification.

Even after the distinction between two kinds of preferences is established, there remains a further basis for argument. As a matter of social understanding, color blindness stands within a cluster of related values, including those associated with merit, efficiency, and autonomy.[169] Acceptance of race as a basis for distribution of

---

[164] See, e.g., BICKEL, note 53 supra, at 133.

[165] For a clear statement, though not an endorsement, of this position, see DWORKIN, TAKING RIGHTS SERIOUSLY 225 (1977).

[166] See note 152 supra.

[167] See, e.g., Wasserstrom, note 140 supra, at 584–87.

[168] See DWORKIN, note 165 supra, at 223–39; Marshall, A Comment on the Nondiscrimination Principle in a "Nation of Minorities," 93 YALE L.J. 1006, 1011–12 (1984).

[169] See Fallon, note 56 supra, at 834–40.

jobs and other benefits might threaten all these values. For the response to this argument, the objector will need to wait. To arguments that other values give rise to moral rights against affirmative discrimination, we shall respond below. Here we claim only that affirmative discrimination offends no right not to be morally derogated on account of race.

2. Racial Preferences and Moral Rights

Opponents sometimes argue that affirmative action and race-conscious remedies violate moral rights held by "dispreferred" whites to achieve whatever benefits their talents and efforts otherwise would bring them.[170] This argument requires one of two assumptions. The first is that people have moral rights—for reasons related to merit, but not uniquely dependent on it—to any job that a freely operating labor market (regulated only by the antidiscrimination principle) would allot them. Alternatively, the argument might assume that there is a moral right to have jobs distributed on the basis of merit itself.

The argument is stronger if premised on the moral sanctity of a free labor market. This position would draw support from the personal autonomy argument for freedom of contract, and it would be buttressed by the widely shared notion that it is desirable to reward individual effort and productivity, as a free market will tend to do. Moreover, there is no doubting the central role of the market as an engine of distribution—and, the argument would run, of distributive justice—in the American economy. Beyond the subsistence provisions of various welfare programs, and a few specific restraints such as the antidiscrimination principle, the sum of freely made economic decisions—decisions to buy and sell, hire and fire, work and invest, give and bequeath—defines the principal features of the economic, and, many would argue, the "just" landscape.[171]

It is not enough, however, to show that the market does in fact

---

[170] See, *e.g.*, BICKEL, note 53 *supra*, at 133–34. Under this argument it also might be wrong to deny employers the right to contract with the most meritorious applicant for a job.

[171] For a celebrated elaboration of a libertarian conception of distributive justice, see NOZICK, ANARCHY, STATE, AND UTOPIA (1974). Reduced to a maxim, Nozick's theory of distributive justice holds: "From each according to what he chooses to do, to each according to what he makes for himself (perhaps with the contracted aid of others) and what others choose to do for him and choose to give him of what they've been given previously (under this maxim) and haven't yet expended or transferred." *Id.* at 160.

have a large role in determining distributions of jobs and other opportunities. To succeed, the argument needs a moral theory that shows the justness of the market itself, such that redistributive intervention is forbidden. This is harder to establish. The concept of merit will not bear the moral weight of demonstrating that justice requires an unalloyed free market. First, merit itself cannot be adequately identified objectively as a standard by which the market could be tested. Although there has been some historical consistency in the traits that society has valued, merit is a concept intrinsically bound up with human interests, desires and purposes that are subject to change.[172] For example, at one time a society might place a high value on the ability to split rails with an axe or to do addition without a computer. In other eras these capacities may count for little. As a result, merit is not a concept external to the market, but, on the contrary, one more often defined within it: merit consists of those talents for which the market is willing to pay. A concept frequently defined by the market, merit cannot provide an independent justification for adherence to market principles.

Second, even within a market—with "merit" defined in terms of ability to satisfy existing societal desires and tastes—there is only an attenuated connection between the principles of "market freedom" and of "rewards to merit." On the whole, the market can be expected to sort people into the jobs for which they are best suited by their relative talents and productivity. If so, it will lure the ablest people into the most important jobs, help to maximize the productive output of the society, and reward people for their personal talents and achievements. But these are the expected by-products of a market, not its governing rules. No legal compulsion demands that talent and effort be rewarded. Nepotism seems a relatively common practice. And other reasons may cause merit to go unnoticed or unrewarded.

If it is to be established at all, the moral inviolability of the market—and the justification for the outcomes that it produces—would need to be justified morally by what Robert Nozick has termed an "historical" or "entitlement" theory of distributive jus-

---

[172] See Fallon, note 56 *supra*, at 823–25.

tice.[173] In contrast with "patterned" or "substantive" theories,[174] an entitlement theory tests the justice of distributive shares—including wealth, jobs, and opportunities—mostly by the process through which the distribution occurs. An entitlement theory posits as its ultimate, justifying value respect for the free, individual choices through which the market functions.[175] Any interference with the natural process of free exchange—including employment decisions providing rewards to merit—is presumptively illegitimate.

Even within an entitlement theory, however, process and liberty do not alone account for patterns of economic distribution. As people begin to exercise autonomy, some are endowed with enormous material and educational advantages, others with none. Entitlement theories lodge no per se objection against unequal starting points; liberty upsets any patterns that a free society might attempt to impose. But, even if it is not required to demonstrate affirmatively that the original distribution is just, if it is to establish that free market choices cannot fairly be interfered with, an entitlement theory must at least require that the structure of starting points not have been reached unjustly.[176] In the absence of just acquisitions, it would be unfair to permit people to exploit assets that confer competitive advantages in the pursuit of scarce opportunities and resources. For example, it would be unfair to allow a thief or the recipient of stolen funds to exploit the stolen wealth to purchase scarce goods in competition with other potential buyers. The unfairness would be measurable not only by its effect on the initial victim of theft, but on his heirs and on others subsequently subjected to a competitive disadvantage.

---

[173] See NOZICK, note 171 supra, at 149–82.

[174] See id. at 155–60. Nozick defines principles of distributive justice as "patterned" if they provide that distributive shares should depend on substantive criteria of desert, such as "moral merit" or "usefulness to society." See id. at 156.

[175] Nozick's objection to patterned or substantive theories is that liberty upsets patterns. See id. at 160–62.

[176] Nozick defines a distribution as just "if it arises from another just distribution by legitimate means." Id. at 151. This formulation presupposes justice in the original acquisition of holdings. Id. at 150. Where past injustices have occurred, Nozick recognizes the need for a theory of rectification of injustice in holdings. Id. at 152. He does not, however, attempt to provide any theory of rectification that would answer such questions as "How far back must one go in wiping clean the slate of historical injustices?" Id.

The most conspicuous asset in a market economy is financial wealth. But similarly important are personal assets such as the testable intelligence and various occupational skills that an individual brings to the labor market. Talents and abilities may seem conceptually difficult to separate from the person possessing them.[177] But premarket experiences, including education and nurture, importantly influence aptitude and employability.[178] Analogously to the transfer of wealth, with which they are correlated if not causally linked, educational and cultural advantages, most visibly manifest in measurable aptitudes, are subject to charges of unjust acquisitions at the beginning of an historical chain.[179]

In the context of American history, past racial injustices have permeated the existing structure of economic and educational advantages that are crucial in the market's apportionments of jobs and material benefits. As passed through the generations, unjust acquisitions continue to give rise to comparative advantages—measurable in disparities between racial groups—in a competitive economic and social community. Citing past racial injustices, many of them having the sanction of law, a group-based argument therefore succeeds at least in showing that an historical theory of distributive justice, even within its own terms, could not establish the necessary predicates to demonstrate the justice of market allocations of jobs.[180] In other words, an entitlement theory cannot establish the

---

[177] See *id.* at 214–31; SANDEL, LIBERALISM AND THE LIMITS OF JUSTICE 77–95 (1982).

[178] See generally JENCKS, note 156 *supra*.

[179] We can imagine, for example, that a thief steals a sum of money, half of which he hides and half of which he spends on education. The education, as much as the money saved, may be traced back to roots in an unjust acquisition. The immediate difference between the hidden money and the education is that the money retains a tangible status, independent of the thief, while the education is now literally inseparable from the thief himself. He has been transformed by his education; it helps to constitute him as he now is. Because this is so, the unjust acquisition of education could not be rectified by taking the thief's education away from him, or by restoring him to the intellectual state that he would have had "but for" his unjust acquisition. But it may be possible, and morally appropriate, to impose limitations on the thief's capacity to "exploit" his educationally fostered talents by, for example, denying him a job or by placing a special tax on his income.

[180] The argument is sometimes made that past injustices have only a relative brief "half-life," after which their effects and significance should be regarded as morally dissipated. Fried, *Is Liberty Possible?* in TANNER LECTURES ON HUMAN VALUES (1982), at 103; *cf.* Sher, *Ancient Wrongs and Modern Rights*, 10 PHIL. & PUB. AFF. 3 (1980). The premise for this argument seems to be that anyone's present circumstances result from some combination of material advantage and of personal character and effort, and that the latter factors progressively overwhelm the significance of past wrongs. If the claim is empirical, its accuracy is dubious with respect to black Americans. Nearly universal discrimination against blacks,

injustice of the intervention into the market that is commended by the Model of Social Justice.[181]

Once the argument for the justice of market distributions is shown to be problematic, it becomes difficult to argue from the second assumption, that people have a moral right to employment or other rewards based on their measurable intelligence or talents or similar merit characteristics. As argued above, merit cannot be identified independently of societal tastes, values, and preferences, such as those that the market reflects. Although society may wish to encourage employment decisions based on traditional merit traits, a person has no moral right to have employers make their decisions on the basis, for example, of measurable intelligence.[182] If employers began instead to favor congeniality, or to hire athletic heroes or military veterans, a rejected applicant would have no valid claim of injustice.

The claim of injustice is no stronger where society, to serve legitimate purposes, makes a political decision to change its structure of opportunities and rewards. For example the nation may decide to give preferences to veterans, in order to recognize the sacrifices that they made for their country.[183] Or a community may decide to give local residents a preference in work projects being funded out of local taxes.[184] Or a poverty program may allot jobs to

---

spread over a long period of time, seems not only to have caused direct economic deprivation but also to have transformed many of the victims' behaviors in self-defeating ways. See Jencks, note 65 *supra*. If the argument is moral, it must rely on harsh and contentious principles that would threaten to trivialize a historical theory of distributive justice; after a few generations, it would justify nearly any structure or advantage and disadvantage.

[181] In contrast to arguments that undertake to trace the individualized consequences of historical deprivations, our argument aspires only to show that the existing structure of distributions is tainted at its foundations by historically unjust acquisitions. In other words, justice does not forbid group-based redistributive policies. This is a group-based argument, and group arguments for corrective justice generally have been thought susceptible to the objection that only individuals are entitled to compensation for past injustices. But this objection does not defeat, because it does not address, our argument that the society's existing structure of distributive starting points, tainted at base by historical injustices, cannot be defended on grounds of distributive justice, and that group-based redistributive programs—justified on other grounds of morality and social policy—therefore ought not to be held impermissible.

[182] See Dworkin, note 165 *supra*, at 225.

[183] See Koelfgen v. Jackson, 355 F. Supp. 243 (D. Minn. 1972), *aff'd. mem.*, 410 U.S. 976 (1973); *cf.* Personnel Adm'n of Mass. v. Feeney, 442 U.S. 256 (1979).

[184] See White v. Massachusetts Council of Constn. Employers, Inc., 103 S.Ct. 1042 (1983); but *cf.* United Trade Council of Camden v. Mayer and Council, 104 S.Ct. 1020 (1984).

the poorest candidates, not the most deserving. Each of these policies may have the effect of excluding the applicant who otherwise would be regarded as the most able. But none offends any individual right to have only traditional merit characteristics count in awarding jobs. If the defeated applicant has a compelling argument, it must be that he has been dispreferred for reasons that are themselves morally impermissible.

C.   THE MODEL OF SOCIAL JUSTICE: WHO BENEFITS?

So far we have asserted a positive case for affirmative discrimination, tied closely to the special status of blacks in American history. We have also rejected three familiar arguments that justice forbids intervention into the market to achieve redistribution along group lines. But an important question left open involves the relationship between our positive and our negative arguments.

From one perspective, the negative arguments may seem to prove unsettlingly more than do the positive ones. If interference with a largely meritocratic labor market cannot be defeated by the arguments considered, have we introduced a regime in which any group-based redistribution whatsoever must be held morally permissible? The answer is no. First, despite our abstract arguments against the moral inviolability of traditional merit criteria and of the labor market, conventional moral norms would hold it unfair to impose excessive costs of rectification on particular individuals, based on a predicate of social instead of individual wrongdoing. We accept limitations arising from this concern. Second, our negative arguments merely show that particular appeals to "justice" fail to demonstrate the moral necessity of the status quo. The negative arguments do not mandate particular redistributions, and, more important, they do not deny that other moral considerations impose limits on the scope of defensible changes. Fairness requires that like cases should be treated alike and that discriminations should be based on morally relevant differences. To the extent that redistribution is mandated by the government, the basis for the prescribed allocations would need to satisfy a standard of moral relevance.[185] Similarly, within the private sector, the normally governing value scheme holds that race and certain other group-based

---

[185] Goldman, note 123 *supra*, at 23.

characteristics represent impermissible criteria for the distribution of jobs. Even if there is no "right" to be hired on the basis of particular talents, other moral concerns—especially to respect expectations that the society has fostered and to honor values to which it generally remains committed—demand a presumption against group-based allocations of employment opportunities.[186] Under what circumstances then are group-based preferences appropriate in the labor market?

In addressing this question, we assume throughout that racial or ethnic preferences would require a modification of selection processes linked to merit or to the ability to perform a particular job. But this assumption will not always be correct, and the bounds of its validity define an important limitation of our argument. There are contexts in which racial or minority status may enhance a person's ability to fulfill a particular function in employment. For example, a black policeman may win the trust of ghetto residents more easily and therefore perform more successfully than a white; a teacher from a minority background may communicate more successfully with, and provide greater inspiration to, minority students. In such contexts, because racial or ethnic background is relevant to job performance, it serves the same function as more traditional indicia of merit and would seem compatible with distribution on the basis of talent and productivity.[187] This, however, is not the type of racial preference with which we are concerned here. Our arguments address the more typical and more problematic case in which group characteristics presumptively provide no valid measure of individual capability.[188]

---

[186] *Cf.* DREYFUSS & LAWRENCE, THE BAKKE CASE: THE POLITICS OF INEQUALITY 96 (1979) ("In a society in which men and women expect to succeed by hard work and to better themselves by making themselves better, it is no trivial moral wrong to proceed systematically to defeat this expectation") (quoting Alexander Bickel).

[187] Race is most likely to be relevant in this sense when a job involves the performance of a service, and the recipients of that service are more comfortable with, or possess greater confidence in, members of some groups than of others. A difficulty about allowing the assimilation of race to more traditional merit traits, even in these contexts, is that some whites may be more comfortable with, or otherwise prefer to be served by, other whites. In response to such attitudes by the white majority, a traditional function of merit criteria has been to affirm the moral and economic irrelevance of racial and similar criteria as indicia of individual talent and productivity. See Fallon, note 56 *supra*, at 837.

[188] Racial or ethnic background is likely to enhance the ability to perform a job only in a relatively narrow range of contexts. It has little if any relevance to the firefighting positions involved in *Stotts*, for example. Where applicable, our justifications for affirmative discrimi-

1. The Justification of Group Selection

Framed initially as an expression of the antidiscrimination principle, Title VII extended its protections broadly, forbidding any discrimination based on race, sex, or national origin. So construed, the statute reflected a moral judgment that group-based bias and animus have no rightful place in the labor market. In the years since 1964, however, Congress, the executive branch, and the courts have moved increasingly from the individualistic values associated with the antidiscrimination principle to a group conception of equality of opportunity, expressed in various forms and programs of affirmative discrimination.

Superimposed on the original structure of Title VII, the group approach to employment discrimination has tended to extend its affirmative preferences as broadly as the antidiscrimination principle establishes prohibitions against prejudiced wrongdoing. It is far from clear, however, that all groups protected by the antidiscrimination principle should receive the benefits of group-based affirmative discrimination. It is possible, of course, to imagine a societal transition from free market and meritocratic principles to a group-based conception of distributive justice, with jobs allotted on proportional bases. But this approach, requiring a general restructuring of the labor market, would also represent a sharp departure from traditional practice and values, which hold race irrelevant to nearly all moral questions and prescribe respect for individual autonomy, talents, and efforts. Indeed, the strongest arguments for affirmative discrimination generally have acknowledged as much. Instead of proffering a general defense of racialism as a theory of distributive justice, they have built upon the intuition that the historical circumstances of black Americans define a morally special case. Consistently with the intuition of moral uniqueness, an extraordinary justification, going beyond that needed to earn the protection of the antidiscrimination principle, should be required before a group qualifies for affirmative discrimination.

The appropriate requirements cannot be defined by any process of logical deduction. Our justification for affirmative action for

nation sweep more broadly. It is possible, however, that an argument founded on the relevance of race to a particular job might justify preference for a nonblack minority applicant who would not qualify for a racial preference within the terms of the argument that we develop.

blacks began with a moral intuition of appropriateness, supported by three arguments. Some clarity may be gained if those arguments are restated as conditions for affirmative discrimination: (i) there has been an historic pattern of legally sanctioned, group-based discrimination; (ii) the legacy of historical discrimination includes a current condition of group disadvantage, resulting in social problems at least partly remediable through affirmative discrimination; and (iii) social and psychological factors give current meaning to the group as more than an arbitrary collection of individuals.

Reflecting an effort to explain and justify the moral intuition that affirmative discrimination represents an appropriate response to historical discrimination against American blacks, these conditions can be used to test the arguments for affirmative discrimination advanced on behalf of other groups. If their application to other cases should yield consequences that seem jarring or intolerable, then the original justifications might need to be modified or abandoned, or the initial intuition possibly reconsidered. In point of fact, however, these conditions do not call for affirmative discrimination of unsettling breadth. When any of these conditions is not satisfied, the case for affirmative discrimination seems to us to be significantly weaker.

a) Japanese and Chinese Americans. Is it justifiable for the advantages of affirmative discrimination to be denied to Japanese and Chinese Americans, racial groups that did suffer from severe and officially sanctioned discrimination in the United States? Historical treatment of these groups has included many wrongs, some of them within the domain of government responsibility. Where the direct victims can be identified, corrective justice would make reparations appropriate. But the argument for group-based affirmative discrimination in the job market is much weaker. Were such programs implemented, the beneficiaries would tend to be the children and grandchildren of those most directly harmed by governmentally perpetrated or sanctioned injustices. And, happily, historical wrongs have not measurably reduced the life prospects of Japanese and Chinese Americans of this generation.[189] In the absence of

---

[189] As of 1970, adult Japanese males earned 104 percent of what white males earned, while the Chinese earned 106 percent. When one controls for the influence of age, residence and schooling, however, the earnings ratios were essentially the same. See Chiswick, *An Analysis of the Earnings and Employment of Asian-American Men,* 1 J. LAB. ECON. 197 (1983).

continuing group deprivation, affirmative discrimination does not seem warranted.

b) Other racial and ethnic groups. Blacks are not the only ethnic group at the lower levels of the economic spectrum. There are Hispanic and Asian groups that may rank even below blacks in current achievements.[190] Some of them exhibit a strong sense of group identity and interdependence. Despite arguments in favor of affirmative discrimination, there is a material difference between these cases and that of American blacks, who suffered centuries of discrimination within the United States, sanctioned if not abetted by government. Successive waves of immigrant groups have come to this country, often predominantly impoverished when they entered, though commonly better off here than in the nations that they left.[191] Upon arrival, newcomers should have access to the array of public programs and services generally available to the poor in this country. They also should enjoy full protection against invidious discrimination based on race, nationality, or religion. But group-based preferences in the job market represent extraordinary action, burdensome to employers and especially to dispreferred individuals. Because their interests are inevitably affected, more should be required to justify affirmative discrimination than present group disadvantage and psychological interdependence.

Who besides blacks should receive the benefits of affirmative action?[192] This is a difficult and important question, the complexity of which we have only tried to suggest. Our effort has been to identify, regrettably only to leave, a set of moral, empirical, and jurisprudential issues that deserve more careful treatment. Ideally, inquiry would proceed at two levels. One would ask whether other groups—for example, Hispanics—or possibly "subgroups"—for example, Chicanos as a subcategory of Hispanics—satisfy all three of the conditions that we framed initially to rationalize special treatment for American blacks.[193] The other line of analysis would

---

[190] See Jencks, note 65 *supra*, at 34.

[191] See generally SOWELL, ETHNIC AMERICA (1981).

[192] We assume that North American Indians also would satisfy the conditions set out above. See Morton v. Mancari, 417 U.S. 535 (1974).

[193] Hispanics represented 6.4 percent of all U.S. residents in 1980 (vs. the 11.7 percent black share), and male Hispanics earned 76 percent of what white males earned in 1975 (vs. 73 percent for blacks), with Chicanos (who were 60 percent of all Hispanics) earning slightly less than the overall Hispanic average. See McManus, Gould, & Welsh, *Earnings of Hispanic*

further test the adequacy of the three conditions themselves to describe and to guide moral and legal choice. Treated as individually necessary to justify affirmative discrimination, the three conditions could yield results that would seem too objectionable to be countenanced. Without close inspection of individual cases, however, we are inclined to believe that a persuasive case for any racial or ethnic group's claim to affirmative discrimination would need to satisfy all of the three conditions.

c) The poor. A somewhat different issue involves claims on behalf of the poor. Invoking the ideal of equality of opportunity for people who encounter the obstacles of a deprived social, economic, or family environment, a familiar argument holds that the benefits of affirmative discrimination—if extended at all—should be based on poverty,[194] not race. Blacks suffer disproportionately more from these conditions than do whites. But because there are more poor whites than there are poor blacks, more whites presumably are denied the opportunity to develop and exercise talents to the fullest. And it is unfair, the argument continues, to deny the white poor the special help afforded to blacks.

Under the conditions that we have identified, it is not morally arbitrary to conclude that affirmative discrimination for blacks finds support in special interests and justifications that are not equally compelling in the case of the poor. Racial injustices have stigmatized blacks as a group, even those who are reasonably well off, in a way that has not happened to the poor. There also is a

---

Men: The Role of English Language Proficiency, J. LAB. ECON. 101, 107–09 (1983). Moreover, at least some of the distinctive ethnic communities within the overall Hispanic population appear to have been the target of sustained discrimination. (For an illuminating review of the relevant history in the case of Chicanos, see Lopez, *Undocumented Mexican Migration: In Search of a Just Immigration Law and Policy*, 28 UCLA L. REV. 615, 641–72 (1981).) However, when one takes account of their relative age, residence, and education, the current disparities in the earnings of Hispanics disappear (although they remain in the case of blacks). See Shapiro, *Wage Differentials among Black, Hispanic and White Young Men*, 37 INDUS. & LAB. REL. REV. 570 (1984). McManus *et al.*, *supra*, at 117–19, therefore conclude that the major obstacle faced by Hispanics is English language deficiency. In justifying affirmative discrimination for any or all Hispanic groups, a central issue is whether current lack of success in the labor market should be viewed as a legacy of discrimination or as a natural feature of their rate of immigration and assimilation. Interestingly, employment preferences for Hispanics under Executive Order 11246 appear not to have produced any significant gains in Hispanic employment (by contrast with the sharp improvement it has worked for blacks). See LEONARD, note 47 *supra*, at 127.

[194] See, *e.g.*, FISHKIN, JUSTICE, EQUAL OPPORTUNITY, AND THE FAMILY 86 (1983); GOLDMAN, note 123 *supra*, at 170–200.

unique contemporary need to surmount racial prejudice and to address race-linked social alienation. Accordingly, the logic of the case for racial preferences for blacks does not require—under the principle of like treatment for like cases—affirmative discrimination for the poor.

It is a further question, however, whether our argument would forbid affirmative discrimination to alleviate the obstacles of poverty in the labor market. We think not.[195] Affirmative discrimination for the poor differs from programs of racial preference in at least two relevant respects. First, in light of their history, racial preferences deserve to be regarded as suspect. This is not to say that affirmative discrimination should never be approved; we have argued precisely the contrary. But racial preferences should be tested against a more stringent standard than those based on other factors.

Second, unlike racial preferences, affirmative discrimination for the poor can be justified in individual terms, without reference to group concepts. If poverty is viewed as a barrier to equality of opportunity, then the purpose of providing equal opportunity justifies a preference for all (or nearly all) individual beneficiaries. There is no need to defend, in group terms, a preference for someone who could not be characterized as individually deserving within the morally legitimate purposes of the program. It is a special problem of racial preferences that they may visit their benefits on persons who seem little disadvantaged by past racial injustice.[196]

2. The Selection of Individual Beneficiaries

While the justifications for affirmative action relate to the situations of blacks as a group, preferences in the labor market confer their benefits on black individuals. Whatever group benefits may ensue, they are attenuated. One form of criticism, which any justification for affirmative discrimination must meet, focuses on the

---

[195] Like preferences based on race, affirmative discrimination for the poor would defeat expectations that hiring will be based on presently demonstrable merit. But these expectations are neither universally respected nor morally inviolable. See notes 170–84 *supra* and accompanying text.

[196] Although the expectations of dispreferred persons may be defeated in either case, it is a weaker expectation that hiring will be based on "pure merit" than that hiring cannot be based on race. See Fallon, note 56 *supra*, at 837.

situations of individual beneficiaries. The distributional difficulty
arises from the nature of the labor market. The bigger and better
employers tend to be the major targets of government policies—
including disparate impact theory under Title VII and the strictures of Executive Order 11246—that virtually require affirmative
discrimination. Since these employers are likely to prefer and bid
for the best qualified blacks to fill the higher-ranking jobs,[197] the
concern is that an excessive share of the benefits will be concentrated on the more advantaged blacks,[198] from whom the historical
burden of race is now largely removed.[199] This is not to deny that
blacks on average still suffer much more from the obstacles to
advancement presented by poverty and family structure.[200] The
point of the argument, rather, is that a sharp economic divide
appears to have opened up within the black community, such that
it is no longer appropriate to treat blacks as an undifferentiated
group.[201] We can no longer be confident, this criticism asserts, that

---

[197] Both LEONARD, note 48 supra, at 131–34, and Smith and Welsh, note 47 supra, at 281–
83, found that the employment impact of the Executive Order among professionals and
managers was more than double that felt by black workers overall, with essentially no impact
on the demand for black laborers or service workers. An intriguing aspect of these trends is
that the differential impact of affirmative discrimination comes in spite of the fact that federal
judges have taken a much less aggressive approach toward "upper-level jobs" under Title
VII. See Bartholet, Application of Title VII to Jobs in High Places, 95 HARV. L. REV. 945
(1982).

[198] See, e.g., FISHKIN, note 194 supra, at 92. There is substantial evidence of this trend.
For example, the differential in black/white earnings of male college graduates shot up from
59 in 1965 to 84 in 1979, whereas the rate for black high school graduates made only modest
improvement, from 67 to 74 in that same period. See Jencks, note 65 supra, at 36. Indeed, by
the early seventies, the young (twenty-five to twenty-nine) black male college graduate (the
person who came into the labor market under the umbrella of Title VII and the Executive
Order) actually earned more (1.09) than his white counterpart, as also did the black, college-
educated couple with both husband and wife working, regardless of age. See SOWELL, CIVIL
RIGHTS: RHETORIC OR REALITY 80 (1982).

[199] Econometric analysis of these statistical trends shows that for young blacks, pre-labor-
market characteristics have essentially the same influence as they have for whites on hourly
earnings (.17 vs. .16) and occupational status (.20 vs. .23). See Freeman, note 159 supra, at
266–67. This is not to deny that black youths suffer disproportionately more from a disadvantaged background. But when one controls for the latter variables, there is very little
difference between the achievement of young blacks and that of whites in occupational status
and weekly earnings, and drastically less than is true of the older blacks whose prospects
were largely fixed before Title VII and Executive Order 11246 came into force (.03 vs. .15
variance in occupational position and .03 vs. .32 in weekly earnings). Ibid.

[200] Freeman found that, on average, black male youths were considerably worse off than
their white counterparts in parental years of schooling (7.9 vs. 10.5), parental median income
(7.7 vs. 8.5), and in female-headed homes (40 percent vs. 12 percent). See id. at 257.

[201] One tangible index is to be found in the difference between the share of black income
going to the upper 40 percent of black families and that going to the bottom 40 percent. This

the benefits of affirmative discrimination will eventually trickle down to the poor black in the urban ghetto,[202] the very black whose interests are so often invoked to justify racial preferences in the first place.

This is a substantial objection, but ultimately it is not persuasive. First of all, at the time the seeds of affirmative discrimination were sown in the late 1960s and early 1970s,[203] it was clear and demonstrable that the bare fact of race, independent of poverty and family background, was a major barrier to black achievement. This powerful index of entrenched racism affected blacks of all economic classes. Against the background of historical discrimination, not yet purged from the economy, there existed ample justification for a vigorous governmental effort to break down the unfavorable link between blackness and life prospects for the black middle and working classes—even if that effort would not necessarily suffice at the lowest levels to elevate the black ghetto classes from abject poverty. The effort that was undertaken took the form of affirmative discrimination in the employment market, a policy that the Supreme Court tacitly ratified in *Weber*. And, viewed from one perspective, affirmative discrimination has been remarkably successful. Now, class variables such as poverty and education explain better than race the occupational and income status of blacks and whites alike. It is far from clear, however, what this evidence "proves." Though often cited in arguments against affirmative discrimination, it surely does not show that programs of racial preference should be condemned as unjustified at their inception. If the assertion is that affirmative discrimination now benefits the "wrong" blacks, the argument must instead be that affirmative discrimination has done its work and should therefore be dismantled, possibly to be replaced by more carefully targeted programs.

---

differential has widened considerably from 1964 (when it was 69 to 15) to 1982 (when it was 72 to 13). The disparity is now significantly greater among blacks than it is among whites where the comparable ratio was 66 to 17 in 1982. See CURRENT POPULATION REPORT, note 2 *supra*, at 47–48.

[202] For a provocative discussion of this issue, and of possible alternative policies, see WILSON, note 43 *supra*, at 144–54; see also MURRAY, LOSING GROUND (1984).

[203] This roughly was the period of *Griggs*, the early court of appeals decisions prescribing quota remedies for Title VII violations, and Congress's seeming approval of both the emerging case law and Executive Order 11246 when it enacted the 1972 amendments to Title VII. See notes 104–11 *supra* and accompanying text.

As to this position, the evidence is not yet strong enough to be persuasive. At most, recent statistics establish that race no longer has a significant influence on the occupational status and hourly earnings of young, employed blacks. Even with respect to these figures, however, there remains a sharp dispute among labor economists,[204] and we are some distance from a final verdict. It is also significant that the statistical trends underlying this debate involve the achievements and relative positions of black workers under the umbrella of Executive Order 11246 and other incentives to affirmative discrimination.[205] Certainly there is no guarantee that current patterns would continue if such support were suddenly removed. Finally, we are not persuaded that class divisions have eroded what we have called the group status of the black community. Recent voting patterns, for example, suggest a widely shared black interest in the success of black candidacies. Similarly in the employment market, the achievements of some blacks may lift the aspirations of others, or may combat group-based alienation and despair associated with systems of racial caste.[206]

Our position does not purport to embody ultimate truths. It is accepted that affirmative discrimination is justifiable only as a temporary corrective device.[207] Its termination should be signaled either by the elimination of the identifiable residues of past discrimination or by the failure of affirmative discrimination as a rational corrector. Candidly, however, our position is to insist on a positive showing that American blacks are no longer held back by the color of their skin.

---

[204] Compare Freeman, note 159 *supra*, and Jud & Walker, *Racial Differences in the Returns to Schooling and Experience among Prime-Age Males*, 17 J. HUM. RESOURCES 622 (1982); Brown, *Black-White Earnings Ratios since the Civil Rights Act of 1964: The Importance of Labor Market Dropouts*, 1984 Q. J. ECON. 33; with Butler and Heckman, *The Goverment's Impact on the Labor Market Status of Black Americans: A Critical Review*, in HAUSMAN et al. (eds.), EQUAL RIGHTS AND INDUSTRIAL RELATIONS 235 (1977); Lazear, *The Narrowing of Black-White Differentials Is Illusory*, 69 AM. ECON. REV. 553 (1979); and Shapiro, note 193 *supra*. However this particular debate is resolved, there remains a clear link between being black and being unemployed, with unemployment statistics causing a considerable difference in annual earnings. Freeman found that while the influence of race on annual earnings is far greater for older black males (.34), there still remains a substantial effect for young blacks (.12), more than he was able to locate for occupational position (.04) and weekly earnings (.03). See Freeman, note 159 *supra*.

[205] See note 48 *supra*.

[206] See Fiss, note 74 *supra*.

[207] See, *e.g.*, Steelworkers v. Weber, 443 U.S. 193, 208 (1979); Regents of the University of California v. Bakke, 438 U.S. 265, 403 (1978) (separate opinion of Blackmun, J.).

V. THE MODEL OF SOCIAL JUSTICE: WHO PAYS?

Even if affirmative discrimination can be justified in principle, there remains within our Model of Social Justice the further
question what burdens reasonably may be imposed on individual
whites. There would be no serious problem if the costs of affirmative discrimination could be discharged collectively: for example,
by raising money through the general tax system to be used as
reparations, as has been suggested for the mistreatment of Japanese-Americans during World War II. But affirmative discrimination is seldom paid for in this way. Employment preferences to
blacks most often come at the expense of individual whites, who
lose jobs that otherwise would be theirs.

In *Stotts* the Supreme Court confronted the problem of assessing
burdens in the context of seniority layoffs. This is a singularly
difficult situation. Layoffs can undoubtedly pose a serious threat
to the maintenance, let alone the momentum, of black progress
achieved through recruitment and hiring. But the remedy usually
endorsed by the Model of Group Justice—the layoff of senior
whites to preserve current levels of black employment within an
employer's work force—exacts enormous costs from displaced
white workers, who have often invested the most productive years
of their lives in attaining the security normally associated with
seniority. Moreover, as a matter of both industrial practice and of
positive law under Title VII's § 703(h), the importance of seniority
is pervasively acknowledged and respected. In light of these factors, insofar as *Stotts* barred the federal courts from simply evicting
innocent senior whites to preserve the jobs of junior blacks, its
holding ought to be approved.

But affirmative discrimination does not ordinarily require the
displacement of white incumbents from their jobs. Even in situations such as that in *Stotts*, the sole choice may not be between
laying off junior blacks or senior whites. Alternative possibilities
include concentration of the burden on the employer, whose statutory violations provided the predicate for judicial action, or distributing the burden across wider segments of the work force or the
community. More importantly, there are compelling differences
between racial preferences that result in seniority layoffs and those
that operate at the level of initial hiring. This distinction between
layoff and hiring preferences was actually reflected in Title VII

case law until the early 1980s,[208] and it is supported by persuasive arguments of policy and public morality. Despite the Supreme Court's contrary dictum in *Stotts*, the rationale that best justifies its holding as to seniority layoffs does not imply that affirmative discrimination is inappropriate at the hiring stage.

A. SENIORITY SYSTEMS AND LAYOFFS

The importance of seniority—the seemingly mundane fact of length of service with a particular employer—is recognized in both industrial practice and in federal law. The vast majority of union contracts stipulate that seniority is the most important factor in deciding which workers are to be laid off.[209] And while management is much less likely to tie its hands through a written policy in nonunion employment, the actual practice even in nonunion firms reveals seniority to be far the most prominent factor in layoff decisions.[210] Unilateral adoption of this policy by nonunion firms shows that the institution of seniority reflects values widely shared by employers and workers alike. Congress echoed these popular sentiments when it inserted explicit protection of seniority systems into § 703(h) of Title VII, a provision that the Supreme Court has

---

[208] Compare the cases collected by Justice Blackmun in *Stotts*, 104 S.Ct. at 2606 n.10, upholding hiring preferences, with, *e.g.*, Chance v. Board of Examiners, 534 F.2d 993 (2d Cir. 1976); Jersey Central Power & Light Co. v. Electrical Workers, 508 F.2d 687 (3rd Cir. 1975); Watkins v. United Steelworkers, 516 F.2d 41 (5th Cir. 1975); and Waters v. Wisconsin Steelworks of International Harvester, 502 F.2d 1309 (7th Cir. 1974), all rejecting racial preferences in layoffs precipitated by the recession of the middle 1970s. Not until the recession of the early 1980s did several of the courts of appeals change direction and mandate layoff quotas overriding seniority rights, most commonly in cases involving public employers. See, *e.g.*, Oliver v. Kalamazoo Bd. of Educ. (6th Cir. 1983); Boston Chapter NAACP v. Beecher, 679 F.2d 965 (1st Cir. 1982); Stotts v. Memphis Fire Dept., 679 F.2d 541 (6th Cir. 1982); and Brown v. Neeb, 6434 F.2d 551 (6th Cir. 1981) (Toledo); Morgan v. O'Bryant, 671 F.2d 23 (1st Cir. 1982) (Boston); Arthur v. Nyquist, 712 F.2d 816 (2d Cir. 1983) (Buffalo). *Cf.* Tangren v. Wackenhut Serv., 658 F.2d 705 (9th Cir. 1981) (upholding voluntary affirmative discrimination in layoffs). For illuminating scholarly discussions of layoffs under Title VII, see Summers & Love, *Work Sharing as an Alternative to Layoffs by Seniority: Title VII Remedies in a Depression*, 124 U. PA. L. REV. 893 (1976); Edwards, *Race Discrimination in Employment: What Price Equality?* 1976 UNIV. ILL. L. FORUM 572 (1976); Poplin, *Fair Employment in a Depressed Economy: The Layoff Problem*, 23 UCLA L. REV. 177 (1975).

[209] A recent review of union contracts found that three-quarters of all collective agreements, including 90 percent of those in manufacturing, singled out seniority as the dominant factor in layoffs. See FREEMAN & MEDOFF, WHAT DO UNIONS DO? (1984).

[210] In one recent study, 86 percent of the surveyed nonunion firms made seniority the dominant factor in layoffs, and 42 percent even responded that they would never lay off a senior employee and keep the junior. See Abraham & Medoff, *Length of Service and Layoffs within Union and Nonunion Work Groups*, INDUS. & LAB. REL. REV. 87 (1984).

expansively and vigorously implemented.[211] The Justices, however, have never sought to explain why seniority rights are so important as a matter of sound policy or moral principle that § 703(h) warrants the expansive interpretation that it has received. The question for us is why seniority—in the layoff context—might deserve to be accorded such respect.

1. Seniority and Equity

Perhaps the most common rationale for the use of seniority[212] is that it furnishes an objective, "bright line" rule—length of service with the firm—that protects employees from arbitrariness and favoritism by lower echelon supervisors[213] and relieves management from having to make and defend contentious judgments about the relative qualifications of employees. But this argument will not suffice as a reason to override affirmative action for blacks. A number of criteria could serve the values of objectivity and nonarbitrariness: in particular, the creation of dual seniority systems—one for blacks and one for whites. Approved by the federal courts in Memphis and Boston, this approach has the added virtue of preserving the benefits of affirmative discrimination.

Another familiar argument holds that length of service with a firm is a fairly reliable rule-of-thumb index of workers' relative productivity, reflecting the degree of training and experience in a particular job. If this were true, one could understand why, when a layoff looms, even nonunion firms voluntarily choose to retain their senior workers.[214] But this argument fails to accord with the

---

[211] See, e.g., International Bhd. of Teamsters v. United States 431 U.S. 324 (1977) (reversing the unanimous view of the courts of appeals that an existing seniority system that perpetuated the effects of past discrimination could not be said to be "bona fide" within the meaning of S.703(h)); American Tobacco Co. v. Patterson, 456 U.S. 63 (1982) (extending the Teamsters ruling to post-1965 seniority systems); California Brewers Ass'n v. Bryant, 444 U.S. 598 (1980).

[212] See Cooper and Sobol, *Seniority and Testing under Fair Employment Laws*, 82 HARV. L. REV. 1589, 1604–05 (1969).

[213] Reliance on objective criteria may be especially important to blacks, because racial prejudice more easily infects subjective evaluation processes. See Bartholet, note 197 *supra*. Significantly, the relative situation of black workers is improved more than that of whites under collective bargaining, not simply in terms of compensation, see Holzer, *Unions and the Labor Market Status of Whites and Minority Youth*, 35 INDUS. & LAB. REL. REV. 392 (1982), but also in terms of tenure and advancement in employment with the firm. See Leigh, *Unions and Nonwage Racial Discrimination*, 32 INDUS. & LAB. REL. REV. 439 (1979).

[214] See Parsons, *Specific Human Capital: An Application to Quit Rates and Layoff Rates*, 80 J. POL. ECON. 1120 (1972).

facts.[215].Recent research shows that younger employees are relatively more productive than those with longer service, especially in light of the increasing cost of compensating more senior employees who typically receive salary increments and enjoy higher-cost fringe benefits based on length of service.[216]

Happily, however, this fact—that the standard compensation package in modern employment is tilted in favor of senior employees even though performance and productivity eventually decline with length of service—suggests a subtler but more powerful explanation. Employers are not irrational in adopting seniority rules, nor are employees irrational in welcoming them. From the employer's perspective, this compensation arrangement enhances productivity by reducing turnover within its work force and reinforcing the employees' commitment to a career with the firm.[217] By the same token, the employee has an interest in attaining the security afforded by the implicit promise of gradual upward progress in earnings, as well as in achieving the stability in his personal life associated with secure employment.

Seniority is the glue that holds together this mutually beneficial arrangement for stable career employment. To the worker, seniority guarantees that his employer, having obtained the benefit of a higher performance/compensation ratio during the early years of employment, will not replace its older employees when that ratio becomes unfavorable. At the same time, a strong commitment to seniority serves the long-run interest of employers, by allowing them to make credible promises of de facto tenure to their newer employees[218] in order to obtain their consent to an overall compensation package.

---

[215] See Cornfield, *Seniority, Human Capital, and Layoffs: A Case Study*, 21 INDUS. REL. 352 (1982).

[216] See Medoff & Abraham, *Experience, Performance and Earnings*, 95 Q. J. ECON. 703 (1980); Medoff & Abraham, *Are Those Paid More Really More Productive? The Case of Experience*, 16 J. HUM. RESOURCES 186 (1982).

[217] Career employment reduces the cost of hiring and training replacements, see OKUN, PRICES AND QUANTITIES 49–80 (1981); it is conducive to the kind of cohesive teamwork essential in a social system of production, see WILLIAMSON, MARKETS AND HIERARCHIES 57–81 (1979); and it enhances the confidence of experienced employees in transmitting their lore to new workers without being concerned about endangering their own personal prospects. See THUROW, DANGEROUS CURRENTS 196–214 (1983). As a result, a system of stable career employment is much more productive than a casual, at-will relationship—a lesson from the Japanese experience.

[218] The promise is subject, of course, to exceptions allowing dismissal for personal misconduct or especially poor performance.

Once a seniority regime is established, an employee working under it knows that in return for staying (rather than accepting or even looking for better jobs elsewhere), he is improving his relative ranking in the system. In a real sense, the added seniority credit for each period worked represents an intangible but crucial aspect of the return on the employee's labor (albeit one he cannot "spend" but rather must invest with the firm). At a certain point, the worker achieves the equivalent of tenure, because he knows that he is sufficiently high on the seniority list to be protected against nearly any risk of permanent job loss.[219] At that point, the rights and expectations surrounding seniority make up what is probably the most valuable capital asset that the worker "owns," worth even more than the current equity in his home.

Although less subject to quantification, a set of psychological concerns also supports the employee's interest in seniority. In American society, a job helps to define who a person is: not merely what the person does at work, but how he thinks of himself and the purposes of his life. As a worker invests the most productive years of his life in a particular job or a particular firm, the stable, continuing employment may play an increasing role in self-definition.

It is true that the traumatic features of a layoff—both economic and psychological—cannot be measured solely by their impact on senior whites. In layoffs where affirmative discrimination is also of concern, less senior black workers also face financial and emotional losses, and their well-being should not be ignored. Under some circumstances a partial accommodation, in which no one loses a job entirely, will be feasible. Sometimes, however, a clear choice must be made, and the question then concerns the appropriate content of the governing legal rule. Three arguments support the choice for seniority. First, whatever the interests of a junior black, the otherwise protected rights of a senior white provide a measure of the sacrifice that a layoff would demand of him to advance the policies of affirmative discrimination. And the burden may be very large indeed. Second, even if the relevant questions are seen as compara-

---

[219] Seniority protection may not be as strong against short-term layoffs, due to shutdowns for maintenance or retooling. Nor is it an absolute guarantee against economic disaster, involving an employer's bankruptcy, the closing of a plant, or the relocation of operations. Nevertheless, by committing a certain part of his working life to one firm, the employee can insure himself against most of the vicissitudes that might affect his job security.

tive—calling for a weighing of the relative stakes of senior white and junior black—seniority probably provides the best available measure. More subjective standards would be impracticable. Finally, seniority defines the best "bright-line" rule for layoff cases of the most serious kind. Seniority layoff cases exhibit two important dimensions, one involving the degree to which integration is threatened if junior blacks are laid off, the other concerning the severity of the invasion of seniority rights if whites instead are displaced. In a case such as *Stotts*, which involved the layoff of only a handful of firefighters, and for a brief period, with the affected persons actually having been hired on the same day, no large sacrifice of values is required. Little is at stake, with respect either to the benefits of integration or the losses of seniority and security. Were this the paradigm case, it would seem nearly a matter of moral indifference what rule was followed. Similarly, important questions of civil rights policy are seldom likely to arise in cases involving long-term layoff choices between relatively senior white and relatively senior black employees. Choices such as this generally will occur only in radically shrinking firms or industries, where affirmative discrimination promises few important social benefits. The true moral dilemma arises when there is a forced choice between a serious setback to integration on the one hand and severe invasion of seniority rights on the other. That is why we have regularly recurred to the situation in Boston.

Consider what affirmative discrimination implies in a serious long-term layoff, such as occurred in the Boston school system. Observing that "there is nothing magical about seniority,"[220] the court of appeals effectively took this "asset" away from hundreds of senior white teachers, all of whom had been hired after intentional discrimination by the school board had ended, and gave the benefits to recently hired black teachers, who had not committed much of their lives to teaching in the Boston schools and probably enjoyed substantial mobility in the early stages of their careers.[221] In the light of the nature and operation of seniority systems in the real world of employment, this judicial evisceration of seniority rights imposed a severe burden that could not reasonably be as-

---

[220] Morgan v. O'Bryant, 671 F.2d 23 (1st Cir. 1982).

[221] This mobility is enhanced by widespread programs of affirmative discrimination in hiring, which are encouraged by both Title VII and the Executive Order.

signed to only a few white workers[222] to rectify historic injustices by American society as a whole.[223]

2. Alternatives to Layoffs

If it is held inequitable to require a senior white worker to give up his job in order to rectify societal injustices, a gap may emerge in the structure of programs of affirmative discrimination. But part of the dilemma may arise from the question who—as between senior white and junior black—is to be selected for a layoff. Perhaps the inquiry should be recast as whether there need be any layoff at all.

One avenue of inquiry would focus on the employer rather than senior white workers, as the appropriate candidate to bear the cost of affirmative discrimination. In *Stotts*, for example, the district judge might have forbidden the layoff of blacks but without authorizing the layoff of senior whites. The employer then would have had either to retain the senior whites in their jobs, or, if he dismissed them, pay compensation for any loss of earnings suffered as a result.[224]

This "full payroll" approach[225] has conspicuous advantages. It offers the benefits of affirmative discrimination without burdening innocent whites with the loss of their job. It also assigns the costs to a legal wrongdoer, thereby creating incentives to future lawful be-

---

[222] Some measure of the burden can be gained by realizing that the expected value to the worker of seniority may exceed the actual value of such tangible assets as his home or accumulated pension benefits. Presumably no one would suggest taking a white teacher's home or pension benefits, either to fund a program of affirmative discrimination or to promote racial equality in post retirement income.

[223] The argument in the text is that the seniority rights of white workers are entitled to protection in a layoff as a matter of sound policy supported by moral principle, independent of whether this was the specific intent of Congress when it enacted Title VII. As such, the argument has force even beyond the context of judicial orders for violations of Title VII or other statutes requiring the federal courts to frame remedies for employment discrimination. It also should apply to "voluntary" private affirmative discrimination, such as was upheld in Steelworkers v. Weber, 443 U.S. 193 (1979). The Court in *Weber* was careful to note that the specific program involved did not "unnecessarily trammel the rights of white employees." Our argument suggests that a voluntary program that deprived whites of substantial seniority rights in a layoff context would violate the interests of whites in a way that ought not to be allowed. But see Tangren v. Wackenhut Services, 658 F.2d 705 (9th Cir. 1981); Wygant v. Jackson Bd. of Educ., 36 Fair Empl. Prac. Cas. 153 (6th Cir. 1984).

[224] The Supreme Court essentially took this approach in *W. R. Grace*, discussed note 23 *supra*.

[225] The label comes from Burke and Chase, *Resolving the Seniority/Minority Layoffs Conflicts: An Employer-targeted Approach*, 13 HARV. C.R.-C.L. L. REV. 81 (1978).

havior. Regrettably, however, the full payroll strategy has significant limitations. One problem is the limited availability of funds. The full payroll approach requires the employer to pay both the senior white and junior black workers. Yet presumably it is the financial difficulty of maintaining an undiminished work force that inspires layoffs in the first place. This financial concern will not always be compelling. In some cases, it may be both feasible and equitable to force a firm to absorb the costs necessary to avoid sliding backward into a segregated work force. Inevitably, though, there will be many situations in which a judicial order forbidding a firm to reduce its labor costs would simply endanger the future viability of the entire enterprise, including all the jobs that it sustains.

Public employers pose a different set of problems. Even where a public employer has scheduled layoffs, the need for public services—for example, fire protection—often will not have diminished. Further, while taxpayer resistance may have decreased the funds immediately available to support those services, financial shortages would not obviate the obligation of public bodies to obey constitutionally valid judicial orders. Therefore, at least prior to *Stotts*, a federal judge might have thought it both equitable in result and supportable under Title VII to meet threatened layoffs by imposing the costs of affirmative discrimination on the public employer.[226] At the same time, however, judicial orders affecting budgetary priorities present a host of problems, involving both the constitutional and the practical competence of the judicial branch.[227] All in all, this is an area where judicial restraint ought to be exercised.

Another alternative to layoffs would seek accommodation of conflicting values through work sharing.[228] The logic of this approach is simple. If an employer experiences a drop in demand and revenues, it need not adjust by paring the number of employees in its

---

[226] The general remedial provision of Title VII, section 703(h), invests the district courts with broad remedial discretion in fashioning appropriate relief. See note 106 *supra*, and accompanying text.

[227] See, *e.g.*, Frug, *The Judicial Power of the Purse*, 125 U. PA. L. REV. 715 (1978).

[228] For a detailed and insightful analysis of this option, see Summers and Love, note 208 *supra*.

work force. Instead it could cut the hours of all its employees.[229] Because this would produce no drop in the number of people employed, many of the benefits of affirmative discrimination would be retained. And the price is spread across the entire complement of employees, not concentrated on a few senior whites who would be deprived entirely of their seniority rights.[230]

From the employer's perspective, work sharing could often be an attractive alternative to the normal layoff. Although there may be additional costs in maintaining fringe benefits,[231] these costs are overshadowed by the employer's ability to retain experienced workers whom it has recruited and trained,[232] and, more important, by significant savings in assessments for unemployment insurance.[233] For many employees, however, this solution may appear less desirable. Unemployment benefits are generally not payable if employees suffer only a reduction in the hours that they work. Yet many workers come to rely on all the earnings that they receive from their regular employment schedule. If there is to be no more than a marginal decrease in the work week, employees may be able

---

[229] For example, instead of cutting the number of workers by one-fifth, it could retain all of its employees but reduce the hours of each by the same proportion, *e.g.*, from forty to thirty-two hours a week.

[230] Under this approach a share of the burden is appropriately borne by older whites, who may have reaped some advantage from the employers' earlier invidious discrimination, and also by the most junior blacks, who may have reaped the benefit of later affirmative discrimination. A variant of the work-sharing approach would respond to financial difficulties by prescribing that all workers simply accept a proportionate cut in pay in order to fund the "full payroll" approach. But this variant would confer a windfall on the employer (or its consumers, shareholders, or taxpayers). Under work sharing, the employees at least get the benefit of some additional leisure as a trade-off for having to accept lower weekly earnings.

[231] While most fringe benefits, such as pension contributions, are wage-related and thus will decline automatically with the hours worked, other benefits, such as employer-paid health insurance, are paid for on a per capita basis, and thus would not decline under work sharing as they would with layoffs. However, empirical research indicates that this additional cost is just a tiny part of the overall wage bill, which is likely to be outweighed by other savings to the employer. See Reid, *U-I Assisted Work Sharing as an Alternative to Layoffs: The Canadian Experience*, 35 INDUS. & LAB. REL. REV. 319, 323 (1982).

[232] Although laid-off employees typically have rights of recall before new workers are hired, they will be under pressure to find other jobs in the interim, and some will therefore not be available for recall. The loss to the employer of this valuable "human capital" has been estimated to be greater than the additional cost in per capita fringe benefits created by work sharing. See Reid, note 231 *supra*.

[233] In most states, levies upon individual firms are influenced by the degree to which their own workers can and do draw on unemployment benefits. See Summers & Love, note 208 *supra*, at 929. Work sharing often will spare the employer higher assessments, because unemployment insurance benefits are not payable when employees suffer only a reduction in their number of hours worked.

to adjust reasonably well, taking into account the effects on after-tax income under a progressive tax system.[234] But if there is to be a substantial cut in paid hours, the result will be a real burden to families that have grown dependent on a certain level of income in every paycheck.

The function of unemployment insurance cannot be overlooked. In a dynamic economy, in which movement and adaptation are expected to occur, it is the role of unemployment insurance to shift much of the economic burden arising from work shrinkages in small economic units to a larger state or national pool financed by a payroll tax. In this social and institutional context, seniority rules ordinarily supply the criterion for deciding which workers are to retain their jobs with regular income and which are to depend on unemployment insurance while looking for other employment. The use of work sharing instead significantly reduces the total income received by the unit of employees immediately affected, as compared with the total income that would be realized from the aggregate of wages and unemployment insurance benefits. For this reason, and because work sharing also confers a windfall on the employer whose potential unemployment insurance assessments will be reduced, judicial imposition of this remedy is likely to be received even less enthusiastically than would a forthright layoff out of seniority order.

The current design of unemployment insurance is not, of course, unalterable. Moreover, there is a strong policy argument for removing artificial economic disincentives to the use of work sharing, rather than layoffs, as the means through which firms and their employees adjust to changes in market demand. Unemployment insurance systems in Europe, in Canada, and most recently in California have been revised to provide benefits in situations where all the employees in a work unit lose some hours of work, not only where some lose their jobs entirely.[235] If such a change were to be

---

[234] *Stotts* was a likely candidate for work sharing. The Memphis Fire Department ended up reducing its staff by only twenty-four firefighters, less than 2 percent of the 1,500-person department, or the equivalent of a reduction of less than one hour of work a week (assuming an average cycle of forty hours a week).

[235] Another alternative to layoffs in order of seniority was explored recently in Vulcan Pioneers v. New Jersey Department of Civil Service, 34 Fair Empl. Prac. Cas. 1239 (D.N.J. 1984). Having overridden the seniority rights of white firefighters in a layoff in order to retain a black presence within the fire departments, the federal district court characterized its own action as effecting a "taking" of the property rights of the senior whites, for which the

accomplished nationally, work sharing often might be the ideal way to secure the benefits of affirmative discrimination in a recession.

We should not be unduly optimistic, however, about the promise of work sharing in those situations in which racial integration is most seriously threatened. This technique is sensible mainly in cases of a relatively small reduction in available work, where the downturn is likely to be sufficiently brief so that most of the laid off employees will not likely find work elsewhere. Yet these are precisely the cases that pose no serious threat to black employment progress. *Stotts* is a good example. As Memphis's budgetary situation improved, the City's seniority system would have triggered a recall to work of all the laid-off blacks and thus a restoration of black representation within the fire department. The real threat to racial integration occurs when there is a major contraction in the business and work available in particular firms or industries (e.g., the auto and steel industries), or occupations (e.g., teaching), and the decline is likely to be long lived, if not permanent. In such settings, neither the "full payroll" nor the work-sharing alternatives to layoffs is a panacea,[236] and the social justice model implies that, however important the policies supporting affirmative discrimination, it would be misguided and inequitable to eviscerate the hard-earned seniority rights of innocent white workers.

B. HIRING PREFERENCES

Many in the civil rights movement view seniority as a major obstacle in the quest for racial justice in employment. They assume that blacks, who have only recently received fair opportunities in much of the labor market, do not have much seniority relative to white workers, and accordingly that blacks will inevitably suffer

---

federal government, as the author of Title VII, was responsible to provide compensation. Whatever its legal footing (after *Stotts* came down, the district court reversed its own ruling, see 35 Fair Empl. Prac. Cas. 25), the court's initial ruling is resonant with our social justice approach, insofar as it rejects the potentially large and unfair burden associated with the evisceration of seniority rights. But while the federal government might appear better able to provide needed funds than financially straitened municipalities, it is not clear why federal taxpayers—and especially those who live in similarly impoverished municipalities to which they already pay taxes—should be made to provide this form of financial assistance to a city wishing to engage in layoffs.

[236] See Best & Mattesich, *Short-Time Compensation Systems in California and Europe*, MONTHLY LAB. REV., July 1980, at 13.

disproportionately under the "last-hired, first-fired" principle.[237] This assumption was certainly valid well beyond the 1960s, when effective civil rights policies first were put in place. But today, two decades after the enactment of Title VII and the implementation of affirmative discrimination under Executive Order 11246, the situation has changed. On average, black workers now have accumulated seniority roughly equal to that of whites.[238] This is an important development. Not subject to undermining by latent prejudice or racial stereotypes, the practice of seniority is now as valuable to black workers as it is to whites.

Appreciation of the facts about seniority encourages a shift of attention from race-based layoffs to affirmative discrimination in hiring. The enlistment of black workers not only puts them in jobs but also places them on the seniority ladder. There they accumulate service with a firm, establish rights of recall during temporary layoffs, and eventually secure the kind of tenure that may insulate them from job loss even if the employer must institute a severe, long-term layoff.

The view that racial preferences were appropriate in hiring but not in layoffs until recently represented a consensus reflected in judicial, executive, and congressional action throughout the 1970s. Since then, this consensus has suffered erosion from both sides: prior to *Stotts*, several courts of appeals had prescribed race-based layoff preferences, and in *Stotts* itself the Supreme Court suggested that quota hiring remedies might be impermissible in Title VII lawsuits.

The earlier law reflected our intuitive judgment that affirmative discrimination in hiring was quite a different matter from racial quotas in the context of layoffs. But the question remains whether there is a principled rationale for this distinction. We have argued

---

[237] See, *e.g.*, U.S. COMMISSION ON CIVIL RIGHTS, LAST HIRED FIRST FIRED: LAYOFFS AND CIVIL RIGHTS (1977).

[238] The May 1979 Current Population Survey asked a representative national sample of 29,000 workers how many years they had worked for their current employer. In the work force as a whole, blacks had accumulated 6.8 years of service vs. 6.6 for whites. In the public sector, blacks led whites by 8.1–7.9 years. Among schoolteachers and police officers, the relative positions were the same. There was insufficient response by blacks to provide an average for firefighters, but other minorities (predominantly Hispanics in this sample) outpaced white firefighters in length of service, and these other minorities trailed blacks in just about every other category. (We are grateful to James Medoff and Alan Krueger for extracting these data from the CPS tapes for us.)

that even as vital a policy as helping blacks overcome the legacy of racial oppression does not justify imposing on innocent whites the burden entailed by the denial of seniority rights in a long-term layoff. Why then does a comparable judgment not hold true in the context of entry-level hiring?

Material differences between layoffs and hiring exist along two dimensions. One involves the defeat of socially fostered expectations. The incumbent white in a layoff context seeks to enforce an explicit or implicit contractual right that he has earned with his labor. Having invested his energies and his aspirations in a firm, he feels—and it is desirable both economically and morally that he should feel—entitled to the security that seniority is designed to provide. Quite different is the situation of the first-time job applicant. He has no individual right to have the selection made in accordance with any particular set of criteria.[239] Undoubtedly there is a general expectation that relative competence ought to be taken into account. But private employers are not required to conduct purely meritocratic hiring competitions, and the community, by law, familiarly establishes nonmerit hiring preferences in a variety of ways and for a variety of reasons.[240] Established to help purge the legacy of historic racism, affirmative discrimination can be fitted into the existing fabric of departures from meritocratic standards.

The same distinction obtains along the dimension of tangible impact. In the layoff context, the senior white loses a currently held job in which he may have invested a good part of his working life (thus foreclosing a variety of other options). By contrast, the unsuccessful applicant for a new job suffers essentially the same loss as anyone else who fails to get a desired position, whatever the selection criteria used, whatever the employer's or the community's aim in designing the process. We do not mean to trivialize the sense of grievance that may be felt by dispreferred whites; nor do we deny that the unsuccessful applicant suffers a palpable economic loss. But the burden of losing an unheld job is not so large that a morally decent community, determined to rectify the legacy of racism, could not reasonably impose that burden on some individual community members. At issue is not the gratuitous infliction of suffer-

---

[239] See notes 170–82 *supra* and accompanying text.

[240] See notes 183–84 *supra* and accompanying text.

ing but a question of appropriate distribution. Absent a policy of affirmative discrimination, there will be many blacks who experience the same disappointment of nonselection. At least some of their losses will occur because sufficient steps were not taken to overcome inherited disadvantages and the unfair head start enjoyed by some white competitors.[241]

C. OTHER ISSUES

The operation of a labor market consists of more than just initial hiring and eventual termination, whether by indefinite layoff or otherwise. In between occurs a continual process of transfers, upgrading, and promotions.[242] Positive action both by private firms and by government is important at this intermediate stage: the goal of affirmative discrimination is not simply to get blacks anywhere inside the firm, possibly in dead-end jobs, but to insure that they have a fair chance at the more attractive and more important positions. How should one assess the burden that affirmative discrimination here might impose on individual whites? On the one hand, promotion resembles hiring in the sense that the dispreferred white does not lose an existing job, but merely fails to progress to a more attractive position. On the other hand, because seniority does play a significant role in promotion decisions, overriding that criterion can produce the same sense of grievance about the denial of an earned right as it does in the layoff setting.[243] We concede that we cannot here sort out the competing considerations and indicate precisely where to strike the balance. Our Model of Social Justice at least clarifies the agenda of issues.

---

[241] There is a further aspect to the evaluation of hiring quotas, involving the adoption by courts of rather ambitious short-term hiring targets (*e.g.*, one black for one white in an area where the black share of the available labor force may be 20 percent or even less). While we note this as a pertinent problem for a fully worked-out theory of affirmative discrimination in employment, see Williams v. City of New Orleans, 34 Fair Empl. Prac. Cas. 1009, 1015–18 (5th Cir. 1984) (*en banc*) (plurality opinion), we are not able to address it here.

[242] United Steelworkers v. Weber, 443 U.S. 193 (1979), the case in which the Supreme Court explicitly approved of affirmative discrimination in employment (albeit, through private voluntary action), involved a program under which employees would be trained for and then promoted to the skilled trades position at Kaiser Steel.

[243] ABRAHAM & MEDOFF, YEARS OF SERVICE AND PROBABILITY OF PROMOTION (Nat. Bur. Econ. Research, November 1983), found that while a substantial majority of firms reported that seniority was a relevant factor in their promotion decisions, it was considerably less important for promotions than it was in layoffs. See note 209 *supra*.

VI. Conclusion

Sometimes, "No answer is what the wrong question begets."[244] On other occasions, a conclusion does emerge, however misbegotten and misguided. *Memphis Firefighters v. Stotts* fits the second category. Conceiving the question before it as requiring a selection between the Model of Individual Justice and the Model of Group Justice, the Supreme Court opted for the individual justice approach. The result was an apparent sacrifice of the values supporting affirmative discrimination.

The issues surrounding affirmative discrimination are better expressed in two questions than, as the *Stotts* Court apparently believed, in one. The first question involves the necessary justifications, in principle, for programs of affirmative discrimination aimed to rectify past, group-based injustices. The second, which assumes that a justification exists, concerns issues of fairness in cost allocation, and more particularly, the reasonableness of placing the burden on particular, dispreferred individuals.

Although the *Stotts* Court's formulation of the question for decision was wanting, its holding as to seniority layoffs was correct. There are important differences between race-based hiring preferences and racial quotas that eviscerate seniority rights. The latter, when causing senior whites to be evicted from their jobs, impose an excessive burden on the displaced individuals. By comparison, because hiring quotas exact a lesser cost, preferences at the entry level ought to be upheld.

Fortunately, the objectionable aspects of *Stotts* fairly can be characterized as dicta. The broader issues—including the permissibility of race-based hiring preferences in the job market—remain open for reconsideration.

---

[244] Ely, *The Supreme Court 1977 Term—Foreword: On Discovering Fundamental Values*, 92 HARV. L. REV. 5 (1978), quoting BICKEL, THE LEAST DANGEROUS BRANCH 103 (1962).

DIANE WOOD HUTCHINSON

ANTITRUST 1984: FIVE DECISIONS IN SEARCH OF A THEORY

I. INTRODUCTION

The 1983 Term held promise of being the most important antitrust term since the 1976 Term, which had produced such decisions as *Continental T.V., Inc. v. GTE Sylvania, Inc.*,[1] *United States Steel Corp. v. Fortner Enterprises, Inc.*,[2] and *Brunswick Corp. v. Pueblo Bowl-O-Mat, Inc.*[3] The Court had five antitrust cases on its docket; each raised significant questions about the reach of the antitrust laws; and in each the United States appeared to urge the Court to adopt the teachings of the consumer welfare school of thought as a coherent approach to antitrust policy.[4] Depending on the reading given the opinions, the Court declined the Administration's invitation in either three or four of the five. Even where the Court accepted the results urged by the Government, it used reasoning that clearly signaled a reluctance to swallow that theory, or any other, hook, line, and sinker.

The 1984 cases raise more questions than they answer. To what extent has the Court adopted the consumer welfare model as the central meaning of the antitrust laws? How willing is the Court to overrule, explicitly or sub silentio, prior antitrust decisions that are

---

Diane Wood Hutchinson is Assistant Professor of Law, The University of Chicago.

[1] 433 U.S. 36 (1977).

[2] 429 U.S. 610 (1977).

[3] 429 U.S. 477 (1977).

[4] Monsanto Co. v. Spray-Rite Serv. Corp., 104 S.Ct. 1464 (1984); Jefferson Parish Hospital Dist. No. 2 v. Hyde, 104 S.Ct. 1551 (1984); Hoover v. Ronwin, 104 S.Ct. 1989 (1984); Copperweld Corp. v. Independence Tube Corp., 104 S.Ct. 2731 (1984); and National Collegiate Athletic Ass'n v. Board of Regents, 104 S.Ct. 2948 (1984).

inconsistent with this model? What has happened to the per se rules of Justice Hugo Black's era, and why? What emerges is an antitrust law that has fewer per se rules, and hence is more hospitable to a variety of business arrangements. The hospitality has come about, however, not by framing clear standards leading to these results but through the application of an open-ended rule of reason that has become the order of the day.

The net result is that antitrust law is caught in a world of uncertainty, halfway between the comforts of the per se rules of *Northern Pacific Railway Co. v. United States,*[5] on the one hand, and the full-blown economic approach to the laws, on the other. The reasons for this may include the Court's substantive preferences, its view of stare decisis, and its notion of the respective roles of Court and Congress. Whatever they are, it is clear that the Court in 1984 did not settle on any one conception of antitrust law, nor does it seem likely that any such theoretical coherence is to be expected soon.

II. The Cases

The 1984 cases ranged over a wide variety of antitrust issues, from the fundamental question whether the antitrust laws apply at all to certain transactions to common questions about the appropriate rules for measuring the legality of conduct. The Court looked at horizontal arrangements, vertical arrangements, and dealings between affiliated companies. It considered the extent to which state regulation or state action overrides the normal operation of federal antitrust laws. The decisions in these cases require individual attention initially, for each was important to its own category of antitrust law.

The variety of issues need not, however, obscure the broader messages the Court was sending. There are a number of possible ways of looking at the Term as a whole: as a study of Supreme Court consistency, asking which cases adhered to precedent most closely and which displayed the most freedom from that constraint; as a study of Chicago school economic analysis, asking which cases used this intellectual and policy approach to antitrust most successfully and which ones eschewed it; or as a jurisprudential study of

---

[5] 356 U.S. 1 (1958).

antitrust law, looking at the Supreme Court's ideas about the role of competition in general, the meaning of competition, and the way to preserve competitive markets. I prefer the last of these approaches. The Court's treatment of its own precedent will be apparent in the consideration of the various cases in any event. Others will be concerned about the successes and failures of various schools of thought in gaining Supreme Court adherence.[6] The focus on the law of antitrust underscores the point that antitrust is still a body of legal doctrine set in motion by several Acts of Congress and still ultimately attached to its legislative roots.

With this organizing principle in mind, the natural order of consideration for the five cases is to begin with the question of antitrust exemption raised in *Hoover v. Ronwin*,[7] to move next to the question raised in *Copperweld Corp. v. Independence Tube Corp.*[8] whether Sherman Act § 1 should apply at all to intra-enterprise agreements, and finally to consider the three "substantive" decisions: the horizontal practices in *National Collegiate Athletic Association (NCAA) v. Board of Regents*,[9] the vertical manufacturer restraints in *Monsanto Co. v. Spray-Rite Service Corp.*,[10] and the vertical relationship between the hospital and the anesthesiologists in *Jefferson Parish Hospital District No. 2 v. Hyde.*[11]

A. HOOVER V. RONWIN: COMPETITION OR STATE ECONOMIC REGULATION?

1. *The* Parker *doctrine.* The tension between a competitive regime and governmental regulation is now so well recognized as to be

---

[6] For a small sample of these articles, see, *e.g.*, Gerhart, *The Supreme Court and Antitrust Analysis: The (Near) Triumph of the Chicago School*, 1982 SUPREME COURT REVIEW 319; Lipner, *Antitrust's Per Se Rule: Reports of Its Death Are Greatly Exaggerated*, 60 DEN. L.J. 593 (1983); *Antitrust Symposium*, 27 ST. LOUIS U.L.J. 287 (1983); Sullivan, *Economic Jurisprudence of the Burger Court's Antitrust Policy: The First Thirteen Years*, 58 NOTRE DAME L. REV. 1 (1982); Handler, *Reforming the Antitrust Laws*, 82 COLUM. L. REV. 1287 (1982); Fox, *The Modernization of Antitrust: A New Equilibrium*, 66 CORNELL L. REV. 1140 (1981); *Antitrust Jurisprudence: A Symposium on the Economic, Political and Social Goals of Antitrust Policy*, 125 U. PA. L. REV. 1182 (1977). See generally BORK, THE ANTITRUST PARADOX (1978); POSNER, ANTITRUST LAW: AN ECONOMIC PERSPECTIVE (1976).

[7] Note 4 *supra.*

[8] *Ibid.*

[9] *Ibid.*

[10] *Ibid.*

[11] *Ibid.*

commonplace.[12] At the federal level, the antitrust laws either coexist with other federal legislation, supersede that legislation or give way to it, depending in every case on legislative language and intent. Normally, when Congress has spoken on a subject, conflicting state laws must give way, by force of the Supremacy Clause. The Supreme Court decided on the first occasion when a state law interfering with competition was challenged as inconsistent with the antitrust laws, however, that preemption would not be the invariable conclusion. Instead, in *Parker v. Brown*,[13] the Court held that the Sherman Act did not invalidate a state-created raisin marketing cartel, even though between 90 and 95 percent of the raisins grown in California were ultimately shipped in interstate commerce, and the effect of the program was clearly to restrict supply and to enhance price.

What saved the program was the fact that "[i]t derived its authority and its efficacy from the legislative command of the state and was not intended to operate or become effective without that command."[14] The Court's examination of the legislative history of the Sherman Act produced no evidence that the Act was intended to restrain state action. Significantly, however, the Court limited its ruling of no preemption: States could not simply authorize violations of the Sherman Act, nor could the state or its municipalities participate in a private agreement in restraint of trade.[15] Since the raisin marketing program in *Parker*, although initiated and governed by state legislation, also involved private parties, it was evident from the outset that some line had to be drawn between the kind of state action that was not covered by the federal antitrust laws and the kind that was.

---

[12] See, *e.g.*, Handler, *Regulation versus Competition*, 43 ANTITRUST L.J. 277 (1974); Baker, *Competition and Regulation: Charles River Bridge Recrossed*, 60 CORNELL L. REV. 159 (1975); *Discussion, Deregulation and the Antitrust Laws—What It's All About*, 45 ANTITRUST L.J. 194 (1976). See generally Stigler, *The Theory of Economic Regulation*, 2 BELL J. ECON. 3 (1971); Peltzman, *Toward a More General Theory of Regulation*, 19 J. LAW & ECON. 211 (1976). Numerous studies of the effects of regulation on price and output have been conducted for specific industries. See, *e.g.*, *Symposium on Antitrust Implications of Deregulation*, 28 ANTITRUST BULL. 1 (1983); Frew, *The Existence of Monopoly Profits in the Motor Carrier Industry*, 24 J. LAW & ECON. 289 (1981); Olson & Trapani, *Who Has Benefited from Regulation of the Airline Industry?* 24 J. LAW & ECON. 75 (1981).

[13] 317 U.S. 341 (1943).

[14] *Id.* at 350.

[15] *Id.* at 351–52.

The Supreme Court did not return to this problem in earnest until 1975, when it decided *Goldfarb v. Virginia State Bar*.[16] *Goldfarb* created a minor stir in its holding that the Virginia State Bar was not immune from Sherman Act liability under the *Parker* doctrine,[17] insofar as it had adopted "advisory" minimum fee schedules for common legal services, backed up by disciplinary sanctions. In the years since *Goldfarb*, the Court has considered two different aspects of the *Parker* doctrine: first, the extent to which it immunizes private parties acting under some scheme of state regulation; and second, the extent to which municipalities are entitled to be treated as "States," either for purposes of immunizing the conduct of others or for purposes of placing their own actions beyond the scope of the antitrust laws. The net result of the immunity decisions was to establish a two-part test that applied when private party action under a state regulatory scheme was involved (often referred to as the *Midcal* test, after the case that summarized it): first, the challenged restraint had to be one clearly articulated and affirmatively expressed as state policy, and second, the policy had to be actively supervised by the State.[18]

One of those decisions, *Bates v. State Bar of Arizona*,[19] is of particular interest here, since the *Hoover* majority's holding rested almost exclusively on *Bates*. Like *Hoover*, *Bates* involved the activities of the State Bar of Arizona, which operates under the general supervision of the Arizona supreme court. In *Bates*, the question concerned the validity of the Arizona supreme court's rule restricting lawyer ad-

---

[16] 421 U.S. 773 (1975). But see Schwegmann Bros. v. Calvert Distillers Corp., 341 U.S. 384 (1951).

[17] The American Bar Association had argued to the Court against a "mechanical application of the antitrust laws to the professions." See Allen, *Do Fee Schedules Violate Antitrust Law?* 61 A.B.A. J. 565, 567 (1975). For reactions to the decision, see, *e.g.*, Shenefield, *Annual Survey of Antitrust Developments 1974–75*, 33 WASH. & LEE L. REV. 259, 279–98 (1976); Francis & Johnson, *The Emperor's Old Clothes: Piercing the Bar's Ethical Veil*, 13 WILLAMETTE L.J. 221 (1977); Branca & Steinberg, *Attorney Fee Schedules and Legal Advertising: The Implications of Goldfarb*, 24 U.C.L.A. L. REV. 475 (1977).

[18] See Cantor v. Detroit Edison Co., 428 U.S. 579 (1976) (state approval of utility rates insufficient to confer *Parker* immunity on tie-in between electricity and light bulbs); Bates v. State Bar of Arizona, 433 U.S. 350 (1977) (discussed in text); New Motor Vehicle Bd. v. Orrin W. Fox Co., 439 U.S. 96 (1978) (state law permitting competing car dealers to protest establishment of new or relocated dealerships not in conflict with Sherman Act); and California Retail Liquor Dealers Ass'n v. Midcal Aluminum, Inc., 445 U.S. 97 (1980) (state involvement in retail price maintenance scheme for wine insufficient for *Parker* immunity because of the lack of adequate state supervision).

[19] Note 18 *supra*.

vertising.[20] The State Bar of Arizona had the initial responsibility for enforcing the disciplinary rules of the Arizona supreme court. When lawyers Bates and O'Steen committed a clear violation of the advertising rule, the State Bar held hearings and ultimately recommended to the Arizona supreme court that each lawyer be suspended (for the trivial time period of one week each). Bates and O'Steen then sought and received review in the Arizona supreme court, which rejected their various challenges to the rule.

On appeal, the Supreme Court relied on several critical facts as it found the State Bar exempt from Sherman Act liability. The challenged restraint was "the affirmative command of the Arizona Supreme Court" and was thus " 'compelled by direction of the State acting as sovereign,' "[21] unlike the loose relationship presented in *Goldfarb*. In addition, "[a]lthough the State Bar play[ed] a part in the enforcement of the rules, its role [was] completely defined by the court; [the Bar] act[ed] as the agent of the court under its continuous supervision."[22] Finally, the Court found that Arizona's regulation of the activities of the bar was "at the core of the State's power to protect the public."[23]

The cases involving municipalities have shown greater hostility to *Parker* immunity.[24] The Court has emphasized the distinction between the State as sovereign and entities created by the State. Federalism concerns arise only in connection with the former, and thus only the State itself is entitled to an "absolute" *Parker* immunity. Municipal regulations must be authorized specifically by the State before the "clearly authorized" prong of the *Midcal* test can be satisfied. The Court has not addressed the question whether municipal supervision may take the place of State supervision.

2. *The* Hoover *decision*. There was nothing complicated about the facts. Arizona, like every State, entrusts the regulation of the legal

---

[20] Although the Court found that this rule was exempt from Sherman Act scrutiny, it eventually struck down the rule as an interference with "commercial speech" prohibited by the First Amendment of the Constitution.

[21] 433 U.S. at 360.

[22] *Id.* at 361.

[23] *Ibid.*

[24] City of Lafayette v. Louisiana Power & Light Co., 435 U.S. 389 (1978) (no automatic *Parker* exemption for municipalities [plurality]; no exemption for proprietary activities of municipalities [Chief Justice]); Community Communications Co. v. City of Boulder, 455 U.S. 40 (1982) (general home rule charter from state did not authorize anticompetitive cable television ordinances).

profession to its supreme court, and the court in turn delegates most of its responsibilities to the State bar. The vital matter of admissions to the bar was at issue here. Rather than deciding individual-by-individual who should be admitted to practice before it, the Arizona supreme court had created a Committee on Examinations and Admissions to examine applicants to the bar and to recommend who should be admitted. Except in cases raising questions of moral character,[25] the Committee recommended for admission all persons who passed the state bar examination. The state supreme court also provided review procedures for persons aggrieved by two kinds of decisions of the Committee: (1) failure to award a satisfactory grade on the examination, and (2) anything else. The general review procedure guaranteed consideration by the court, but the right to court review of a failing examination grade was not absolute. Only if three members of the seven-member Committee agreed with the petitioner that he or she had not received an appropriately high grade would the court even consider reviewing a grade dispute, and even then, supreme court review was discretionary. With those qualifications, the Arizona supreme court was the final authority for all decisions to admit or to refuse to admit applicants to the bar.[26]

Ronwin took the Arizona bar examination in February, 1974, and failed it. When he was not recommended for admission to the bar, he invoked both the general review provisions and the grading review provisions. Instead of emphasizing the challenge to his grade, Ronwin claimed that the exam had not been conducted in a lawful manner. He argued that the Committee had tried to control the number of applicants who would be permitted to practice law. He specifically alleged in the review proceeding that this course of action violated the Sherman Act. The Arizona supreme court was unpersuaded, and the United States Supreme Court denied Ronwin's petition for certiorari.[27]

After Ronwin failed to gain admission to the Arizona bar in other ways, he filed an antitrust suit against the State Bar of Arizona, the

---

[25] This issue actually came up at one point in Ronwin's saga, but it is not germane to the *Parker* issue or to either the majority or the dissenting Supreme Court opinion.

[26] See Hunt v. Maricopa County Employees Merit System Comm'n, 127 Ariz. 259, 261, 619 P.2d 1036, 1038–39 (1980); Ariz. Rev. Stat. Ann. § 32–275 (1956); Arizona Supreme Court Rule 28(c), 110 Ariz. xxxv–xxxvii (1974). See also 104 S.Ct. at 1991.

[27] 419 U.S. 967 (1974).

individual members of the Committee on Examinations and Admissions, and their spouses. He claimed that the Committee members had conspired to restrain trade in violation of Sherman Act § 1 by "artificially reducing the numbers of competing attorneys in the State of Arizona." The Committee allegedly did this by manipulating the grading process: it would assign a "raw score" to each examination, decide how many new lawyers it wanted, and then find the raw score equivalent of the pass/fail point that yielded the desired number of new lawyers. Thus, the Committee used its examination powers not to screen out the unqualified, but to restrict entry into the profession.

The defendants moved to dismiss the complaint on a number of grounds, including failure to state a claim on which relief could be granted, because of their immunity from Sherman Act liability under *Parker v. Brown*.[28] The district court granted the motion without explaining its reasons. On appeal, the Court of Appeals for the Ninth Circuit reversed on the critical question of *Parker* immunity for the Committee members.[29] The court of appeals found nothing in the Arizona supreme court's general delegations of authority to the Committee that addressed the question of the number of new lawyers. The relevant court rules all concerned testing for qualifications. Furthermore, the appellate court found nothing in the record indicating that the Committee had informed the supreme court that it was scoring the examination in such a way as to admit a predetermined number of applicants. At least on the pleadings, the testing scheme failed both branches of the *Midcal* test: there was no clearly articulated and affirmatively expressed policy of the state supreme court to restrict entry for reasons unrelated to competence, and there was no active supervision of the anticompetitive aspect of the Committee's work. The court of appeals therefore ordered a remand for further proceedings, over one dissent.

The Supreme Court, with Justices Rehnquist and O'Connor out of the case, reversed the court of appeals and reinstated the district

---

[28] The other grounds were lack of jurisdiction because of an insufficient effect on interstate commerce, and failure to state a claim because Ronwin had suffered no damage from the conduct of which he complained. See Ronwin v. State Bar of Arizona, 686 F.2d 692 (9th Cir. 1982).

[29] *Ibid.* The court of appeals affirmed the dismissals of the State Bar and the committee members' spouses. It found the allegations of effect on interstate commerce and injury adequate to survive the motions to dismiss. *Id.* at 699, 700.

court's dismissal of the complaint on a four-to-three vote.[30] Justice Powell, writing for the majority, took a broad and formalistic view of the *Parker* doctrine. From *Parker* and *Bates*, he distilled the principle that "a decision of a state supreme court, acting legislatively rather than judicially, is exempt from Sherman Act liability as state action."[31] When the challenged activity is carried out by others pursuant to state authorization, whether municipal actors or private individuals, the *Midcal* test applies.[32] Since the issues of clear articulation and active supervision need not be addressed where the conduct at issue is that of the state legislature or supreme court, Justice Powell decided that the case turned on who denied Ronwin admission to the bar: the Arizona supreme court, or the defendant members of the Committee.

The decision in *Bates*, he concluded, revealed the Arizona supreme court to be the true actor. A unanimous Court in *Bates* had agreed that the "Arizona supreme court [was] the real party in interest,"[33] since the court had adopted the advertising rules and was the ultimate trier of fact in the enforcement process. Here, the court had selected members of its bar to serve on the Committee and had given them discretion in "compiling and grading the bar examination, but it had "retained strict supervisory powers and ultimate full authority over its actions."[34] In support of this conclusion, the Court noted that the Arizona court had told the Committee to establish a grading or scoring system and to file it with the court. Furthermore, Arizona case law established that the supreme court had the final authority to determine who should be admitted to practice law in the state.[35] In rejecting Ronwin's argument that the supreme court had never approved or even been aware of the

---

[30] Justice Powell wrote for himself, the Chief Justice, and Justices Brennan and Marshall. Justice Stevens led Justices White and Blackmun in dissent.

[31] 104 S.Ct. at 1995.

[32] The majority thus rejected the Solicitor General's argument that municipalities and state agencies fall in a "middle tier" for *Parker* purposes. It did, however, rephrase the *Midcal* "active supervision" test in a way that softened the requirement, simply saying that "the degree to which the state legislature or supreme court supervises its representative [is] . . . relevant to the inquiry." *Ibid.*

[33] 433 U.S. at 361.

[34] 104 S.Ct. at 1997.

[35] Note 26 *supra*.

anticompetitive manner in which the Committee was allegedly exercising its discretion, Powell responded:[36]

> The Court did not suggest in *Parker*, nor has it suggested since, that a state action is exempt from antitrust liability only if the sovereign acted wisely after full disclosure from its subordinate officers. The only requirement is that the action be that of "the State acting as sovereign."

Although he might have stopped writing at that point, Powell was obviously bothered enough by the dissenters' argument to add a lengthy response. The dissenters essentially refused to ignore the Committee's role in determining admissions to the bar. The suit was against the Committee members, and it was unquestionable that they played a decisive role in the vast majority of bar admission cases. Justice Powell, for the majority, expressed great fear of the consequences of looking behind the formal apparatus of Arizona bar admissions to the reality of the Committee's role. First, displaying a certain disregard for the facts of *Bates*, he suggested that the claim against the State Bar in *Bates* had failed because the state supreme court was the real actor there, not because the State Bar was acting pursuant to clearly articulated standards and was actively supervised by the State. Second, and more importantly, he warned that a focus on the committee members' actions[37]

> would allow Sherman Act plaintiffs to look behind the actions of state sovereigns and base their claims on perceived conspiracies to restrain trade among the committees, commissions, or others who necessarily must advise the sovereign. Such a holding would emasculate the *Parker v. Brown* doctrine.

In short, any time a state acted on the advice of a committee whose members might have been secretly plotting to restrain trade, an antitrust plaintiff could draft a complaint against the committee members that would survive a motion to dismiss. *Parker* would become a nullity. Rather than fall into that trap, the majority elected to remain on the safe ground of the formal ultimate responsibility of the state supreme court.

Justice Stevens's dissenting opinion assumed that the Arizona supreme court had indeed delegated real power to the Committee and that the Committee's decisions to pass or fail bar applicants had

---

[36] 104 S.Ct. at 1998.

[37] *Id.* at 2001.

a direct effect on the number of persons admitted to practice law in the state. Stevens placed the dispute in the general context of the common law of restraints of trade, as he has done before.[38] He agreed that *Parker* immunized activities of the state itself, for the reason that "[w]hen the State itself governs entry into a profession, the evils associated with giving power over a market to those who stand to benefit from inhibiting entry into that market are absent."[39] Different competitive risks are present, he argued, when the State's power is delegated:[40]

> When that authority [to formulate the standards and to determine the qualifications of particular applicants] is delegated to those with a stake in the competitive conditions within the market, there is a risk that public power will be exercised for private benefit. To avoid, or to minimize that risk state policies displacing competition must be "clearly and affirmatively expressed" and must be appropriately supervised.

Since this was a case of delegated authority to those with a competitive stake in the outcome, Stevens applied the *Midcal* test to the Committee's decisions.

He had a number of answers to the majority's assertion that the Arizona supreme court, and only the court, made the final decisions. First, in a footnote, he said that the Committee members themselves did not argue that their functions were totally advisory.[41] Second, he noted that the Arizona supreme court was not a party to the case, and that the complaint alleged that it was the committee members who had made the decision to limit the number of attorneys in Arizona, not the court. Next, he said that

---

[38] See National Soc'y of Professional Eng'rs v. United States, 435 U.S. 679, 688–89 (1978).

[39] 104 S.Ct. at 2004.

[40] *Ibid.*

[41] *Id.* at 2006 n.12. This is not a fair representation of the Committee's brief. The committee members argued, *inter alia*, that they were entitled to *Noerr-Pennington* immunity from the antitrust laws. See California Motor Transp. Co. v. Trucking Unlimited, 404 U.S. 508 (1972); United Mine Workers of America v. Pennington, 381 U.S. 657 (1965); Eastern Railroad Presidents Conf. v. Noerr Motor Freight, Inc., 365 U.S. 127 (1961). In the course of that argument, they said that "[f]irst, the Examiners' action did not injure Ronwin. They did not have the power to admit or deny his admission. Only the Arizona Supreme Court has such power." Brief for Petitioners at 80. It is true that the petitioners argued at greater length that they were state officials whose conduct was to be judged by a standard more lenient than *Midcal*'s, and in the alternative that they satisfied the *Midcal* standard. That, however, does not negate the fact that they raised the point deemed critical by the majority, even if in a different section of the brief.

Arizona had not specifically required the particular anticompetitive conduct here—that is, a limitation on total numbers of new lawyers. *Bates* provided a useful contrast, since there the state supreme court had specifically required attorneys to refrain from the challenged types of advertising. Finally, Stevens relied on the fact that the Arizona court had never issued a particular order denying anyone admission to the bar, including Ronwin. The Committee weeded out the first group of unsuccessful applicants by determining who passed and who failed the examination. Then, among those who passed, the Committee decided whom to recommend. People who passed the examination but who were not recommended for admission were normally the ones who petitioned the court for review.

Stevens concluded that, on the pleadings alone, the *Midcal* test was not satisfied. He showed no real concern about the majority's fears of crippling the *Parker* doctrine. Ronwin's case would vanish quickly on remand.[42] The majority's fears about spurious suits against persons who advise legislators were unfounded. A decision not to give absolute *Parker* immunity to the Committee did nothing more than place the legal profession on an even footing with all other professions. Doctrines exist for weeding out frivolous antitrust suits, and if they are inadequate, it is they that should be revised. Stevens, in summary, saw the majority decision as a retreat from "[t]he commitment to free markets and open competition that has evolved over the centuries and is embodied in the Sherman Act."[43]

3. *The choice of a bright-line rule.* Before *Hoover* was decided, there was no lack of theory about the appropriate contours of the *Parker* doctrine. The amicus brief for the United States offered a rather traditional analysis of the post-*Goldfarb* line of cases.[44] According to its system, the level of scrutiny required should vary according to the type of entity acting for the State: virtually complete Sherman

---

[42] He predicted that Ronwin would lose on summary judgment. 104 S.Ct. at 2010. The Solicitor General was similarly confident that Ronwin would not last long. The final section of the Brief for the United States offers several possible grounds for disposing of Ronwin's complaint on remand. See Brief for the United States at 26–30. Not the least of Ronwin's problems was the fact that the Sherman Act claim had already been raised and rejected in the direct review proceedings. See note 27 *supra,* and accompanying text. The Committee therefore had a serious issue preclusion defense.

[43] 104 S.Ct. at 2012–13.

[44] Brief for United States at 6–7.

Act immunity for "the State itself"; a more qualified immunity for state agencies or municipalities, if the policy to displace competition is clear; and the most limited immunity for private actors, who must also be supervised actively by the State.

Other commentators, in some instances writing before all these cases had been decided, opt for a unified test. Philip Areeda and Donald Turner, for example, propose that *Parker* immunity should exist only if two conditions are satisfied: adequate state supervision, and authorized state action clearly intended to displace antitrust law.[45] In their view, it is unnecessary to require State compulsion of the anticompetitive activity, as long as the other requirements are satisfied. Judge Robert Bork seems to emphasize the State's commitment to substitute regulation for competition.[46] Frank Easterbrook, in contrast, would dispense entirely with the traditional structure of *Parker* analysis and ask instead whether the State is trying to export a monopoly overcharge to other jurisdictions.[47] The "correct" result in *Hoover* would vary depending upon which of these approaches is adopted: the Solicitor General, Areeda and Turner, and possibly Bork would require a remand because of the indefiniteness of the Arizona supreme court's position on limitation of entry into the legal profession for its own sake; Easterbrook would find immunity as a matter of law for the same reason as in *Bates*, namely, that any overcharges suffered due to a restriction in the supply of lawyers would be borne exclusively by Arizona residents.

It is appropriate here to mention one other doctrine of antitrust immunity: the *Noerr-Pennington* doctrine.[48] The committee members in *Hoover* had also argued that their actions were beyond the reach of the Sherman Act because they were the equivalent of lobbying the state supreme court for political action. *Noerr* puts this kind of activity outside the antitrust laws, even if competitors join together for this purpose and even if their motive is strictly to hurt

---

[45] 1 Areeda & Turner, Antitrust Law ¶¶ 211–14, at 66–92 (1978); *cf.* California Retail Liquor Dealers Ass'n v. Midcal Aluminum, Inc., note 18 *supra*.

[46] Bork, The Antitrust Paradox, note 6 *supra*, at 350 n.*.

[47] Easterbrook, *Antitrust and the Economics of Federalism*, 26 J. Law & Econ. 23, 45–46 (1983).

[48] See note 41 *supra*. See generally Fischel, *Antitrust Liability for Attempts to Influence Government Action: The Basis and Limits of the Noerr-Pennington Doctrine*, 45 U. Chi. L. Rev. 80 (1977).

their rivals. The Court in *Noerr* expressed the concern, also raised in *Hoover*, that a contrary holding would "substantially impair the power of government to take actions through its legislature and executive that operate to restrain trade."[49] Thus, the Court in *Hoover* could have considered the Committee's actions in the light of this doctrine, although, as the majority noted, its view of *Parker* made this unnecessary.[50]

For purposes of analysis, four factual variations may be suggested:

1. The Arizona supreme court is the only entity with any authority to admit or to deny admission to the bar. The Committee is a purely advisory body, not unlike a trade association. It "lobbies" for the admission of certain applicants and against the admission of others.

2. The Arizona supreme court is the only entity with any authority to admit or deny admissions to the bar. It seeks assistance in this task from a number of different groups, including its law clerks, its secretaries, and the Committee. The Committee's status is no different from that of those other state employees, whether or not its members receive remuneration. Similarly, the Committee has no more power over final decisions than do the clerks.

3. The Arizona supreme court, while possessing the final say over bar admissions, has delegated most of this work to the Committee. Although the Committee is composed of private lawyers, for this purpose they have the status of state officials. Most of their decisions are final, but the court reviews specified cases.

4. The same as model 3, except that the Committee, since it is composed of private lawyers, must be viewed as a private group attempting to restrict entry into its guild.

It is worth noting that all these models rely on the identity of the actors rather than the degree to which the activity itself interferes with competition. This is consistent with *Parker*, but not with an approach like Easterbrook's.

The majority's opinion viewed the facts to be as model 2 describes them. The difference between model 1 and model 2 is important in law. If Ronwin had sued the Committee and the Court had followed model 1, the correct ruling on a motion to

---

[49] 365 U.S. at 137.

[50] 104 S.Ct. at 1998 n.25.

dismiss would be that the Committee was immune from Sherman Act liability under *Noerr*. Ronwin would then have been entitled to allege and prove one of the exceptions to the *Noerr* doctrine, such as fraud on the court or abuse of process.[51] Model 2, on the other hand, treats the legal status of the Committee exactly as the status of other court helpers. Ronwin conceivably could have sued the justices' law clerks, claiming that they were trying to keep potential competitors out of the bar. The law clerks, although obviously persons separate from the justices, effectively "merge" into the court for this purpose. If this type of state employee could be liable under the Sherman Act, the State's own immunity would be a dead letter; thus, the clerks would plead *Parker* immunity derivatively and a motion to dismiss would be granted unless one of *Parker*'s own limits could be proved. Model 2 requires no clear statement from the supreme court that competition is being displaced, for the simple reason that the court is the only real actor.

The dissenters viewed the facts to be somewhere between model 3 and model 4. The difference would be important if Justice Stevens had accepted the analysis in the brief for the United States that varied the state supervision requirement in those two cases, but he did not differentiate in that way. Using either model, the clear statement of intent to displace competition with regulation is a critical requirement, and such a statement from the Arizona supreme court was undoubtedly missing. Justice Powell's efforts to find one in the court's general directives about the examination process are unavailing at best and a vast expansion of *Parker* immunity at worst. Time and again the Court has rejected just such general authorizations as insufficient: the home rule charter in *Community Communications Co. v. City of Boulder*[52] and the utility rate approval in *Cantor v. Detroit Edison Co.*[53] illustrate the point. It seems quite unlikely that the Court intended to disrupt the law so dramatically, especially in the direction of broader antitrust immunity.

In order to avoid case-by-case adjudications of the various court rules that affect competition in the legal profession, the majority chose an interpretation of the facts and of the law that yielded a

---

[51] See California Motor Transp. Co. v. Trucking Unlimited, note 41 *supra*.

[52] See note 24 *supra*.

[53] See note 18 *supra*.

simple, easily administered rule for this minimal context. *Hoover* itself will probably have little effect on the scope of the *Parker* doctrine.[54] It will be cited for the proposition that actions of the State itself are immune and thus will not contribute much to the broader problems of state agency action, municipal action, and private action authorized by the State.

The approach of the *Hoover* majority gives more food for thought. The Court's straining to find a rule of law that would enable district courts to dismiss these cases on the pleadings, instead of engaging in even the limited additional fact-finding that would have been required here, reveals a concern for the methodology of antitrust litigation that has drifted in and out of the cases of recent years.[55] In *Hoover*, this approach required the Court to bury its head in the sand rather than confront the reality of the Committee's relationship to the state court. In the next case, a similar clearcut rule resulted from the most sophisticated analysis the Court used all Term.

B. COPPERWELD CORP. V. INDEPENDENCE TUBE CORP.: THE DOWNFALL OF INTRA-ENTERPRISE CONSPIRACIES

The state action doctrine is one that potentially applies to any antitrust case. Federalism concerns do not depend on whether the statute is Sherman Act § 1 or § 2 or some section of the Clayton Act or the Federal Trade Commission Act.[56] In contrast, for the intra-enterprise conspiracy doctrine at issue in *Copperweld*, two or more actors are essential to a finding of liability. In practical terms, the significance of intra-enterprise conspiracy is limited to Sherman Act § 1. The decision to recognize intra-enterprise conspiracies nevertheless bears directly on the general scope of the antitrust

---

[54] The Court has acknowledged as much, in that it has on its docket for the 1984 Term two cases raising issues about the scope of the *Parker* doctrine: Town of Hallie v. City of Eau Claire, 700 F.2d 376 (7th Cir. 1983), *cert. granted*, 104 S.Ct. 3508 (1984); Southern Motor Carriers Rate Conf., Inc. v. United States, 702 F.2d 532 (5th Cir., Unit B 1983) (*en banc*), *cert. granted*, 104 S.Ct. 3508 (1984).

[55] Compare Broadcast Music, Inc. v. Columbia Broadcasting Sys., Inc., 441 U.S. 1 (1979), with Arizona v. Maricopa County Medical Soc'y, 457 U.S. 332 (1982).

[56] This last point is not without some controversy. See, *e.g.*, AREEDA & TURNER, note 45 *supra*, ¶ 218. I agree with their conclusion that the Federal Trade Commission Act also contains a *Parker*-type exemption, for the federalism reason noted in the text.

laws, no less than the state action immunity doctrine. As in *Hoover*, the Court chose in *Copperweld* to narrow the substantive reach of antitrust law.

1. *The intra-enterprise conspiracy doctrine.* Violation of § 1 of the Sherman Act requires a "contract, combination, or conspiracy" in restraint of trade. Section 2, in contrast, reaches either single-firm monopolization or attempts to monopolize, or multiple-actor conspiracies to monopolize. Over time, the idea has developed that the standards embodied in § 2 for single-firm conduct are less intrusive, or more tolerant, than the standards of § 1 for concerted conduct.[57] The distinction between single-firm conduct and multiple-firm conduct is therefore of great importance.[58]

The question arises which individuals or firms are capable of conspiring with one another, bringing their conduct within the stricter § 1 standards. The definition of the word "person" for the Sherman Act is unhelpful: it simply states that "[t]he word 'person,' or 'persons,' wherever used in this act shall be deemed to include corporations and associations" properly constituted under federal, state, or foreign law.[59] The Court has never read this language literally, for to do so would be to condemn the agreements of a corporate manager with his superiors, or the agreements of two members of a partnership, since even these agreements restrain some trade. The same recognition of the absurdity of overliteral interpretation has caused some courts to refuse to find a plurality of actors when one division of a corporation combines with another to

---

[57] See, *e.g.*, AREEDA, ANTITRUST ANALYSIS: PROBLEMS, TEXT, CASES ¶ 334(d) (3d ed. 1981); Handler & Smart, *The Present Status of the Intracorporate Conspiracy Doctrine*, 3 CARDOZO L. REV. 23, 67–72 (1981); *cf.* NATIONAL COMMISSION FOR THE REVIEW OF ANTITRUST LAWS AND PROCEDURES 141–42 (1979) (recommending an expansion of the Sherman Act § 2 attempt to monopolize offense to reach more unilateral conduct than at present). The opinion in Standard Oil Co. v. United States, 221 U.S. 1 (1911), described the relationship between §§ 1 and 2 in a slightly different way. Section 1 was "an all-embracing enumeration to make sure that no form of contract or combination by which undue restraint" was created would be legal; § 2 supplemented § 1, in the sense that it prohibited the acts that would produce the results of monopoly. *Id.* at 59–60. It was in later years, as the Court developed doctrines that dispensed with the need to prove market power in certain § 1 cases, *e.g.*, United States v. Socony-Vacuum Oil Co., 310 U.S. 150 (1940), and that required sophisticated proof of such power in § 2 cases, *e.g.*, United States v. E.I. du Pont de Nemours & Co., 351 U.S. 377 (1956), that the distinction noted in the text became apparent.

[58] See, *e.g.*, *Monsanto*, note 4 *supra*, 104 S.Ct. at 1469; *Copperweld*, note 4 *supra*, 104 S.Ct. at 2740–41.

[59] Sherman Act § 8, 15 U.S.C. § 7 (1982); see also Clayton Act § 1, 15 U.S.C. § 12 (1982).

fix prices, allocate markets, or otherwise to "restrain trade" for the greater corporate good.[60]

The problem has been how to treat concerted behavior of two corporations that are affiliated in some way: parent and wholly owned subsidiary, parent and partly owned subsidiary, sister corporations, and so forth. *United States v. Yellow Cab Co.* is generally recognized as the case that created the rule that related corporations may provide the plurality of actors necessary for § 1 liability.[61] In *Yellow Cab*, however, a broader course of conduct was attacked. One individual, Markin, who was the president, general manager, and controlling shareholder of Checker Cab Manufacturing Corporation, set out to acquire control of important taxicab operating companies in Chicago, New York, and other cities. He achieved this goal through the purchase of controlling interests in the target companies. Thereafter, Markin allegedly foreclosed other manufacturers of taxicabs from the trade of the controlled companies. When the United States sued to break up the combination under § 1 of the Sherman Act, and the defendants responded that their conduct was not covered by the Act because they were a vertically integrated enterprise, the Court responded with the language that gave birth to the doctrine:[62]

> The fact that these restraints occur in a setting described by the appellees as a vertically integrated enterprise does not necessarily remove the ban of the Sherman Act. The test of illegality under the Act is the presence or absence of an unreasonable restraint on interstate commerce. Such a restraint may result as readily from a conspiracy among those who are affiliated or integrated under common ownership as from a conspiracy among those who are otherwise independent. Similarly, any affiliation or integration flowing from an illegal conspiracy cannot insulate the conspirators from the sanctions which Congress has imposed. The corporate interrelationships of the conspirators, in other words, are not determinative of the applicability of the Sherman Act. That statute is aimed at substance rather than form.

---

[60] *E.g.*, H&B Equip. Co. v. International Harvester Co., 577 F.2d 239 (5th Cir. 1978); Ark Dental Supply Co. v. Cavitron Corp., 461 F.2d 1093 (3d Cir. 1972); Joseph E. Seagram & Sons v. Hawaiian Oke & Liquors, Ltd., 416 F.2d 71 (9th Cir. 1969), *cert. denied*, 396 U.S. 1062 (1970).

[61] 332 U.S. 218 (1947).

[62] *Id.* at 227.

Although it is easy to see distinctions between the fact pattern of
Yellow Cab and a broad intra-enterprise conspiracy doctrine that
would require a finding of separateness every time affiliated corporations acted in concert, the quoted language from the opinion took
on a life of its own. In *Kiefer-Stewart Co. v. Joseph E. Seagram &
Sons*,[63] the Court found two affiliated liquor manufacturers liable
for a § 1 conspiracy to fix maximum resale prices for their wholesalers. The manufacturers argued that their status as " 'mere instrumentalities of a single manufacturing-merchandising unit' [made]
it impossible for them to have conspired in a manner forbidden by
the Sherman Act."[64] Unimpressed by the argument, the Court dismissed it with the following comment:[65]

> But this suggestion runs counter to our past decisions that com-
> mon ownership and control does not liberate corporations from
> the impact of the antitrust laws. *E.g. United States v. Yellow Cab
> Co.*, 332 U.S. 218. The rule is especially applicable where, as
> here, respondents hold themselves out as competitors.

Perma Life Mufflers, Inc. v. International Parts Corp.,[66] which dealt
with restrictions imposed by manufacturers and their subsidiaries
on franchised dealers, added a final twist to the doctrine. Those
who "avail[ ] themselves of the privilege of doing business through
separate corporations" cannot for § 1 purposes claim that they are
single entities.[67]

From these and other Supreme Court decisions, a number of
approaches to intra-enterprise conspiracy questions emerged.[68] It is
worth emphasizing that no court and no commentator ever flatly
said that all agreements between affiliated companies that could
restrain trade were illegal to the precise extent that they would be
in the absence of the affiliation. To the contrary, the Supreme
Court had spoken disparagingly in a case concerning agricultural
cooperatives of "impos[ing] grave legal consequences upon organi-

---

[63] 340 U.S. 211 (1951).

[64] *Id.* at 215.

[65] *Ibid.*

[66] 392 U.S. 134 (1968).

[67] *Id.* at 141–42.

[68] See, *e.g.*, United States v. Griffith, 334 U.S. 100 (1948); Schine Chain Theatres, Inc. v.
United States, 334 U.S. 110 (1948); Timken Roller Bearing Co. v. United States, 341 U.S.
593 (1951); and Albrecht v. Herald Co., 390 U.S. 145 (1968). See generally Handler &
Smart, note 57 *supra*.

zational distinctions that are of de minimis meaning and effect."[69] The effort on all sides was to limit the doctrine. One suggestion, from the Attorney General's National Committee to Study the Antitrust Laws, was to condemn only "concerted action between a parent and subsidiary or between subsidiaries which has for its purpose or effect coercion or unreasonable restraint on the trade of strangers to those acting in concert."[70] This test sounded more limiting than it actually was, since restraint or effect on third parties or strangers to the corporate group was not hard to find, if the enterprise was competing successfully.

Other suggested limitations included various elaborations of the "holding out" suggestion from *Kiefer-Stewart* (that is, what did the affiliated companies look like from the outside), and efforts to see how separately or independently the two companies were run (an inside perspective).[71] The trouble with all of these was their inherent arbitrariness. If one postulates a wholly owned subsidiary, the degree of independence permitted by the parent, or the outside appearances, are a thing of the moment. As soon as business judgment dictates a change, the change is made. In *Copperweld*, yielding to a growing tide of opposition to the doctrine, and at the Solicitor General's urging, the Supreme Court decided to take one more look at it.

2. *The* Copperweld *case. Copperweld* was the perfect vehicle for the Court's reconsideration of the intra-enterprise conspiracy doctrine, because the availability of antitrust treble damages to the plaintiff turned on a jury finding that two related corporations had conspired with one another. Copperweld Corporation had a wholly owned subsidiary, Regal Tube Company, which it had purchased from Lear Siegler, Inc., in 1972. Founded in 1955, Regal had originally been a wholly owned subsidiary of C. E. Robinson Company, in the business of manufacturing steel tubing for use in heavy equipment, cargo vehicles, and construction. In 1968, Lear Siegler

[69] Sunkist Growers, Inc. v. Winckler & Smith Citrus Prods. Co., 370 U.S. 19, 29 (1962).

[70] THE ATTORNEY GENERAL'S NATIONAL COMMITTEE TO STUDY THE ANTITRUST LAWS 34 (1955) (hereinafter referred to as 1955 ATTORNEY GENERAL'S REPORT).

[71] See generally Areeda, *Intraenterprise Conspiracy in Decline*, 97 HARV. L. REV. 451 (1983); Handler & Smart, note 57 *supra*; Note, *Intra-Enterprise Conspiracy under Section 1 of the Sherman Act: A Suggested Standard*, 75 MICH. L. REV. 717 (1977); Stengel, *Intra-Enterprise Conspiracy under Section 1 of the Sherman Act*, 35 MISS. L.J. 5 (1963); McQuade, *Conspiracy, Multicorporate Enterprises, and Section 1 of the Sherman Act*, 41 VA. L. REV. 183 (1955).

acquired Regal and operated it as an unincorporated division. David Grohne, who had been vice president and general manager of Regal under Robinson's ownership, became the president of the Regal Division under Lear Siegler's ownership. When Copperweld acquired Regal, the sales agreement included a covenant requiring Lear Siegler and its subsidiaries not to compete with Regal in the United States for a period of five years. The covenant was apparently silent about competition from Regal's Lear Siegler employees. After the sale, Copperweld transferred Regal's assets to a newly formed corporation wholly owned by Copperweld.

Grohne, meanwhile, initially stayed with Lear Siegler. Within a matter of months, he made a move to establish his own steel tubing business, which would compete with Regal. Toward that end, he formed the Independence Tube Corporation in May 1972. In preparation for business, Independence placed a machinery order with the Yoder Company, which promised to have the machinery delivered by December 1973. The executives at Regal and Copperweld, upon hearing of Grohne's plans, set out to stop him. They were evidently disappointed to learn that the noncompetition covenant was not binding on Grohne, but 'they were advised that Grohne could be stopped if he tried to use any of Regal's trade secrets or proprietary information (an unlikely event in that business). On this somewhat flimsy basis, they sent a letter to Yoder warning it that Copperweld would take "any and all steps which are necessary to protect our rights."[72] Two days later, Yoder voided its acceptance of Independence's purchase order for the machinery. Independence eventually found an alternate supplier, but its entry into the market was delayed some nine months by Yoder's backing out.

Independence then sued Copperweld, Regal, and Yoder, claiming among other things that they had violated Sherman Act § 1 and that Copperweld and Regal had interfered with Independence's contractual relations with Yoder.[73] After trial, the jury found that

---

[72] See 104 S.Ct. at 2734.

[73] Independence also named Phillip H. Smith, the chief executive officer of Copperweld, as a defendant, but he was dropped from the case before trial. In addition to the Sherman Act § 1 claims and contractual interference claims, Independence also charged that Copperweld and Regal had attempted to monopolize the market for steel tubing in violation of Sherman Act § 2, that Yoder had breached its contract to supply a tube mill to Independence, and that Copperweld and Regal had slandered and libeled Independence with a third company. See Independence Tube Corp. v. Copperweld Corp., 691 F.2d 310, 315 (7th Cir. 1982). Independence dropped the § 2 charges before trial. It settled the breach of contract claim with Yoder. The jury returned verdicts in its favor on the remaining counts. *Id.*

Copperweld and Regal, but not Yoder, had conspired to violate Sherman Act § 1, and that Copperweld alone had interfered with Independence's contractual relations with Yoder. The jury also found, following the judge's instructions, that the damages for the contractual interference and the antitrust violation were identical— $2,499,009. The presence of the antitrust claim meant that this figure was trebled to $7,497,027. The net result was to place a very clear price tag on the intra-enterprise conspiracy doctrine of $4,998,018, the punitive two-thirds of the antitrust damages. If Copperweld and Regal were legally incapable of combining with one another for purposes of Sherman Act § 1, the antitrust award would vanish, and Copperweld would be left with a significantly lower liability.

On appeal to the Seventh Circuit, Copperweld and Regal argued that they were not sufficiently distinct to qualify as separate entities under that court's test.[74] The court of appeals rejected this argument, but not before it expressed frustration with the intra-enterprise conspiracy doctrine. In the end, however, it felt constrained as a lower court not to abandon the doctrine altogether, but to apply it as well it could. Focusing on the question "when the distinction between affiliation and integration is trivial and when it is significant,"[75] the court affirmed the jury's verdict. Copperweld and Regal then petitioned for certiorari on the question (among others) "[w]hether a parent corporation and its wholly-owned subsidiary are capable of conspiring together in violation of the Sherman Act."[76] At the Court's invitation, the Solicitor General also appeared, taking the position that the answer to the question was no.

Despite the near unanimity of academic criticism directed against the doctrine, the Supreme Court split narrowly in its decision. Five members of the Court, led by the Chief Justice, voted to

---

[74] The Seventh Circuit's test had been elaborated in Photovest Corp. v. Fotomat Corp., 606 F.2d 704, 726–27 (7th Cir. 1979), *cert. denied*, 445 U.S. 917 (1980). It focused on a number of factors, in order to determine when there was enough separation between the two entities to justify treating them as distinct companies. The factors included the extent of the integration of ownership, whether there were two separate managerial staffs, efficiencies of the combination, their history, and so forth.

[75] 691 F.2d at 318.

[76] Brief for Copperweld Corporation and Regal Tube Company at i. The grant of certiorari was limited to the question quoted in the text.

repudiate intra-enterprise conspiracies as a basis for § 1 liability, at least in those cases involving a parent and its wholly owned subsidiary. Justice White did not participate.[77] This left Justice Stevens, joined by Brennan and Marshall, to write the dissenting opinion.

The Chief Justice's opinion for the Court opened with the comment that the Court had neither considered the implications of intra-enterprise conspiracies seriously in the past nor had it needed to use the doctrine to achieve any of its prior results.[78] The opinion then undertook to distinguish such cases as *Yellow Cab*, *Kiefer-Stewart*, and *Perma Life Mufflers*. It admitted that *Kiefer-Stewart* did not readily lend itself to a reading making the intra-enterprise conspiracy finding irrelevant, but it suggested that "were the same case decided today, the same result probably could be justified on the ground that the subsidiaries conspired with wholesalers other than the plaintiff."[79] In emphasizing this entirely hypothetical alternate ground for *Kiefer-Stewart*, the Court relied implicitly on its recent decision in *Monsanto Co. v. Spray-Rite Service Corp.*, considered in Section IID below, which found a similar conspiracy between a manufacturer and some of its wholesalers.

After this attempt to show that intra-enterprise conspiracies had never mattered very much anyway—a demonstration that even the majority did not find completely persuasive, since it took the precaution at the end of the opinion of overruling and disapproving all prior cases to the extent that they had used the doctrine—the Court came to the heart of the problem: Are intra-enterprise conspiracies the conduct of one economic actor or two? Relying again on *Monsanto*, the Court reaffirmed its view that the Sherman Act contains a "basic distinction between concerted and independent action."[80]

---

[77] For those who like to speculate about a nonparticipant's probable vote, it may be interesting to note that Justice White's separate concurrence in *Perma Life* made no mention of the intra-enterprise conspiracy aspect of the majority's opinion. He authored Albrecht v. Herald Co., note 68 *supra*, a decision in which the necessary conspiracy was found among a newspaper, a firm hired by the paper to solicit customers, and one of the paper's carriers. It is not unlikely that White would have been on the dissenting side, although naturally one can never say for sure.

[78] The opinion put it like this: "In short, while this Court has previously seemed to acquiesce in the intra-enterprise conspiracy doctrine, it has never explored or analyzed in detail the justifications for such a rule; the doctrine has played only a relatively minor role in the Court's Sherman Act holdings." 104 S.Ct. at 2739.

[79] 104 S.Ct. at 2738.

[80] 104 S.Ct. at 2740, citing *Monsanto*, 104 S.Ct. 1464, 1469.

For the first time, in so many words, the Court put its imprimatur on the theory that antitrust law judges single-firm conduct more leniently than the concerted behavior of more than one firm.[81] Single-firm conduct, the Court flatly stated, "is unlawful only when it threatens actual monopolization."[82] This is so for important reasons:[83]

> In part because it is sometimes difficult to distinguish robust competition from conduct with long-run anti-competitive effects, Congress authorized Sherman Act scrutiny of single firms only when they pose a danger of monopolization. Judging unilateral conduct in this manner reduces the risk that the antitrust laws will dampen the competitive zeal of a single aggressive entrepreneur.

The Court thus recognized the detriment to competition imposed by overenforcement of the antitrust laws, and the fine line that exists between healthy competition (which can hurt rivals) and impermissible exclusionary behavior (which can also hurt rivals).

Concerted activity, the Chief Justice wrote, is subject to the broad § 1 prohibition against unreasonable restraints of trade and is thus judged more sternly. Some agreements are judged so sternly that the Court will hear no justifications for them—those within the per se group. Other combinations do not lend themselves to such ready condemnation: "mergers, joint ventures, and various vertical agreements [ ] hold the promise of increasing a firm's efficiency and enabling it to compete more effectively."[84] Those

---

[81] This has been implicit for years, as many persons have noted. Note 57 *supra*. Still, the Court had never expressly endorsed this reading of the law. Its opinion in *Copperweld* has thus resolved the controversy over the scope of § 2's attempt to monopolize prohibition, which was generating substantial controversy several years ago. See, *e.g.*, NATIONAL COMMISSION FOR THE REVIEW OF ANTITRUST LAWS AND PROCEDURES, note 57 *supra*, ch. 8 & app. B (majority recommending that proof of a high probability of actual monopoly should not be required for the attempt offense, but rather only a determination of whether the defendant had significantly threatened competition; dissenting views expressed); 3 AREEDA & TURNER, note 45 *supra*, ¶¶ 832–34 (retaining most of the "dangerous probability of success" requirement); *Debate, Should the Sherman Act Be Amended to Broaden the Offense of Attempt to Monopolize?* 48 ANTITRUST L.J. 1433 (1979); Cooper, *Attempts and Monopoly: A Mildly Expansionary Answer to the Prophylactic Riddle of Section Two*, 72 MICH. L. REV. 373 (1974). The emphasis here on a stricter standard for single-firm conduct and the importance of the link to actual monopolization preclude interpretation of § 2 attempt as an offense designed to reach single-firm anticompetitive acts.

[82] 104 S.Ct. at 2740.

[83] *Ibid*.

[84] *Id*. at 2741.

"are judged under a rule of reason, an inquiry into market power and market structure designed to assess the combination's actual effect."[85] Whether the conduct is subject to the per se rule or the rule of reason, effects short of threatened monopolization are prohibited by § 1.

On the fundamental question why concerted activity should be "worse," the Court gave two answers. First, it noted that concerted activity "deprives the marketplace of the independent centers of decisionmaking that competition assumes and demands."[86] In other words, Congress thought that the change from two units in the marketplace to one is suspect; other things being equal, it prefers an unconcentrated market. Antitrust scrutiny is required to find out if the concerted activity might lead to efficiencies that benefit consumers or if it is anticompetitive. Second, the Court seemed to suggest that a "sudden" combining of previously independent units was particularly bad. It never explained what "sudden" meant in this context, unless it intended only to distinguish any new kind of concerted activity from day-to-day cooperation within a business unit.[87] Both the act of combining several independent business units and the behavior of loosely combined units that retain real independence from one another are judged under the stricter § 1 standard, because of the legislative preference for separate decision-making centers.

Affiliated corporations—at least a parent and a wholly owned subsidiary—are not independent decision-making centers, the Court concluded, no matter how much or how little independence from one another they may display on the surface. Coordination within a firm may take many forms: two officers or employees, two divisions of a single firm, or two affiliated corporations. To make antitrust liability turn upon which of these functionally identical forms was selected by the particular enterprise would be an unjustified elevation of form over substance. No intent to violate the antitrust laws can be inferred from the decision to use separate corporations instead of divisions, since "the economic, legal, or other

---

[85] *Ibid.*

[86] *Ibid.* ·

[87] The way the Court distinguished *Yellow Cab* gives some support to this reading, since it "saved" that result by noting the illegality of the initial acquisitions. The majority also commented that "[a] corporation's initial acquisition of control will always be subject to scrutiny under § 1 of the Sherman Act and § 7 of the Clayton Act." 104 S.Ct. at 2745.

considerations that lead corporate management to choose one structure over the other are not relevant to whether the enterprise's conduct seriously threatens competition."[88] The Court conceded that its result left a "gap" in antitrust coverage, in that a single enterprise might engage in restraints of trade short of attempted monopolization without antitrust liability. This gáp, it said, was not of the Court's making, but of Congress's. Any other result would thwart congressional intent and harm competition in the final analysis.

Justice Stevens, again writing for the dissenters, fired a barrage of accusations at the Court: the majority, not the dissent, was elevating form over substance; the majority was irresponsibly creating a new per se rule of legality; the majority was cavalierly disregarding established precedent and implicit legislative approval of that precedent; and the majority was blind to the anticompetitive potential of combinations between members of the same corporate family. In his view, the rule of reason saved any intra-enterprise dealings that improve the integration between parent and subsidiary, and at the same time it condemned the two corporations when they acted together to exclude others from the market, as in the case at bar, or otherwise engaged in anticompetitive behavior. He found support for this position in the common law (which did not disregard separate corporate form), the legislative history of the Sherman Act (which was directed against the affiliated corporations known as "trusts"), precedent (which contained "at least seven" prior decisions relying wholly or in part on intra-enterprise conspiracies), and economic justifications.[89] The first three arguments require no elaboration; the fourth does.

Justice Stevens found the *Yellow Cab* rule to be economically justified precisely because it addressed the gap in antitrust enforcement recognized and tolerated by the majority: agreements between affiliated corporations that have sufficient market power to affect competition, but not sufficient power to be considered monopolists under § 2. By "economically justified," Stevens meant something like "useful," for his next point was that the doctrine at issue helps to establish liability where an agreement is difficult to

---

[88] 104 S.Ct. at 2743.

[89] See 104 S.Ct. at 2750 (common law); 2751 (legislative history); 2746–48 (precedent); 2752 (economic justifications).

prove, such as when a third party declines to join a conspiracy and is punished for its behavior, or when organized crime attempts to build an empire of affiliated corporations. He did not explain why he could tolerate different treatment for divisions and subsidiaries. Instead, he suggested several ways in which corporate affiliation could operate to restrain trade: affiliation could increase entry barriers for others, it could help to conceal the true ownership of brands or products, and it could make predatory conduct more effective (presumably through practices such as cross-subsidization). Finally, he had an interesting comment on the usefulness of the economic theory that lay behind the Court's opinion:[90]

> Use of economic theory without reference to the competitive impact of the particular economic arrangement at issue is properly criticized when it produces overly broad per se rules of antitrust liability; criticism is no less warranted when a per se rule of antitrust immunity is adopted in the same way.

Where the antitrust laws can be read to reach undesirable conduct, they should be so read, he concluded. As in *Hoover*, he found a rule of antitrust exemption inappropriate.

3. *The effect of the decision.* As *Copperweld* was argued, both sides accused the other of elevating form over substance. Those in support of the intra-enterprise conspiracy doctrine noted, correctly enough, that its abolition would lead to an automatic exemption from Sherman Act § 1 liability for affiliated corporations (though not, of course, to any § 2 exemption). Those who urged the Court to overrule the doctrine emphasized the lack of economic substance behind a company's decision to operate through divisions rather than subsidiaries. Which was the better argument? The answer again depends upon the purpose and scope of the antitrust laws. If antitrust is viewed as a body of laws designed to preserve competitive market structures, along the lines of the Kaysen and Turner model of the late 1950s,[91] then formal multiplicity of actors may be of some significance. Justice Stevens tried to suggest some benefits of subjecting affiliated corporations to § 1 rule of reason analysis in each case, and in so doing, he relied heavily on Lawrence Sullivan's

---

[90] *Id.* at 2755.

[91] See KAYSEN & TURNER, ANTITRUST POLICY: AN ECONOMIC AND LEGAL ANALYSIS (1959).

contributions to this vision of antitrust.[92] If, on the other hand, antitrust is directed exclusively toward the prevention of the kind of market power that can result in the restriction of output and the enhancement of prices, to the detriment of consumers, then it makes no sense to treat related companies as individual actors.

The fact that the Court adopted both the result and much of the reasoning consistent with the consumer welfare conception of antitrust is important. It adds *Copperweld* to the ever-lengthening list of, decisions in which the Court has expressly or implicitly endorsed this concept of the antitrust laws. Moreover, in *Copperweld* the Court did not simply mouth the words of consumer welfare analysis while reaching a perverse result, as it did in the *Monsanto* and *NCAA* decisions. With the qualifications noted above, the reasoning and result were congruent with one another.

Even so, the Court was at pains to limit the rejection of the intraenterprise conspiracy doctrine to the narrow case of the parent and wholly owned subsidiary presented on the facts. Its care in doing so may reflect judicial prudence: the Court usually does not render advisory opinions, and statements beyond the case at hand would have been dicta in any event. It is legitimate to hazard guesses about what *Copperweld* means for the next cases in this line: the parent and a 51–99 percent owned subsidiary; two subsidiaries wholly owned by the same parent; two subsidiaries 51–99 percent owned by the same parent; and two corporations, one of which controls the other with a less than 50 percent ownership block. The logic of *Copperweld* seems to lead to the same finding in each of those cases: no § 1 conspiracy, because no destruction of competition that was otherwise in the market. The more complex cases of corporate control with less than a majority stock interest would require factfindings on the control issue, but that should not affect the underlying antitrust issue. Problems of unfairness to minority interests, if the *Copperweld* approach is extended, would have to be handled by reference to the appropriate body of state corporate law or federal law.

---

[92] See 104 S.Ct. at 2749 n.9 (citing SULLIVAN, HANDBOOK OF THE LAW OF ANTI-TRUST § 114 (1977) (hereinafter cited as SULLIVAN, ANTITRUST)), and at 2752–53 n.22, 2753 n.25, 2754 n.28, and 2754–55 n.29, for Stevens's citations to Sullivan. See also note 192 *infra*.

It is impossible to predict what the Court will actually do in these future cases. Logic may not provide the answer. The Court also reserved the issue of the legality of vertical price restrictions in its *Sylvania* decision, where it placed nonprice vertical restrictions under the rule of reason. It is practically undisputed that the arguments in favor of rule of reason treatment for nonprice restraints are equally cogent for price restraints,[93] but the Court passed up the opportunity in *Monsanto* to say so once and for all. This Court does nothing so consistently as it refuses to adopt clear, broad, and easily administered rules.

One point about *Copperweld* is of broader significance. The Court's decision has the effect of returning some ground to state tort or contract law, which the ever-widening scope of federal antitrust had swallowed for a time. In the case itself, the fortuity of Copperweld's decision to place Regal's assets in a corporation instead of a division transformed a case of contractual interference into a fifty-megaton antitrust suit. By refusing to use the intra-enterprise conspiracy doctrine, the Court was effectively leaving the regulation of one class of business behavior to other bodies of law, principally state law. The end result was the same in *Hoover*, although *Copperweld* rested on the conclusion that no substantive antitrust problem existed in the concerted behavior of parent and wholly owned subsidiary (apart from § 2 concerns), while the anti-competitive character of the alleged activity in *Hoover* was apparent but for the *Parker* exemption. The remaining three cases of the Term—*NCAA*, *Monsanto*, and *Hyde*—also turned on substantive conclusions about the scope of the laws. Unlike *Copperweld*, the opinions in each of the remaining cases lacked theoretical consistency and failed to resolve much beyond the immediate case.

---

[93] See, *e.g.*, Liebeler, *1983 Economic Review of Antitrust Developments: The Distinction between Price and Nonprice Distribution Restrictions*, 31 U.C.L.A. L. REV. 384 (1983); Baker, *Interconnected Problems of Doctrine and Economics in the Section One Labyrinth: Is Sylvania a Way Out?* 67 VA. L. REV. 1457, 1465 (1981); Bork, *Vertical Restraints: Schwinn Overruled*, 1977 SUPREME COURT REVIEW 171 (1977); Posner, *The Rule of Reason and the Economic Approach: Reflections on the Sylvania Decision*, 45 U. CHI. L. REV. 1 (1977). See generally Telser, *Why Should Manufacturers Want Fair Trade?* 3 J. LAW & ECON. 86 (1960). But see Pitofsky, *In Defense of Discounters: The No-Frills Case for a Per Se Rule against Vertical Price Fixing*, 71 GEO. L.J. 1487 (1983); Stewart & Roberts, *Viability of the Antitrust Per Se Illegality Rule: Schwinn Down, How Many to Go?* 58 WASH. U.L.Q. 727 (1980) (the latter two articles arguing not so much that logic compels a distinction between price and nonprice restrictions as that policy demands that the effort be made to distinguish the two).

C. NCAA V. BOARD OF REGENTS: THE UNCERTAIN WORLD
   OF HORIZONTAL ARRANGEMENTS

Perhaps better than any other decision of the Term, the *NCAA* case illustrates the present Court's typical reluctance to adopt hard and fast rules for antitrust. Although the case initially involved a laundry list of antitrust charges,[94] the Supreme Court focused on two questions: First, when should a per se rule apply to business behavior and when should the rule of reason apply? And second, was the NCAA's horizontal arrangement for televising college football games illegal? The Court's opinion left the per se rule narrower than it had been before, while it imposed liability under a confused and internally inconsistent application of the rule of reason.

1. *Per se rules and cooperation among competitors.* The question of the substantive scope of the Sherman Act and the question how to prove a violation have been intertwined since its earliest days. Whether one looks to Judge Taft's famous decision in *United States v. Addyston Pipe & Steel Co.*,[95] or to the Supreme Court's 1911 decision in *Standard Oil Co. v. United States*,[96] or to other prominent early cases such as *United States v. Trans-Missouri Freight Association*,[97] one finds consensus on the substantive proposition that the Act did not condemn all restraints of trade. Such a broad condemnation, all recognized, would be absurd, since it would sweep in productive arrangements like the partnership, the corporation, and the joint venture. Therefore, in the *Standard Oil* decision, the Court concluded that the statute had to be interpreted in the "light of reason," to prohibit those acts, but only those acts, that Congress intended to ban—all "undue restraints."[98] Sixty-seven years later,

---

[94] Plaintiffs alleged that the NCAA had fixed prices in violation of Sherman Act § 1 (either a per se violation or in the alternative a rule of reason offense), that it had conducted a group boycott that was illegal under § 1, and that it had monopolized college football televising in violation of Sherman Act § 2. The NCAA raised various defenses, including antitrust standing.

[95] 85 F. 271 (6th Cir. 1898), *modified and aff'd*, 175 U.S. 211 (1899).

[96] 221 U.S. 1 (1911).

[97] 166 U.S. 290 (1897). Although the Court wrote broadly in *Trans-Missouri*, to the effect that the Sherman Act condemned "all" restraints, the opinion went on to admit that covenants not to compete that were collateral to a sale of property "might not be included, within the letter or spirit of the statute in question." *Id.* at 329. Thus, even in *Trans-Missouri*, the most absolute of the Court's decisions, limits were recognized.

[98] ". . . [I]t follows that it was intended that the standard of reason which had been applied at the common law and in this country in dealing with subjects of the character embraced by the statute, was intended to be the measure used for the purpose of determining whether in a

the Court reaffirmed this substantive Rule of Reason in *National Society of Professional Engineers v. United States*,[99] in which it condemned the engineering society's rule against competitive bidding. Just as the early cases had rejected defenses to price-fixing and market allocation that relied on the reasonableness of the particular price or the danger of "ruinous competition," *Professional Engineers* rejected the defense that competition itself would be injurious to safety and quality in designs. The sole focus of the substantive Rule of Reason is on the competitive process: anything that injures competition is prohibited by the statute. This leaves open the question what exactly is meant by "competition": antitrust law would prohibit far more exclusionary behavior if "rivalry" is the correct synonym than if "allocative efficiency" is. In either case, however, *Professional Engineers* is best understood as a substantive decision.

The more common use of the phrase "rule of reason" today connotes the lack of a presumption against a particular practice. When such a presumption exists, the practice is said to be per se illegal. Justice Hugo Black provided the classic description and justification for the per se offenses in the *Northern Pacific Railway* case:[100]

> However, there are certain agreements or practices which because of their pernicious effect on competition and lack of any redeeming virtue are conclusively presumed to be unreasonable and therefore illegal without elaborate inquiry as to the precise harm they have caused or the business excuse for their use. This principle of per se unreasonableness not only makes the type of restraints which are proscribed by the Sherman Act more certain to the benefit of everyone concerned, but it also avoids the necessity for an incredibly complicated and prolonged economic investigation into the entire history of the industry involved, as well as related industries, in an effort to determine at large whether a particular restraint has been unreasonable—an inquiry so often fruitless when undertaken. Among the practices which the courts have heretofore deemed to be unlawful in and of themselves are price fixing, . . . division of markets, . . . group boycotts, . . . and tying arrangements. . . .

---

given case a particular act had or had not brought about the wrong against which the statute provided." 221 U.S. at 60.

[99] 435 U.S. 679 (1978). I will capitalize "Rule of Reason" when I use it in the substantive sense, and use lower-case "rule of reason" to describe the nonpresumptive sense discussed below.

[100] Note 5 *supra*, 356 U.S. at 5 (citations omitted).

Although Black wrote about per se rules as if they had always existed, the fact is that the terminology if not the substance was relatively recent even for price-fixing, and that many of the per se categories originated only after World War II.[101] The administrative convenience of the rules was premised upon a court's ability to take a quick look at the business practice and to place it in the appropriate category. When the structuralist view of antitrust was the prevailing theory, this premise was satisfied. However, as the Supreme Court and the lower courts began to apply the teachings of microeconomic theory to antitrust law, the per se rules lost much of their simplicity, and hence, their raison d'etre.[102]

Per se analysis requires two steps: characterization of the practice and application of the rule. During the Black era, characterization was almost automatic. If, for example, a group of persons in direct competition with one another combined to fix or to affect price, they were characterized as price-fixers, and condemnation followed. Since the mid-1970s, the characterization step has expanded so dramatically that it is no longer possible to assume administrative convenience from the use of per se rules. The Court recognized the new significance of characterization in its 1979 decision in *Broadcast Music, Inc. v. Columbia Broadcasting System, Inc.*:[103]

> More generally, in characterizing this conduct under the per se rule, our inquiry must focus on whether the effect and, here because it tends to show effect, . . . the purpose of the practice are to threaten the proper operation of our predominantly free-market economy—that is, whether the practice facially appears to be one that would always or almost always tend to restrict

---

[101] Although a per se approach against price fixing can be detected in Supreme Court cases as early as United States v. Trenton Potteries, 273 U.S. 392 (1927), the Court first used the terminology in United States v. Socony-Vacuum Oil Co., 310 U.S. 150 (1940), fully fifty years after the passage of the Act. The identification of group boycotts as presumptively illegal dates from either Fashion Originators' Guild of America, Inc. v. Federal Trade Comm'n, 312 U.S. 457 (1941), or more accurately, Klor's, Inc. v. Broadway-Hale Stores, Inc., 359 U.S. 207 (1959). The general per se rule against tying arrangements, as the Court noted in *Hyde*, dates only from the decision in International Salt Co. v. United States, 332 U.S. 392 (1947). If nothing else, the fact that the per se rules to which Black referred arose for the most part no earlier than the 1940s shows how quickly something can appear to be part of the natural order of things.

[102] See Lipner, note 6 *supra;* Note, *Fixing the Price Fixing Confusion: A Rule of Reason Approach*, 92 YALE L.J. 706 (1983); Redlich, *Burger Court and the Per Se Rule*, 44 ALBANY L. REV. 1 (1979).

[103] Note 55 *supra*, 441 U.S. at 19–20 (quoting United States v. United States Gypsum Co., 438 U.S. 422, 441 n.16 (1978) (footnotes and citations omitted).

competition and decrease output, and in what portion of the market, or instead one designed to "increase economic efficiency and render markets more, rather than less, competitive."

Even so, the Court was less than fully committed to the characterization approach. In 1982, in *Arizona v. Maricopa County Medical Society*, it eschewed the type of analysis suggested in *Broadcast Music* in favor of a Black-style condemnation of a maximum price-fixing arrangement among doctors.[104] Thus, when the *NCAA* case came before the Court, the Justices could look to one recent decision that reaffirmed the traditional per se approach for horizontal arrangements and to another that stripped the per se rules of their advantages by requiring sophisticated economic analysis of the output effects of a practice prior to condemnation.

The alternative to the per se rule, the rule of reason (in a lack-of-presumption sense), has implied until now an extensive list of factors that courts were supposed to throw at juries, in the hope that the juries would end up imposing liability on the trade restrainers and exonerating those who stayed on the right side of the law. The lists, epitomized by Justice Brandeis's decision in *Board of Trade of City of Chicago v. United States*,[105] include facts such as the nature of the business to which the restraint was applied, its condition before and after the restraint, the history of the restraint, the purpose of the restraint, and so on. The law has provided little if any guidance to lower courts or to juries on the relative weights to be attached to the various factors—a state of affairs making the rule of reason tantamount to a game of craps and making review of jury verdicts difficult.[106] In particular, although the idea of connecting reason-

---

[104] Note 55 *supra*, 457 U.S. 332. See also Gerhart, note 6 *supra;* Easterbrook, *Maximum Price Fixing*, 48 U. CHI. L. REV. 886 (1981). Judge Posner has suggested that *Maricopa* may be explained as a case in which a cartel-facilitating practice (maximum prices) was condemned. See Vogel v. American Soc'y of Appraisers, 744 F.2d 598 (7th Cir. 1984). If he is right, then a full-blown characterization analysis would have led to the same result. Still, the language of *Maricopa* implies that the arrangement would have been condemned regardless of the likelihood of a physicians' cartel.

[105] 246 U.S. 231 (1918). See Continental T.V., Inc. v. GTE Sylvania Inc., note 1 *supra.* Cf. United States v. Penn-Olin Chemical Co., 378 U.S. 158 (1964) (lengthy list of criteria suggested for assessing effect on competition of proposed joint venture, under Sherman Act § 1 and Clayton Act § 7).

[106] Not surprisingly, the rule of reason has been criticized in the literature for these flaws. See Easterbrook, *Vertical Arrangements and the Rule of Reason*, 53 ANTITRUST L.J. 135, 153–57 (1984); Posner, *The Next Step in the Antitrust Treatment of Restricted Distribution: Per Se Legality*, 48 U. CHI. L. REV. 6, 14–18 (1981); Pitofsky, *The Sylvania Case: Antitrust Analysis of Non-Price Vertical Restrictions*, 78 COLUM. L. REV. 1, 34 (1978).

ableness with market power (and thus with market definition in the usual case) has lurked around the edges of court descriptions of the rule, the Supreme Court had never said that a restraint had to enhance or create market power in order to be illegal under the rule of reason.

Imperfect as both the per se rule and the rule of reason were, the consequences of assigning conduct to one or the other were obviously great—plaintiffs had a built-in advantage if they succeeded in placing their claim within a per se category. Almost equally significant was the characterization of conduct as horizontal or vertical. Arrangements among competitors have since the earliest days of antitrust been subject to stricter legal scrutiny than vertical arrangements, and the gap has widened in recent years.[107] The *NCAA* case presented the Supreme Court with an opportunity to consider again the respective spheres of the per se rule and the rule of reason, as well as to refine the rules that define and regulate horizontal cooperation or collusion.

2. *The decision.* For nearly eighty years, the National Collegiate Athletic Association has existed to regulate amateur intercollegiate sports, including football, basketball, and baseball. Its regulations cover everything from rules of play and standard specifications for playing fields and equipment, to recruitment of student athletes and size of coaching staffs, to the matters close to the heart of this case: the number of games played and the televising of those games. During the time that television has been a significant factor in American life, the NCAA's members have regulated the televising of college football games. The various Television Plans that it has adopted over the years have restricted the number of college games on television, the number of times any given school could appear, and the compensation each school would receive for a television appearance.[108]

---

[107] For example, Addyston Pipe & Steel, note 95 *supra*, United States v. Sealy, Inc., 388 U.S. 350 (1967), and United States v. Topco Associates, Inc., 405 U.S. 596 (1972), established the per se illegality of territorial allocations among competitors, but the Court imposed the analogous per se rule against vertical territorial or other nonprice restrictions only for the ten-year period between United States v. Arnold, Schwinn & Co., 388 U.S. 365 (1967), and *Sylvania*, note 1 *supra*.

[108] The NCAA now has 785 college and university members and about 100 institutional members. Each member has an equal vote on the Television Plan. Brief for NCAA at 2. The NCAA has not chosen to regulate the televising of games in other sports, other than contests that it sponsored.

The NCAA asserted a number of reasons for adopting the television rules. To a greater or lesser degree, all the reasons flowed from the ideal of college football as amateur rivalry, subordinate to the educational activities of the student athletes. For example, the restrictions on the number of games shown as a whole and on the number of times any given institution could appear on television were adopted to preserve the amateur status of the sport. (If the NCAA thought it could have gotten more revenue for its members by more televising of games, it was thus intentionally forfeiting profit for noneconomic goals. If, on the other hand, it believed that more games would lead to less revenue, then it was acting in the aggregate economic interest of its members, although not necessarily in the individual interest of a particular school.) The NCAA also expressed concern about the effect of televised games on gate attendance. Finally, the rules governing allocation of television revenues among teams that appeared were adopted to prevent any one team or small group of teams from dominating the sport. The NCAA hoped that balance among schools would result over time from this system.

The Television Plan at issue before the Supreme Court covered the 1982–85 seasons. The important terms were spelled out in separate agreements with ABC Television Network, Columbia Broadcasting System, and Turner Broadcasting System (a cable network). ABC and CBS were each given the right to telecast fourteen live "exposures," or time slots in which either a national telecast or several regional telecasts could be inserted. The contracts obligated ABC and CBS each to pay to the NCAA institutions a "minimum aggregate compensation" of $131,750,000 over the four-year life of the contract. As a practical matter, the monies were allocated among institutions depending upon whether the telecast was national or regional, and whether the team was in division 1 (*i.e.* a major football school) or the smaller divisions 2 or 3, although this was not written in the contract. Significantly, the amount a school received did not vary by the size of the viewing audience the broadcast was likely to command, the number of markets in which it was to be telecast, or any other individuating factors. Consequently, for example, when ABC televised a 1981 game between the University of Oklahoma and the University of Southern California on the vast majority of its stations, and a game between Citadel and Appalachian State on four local affiliates, all four schools received exactly the same amount of money.[109]

The major football powers were unhappy with this situation, since their games were attracting much greater television audiences than the Citadel–Appalachian State type of game, and they wanted the revenues that normally correspond to the larger audience. When other steps to achieve this end were unsuccessful, the Board of Regents of the University of Oklahoma and the University of Georgia Athletic Association sued the NCAA under Sherman Act §§ 1 and 2, claiming that its football television controls constituted a horizontal agreement among competitors to fix prices and to reduce output in violation of § 1, that the NCAA was engaged in a group boycott in violation of § 1, and that the NCAA was monopolizing college football television in violation of § 2. The plaintiffs asked only for injunctive relief.

The district court found, in a bench trial, in favor of the plaintiffs on all issues.[110] It entered an injunction banning the NCAA from enforcing the 1982–85 television contracts, from acting as the exclusive agent for its members for the sale of telecasting rights, from making any future contracts that granted any telecaster the right to televise the football games of any member institutions, and generally from regulating the televising of its members' games. The Court of Appeals for the Tenth Circuit affirmed only on the horizontal price-fixing and output-reduction point.[111] The appellate court overturned the finding of an illegal group boycott, and it found it unnecessary to consider the § 2 monopolization holding.[112] Curiously, the Tenth Circuit seemed to agree with the NCAA that the district court's injunction was overly broad, since the district court apparently had prohibited even actions such as the use of television sanctions for violation of other, presumptively legitimate, rules, but the court of appeals declined to vacate the injunction and remand for further proceedings. It suggested only that the NCAA should seek modifications in the district court. Judge Barrett dissented, on the ground that the NCAA plan was not anticompetitive

---

[109] See 104 S.Ct. at 2964 n.33.

[110] 546 F. Supp. 1276 (W.D. Okla. 1982).

[111] 707 F.2d 1147 (10th Cir. 1983).

[112] *Id.* at 1160 (group boycott), 1159 n.16 (monopolization).

in purpose and that under rule of reason scrutiny the justifications offered in support of the plan were sufficient to save it.

With Justice Stevens this time heading a majority of seven, the Supreme Court affirmed the two lower courts, on precedent-breaking grounds. The majority found that the per se rule should not apply to the NCAA's television regulations, but that the NCAA was nevertheless in violation of the Sherman Act under the rule of reason. This is the first time the Supreme Court has imposed § 1 liability on rule-of-reason evidence,[113] although Justice Stevens would have done the same thing in *Broadcast Music*. The two dissenters, led by Justice White (the author of *Broadcast Music*), relied on both the nonbusiness nature of the NCAA and various flaws in the majority's market analysis.

The Court's opinion addressed three questions: (1) whether the per se rule or the rule of reason should apply; (2) whether there was any anticompetitive potential in the NCAA contracts; and (3) whether the NCAA's justifications for its arrangements were sufficient to save their legality. Analysis requires first a look at the market in which the NCAA contracts operated. Five types of actors produce college football games on television: the colleges and universities (producers of football games), the NCAA (common selling agent for the producers and regulator of the sport), the television networks (direct purchasers from the NCAA, with contractual commitment to pay negotiated amount of money to colleges), television viewers (except in the case of cable, persons who pay nothing but are a "commodity" in the aggregate that the networks deliver to advertisers), and advertisers (persons who buy time on the football program, paying according to the size and demographics of the expected audience). To an important degree, the difference between the majority and the dissenters can be reduced to a different focus within this complex market—what is the relevant market, who are the consumers, and what is the best measure of output?

Justice Stevens had no trouble characterizing the NCAA's television practices as a horizontal restraint, which he defined as "an agreement among competitors on the way in which they will com-

---

[113] I place *Professional Engineers* in the substantive Rule of Reason category. There was no question of a per se rule for that case, and the proffered defense went to the substantive conduct, not to the usefulness of a presumption. In essence, the engineers argued that competition was a bad thing for their profession, and the Court rejected this.

pete with one another."[114] The member institutions competed off
the football field in a number of ways: for television revenues, for
fans, and for athletes. The Television Plan, by placing a ceiling on
the number of games that would be shown, put an artificial limit on
output, which Stevens defined as the quantity of televised college
football that is available to broadcasters and consumers. The Plan's
minimum aggregate price operated to preclude any price negotia-
tion between broadcasters and institutions—that is, it fixed the
price per telecast for each NCAA member. Twenty years ago, the
Court's opinion would probably have stopped right there: to
characterize conduct plausibly as horizontal output limitation and
price-fixing was to state a per se violation of the Sherman Act.
Nothing more need be said.

Stevens gave an intriguing reason for refusing to take the conventional approach. He did not rely on the usual arguments for
avoiding the per se rule, such as lack of judicial experience with the
type of arrangement, the nonprofit status, or the history of the
NCAA. Rather, he said, "what is critical is that this case involves
an industry in which horizontal restraints on competition are essential if the product is to be available at all."[115] He thereby likened the
NCAA's television controls to the blanket license for copyrighted
music that the Court had held subject to the rule of reason in
Broadcast Music, although the blanket license was not "necessary"
for the composers. In this context, he recognized that the NCAA
was trying to create a particular product—college football—that
would be different from and "more popular than professional sports
to which it might otherwise be comparable, such as, for example,
minor league baseball."[116] This, the majority recognized, was procompetitive action. Because the NCAA's football controls taken
together were not uniformly anticompetitive, the Court concluded
that a full consideration of the justifications for the Television Plan
was necessary, under the rule of reason. The essential inquiry, it
stressed, was "whether or not the challenged restraint enhances
competition."[117]

The Court found a number of anticompetitive aspects to the

[114] 104 S.Ct. at 2959 (footnote omitted).

[115] 104 S.Ct. at 2961.

[116] *Ibid.*

[117] *Id.* at 2962 (footnote omitted).

Television Plan. Without the Plan, more games would be shown on television, which would mean an increase in output measured by television appearance time. The NCAA plan had the effect of increasing the price paid by the networks for the series; its abolition would bring prices down to market levels.[118] Finally, the Court found the method of allocating compensation among schools to be anticompetitive, insofar as it ignored viewer demand for particular games. A number of anticompetitive consequences followed from these facts. First, the Court noted that individual competitor schools lost their freedom to compete (*i.e.* their ability to sell rights to football games to the television station of their choice, in the amount they could command). Second, it stated that prices were higher and output lower than they would otherwise be. (Here the Court lost the thread of its own argument, for it is difficult to see how the colleges were injured by receiving too much money for too little effort. The injured parties would have been the networks, or other purchasers of games.) The Court also noted that both price and output were unresponsive to consumer preference, apparently referring to the fact that the games shown on television were not always the games demanded by viewers and that the networks did not pay a higher price, and the colleges did not receive more money, for the more popular games. This point went more to internal NCAA affairs, since the powerhouse universities wanted a larger share of the pie and more of their own games on the air, but not necessarily more of anyone else's games. Finally, the Court criticized the fact that only the television broadcasters that were large enough to submit a bid on the entire NCAA package were able to enter the market. The exclusion of the small stations hurt potential viewers of games that would not command a national audience, but that were popular locally.

---

[118] The Court's prediction in this respect has come to pass. For several reasons, the prices that the networks and stations are paying for college football games for the 1984 season are considerably lower in the aggregate than the NCAA contract would have guaranteed. See NEW YORK TIMES, Sunday, August 26, 1984, sec. 5, at 9, col. 1. It appears that the victory of Oklahoma and Georgia in the Supreme Court was a Pyrrhic one: national telecasts under the voided NCAA contract were worth $700,000 for each team, while the new contract between ABC and the College Football Association (to which both Oklahoma and Georgia belong) will bring only $300,000 per team. *Id.* SPORTS ILLUSTRATED reported that Oklahoma may have to rent out its stadium to the U.S. Football League in the spring of 1985 to raise revenue. "A Supremely Unsettling Smorgasbord," SPORTS ILLUSTRATED, Sept. 5, 1984, at 151.

The NCAA argued against the Court's perception of the anti-competitive effects, since the NCAA had no market power to begin with. The Court rejected the relevance of market power to this sort of restraint, apparently even in a rule-of-reason case. In so doing, and in characterizing the Television Plan as a naked restraint on price and output, the Court undercut its own reasons for rejecting per se condemnation. It seems inconceivable that the Court meant here to permit competitive justifications for all "naked restraints," though the language of the opinion fails to exclude that possibility. To the antitrust lawyer, naked restraint is a synonym for per se violation, yet nothing in the *NCAA* opinions suggests that the Court was utterly abandoning per se analysis. In context, the expression must either be ignored or read to mean noncovert horizontal restraint. The Court was willing to assume in the alternative that the NCAA had market power, but its approach to market definition was to assume the answer before the analysis took place. Because Saturday afternoon college football broadcasts are uniquely attractive to television viewers, the Court agreed with the district court that those broadcasts made up a distinct market, relying on *International Boxing Club v. United States.*[119] This conclusion relied implicitly on the assumption that the "consumers" in this market were viewers, not television networks or advertisers.

The Court rejected all of the NCAA's proffered justifications for its Plan. It refused to see the organization as a cooperative joint venture, marketing college football as a television series in competition for advertising dollars with other series, such as "Hill Street Blues," "60 Minutes," and "Dallas." It also refused to see the limitation on number of games and the partial network exclusivity as a way of increasing output measured by aggregate number of viewers of college football. Once the market was defined as Saturday afternoon college football, the relevance of these defenses was impossible to sustain. Finally, the Court was unpersuaded by the NCAA's amateurism defenses, including the protection of gate attendance and the preservation of competitive balance among teams. It placed the burden of proof on the NCAA to show that these goals

---

[119] 358 U.S. 242 (1958). The Court referred to Times-Picayune Publishing Co. v. United States, 345 U.S. 594 (1953), in the same passage, but *Times-Picayune* actually supports the NCAA's case more than the reverse. The Court recognized there that advertisers buy readership (or viewership), and it held that it was meaningless to claim a tie between the readers of a morning paper and (the same) readers of an evening paper. The same approach in *NCAA* would have led a majority to the position expressed by Justice White.

were actually achieved, at the least possible competitive cost, by the means the NCAA adopted, and the NCAA failed to meet that burden. With the anticompetitive potential of the arrangement established to the Court's satisfaction, and the justifications rejected, the Court thus condemned the Television Plan under a rule-of-reason analysis.

Justice White's dissent gave more prominence to the noncommercial nature of the NCAA than to the economic analysis of the Plan, although he offered both reasons for disagreeing with the majority's conclusions. The NCAA's controls were necessary to correct the free market's inability to provide high quality amateur athletics in the college setting. All its rules, including the television rules, worked together to accomplish this end. Justice White expressly stated that the noneconomic goals of the NCAA legitimately could be taken into account in assessing the legality of the association's plans. He rejected the reading of *Professional Engineers* that precluded reliance in a rule-of-reason analysis on anything other than effects on competitive conditions.

White was also willing to meet the majority on its own economic grounds. He noted that the district court had used the wrong measure of output when it asked the question whether more football games would appear on television in the absence of the restraint. The proper measure was total viewership, which White found was expanded by the NCAA's plan. Second, he questioned whether any anticompetitive increase in the price for television rights had resulted from the plan. The exclusivity that the NCAA was able to guarantee made the rights sold more valuable. Without exclusivity, the networks, stations, and advertisers would have paid less, and the colleges would have received less. Next, he addressed squarely the universities' principal complaint, namely, the distribution of revenues among NCAA members. No court had found this to be illegal, in itself, unless the majority's comments about the need to achieve a correspondence between viewer preference and televised games were read to require a distribution of total revenue that corresponded to Nielsen ratings of each broadcast. The problem with the plaintiffs' complaints at that point was characterization: if the NCAA is truly a cartel, no court would intervene solely to redistribute cartel profits more to the liking of the dominant members; if the NCAA is a joint venture, then its internal distribution of profits is of no concern to the law.

Finally, White offered a different approach to the question of market definition. In conducting his own rule-of-reason analysis, he looked to the market in which NCAA telecasts competed—that is, the entertainment market. NCAA football competes with other television offerings for advertising dollars, and television itself competes with other forms of entertainment for viewer time. In that context, the NCAA has no market power, and its Television Plan has no adverse effect on competitive conditions anywhere. By keeping clearly in mind whose interests were being served where, White was able to evaluate the NCAA arrangement to his own satisfaction and to conclude that the plan did not injure competition and that the antitrust laws were not designed to impede organizations such as the NCAA in any event.

3. *The rule of reason of the future.* By rejecting the per se rule and nevertheless condemning the Television Plan, the Court signaled a greater role for the rule of reason and just as clearly indicated that the rule of reason will no longer be a synonym for "defendant wins." *NCAA* thus joins decisions such as *Broadcast Music* and *Sylvania*, which refuse to lump superficially similar arrangements (either horizontal or vertical) together for the purpose of condemning them. In other words, the Court increasingly is taking the position that the administrative simplicity offered by the traditional per se rule is being purchased at too high a cost. In markets such as the market for college football television, which require some horizontal cooperation to exist, the Court is no longer afraid to undertake the complex economic analysis that Justice Black wished to avoid in *Northern Pacific*. At the same time, it is very difficult to tell when the Court will conclude that such an imperfect market exists, because everything depends upon the definition of the market adopted for the case. In *Maricopa*, for instance, the Court could have emphasized the market imperfections that exist for health care and defined the market as one for guaranteed cost medical services, and it would have been in the same position as it was in *NCAA*— needing to go to a full rule-of-reason analysis of the practice. Instead, it applied an old-fashioned per se rule to the Medical Society's plan while openly recognizing that the practice at issue might have been procompetitive.

If the rule of reason is to assume the central position in antitrust that has been occupied up to now by the per se rule, then it becomes critical to understand what content the rule has. The Court's

NCAA opinion gives the most direct guidance, since the rule of reason was actually applied there. A number of points are clear. First, the Court explicitly rejected the argument that proof of market power was necessary to a finding of liability under the rule of reason.[120] Second, the Court endorsed the placement of the burden on defendants to show the necessity of adopting a particular practice that could have anticompetitive consequences, and to show that the practice was effective in achieving the desired end.[121] These aspects of the opinion represent a fairly conservative approach to the rule of reason—that is, an approach under which defendants will find it hard to prevail.

On the other hand, the Court's opinion uses much of the language of economic analysis. Taking the district court's fact-finding at face value (and implicitly rejecting the NCAA's burden-of-proof argument), the opinion makes a valiant effort to analyze the price and output effects of the NCAA's controls. It places "consumer demand" at the center of the antitrust laws, and it criticizes the Television Plan for disrupting the operation of a free market insofar as it fails to provide the number of games and the matches between schools that television viewers would prefer to have. All these questions—price, output, consumer welfare—are precisely the questions that should be asked in this kind of case. The problem with the Court's opinion is that it answers the questions without a clear conception of the market in which these factors are operating. By refusing to take the first step, market definition, the Court made it impossible for itself to provide an intellectually consistent answer to the other questions. If the Court had looked more carefully at the market, one of two results would probably have occurred. Either the Court still would have condemned the NCAA's arrangements, but would have grappled with the problem of the standing of the beneficiary universities to raise these points, or it would have taken the dissent's approach and upheld the Plan, on the theory that college football is only a small part of the overall television market and that it is the latter market that is relevant for the advertisers who underwrite the programs in the end.

The NCAA opinion is also important for the light it throws on the growing antitrust problems of professionals and nonprofit in-

---

[120] 104 S.Ct. at 2965.

[121] *Id.* at 2967–68 (necessity); 2969–70 (effectiveness).

stitutions. Justice Stevens adhered to his own formulation of the content of the rule of reason in *Professional Engineers:* only effect on competition is relevant, no matter how worthy the noneconomic goals of the organization may be. Stevens unfortunately has never spelled out what he means by "competition" in this context: maximum rivalry, the allocation of resources in which prices are set equal to full cost, or something else. If consensus existed on this pivotal point, the *Professional Engineers* approach could simplify the rule of reason, since it provides a single focus for juries and appellate courts. As it is, the different results the Court has reached over the years in antitrust may be due in large part to different conceptions of the "competition" that the antitrust laws protect.

NCAA, in the end, shows the Court attempting to adopt a sophisticated approach to horizontal restraints, refusing to apply the per se rule, and trying to protect the interest of "consumers." Both majority and dissent thought that they were accomplishing these worthy goals. The trouble is that the fact-bound analysis of the NCAA's Television Plan, and the description of some parts of the plan as procompetitive and others as anticompetitive, took place outside any general framework. The Court's rejection of market analysis—even a truncated version of market analysis such as the Solicitor General suggested[122]—led to its confusion over the proper measure of output, the ultimate consumers in the market, and the significance of the restrictions on which games, and how many games, were televised. This tension between the statement of the rules and their application was repeated in the most important case on vertical restrictions of the Term, *Monsanto;* the other decision, *Hyde*, was a textbook example of rhetoric run amok.

D. MONSANTO V. SPRAY-RITE SERVICE CORPORATION:
MANUFACTURERS AND DISTRIBUTORS REVISITED

A number of different antitrust doctrines converged in *Monsanto*. As presented to the Supreme Court, it was popularly perceived as a case that invited the Court to overrule the venerable decision in *Dr. Miles Medical Co. v. John D. Park & Sons Co.*,[123] which had estab-

---

[122] See Brief for the United States at 7. Compare the approach taken by the Seventh Circuit to per se illegality in General Leaseways, Inc. v. National Truck Leasing Ass'n, No. 83-3173. Sept. 18, 1984 ("quick look" reveals probable per se offense, on review of a preliminary injunction).

[123] 220 U.S. 373 (1911).

lished the per se rule against so-called vertical price-fixing (otherwise known as resale price maintenance, or RPM). In addition, the case included a conspiracy issue reminiscent of *Copperweld:* on what evidence is a jury entitled to infer a conspiracy among a manufacturer and its distributors to maintain fixed retail prices. Without that essential concert of action, the manufacturer's dictation of a price to his resellers would fall within the protected sphere of the *Colgate* doctrine,[124] which guarantees firms the right to deal with whom they wish, on the terms they wish, as long as those terms (including required resale prices) are dictated in a purely unilateral manner. If the Court had found the required conspiracy missing in *Monsanto*, it could nevertheless have decided to reconsider *Colgate*, although none of the parties urged this. While *NCAA* may have been the decision to attract the most public attention, *Monsanto* easily attracted the most legislative and legal attention.

1. *The law of vertical restrictions.* The history of the law concerning vertical restrictions—that is, those between different levels of the distributional chain, such as manufacturer to wholesaler, or distributor to retailer—has been well documented elsewhere.[125] In brief, the Court has vacillated between treating vertical restrictions just as strictly as horizontal restrictions, and treating the former as a different, and more defensible, economic phenomenon. At present, an agreement between a manufacturer and its dealer on the price at which an item is to be sold is condemned as vertical price-fixing, subject to a per se rule established in the 1911 *Dr. Miles* decision. Although the economically indistinguishable practice of vertical territorial division was at one time also subject to a per se prohibi-

---

[124] United States v. Colgate & Co., 250 U.S. 300 (1919).

[125] Recognizing both the impossibility and, in limited space, the undesirability of referring to everything written on this subject, a few principal references follow. See, *e.g.*, Bork, *The Rule of Reason and the Per Se Rule: Price Fixing and Market Division* (Pts. 1 & 2), 74 YALE L.J. 775 (1965), 75 YALE L.J. 373 (1966); Posner, *Antitrust Policy and the Supreme Court: An Analysis of the Restricted Distribution, Horizontal Merger and Potential Competition Decisions,* 75 COLUM. L. REV. 282 (1975); Pitofsky, note 106 *supra;* Williamson, *Assessing Vertical Market Restrictions: Antitrust Ramifications of the Transaction Cost Approach,* 127 U. PA. L. REV. 953 (1979); Scherer, *The Economics of Vertical Restraints,* 52 ANTITRUST L.J. 687 (1983); BORK, ANTITRUST PARADOX, note 6 *supra,* at 280–98; POSNER, ANTITRUST LAW, note 6 *supra,* at 147–66; Easterbrook, *Vertical Arrangements and the Rule of Reason,* note 106 *supra.* Compare with the more recent treatments of this issue the discussion in the 1955 ATTORNEY GENERAL'S REPORT, note 70 *supra,* which assumed the identity of horizontal and vertical price fixing without discussion, at 12–16, and which similarly assumed that horizontal nonprice restraints were different in important ways from exclusive territorial dealerships, at 27–29. See also Levi, *The Parke, Davis–Colgate Doctrine: The Ban on Resale Price Maintenance,* 1960 SUPREME COURT REVIEW 258, for a thorough treatment of the early law in this area.

tion,[126] in the 1977 *Sylvania* decision the Supreme Court decided that location clauses imposed by a manufacturer upon its distributors should be judged under the rule of reason.[127]

Sylvania created a serious tension in the law concerning vertical restrictions. The usual rule for "price-fixing" of any kind had been established in *United States v. Socony-Vacuum Oil Co.*,[128] which had held that "[u]nder the Sherman Act a combination formed for the purpose and with the effect of raising, depressing, fixing, pegging, or stabilizing the price of a commodity in interstate or foreign commerce is illegal per se."[129] Under this standard, territorial divisions imposed by a manufacturer upon its retailers would clearly be illegal, since the whole purpose of such divisions is to guarantee less "intrabrand" competition for the dealers and hence a higher price. In *Sylvania*, however, the Court explicitly decided to live with this tension for the time being, as it declined to reexamine the per se rule against vertical price restrictions.[130]

Sylvania's imposition of a different legal standard for price and nonprice vertical restrictions naturally placed a new premium upon the distinction between the two sorts of distributional restraints. Cases following *Sylvania* in the lower courts, including *Monsanto* in the district court, tended to focus upon whether the manufacturer practice in question was a "price" or a "nonprice" restriction.[131] Since all nonprice restrictions have a price effect, some standard other than effect on price was necessary in order to give the distinction any meaning. In essence, the lower courts were faced with the dilemma of reading all meaning out of the recent *Sylvania* decision, if they characterized everything as a price restraint, or reading all meaning out of the old *Dr. Miles* rule, if they refused to find price

---

[126] See United States v. Arnold, Schwinn & Co., 388 U.S. 365 (1967).

[127] Continental T.V., Inc. v. GTE Sylvania, Inc., note 1 *supra*.

[128] Note 101 *supra*.

[129] 310 U.S. at 223.

[130] 433 U.S. at 51 n.18.

[131] See, *e.g.*, Eastern Scientific Co. v. Wild Heerbrugg Instruments, Inc., 572 F.2d 883 (1st Cir.), *cert. denied*, 439 U.S. 833 (1978); Carlson Machine Tools, Inc. v. American Tool, Inc., 678 F.2d 1253 (5th Cir. 1982); General Cinema Corp. v. Buena Vista Distribution Co., 681 F.2d 594 (9th Cir. 1982); AAA Liquors, Inc. v. Joseph E. Seagram & Sons, Inc., 705 F.2d 1203 (10th Cir. 1982), *cert. denied*, 103 S.Ct. 1903 (1983). *Cf.* Davis-Watkins Co. v. Service Merchandise, 686 F.2d 1190 (6th Cir. 1982), *cert. denied*, 104 S.Ct. 1718 (1984) (distinguishing between vertical nonprice restrictions, judged under the rule of reason, and horizontal nonprice restrictions, judged under the per se rule).

restraints in the absence of printed words in the distributorship contract such as "This Is a Resale Price Restriction."

The basic agreement requirement of Sherman Act § 1 also posed problems in the vertical context. *Colgate*, as noted above, had assured manufacturers the freedom to announce required resale prices to their dealers, and to terminate the dealers if they did not adhere to the announced prices. However, anything that went beyond a unilateral announcement was taken by the Court to connote "agreement," in the technical § 1 sense. Thus, in *United States v. Parke, Davis & Co.*,[132] the Court found a § 1 violation in Parke, Davis's efforts to ensure that its wholesalers and retailers followed its suggested prices. Parke, Davis, "[i]n . . . involving the wholesalers to stop the flow of Parke Davis products to the retailers, thereby inducing retailers' adherence to its suggested retail prices, . . . created a combination with the retailers and the wholesalers to maintain retail prices and violated the Sherman Act."[133] This could be described as the coercion theory of agreement which, however illogically, sufficed to bring this type of manufacturer price restriction within the ambit of § 1. The Court found a similarly strained combination in *Albrecht v. Herald Co.* between a newspaper, a circulation firm, and a carrier who replaced a renegade who had refused to adhere to suggested maximum resale prices.[134]

This left very little room for the manufacturer that wished to exercise its *Colgate* rights—so little room, indeed, that some wondered if *Colgate* had become a dead letter.[135] The problem was the same as the one considered in the conspiracy line of antitrust cases: how to distinguish between independent action on the part of manufacturers and dealers and action that results from agreement of some sort.[136] If, as the Court chose to do in *Copperweld*, the

---

[132] 362 U.S. 29 (1960).

[133] *Id.* at 45.

[134] Note 68 *supra*, 390 U.S. at 149.

[135] See In the Matter of Russell Stover Candies, Inc., 100 F.T.C. Decisions 1 (1982), *rev'd*, 718 F.2d 256 (8th Cir. 1983); Yentsch v. Texaco, Inc., 630 F.2d 46 (2d Cir. 1980); Pitofsky & Dam, *Is the Colgate Doctrine Dead?* 37 ANTITRUST L.J. 772 (1968) (Pitofsky arguing yes, Dam arguing no).

[136] For the conspiracy cases, see Interstate Circuit, Inc. v. United States, 306 U.S. 208 (1939); Theatre Enterprises, Inc. v. Paramount Film Distributing Corp., 346 U.S. 537 (1954). See also Turner, *The Definition of Agreement under the Sherman Act: Conscious Parallelism and Refusals to Deal*, 75 HARV. L. REV. 655 (1962); compare POSNER, ANTITRUST LAW, note 6 *supra*, at 42–55.

combination requirement of Sherman Act § 1 is to be taken seriously, then the law of vertical restraints had to develop some way of drawing the line between independent action and agreement. *Monsanto* provided the Court with a good vehicle for doing so.

2. *The decision*. In 1956, the Monsanto Company decided to enter the agricultural herbicide market with a new type of product that prevented weeds from germinating instead of killing them after emergence. It introduced a product, Randox, which was effective to protect both corn and soybeans. In 1966, it introduced a "second generation" corn herbicide, Ramrod, which caused its market share for corn herbicides to jump from 8.6 percent in 1965 to 15 percent in 1968. Its 1968 soybean herbicide market share was a low 3 percent. At the time, Monsanto marketed through nonexclusive wholesale distributors, who resold to retailers and to other customers.

In 1967, Monsanto decided to adopt a new marketing program, which included technical educational programs, an expansion of technical support staff, and increased promotional and educational activities by both Monsanto and its distributors. It imposed a number of new requirements on its distributors, including a focus on sales to dealers, use of trained salesmen, and full exploitation of the dealer's area of primary responsibility. The next year, Monsanto took even more steps to improve its market position: it introduced yet another product, it reduced some distributor prices and suggested retail prices, it suggested that distributor profit margins be reduced, it changed its shipping policies, and it began to give cash bonuses to distributors who participated in its technical schools or made technical presentations to retail dealers and farmers. By 1972, Monsanto's market share for corn herbicides had nearly doubled, to 28 percent, while its soybean herbicide share had increased to 19 percent.

The dealers to whom Monsanto's distributors sold did not always adhere to the suggested resale prices. Spray-Rite Service Corporation in particular, which had been an authorized Monsanto distributor since 1957, was known as a price-cutter. It operated a low-overhead business and by 1968 was Monsanto's tenth largest distributor out of more than a hundred. Other Monsanto distributors complained from time to time to the company about Spray-Rite's pricing policies. Monsanto distributors discussed Spray-Rite and its low prices among themselves at two Chicago district meetings. The last documented price complaint Monsanto received concerning Spray-Rite occurred in May 1967. Four months later, Monsanto renewed Spray-Rite's distributorship for a one-year period, but it warned Spray-Rite that adherence to the full Monsanto marketing plan was a requirement of renewal.

In the fall of 1968, Monsanto chose not to renew Spray-Rite's distributorship, for the asserted reason that Spray-Rite had failed to hire additional salesmen and to conduct the type of promotional activity that Monsanto desired. Spray-Rite had continued to price the Monsanto herbicides considerably lower than the other distributors, well below Monsanto's suggested prices. Early in 1969, Monsanto told other price-cutting distributors that if they did not change their ways, they would not receive adequate supplies of the new corn herbicide that Monsanto had developed. When one distributor did not agree to follow the suggested prices, Monsanto complained to its parent company. The parent instructed the distributor to comply with Monsanto's request, and the distributor then informed Monsanto that it would charge the suggested prices.[137] Monsanto took similar action with respect to other price-cutting distributors—a fact which was reported in a newsletter from one of the distributors to his dealer-customers. The newsletter commented that "harmony can only come from following the rules of the game and . . . in case of dispute, the decision of the umpire is final."[138]

Spray-Rite's termination as a Monsanto dealer, and Monsanto's subsequent successful efforts to block all supplies of its products to Spray-Rite, were devastating to the company. By 1968, Spray-Rite claimed, Monsanto products had become necessary to a dealer's line. Without them, Spray-Rite's sales dropped 70 percent between 1968 and 1972, and its bottom line quickly went from profits to losses. In 1972, Spray-Rite went out of business.

Spray-Rite brought this suit early in 1972, claiming that Monsanto had violated § 1 of the Sherman Act by conspiring with some of its distributors to fix the resale prices for Monsanto herbicides, to impose restrictions on customers and territories, and to terminate Spray-Rite as a competitor. It also alleged that Monsanto had organized a group boycott against Spray-Rite after the termination and

---

[137] 104 S.Ct. at 1471; Brief for Resp. at 29–30.

[138] 104 S.Ct. at 1472.

that Monsanto had violated the Robinson-Patman Act,[139] although the latter two claims were of no importance by the time the case reached the Supreme Court. The case was tried to a jury, and the jury returned a verdict against Monsanto for $3,500,000, which the court trebled to $10,500,000 plus interest, costs, and attorneys' fees. The Court of Appeals for the Seventh Circuit affirmed in all material respects.[140] Monsanto filed a petition for certiorari that raised two questions: (1) whether nonprice vertical restrictions should be subject to a per se rule because they are alleged to be part of a vertical price-fixing scheme, and (2) whether the necessary conspiracy could be inferred solely from evidence that a manufacturer received price complaints from other distributors and, at a later date, terminated the price-cutter's distributorship. The Solicitor General filed a controversial brief in support of Monsanto, arguing first in support of Monsanto's two points, and in the alternative inviting the Court to reconsider the *Dr. Miles* per se rule.[141]

Unlike the first three cases discussed here, *Monsanto* did not split the Court. Justice Powell wrote the opinion for a unanimous Court; Justice White recused himself; and Justice Brennan wrote a concurring paragraph. Unlike Solomon, Powell tried in earnest to cut the baby in half. Taken alone, his reasoning seems to support a ruling on this evidence in favor of Monsanto. As the Court read the opinion of the appellate court, the ruling of law on the conspiracy issue had been that an antitrust plaintiff can survive a motion for directed verdict if it shows that "a manufacturer terminated a price-cutting distributor in response to or following complaints by other distributors."[142] The Court rejected this standard, but affirmed the jury's verdict under the new standard that it announced.

The opinion proceeded ambivalently. Initially, Powell proclaimed that two important distinctions stand at the center of this

---

[139] 15 U.S.C. §§ 13(a), (c), (d), and (e).

[140] The court ordered a minor remittitur of $172,412, and ordered recomputation and reduction of the attorneys' fees award. See 684 F.2d 1226, 1251 (7th Cir. 1982).

[141] After the brief was filed, Congress passed an appropriations rider forbidding the Government from arguing in support of any modification to the rule against resale price maintenance. Appropriations Act of 1984 for the Departments of Commerce, Justice, and State, the Judiciary and Related Agencies, Pub. L. No. 98-166, § 510, 97 Stat. 1102 (1983). Thus, when Assistant Attorney General William Baxter appeared to argue for the United States, he made no mention of this part of the brief—a fact which the Court acknowledged obliquely in its opinion. 104 S.Ct. at 1469 n.7.

[142] 104 S.Ct. at 1468.

and every other distributor termination case: that between concerted and independent action and that between price and nonprice
restraints. Independent action is perfectly legal; concerted action is
prohibited by Sherman Act § 1. Price restrictions are per se illegal;
nonprice restrictions are subject to rule-of-reason scrutiny. After
establishing these fundamental categories of antitrust jurisprudence, Powell criticized both of them as being without real substance. First, he noted that they were often difficult to apply in
practice.[143] This, however, was just the beginning:[144]

> But the economic effect of all of the conduct described above—
> unilateral and concerted vertical price-setting, agreements on
> price and non-price restrictions—is in many, but not all, cases
> similar or identical. . . . And judged from a distance, the conduct
> of the parties in the various situations can be indistinguishable.

Rather than abandon these practically meaningless distinctions, as
Copperweld suggests the Court would have done, Powell decided to
retain them. With wonderfully circular reasoning, he said that the
reason the different types of conduct he had identified had to be
distinguished was because the law imposed different sanctions on
each. The majority resolutely refused to acknowledge that the
creator of the distinctions was the Court itself, and that the Court
had sub judice at the time another case in which it was to abandon
just such classifications.

The Court expressly declined to reconsider *Dr. Miles*, since
neither party had argued to the district court that the rule of reason
should apply to a vertical price-fixing conspiracy.[145] Instead, it
concluded that evidence of complaints about price to a manufacturer, followed by a distributor's termination, was not sufficient to
refute the normal inference of independent action. As *Sylvania* had
recognized, manufacturers have a legitimate interest in knowing
what prices their distributors are charging, what services they are
performing, and how the products are being received, in order to
ensure sufficient profits for the desired services and to prevent free
riders. Distributors who may be hurt by price-cutting free riders
are the most natural source of information for the manufacturer.
Thus, both the distributors and the manufacturers could be acting

---

[143] *Id.* at 1470.

[144] *Ibid.* (citations omitted).

[145] *Id.* at 1469–70 n.7.

unilaterally when complaints are made and the offender is terminated. The Court, in order to preserve the integrity of the *Colgate* doctrine, adopted the following evidentiary standard in place of the one used by the court of appeals:[146]

> There must be evidence that tends to exclude the possibility that the manufacturer and nonterminated distributors were acting independently. . . . [T]he antitrust plaintiff should present direct or circumstantial evidence that reasonably tends to prove that the manufacturer and others "had a conscious commitment to a common scheme designed to achieve an unlawful objective."

Up to this point in the opinion, Monsanto's lawyers must have been ecstatic, since everything sounded as if the jury's verdict would be overturned for lack of the right evidence, or at least a remand would be ordered. The Court's application of its new standards to the evidence outlined above, however, cast a shadow over how great a change in the law it was actually effecting.

The Court concluded, on the evidence of the distributor who was pressured into coming into line on price and the evidence of the newsletter, that Spray-Rite had won the right to go to the jury on the conspiracy issue. The Court also found vague evidence that Spray-Rite's termination was pursuant to the agreement between Monsanto and its other distributors, since competing distributors deciding whether or not to follow suggested prices would know that termination would result from noncompliance, and circumstantial evidence that Spray-Rite's termination was due to its pricing policies. Content that the evidence raised a jury issue on both critical points—existence of conspiracy, and causal link between conspiracy and termination—the Court applied the per se rule and affirmed the jury's verdict. Justice Brennan's concurring paragraph was limited to a reaffirmation of the *Dr. Miles* rule.

3. *The Court takes away, the Court gives. Monsanto* clarified several points. First, whatever doubts may have existed about the continuing validity of the *Colgate* doctrine should have been erased. The Court's rejection of the evidentiary standard of the Seventh Circuit for finding a vertical combination, and its expressed concern for the need to rule out the possibility of independent action, did as much to resuscitate *Colgate* as a decision limited to that issue would have. Taking together *Monsanto*, for vertical cases, and *Copperweld*, for

---

[146] *Id.* at 1471 (citations omitted).

any type of case, the Court breathed considerable life into the § 1 conspiracy requirement. Decisions such as *Parke, Davis* and *Albrecht*, if not overruled on this point, could retain very little vitality, since the burden to refute what the Court considered to be the normal inference—independent action—is now squarely on the plaintiff. On the other hand, if plaintiff need only discover a damning memorandum or two to meet that burden, practically nothing has changed but the window dressing.

Whether the *Monsanto* decision did anything at all to the *Dr. Miles* per se rule is doubtful. The Court itself took the trouble to say that it was not expressing any opinion on the point. It is not uncommon for the Court to reopen a previously closed legal point by a comment of this sort and then to change positions in a later opinion.[147] It is impossible, however, to read the tea leaves here. The undeniable fact is that Monsanto was found liable to Spray-Rite in the whopping amount of $10,500,000 plus miscellaneous other fees, for the practice of resale price maintenance. The Court's prim complaint that Monsanto had not asked the district court to overrule *Dr. Miles* is not persuasive, even acknowledging that the Federal Rules of Civil Procedure permit pleading in the alternative and that Monsanto would have been entitled to argue that resale price maintenance was not a per se offense. Such an argument would not have detained either the district court or the court of appeals for long. The issue was fully briefed and then some in the Supreme Court.[148]

---

[147] For example, in Brown v. Board of Educ., 347 U.S. 483 (1954), the Court assumed without addressing the question that a school board was subject to suit under 42 U.S.C. § 1983. Seven years later, in Monroe v. Pape, 365 U.S. 167 (1961), the Court held squarely that municipal corporations were not within the definition of "person" for purposes of § 1983. Then, in 1977, the Court announced in Mt. Healthy City School Dist. Bd. of Educ. v. Doyle, 429 U.S. 274, 279 (1977), that "the related question of whether a school district is a person for purposes of § 1983 is likewise not before us. We leave those questions for another day. . . ." Finally, in Monell v. Department of Social Servs., 436 U.S. 658 (1978), the Court overruled *Monroe* to the extent that it had held municipalities outside § 1983. The Court went through a similar process with respect to the right to free speech on private property, in the group of cases including Amalgamated Food Employees Union Local 590 v. Logan Valley Plaza, Inc., 391 U.S. 308 (1968), Lloyd Corp. v. Tanner, 407 U.S. 551 (1972), and Hudgens v. N.L.R.B., 424 U.S. 507 (1976).

[148] See, *e.g.*, Brief for the United States as Amicus Curiae in Support of Petitioner, Brief of the National Association of Manufacturers as Amicus Curiae in Support of Petitioner, Brief Amicus Curiae of National Agricultural Chemicals Association in Support of Reversal, Brief of the Small Business Legal Defense Committee as Amicus Curiae in Support of Respondent, Brief of the Association of General Merchandise Chains, Inc. as Amicus Curiae in Support of Respondent, and Brief of the National Association of Catalog Showroom Merchandisers as Amicus Curiae in Support of Respondent. Thus, although Monsanto itself

The reasons that lie behind the Court's normal rule requiring issues to be raised below were largely missing here: no facts needed to be developed in the district court, for the issue was purely one of law; the case arose within the federal court system, not the state courts, so there was no problem of a properly presented federal question below; and the Court had the benefit of a full adversarial presentation on the issue. The question, had the Court decided it, would have determined the outcome of the case and thus would certainly not have amounted to an advisory opinion. Instances where the Court has not followed this prudential rule of self-governance abound, from cases as prominent as *Erie Railroad v. Tompkins*[149] to the 1984 decision in *Bacchus Imports, Ltd. v. Dias.*[150] The Court's refusal to reexamine the *Dr. Miles* rule may therefore have meant that the Court agreed with the argument that the rule is so firmly fixed in the common law of antitrust that Congress should be the one to modify it. For the time being, the only safe thing to do is to take the Court at its word and continue to assume that a per se rule applies to RPM.

It is more difficult to come to any clear conclusion with respect to the issue *Monsanto* actually decided: the standard of proof for conspiracy. On the one hand, plaintiffs will find it more difficult to win a directed verdict on this point, since the most readily available evidence will no longer suffice. On the other hand, since Monsanto lost on evidence that seemed perfectly consistent with the hypothesis of independent action, it is obvious that the Court intended to give juries great latitude on this question. This means that defendants will also find it difficult to win directed verdicts or summary judgments on the conspiracy issue.[151] With neither side

---

steered clear of the position that *Dr. Miles* had to be overruled, the issue was fully explored in briefs to the Court.

[149] 304 U.S. 64 (1938).

[150] 104 S.Ct. 3049 (1984) (majority of Court reaches question of constitutionality of state liquor tax exemption under Twenty-first Amendment, despite the fact that the question was not properly preserved in the state courts, and hence probably not even within the Court's jurisdiction).

[151] This is already happening in the lower courts. See, *e.g.*, Buckingham Corp. v. Odom Corp., reported in 47 ANTITRUST & TRADE REG. REP. (BNA) 478 (reaffirming in the light of *Monsanto* earlier decision overturning directed verdict for manufacturer; evidence of conspiracy makes out jury issue); James Julian, Inc. v. Raytheon Co., No. 80-30 MMS, D. Del., Aug. 31, 1984 (defendants lose on summary judgment because enough evidence exists for the plaintiff to go to trial); Jeanery, Inc. v. James Jeans, Inc., No. 82-6359, D. Ore., Oct. 1, 1984 (jury issue on conspiracy).

able to win without a trial, the question then becomes, Who is helped by going to trial? In the past, the need for a trial favored the defendant overwhelmingly, because it prolonged and increased the risk for plaintiffs, the rule of reason was normally involved, and defendants won under the rule of reason. After *NCAA*, however, the Court has changed at least the last part of that reasoning—plaintiffs may now prevail in more rule-of-reason cases. *Monsanto* itself, of course, was a plaintiff victory on the conspiracy issue. Plaintiffs therefore won on two critical § 1 points: combination and the merits. The calculus of costs and benefits that plaintiffs' counsel assess when deciding whether a trial is worth the risks must have moved in the direction of taking their chances before a jury.

In the end, the degree to which *Monsanto* tightened the requirements for prevailing in a distributor termination case will depend upon which is more important over time, the words of the opinion or its outcome. This Court has shown no hesitation in other areas in distinguishing its own opinions so that neither language nor outcome controls apparently similar cases.[152] As long as the conspiracy question is within the province of the jury, and plaintiffs' counsel can adjust the proof to show something more than distributor complaints and subsequent termination, it is most likely that terminated price-cutters will still be a significant factor in antitrust litigation. In this area, as in *NCAA* but in contrast to *Hoover* and *Copperweld*, the Court opted for almost no legal rules. Just to keep things interesting, it ended up somewhere in the middle in the remaining decision of the Term. In *Hyde*, the Court announced a rule that appeared simultaneously to depend on large amounts of fact-finding and to preserve a per se approach, but that in substance overruled a per se rule of illegality and came close to substituting for it a per se rule of legality.

---

[152] See, *e.g.*, Rummel v. Estelle, 445 U.S. 263 (1980) (whether Texas statute providing for mandatory life imprisonment for the third conviction of a noncapital felony violated Eighth Amendment when applied to three convictions for felonies involving $80, $28.36, and $120.75—Court says no), and Solem v. Helm, 103 S.Ct. 3001 (1983) (whether Eighth Amendment is violated by life sentence without possibility of parole for a seventh nonviolent felony—Court says yes); *cf.* General Electric Co. v. Gilbert, 429 U.S. 125 (1976) (disability plan that excludes pregnancy benefits does not violate Title VII, 42 U.S.C. § 2000e-2(a)(1), as sex discrimination) and City of Los Angeles, Dep't of Water & Power v. Manhart, 435 U.S. 702 (1978) (pension plan requiring women to make larger contributions than men because women actuarially live longer violates Title VII).

E. JEFFERSON PARISH HOSPITAL DISTRICT NO. 2. V. HYDE:
   THE CONFUSED LAW OF TIE-INS

Tying arrangements and, to a lesser extent, exclusive dealing contracts were the subject of the dispute between a public hospital and an anesthesiologist in *Hyde*. Again, the scope, meaning, and applicability of the traditional per se rules captured most of the Court's attention. Practices such as tying arrangements have never enjoyed quite the clarity of treatment in antitrust jurisprudence that horizontal price-fixing and market division or vertical price and nonprice controls have had. In this area, however, the Court has been nudging the law in the direction of rule-of-reason treatment for some years. *Hyde* pushed it a bit further.

1. *Tying arrangements and exclusive dealing contracts.* The year 1947 was a prolific one for antitrust law. As noted above, that was the year in which the Court first enunciated the intra-enterprise conspiracy doctrine, in *Yellow Cab*. It was also the year to produce the first clear statement that tying arrangements amounted to a per se violation of the Sherman Act, in *International Salt Co. v. United States*.[153] Tying arrangements involve a seller's conditioning the availability of one (desirable) item, the tying product, on the buyer's agreement to take a second (less desirable) item, the tied product. In *International Salt*, the Salt Company refused to lease its salt machines unless the lessee also agreed to purchase from it all the salt used in the machines. The Court saw this as an effort by the company to "close this market for salt against competition."[154] Presumably, it meant the market for salt used in International Salt's machines, not the nationwide market for salt. The machines were patented, and the volume of business affected by the offending contracts was about $500,000—an amount that the Court deemed not insignificant or insubstantial. Just as price-fixing was unreasonable, per se, the Court announced that "also it is unreasonable, per se, to foreclose competitors from any substantial market,"[155] citing

---

[153] 332 U.S. 392, 396 (1947). Tying arrangements in particular factual settings, particularly ties between the availability of patented machines and products used with those machines had been condemned earlier. See Motion Picture Patents Co. v. Universal Film Mfg. Co., 243 U.S. 502 (1917); Carbice Corp. v. American Patents Development Corp., 283 U.S. 27 (1931); International Business Machs. Corp. v. United States, 298 U.S. 131 (1936). Congress had also condemned tying arrangements in Clayton Act § 3, 15 U.S.C. § 14 (1982), which was added to the antitrust laws in 1914.

[154] 332 U.S. at 396.

[155] *Ibid.*

the Federal Trade Commission group boycott case of *Fashion Originators Guild v. FTC.*[156]

During the years between 1947 and 1977, the Supreme Court
followed the per se rule against tying arrangements with vigor. In
1956, it concluded that the Northern Pacific Railway Company had
illegally tied preferential routing clauses that compelled the use of
its rail facilities to leases of its lands.[157] The Court there specifically
rejected the argument that the defendant had to have monopoly
power over a tying product, such as the land in that case. Only
"sufficient economic power to impose an appreciable restraint on
free competition in the tied product" was necessary to bring a
practice within the condemnation of the Sherman Act.[158] This
standard meant that almost any desirable product could be found to
be a tying product, and hence that the packaging of such a product
with another item could be found to be an illegal tying arrangement. Consequently, in *Fortner Enterprises, Inc. v. United States Steel
Corp.,*[159] the Court found that summary judgment against Fortner
had been inappropriate because Fortner had alleged enough to get
to a jury on a tying claim. In brief, Fortner had claimed that U.S.
Steel had tied credit from its Credit Corporation to the purchase of
its prefabricated houses. The Credit Corporation's loans were particularly desirable, because they equaled 100 percent of the acquisition price of the houses (and then some, in Fortner's case), and
100 percent financing was generally unavailable from other local
credit sources. The case was therefore sent back for a trial on the
question whether U.S. Steel in fact possessed the necessary appreciable economic power in the credit market.

On remand, the lower courts eventually concluded that U.S.
Steel indeed possessed such power, and the Supreme Court agreed
to hear the case again. The winds had shifted, however, and the
1977 decision (known as *Fortner II*) came close to overruling *Fortner
I*, while maintaining the facade of adhering to the law of the case.[160]
The Court focused on the question whether the credit offered by

---

[156] See 312 U.S. 457 (1941).

[157] Northern Pac. Ry. Co. v. United States, note 5 *supra*, 356 U.S. at 7.

[158] *Id.* at 11.

[159] 394 U.S. 495 (1969). See Dam, *Fortner Enterprises v. United States Steel: "Neither a
Borrower, Nor a Lender Be,"* 1969 SUPREME COURT REVIEW 1.

[160] Note 2 *supra*.

U.S. Steel was unique and decided that the answer was no. In the final analysis, uniqueness depended upon "whether the seller has some advantage not shared by his competitors in the market for the tying product."[161] Evidence showing only that the seller is willing to accept a lower profit or to incur greater risks was specifically found to be insufficient to prove this new kind of uniqueness.[162] Since the *Fortner* record showed only the latter kind of difference between U.S. Steel and other credit suppliers in the market, the Court reversed the decision in favor of Fortner.

Thus, by 1977, the Court had imposed a new and potentially more stringent requirement for proving the existence of a tying arrangement: mere popularity of a product would not be enough unless it flowed from a special advantage of the seller that could not be duplicated by the seller's competitors.[163] This required economic analysis of the tying product market and the seller's power within that market—something that looked much more like a rule-of-reason inquiry than a per se rule. Furthermore, the rule against tying arrangements was less than absolute in other ways. It was always necessary to find two products that could be tied together. If only one product was involved, a tie was impossible. Nice questions about product characterization accordingly abounded in the lower courts, such as whether a franchise and a lease were one or two products,[164] or whether a car and its air conditioner involved one or two products.[165] The analysis necessary in order to decide the one-product/two-product question took the rule further away from per se simplicity. Finally, ties occasionally could be justified on quality control grounds, although courts normally required "less restrictive alternatives" in this context.[166]

In the tying cases, the Court had identified a number of evils

---

[161] 429 U.S. at 620.

[162] *Id.* at 621.

[163] See Jones, *The Two Faces of Fortner: Comment on a Recent Antitrust Opinion*, 78 COLUM. L. REV. 39 (1978); Baker, *The Supreme Court and the Per Se Tying Rule: Cutting the Gordian Knot*, 66 VA. L. REV. 1235 (1980).

[164] *E.g.*, Principe v. McDonald's Corp., 631 F.2d 303 (4th Cir. 1980), *cert. denied*, 451 U.S. 970 (1981).

[165] *E.g.*, Heatransfer Corp. v. Volkswagenwerk, A.G., 553 F.2d 964 (5th Cir. 1977), *cert. denied*, 434 U.S. 1087 (1978).

[166] United States v. Jerrold Elec. Corp., 187 F. Supp. 545 (E.D. Pa. 1960), *aff'd per curiam*, 365 U.S. 567 (1961); Kentucky Fried Chicken Corp. v. Diversified Packaging Corp., 549 F.2d 368 (5th Cir. 1977). See also Baker, note 163 *supra*.

attendant to tying arrangements, which generally focused on foreclosure of other sellers in the tied product market or deprivation of
buyer choice in that market.[167] In the *Standard Stations* case, which
refused to adopt a per se rule for an exclusive dealing arrangement
between an oil company and its independent dealers, the Court
declared without explanation that "[t]ying agreements serve hardly
any purpose beyond the suppression of competition."[168] Commentators discussing tying arrangements suggested a number of evils
that are supposed to exist. Under the foreclosure approach, the
tying arrangement raises barriers to entry in the tied product market and thus insulates the seller from competition in that market;
under the leverage theory, the seller tries to extend whatever power
it has in the tying product market to the tied product market and in
the process reaps greater profits through the tied sales than it could
through individual sales. Tie-ins could also facilitate price discrimination, although the effects of this on consumer welfare are difficult
to predict in the abstract, and they could permit a company operating in a regulated market to evade price controls by shifting the
higher price to the unregulated product.[169] On the other hand, for
years there has been a substantial body of academic literature that
has condemned the per se rule against tie-ins, because the perceived
evils are rarely, if ever, likely to occur, and procompetitive results
will obtain in many cases.[170] Thus, when *Hyde* arose, this area was
also considered ripe for reconsideration.

2. *The decision.* The case was an odd one to consider under the
tying rubric, since it involved an alleged tie between a hospital's
operating rooms and the services of an anesthesiologist—two items
that most people would want to purchase together. The hospital
was East Jefferson General Hospital, a large public facility located

---

[167] International Salt Co. v. United States, *supra* note 153, 332 U.S. at 396, 398 (competitor foreclosure); Northern Pacific Railway Co. v. United States, *supra* note 5, 356 U.S. at 6,
10 (competitor foreclosure and interference with independent buyer judgment, citing Times-
Picayune Publishing Co. v. United States, 345 U.S. 594 (1953)).

[168] Standard Oil Co. of Cal. v. United States, 337 U.S. 293, 305–06 (1949).

[169] See, *e.g.*, 1955 ATTORNEY GENERAL'S REPORT, note 70 *supra*, at 144–45; Turner, *The
Validity of Tying Arrangements under the Antitrust Laws*, 72 HARV. L. REV. 50 (1958); Bauer, *A
Simplified Approach to Tying Arrangements: A Legal and Economic Analysis*, 33 VAND. L. REV.
283 (1980); Slawson, *A Stronger, Simpler Tie-in Doctrine*, 25 ANTITRUST BULL. 671 (1980);
SULLIVAN, ANTITRUST, note 92 *supra*, § 156, at 445–54.

[170] See generally Bowman, *Tying Arrangements and the Leverage Problem*, 67 YALE L.J. 19
(1957); POSNER, note 6 *supra*, at 171–84; BORK, note 6 *supra*, at 365–81.

on the East Bank of Jefferson Parish, Louisiana, in the greater New Orleans area. It opened for business in 1971 with an arrangement between itself and Roux & Associates, a group of anesthesiologists, that gave Roux the exclusive right to provide anesthesiology services at the hospital and obligated Roux not to work elsewhere. The contract was for a term of one year, renewable for additional yearly periods; either party could terminate it on ninety days' notice.

In 1976, the contract with Roux was renegotiated, and a new, longer-term agreement was substituted. The new contract no longer specifically gave Roux exclusive rights, although the hospital continued in practice to use Roux's group exclusively. It ran for five years and called for Roux to supply all anesthesiology services needed at the hospital and to supervise the anesthesia department. The hospital performed billing services, listing the anesthesiology services as a separate item on its bills and paying an agreed amount as a fee to Roux.

Dr. Edwin G. Hyde was another anesthesiologist, not affiliated with Roux, who wished to practice at East Jefferson. In 1977, he submitted an application for an appointment to the hospital's medical staff. The appropriate committees of doctors recommended to the hospital's Board of Directors that he be appointed, but the Board denied the application. The Board's letter notifying Hyde of the rejection explained that "in view of the exclusive nature of the contract between the hospital and Roux & Associates and due to the fact that we have no openings in the Department of Anesthesia," he would not receive staff privileges.[171] Hyde then filed his suit under the Sherman Act, claiming that the contract between the hospital and Roux constituted a tying arrangement illegal per se under § 1 and that it constituted a conspiracy in restraint of trade also prohibited by § 1.[172]

The district court entered judgment for the hospital after a bench trial.[173] It assumed that the hospital services had been tied to the use of Roux & Associates, but it applied the rule of reason to the contract because the hospital did not have sufficient economic power over the tying product—hospital services—to make the tie

---

[171] Brief for Respondent at 5.

[172] Joint Appendix at 8. The complaint also contained allegations of violations of Louisiana law and federal civil rights laws not material here.

[173] 513 F. Supp. 532 (E.D. La. 1981).

per se illegal. The evidence showed that 70 percent of the patients from the East Bank of Jefferson Parish went to hospitals other than East Jefferson, which indicated that East Jefferson was in active competition with other New Orleans area hospitals. On the other hand, 70 percent of the hospital's patients were from the East Bank. The district court concluded nevertheless that the use of East Jefferson by the local residents in itself did not prove that the hospital was a strong economic power in its market.[174] Furthermore, the fact that East Jefferson was a public hospital did not give it any advantage over other hospitals in the area. The district court concluded that "[n]o evidence was presented that East Jefferson imposes any higher prices or imposes any more burdensome terms on its patients than other hospitals in the area."[175] To the contrary, the district court found a number of advantages to the hospital from the use of the exclusive contract. The arrangement efficiently ensured twenty-four hour anesthesiology care, it aided in the control and standardization of procedures, it lent flexibility to the scheduling of operations, and it facilitated monitoring by the Board, because fewer individuals were involved in anesthesiology operations. The absence of market power on the hospital's part, coupled with these benefits, led the court to conclude that the contract on balance was reasonable.

The Court of Appeals for the Fifth Circuit reversed, declared the exclusive contract to be an illegal tying arrangement, and ordered Hyde admitted to the anesthesiology staff.[176] The appellate court concluded readily that two distinct services were involved. It rejected the district court's approach to the economic power question for an interesting reason: market imperfections within the health care industry skewed the operation of the markets defined by the lower court so as to understate the hospital's true power.[177] The existence of third party (insurance company) payment of hospital bills, the patients' ignorance about the quality of medical care, and the patients' preference for hospitals close to home, combined to give the hospital the kind of economic power over the tying product that was needed to brand the contract per se illegal. The court

---

[174] *Id.* at 543.

[175] *Ibid.*

[176] 686 F.2d 286, 294 (5th Cir. 1982).

[177] *Id.* at 290.

rejected all justifications for the contract for the reason that less restrictive alternatives existed in every case.

The petition for certiorari raised only the question of the per se unlawfulness of the contract, within the framework of the Supreme Court's tying decisions. The Solicitor General, again an amicus curiae, suggested to the Court that it should abandon the per se label for tying arrangements, in favor of an approach that explicitly considered cost justifications for product packaging and true market power over the tying product. As in *Monsanto*, a large number of organizations also appeared as amici curiae to argue the pros and cons of the per se rule against tie-ins.[178]

Although the Supreme Court was unanimous in its conclusion that the Roux contract was not illegal, it split narrowly on the reasoning. Justice Stevens, for a bare majority, wrote to preserve the per se rule but to condemn its application to the hospital's agreement with Roux. Justices Brennan and Marshall joined in a concurring opinion that expressed the view that only Congress should change the rule against tying arrangements. Finally, Justice O'Connor, in her first antitrust opinion, wrote for herself and three others that the time has come to abandon the remnants of the per se rule against tie-ins and to adopt an open rule-of-reason test for the practice.

It is hard to summarize Stevens's opinion for the Court, because the opinion strains so hard to preserve the per se rule and at the same time to adopt a sophisticated market analysis of the arrangement in question. "It is far too late in the history of our antitrust jurisprudence," wrote Stevens, "to question the proposition that certain tying arrangements pose an unacceptable risk of stifling competition and therefore are unreasonable 'per se.' "[179] This is a noteworthy statement, both because it concedes that all tying arrangements do not deserve this harsh treatment, and because Stevens had made the same comment in dissent in *Copperweld* about a

---

[178] *E.g.*, Brief Amicus Curiae of the American Hospital Association in Support of Petitioners, Brief Amicus Curiae of the College of American Pathologists in Support of Petitioners, Brief Amicus Curiae of Louisiana Hospital Association in Support of Petitioners, Amicus Curiae Brief of Louisiana State Medical Society on Behalf of Respondent, Brief Amicus Curiae of the American Society of Anesthesiologists, Inc., in Support of Respondent, and Brief Amicus Curiae of the Association of American Physicians & Surgeons, Inc., in Support of Respondent.

[179] 104 S.Ct. at 1556.

doctrine that had arisen in precisely the same year as the tie-in rule. Justice White, who had not participated in *Copperweld*, joined Stevens in *Hyde*; Justice Blackmun, without offering any explanation of his reasoning, was content to overrule the 1947 *Yellow Cab* rule but not the 1947 *International Salt* rule.

Having announced that he intended to follow stare decisis for tying arrangements, Stevens next addressed the question which tying arrangements posed the unacceptable risk of which he spoke and which did not. Tying arrangements were not illegal, the majority agreed, when "each of the products may be purchased separately in a competitive market."[180] Tie-ins were also outside the per se rule when the packaging of two products together resulted only in the enhancement of the price of the tying product, but no harm to competition on the merits for the tied product. Finally, the per se rule would not be appropriate without "a substantial potential for impact on competition."[181] If only one purchaser were forced to buy the two items together, or if purchasers in general were forced to buy an item that they would not have bought from anyone, no adverse effect on competition in the tied product market results— in the first case because of the triviality of the impact, and in the second case because the buyers in question were not potential customers of sellers in the tied product market and hence foreclosure is impossible.

This left the case of two products, tied together, both of which the buyer wants, for which there are not two independent competitive markets, in which the tie does something more than enhance the price for the tying product, still under the per se rule. Although Stevens wrote that the Court's cases condemned tying arrangements when the seller exploited its control over the tying product "to force the buyer into the purchase of a tied product that the buyer either did not want at all, or might have preferred to purchase elsewhere on different terms,"[182] his conclusion three paragraphs later in the opinion that the first situation forecloses no real competition leads to the conclusion that he meant only to condemn the second kind of tie—the tie that forces the buyer to take the tied product on unfavorable terms. Relying on all the traditional reasons

---

[180] *Id.* at 1558.

[181] *Id.* at 1560.

[182] *Id.* at 1558.

for prohibiting tying arrangements, Stevens wrote that ties that fall
within this limited compass are anticompetitive because they interfere with the buyer's independent judgment, because they hurt the
seller's competitors in the tied product market, and because they
can increase the social costs of market power by facilitating price
discrimination.[183]

Tying arrangements of this sort could arise only when the seller
has "some special ability—usually called 'market power'—to force
a purchaser to do something that he would not do in a competitive
market."[184] Stevens made clear in a number of ways that he was not
referring to market power in the economic sense: first, by putting
the term in quotes when he introduced it, and again, by following
the conclusions in prior decisions that a patent or copyright over a
tying product sufficed to show market power, and by asserting that
a unique product (as defined in *Fortner I* and *Northern Pacific*) can
give the seller the necessary power. In the case at hand, he concluded that the hospital did not have the necessary market power,
despite the court of appeals' conclusions about the various market
imperfections for hospital services. The fact that 70 percent of the
patients residing in Jefferson Parish went to other hospitals showed
East Jefferson not to be dominant. Astonishingly, Stevens claimed
in a footnote that the Court's decision in the bank merger case of
United States v. Connecticut National Bank[185] supported this conclusion, even though that case principally found fault with the Government's market definitions and it distinguished *United States v.
Philadelphia National Bank*,[186] in which the Court had explicitly said
that a 30 percent share of the market was threatening to competition. Since the hospital lacked the right sort of power over the tying
product (hospital services), the arrangement was not per se illegal.

The majority specifically rejected the functional relation between
the two items in a package as the correct test for distinguishing one
product from two.[187] Products might be related functionally and
still be the necessary components of a tying arrangement. The

---

[183] See *id.* at 1558–59.

[184] *Id.* at 1559.

[185] 418 U.S. 656 (1974).

[186] 374 U.S. 321 (1963).

[187] 104 S.Ct. at 1562.

proper focus, according to the Court, was on "the character of the demand for the two items."[188] While it sounds nice to rely on a demand-oriented test, in practice the approach solves little. Buyers surely distinguish between tires and automobiles: the demand for the two products differs, since there is a replacement need for tires but the purchase of a car equipped with tires is normally considered to be the purchase of only one "product." In addition, the call for a link between two distinguishable product markets was inconsistent with the Court's assumption that no tie was possible if there were two independent markets for the two products, unless Stevens meant to postulate distinguishable product markets that were only imperfectly competitive. If the latter is the case, the question arises how much competition in the tied product, and how much separate demand for that product, are necessary in order to make it distinct for the two-product issue, but susceptible to foreclosure or leverage for the "forcing" issue.

Once the Court had established that the rule against tying arrangements did not apply to the Roux contract, it turned to a general unreasonableness analysis (presumably because the contract surely was an exclusive dealing arrangement, and such things are tested under the rule of reason). For this purpose, it focused on the effect of the exclusive contract on competition among anesthesiologists. The record did not support any of Hyde's assertions to the effect that competition in the anesthesiologist market had been harmed, or even what that market was. The Court concluded that "[w]ithout a showing of actual adverse effect on competition, respondent cannot make out a case under the antitrust laws, and no such showing has been made."[189]

Justice O'Connor's opinion concurring in the judgment exposed the numerous qualifications of the majority's opinion as an unsuccessful effort to save the per se rule in name, but to abolish it in substance. She argued that the Court had long since legitimized inquiry into the economic effects of tying arrangements, and that nothing but confusion and occasional lower court error resulted from the retention of the per se label:[190]

---

[188] *Ibid.*

[189] *Id.* at 1568.

[190] *Id.* at 1570.

The time has therefore come to abandon the "per se" label and refocus the inquiry on the adverse economic effects, and the potential economic benefits, that the tie may have. The law of tie-ins will thus be brought into accord with the law applicable to all other allegedly anticompetitive economic arrangements, except those few horizontal or quasi-horizontal restraints that can be said to have no economic justification whatsoever. This change will rationalize rather than abandon tie-in doctrine as it is already applied.

O'Connor suggested her own test for identifying which tying arrangements would have a demonstrable exclusionary impact in the tied product market or would enhance the seller's power in the tying product market. First, the seller had to have real market power in the tying product market. Second, there had to be a substantial threat that the tying seller would acquire market power in the tied product market. Third, there must be a coherent economic basis for treating the tying and tied products as distinct. Arrangements that do not meet these three criteria are not even subject to rule-of-reason analysis; they are per se legal. If all three requirements are met, O'Connor proposed that rule-of-reason inquiry would begin, including an evaluation of the benefits made possible by the arrangement. She specifically rejected Stevens's effort to distinguish between the seller who exploited power over a tying product by raising its price and the seller who forced the purchase of a tied product.

In applying her test, she assumed that the hospital had market power in the New Orleans area and that a threat existed that it would attain market power over the provision of anesthesiology services. However, she could find no sound economic reason for treating surgery and anesthesia as separate services, and she thus found for the hospital on that ground. Furthermore, she found so many benefits from the arrangement that she would have upheld it even assuming the existence of two services. She also found nothing in the exclusive dealing feature of the contract that raised antitrust concerns. Thus, on grounds that had the virtue of analytical clarity, O'Connor and three other members of the Court also found in favor of the hospital.

3. *The future of tie-ins.* As the account of *Hyde* indicates, it is hard to imagine what tying arrangements will fall within the narrow and

internally inconsistent test that Justice Stevens created for the per se rule. The question really becomes why he and four other members of the Court chose to preserve the per se rule at all, and when they might apply it. This per se rule has none of the virtues of simplicity, ease of administration, and likely correctness that Justice Black envisioned when he wrote *Northern Pacific*. Instead, it is a convoluted, apologetic sort of rule that creates the kind of trap for the unwary that the courts are always criticizing. Inertia cannot be the explanation, because Justice O'Connor offered the Court a thoughtful, well-reasoned opinion that, as she suggested, did the same thing the majority was doing but in a more straightforward manner.

Two forces seem to be at work in the *Hyde* majority, as the concurring opinion from Justice Brennan hints. It is probable that Brennan and Marshall would have been far happier with a *Northern Pacific*–style restatement of the rule against tie-ins, and a decision that exonerated East Jefferson on more traditional grounds, such as a rejection of the two-product finding or a finding that this had been mischaracterized in the first place as a tying arrangement instead of an exclusive dealing contract. Justice Stevens, however, has tried to take a more complex approach to antitrust cases. For tying arrangements in particular, he authored the influential *Fortner II* opinion that put the Court on the road toward the O'Connor position. Stevens wants to have things both ways: in cases like *Maricopa*, he has extolled the virtues of per se rules and has reiterated their usefulness in ringing tones; in cases like *Broadcast Music*, *NCAA*, and *Hyde*, he has plunged into rule-of-reason fact-by-fact analysis with a vengeance. Stevens, White, and Blackmun have shown favor toward a greater role for economic analysis in antitrust cases, but they do not want to take the final step away from the rules of the 1950s and 1960s. It is an odd way to respect precedent, however, when teachings are followed in name and rejected in reality.

The Court will surely have more cases concerning tying arrangements, since *Hyde* leaves the impression that there is still a per se rule in the area, but defendants have every incentive to test its limits. One possible candidate is *Digidyne Corp. v. Data General Corp.*, which raises among other things the question whether a copyright over the tying product is still enough to support a finding of "economic power," as *Loew's* had held, or if this rule did not survive *Fortner II* and *Hyde*.[191] The question is posed nicely in that case, for the state-conferred monopoly over computer software gives no information whatsoever about the degree of competition faced by that software in the broader market. Only two outcomes seem likely, although there is a third in theory. The two most probable are that the Court will continue to leave matters in their present unresolved state, at least until its membership shifts, or that the Court will take another look at O'Connor's opinion and adopt it by a majority next time. Theoretically, it is possible that the Court will move back in the direction of the Black per se rule against tying, but to do so it would have to reject most of its current emphasis on consumer welfare and replace it with the focus on competitors in the tied product market and foreclosure of new competitors that accompanied the Black approach. Nothing is impossible, of course, but at this time such a shift in the Court's antitrust policy seems doubtful.

III. General Themes of the Term

It might seem impossible to draw any general conclusions about the five decisions of October Term 1983, since they touch upon so many different aspects of antitrust law. That, however, reflects too narrow a vantage point on the Court's opinions. The truth of the matter is that the Court returned again and again to basic questions about the scope of antitrust law, its theoretical underpinnings, and the role of the Court itself in determining these matters. Four general themes run through the 1984 cases: (1) the theoretical choices the Court is making about antitrust law; (2) the place in which antitrust law operates, and conversely the area left to other regulation, federal or state; (3) the place for per se rules and the place for the rule of reason (including the characterization question); and (4) the relevance of legislative constraints on the Court's antitrust jurisprudence (both the legislative history of the original acts and subsequent congressional action), on the one hand, and the Court's treatment of its own precedents, on the other. There are no

---

[191] 734 F.2d 1336 (9th Cir. 1984). See also Northwest Wholesale Stationers, Inc. v. Pacific Stationery and Printing Co., 715 F.2d 1393 (9th Cir. 1983), *cert. granted*, 105 S.Ct. 77 (1984) [53 U.S.L.W. 3235 (U.S. Oct. 2, 1984) (No. 83-1368)]. The Court's decision in *Northwest Wholesale Stationers*, which concerns the per se rule for group boycotts, may throw some light on the *Hyde* per se rule.

final answers for antitrust, any more than such answers exist for any other area dominated by the Supreme Court. Still, this portrait of the 1983 Term throws light on the process the Court uses and what is likely to follow in the coming years.

A. THEORETICAL CHOICES

The literature about antitrust theory is encyclopedic.[192] Three broad schools of thought can be identified: the pure industrial organization or structuralist school (known sometimes as the "Harvard School"), the political antitrust school (or the revised Harvard School), and the pure consumer welfare or economic analysis school (known as the "Chicago School"). The industrial organization school was typified by the study of antitrust policy conducted by Carl Kaysen and Donald Turner in 1959.[193] It postulates that threats to the competition protected by the Sherman Act can be ascertained by examining the type of market structure in which the parties are acting—monopolistic, oligopolistic, or competitive. The focus on market structure leads naturally to a concern for the number of actors participating in any particular industry, and hence for some need to protect competitors directly. Foreclosure of competitors from the market, exclusionary practices, and practices that lead to an increase in concentration can be condemned without examination of the price and output effects that result, because by assumption the market structure itself—the organization of the industry—is the critical factor. This intellectual approach underlay the per se rules, making it possible to condemn the practices listed in *Northern Pacific* without extensive economic inquiry. It is not an attitude that ignores economic analysis so much as an approach that chooses to

---

[192] See generally, *e.g.*, KAYSEN & TURNER, note 91 *supra*; NEALE, THE ANTITRUST LAWS OF THE UNITED STATES OF AMERICA (1970); ARMENTANO, ANTITRUST AND MONOPOLY: ANATOMY OF A POLICY FAILURE (1982); BORK, note 6 *supra*; POSNER, note 6 *supra*; *Symposium: Bork & Bowman, The Crisis in Antitrust*, 65 COLUM. L. REV. 363 (1965); Blake & Jones, *In Defense of Antitrust*, 65 COLUM. L. REV. 377 (1965); Bork, *Contrasts in Antitrust Theory: I*, 65 COLUM. L. REV. 401 (1965); Bowman, *Contrasts in Antitrust Theory: II*, 65 COLUM. L. REV. 417 (1965); Blake & Jones, *Toward a Three-dimensional Antitrust Policy*, 65 COLUM. L. REV. 422 (1965); *Antitrust Jurisprudence*, note 6 *supra*, esp. Elzinga, *The Goals of Antitrust: Other Than Efficiency, What Else Counts?* 125 U. PA. L. REV. 1191 (1977); Sullivan, *Economics and More Humanistic Disciplines: What Are the Sources of Wisdom for Antitrust?* 125 U. PA. L. REV. 1214 (1977); Dorsey, *Free Enterprise vs. The Entrepreneur: Redefining the Entities Subject to the Antitrust Laws*, 125 U. PA. L. REV. 1244 (1977).

[193] KAYSEN & TURNER, note 91 *supra*.

emphasize industry characteristics rather than the particular firm's market power.

The second theoretical option, the political content measure, was at the same time a response to criticism of the industrial organization school and a refusal to accept the implications of the consumer welfare school. Lawrence Sullivan and Dean Robert Pitofsky are two prominent advocates of this approach.[194] Essentially, they recognize that practices which have the effect of lowering price or increasing output ought not to be prohibited by a law protecting competition. The legislative history of the Sherman Act reflects several purposes, as they see it, including the protection of consumers (by ensuring that no one has the power to restrict output or to enhance price, either through a cartel or a monopoly position), and the avoidance of extreme concentrations of economic power in organizations that become too big. This group thus tries to have it both ways—it tries to ensure a certain type of market structure and at the same time to use the microeconomic approach characteristic of the consumer welfare school. Its advocates recognize the impossibility of serving both masters all of the time. They therefore suggest that the consumer welfare approach should govern most of the time, and that the political goals of the antitrust laws should function principally as "tie-breakers."[195]

The approach of the consumer welfare school is easy to state.[196] Any practice or act that does not lead to an increased ability on the part of a firm or firms to increase price or (which is to say the same thing) to reduce output is not prohibited by the Sherman Act. Nothing in the Act requires the Court to adopt a model of atomistic competition as the final goal of the antitrust laws, and such a model would quickly lead to absurd results. Firms commonly can achieve efficiencies by combining the efforts of many persons, and consumers would be the ones who suffered if these efficiencies were forbidden by the law. The Court has said, correctly, that the antitrust

---

[194] See, e.g., Pitofsky, *In Defense of Discounters*, note 93 *supra;* Pitofsky, *The Political Content of Antitrust*, 127 U. PA. L. REV. 1051 (1979); SULLIVAN, ANTITRUST, note 92 *supra;* Sullivan, *Economics and More Humanistic Disciplines*, note 192 *supra.*

[195] See, e.g., Pitofsky, *The Political Content of Antitrust*, note 194 *supra;* Schwartz, *"Justice" and Other Non-economic Goals of Antitrust*, 127 U. PA. L. REV. 1076 (1979).

[196] Two of the leading proponents of this school are Judge Robert Bork and Judge Richard Posner. See BORK, note 6 *supra;* POSNER, note 6 *supra.*

laws protect "competition, not competitors."[197] It follows from this that normally only after a sophisticated analysis of the practice in question can any conclusion be drawn about its lawfulness for antitrust purposes. More often than not, it will be possible to say immediately that no antitrust problem exists.[198] Applying the teachings of the consumer welfare school, its proponents have concluded that the costs of condemning practices such as vertical distributional restraints (price or nonprice), tying, exclusive dealing, vertical integration, and a host of others far exceed the benefits, and the practices should therefore be free from antitrust condemnation.[199] The Supreme Court was right when, in *Broadcast Music*, it focused upon the output and efficiency effects of challenged practices.[200] It is the Court's choice not to follow this rule consistently that makes the 1984 cases worth examining.

The *Hoover* majority opinion does not fit neatly into any of the three schools of thought described above. The majority worked hard to avoid doing anything but simplifying the facts and purporting to follow prior decisions. Justice Stevens's dissent, in contrast, invoked the political and legislative bases for antitrust and justified finding a claim stated by referring to the Sherman Act's condemnation of private regulation of markets and of guilds in particular.[201] Stevens continued this approach in his majority opinions for the Court in *NCAA* and *Hyde*. Both those opinions are full of the words of economic analysis, yet in neither of them did a majority of the Court adopt the consumer welfare approach. In *NCAA*, Stevens and the majority failed to appreciate White's point about the necessity of clearly understanding the proper measure of output before deciding whether a practice helped or harmed allocative efficiency. They assumed instead, much too readily, that the consumers in

---

[197] See Brown Shoe Co. v. United States, 370 U.S. 294, 320 (1962); Brunswick Corp. v. Pueblo Bowl-O-Mat, Inc., 429 U.S. 477, 488 (1977).

[198] See Easterbrook, *Vertical Arrangements and the Rule of Reason*, note 106 *supra*, at 157–168 (five "filters" proposed for vertical arrangements: (1) the firm employing the arrangement lacks market power; (2) firms use different methods of distribution; (3) the arrangement in question has led to an increase in output by the defendants; (4) the arrangement in question has been in use longer than five years; or (5) the firm cannot increase its profits by harming consumers—*id*. at 159).

[199] *E.g.*, BORK, note 6 *supra*; POSNER, note 6 *supra*; Easterbrook, note 106 *supra*.

[200] Note 55 *supra*.

[201] 104 S.Ct. at 2003–04.

question were the television viewers—the "little guys"—instead of asking whether the buck stopped there. In *Hyde*, Stevens and the majority explicitly refused to overrule the per se rule against tying arrangements, in the face of the Solicitor General's invitation to do so and in spite of the opinion O'Connor offered to them.

One explanation for this is that a majority of the Court simply does not understand economic analysis and so "gets it wrong" some of the time. According to this view, the Court has at least taken a step forward in realizing that questions about price and output effects must be asked. In time, it will learn from informed advocates and others how to apply consumer welfare analysis more perfectly. More and more cases have already achieved this goal, including *Copperweld* from the 1983 Term, *Broadcast Music*, *Reiter*, and *Sylvania*.[202] *Monsanto* fits into this model insofar as the Court explicitly recognized the legitimacy of manufacturer concern over prices, manufacturer communication with dealers about price and other related matters, and the manufacturer's right unilaterally to impose any kind of restraint it desires.

The trouble with this explanation is that it sometimes reads too much into isolated pieces of language in the Court's opinions, and it implies (possibly unintentionally) a rather patronizing attitude toward the Court. Another explanation, which has the merit of incorporating decisions such as *Maricopa*, *NCAA*, the *Hyde* majority, and the *Monsanto* result just as readily as the consumer welfare decisions mentioned above, is that a majority of the Justices have knowingly rejected the consumer welfare school of antitrust analysis in favor of something closer to the political content approach. These Justices readily concede not only the relevance but the importance of economic analysis to antitrust law, but they continue to perceive political goals such as maintenance of relatively unconcentrated market structures, elimination of exclusionary practices, and restrictions on manufacturers' ability to dictate consumer choices. Thus, Justice Stevens in *NCAA* noted as a flaw of the television plan the fact that only the big networks could compete for the contract—the smaller stations were foreclosed.[203] In *Hyde* he openly invoked foreclosure of competitors in the tied product mar-

---

[202] *Copperweld*, note 4 *supra*; *Broadcast Music*, note 103 *supra*; Reiter v. Sonotone Corp., 442 U.S. 330 (1979); *Sylvania*, note 1 *supra*.

[203] 104 S.Ct. at 2964.

ket as a reason for continuing some sort of per se rule.[204] Justice Powell was content in *Monsanto* to live with the rule prohibiting manufacturer resale price maintenance, even though he conceded that nonprice restrictions were the same in economic purpose and effect.

If the second explanation is correct, one would expect to see the Court sometimes deciding cases purely on economic analysis and sometimes refusing to do so, which is of course what is happening. The problem then arises how to use these "other factors" as tie-breakers. There is no intellectually clean way to do so. It is therefore also not surprising that the Court is throwing the messier cases to the jury. As long as the relative weight of all the evidence is hidden within the jury room, no one can complain that competitor foreclosure in a given case played a greater role than considerations of economic efficiency. One can only say that it should not have been a jury issue, or that the jury's discretion should have been confined to make the relative weights fixed from case to case. In cases without juries, the protection of the district judge's fact-findings afforded by the "clearly erroneous" rule operates almost as effectively to avoid fixing relative weights. The judge need only enumerate all the factors that he took into account, as judges commonly do when applying balancing tests, and refrain from assigning conclusive weight to any particular point. In the end, the unconstrained fact-finder seems to be the only way out of the difficulties the political content school has brought upon itself by attempting to sit halfway between the industrial organizationalists and the consumer welfarists. The Court's treatment of the other general themes mentioned above lends support to this perspective.

B.   FEDERAL ANTITRUST OR OTHER REGULATION?

This question was prominent only in *Hoover* and *Copperweld*. It is implicit, however, in both *Hyde* and *Monsanto*, since no one denies the possibility of abusive business practices, but it is a legitimate question whether federal antitrust law is the proper legal vehicle for their regulation. In both *Hoover* and *Copperweld*, the Court decided to keep antitrust law out of a particular area: in *Hoover*, out of the regulation of the number of lawyers admitted to practice in the

---

[204] 104 S.Ct. at 1559.

state, and in *Copperweld*, out of the business of regulating most activities undertaken by members of the same corporate family. In neither case did it mean that the activity would be unregulated. Following the *Parker* doctrine, the *Hoover* decision represented the Court's willingness to keep this regulation within the sphere of state law, even if the activity was anticompetitive. *Copperweld* was only slightly different. It assumed that the activity was not anticompetitive in itself, and thus that only state tort or contract law was needed to remedy the general abuses short of attempted monopolization that could exist.

Monsanto and *Hyde* present more complicated situations, for no ready body of state law is waiting in the wings to regulate either tying arrangements or vertical conspiracies to maintain price. Instead, the choice is largely between regulation through federal antitrust or business freedom. In *Monsanto*, the Court chose to maintain federal antitrust regulation; in *Hyde*, the majority made a similar choice when it decided to retain the per se rule and found only that the practice at bar did not deserve se treatment. The Court appears unwilling to cede its authority over these practices to the open marketplace; as long as per se rules exist in name, some people will continue bringing cases to the Court's attention, and it can continue to monitor business behavior as it chooses. This incentive would continue to exist in a reduced way if the Court placed these and other similar arrangements under a rule of reason. Only if the Court accepted the most extreme consumer welfare arguments and declared such practices to be per se legal would its authority disappear. It is this sort of pronouncement that is most conspicuously missing from the Court's decisions up to now. Even *Sylvania* was only willing to place nonprice vertical restrictions under the rule of reason.

The Court's treatment of the general applicability of antitrust law therefore shows some inconsistency. When it compared federal antitrust regulation to regulation by other laws, it opted for the other laws. This is consistent with its decisions in other recent cases involving state economic regulation, such as *Rice v. Norman Williams Co.*,[205] *New Motor Vehicle Board of California v. Orrin W. Fox Co.*,[206]

---

[205] 458 U.S. 654 (1982) (California statute requiring liquor importers to be designated as authorized by the brand owner not invalid on its face as being preempted by Sherman Act).

[206] 439 U.S. 96 (1978) (California statute requiring automobile manufacturers to obtain approval of Board before opening or relocating retail dealership not in conflict with Sherman Act).

and *Exxon Corp. v. Governor of Maryland.*[207] Similarly, in *H. A. Artists & Associates, Inc. v. Actors' Equity Association,*[208] the Court found that the federal statutory labor exemption from the antitrust laws applied to the actors' system of regulating theatrical agents. Although the Court has been less charitable to other groups relying on federal exemptions to the antitrust laws,[209] the federal cases are in a sense less important than the state cases, since the Court is always reconciling two congressional enactments in a federal claim. When the Court was faced, in essence, with a claim for partially or wholly "deregulating" part of federal antitrust, it refused to do so. In the end, it seems that the Court is willing to live with state regulation over economic activity, or antitrust regulation, but not with a laissez-faire approach.

C. THE SCOPE OF THE PER SE RULE

The extent to which the Court retains power over economic activity depends in part on the breadth of the per se rule, since plaintiffs will be most likely to sue when they have a chance of prevailing under the per se rule. Whether per se rules are a good idea or not is a topic that has been discussed widely.[210] The concern here is somewhat different: it is limited to what the Court is actually doing with its per se rules. The short answer clearly seems to be that it is reducing their scope at every turn—through expansion of the characterization process, through contraction of the sorts of conduct to which they apply, and through refinements of the alternative approach, the rule of reason.

---

[207] 437 U.S. 117 (1978) (Maryland statute prohibiting gasoline producers or refiners from operating retail service stations within the state not preempted by federal antitrust statutes).

[208] 451 U.S. 704 (1981).

[209] See, *e.g.*, St. Paul Fire & Marine Insurance Co. v. Barry, 438 U.S. 531 (1978), Group Life & Health Insurance Co. v. Royal Drug Co., 440 U.S. 205 (1979), and Union Labor Life Insurance Co. v. Pireno, 458 U.S. 119 (1982) (all finding that the McCarran-Ferguson Act exemption from antitrust liability did not apply); National Broiler Marketing Ass'n v. United States, 436 U.S. 816 (1978) (rejecting a claim of Capper-Volstead Act immunity for agricultural association that contained nonfarmer members); and National Gerimedical Hospital and Gerontology Center v. Blue Cross, 452 U.S. 378 (1981) (refusing to find implicit antitrust exemption in the National Health Planning and Resources Development Act of 1974, Pub. L. No. 93-641, 88 Stat. 2229, 42 U.S.C. § 300ℓ).

[210] Redlich, *The Burger Court and the Per Se Rule*, note 102 *supra*; Note, *Fixing the Price Fixing Confusion: A Rule of Reason Approach*, note 102 *supra* (recommending abandonment of the per se rule against price fixing); Lipner, note 6 *supra*. For discussions of specific per se rules, such as rules against vertical arrangements, see note 123 *supra*; note 191 *supra*. Justice Hugo Black's statement in *Northern Pacific*, note 100 *supra* and accompanying text, remains the best statement of the traditional rationale for per se rules.

At least since *Broadcast Music* was decided, the characterization step in an antitrust case has been recognized as crucial to the choice of legal rule. In a sense, it poses the ultimate question, whether the activity at hand is the type with which the antitrust laws are concerned. The 1983 Term continued to place greater emphasis on this ultimate question, almost to the point of abandoning all categories. In *Monsanto*, Justice Powell complained that the traditional categories for measuring the legality of manufacturer conduct were artificial and difficult to apply. In both *NCAA* and *Hyde*, Justice Stevens stressed that the real problem was to form a judgment about the competitive significance of the practice in question.[211] In *Hyde*, he went so far as to say that "the question whether this case involved 'tying' is beside the point. The legality of petitioners' conduct depends on its competitive consequences, not whether it can be labeled 'tying.' If the competitive consequences of this arrangement are not those to which the per se rule is addressed, then it should not be condemned irrespective of its label."[212]

The Court's decision in *NCAA* not to apply the per se rule, and in *Hyde* to narrow it almost beyond perception, is consistent with the suggestion that the only serious question is the ultimate one about competitive consequences. *Monsanto* had a similar effect, even if one assumes that the Court did not intend to signal an impending change of the *Dr. Miles* rule. *Monsanto* certainly made it more difficult for dealers to prove the forbidden resale price maintenance, by making the underlying conspiracy harder to prove. Thus, at the least *Monsanto* did the same thing as *Hyde*, namely, preserved a per se rule in name but chipped away at it in substance. At the most, it may indeed have been the first step toward abandoning the rule altogether.

If characterization has swallowed up the whole of antitrust inquiry, and if the only question has become the effect on competitive conditions, then the old rule of reason assumes enormous importance. The rule of reason, as noted above, has been criticized as being without sufficient content to mean anything. At least in dictum, the Court took some steps this Term to change that.

Although *Copperweld* was not about the rule of reason, the Chief Justice's definition of rule-of-reason inquiry as one "into market

---

[211] *NCAA*, 104 S.Ct. at 2962 & n.26; *Hyde*, 104 S.Ct. at 1563 & n.34.

[212] *Hyde*, note 211 *supra*.

power and market structure designed to assess the combination's actual effect" inserted more content into the rule than the old lists provided.[213] Justice Stevens chose the rule of reason in *NCAA* because he believed that the product in question—televised college football games—would not exist in the absence of any cooperation among the schools. He too called for "market analysis" under the rule of reason,[214] even though he also specifically rejected a requirement of proof of market power.[215] The Solicitor General in *NCAA* had suggested a sort of truncated rule-of-reason analysis, which the Court apparently adopted. The only requirement of the Solicitor General's test, and the test used by the Court, is that some consensus exist as to the type of consequences that deserve to be labeled "anticompetitive." It is that consensus that I suggest is lacking among the Justices, since their theoretical preferences appear to diverge at this time. That leaves the rule of reason of paramount importance for antitrust, but still rather shapeless. As before, and as *Monsanto* illustrates most graphically, the only answer the Court has found over the short run to the problem of shapeless policy is to throw questions to the fact-finder.

D. CONGRESS AND THE COURT

Questions relating to legislative purpose and intent are generally distinct from questions relating to stare decisis, but that is not the case in antitrust. For one thing, as the Court has recognized, Congress deliberately gave the Court a role in elaborating the antitrust laws. At times, the Court seems quite conscious of the delegation of power and quite careful not to overstep the bounds that Congress set.[216] At other times, the Court has emphasized its common-law powers over antitrust.[217] Congress has also given implicit legislative recognition to the court-created rules. For example, the 1937 Miller-Tydings Act exempted agreements prescribing minimum resale

---

[213] 104 S.Ct. at 2741. See note 105 *supra.*

[214] 104 S.Ct. at 2962.

[215] *Id.* at 2965.

[216] See, *e.g.*, Texas Industries, Inc. v. Radcliff Materials, Inc., 451 U.S. 630, 643–46 (1981).

[217] *E.g.*, National Society of Professional Engineers v. United States, 435 U.S. 679, 688 (1978). See generally Bork, *Legislative Intent and the Policy of the Sherman Act*, 9 J. LAW & ECON. 7 (1966); Baxter, *Separation of Powers, Prosecutorial Discretion, and the "Common Law" Nature of Antitrust Law*, 60 TEX. L. REV. 661 (1982).

prices from the Sherman Act when such agreements were lawful under state law, even though the only source of a need for such an exemption was the Court's *Dr. Miles* rule.[218] Thus, the argument Justice Brennan made in his concurring opinions in *Monsanto* and *Hyde*, and that Justice Stevens emphasized in the 1982 *Maricopa* decision, that only Congress should change rules so well established as the per se rules against resale price maintenance and tying arrangements, had some force behind it.[219]

The Court has been more than sparing in the antitrust field with the exercise of its power to overrule prior decisions. *Sylvania* and *Copperweld* are the only two decisions that expressly and in terms overrule other antitrust cases. In *Copperweld*, the majority felt constrained to legitimize its decision to overrule the intra-enterprise conspiracy doctrine with repeated insistence that the doctrine had failed to do justice to Congress's intent in the Sherman Act to create one set of rules for concerted behavior and another for unilateral activity. Its discovery almost one hundred years after the passage of the Sherman Act of this important distinction did not come about because of new revelations about the legislative history of the Act. The majority had simply accepted a structural argument about the Act that had been well known among academics for some time. The Court also justified its decision to set aside stare decisis considerations by claiming first that the doctrine was unimportant anyway, and second that its adoption had been rather inadvertent.

The infrequency of overrulings does not mean that the Court has created consistent rules and has followed them, either out of deference to the quasi-legislative role that Congress gave to it or out of some general respect for the doctrine of stare decisis. To the contrary, it has shown no hesitation in effecting changes in antitrust doctrine through the well-worn device of distinguishing or ignoring prior decisions—a practice it employed in *Hyde, Monsanto, Hoover,* and *NCAA. Hyde* and *Monsanto* are particularly noteworthy, since

---

[218] The Miller-Tydings Act and its companion, the McGuire Act, were repealed in 1975, in the Consumer Goods Pricing Act of 1975, Pub. L. No. 94-145, 89 Stat. 801, 15 U.S.C. §§ 1, 45(a).

[219] See 104 S.Ct. at 1473 (Brennan, J., concurring in *Monsanto*); 104 S.Ct. at 1569 (Brennan, J., concurring in *Hyde*); Arizona v. Maricopa County Medical Soc'y, 457 U.S. 332, 354–55 (1982) ("By articulating the rules of law with some clarity and by adhering to rules that are justified in their general application, however, we enhance the legislative prerogative to amend the law").

the Court went out of its way in each of those opinions to insist that it was following its precedents, while quietly draining most of the substance from those same prior decisions. It may or it may not be legitimate to insist that the Court be consistent in its adjudications,[220] but it surely is fair to ask that the Court be frank in admitting how much it is doing. The doctrine of stare decisis becomes empty indeed when nominally respected precedents upon closer examination turn out to be Cheshire cats.

IV. CONCLUSION

The 1983 Term did not bring the end of the per se rules against resale price maintenance and tying arrangements, as the Solicitor General had urged, nor did it result in the adoption of the consumer welfare approach to the field. Instead, it left the Court halfway between the certainties of the Hugo Black per se rules and the opposing clarity of consumer welfare analysis. A majority of the Court, although not ready to jettison the formal per se rules, has recognized the complexity of most economic arrangements in the modern world. Despite the fact that swings of the pendulum have occurred before in antitrust and doubtless will occur again, it seems unlikely that the Court will ever retreat from this realization. Two possible routes for the future seem plausible: either an adoption of the consumer welfare analysis, which gives the greatest weight to the subtleties of business arrangements, or a refinement and elaboration of the rule of reason. It is possible, of course, that the Court will not move at all from its present position, which is to give nearly all hard questions to the trier of fact, but the unpredictability of that course of action would lead to great pressure on the institution to change.

Perhaps the most important message of the 1984 cases lies in the freedom with which this Court manipulates the law. *Copperweld* flatly overruled a line of cases; *Hoover* insisted that it was following *Bates* even as it twisted the rationale of the earlier decision beyond recognition; *NCAA* broke new ground by finding liability under the rule of reason; *Monsanto* confusingly switched back and forth between statements that reiterated the holdings of old cases and statements that radically changed those holdings; and *Hyde* won the

---

[220] See Easterbrook, *Ways of Criticizing the Court*, 95 HARV. L. REV. 802 (1982).

prize for saying one thing and doing another. This practice is by no means confined to antitrust law. One need only think of the Court's recent record in areas such as the Eighth Amendment's prohibition against cruel and unusual punishment,[221] the Fourth Amendment's warrant requirement for searches and seizures,[222] and the Establishment Clause of the First Amendment[223] to recognize the pervasiveness of the approach.

If it is true that the Court has special responsibilities in antitrust to articulate the law, just as it does in other quasi-common-law areas such as constitutional law, then its obligation to be forthright and to be sensitive to the predictability of its rules is especially great in antitrust. The approach that the majority of the Court has adopted for antitrust, whether one calls it a political content theory, or standardless jury discretion, or anything else, leaves much to be desired by these criteria. It places a great burden on antitrust counselors, who are far more important to the enforcement of the laws than any judges or agencies. The uncertainty in itself dampens competition, as the Court appeared to recognize in *Copperweld*. In the end, the lack of an overriding vision of the antitrust laws is more costly for the system than either Black's per se rules or the consumer welfare school. The time is ripe for the Court to decide whether per se rules make any sense any longer, in the light of a shared understanding of the goals of the antitrust laws, and to adopt clear standards for its rule of reason. If that is asking too much of the institution, perhaps, as the hundredth anniversary of the Sherman Act approaches, there is no alternative to sending the issue back to Congress for a renewed political statement on what the antitrust laws are supposed to be about.

---

[221] Note 152 *supra*.

[222] Illinois v. Gates, 103 S.Ct. 2317 (1983); United States v. Leon, 104 S.Ct. 3405 (1984); Massachusetts v. Sheppard, 104 S.Ct. 3424 (1984).

[223] Compare, *e.g.*, Lemon v. Kurtzman, 403 U.S. 602 (1971), with Mueller v. Allen, 103 S.Ct. 3062 (1983).

DAVID P. CURRIE

SOVEREIGN IMMUNITY AND SUITS AGAINST GOVERNMENT OFFICERS

When the Supreme Court in *Chisholm v. Georgia* held that the Constitution authorized an action against one state by a citizen of another,[1] the country immediately registered its disapproval by adopting the Eleventh Amendment: "The Judicial power of the United States shall not be construed to extend to any suit in law or equity, commenced or prosecuted against one of the United States by Citizens of another State, or by Citizens or Subjects of any Foreign State." Influenced by the spirit of this amendment, the Supreme Court went beyond its terms to conclude that the judicial power did not extend to a suit by a citizen against his own state either,[2] or against the United States,[3] in the absence of consent.

Not long after the establishment of these limitations the question arose to what extent they applied to suits filed against state or federal officers rather than against the government itself. The Court's answer has been that sometimes the officer may be sued and sometimes he may not.[4] Last Term's decision in *Pennhurst State*

David P. Currie is Harry N. Wyatt Professor of Law, University of Chicago.

AUTHOR'S NOTE: My thanks to Frank Easterbrook, Paul Mishkin, Cass Sunstein, and David Shapiro for helpful criticism, to Karla Kraus for valuable research assistance, and to the Jerome S. Weiss Faculty Research Fund for helping to make this study possible.

[1] 2 U.S. (2 Dall.) 419 (1793), discussed in Currie, *The Constitution in the Supreme Court: 1789–1801*, 48 U. CHI. L. REV. 819 (1981).

[2] Hans v. Louisiana, 134 U.S. 1 (1890).

[3] See, *e.g.*, United States v. McLemore, 45 U.S. (4 How.) 286 (1846) (not identifying the source of the limitation); Monaco v. Mississippi, 292 U.S. 331–32 (1934) (dictum).

[4] The Court has never distinguished in this respect between state and federal officers. See Larson v. Domestic v. Foreign Commerce Corp., 337 U.S. 682 (1947).

School & Hospital v. Halderman[5] is only the latest example of the inconstancy and confusion that have long characterized this field. To straighten it all out is more than can be expected; my aim is to suggest various points where the Court's analysis has gone astray.

I. OSBORN AND OTHER MARSHALL DECISIONS

The issue first appeared in *United States v. Peters*[6] in 1809, where the Court without much ado rejected the contention that an action against representatives of a deceased state treasurer to recover "the proceeds of a vessel condemned in the court of admiralty" was a suit against the state: "[T]he suit was not instituted against the state, or its treasurer, but against the executrices of David Rittenhouse"; the state "had neither possession of, nor right to, the property"; and "a mere suggestion of title in a state, to property in possession of an individual," could not destroy jurisdiction."[7] Which of these various considerations were sufficient in themselves to justify the action was left unclear, but the Court does not seem to have established that the sole test was whether the state had been formally named as defendant.[8]

The Court came very close to saying just that in *Osborn v. Bank of the United States*[9] in 1824, upholding an order directing state officers to return a trunkful of money they had taken from the Bank in violation of a federal injunction. The Eleventh Amendment, wrote Marshall, was "limited to those suits in which a state is a party on the record."[10] Since the officers held the money on behalf of the state, however, the order of restitution deprived the state of possession just as effectively as if the state itself had been named as defendant. Whatever the purpose of the Eleventh Amendment, it

---

[5] 104 S.Ct. 900 (1984).

[6] 9 U.S. (5 Cranch) 115 (1809).

[7] *Id.* at 139–41.

[8] See Justice Gray's later explanation, United States v. Lee, 106 U.S. 196, 242 (1882) (Gray, J., dissenting), stressing Marshall's statement that the property in Peters had not been in the state's possession. In such a case, as in the case of an award of damages payable by the officer personally, Scheuer v. Rhodes, 416 U.S. 232, 238 (1974), the effect of the order is not to take money out of the hands of the government.

[9] 22 U.S. (9 Wheat.) 738 (1824), discussed in Currie, *The Constitution in the Supreme Court: The Powers of the Federal Courts, 1801–1835*, 49 U. CHI. L. REV. 646 (1982).

[10] 22 U.S. (9 Wheat.) at 847–58.

demanded that *Osborn* be regarded as what it was in effect: a suit against the state.[11]

Marshall did leave room for salvaging something of the amendment's purpose when he added that the "true question" was "not one of jurisdiction, but whether [the defendants] are to be considered as having a real interest, or as being only nominal parties."[12] Four years later, moreover, Marshall found a case in which, despite *Osborn*, a state officer was not subject to suit. The case was *Governor of Georgia v. Madrazo*,[13] an action for possession of certain slaves seized when allegedly imported in violation of federal law and for the proceeds obtained by the sale of others. The reasoning was sketchy and in part purely formal: The governor was sued "not by his name, but by his title. The demand made upon him, is not made personally, but officially." Thus "the state itself may be considered as a party on the record."[14] Marshall went on, however, to suggest that the flaw was not merely one of pleading:[15]

> But were it to be admitted, that the governor could be considered as a defendant, in his personal character, no case is made which justifies a decree against him personally. He has acted in obedience to a law of the state, made for the purpose of giving effect to an act of congress; and has done nothing in violation of any law of the United States.

Thus *Madrazo* demonstrated that even Marshall did not believe that the Eleventh Amendment could always be avoided by naming an officer as defendant in his individual capacity. Moreover, he gave us a perfectly good reason why it could not: The mere fact that the suit is not against the state is no reason to hold liable on the merits a person who has committed no actionable wrong.[16]

---

[11] This remains true even if it should be established, as has sometimes been argued, that the English law of sovereign immunity was only a formality. People are not likely to amend constitutions just to change captions on complaints.

[12] 22 U.S. (9 Wheat.) at 858.

[13] 26 U.S. (1 Pet.) 110 (1828).

[14] *Id.* at 123.

[15] *Id.* at 124.

[16] Just why compliance with federal and state statutes meant the governor was not liable for tortious possession of the plaintiff's property Marshall did not say. The simplest explanation would be that it cannot be tortious for an official to act "in obedience to a law of the state." See PROSSER, TORTS 127 (4th ed. 1971). An alternative possibility is that the governor did not have actual custody of any property belonging to the plaintiff. *Cf.* Elliot v. Swartwout, 35 U.S. (10 Pet.) 137 (1836), declaring that under ordinary agency principles an

II. FROM THE CIVIL WAR TO IN RE AYERS

In *Davis v. Gray*,[17] in 1873, the Court allowed a suit to enjoin an officer from selling to someone else land granted or promised to the plaintiff. In *United States v. Lee*,[18] in 1882, it permitted an action to eject government officers from land illegally seized for nonpayment of taxes. Both cases were treated as simple applications of *Osborn*, and so at least the *Lee* case appeared to be.[19] There were, however, dissents in both cases.[20] The dissenters gave no reasons in *Davis*, and Justice Gray's principal arguments against *Lee* could have been made as effectively against *Osborn*. But not long after *Lee* the Court reaffirmed that there were limits to the ability to evade immunity by suing an officer.

Most of the limiting cases of this period involved efforts to obtain payment of obligations that the states had repudiated in violation of the Contracts Clause. In *Louisiana v. Jumel*,[21] for example, the Court refused to entertain an action that among other things would have required the State treasurer to levy taxes in order to pay the interest on bonds. The opinion did not clearly say why. It called attention to the sweeping nature of the relief requested[22] and distinguished *Lee* on the ground that the State in *Jumel* had title to the contested funds as well as possession.[23] It neglected to say why that made a difference, and it nowhere said the suit was one against the state. That *Jumel* had not abandoned *Osborn* and *Lee*, however, was

---

officer would not be personally liable for money had and received if he had paid it over to his principal before notice of the claim that it had been unlawfully acquired.

[17] 83 U.S. (16 Wall.) 203 (1873).

[18] 106 U.S. 196 (1882). This and the other decisions in this section will be discussed in detail in CURRIE, THE CONSTITUTION IN THE SUPREME COURT: THE FIRST HUNDRED YEARS (forthcoming, University of Chicago Press, 1985).

[19] Later cases would suggest that the officer's liability in *Davis* should have depended on whether title to the land had already passed. If it had, the officer was wrongfully interfering with the plaintiff's property; if it had not, he could not be held for breach of a contract to which only the state was a party. See the discussion of *In re Ayers, infra*. Since the property involved in *Davis* was land, the distinction may be blurred by the notion that equitable title passes when the contract is made, and in any event the second sale might arguably have been tortious on the theory of interference with contractual relations.

[20] 83 U.S. (16 Wall.) at 233 (Davis, J., joined by Chase, C.J.); 106 U.S. at 223 (Gray, J., joined by Waite, C.J., and by Bradley and Woods, JJ.).

[21] 107 U.S. 711 (1883).

[22] *Id.* at 721–22.

[23] *Id.* at 724–27.

shown by the *Virginia Coupon Cases*,[24] in which the Court allowed injunctions and restitution as well as damages against officers who had seized or threatened to seize property in satisfaction of taxes already discharged by the tender of interest coupons, even though the basis of objection to the state's action was, as in *Jumel*, the Contract Clause.

The basis for these distinctions was made explicit in Justice Matthews's 1887 opinion in *In re Ayers*,[25] holding an officer could not be enjoined from suing to collect a tax under circumstances otherwise identical to those of the *Virginia Coupon Cases:*[26]

> The action has been sustained only in those instances where the act complained of, considered apart from the official authority alleged as its justification, and as the personal act of the individual defendant, constituted a violation of right for which the plaintiff was entitled to a remedy at law or in equity against the wrongdoer in his individual character. . . .
>
> The present case stands upon a footing altogether different. . . . The acts alleged in the bill as threatened by the defendants . . . are violations of the assumed contract between the State of Virginia and the complainants, only as they are considered to be the acts of the State of Virginia. The defendants, as individuals, not being parties to that contract, are not capable in law of committing a breach of it. . . .

This explanation does serve to rationalize the cases. Under traditional agency principles, an agent is liable for his own torts (as in *Osborn, Lee*, and the *Virginia Coupon Cases*), even though committed in the course of his employment; but he is not liable for breach of his employer's contracts (as in *Jumel*), to which he is not a party.[27] Nor, in *Ayers*, was it a tort to file a losing lawsuit; if there was a defense to the action, the court could simply deny relief.[28] Moreover, the distinction invoked in *Ayers* could be traced all the way back to Marshall's opinion in *Madrazo*. For in that case the Court had said, among other things, that even if the governor had been sued in his individual capacity he could not have been held liable,

---

[24] 114 U.S. 269 (1885).

[25] 123 U.S. 443 (1887).

[26] *Id.* at 502–03 (emphasis added).

[27] See 1 MECHEM, A TREATISE ON THE LAW OF AGENCY, §§ 1357, 1406, 1455, 1457 (2d ed. 1914).

[28] 123 U.S. at 494. Apparently the tort of malicious prosecution had not yet generally been extended to civil cases. See PROSSER, note 18 *supra*, at 850–53.

because he had committed no wrong.[29] Finally, as noted above, the distinction makes eminent sense: The fact that a suit may not be against the state is no excuse for holding liable a person who has committed no wrong.[30]

Unfortunately, Matthews proceeded in the next breath to obscure the correctness of his distinction by announcing that because the officer was not himself liable the suit was against the state and thus barred by the Eleventh Amendment.[31] This explanation had the practical consequence of making the defect jurisdictional and thus outside the usual rules limiting the time in which the objection could be made.[32] It also made the distinction seem absurd. The officer's own responsibility was irrelevant to the purposes of the amendment, and the suit was neither more nor less against the state than it would have been if the officer had himself been liable.

III. Ex parte Young

In 1908, in *Ex parte Young*,[33] the Court held that a state official could be enjoined from suing to enforce an unconstitutional law. As the dissenters protested, this was contrary to *In re Ayers*.[34] But the majority had other precedent on its side, and of more recent vintage, for without facing up to the inconsistency the Court in a series of cases decided since *Ayers* had already allowed suits against officers who had done nothing more than threaten suit under statutes attacked as unconstitutional.[35] On the basis of those essentially unreasoned departures, the Court was able to assimilate *Young* to the category of cases in which officers "specifically charged with the

---

[29] See text at note 16.

[30] The Contract Clause may have required the state itself to honor its promises, but it did not appear to impose duties on any particular state officer.

[31] 123 U.S. at 507.

[32] In *Ayers* itself, for example, it permitted a collateral attack on a contempt judgment by means of habeas corpus. *Id.* at 485–87.

[33] 209 U.S. 123 (1908).

[34] *Id.* at 190; see text at note 25 *supra*. The majority, correctly describing *Ayers* as a case in which the officers had had "no personal interest in the subject-matter of the suit" (*id.* at 151), ignored its holding that they had had no personal interest in suing to enforce the tax laws.

[35] Reagan v. Farmers' Loan & Trust Co., 154 U.S. 362 (1894); Smyth v. Ames, 169 U.S. 466 (1898); Prout v. Starr, 188 U.S. 537 (1903); McNeil v. Southern Ry., 202 U.S. 543 (1906). But see Fitts v. McGhee, 172 U.S. 516 (1899), following *Ayers*. For exposition of these cases see Note, 50 HARV. L. REV. 956 (1937).

execution of a state enactment alleged to be unconstitutional . . . commit under its authority some specific wrong or trespass to the injury of plaintiff's rights."[36]

By effectively concluding that the filing of suit seeking an unconstitutional judgment was itself a wrong, *Ex parte Young* substantially expanded the ability to sue officers in federal court. It did not, however, require a significant modification of the theory that lay behind *Ayers* and the other Contract Clause cases. For it could still be said after *Young* that the official was subject to suit only if he himself had committed an actionable wrong.[37]

One additional fact about *Ex parte Young* should be noted: The parties were not of diverse citizenship.[38] That meant that jurisdiction had to be based on the ground that the case arose under federal law, and so the Court held: the case involved questions under the Due Process, Equal Protection, and Commerce Clauses.[39]

The most straightforward interpretation of this conclusion is that the Court found that the officer himself had threatened to take property without due process of law. In explaining why the suit was not one against the state, however, the Court repeated a thesis first expounded in the *Virginia Coupon Cases*:[40]

> If the act which the state Attorney General seeks to enforce be a violation of the Federal Constitution, the officer in proceeding under such enactment comes into conflict with the superior authority of the Constitution, and he is in that case stripped of his official or representative character and is subjected in his person to the consequences of his individual conduct.

In other words, the reason the officer was not treated as the state was that he had acted outside his authority. But if that was true, it should have followed that he had not violated the Constitution either, since its relevant provisions limit only the state.[41] There had

---

[36] 209 U.S. at 158.

[37] Indeed, the Court expressly reaffirmed that he could not be sued for specific performance of the state's contract. *Id.* at 151.

[38] See *id.* at 129, 143.

[39] *Id.* at 144–45.

[40] *Id.* at 144–45, 160. See also 114 U.S. at 288.

[41] See Note, 50 HARV. L. REV. at 960–61. The alternative explanation that the due process clause entered the case only to invalidate the defense that the state had immunized the officer by giving him authority appears to contradict the Court's contemporaneously announced rule that a case arises under federal law only if the federal claim is an element of

been no such inconsistency in the original theory. The reason the officer was liable in *Osborn* was not that he had violated constitutional provisions limiting only the state; it was that he had committed a common-law tort.[42]

Thus, in apparently redefining the basis of the officer's liability as one of federal law, *Young* seems to have effected a significant expansion of federal jurisdiction. Moreover, in so doing it contradicted its simultaneous explanation of why the suit was not barred by sovereign immunity. Finally, that explanation itself, in departing from Marshall's simpler position that the suit was not against the state because the state had not been named as defendant, was yet another consequence of the Court's unfortunate decision to rephrase the objection to suits like *Jumel* and *Ayers* as one of immunity. As we shall see, this apparently stylistic change was to contribute significantly to an important substantive determination as well.

IV. LARSON V. DOMESTIC & FOREIGN COMMERCE CORP.

Cases decided during the forty years after *Ex parte Young* were basically faithful to its distinctions and thus to the fundamental principle underlying the cases leading to *In re Ayers:* An officer could be sued when he himself had committed a wrong,[43] but not when the only duty was that of the government.[44] In 1949, how-

---

the plaintiff's original case. Louisville & N.R.R. v. Motley, 211 U.S. 149 (1908); see 50 HARV. L. REV. at 961 n. 40. Indeed in one of the *Virginia Coupon Cases* the Court had expressly held that a suit to enjoin an officer from collecting taxes in violation of the Contract Clause was not one seeking relief for infringement of a right secured by the Constitution under what is now 42 U.S.C. § 1983. Carter v. Greenhow, 114 U.S. 317, 322 (1885).

[42] Nor was the original theory inconsistent with the holding in Ex parte Virginia, 100 U.S. 339 (1879), that the act of a state officer can be attributed to the state under the Fourteenth Amendment although he has acted beyond the scope of his authority. It is hornbook agency law that the act of an agent may bind his principal even though not actually authorized, but that does not make a suit against the agent one against his principal or render the agent liable for breach of a contract to which he is not a party.

[43] *E.g.*, Truax v. Raich, 293 U.S. 33 (1915) (injunction against prosecution under unconstitutional statute); Houston v. Ormes, 252 U.S. 469 (1920) (mandamus where officer had ministerial duty toward plaintiff); Land v. Dollar, 330 U.S. 731 (1947) (return of property unlawfully held by officers).

[44] *E.g.*, Lankford v. Platte Iron Works, 235 U.S. 498 (1915) (no mandamus when state law imposed no duty on officer toward plaintiff); Great Northern Life Ins. Co. v. Read, 322 U.S. 47 (1944) (no order to pay tax refund out of state funds); Mine Safety Appliances Co. v. Forrestal, 326 U.S. 371 (1945) (no injunction against instructions not to pay government debt). The case last cited, ignoring the possibility that the officer had tortiously interfered

ever, in professing to apply settled law, the Court significantly changed direction over a biting dissent by Justice Frankfurter.[45]

The suit was brought to enjoin an officer from selling coal that had allegedly already been sold to the plaintiff.[46] The Court held immunity a bar. A suit seeking relief effectively against the government, Chief Justice Vinson wrote, was permissible only when the plaintiff alleged that the officer had exceeded his authority or that the statute granting him authority was unconstitutional.[47]

It is easy to see where the Court's argument came from; it is a logical result of the unfortunate terminology of lack of authority employed in *Ex parte Young*.[48] But that terminology, while helping to explain why immunity was no bar even after *Osborn*'s formal party doctrine had been abandoned, had subtly restated the principle that underlay the Court's earlier decisions. The basic question had originally been whether the officer had committed a wrong. To be sure, there had been language in early opinions suggesting that a showing of actual authority would negate the existence of wrong,[49] and one view of the matter is that it cannot be a tort to do what the legislature has made lawful.[50] The modern view, however, is that executive authority is a defense only when the risk of suit will deter the official from performing his duty by threatening his own pocketbook.[51] None of the early precedents appears clearly to have

---

with the plaintiff's contractual relations, found the United States an indispensable party on the express ground that the officer himself had done no wrong. See also Worcester County Trust Co. v. Riley, 302 U.S. 292 (1937) (no interpleader of officers of two states threatening to tax same estate), applying the *Ayers* reasoning that the filing of a tax suit would not be a wrong even if the tax proved unconstitutional. This reasoning seemed to contradict the specific holding of Ex parte Young but certainly was consistent with its general theory.

[45] 337 U.S. 682.

[46] *Id.* at 684.

[47] *Id.* at 689–95. Justices Frankfurter, Burton, and Jackson dissented and Justice Rutledge concurred only in the result. Thus the indispensable fifth vote was provided by Justice Douglas, who agreed only that the principles the Chief Justice had announced were the ones governing "the selling of government property." *Id.* at 705. Vinson's reasoning, however, was followed by a majority in Malone v. Bowdoin, 369 U.S. 643 (1962), and in Dugan v. Rank, 372 U.S. 609 (1963).

[48] See text at note 40 *supra*.

[49] *E.g.*, The Flying Fish, 6 U.S. (2 Cranch) 170, 177–79 (1804); Spalding v. Vilas, 161 U.S. 483 (1896); Osborn v. Bank of the United States, *supra*, at 836–37; United States v. Lee, 106 U.S. at 219–20; and see the discussion of Ex parte Madrazo, *supra*.

[50] See Note, 70 HARV. L. REV. at 832.

[51] Supreme Court of Va. v. Consumers Union, 446 U.S. 719 (1980) (prosecutor may be sued for injunction).

extended the defense of authority beyond pocketbook injury to an injunctive suit like *Larson*;[52] and to reach its conclusion the Court had to explain away decisions that had entertained claims for restoration of property erroneously held in the exercise of granted authority.[53]

Whether the officer had committed a wrong in *Larson* seemed to depend, as Justice Frankfurter said in dissent,[54] on whether title to the coal had passed to the plaintiff. If it had, it was a tort for the officer to withhold the plaintiff's property, as in *Osborn* and *Lee*; if it had not, the claim was for breach of a contract that, as in *Ayers*, could be broken only by the government itself.[55] On the Court's reasoning, however, there could be no suit even if title had passed. Thus the Court's unnecessary and ostensibly formal conclusion in *Ayers* that the officer's lack of responsibility on the merits meant the government was the real defendant had led to a decision arguably narrowing the substantive scope of suability as well.

In a footnote in *Larson* the Court added yet another important limitation:[56]

> [A] suit may fail, as one against the sovereign, even if it is claimed that the officer being sued has acted unconstitutionally or beyond his statutory powers if the relief requested can not be granted by merely ordering the cessation of the conduct complained of but will require affirmative action by the sovereign or the disposition of unquestionably sovereign property.

There was a grain of truth in this wholly gratuitous dictum, but its principal effect was to sow confusion. The sole case cited in support of the supposed ban on affirmative action was an 1890 case

---

[52] *The Flying Fish* and *Spalding* were damage actions; in *Osborn* and *Lee* the action was allowed. The better explanation of Madrazo may be that the governor was not personally responsible for property not in his own possession.

[53] *E.g.*, United States v. Lee and Land v. Dollar, note 43 *supra*, where the Court entertained not only claims that the defendants had exceeded their constitutional authority but also claims that they had committed simple torts; Goltra v. Weeks, 271 U.S. 536 (1926), which *Larson* expressly discredited, 337 U.S. at 701. For good discussions of *Land* and *Larson* see Note, 65 HARV. L. REV. 466 (1900).

[54] 337 U.S. at 725.

[55] But see the argument of interference with contract in note 19 *supra*, discussing Davis v. Gray.

[56] 337 U.S. at 691 n.11.

refusing to order an officer to levy taxes to satisfy outstanding state bonds.[57] The relief there sought had indeed been affirmative, but in its usual sense that could hardly have been the basis of the decision. For the Court did not purport to disturb either earlier precedents like *Osborn* and *Lee*, which had gone beyond the mere enjoining of unlawful acts to order the return of property illegally held, or repeated dicta that immunity did not bar mandamus, which by definition entailed affirmative action.[58] The case had rather been decided simply by citation of *Jumel*, *Ayers*, and another case seeking specific performance of a state contract;[59] the apparent reason for dismissal was thus, as in *Ayers*, that the officer was not personally liable for the government's breach. In short, the 1890 decision was not evidence of an independent rule against affirmative relief, but just another application of the same rule the *Larson* opinion was trying to explain by its conclusion that the officer could be enjoined only if he acted beyond his authority. A single rule had become two rules; and neither of the two new tests made as much sense as the one they had replaced.

V. EDELMAN V. JORDAN

We come now to the modern cases. The most significant is *Edelman v. Jordan*,[60] in which a lower court had ordered an officer to pay from the State treasury money that had been withheld from the plaintiffs in violation of federal law.[61] In an opinion by Justice Rehnquist, the Court quite rightly reversed. It would have sufficed to say that federal law imposed the duty of payment only on the State, not on any particular official; just as the State treasurer had committed no wrong in failing to pay off Louisiana's bonds in

---

[57] *Ibid.*, citing North Carolina v. Temple, 134 U.S. 22 (1890).

[58] *E.g.*, Board of Liquidation v. McComb, 92 U.S. 531, 541 (1876). I put to one side cases actually upholding mandamus against federal officers, which could have been based upon congressional consent to suit, although the Court seldom addressed the immunity question in those terms. See Kendall v. United States ex rel. Stokes, 37 U.S. (12 Pet.) 524 (1838); Currie, note 7 *supra*, at 652, discussing Marbury v. Madison.

[59] 134 U.S. at 30. The third case was Hagood v. Southern, 117 U.S. 52 (1886), which had used the term "affirmative" relief in the context of specific performance while restating the traditional question whether the officer had committed an actionable wrong.

[60] 415 U.S. 651 (1974).

[61] See *id.* at 658.

Jumel, the individual officer had committed no wrong in *Edelman*. Unfortunately, that was not quite how the Court put it.

The opinion began by declaring flatly that a suit "seeking to impose a liability which must be paid from public funds in the state treasury is barred by the Eleventh Amendment."[62] This statement, based upon an analogous decision refusing to hear a suit seeking repayment of taxes from the State treasury,[63] was overly broad, for it overlooked the Court's long-standing and correct conclusion that mandamus would lie to compel an official to perform a duty imposed upon him individually by state statute.[64] When payment from the treasury had been denied, it had been for want of any duty on the official himself to pay it, not for the mere fact that the money belonged to the State.

More important, however, were later passages in the *Edelman* opinion that further unsettled the law by suggesting new criteria for determining the officer's suability. Earlier decisions, the Court conceded, had permitted significant effects upon state treasuries by enjoining officials from discriminating against plaintiffs in the distribution of government benefits.[65] But those cases, in the Court's opinion, were different:[66]

> [T]he fiscal consequences to state treasuries in these cases were the necessary result of compliance with decrees which by their terms were prospective in nature. . . . Such an ancillary effect on the state treasury is a permissible and often an inevitable consequence of the principle announced in *Ex parte Young*. . . .
>
> But that portion of the District Court's decree which petitioners challenge . . . goes much further than any of the cases cited. It requires payment of state funds, not as a necessary consequence of compliance in the future with a substantive federal question determination, but as a form of compensation to those whose applications were processed on the slower time schedule at a time when petitioners were under no court-imposed obligation to conform to a different standard.

---

[62] *Id.* at 663. Since suit was by Illinois citizen and the state in question was Illinois, the amendment was not in fact the source of the immunity. For the proper explanation see Hans v. Louisiana, 134 U.S. 1 (1890).

[63] Ford Motor Co. v. Department of Treasury, 323 U.S. 459 (1945).

[64] See note 58 *supra*.

[65] 415 U.S. at 667, citing Graham v. Richardson, 403 U.S. 365 (1971) (forbidding discrimination against aliens in distributing welfare benefits); and Goldberg v. Kelly, 397 U.S. 254 (1970) (holding unconstitutional the termination of individual welfare benefits without prior hearing).

[66] 415 U.S. at 667–68.

A cursory reading of this passage might lead one to the conclusion that the Court would allow an order to pay state funds so long as they were not meant as compensation for a past wrong. Such a distinction would not only be irrelevant to the original question whether the official was responsible for the plaintiff's injury, it would also contradict the opinion's own insistence that an officer could not be ordered to take money from the treasury.[67] Moreover, the cases the Court was distinguishing had established no such principle. Apart from the fact that neither had considered the immunity question, an order to pay money to the plaintiffs would have been inappropriate under the circumstances of either case. When payment has been denied for an illegitimate reason such as discrimination against aliens, there is no obligation to pay future benefits but only a duty to stop discriminating; the state can comply by dropping the program as well as by including aliens.[68] If the Court did not mean to contradict itself, it must have meant that earlier cases had allowed orders not directing the payment of state funds but having an "ancillary effect" on the treasury.[69] But it was obvious that additional litigation was in store to determine the meaning of the new criteria.

VI. MILLIKEN, HUTTO, AND QUERN

In *Milliken v. Bradley*,[70] in reliance on the loose language of *Edelman*, State officers were ordered to spend money from the State treasury in order to finance remedial programs to counteract the effects of past school segregation. This decree, the Court held without dissent, "fits squarely within the prospective-compliance exception reaffirmed by *Edelman*."[71]

---

[67] See text at note 62 *supra*.

[68] See Iowa–Des Moines Nat'l Bank v. Bennett, 284 U.S. 239, 247 (1931) (Brandeis, J.). Ex parte Young's apparent conclusion that the officer himself had violated the fourteenth amendment, see text at note 39 *supra*, may dispose of the argument that the benefits cases themselves had been wrongly decided because the officers had committed no personal wrong in failing to fulfill the state's obligation not to discriminate or to provide a hearing before terminating benefits.

[69] This interpretation is supported by the further statement that in the benefits cases the order had made it "more likely" that the state would pay, 415 U.S. at 668.

[70] 433 U.S. 267 (1977).

[71] *Id.* at 289.

There were two serious flaws in this reasoning. First, as already stated, *Edelman* had not established any blanket exception for prospective orders. Quite the contrary, it had announced an absolute bar to actions "seeking to impose a liability which must be paid from public funds in the State treasury."[72] Far from following authority, *Milliken* seems to have been the first case outside the traditional mandamus area consciously to order payment out of the treasury.

The second problem was in applying the supposed distinction, for the order in *Milliken* was no more "prospective" than that condemned in *Edelman* itself. In both cases the money was to be paid in the future in order to right a past wrong. If that is enough to make the order "prospective," there is no such thing as a retrospective order; nobody is ever ordered to have paid yesterday.

In an apparent reference to *Edelman*'s observation that the order there requested was "compensation" for the past wrong, the Court in *Milliken* seized upon the fact that in the latter case the money was not to be paid directly to the victims of discrimination.[73] But *Edelman* had not made direct monetary compensation requisite to a holding of immunity; it had condemned compensatory orders as one example of those ordering payment from government funds. The Court in *Milliken* gave no hint of why it thought the distinction material, and it appeared to have nothing to do either with precedent or with any conceivably relevant policy.

The year after *Milliken*, in *Hutto v. Finney*,[74] the Court extended suability still further by upholding an order to pay attorneys' fees out of the State treasury on the ground that it was merely "ancillary" to the issuance of a negative and prospective injunction.[75] This ruling completely transformed the "ancillary" concept employed in the *Edelman* opinion. *Edelman* had spoken not of ancillary orders to pay money but of orders having ancillary effects on the treasury, and the rest of the opinion shows it was referring to orders that did not direct the payment of money at all.

The Court attempted to buttress its conclusion in *Hutto* by

---

[72] See text at note 62 *supra*.

[73] 433 U.S. at 290 n.22.

[74] 437 U.S. 678 (1978).

[75] *Id.* at 690–91.

analogizing the fee order to a fine for violating a negative injunction and argued that such a fine might even be so framed as to "compensate [ ] the party who won the injunction for the effects of . . . noncompliance."[76] Unlike a fine, however, a fee award is given to the plaintiff to pay his attorneys; and it was the fact that the money ordered to be spent in *Milliken* was not given to the plaintiffs that, for better or worse, had been the reason for upholding the order in that case.[77] More fundamentally, the reason a fine against the officer who disobeyed an injunction would be permissible is that he would pay it himself. Like a damage award to be paid out of the officer's pocket,[78] the fine would not have the same effect as if the state had been ordered to pay it. The fee in *Hutto*, in contrast, was ordered to be paid out of the State treasury; and that, *Edelman* had said, could not be done.

Finally, in *Quern v. Jordan*[79] in 1979 the Court held a federal court could order a state official to notify members of the class that had been denied retroactive relief in *Edelman* that they might seek back benefits by invoking state administrative procedures. Unlike the order in *Edelman*, Justice Rehnquist properly emphasized, the requirement of notice left it "entirely with the State" to determine whether or not retroactive benefits would be awarded. Thus, the Court concluded, the order in *Quern* did not offend *Edelman*'s strictures against requiring the payment of money from the State treasury.[80]

The trouble with this reasoning is that treasury payments did not exhaust the category of impermissible orders but were only one example of the more general principle that an officer may be ordered to perform only his own duties and not those of the state; federal law no more required the individual officer to give notice of state remedies than to pay out state money in *Edelman* itself.[81] The Court added that the order to give notice was "ancillary to the

---

[76] *Ibid.*

[77] See text at note 73 *supra.*

[78] Scheuer v. Rhodes, note 8 *supra.*

[79] 440 U.S. 332.

[80] The Court specifically noted that the officer "makes no issue of the incidental administrative expense connected with preparing and mailing the notice," *id.* at 347, which although described as "de minimis," *id.* n.19, would appear to create a serious objection in principle if it had been properly asserted.

[81] *Cf.* Hawaii v. Gordon, 373 U.S. 57 (1963) (conveyance of government land).

prospective relief already ordered,"[82] but, like the similar argument in *Hutto*, this was not what Justice Rehnquist himself had meant by an "ancillary effect" in *Edelman*. Finally, in discussing the general principles of immunity, the *Hutto* opinion flatly declared that "the distinction between that relief permissible under the doctrine of *Ex parte Young* and that found barred in *Edelman* was the difference between prospective relief on one hand and retrospective relief on the other."[83] If taken seriously, this dictum would authorize suits to compel officers to pay future interest installments on state obligations, contrary to *Edelman*'s flat statement that no money could be ordered paid from the State treasury, and despite the fact that it remains as difficult as today as it was at the time of *In re Ayers* to justify holding an agent for breach of a contract to which only his principal is a party.

VII. PENNHURST

In an action involving both federal and state challenges, the district court entered an injunction against the continuance of existing conditions in a public institution for the mentally retarded. After the Supreme Court held that a federal statute on which the court below had partly relied created no private right of action,[84] the court of appeals reaffirmed the injunction on state-law grounds without reaching the remaining arguments based on federal law. Last Term, in *Pennhurst State School and Hospital v. Halderman*,[85] the Supreme Court reversed, five to four.

Ex parte Young, wrote Justice Powell for the majority, had been based on the necessity of "permit[ting] the federal courts to vindicate federal rights"; there was no such necessity "when a plaintiff alleges that a state official has violated state law."[86] As Justice Stevens observed in dissent,[87] however, the Court had entertained state-law claims against state officers since long before *Young* itself, and it had never before suggested that *Young* was limited to federal

---

[82] 440 U.S. at 349.

[83] *Id.* at 337.

[84] 451 U.S. 1 (1981).

[85] 104 S.Ct. 900 (1984).

[86] *Id.* at 910–11.

[87] *Id.* at 922–44.

claims.[88] Nor had the question invariably passed unnoticed. As early as 1887, for example, in expressly rejecting the Eleventh Amendment objection, the Court had said the litigation was "with the officer, not the State" because "the suit was to get a state officer to do what a statute requires of him."[89] In a case decided during the same Term as *Young*, the Court had expressly said a suit charging an official only with what the opinion called "dereliction of duties enjoined by the statutes of the State" was "not a suit against the State."[90] Five years later, in a case presenting both federal and State claims, the Court had proceeded directly to the latter after declaring that the question of sovereign immunity had been settled by decisions like *Ex parte Young*;[91] and eight Justices had reaffirmed the principle not two years before *Pennhurst*.[92] The majority's efforts to get around the precedents were unconvincing.[93]

Apart from precedent, the Court's explanation of *Ex parte Young* confuses the theory of that decision with its motivation. It is no doubt true that a desire to find an effective means of enforcing the Constitution influenced the Court in its narrow construction of the state's immunity in suits against officers.[94] But the theory the Court developed to accomplish that goal was not limited to federal claims.

---

[88] Indeed, it had long been the Court's explicit rule that state-law claims in suits against state officers should be decided first in order to avoid unnecessary constitutional questions. Siler v. Louisville and N.R.R., 213 U.S. 175 (1917).

[89] Rolston v. Missouri Fund Commissioners, 120 U.S. 390, 411 (1887).

[90] Scully v. Bird, 209 U.S. 481, 490 (1908).

[91] Greene v. Louisville and I.R.R., 244 U.S. 499, 506–08 (1917).

[92] Florida Department of State v. Treasure Salvors, Inc., 458 U.S. 670, 696–97, 714 (1982). For the four dissenting Justices, this conclusion was dictum. See also Cory v. White, 457 U.S. 85, 91 (1982), reaffirming that immunity barred interpleading officials of two states taxing a single estate: "Thus, there was no occasion in [*Edelman*] to discuss the unanimous opinion in *Worcester* [note 44 *supra*] that the Eleventh Amendment bars suits against state officers unless they are alleged to be acting contrary to federal law or against the authority of state law."

[93] As the majority noted, 104 U.S. at 913 n.19, *Greene* did not expressly say it was rejecting "the Eleventh Amendment" argument as to both state and federal grounds. But it said nothing to support the unnatural inference that it meant to limit its discussion to the federal claim and then to enter an order on state-law grounds without determining its authority to do so. The majority's only response to *Scully* was that since it had allowed suit against an officer who had not violated state law it had been overruled by *Larson*, see text at note 100 *infra*, but *Larson* contained nothing to impair *Scully*'s clear holding that *Young* applied although the claim was not based on federal law. *Rolston* was distinguished, 104 S.Ct. at 913 n.18, on the unresponsive ground that the state statute in the case had imposed a " 'plain ministerial duty.' "

[94] See, *e.g.*, Osborn v. Bank of the United States, 22 U.S. (9 Wheat.) at 847–48 (1824).

As *Young* itself said, the Constitution "stripped" the official of any authority the State may have attempted to give him to commit an act otherwise actionable;[95] he was left in the same position as if the state had given him no authority at all.[96]

A closer look at the *Pennhurst* opinion, indeed, suggests that the questionable conclusion that *Young* was limited to federal claims was not the basis of the decision after all. For near the end of his opinion Justice Powell appended a footnote declaring that "it may well be wondered" whether it was really consistent with state immunity to permit suits against officers on the ground that they had acted "without any statutory authority."[97] One would have thought the extended passages devoted to showing that *Young* applied only to federal claims had already settled the issue about which the footnote "wondered."[98] But the footnote added explicitly: "[w]e hold only that to the extent the doctrine is consistent with the analysis of the opinion, it is a very narrow exception" not satisfied on the facts of the *Pennhurst* case.[99]

In other words, the distinction between federal and State claims was unnecessary to the decision; there was a narrower ground on which the Court relied instead. That ground was the one taken in *Larson:* even the *ultra vires* theory did not justify suing an officer if he was acting within his authority.[100] As Justice Stevens again pointed out,[101] the trouble with this argument was that, in contrast to *Larson*, where the plaintiff had alleged merely a common-law tort, the complaint in *Pennhurst* seemed to satisfy the *Larson* criterion by alleging that the officers had violated statutory require-

---

[95] See text at note 40 *supra*.

[96] There are many similar statements of the governing principle. *E.g.*, Cunningham v. Macon and Brunswick R.R., 109 U.S. 446, 452 (1883): "To make out his defence he must show that his authority was sufficient in law to protect him." See *Pennhurst*, 104 S.Ct. at 933 (Stevens, J., dissenting): "since a state officer's conduct in violation of state law is certainly no less illegal than his violation of federal law, in either case the official, by committing an illegal act, is 'stripped of his official or representative character.'"

[97] *Id.* at 916 n.25.

[98] See also *id.* at 911: "We conclude that Young and Edelman are inapplicable in a suit against state officials on the basis of state law." In context, this may only mean that the analysis is different in respect to state-law claims, not that the bar is absolute.

[99] *Id.* at 916 n.25.

[100] *Id.* at 911–17. This discussion gives every appearance of having been tacked on as an afterthought in response to Justice Stevens's overpowering dissent.

[101] *Id.* at 928, 936–39.

ments defining their official duties.[102] If *Larson* meant an officer could not be sued on grounds like those in *Pennhurst*, it seemed inconsistent with its own express affirmation that, "where the officer's powers are limited by statute," he could be sued for "actions beyond those limitations."[103]

VIII. CONCLUSION

The Supreme Court's course in determining when officers may be sued has not been steady. With respect to federal officers the problem has become largely one of statutory construction, for in 1976 the Administrative Procedure Act was amended to eliminate both sovereign immunity and the defense that the United States was an indispensable party in actions seeking relief "other than money damages" on account of the action or inaction of a federal officer.[104] The precedents remain important, however, in actions against state officials.

The first mistake was made in *Osborn*, for no one taking the trouble to amend the Constitution to protect states from suit would have permitted this protection to be circumvented by the simple device of changing the name of the defendant. Once *Osborn* was decided, however, the distinctions drawn in the early Contract Clause cases made eminent sense, for the decision to pretend the

---

[102] Indeed, that is what both the District Court and the Court of Appeals had held, 446 F. Supp. 1295, 1322–23 (E.D. Pa. 1977) ("both the Commonwealth and the county have violated their statutory obligation to provide minimally adequate habilitation"); 673 F.2d 647, 651–56 (3d Cir. 1982). Contrast *Larson*, 337 U.S. at 691: "Nor was there any allegation of a limitation in the Administrator's delegated power to refuse shipment in cases in which he believed the United States was not obligated to deliver." Whether all relief granted in *Pennhurst* was consistent with the distinctions made in Edelman v. Jordan, text at notes 66–69 *supra*, see 612 F.2d at 109, the Supreme Court did not have to determine.

[103] 337 U.S. at 689. See also the next sentence of the *Larson* opinion, arguing that in such a case "the officer is not doing the business which the sovereign has empowered him to do or he is doing it in a way which the sovereign had forbidden"; *id.* at 695, declaring the suit barred "if the actions of an officer do not conflict with the terms of his valid statutory authority." The majority in *Pennhurst* argued that the defendants had not acted "beyond their delegated authority" because the statute "gave them broad discretion to provide 'adequate' mental health services" and the claim was "that petitioners have not provided such services adequately." 104 S.Ct. at 909 n.11. But the courts below had held the defendants had contradicted a statutory limitation on that discretion. See note 102 *supra*. Official immunity from damages in cases of violations of law (see 104 S.Ct. at 912) is not a good analogy; an official may be free from damage liability, for reasons inapplicable to injunctive cases, even when he has acted unconstitutionally and thus is clearly not treated as the State under the Court's own test. See Scheuer v. Rhodes, note 8 *supra*.

[104] 5 U.S.C. § 702.

action was not against the state did not justify holding an officer liable when he had committed no actionable wrong.

The Court's unfortunate explanation that the reason for dismissal when the officer had done no wrong was that the suit was against the government not only obscured the original basis of these distinctions but had more practical consequences as well. In the first place, immunity was a jurisdictional matter that could be raised tardily,[105] even in a collateral attack on a judgment for want of jurisdiction.[106] More important, the characterization of the question as one of immunity led to the inconsistency of finding the same act to be official for substantive but not for jurisdictional purposes and to *Larson*'s refusal to hear cases where the officer had acted within his authority even if he had committed an actionable wrong. *Larson*'s allegedly independent prohibition of "affirmative" relief, which similarly made no sense in terms of immunity policy and departed from a number of sound precedents, was yet another result of the Court's refusal to ask the basic question whether the officer himself was legally responsible for the plaintiff's harm.

In its most recent cases the Supreme Court has deviated increasingly from the original landmarks, muddying the waters in *Edelman* by suggesting the relevance of new criteria such as ancillariness, compensation, and prospectivity, and taking liberties in *Milliken* and *Hutto* with *Edelman* itself. Finally, *Pennhurst* expanded *Larson*'s category of actions within the officer's authority without admitting it and unpersuasively called into question whether an officer could ever be sued on a state law claim.

Sovereign immunity in an unattractive doctrine that does not belong in an enlightened constitution. Unfortunately, however, it is a part of ours. Marshall's effort to sabotage the Eleventh Amendment in *Osborn* was one of his least attractive moments. But it is equally undesirable for his successors to compound his error by ordering officers who are suable only on the theory that they are not the state to pay money that only the state has a duty to pay; and one cannot help wondering why the Court thought it would improve the acceptability of its decision in *Pennhurst* by going to such lengths to disguise the fact that it was taking a new tack that, as the ultimate interpreter of a less than pellucid provision, it had a perfect right to take.

---

[105] Edelman v. Jordan, 415 U.S. 651, 677–78 (1974).

[106] See note 32 *supra*, discussing In re Ayers.

ROBERT C. POST

THE MANAGEMENT OF SPEECH:
DISCRETION AND RIGHTS

Discretion is pervasive in our legal system, and yet we scarcely know what it is. Ronald Dworkin, for example, has compared discretion to "the hole in the doughnut."[1] Dworkin's metaphor is unsettling because it so precisely captures our instinctive sense of discretion as dead analytic space.

Discretion most often appears to us as merely the negative reflection of the law. It subsists in the interstices of the law. "Where the law ends," Kenneth Davis writes, "discretion begins."[2] It is as if law and discretion were binary opposites, as if the presence of one signaled the absence of the other. We can have law or discretion, but not both. And this is because, as Herbert Packer put it, "The basic trouble with discretion is simply that it is lawless, in the literal sense of that term."[3]

The difficulty with this view is that it blinds us to the subtle and various ways in which law and discretion are in fact related. Discre-

---

Robert C. Post is Acting Professor of Law, University of California, Berkeley.

AUTHOR'S NOTE: I wish to thank Jan Vetter, Paul Mishkin, Owen Fiss, and David Cope for their patience, advice, and assistance. The usual disclaimer that all errors are the author's own is more than usually applicable.

[1] DWORKIN, TAKING RIGHTS SERIOUSLY (1978).

[2] DAVIS, DISCRETIONARY JUSTICE: A PRELIMINARY INQUIRY 3 (1969).

[3] PACKER, THE LIMITS OF THE CRIMINAL SANCTION 290 (1978). The notion that law and discretion are simply binary opposites has a long intellectual pedigree. In modern times it can be traced to sources as diverse as Dicey's vision of the Rule of Law, see DICEY, THE LAW OF THE CONSTITUTION 215 (1885), and Weber's conception of "rational-legal" authority, see NONET & SELZNICK, LAW AND SOCIETY IN TRANSITION 64 (1978). See, e.g., Gr. Brit. Committee on Administrative Tribunals (Franks Committee), Report, Comd. No. 218, at 6 (1957); HAYEK, THE ROAD TO SERFDOM 72–73 (1944); DICKINSON, ADMINISTRATIVE JUSTICE AND THE SUPREMACY OF LAW IN THE UNITED STATES 126 (1927); MASHAW, BUREAUCRATIC JUSTICE 1–2 (1983).

tion is not simply the negative reflection of law, and if we persist with such a vision, we truncate our understanding of important and complicated occasions when law authorizes the exercise of discretion. This is particularly true when litigants seek to curb the management of government institutions by the assertion of constitutional rights. In such circumstances the demands of law and of discretion are at their greatest, as is the necessity of accurately comprehending the relationship of one to the other.

This was demonstrated in the 1983 Term in *Seattle Times Co. v. Rhinehart*,[4] a case concerned with the constitutional rules governing protective orders that prohibit the disclosure of information received in civil discovery. On one side was the First Amendment right to be free from restraints on speech. On the other was the need for flexibility in the management of pretrial discovery. The Supreme Court perceived the case as a choice between law, with its attendant rules and rights, and discretion, with its attendant flexibility and effectiveness. The Court opted for discretion.

The decision placed the Court at odds with a long line of precedents holding that discretion in the suppression of First Amendment rights is particularly suspect. The most striking aspect of the Court's opinion is its refusal to address this tension, which suggests that the Court lacked an underlying theory of the relationship between First Amendment rights and government discretion. If law and discretion are viewed as irreconcilable, such a theory is impossible. But if law and discretion are instead seen as complementary, one can develop what the Court in *Rhinehart* so clearly needed: a theory of the management of speech.

I. Prologue: A Brief Introduction to Civil Discovery, Restraining Orders, and the First Amendment

Modern civil discovery was created by the Federal Rules of Civil Procedure of 1938. In a "striking and imaginative departure from tradition,"[5] the Rules divested pleadings of their previous functions of "issue-formulation and fact-revelation," and assigned

---

[4] 104 S.Ct. 2199 (1984).

[5] Proposed amendments to the Federal Rules of Civil Procedure, Advisory Committee's Explanatory Statement concerning Amendments of the Discovery Rules, 48 F.R.D. 487 (1970).

these functions instead to a new pretrial "deposition-discovery process."[6] This process was to be conducted in the first instance by the litigants themselves,[7] who were to be provided with powerful "instruments" of information acquisition.[8] It was to be supervised by the trial judge, who was clothed "with full discretionary power to stop the use of the discovery weapons for harassment or other ulterior motives."[9]

Included in this discretionary authority was the power to issue protective orders prohibiting disclosure of information gained through discovery.[10] Such restraining orders[11] had many uses. They could prevent unnecessary disclosure of trade secrets or other confidential information; they could reduce the incentive to abuse discovery processes by seeking information for purposes unrelated to the litigation. As the philosophy of the Rules grew nationally predominant,[12] restraining orders became commonplace in both state and federal courts.[13]

---

[6] Hickman v. Taylor, 329 U.S. 495, 500–01 (1947). See Pike & Willis, *The New Federal Deposition-Discovery Procedure*, 38 COLUM. L. REV. 1179, 1436 (1938).

[7] "To the extent possible, discovery should take place through procedures instituted and carried out by the parties without judicial intervention." Advisory Committee on Civil Rules, "Topic Disc.—3, The Extrajudicial Operation of Discovery: A Tentative Approach toward Improvement" (Oct. 8, 1963), at 1. See Brazil, *Improving Judicial Controls over the Pretrial Development of Civil Actions: Model Rules for Case Management and Sanctions*, A.B.F. RESEARCH J. 873, 881–82.

[8] Hickman v. Taylor, 329 U.S. at 501.

[9] Holtzoff, *The Elimination of Surprise in Federal Practice*, 7 VAND. L. REV. 576, 580 (1954). The first circulated draft of the federal rules contained "practically no provisions for protection" against discovery abuse, but, after "a storm of protest arose all over the country," "novel" powers to supervise discovery were incorporated into Rule 30(b). Federal Rules of Civil Procedure: Proceedings of the Institute at Washington, D.C. 138 (1938); *id.* at Cleveland, at 287; Preliminary Draft of Rules of Civil Procedure for the District Courts of the United States and the District of Columbia (May 1936). Rule 30(b) was thought to give trial courts "sufficient control" to protect the discovery process from misuse. Institute at Washington, at 99.

[10] Authority to issue such protective orders is currently found in Rule 26(c).

[11] In discovery systems modeled on the federal rules, the term "protective order" is ordinarily used to refer to the various orders, authorized by Fed. R. Civ. P. 26(c), by which a trial judge exercises control over the discovery process. Such orders can range from limiting or curtailing discovery to placing specified terms and conditions on discovery. For the sake of clarity, I shall use the term "restraining order" to refer to the specific kind of protective order that prohibits litigants and their attorneys and agents from disclosing to third parties information received in discovery.

[12] LOUISELL, HAZARD, & TAIT, PLEADING AND PROCEDURE 27 (5th ed. 1983).

[13] See Marcus, *Myth and Reality in Protective Order Litigation*, 69 CORNELL L. REV. 1 (1983). Judge Edward Becker recently observed that he was "unaware of any case in the past half-

Under the Rules the power to issue restraining orders was circumscribed only by the vague legal requirement of "good cause,"[14]
which freed trial judges from "hard and fast rules"[15] and thus permitted "complete control" over the discovery process through the
exercise of "enlightened discretion . . . to decide what restrictions
may be necessary in a particular case."[16] Although restraining orders were designed to suppress speech by litigants and their attorneys, they were not thought to pose any particular First Amendment problem.[17]

This comfortable system of judicial management became suspect
in 1979, when the District of Columbia Circuit, speaking through
Judge David Bazelon, decided *In re Halkin*.[18] In a closely reasoned
opinion, Judge Bazelon argued that restraining orders pose "many
of the dangers of a prior restraint" and thus require "close scrutiny
of [their] impact on protected First Amendment expression."[19] *Halkin* transposed conventional First Amendment principles into the

---

dozen years of even a modicum of complexity where an umbrella protective order . . . has not
been agreed to by the parties and approved by the court." Zenith Radio Corp. v. Matsushita,
529 F. Supp. 866, 889 (E.D. Pa. 1981). For examples of restraining orders issued in state
courts, see Curtis, Inc. v. District Court, 186 Colo. 226, 526 P.2d 1335 (1974); Professional
Microfilming, Inc. v. Houston, 661 S.W.2d 767 (Tex. Ct. App. 1983); Wagner Iron Works
v. Wagner, 4 Wis. 2d 228, 90 N.W.2d 110, 117 (1958); Bee Chemical v. Service Coatings,
Inc., 116 Ill. App. 2d 217, 253 N.E.2d 512, 514 (1969). Restraining orders can vary widely
in their provisions. Compare Tavoulareas v. Prio, 93 F.R.D. 24, 33–35 (D.D.C. 1981), with
MANUAL FOR COMPLEX LITIGATION, pt. 2, § 2.50, at 357 (5th ed. 1982), reprinted in 1
MOORE'S FEDERAL PRACTICE, pt. 2, at 354–59 (2d ed. 1982) (hereinafter cited as MANUAL
FOR COMPLEX LITIGATION), with In Re Coordinated Pretrial Proceedings in W. Liquid
Asphalt Cases, 18 Fed. R. Serv. 1251 (N.D. Cal. 1974).

[14] See Fed. R. Civ. P. 26(c). Virtually every state permits restraining orders to be issued
upon a showing of "good cause."

[15] Zenith Radio Corp. v. Matsushita, 529 F. Supp. at 891.

[16] WRIGHT & MILLER, FEDERAL PRACTICE AND PROCEDURE: CIVIL § 2036 (1970).

[17] In 1963, for example, the Second Circuit, speaking through Friendly, J., summarily
rejected a First Amendment challenge to a protective order enjoining litigants from "publishing or disclosing to any third party" certain information acquired in discovery. International
Products Corp. v. Koons, 325 F.2d 403. See also Rodgers v. U.S. Steel Corp., 536 F.2d
1001, 1006 (3d Cir. 1976). Judge Friendly stated simply: "[W]e entertain no doubt as to the
constitutionality of a rule allowing a federal court to forbid the publicizing, in advance of
trial, of information obtained by one party from another by use of the court's processes." 325
F.2d at 407.

[18] 598 F.2d 176 (D.C. Cir. 1979).

[19] *Id.* at 186. The holding in *Halkin* was anticipated by a decision in the Southern District
of New York to the effect that a restraining order was a "prior restraint" and thus unconstitutional. Reliance Ins. Co. v. Barron's, 428 F. Supp. 200 (S.D.N.Y. 1977). See also Davis v.
Romney, 55 F.R.D. 337 (E.D. Pa. 1972).

context of civil discovery, and concluded that the constitutionality of a restraining order should rest on three requirements: "the harm posed by dissemination must be substantial and serious; the restraining order must be narrowly drawn and precise; and there must be no alternative means of protecting the public interest which intrudes less directly on expression."[20]

Halkin provoked immediate and vigorous reaction.[21] The impact of the decision stemmed from its conclusion that restraining orders could not be analyzed independent of the First Amendment. The opinion was controversial because the "rigorous standard" it established was thought to curtail the ability of trial judges "to regulate abuses once the discovery process has started."[22] Precisely at the moment when a growing perception of a discovery "crisis"[23] was provoking calls for greater "personal supervision and management by the trial Judge,"[24] *Halkin* appeared to deny judges the flexibility necessary for such management.[25]

The logic of *Halkin*, however, proved difficult to fault. One line of attack was to redefine and diminish the First Amendment interests at issue. But there did not seem to be a convincing alternative analysis of litigants' First Amendment interests, and widely varying and implausible approaches were advanced. The nature of First

---

[20] 598 F.2d at 191.

[21] For discussion of the case, see Marcus, note 13 *supra;* Note, *Rule 26(c) Protective Orders and the First Amendment*, 80 COLUM. L. REV. 1645 (1980); Note, *The First Amendment Right to Disseminate Discovery Materials: In Re Halkin*, 92 HARV. L. REV. 1550 (1979); Comment, *Protective Orders Prohibiting Dissemination of Discovery Information: The First Amendment and Good Cause*, 1980 DUKE L.J. 766; Recent Decision, 48 CIN. L. REV. 900 (1979); Note, *First Amendment Interests in Trade Secrets, Private Materials, and Confidential Information: The Use of Protective Orders in Defamation Litigation*, 69 IOWA L. REV. 1011 (1984); Note, *Constitutional Standards Governing Issuance of Protective Orders Pursuant to Fed. R. Civ. P. 26(c) When Freedom of Speech Is Restrained—In Re Halkin 598 F.2d 176 (D.C. Cir. 1979)*, 52 TEMP. L.Q. 1197 (1979).

[22] Note, *The First Amendment Right to Disseminate Discovery Materials*, note 21 *supra*, at 1559.

[23] See Herbert v. Lando, 441 U.S. 153, 176–77 (1979); Amendments to Federal Rules of Civil Procedure, 85 F.R.D. 521 (1980) (Powell, J., dissenting). For a narrative of the development of the discovery "crisis," see Nordenberg, *The Supreme Court and Discovery Reform: The Continuing Need for an Umpire*, 31 SYRACUSE L. REV. 543 (1980).

[24] Pollack, *Discovery—Its Abuse and Correction*, 80 F.R.D. 219, 223 (1977). See Schwarzer, *Managing Civil Litigation: The Trial Judge's Role*, 61 JUDICATURE 400 (1978); Rosenberg & King, *Curbing Discovery Abuse in Civil Litigation: Enough Is Enough*, 1981 B.Y.U. L. REV. 579; MANUAL FOR COMPLEX LITIGATION, § 1.10 ("Judicial Control of Complex Cases"), at 17–19.

[25] See Marcus, note 13 *supra*, at 23–27; Koster v. Chase Manhattan Bank, 93 F.R.D. 471, 475–80 (S.D.N.Y. 1982). For a contrary view, see Brink v. DaLesio, 82 F.R.D. 664, 677 (D. Md. 1979).

Amendment interests was said to turn on whether discovered information was admissible at trial;[26] on whether information was discovered from the government or from a private party;[27] on whether information discovered was "commercial" or "near the heart of the information protected by the First Amendment."[28] It was also said that since discovery itself was a matter of grace which could be terminated at the discretion of the trial judge, litigants had only *de minimis* First Amendment rights in disseminating information gained through discovery.[29] Although the last approach was compatible with great judicial flexibility, it was not widely accepted because of its apparent resurrection of the "right-privilege" distinction putatively discarded by the Supreme Court.[30]

An alternative line of attack was to emphasize the importance of the government's interests in maintaining discretionary control over the discovery process. This approach, taken in tandem with the first, led some courts to an amorphous "balancing test" in which "the trial court's broad discretion to impose protective orders for good cause" was preserved.[31] It led one circuit to a "standard of 'good cause' that incorporated a 'heightened sensitivity' to the First Amendment concerns at stake."[32] Tests proliferated,[33] and it soon

---

[26] See In re San Juan Star Co., 662 F.2d 108, 115 (1st Cir. 1981).

[27] See In re Agent Orange Product Liability Litigation, 99 F.R.D. 645, 649 (E.D.N.Y. 1983).

[28] See Magnavox Co. v. Mattell, Inc., No. 80-C-4124, slip op. (March 24, 1981, N.D. Ill.).

[29] See In re Halkin, 598 F.2d at 206–07 (Wilkey, J., dissenting); Note, *The First Amendment Right to Disseminate Discovery Materials*, note 21 *supra*, at 1552–57.

[30] See In re Halkin, 598 F.12d at 190; In re San Juan Star, 662 F.2d at 114; Zenith Radio Corp. v. Matsushita, 529 F. Supp. at 911; Recent Decision, 48 GEO. WASH. L. REV. 486, 502–04 (1980). So great was the divergence of approaches, that a consensus emerged only for the propositions that litigants' First Amendment rights did not terminate automatically with the commencement of litigation; that such rights were not "waived" simply by choosing to engage in discovery; and that attorneys retained First Amendment rights despite their positions as officers of the court. See Koster v. Chase Manhattan Bank, 93 F.R.D. at 475–76. *Halkin*'s reasoning on these points was persuasive. See 598 F.2d at 186–90.

[31] Zenith Radio Corp. v. Matsushita, 529 F. Supp. at 911; Air Tec Associates, Inc. v. Cottman Transmission Systems, Inc., 1980–2 Trade Cases, ¶ 63,560 (E.D. Pa. 1980).

[32] In re San Juan Star, 662 F.2d at 116.

[33] One commentator, for example, found guidance in the Court's decision in Pickering v. Board of Education, 391 U.S. 563 (1968), and proposed a "*Pickering*-type balancing test." Comment, note 21 *supra*, at 791. Another, with some prescience, found Procunier v. Martinez, 4167 U.S. 396 (1974), controlling and offered a different balancing test. Note, *Rule*

became apparent that the problem was the absence of an underlying theoretical framework within which a convincing analysis could be developed.

In the midst of this disarray the Supreme Court granted certiorari in a case that exemplified the confusion, *Rhinehart v. Seattle Times Co.*[34] *Rhinehart* was an en banc decision of the Supreme Court of Washington, holding that under state rules of civil procedure trial judges had "broad discretion" to issue restraining orders.[35] The Washington Court had concluded that even if a restraining order were assumed to constitute a "prior restraint of free expression" requiring a " 'heavy burden' of justification," discretionary authority to issue such an order was nevertheless justified by the "interest of the judiciary in the integrity of its discovery processes."[36]

II. SEATTLE TIMES CO. V. RHINEHART: THE REASONING AND STRUCTURE OF THE COURT'S OPINION

Rhinehart was an eccentric case. It involved the Aquarian Foundation, a "spiritualist Church" that believed in "the ability to communicate with deceased persons through a medium."[37] The

---

26(c) *Protective Orders and the First Amendment*, note 21 *supra*. Several courts and commentators approved the strict *Halkin* test. See, *e.g.*, National Polymer Products, Inc. v. Borg-Warner, 641 F.2d 418, 424–25 (6th Cir. 1981); Farnum v. G. D. Searle & Co., 339 N.W.2d 384, 389–90 (Iowa 1983); Comment, 55 NOTRE DAME LAW. 424, 434–35 (1980); Comment, 21 WM. & MARY L. REV. 331, 354–55 (1979); Note, 56 CHI. KENT L. REV. 943 (1980); *cf.* Kuiper v. District Court, 632 P.2d 694, 697–98 (Mont. 1981). Some commentators advocated a test stricter than *Halkin*. See Recent Decision, note 30 *supra*, at 506–08; Note, *Constitutional Standards Governing Issuance of Protective Orders*, note 21 *supra*, at 1218. Two decisions, both involving newspapers, appear to have adopted an absolute standard, striking down restraining orders as prior restraints. Georgia Gazette Pub. Co. v. Ramsey, 248 Ga. 528, 284 S.E.2d 386, 387 (1981); Vara v. Gore Newspapers, 8 Med. L. Rptr. 2231 (Fla. Cir. 1982).

[34] 98 Wash. 2d 226, 654 P.2d 673 (1982).

[35] *Id.* at 677.

[36] *Id.* at 690. This conclusion was almost certainly incorrect. If even in time of war the federal government could not overcome the "heavy presumption" against prior restraints to have enjoined the publication of stolen classified documents, *New York Times Co. v. United States*, 403 U.S. 713, 714 (1971), then surely this presumption could not be overcome by the trial judge's restraining order in *Rhinehart*, which had been issued without findings and in response to only the most general claims of confidentiality.

[37] The Seattle Times Co. v. Rhinehart, No. 82-1721 (U.S. Sup. Ct.), Brief of Resp., at 2–3.

"primary mental and physical medium" of the Church was Reverend Rhinehart, who claimed to "transfer . . . objects from one place or time" to another[38] and to "apport" precious stones from his body.[39] Aggrieved by a series of skeptical articles published in the *Seattle Times* and the *Walla Walla Union-Bulletin*, Rhinehart, the Foundation, and several church members brought an action in Washington Superior Court for libel and invasion of privacy.[40] Alleged injuries included declining donations and membership.[41]

Defendants in the suit sought discovery concerning the Foundation's financial condition and the identity of its members.[42] Plaintiffs resisted, claiming that as a small and unpopular religion they were subject to persecution in the community at large, and hence that forced disclosure of the requested information would infringe their constitutional rights of association and religion.[43] In the alternative, plaintiffs moved for the issuance of a restraining order prohibiting dissemination of the requested information.[44] After receiving affidavits alleging that violent threats and incidents had been caused by prior articles in the newspapers, the trial judge compelled the discovery and issued the restraining order.[45] The order

---

[38] *Ibid.*

[39] The Seattle Times v. Rhinehart, No. 82-1721 (U.S. Sup. Ct.), Joint Appendix (hereinafter cited as J.A.), at 20a.

[40] Named as defendants were the Seattle Times Company, which published both the Seattle Times and the Union-Bulletin, and several individual reporters associated with the articles.

[41] J.A. at 11a; 104 S.Ct. 2199, 2203 n.2 (1984).

[42] The discovery provisions of the Washington rules, like those of most states, are modeled after the Federal Rules of Civil Procedure. Liberal discovery is permitted not only of directly relevant information likely to be admissible at trial, but also of information "reasonably calculated to lead to the discovery of admissible evidence." See Wash. Super. Ct. Rule 26(b)(1); Trust Fund Services v. Aro Glass Co., 89 Wash. 2d 758, 575 P.2d 716, 719 (1978).

[43] At the time they made this claim, plaintiffs had already produced to defendants Rhinehart's tax returns, as well as a number of other financial documents. 104 S.Ct. at 2203.

[44] The basis for plaintiffs' motion for a restraining order was Wash. Super. Ct. Rule 26(c), which is virtually identical to its federal counterpart Rule 26(c).

[45] Although the trial judge's opinion is rather ambiguous, it appears that he decided to issue the restraining order because he concluded that it would constitute an "abuse of discovery" to use the court's processes to acquire information that would "normally be kept confidential" and then to publish that information in the news media. J.A. at 51a–54a. In issuing the order, the judge did not refer to plaintiffs' affidavits, or to any other facts in the record. He apparently believed that the only factual predicate necessary for the issuance of the order was that the newspapers intended to publicize information that plaintiffs regarded as confidential.

was ambiguous as to its scope,[46] and the judge made no effort to support it by findings of fact.[47]

The order was affirmed by the Supreme Court of Washington in an opinion which strongly argued that restraining orders were a necessary concomitant of a system of liberal discovery. The court noted that without the assurance provided by restraining orders, information produced in discovery "will be used only for the legitimate purposes of litigation," litigants concerned with publicity might be tempted to "withhold information" or "to shade the truth," or even to "forego the pursuit of their just claims."[48]

Even the *Halkin* decision, however, had acknowledged that restraining orders were important for "the effective functioning of the civil discovery system."[49] But the Washington court, unlike the D.C. Circuit, believed that "the integrity of the discovery process" could be protected only if trial judges were free to exercise "a broad discretion to manage the discovery process in a fashion that will implement the goal of full disclosure of relevant information and at the same time afford the participants protection against harmful side effects."[50] Thus while the *Halkin* court would permit the is-

---

[46] The relevant provisions of the restraining order state: "2. Plaintiffs' motion for a protective order is granted with respect to information gained by the defendants through the use of all of the discovery processes regarding the financial affairs of the various plaintiffs, the names and addresses of Aquarian Foundation members, contributors, or clients, and the names and addresses of those who have been contributors, clients, or donors to any of the various plaintiffs. 3. The defendants and each of them shall make no use of and shall not disseminate the information defined in paragraph 2 which is gained through discovery, other than such use as is necessary in order for the discovering party to try the case. As a result, information gained by a defendant through the discovery process may not be published by any of the defendants or made available to any news media for publication or dissemination. This protective order has no application except to information gained by the defendants through the use of discovery processes." 104 S.Ct. at 2204 n.8. The restraining order is thus ambiguous with respect to scope, because it is not clear whether it applies only to information "regarding the financial affairs of the various plaintiffs [and] the names and addresses of [plaintiffs'] members, contributors or clients," as described in paragraph 2 of the order, or whether it applies to all "information gained by a defendant through the discovery process," as described in paragraph 3 of the order. The Washington Supreme Court referred to the order twice, once as if it applied to all information received in discovery, 654 P.2d at 675, and once as if it applied only to the specific information described in paragraph 2. 654 P.2d at 690.

[47] See note 45 *supra*.

[48] 654 P.2d at 689. Apart from the instrumental effects of restraining orders on the system of pretrial discovery, the court also noted that they served to implement the state's interest in protecting "citizens in their legitimate expectations of privacy." *Id.* at 688. See *id.* at 679–80.

[49] 598 F.2d at 192.

[50] 654 P.2d at 689, 677.

suance of a restraining order only if a trial judge considered and made "the necessary findings on each element" of the appropriate First Amendment standard,[51] the Washington Supreme Court found these restrictions "unduly complex and onerous" to achieve "the objectives of pretrial discovery."[52] It disparaged "the difficulties which . . . trial courts create for themselves when they attempt to enunciate restrictive criteria for the exercise of their discretion."[53] The Washington court concluded that the management of pretrial discovery could constitutionally be accorded the flexibility necessary to attain its ends. The issuance of restraining orders was to be "singularly within the discretion of the trial court" and reversible "only on a clear showing of abuse of discretion."[54]

As the case came to the Supreme Court of the United States, therefore, it was susceptible to several narrow resolutions. The Court could have found the restraining order before it justified because of plaintiffs' constitutional interests in freedom of association and religion, or because the affidavits in the record graphically detailed dangers of actual physical harm. Conversely, the Court could have found the restraining order constitutionally unjustified because of its ambiguity, or because it was not grounded in findings of fact.[55] But the Court avoided these narrow approaches and instead affirmed the Washington court on the broadest possible grounds.

In a terse and unanimous opinion, the Court, speaking through Justice Powell, held that although litigants had First Amendment rights in the dissemination of information gained through discovery, the State's "substantial interest in preventing . . . abuse of its

---

[51] 598 F.2d at 192.

[52] 654 P.2d at 685.

[53] Id. at 684.

[54] Id. at 678.

[55] There is a developing case law interpreting the "good cause" requirement of Fed. R. Civ. P. 26(c) to require "a particular and specific demonstration of fact, as distinguished from stereotyped and conclusory statements." WRIGHT & MILLER, note 16 supra, § 2035 at 265. See Gulf Oil Co. v. Bernard, 452 U.S. 89, 102 n.16 (1981); General Dynamics Corp. v. Selb Mfg. Co., 481 F.2d 1204, 1212 (8th Cir. 1973); Zenith Radio Corp. v. Matsushita, 529 F. Supp. at 891; United States v. Hooker Chemical & Plastics Co., 90 F.R.D. 421, 425 (W.D.N.Y. 1981); Parsons v. General Motors Corp., 85 F.R.D. 724, 726 (N.D. Ga. 1980); Argonaut Ins. Co. v. North American Co. for Property and Casualty Ins., slip op., No. 76 Civ. 802 (Dec. 9, 1980, S.D.N.Y.). These holdings, however, are not constitutional in nature.

processes" justified delegation of "broad discretion on the trial court to decide when a protective order is appropriate and what degree of protection is required." There was to be "no heightened First Amendment scrutiny."[56]

This conclusion was clearly designed to terminate the turmoil created by *Halkin*. But the price of this achievement was to place the Court at odds with a long line of precedents holding that the First Amendment deeply disfavors "official discretionary power to control" speech[57] in the absence of "narrowly drawn, reasonable and definite standards for the officials to follow."[58] Only six days before *Rhinehart*, the Court had reaffirmed its commitment to the rule that statutes creating discretionary authority to suppress speech are facially unconstitutional, since "every application of the statute create[s] an impermissible risk of the suppression of ideas."[59]

This tension between First Amendment rights and official discretion is never acknowledged in Justice Powell's opinion. The silence is strange, and gives the impression that the issue was avoided because the Court lacked a conceptual scheme within which it could be analyzed. Instead the Court struggled to justify its conclusion using conventional doctrinal formulations that were inconsistent with the exercise of official discretion.

A. THE PROCUNIER TEST

At the outset of its opinion the Court announced, without further explanation, that the constitutionality of Washington's Rule 26(c), which authorizes the issuance of restraining orders,[60] would turn on[61]

---

[56] Seattle Times Co. v. Rhinehart, 104 S.Ct. 2199, 2209 (1984). Although Justice Brennan joined Justice Powell's opinion, he also wrote two brief concurring paragraphs in which he said that he would affirm the judgment of the Washington court because plaintiffs' "interests in privacy and religious freedom are sufficient to justify this protective order and to overcome the protections afforded free expression by the First Amendment." 104 S.Ct. at 2210. Justice Brennan's opinion was joined by Justice Marshall.

[57] Kunz v. New York, 340 U.S. 290, 293 (1951).

[58] Nietmotko v. Maryland, 340 U.S. 268, 271 (1951). See Shuttlesworth v. City of Birmingham, 394 U.S. 147, 150–51 & n.2 (1969); Saia v. New York, 334 U.S. 558 (1948); Hague v. CIO, 307 U.S. 496 (1939); Lovell v. Griffin, 303 U.S. 444 (1938).

[59] Members of City Council v. Taxpayers for Vincent, 104 S.Ct. 2118, 2125 & n.15 (1984).

[60] See note 44 *supra*.

[61] 104 S.Ct. at 2207.

whether the "practice in question [furthers] an important or substantial governmental interest unrelated to the suppression of
expression," and whether "the limitation of First Amendment
freedoms [is] no greater than is necessary or essential to the
protection of the particular governmental interest involved."
Procunier v. Martinez, 416 U.S. 396, 413 (1974); see *Brown v.
Glines*, 444 U.S. 348, 354–55 (1980); *Buckley v. Valeo*, 424 U.S.
1, 25 (1976).

The two-part test derives from *Procunier v. Martinez*, an early Powell opinion dealing with the censorship of prisoners' mail. In fashioning the *Procunier* test, Powell relied explicitly on Chief Justice
Warren's opinion in *United States v. O'Brien*.[62]

The first element of the test concerns whether Rule 26(c) furthers
a substantial government interest unrelated to the suppression of
expression. The Court argued that Rule 26(c) furthers a substantial
government interest in the protection of the "privacy interests of
litigants and third parties."[63] As a preliminary matter, this interest
does not appear to be "unrelated to the suppression of expression."
Every suppression of speech can be justified in terms of an interest
that is speech neutral. A ban on the teaching of anarchy, for example, can be justified on the grounds of domestic security. Therefore a sensible interpretation of the requirement that a government
interest be "unrelated to the suppression of expression" must ask, as
John Ely does in his discussion of *O'Brien*, "whether the harm that
the state is seeking to avert is one that grows out of the fact that the
defendant is communicating, and more particularly out of the way
people can be expected to react to his message, or rather would
arise even if the defendant's conduct had no communicative significance whatever."[64]

In *Rhinehart* the Court stated that restraining orders were
justified because of the government's interest in the protection of
privacy interests. But this justification turns precisely on the fact
that litigants are communicating. The purpose of Rule 26(c) is to

---

[62] See Procunier v. Martinez, 416 U.S. 396, 411–14 (1974).

[63] 104 S.Ct. at 2208.

[64] Ely, *Flag Desecration: A Case Study in the Roles of Categorization and Balancing in First Amendment Analysis*, 88 HARV. L. REV. 1482, 1497 (1975). See TRIBE, AMERICAN CON-STITUTIONAL LAW 580–88 (1978). This is the approach implicitly adopted by the Court in Buckley v. Valeo, 424 U.S. 1 (1976). See also Consolidated Edison Co. v. Public Service Comm'n, 447 U.S. 530, 540 n.9 (1980).

eliminate the consequences of speaking about certain kinds of subjects; if litigants spoke gibberish, so that no one could understand them, privacy interests would not be endangered. For this reason the government's interest cannot be said to be unrelated to the suppression of expression.[65]

More important, however, the Court was unable to employ the *Procunier* test in an internally consistent manner. This is true for two reasons. First, the *Procunier* test requires that the "practice in question" further a "substantial" government interest. To justify the issuance of a restraining order, therefore, the privacy interest to be protected must be "substantial." At a minimum this required the Court to create standards by which "substantial" privacy interests could be identified and distinguished from "nonsubstantial" privacy interests. In previous cases the Court has been quite strict in specifying the kinds of privacy interests that could justify suppression of speech. In *Cox Broadcasting Corp. v. Cohn*, for example, where the Court faced a similar "collision between claims of privacy and those of" freedom of speech, the Court recognized the need for "caution" and carefully crafted a narrow decision stressing the exact nature of the privacy interest sought to be protected by state law.[66] But the Court made no such effort in *Rhinehart*. It refused to identify which privacy interests were "substantial" and hence would constitutionally justify the issuance of a restraining order. For this reason the Court could not claim that Rule 26(c) authorized only those restraining orders necessary to protect "substantial" privacy interests.[67] Consequently, its conclusion that Rule 26(c) satisfied the first element of the *Procunier* test is simply unsustainable.

Second, the *Procunier* test required that "the limitation of First Amendment freedoms" be "no greater than is necessary or essential to the protection of the particular governmental interest involved." But if the Court has not specified the nature of the privacy interests

---

[65] Powell's handling of this question recalls his treatment of the same issue in *Procunier*. See 416 U.S. at 413. In that case the regulation at issue sought to suppress the results of intended communications, and yet Powell viewed it as "speech neutral," thus eviscerating the requirement that the regulation be "unrelated to the suppression of expression."

[66] 420 U.S. 469, 491 (1975).

[67] The requirement that restraining orders only issue to protect substantial privacy interests is not implicit in the "good cause" standard of Rule 26(c), because that standard simply confers discretion on trial courts. See text at notes 14–16 *supra*.

to be protected, then it would seem in principle impossible to know whether limitations on First Amendment freedoms will be "necessary or essential." The Court's conclusion, moreover, was that it is constitutional to commit the issuance of restraining orders to the broad discretion of trial judges. The Court did not restrict that discretion by requiring trial judges to consider litigants' First Amendment interests. Thus where litigants' First Amendment interests can be accommodated without impairment of government interests, as, for example, where a narrower or more precise restraining order would adequately protect pertinent privacy interests, the issuance of a broader or vaguer restraining order would be both constitutionally proper and inconsistent with the second element of the *Procunier* test. In the face of these contradictions the Court did not even attempt to claim or argue that Rule 26(c) creates only necessary or essential limitations on the First Amendment rights of litigants. It simply proposed and then abandoned the second element of the *Procunier* test.

The Court's difficulties in applying the *Procunier* test ultimately follow from its conclusion that trial courts should have "broad discretion" to decide "when a protective order is appropriate." The *Procunier* test requires that each decision to issue a restraining order be subject to First Amendment standards designed to measure the weight or importance of the privacy interests to be protected. The Court's refusal to impose such standards is explicable only as a judgment that they would be incompatible with the "broad discretion" that the Court wished to confer on trial courts.

This dilemma could have been softened somewhat if the Court had attempted to justify restraining orders on the basis of a "substantial" government interest that was systemic in nature, as, for example, the government's interest in the supervision of pretrial discovery. Since the importance of such a systemic interest need not be determined on a case-by-case basis, the tension between the application of standards and the exercise of discretion would diminish. But the tension would not disappear altogether, since the question would nevertheless remain whether any particular restraining order was "necessary or essential" to the asserted government interest.

The Court's abandonment of the second element of the *Procunier* test is thus particularly revealing, for it evinces the Court's extreme reluctance to trammel the exercise of trial court discretion by the application of any legal standards. This reluctance is evidence that the Court shared the common belief, "buried deep in the hearts of various constitutional theorists and judges,"[68] that there is an "essential incompatibility" between law and discretion.[69] The Court evidently believed it had to choose between "heightened First Amendment scrutiny" and the "broad discretion" of "the trial court to decide when a protective order is appropriate." It could have one or the other, but not both.

From this perspective, First Amendment rights and government discretion are irreconcilable. "To discipline . . . discretion by rule and rote is somehow to denature it."[70] One way to break out of this impasse is to reject its premise and to view law and discretion as complementary rather than incompatible. The Court, however, chose not to follow this approach, and instead sought to bolster its opinion by arguing, first, that unfettered trial court discretion was justifiable, and, second, that litigants retained only diminished First Amendment rights in the dissemination of discovery information.

B. THE COURT'S JUSTIFICATION FOR DISCRETION

Official discretion to suppress speech has generally been viewed as presumptively unconstitutional. In view of the Court's "long line" of decisions consistently striking down as "unconstitutional censorship" those statutes making the exercise of First Amendment rights "contingent" upon the "discretion" of a public official,[71] one would expect the Court carefully to analyze the particular features of restraining orders that would justify trial court discretion in their issuance. But the Court devoted only one short paragraph to the issue:[72]

> We also find that the provision for protective orders in the Washington Rules requires, in itself, no heightened First Amendment scrutiny. To be sure, Rule 26(c) confers broad discretion on the trial court to decide when a protective order is appropriate and

---

[68] Galligan, *The Nature and Function of Policies within Discretionary Power*, 1976 PUB. L. 332.

[69] Smith, *Thoughts on a British Conseil d'Etat*, 23 PUB. AD. 23, 30 (1945).

[70] *Ibid.*

[71] Staub v. City of Baxley, 355 U.S. 313, 322 (1958).

[72] 104 S.Ct. at 2209.

what degree of protection is required. The legislature of the State of Washington, following the example of the Congress in its approval of the Federal Rules of Civil Procedure, has determined that such discretion is necessary, and we find no reason to disagree. The trial court is in the best position to weigh fairly the competing needs and interests of the parties affected by discovery. The unique character of the discovery process requires that the trial court have substantial latitude to fashion protective orders.

The passage is disappointing. The rhetoric of "deference" is misleading. Neither Congress nor the Washington legislature had anything to do with the formulation of Rule 26(c). The Washington Rule was in fact issued by the Supreme Court of Washington, which simply copied it verbatim from the federal rule promulgated by the United States Supreme Court.[73] Ultimately, the Court was simply "deferring" to itself. Moreover, even if the fiction were indulged that the Court were "deferring" to the independent judgment of the Supreme Court of Washington in deciding to reissue Rule 26(c), such deference is inappropriate in a First Amendment context, where the Court has repeatedly held that "deference to a legislative finding cannot limit judicial inquiry when First Amendment rights are at stake."[74]

The Court's observation that trial judges are in the best position to weigh the "competing needs and interests of the parties" is equally unhelpful. The fact that there are competing interests to be balanced has never, by itself, been thought to require the delegation of "broad" discretion.[75] And the fact that a trial judge is in the best position to assess the particular situation before him would also

---

[73] See note 44 *supra*. Pursuant to Wash. Rev. Code § 204.190, Washington rules of civil procedure are promulgated directly by the Supreme Court of Washington and are immediately effective. See Ashley v. Superior Court, 83 Wash. 2d 630, 521 P.2d 711, 715 (1974). Rule 26(c) was ordered into effect by the Washington court in 1972. 80 Wash. 2d 1191–92 (1972). Pursuant to 28 U.S.C. § 2072, federal rules of civil procedure are prescribed by the Supreme Court, and become effective ninety days after they have been "reported to Congress by the Chief Justice." Congress has never altered the formulation of Rule 26(c) or any of its predecessors.

[74] Landmark Communications, Inc. v. Virginia, 435 U.S. 829, 843 (1978). The Court has also noted that in First Amendment cases, less deference is due to the judgments of lower courts than to legislative decisions, since the "judgments below . . . do not come to us encased in the armor wrought by prior legislative deliberation." Bridges v. California, 314 U.S. 252, 261 (1941).

[75] Press-Enterprise Co. v. Superior Court, 104 S.Ct. 819, 824 (1984); Nebraska Press Assn. v. Stuart, 427 U.S. 539, 570 (1976).

not seem to be distinctive, since the same could be said in defense of the numerous licensing statutes that the Court has struck down because of their impermissible delegation of discretionary power to local officials.[76] In each of these cases local officials could, with some plausibility, have claimed to be in the best position to evaluate the competing claims of local interests, and yet the Court has consistently refused to defer to such claims.

One might defend the Court's position on the grounds that discretion in the hands of a trial judge is quite different from and more acceptable than discretion in the hands of a local sheriff. But this argument ultimately rests on the notion that discretion for the local sheriff constitutes a license to engage in political discrimination, whereas discretion for the trial judge is the freedom to obey the law. Thus the argument fails precisely to the extent that the law simply authorizes a judge to exercise discretion, without providing further standards for guidance. Within the field of discretion authorized by law, a judge, like a sheriff, is free to use the suppression of speech as a tool of policy. And while judicial policy, unlike that of local sheriffs, may not involve hostility to unpopular religious sects, it may well involve exaggerated respect for law and social stability.[77]

For this reason the Court has traditionally viewed with disfavor judicial discretion to suppress speech. In *Cantwell v. Connecticut*,[78] for example, a Jehovah's Witness who had played a religious phonograph record on the street was convicted of the common-law offense of inciting a breach of the peace. The Court noted that since the conviction was "based on a common law concept of the most general and undefined nature," there was a danger that the government could "unduly suppress free communication of views, religious or otherwise, under the guise of conserving desirable condi-

---

[76] Thus, for example, in his separate opinion in Kunz v. New York, 340 U.S. 290, 273 (1951), Justice Frankfurter knew the arguments for deference and stated that "this Court should not substitute its abstract views for the informed judgment of local authorities confirmed by local courts." *Id.* at 284. Frankfurter found these considerations insufficient, however, to sustain the constitutionality of a statute giving local officials broad discretion to grant or deny permits to speak.

[77] It has been said that underlying much First Amendment theory and doctrine is the perception "that judges tend to be unduly risk averse in ruling upon the claims of speakers." Blasi, *Towards a Theory of Prior Restraint: The Central Linkage*, 66 MINN. L. REV. 11, 52 (1981). But see Jeffries, *Rethinking Prior Restraint*, 92 YALE L.J. 409, 426–27 (1983).

[78] 310 U.S. 296 (1940).

tions."[79] The diffuse common-law standard left "to the executive and *judicial* branches too wide a discretion in its application."[80] In the absence "of a statute narrowly drawn to define and punish specific conduct," therefore, judicial discretion was to be controlled by the strict requirements of the clear and present danger test.[81]

A similar distrust of judicial discretion underlies *Bridges v. California*,[82] in which, relying in part on *Cantwell*, the Court used the clear and present danger test sharply to curtail common-law judicial discretion to punish by contempt out of court publications tending to interfere with the fair and orderly administration of justice. This same distrust explains the Court's tendency to view with disfavor judicial injunctions that suppress speech and that are based not on specific statutory authorization, but on vague common-law or constitutional norms.[83] In this respect, the broad discretion given to trial judges to decide "when a protective order is appropriate and what degree of protection is required" creates close structural similarities between restraining orders and those injunctions which the Court has in the past struck down as unconstitutional prior restraints.[84]

---

[79] *Id.* at 308.

[80] *Ibid.* (emphasis added). See Smith v. Goguen, 415 U.S. 567, 573 (1973).

[81] 310 U.S. at 311.

[82] 314 U.S. 252 (1941).

[83] Compare *Nebraska Press*, note 75 *supra*, New York Times v. United States, 403 U.S. 713 (1971), and Organization for a Better Austin v. O'Keefe, 402 U.S. 415 (1971), with Kingsley Books v. Brown, 354 U.S. 436 (1957), and Pittsburgh Press Co. v. Human Relations Comm'n, 413 U.S. 376 (1973). *Cf.* United States v. The Progressive, Inc., 467 F. Supp. 990 (W.D. Wis. 1979).

[84] The Court in *Rhinehart* had a great deal of difficulty distinguishing restraining orders from "the kind of classic prior restraint that requires exacting First Amendment scrutiny." 104 S.Ct. at 2208. The difference, the Court said, lay in the fact that restraining orders prohibit the dissemination only of "that information obtained through use of the discovery process," and permit the publication of "identical information" if "gained through means independent of the court's processes." *Ibid.* The Court's distinction was an apparent attempt to build on Justice Powell's concurring opinion in Gannett Co. v. DePasquale, 443 U.S. 368 (1979), in which he argued that a judicial order closing a pretrial hearing differed from a "classic prior restraint" because the latter "applied to information irrespective of its sources." *Id.* at 399. In *Rhinehart* the Court makes the similar argument that restraining orders are unlike classic prior restraints because the former prohibit speech based on only one source— discovery information—and leave the parties free to speak about the same subject based on information "gained through means independent of the court's processes." The trouble with this argument is that judicial injunctions prohibiting speech based on a single source of information have been viewed traditionally as classic prior restraints. See New York Times v. United States, 403 U.S. 713, 714 (1971).

There might, of course, be government interests implicit in the functioning of pretrial discovery that are sufficiently substantial to justify the discretionary suppression of speech. But they must be identified and analyzed, so that their implications can be carefully assessed. For these purposes the Court's casual reference to "the unique character of the discovery process" is clearly insufficient.

C. THE FIRST AMENDMENT RIGHTS OF LITIGANTS

One method of resolving the tension between First Amendment rights and government discretion is to deny or diminish the First Amendment rights. The Court in *Rhinehart* appeared to employ this method. Although the Court stated that "litigants do not 'surrender their First Amendment rights at the courthouse door,' "[85] it also implied that these rights were of a somewhat diminished constitutional significance.[86] Since restraining orders plainly forbid speech, the cogency of this conclusion is less than obvious.

The Court justified its conclusion on the ground that restraining orders apply only to speech about information provided to the litigants as a matter of "legislative grace":[87]

> [I]t is important to recognize the extent of the impairment of First Amendment rights that a protective order, such as the one at issue here, may cause. As in all civil litigation, petitioners gained the information they wish to disseminate only by virtue of the trial court's discovery processes. As the rules authorizing discovery were adopted by the state legislature, the processes thereunder are a matter of legislative grace. A litigant has no First Amendment right of access to information made available

---

[85] 104 S.Ct. at 2207 n.18. The Court candidly acknowledged that defendants' speech did not fall "within the classes of unprotected speech" such as "fighting words" or obscenity, and that "there certainly is a public interest in knowing more about" the plaintiffs, an interest that "may well include most—and possibly all—of what has been discovered as a result of the court's order." 104 S.Ct. at 2206–07. These acknowledgments must be understood as an implicit rejection of the approach of the Supreme Court of Washington, which had argued that there was only a minimal public interest in the conduct of "civil actions," and that defendants' First Amendment rights were somehow diminished because their speech did not involve "advocacy or abstract discussion," but "only the reporting of supposed facts elicited in discovery." 654 P.2d at 686–88.

[86] The Court was somewhat unclear on this point, but concluded its discussion of litigants' First Amendment interests with the observation that "judicial limitations on a party's ability to disseminate information discovered in advance of trial implicates the First Amendment rights of the restricted party to a far lesser extent than would restraints on dissemination of information in a different context." 104 S.Ct. at 2208.

[87] 104 S.Ct. at 2207.

to him only for purposes of trying his suit. . . . Thus, continued court control over the discovered information does not raise the same spectre of government censorship that such control might suggest in other situations. See *In re Halkin*, 598 F.2d, at 206–07 (Wilkey, J., dissenting).

The Court's reasoning is open to several interpretations. The first, suggested by the Court's reference to Judge Wilkey's dissenting opinion in *In re Halkin*, is that litigants receiving discovery information have only a "limited" First Amendment right in its dissemination, since they receive it "already *subject to* the courts' exercise of [a] discretionary power" of restraint.[88] As Judge Wilkey forthrightly acknowledged, however, this reasoning is "very analogous to the view taken by Mr. Justice Rehnquist in *Arnett v. Kennedy* with respect to one's property interest in a government job. Therein Mr. Justice Rehnquist concluded that 'the property interest which appellee had in his [nonprobationary federal] employment was itself conditioned by the procedural limitations which had accompanied the grant of that interest.' "[89]

The difficulty with this argument is that Rehnquist's position in *Arnett* was specifically rejected by six other Justices,[90] including Justice Powell, who noted that Rehnquist's reasoning failed to perceive that even if benefits are received as a matter of "legislative grace," constitutional rights are not.[91] Later decisions of the Court have reiterated this rejection of Rehnquist's position,[92] and it is

---

[88] In re Halkin, 598 F.2d at 206 (Wilkey, J., dissenting).

[89] *Id.* at 207.

[90] Arnett v. Kennedy, 416 U.S. 153, 166–67 (1974) (opinion of Powell, J., joined by Blackmun, J.); 177–78 (opinion of White, J.); 210–11 (opinion of Marshall, J., joined by Douglas and Brennan, JJ.).

[91] 416 U.S. at 166–67 (Powell, J., concurring). But see Goss v. Lopez, 419 U.S. 565, 586–87 (1975) (Powell, J., dissenting). For recent studies of the vagaries of the Court's approach to the "right-privilege" distinction, and to its first cousin, the doctrine of "unconstitutional conditions," see Kreimer, *Allocation Sanctions: The Problem of Negative Rights in a Positive State*, 132 U. PA. L. REV. 1293 (1984); Smolla, *The Reemergence of the Right-Privilege Distinction in Constitutional Law: The Price of Protesting Too Much*, 35 STAN. L. REV. 69 (1982); Easterbrook, *Substance and Due Process*, 1982 SUPREME COURT REVIEW 85; Terrell, *"Property," "Due Process," and the Distinction between Definition and Theory in Legal Analysis*, 70 GEO. L.J. 861 (1982); Westin, *Incredible Dilemmas: Conditioning One Constitutional Right on the Forfeiture of Another*, 66 IOWA L. REV. 741 (1981); Easterbrook, *Insider Trading, Secret Agents, Evidentiary Privileges, and the Production of Information*, 1981 SUPREME COURT REVIEW 309, 348.

[92] See Logan v. Zimmerman Brush Co., 455 U.S. 422, 431–32 (1982); Vitek v. Jones, 445 U.S. 480, 490 n.6 (1980).

implausible that Justice Powell meant by his unelaborated reference to Judge Wilkey suddenly to revive Rehnquist's approach.

A second interpretation of the Court's reasoning is that the legislature can condition production of discovery information on the sacrifice of First Amendment interests in the dissemination of such information.[93] So characterized, however, this interpretation would appear to conflict with the doctrine of unconstitutional conditions. In its most extreme formulation, the doctrine holds that First Amendment rights may not "be infringed by the denial of or placing of conditions upon a benefit or privilege."[94] A more realistic view of the doctrine is that it functions primarily to deny that conditions placed upon the receipt of government benefits are constitutional simply because the benefits are a matter of legislative grace. The work of constitutionally analyzing such conditions must proceed free of any such conclusive arguments.[95] Even in this more restricted form, however, the doctrine is in tension with the Court's opinion, which attempts to make just such a conclusive argument.

The Court's position may nevertheless be defended on the grounds that the doctrine of unconstitutional conditions ought not to apply to speech about discovery information. The argument could be made that the doctrine should only be applied to cases in which government conditions the receipt of state benefits on the sacrifice of constitutional rights that individuals would otherwise be free to exercise. Since there is no right or ability to speak about discovery information before it is provided by the government, the

---

[93] This interpretation differs from the first in that it is not, like Justice Rehnquist's view in *Arnett*, predicated on the assumption that constitutional rights can be defined by legislative benefits. It is noteworthy, in this regard, that Justice Powell quoted without expressly approving the Washington Supreme Court's observation that participation in discovery constitutes a "waiver" of First Amendment rights. See 104 S.Ct. at 2205 n.9. That observation is untenable. See Curtis Publishing Co. v. Butts, 388 U.S. 130, 145 (1967); Johnson v. Zerbst, 304 U.S. 458, 464 (1938). See also Schlagenhauf v. Holder, 379 U.S. 104, 114 (1964) ("constitutional problems" resulting from any theory that constitutional rights are waived merely from exercising "right of access to the federal courts").

[94] Sherbert v. Verner, 374 U.S. 398, 404 (1963).

[95] The *Sherbert* Court recognized that the benefits at issue were a matter of legislative grace, but nonetheless examined the conditions on their receipt to determine if they were supported by a "compelling state interest." 374 U.S. at 403, 406–09. There was thus no conclusive presumption of either constitutionality or nonconstitutionality. See generally Westin, note 91 *supra*, at 748–51; Linde, *Justice Douglas on Freedom in the Welfare State: Constitutional Rights in the Public Sector*, 40 WASH. L. REV. 10 (1965); Van Alstyne, *The Constitutional Rights of Public Employees: A Comment on the Inappropriate Uses of an Old Analogy*, 16 U.C.L.A. L. REV. 751 (1969).

doctrine should have no application. In *Sherbert v. Verner*, for example, a Seventh-Day Adventist who believed as an article of religious faith that Saturday labor was forbidden, was required to work on Saturday as a condition of receiving unemployment compensation benefits.[96] The premise of the Court's decision was that in the absence of government action, the Adventist was free to exercise her religious beliefs by refraining from Saturday labor. Conditioning unemployment benefits on Saturday labor functioned to "compel" her to violate these beliefs. There does not seem to be a similar compulsion operating on litigants, who cannot exercise their right to speak about discovery information until the government has acted to provide it to them.

This approach does seem to capture something of the unique character of restraining orders. Underlying it are two distinct lines of thought that need to be separately addressed. The first is that placing conditions on the receipt of discovery information does not compel litigants to sacrifice a preexisting constitutional right, since litigants cannot speak about information they do not yet have. This argument is unsatisfactory because it would make the constitutional analysis of a restraining order turn on the arbitrary circumstance of whether the order was issued before or after the receipt of discovery information. In *Halkin*, for example, the restraining order was issued only after litigants had received discovery information and had given written notice that they intended to release it to the press.[97] Therefore the restraining order did in fact deprive litigants of a constitutional right to speak that they otherwise could have exercised.[98] Similarly, the restraining order in *Rhinehart* was issued after some discovery information had already been produced.[99] To apply a different constitutional analysis to this information would be bizarre, and it certainly does not appear to have been the Court's intention. Indeed, by strongly indicating its disapproval of *Halkin*, the Court signaled that its analysis could not be predicated upon

---

[96] 374 U.S. at 399–401.

[97] 598 F.2d at 180–81.

[98] It is thus doubtful that Judge Wilkey, in his *Halkin* dissent, meant to rest his argument on the absence of any preexisting constitutional right. Wilkey emphasized that it made no difference to his analysis of the *de minimis* nature of litigants' First Amendment rights whether a restraining order was issued "*before* or *after* the litigant's receipt of information." *Id.* at 207.

[99] See note 43 *supra*.

whether a restraining order was issued before or after the production of discovery information.

The Court's point, therefore, must be interpreted more broadly to mean that conditioning discovery on the sacrifice of First Amendment rights is permissible whenever the provision of the information makes possible the very exercise of these rights. The argument for this position is that the "spectre of government censorship" is reduced in such circumstances because the government retains the option to withhold the information that makes the rights exist at all.

This argument is both inconsistent with precedent and practically unsound. Indeed, little more than a month after *Rhinehart* the Court decided *FCC v. League of Women Voters*,[100] which held that government contributions to noncommercial educational stations could not be conditioned upon a prohibition of the stations' editorial speech, even if such speech were made possible by the contributions. *League of Women Voters* is simply the latest in a line of decisions rejecting the contention that First Amendment rights made possible by government action can be prohibited by the government. Although the federal government created the United States mail as a matter of legislative grace, for example, it may not condition access to the mails upon the sacrifice of those First Amendment rights made possible by the use of the mail. The Court has held that "grave constitutional questions are immediately raised once it is said that the use of the mails is a privilege which may be extended or withheld on any grounds whatsoever."[101] Similarly, even if a local government builds a municipal auditorium that makes possible the exercise of First Amendment rights associated with theatrical productions, the availability of the auditorium must be "bounded by precise and clear standards," since, "the danger of censorship and of abridgment of our precious First Amendment freedoms is too great where officials have unbridled discretion over a forum's use."[102]

Viewed from this perspective, it is false to say, as the Court

---

[100] 104 S.Ct. 3106 (1984).

[101] Hannegan v. Esquire, Inc., 327 U.S. 146, 156 (1946).

[102] Southeastern Promotions v. Conrad, 420 U.S. 546, 553, 556 (1975). See also Madison School District v. Wisconsin Employment Rel. Comm'n, 429 U.S. 167, 176 (1976); Healy v. James, 408 U.S. 169, 181–83 (1972).

implies, that the "spectre of government censorship" is less when government action makes possible the exercise of First Amendment rights. It does not take much imagination, for example, to envision the government's making the mail service selectively available to presidential candidates on the basis of their political views, or judges' imposing restraining orders on the basis of litigants' political affiliations. It is not, therefore, that the specter of censorship is reduced; it is rather that the Court believed the risk of censorship to be justifiable in the context of civil discovery. But at bottom this is a belief about the process of discovery, rather than about the nature of litigants' First Amendment rights.

The Court might have believed that the concept of a "diminished" First Amendment right would function both to permit the exercise of official discretion and to prohibit flagrant abuse such as overt political discrimination. But this use of the concept appears arbitrary and unsupported, since it is not clear why the concept would function in this manner. The Court made no effort to derive this function from traditional theories of freedom of expression, and it is unlikely that any such effort would have proved successful. The Court has repeatedly stressed that "the operations of the courts and the judicial conduct of judges are matters of utmost public concern,"[103] and reference to discovery information can often be necessary to litigants' public evaluation of the judicial management of a case. Whether one examines such speech from the perspective of the "marketplace of ideas,"[104] or of the information flow necessary for democratic self-governance,[105] or of the "self-fulfillment" of the speaker,[106] or of the "autonomy" of the listener,[107] there does not appear to be any reason to conclude that litigants' rights in the dissemination of discovery information are in any respect diminished.

In prior cases, moreover, the Court has properly and carefully distinguished between a right of access to information and a right to

---

[103] Landmark Communications v. Virginia, 435 U.S. 829, 839 (1978). See note 85 *supra*.

[104] See, *e.g.*, SCHAUER, FREE SPEECH: A PHILOSOPHICAL ENQUIRY 15–34 (1982); Abrams v. United States, 250 U.S. 616, 630 (1919) (Holmes, J., dissenting).

[105] See, *e.g.*, MEIKLEJOHN, POLITICAL FREEDOM: THE CONSTITUTIONAL POWERS OF THE PEOPLE (1948); De Jonge v. Oregon, 299 U.S. 353, 364–65 (1937).

[106] See, *e.g.*, EMERSON, THE SYSTEM OF FREEDOM OF EXPRESSION 6 (1970).

[107] See, *e.g.*, Scanlon, *A Theory of Freedom of Expression*, 1 PHIL. & PUB. AFF. 204 (1972).

disseminate such information once access has been obtained. Thus even in situations where government may legitimately bar access to information, the Court has found that First Amendment rights of dissemination can continue undiminished.[108] In particular circumstances, of course, such rights may be subordinated to appropriate government interests in regulation. But in these circumstances it is more productive to focus on the nature of the asserted government interests, rather than on an undefined and intuitive diminution of First Amendment rights. Government interests in regulation are public and can provide the basis for constitutional dialogue. Thus, for example, if the Court were to have asserted that specific characteristics of the discovery process justify the need for trial court discretion to suppress speech, such an assertion could be made the subject of salutory and rational discussion. But discussion is ended by the deus ex machina appearance of a "diminished" First Amendment right that is unrelated to First Amendment theory or precedent, and that has content and contours that are neither described nor explained.

III. THE MANAGEMENT OF SPEECH AND THE ADMINISTRATION OF DISCOVERY

The Court in *Rhinehart* was determined to reach a result that would insulate discretionary control over pretrial discovery from First Amendment challenge. The Court's difficulty in justifying this result can be explained in part by its reliance on traditional doctrinal formulations that embody values peripheral to the interests the Court was actually trying to protect. The Court never articulated these interests, but it provided us a clue to their nature by its reference to *Procunier* as the appropriate framework for First Amendment analysis. At first blush this reference seems peculiar: the First Amendment rights of prisoners do not seem an obvious standard for those of litigants. But the justification for the reference is made somewhat clearer by the subsequent citation of *Brown v. Glines*,[109] in which the Court discussed the discretionary suppres-

---

[108] See, *e.g.*, Landmark Communications, Inc. v. Virginia, 435 U.S. 829 (1978); New York Times v. United States, 403 U.S. 713 (1971).

[109] 444 U.S. 348 (1980).

sion of First Amendment rights in the military.[110] What *Procunier* and *Brown* have in common is that both address the relationship between First Amendment rights and the internal management of a government institution.

The citation of these cases implies that underlying the Court's decision is the notion that pretrial discovery is a regime of judicial administration, rather than adjudication. From this perspective, the rules of civil procedure do not give litigants "rights" to information that must be adjudicated before a neutral and umpireal judge, but rather create a system of information exchange to be actively managed by a judge so as to secure "the just, speedy, and inexpensive determination of every action."[111] This perspective, of course, was explicitly adopted by the drafters of the 1983 amendments to the Federal Rules, which "encourage forceful judicial management" of "the entire pretrial phase, especially motions and discovery."[112] In his role as manager, the trial judge must consult not merely the interests of the particular parties before him, but the needs of the entire institution of pretrial discovery. He must make decisions based upon their effects on "other parties to other lawsuits."[113]

Administration of the system of pretrial discovery requires the continual exercise of judgment: judgment about whether "a party's aim is to delay bringing a case to trial, or embarrass or harass the person from whom he seeks discovery";[114] judgment about how to

---

[110] The citations to *Procunier* and to *Glines* are followed by a reference to "Buckley v. Valeo, 424 U.S. 1, 25 (1976)." 104 S.Ct. at 2207. This reference seems to be a mistake. The Court in *Buckley* explicitly refused to employ the test of United States v. O'Brien, upon which the formulations in both *Procunier* and *Glines* are based. The language in *Buckley* cited by the *Rhinehart* Court is instead an effort to apply the "closest scrutiny," which is not the Court's intention in *Rhinehart*, and which was not its purpose in either *Procunier* or *Glines*.

[111] Wash. Super. Ct. C.R. 1; Fed. R. Civ. P. 1. For a discussion of the emerging contrast between the managerial and umpireal images of the judge, see Resnik, *Managerial Judges*, 96 HARV. L. REV. 374 (1982); Kritzer, *The Judge's Role in Pretrial Case Processing: Assessing the Need for Change*, 66 JUDICATURE 28, 30 (June–July 1982).

[112] Advisory Committee Notes to Rule 16, 97 F.R.D. 207, 213 (1983). Justice Powell has stressed the "pressing need for judicial supervision" of discovery to prevent abuse. ACF Industries, Inc. v. EEOC, 439 U.S. 1081, 1087 (1979) (Powell, J., dissenting from denial of certiorari).

[113] National Hockey League v. Metropolitan Hockey Club, Inc., 427 U.S. 639, 643 (1976). See Advisory Committee Notes to Rule 26, 97 F.R.D. 220 (1983). To adopt the language of the sociologist Philip Selznik, one might say that the judge's objective in administering pretrial discovery is "to achieve a desired outcome" rather than to attain "justice" between the parties. SELZNICK, LAW, SOCIETY, AND INDUSTRIAL JUSTICE 16 (1969).

[114] Oppenheimer Fund, Inc. v. Sanders, 437 U.S. 340, 353 n.17 (1978).

instill "in counsel a sense of responsibility that will serve as a policing agent against harassment and oppression";[115] judgment about when discovery has become financially oppressive;[116] judgment about when to teach counsel a lesson.[117] No set of rules could comprehend the exercise of such judgment,[118] and for that reason "flexibility and experience are the keys to efficient management" of pretrial discovery.[119] Need for this flexibility has traditionally been recognized in the expansive authority and broad discretionary control to supervise the discovery process given to trial judges by both the Federal and Washington rules.[120] "A judge must have discretion," as one jurist put it in a different context, "because without it the business could not go on."[121]

---

[115] Pollack, note 24 *supra*, at 225.

[116] SCM Societa Commerciale S.P.A. v. Industrial and Commercial Research Corp., 72 F.R.D. 110, 112 (N.D. Tex. 1976); GLASER, PRETRIAL DISCOVERY AND THE ADVERSARY SYSTEM 182–85 (1968); Amendments to the Federal Rules of Civil Procedure, 85 F.R.D. 521, 523 (1980) (Powell, J., dissenting).

[117] Note, *The Emerging Deterrence Orientation in the Imposition of Discovery Sanctions*, 91 HARV. L. REV. 1033, 1047 (1978).

[118] The trial judge is somewhat in the position of the police officers described by James Q. Wilson, for whom "no very useful—certainly no complete—set of instructions can be devised as to what the officer *should* do with, say, quarreling lovers. Defining a policy in such matters is difficult, not because the police have not given much thought to the matters or because they do not know how they should be handled, but because so much depends on the particular circumstances of time, place, event, and personality. Psychiatrists do not use 'how to do it' manuals, and they have the advantage of dealing with people at leisure, over protracted periods of time, and in periods of relative calm." WILSON, VARIETIES OF POLICE BEHAVIOR 65–66 (1968).

[119] Advisory Committee Notes to Rule 16, 97 F.R.D. 211 (1983).

[120] See text at notes 14–16 & note 44 *supra*. The managerial perspective of pretrial discovery has been explicitly articulated primarily by those who have recently commented on the Federal Rules. The fact that this perspective has not been articulated in Washington law may have been one source of the Court's indirection in specifying the government interests at stake in Rule 26(c). But it is fair to say that from their promulgation in 1938, the Federal Rules of discovery implicitly envisioned the trial judge as a manager engaged in the "efficient administration" of justice, and to this end created a "judge-centered procedural model" which left trial judges "unfettered by rules" and able to meet "various situations . . . by wide exercise of judicial discretion." Fish, *Guarding the Judicial Ramparts: John J. Parker and the Administration of Federal Justice*, 3 JUST. SYS. J. 105, 113 (1978). See Resnik, note 111 *supra*, at 391; Cutner, *Discovery—Civil Litigation's Fading Light: A Lawyer Looks at the Federal Discovery Rules after Forty Years of Use*, 52 TEM. L. Q. 933, 936–37 (1979). Since Washington has essentially adopted all of the federal rules of discovery, with their philosophy of liberal information exchange and discretionary judicial control, it might also be said to have adopted the managerial perspective underlying these rules. At least, so the Court might have thought, Washington should constitutionally be free to adopt such a perspective if it should choose to do so.

[121] Reg. v. Winsor, 10 Cox C.C. 276, 321 (1866). See, *e.g.*, Otero v. Buslee, 695 F.2d 1244, 1248 n.1 (10th Cir. 1982).

On this account, the crux of *Rhinehart* is neither the protection of privacy interests nor the diminishment of litigants' First Amendment interests, but rather the Court's perception that discretionary authority to issue restraining orders is essential for the administration of pretrial discovery. In this sense, the government's interests in restraining orders may be analogous to its interests in the management of other government institutions such as schools or prisons. These interests are quite different from those at stake when the government regulates the speech of the general public, as in the many cases where the Court has struck down discretionary authority to suppress speech.

The Court adverted to these management interests by its citation of precedents such as *Procunier* and *Glines*. Whether these precedents actually bear on the issues presented in *Rhinehart*, however, depends upon whether the government can be said to have generic interests in the regulation of state institutions, and whether these interests significantly affect applicable First Amendment standards.

A. THE FIRST AMENDMENT AND THE MANAGEMENT OF GOVERNMENT INSTITUTIONS

Although the Court has several times noted that "First Amendment guarantees must be 'applied in light of the special characteristics of the . . . environment,' "[122] the Court has not developed a systematic approach for the application of First Amendment standards to the management of government institutions. The Court has decided cases dealing with the assertion of First Amendment rights in the context of prisons,[123] the military,[124] government employment,[125] and schools,[126] but it has yet to provide any articulation of the structural similarities that unite these decisions.

---

[122] Procunier v. Martinez, 416 U.S. 396, 410 (1974), quoting Tinker v. Des Moines School District, 313 U.S. 503, 506 (1969). See Healy v. James, 408 U.S. 169, 180 (1972).

[123] See Jones v. North Carolina Prisoners' Union, 433 U.S. 119 (1977); Pell v. Procunier, 417 U.S. 817 (1974); Procunier v. Martinez, 416 U.S. 396, 410 (1974).

[124] Brown v. Glines, 444 U.S. 348 (1980); Greer v. Spock, 424 U.S. 828 (1976); Parker v. Levy, 417 U.S. 733 (1974).

[125] Connick v. Myers, 103 S.Ct. 1684 (1983); Givhan v. Western Line Consolidated School District, 439 U.S. 410 (1979); Pickering v. Board of Education, 391 U.S. 563 (1968); *cf.* Snepp v. United States, 444 U.S. 507 (1980).

[126] Healy v. James, 408 U.S. 169 (1972); Tinker v. Des Moines School District, 313 U.S. 503 (1969).

These similarities derive from the nature of government institutions, which are organizations "formally established for the explicit purpose of achieving certain goals."[127] The goal of the military is the national defense; the goal of the school system is education. Government institutions, like most formal organizations, have explicit authority structures that are integral to their capacity to attain institutional goals.[128] Authority in government institutions typically extends to the speech as well as to the conduct of those subject to the management of the organization. For this reason speech that is insubordinate, that is expressed by those within an organization in defiance of its authority structure, threatens the ability of the institution to function.

The government's interests in the effective management of an institution are essentially its interests in the attainment of the institution's goals. The government therefore has rather strong interests in the regulation of insubordinate speech. These interests have three characteristics pertinent to the present inquiry. First, as the management of speech becomes more detailed and comprehensive, it makes little sense to distinguish between "prior restraints" and "subsequent punishments." Government organizations, for example, often require subordinates to clear with their superiors work-related memoranda before distribution. Constitutional analysis of such requirements should not turn on whether they can be characterized as imposing "prior restraints."

Second, within government institutions the distinction between permissible and impermissible speech routinely and necessarily turns on content. School boards, for example, characteristically instruct teachers that they are to use one curriculum rather than another; superiors characteristically instruct subordinates that they are to support at staff meetings one position rather than another;

---

[127] BLAU & SCOTT, FORMAL ORGANIZATIONS 5 (1962). On the ambiguities of the concept of a "goal," see SCOTT, ORGANIZATIONS: RATIONAL, NATURAL AND OPEN SYSTEMS 261–64 (1981). In this article I will refer to an institution's "public" rather than "actual" goals. Public goals legitimate the institution in the eyes of the general society. ETZIONI, A COMPARATIVE ANALYSIS OF COMPLEX ORGANIZATIONS 72 n.1 (1961). I do not mean to use the term "goal" to refer in any sense to the process of an organization's internal legitimation, or to imply that government organizations have become "infused with value" and hence have undergone what Selznick has described as a transition from organization to institution. SELZNICK, LEADERSHIP IN ADMINISTRATION: A SOCIOLOGICAL INTERPRETATION 40, 134–42 (1957). See PERROW, COMPLEX ORGANIZATIONS: A CRITICAL ESSAY 186–89 (1979).

[128] See, *e.g.*, SIMON, ADMINISTRATIVE BEHAVIOR 134–35 (1958); MARCH & SIMON, ORGANIZATIONS 194 (1958); BARNARD, THE FUNCTIONS OF THE EXECUTIVE 159–84 (1968).

generals characteristically instruct colonels that they are to formulate one kind of defensive plan rather than another. The management of speech within government institutions is thus an exception to the Court's often stated principle that "the First Amendment means that government has no power to restrict expression because of its message, its ideas, its subject, or its content."[129]

Third, government interests in the management of speech extend not merely to avoidance of damage caused by the particular speech regulated, but also to the integrity of the authority structure by which the speech is regulated. If insubordinate speech is constitutionally protected, the government will suffer not only the impact of the speech itself, but also a corresponding impairment of its authority, which may well have implications for its ability to manage other kinds of speech and conduct.

Although the government has a strong interest in the regulation of insubordinate speech, there may nevertheless be good reasons to extend constitutional protection to such speech. First Amendment values of individual "self-realization"[130] do not disappear simply because individuals choose to speak within the context of a government organization. Insubordinate speech may also provide a source of information that is important for the democratic supervision of government institutions. Although there is thus a tension between government interests and First Amendment values, the tenor of the Court's decisions in this area is that government institutions may discipline insubordinate speech that interferes with the accomplishment of institutional purposes.[131] The Court's remarks in *Tinker v. Des Moines School District* are illustrative: "[C]onduct by the student, in class or out of it, which for any reason—whether it stems from

---

[129] Police Department of Chicago v. Mosley, 408 U.S. 92, 95 (1972). See, *e.g.*, Consolidated Edison Co. v. Public Service Comm'n, 447 U.S. 530, 537–41 (1980).

[130] See, *e.g.*, Baker, *Commercial Speech: A Problem in the Theory of Freedom*, 62 IOWA L. REV. 1, 5–9 (1976).

[131] See, *e.g.*, Brown v. Glines, 444 U.S. 348, 356–57 (1980); Parker v. Levy, 417 U.S. 733, 758 (1974); Pell v. Procunier, 417 U.S. 817, 822 (1974); Jones v. North Carolina Prisoners' Union, 433 U.S. 119, 129–33 (1977); Healy v. James, 408 U.S. 169, 189 (1972). In its most recent discussion of the power of the government to regulate the speech of its employees, the Court stated that the Constitution "requires full consideration of the government's interest in the effective and efficient fulfillment of its responsibilities to the public." Connick v. Myers, 103 S.Ct. 1684, 1692 (1983). The Court also added a threshold test, to the effect that if employee expression "cannot be fairly characterized as constituting speech on a matter of public concern," government sanctions for the expression would not be subject to constitutional review. *Id.* at 1689–90.

time, place, or type of behavior—materially disrupts classwork or involves substantial disorder or invasion of the rights of others, is, of course, not immunized by the constitutional guarantee of freedom of speech."[132]

Although the Court is unlikely to immunize insubordinate speech that impairs the ability of a government institution to function, it will undertake its own independent inquiry into whether an institution's regulation of speech is necessary for attainment of organizational goals. This inquiry characteristically examines the authority structure of the relevant institution to determine the effect of constitutionally restricting its capacity to define and discipline the kind of insubordinate speech at issue. If the Court determines that the institution's legitimate authority structure will not be unduly damaged, it will then proceed to assess the impact of the particular speech at issue. These two aspects of constitutional inquiry are nicely illustrated in the contrast between *Brown v. Glines* and *Tinker v. Des Moines School District.*

In *Glines*, the Court upheld a military regulation prohibiting Air Force members from circulating petitions on military bases without prior approval of their commander.[133] The regulation permitted base commanders to censor any petition they felt would create "a clear danger to the loyalty, discipline, or morale" of their troops.[134] The Court did not consider it to be important that the regulation was a prior restraint and that it allowed censorship on the basis of the content of speech. The Court also did not ask whether the specific speech at issue would in fact have created a danger to loyalty, discipline or morale. Instead the Court rested its conclusion on the importance to the institution of the military to maintain "a respect for duty and a discipline without counterpart in civilian life":[135] "The rights of military men must yield somewhat 'to meet certain overriding demands of discipline and duty. . . .' Speech likely to interfere with these vital prerequisites for military effectiveness therefore can be excluded from a military base." In the Court's view "the military mission" required creation of a form of

---

[132] 393 U.S. 503, 513 (1969).

[133] 444 U.S. at 349.

[134] *Id.* at 350.

[135] *Id.* at 354.

authority founded on "instinctive obedience."[136] The overriding constitutional concern was the maintenance of this kind of authority,[137] regardless of the effects of the particular speech at issue.

In *Tinker v. Des Moines School District*, on the other hand, the Court was unwilling to place a constitutional imprimatur on this kind of authority. In *Tinker* the Court struck down a school regulation prohibiting the wearing of black armbands to protest the Vietnam war. The Court rested its conclusion on the premise that "[i]n our system, state-operated schools may not be enclaves of totalitarianism. School officials do not possess absolute authority over their students."[138] Hence school officials, unlike military commanders, could not prohibit expression on the basis of an "undifferentiated fear or apprehension of disturbance," but could only act on the basis of "facts which might reasonably have led [them] to forecast substantial disruption of or material interference with school activities."[139] Since these facts were absent in *Tinker*, the Court found the regulation unconstitutional.

The difference between the First Amendment standard applied in *Tinker* and that applied in *Glines* rests on a form of constitutional sociology, on the Court's judgment about the structure of authority appropriate and necessary for different government institutions. In *Tinker* the Court believed that schools could continue to function even though they were prevented from regulating certain kinds of speech in the absence of evidence sufficient to convince a reviewing court that censorship was necessary to avoid disruption. In *Glines* the Court believed that the need for unquestioned military authority was more important than the propriety of any particular exercise of that authority. In both *Tinker* and *Glines*, government officials were empowered to suppress speech that interfered with the effective functioning of their institutions, but the needs of military authority, unlike those of school officials, were deemed to require

---

[136] *Id.* at 354, 357.

[137] The Court indicated that such authority was not unlimited, stating that "commanders may sometimes apply these regulations 'irrationally, invidiously, or arbitrarily,' thus giving rise to legitimate claims under the First Amendment." *Id.* at 357 n.15. The qualification should be understood as the Court's reservation of ultimate authority to determine whether the purpose of military censorship is the achievement of institutionally legitimate ends.

[138] 393 U.S. at 511.

[139] *Id.* at 508.

that the military retain "substantial discretion over its internal discipline" in the regulation of insubordinate speech.[140]

When it comes to the regulation of insubordinate speech, therefore, the ordinary relationship between the First Amendment and discretion is inverted. If government officials act to regulate the speech of the general public, the First Amendment usually imposes strict limitations on the administrative discretion that can be delegated to such officials. But when these same officials act to manage speech within the context of a government institution, the administrative discretion constitutionally deemed necessary for effective management determines the First Amendment standard to be applied.[141]

B. RESTRAINING ORDERS AND THE MANAGEMENT OF PRETRIAL DISCOVERY

The relationship between the First Amendment and discretion is thus significantly affected by the context of the government regulation at issue. If the regulation occurs in the context of the internal management of a state institution, the First Amendment will permit such discretion as is necessary for the effective management of the institution. The question, therefore, is whether restraining orders should constitutionally be viewed as involving the internal management of the court system.

We ordinarily think of trial courts as adjudicative institutions which govern litigants by law rather than by "managerial direc-

---

[140] 444 U.S. at 357.

[141] In Snepp v. United States, 444 U.S. 507 (1980), the Court endorsed the use of a contract, "voluntarily signed" without "duress," as a basis for regulating the speech of a former CIA employee. *Id.* at 509 n.3. *Snepp,* however, provides a poor basis from which to generalize about government regulation of insubordinate speech. This is because the decision ultimately rests on the concept of "consent." But consent is not present in various management situations, as, for example, those in schools, prisons, or the military. See note 93 *supra.* Moreover the line between voluntary and involuntary consent is difficult to draw in management situations. For example, when government requires as a condition of employment that employees sign explicit contracts forgoing First Amendment rights, serious questions can and should arise concerning the validity of such "consent." See, *e.g.*, National Security Decision Directive 84, Hearing Before the Committee on Governmental Affairs of the United States Senate, 98th Cong., 1st Sess. 85 (September 13, 1984); Powe, *The Constitutional Implications of President Reagan's Censorship Directive* 84, THE CENTER MAGAZINE 8 (March/April 1984). The issue, therefore, is more directly addressed by asking whether government has the power to regulate insubordinate speech, rather than whether it can wring "consent" to such regulation from its employees.

tion."[142] But the judicial system, like any other government institution, needs to accomplish its goals, which may for convenience be taken to be those specified in both the Federal and Washington rules: the securing of "the just, speedy, and inexpensive determination of every action."[143] To accomplish these ends, trial courts are traditionally vested with administrative authority. This can plainly be seen in a trial court's supervision of its courtroom. The trial judge has been accurately described as "the executive of the courtroom. Among his duties and powers are those of presiding, of preserving order and decorum, of regulating the conduct of those who participate in the proceedings, and of directing and guiding such proceedings . . . to the end that there may be such economy of time, effort, and expense as is commensurate with the rights of the parties to present their claims and defenses."[144]

The trial judge's management of the courtroom extends to the regulation of speech. Even in *Bridges v. California*, when the Court, speaking through Justice Black, imposed strict limitations on a trial judge's capacity to punish by contempt the out-of-court speech of nonparties, the Court made a point of strongly reaffirming the constitutional power of trial judges "to protect themselves from disturbances and disorder in the court room by use of contempt proceedings."[145] Courtroom speech can be regulated on the basis of its content, as, for example, when courts permit argument on certain points rather than others, or punish by contempt remarks they

---

[142] FULLER, THE MORALITY OF LAW 210 (1969). Fuller views the "basic difference between law and managerial direction" to be that "law is not, like management, a matter of directing other persons how to accomplish tasks set by a superior, but is basically a matter of providing the citizenry with a sound and stable framework for their interactions with one another." *Ibid.*

[143] Fed. R. Civ. P. 1; Wash. C. R. 1.

[144] BOWERS, THE JUDICIAL DISCRETION OF TRIAL COURTS 10 (1931). See Smith v. Smith, 17 N.J. Super. 128, 85 A.2d 523 (1951); Amo v. Genovese, 17 N. J. Super. 109, 85 A.2d 529 (1951). Trial courts have traditionally been accorded "discretion" in the exercise of these administrative responsibilities. See BOWERS, at 267–492; McKean, *Some Aspects of Judicial Discretion*, 40 DICK. L. REV. 168, 170–71 (1936).

[145] Bridges v. California, 314 U.S. 252, 266 (1941). In Wood v. Georgia, 370 U.S. 375, 383 (1962), a case concerned with the trial court punishment of out-of-court speech, the Court states: "We start with the premise that the right of courts to conduct their business in an untrammeled way lies at the foundation of our system of government and that courts necessarily must possess the means of punishing for contempt when conduct tends directly to prevent the discharge of their functions . . . [C]ourts have continuously had the authority and power to maintain order in their courtrooms and to assure litigants a fair trial . . ."

consider insulting.[146] And courtroom speech is commonly regulated in ways that in other contexts would constitute prior restraints, as, for example, when a judge reviews evidence to decide whether it can be given to the jury. Such regulation is not thought to raise particular First Amendment problems, and this is what one would expect if the regulation were an issue of internal managerial authority.

The premise of the movement toward "case management"[147] is that this same kind of managerial authority should extend to the pretrial process. This is consistent with the original design of the Federal Rules of Civil Procedure, which "vindicated a particular version of judicial administration that sharply modified the preexisting adversary control over all aspects of litigation" and "established on a secure footing the power of the judge as the manager of the case."[148] In complex cases this pretrial managerial power has long been self-consciously exercised. The epigraph to the *Manual for Complex Litigation*, for example, states: "There are no inherently protracted cases, only cases which are unnecessarily protracted by inefficient procedures and management."[149] And in 1983 the pretrial managerial authority of the trial judge was strongly emphasized in the amendments to the federal rules, which explicitly encourage "forceful judicial management" of "the entire pretrial phase, especially motions and discovery."[150]

---

[146] "Courts of justice are universally acknowledged to be vested . . . with power to impose silence, respect and decorum in their presence, . . . and as a corollary to this proposition, to preserve themselves and their officers from the approach and insults of pollution." Anderson v. Dunn, 19 U.S. (6 Wheat.) 204, 227 (1821). See Consolidated Edison Co. v. Public Serv. Comm'n, 447 U.S. 530, 544–46 (1980) (Stevens, J., concurring); Dobbs, *Contempt of Court: A Survey*, 56 CORNELL L. REV. 185, 186–207 (1971).

[147] FLANDERS, CASE MANAGEMENT AND COURT MANAGEMENT IN UNITED STATES DISTRICT COURTS (1977). For a good survey of the literature on case management, see Resnik, note 111 *supra*.

[148] Horowitz, *Decreeing Organizational Change: Judicial Supervision of Public Institutions*, 1983 DUKE L.J. 1265, 1271. See CONNOLLY, HOLLEMAN, & KUHLMAN, JUDICIAL CONTROLS AND THE CIVIL LITIGATION PROCESS: DISCOVERY 14 (1978). Since Washington has adopted the federal rules, it might also be viewed as having adopted the managerial perspective underlying these rules. See note 120 *supra*.

[149] MANUAL FOR COMPLEX LITIGATION, at v.

[150] 97 F.R.D. 207, 213. "[C]lose supervision of discovery" has been termed "the most widespread and urgent policy concern today about the way that the litigation system functions." Flanders, *Blind Umpires—a Response to Professor Resnik*, 35 HAST. L.J. 505, 514–15 & n.49 (1984).

When a trial court exercises managerial control of the courtroom, however, there is little chance for confusion about whether an individual is within its administrative authority. In this respect a trial judge's courtroom governance is like that of a school administrator: it is generally clear enough whether a student is or is not subject to school regulation. But managerial and nonmanagerial authority cannot be so clearly distinguished during the pretrial phase of litigation. If a school were to promulgate a dress code that forbade the wearing of jeans while at home, we would say that the code was not an exercise of managerial authority, since it had nothing to do with the running of the school.[151] But a trial judge can issue a restraining order that prohibits litigants from speaking even though they are not in the actual or constructive presence of the court. The question is whether such an order is an exercise of managerial authority.

The question is illuminated by the Court's decisions in the area of government employment. Government agencies sometimes attempt to extend their managerial authority to employee speech that occurs out of the office. In *Pickering v. Board of Education*,[152] for example, a teacher had been dismissed for sending a letter to a newspaper that was critical of the school board. Since the teacher's speech neither "impeded [his] proper performance of his daily duties in the classroom" nor "interfered with the regular operation of the schools generally," the Court concluded that "the interests of the school administration" in controlling the speech were "not significantly greater than its interest in limiting a similar contribution by any member of the general public."[153] The government, in other words, could not invoke its interests as a manager to justify regulation of the speech, even though the speech may have adversely affected the school administration's ability to achieve institutional goals.[154]

---

[151] See, *e.g.*, Thomas v. Bd. of Educ., 607 F.2d 1043 (2d Cir. 1979), *cert. denied*, 444 U.S. 1081 (1980).

[152] 391 U.S. 563 (1968).

[153] *Id.* at 572–73.

[154] In a recent line of cases, the Court has used the "public forum" doctrine to develop First Amendment standards concerning the capacity of government institutions to regulate members of the general public seeking to use the instrumentalities of the institution to assist them in their speech. See Perry Education Ass'n v. Perry Local Educators' Ass'n, 103 S.Ct. 948 (1983); Greer v. Spock, 424 U.S. 828 (1976).

When a trial court issues a gag order prohibiting the press from writing about a pending criminal trial, the court is in a similar position to the school board in *Pickering*. It is attempting to regulate speech that will adversely affect the operation of the judicial system, but over which it has no specifically managerial interests. The court's regulation of the press must therefore be viewed as an attempt to govern the general public.

The situation is different, however, when a trial court issues a restraining order prohibiting a litigant from speaking about discovery information obtained through the court's own processes. The court is directly engaged in the supervision of the pretrial activities of the litigant, and its decisions in the course of that supervision will directly depend on whether the litigant can speak about discovery information. In cases involving commercially sensitive information, for example, a court may be willing to order discovery only if it can be assured that the information will remain confidential. If a court is uncertain whether pertinent information is being sought for proper or improper purposes, it may choose to order production of the information only if it can ensure that the information will be properly used. In such situations restraining orders are necessary to achieve the pretrial exchange of information thought prerequisite for the effective functioning of the judicial system.

To view restraining orders as an exercise of managerial authority is essentially to see them as ancillary to a trial court's task of declaring the law between the parties. They are a tool used by the trial court to control the behavior of parties so as to create the conditions of achieving a just resolution of their dispute.[155] The First Amendment will permit employment of this tool if it is necessary to attain the legitimate objectives of the judicial system.[156] And, more im-

---

[155] This is the manner in which the Court viewed the old "bill of discovery" that was superseded by the modern federal rules. The bill was seen as "an auxiliary process in aid of trial at law" whose function was "to give facility to proof." Sinclair Refining Co. v. Jenkins Petroleum Process Co., 289 U.S. 685, 693 (1933).

[156] The Court has clearly indicated that the First Amendment will not protect insubordinate speech that interferes with the ability of the judicial system to attain its institutional ends. See note 145 *supra*. In 1966 the Court, speaking in the context of prejudicial pretrial publicity, concluded that a trial court could prohibit the out-of-court speech of "prosecutors, counsel for defense, the accused, witnesses, court staff [and] enforcement officers coming under the jurisdiction of the court" if such speech would "frustrate its function." Sheppard v. Maxwell, 384 U.S. 333, 363 (1966). See Gulf Oil Co. v. Bernard, 452 U.S. 89, 104 n.21 (1981).

portant, the First Amendment will also cede to trial judges discretion to determine if a particular restraining order is necessary to attain such legitimate objectives, but only if it can also be demonstrated that such discretion is essential for effective management of pretrial discovery.

The constitutionality of the "broad discretion" authorized by Rule 26(c) will thus depend upon an inquiry into the nature and extent of the discretion necessary to control pretrial discovery. But the Court's implicit premise that law and discretion are incompatible makes such an inquiry impossible, for it implies that all legal restraint on judicial discretion is unacceptable. The premise renders trial court discretion constitutional by definition. It is thus inconsistent with sensitive constitutional analysis, and with any serious investigation into the means whereby rights and discretion may be accommodated. The premise is, moreover, factually false.

IV. THREE PERSPECTIVES ON DISCRETION

Without doubt the prevailing conception of discretion is that it "signifies choice."[157] Maurice Rosenberg, for example, has written that "if the word discretion conveys to legal minds any solid core of meaning, one central idea above all the others, it is the idea of *choice*."[158] And Kenneth Davis has defined an official as having discretion if "the effective limits on his power leave him free to make a choice among possible courses of action or inaction."[159]

This view of discretion prevails in Supreme Court opinions. Whenever the Court speaks, as it often does, of the "deference

---

[157] Johnson v. United States, 398 A.2d 354, 361 (D.C. App. 1979). See Smith v. Smith, 17 N.J. Super. 128, 85 A.2d 523, 524 (N.J. App. 1951) (" '[J]udicial discretion' is the option which a judge may exercise between the doing and the not doing of a thing which cannot be demanded as an absolute legal right . . ."); Wendel v. Swanberg, 384 Mich. 468, 185 N.W.2d 348, 351 (1971) ("The term discretion itself involves the idea of choice . . .").

[158] Rosenberg, *Judicial Discretion of the Trial Court, Viewed from Above*, 22 SYRACUSE L. REV. 635, 636 (1971). See Dworkin, *Judicial Discretion*, 60 J. PHIL. 624, 625 (1963); Vorenberg, *Decent Restraint of Prosecutorial Power*, 94 HARV. L. REV. 1521, 1523–24 (1981).

[159] DAVIS, note 2 *supra*, at 4. See DESMITH, JUDICIAL REVIEW OF ADMINISTRATIVE ACTION 278 (4th ed. 1980) ("The legal concept of discretion implies power to make a choice between alternative courses of action"); JAFFE, JUDICIAL CONTROL OF ADMINISTRATIVE ACTION 359 (1965) ("We may . . . define discretion as a power to make a choice within a class of actions"); HART & SACHS, THE LEGAL PROCESS 162 (1958) (unpublished manuscript) ("discretion means the power to choose between two or more courses of action each of which is thought of as permissible"); Wexler, *Discretion: The Unacknowledged Side of the Law*, 25 TORONTO L.J. 120, 123 n.8 (1975).

federal courts should pay to the informed discretion" of public officials,[160] it has in mind the notion that officials have a certain freedom of choice that must be respected. This same freedom of choice is undoubtedly what the Court meant to preserve with its concept of "discretion" in *Rhinehart*.

The difficulty with viewing discretion in this manner is that it reinforces the notion that law and discretion are mutually exclusive. Law, after all, "imposes an environment of constraint, of tests to be met, standards to be observed, ideals to be fulfilled."[161] And if discretion is viewed as choice, it is all too easy to begin to think of it as that "residue" of pure free choice which remains after all forms of legal control are eliminated.[162] This way of thinking can lead directly to the image of discretion as "the hole in the doughnut, . . . an area left open by a surrounding belt of restriction."[163] The area of discretion expands or contracts, as surrounding legal restrictions grow or diminish; but by definition discretion (choice) and law (restraint) cannot occupy the same space at the same time. It is this image that appears to underlie the Court's opinion in *Rhinehart*.

It is a misleading image, however, for it focuses attention on the presence or absence of discretion, rather than on the intricate ways in which discretion and law interact in the process of decision making. It invites us to conceptualize choice as a single, unitary act that is either free or constrained, rather than as a complex process. Our judicial system contains numerous examples of decision making that is both discretionary and guided by legal standards. But since we have no disciplined method to bring these examples easily to mind, we do not use them in analysis of unfamiliar circumstances, such as *Rhinehart*.

These examples suggest that trial court discretion to manage pretrial discovery can be analyzed in at least three distinct dimensions. Trial courts can have discretion with respect to controlling

---

[160] Jones v. North Carolina Prisoners' Union, 433 U.S. 119, 136 (1977). See, *e.g.*, Block v. Rutherford, 104 S.Ct. 3227, 3235 (1984); Curtiss-Wright Corp. v. General Electric Co., 446 U.S. 1, 10 (1980); Bell v. Wolfish, 441 U.S. 520, 546 n.28 (1979); Hutto v. Finney, 437 U.S. 678, 688 (1979).

[161] SELZNICK, note 113 *supra*, at 11.

[162] See SIMON, SMITHBURG, & THOMPSON, PUBLIC ADMINISTRATION 514 (1950); *cf.* Stewart, *The Reformation of American Administrative Law*, 88 HARV. L. REV. 1669, 1697 (1975).

[163] DWORKIN, note 1 *supra*, at 31.

legal standards, with respect to the reviewing power of appellate courts, and with respect to structural characteristics of their decision-making process, such as the obligation to articulate reasons for their decisions. Trial court discretion can exist in various degrees in each of these dimensions, and it can exist in some dimensions and not in others.

A. DISCRETION AND APPLICABLE LEGAL STANDARDS

The common law traditionally distinguished between "the incertain and crooked cord of discretion" and "the golden and straight mete-wand of the law."[164] Accustomed to view the law as a system of general rules imposing "restraint and regulation" on judicial decision,[165] the common law distrusted judicial discretion,[166] since a discretionary decision was one in which there were "no fixed principles by which its correctness may be determined."[167] The classic statement, often repeated in nineteenth-century American cases, is by Lord Camden, who said that "[t]he discretion of a judge is the law of tyrants; it is always unknown; it is different in different men; it is casual and depends upon constitution, temper, and passion."[168] American judges embroidered the theme. A justice of the Alabama Supreme Court, for example, inveighed against "the uncertainty of a power, so uncontrollable and liable to error as mere judicial discretion—a power that may possibly be misdirected by a fit of temporary sickness, an extra mint julep, or the smell of a peculiar overcoat."[169]

The primary means by which nineteenth-century American courts reconciled themselves to judicial discretion was to view it, in the manner of Chief Justice Marshall, as a term of art. "Courts are

---

[164] See Smith, note 69 *supra*, at 30; Conway v. The Queen, 1 Cox C.C. 210, 216 (1845).

[165] Pound, *The Causes of Popular Dissatisfaction with the Administration of Justice*, 35 F.R.D. 273, 275–76, 278 (1964) (originally published at 29 A.B.A. REP. (1906)).

[166] Pound, *Discretion, Dispensation and Mitigation: The Problem of the Individual Special Case*, 35 N.Y.U. L. REV. 925, 926–28 (1960).

[167] Palliser v. Home Telephone, 170 Ala. 341, 54 S. 499, 500 (1911).

[168] Doe v. Kersey (1765) (C.P.) (Unreported), quoted in FEARNE, CONTINGENT REMAINDERS AND EXECUTORY DEVISES 535 n.(t) (3d Am. ed. 1826). See State v. Cummings, 36 Mo. 263, 279 (1965), rev'd, 71 U.S. 277 (1866). Hence the proverb: "That system of law is best which confides as little as possible to the discretion of the judge; that judge is best who trusts as little as possible to himself." OSBORN, A CONCISE LAW DICTIONARY 198 (1927).

[169] Ex parte Chase, 43 Ala. 303, 311 (1869).

the mere instruments of the law," he said, "and can will nothing."[170]

> When they are said to exercise a discretion, it is a mere legal discretion, a discretion to be exercised in discerning the course prescribed by law; and, when that is discerned, it is the duty of the court to follow it. Judicial power is never exercised for the purpose of giving effect to the will of the judge; always for the purpose of giving effect . . . to the will of the law.

While this perception could be readily assimilated to a traditional view of law as a system of restraints, it also seemed to deny the very existence of judicial discretion. Frustration with this apparent paradox led one nineteenth-century jurist to exclaim that "when applied to public functionaries" the term discretion means[171]

> a power or right conferred upon them by law, of acting officially in certain circumstances, according to the dictates of their own judgment and conscience, uncontrolled by the judgment or conscience of others. But what is to be understood by a discretion that *is* governed by fixed legal principles is, I must be allowed to say, something that I have not found satisfactorily explained, and what it is not easy for me to comprehend, Poetry may be indulged the license of saying,
>
> > We have a power in ourselves to do it, but it is
> > A power which we have no power to do.

The paradox that so troubled the jurist is to modern eyes easily resolved once it is understood that the attribution of discretion can be relative. From the viewpoint of an appellate court, for example, a trial judge may have discretion with respect to the determination of a defendant's sentence, since the judge can (within limits) choose the standards that will guide the sentencing process, and the appellate court will not interfere.[172] With respect to the appellate court, the sentencing judge is not bound by enforceable legal rules, and can act according to the dictates of judgment and conscience.

From the viewpoint of the sentencing judge, however, there is nevertheless an official decision to be made according to legal crite-

---

[170] Osborn v. Bank of the United States, 22 U.S. (9 Wheat.) 326, 381 (1924). See, *e.g.*, Langnes v. Green, 282 U.S. 531, 541 (1931); Lent v. Tillson, 140 U.S. 316, 329 (1891); Tingley v. Dolby, 13 Neb. 371, 14 N.W. 146, 147–48 (1882); Scott v. Marley, 124 Tenn. 388, 1317 S.W. 492, 493 (1911).

[171] Judges v. People, 18 Wend. 79, 99 (1837).

[172] United States v. Mejias, 552 F.2d 435, 447 (2d Cir.), *cert. denied*, 434 U.S. 847 (1977).

ria. The sentencing judge does not perceive himself as free to act on purely personal motives or private desires. He cannot decide the proper sentence by flipping a coin. He might instead feel himself bound to choose the appropriate legal policies—whether they be deterrence, punishment, or rehabilitation—and to do his best to implement them. He can be, from his own perspective, an "instrument of the law."

It is rather common for trial court decisions to be governed by legal standards, even though the decisions are "discretionary" from the point of view of an appellate court. This is typical of the structure of the Federal Rules of Civil Procedure. Rule 26(b), for example, provides that the decision with respect to permissive intervention should lie within the "discretion" of the trial court, meaning that the decision "is not reviewable by an appellate court unless clear abuse is shown."[173] Yet the Rule also states explicit criteria to guide the trial judge's decision even in the absence of appellate review.[174] From the point of view of the trial judge, then, the decision whether to permit intervention is governed by authoritative legal standards. This combination of discretion and constraint characterizes the Court's treatment of discretion in a variety of areas. The decision whether to dismiss an action for *forum non conveniens*, for example, "is committed to the sound discretion of the trial court" and "may be reversed only when there has been a clear abuse of discretion."[175] Yet the Court has promulgated a list of no less than twelve "factors" to be evaluated by the trial court in the exercise of its discretion.[176]

There can, of course, be situations in which a trial court is, from its own perspective, free from guiding legal standards. An example offered by an early writer is a judge's control of the court calendar. In the decision to fix "a day for appearance," the judge is not bound to act "according to his ideas of right," but rather may act "as he pleases."[177] In such circumstances, we might say, there is no law to

[173] Allen Calculators, Inc. v. National Cash Register Co., 322 U.S. 137, 142 (1944).

[174] Rule 24(b) states: "In exercising its discretion the court shall consider whether the intervention will unduly delay or prejudice the adjudication of the rights of the original parties."

[175] Piper Aircraft Co. v. Reyno, 454 U.S. 235, 257 (1981).

[176] *Id.* at 241 n.6.

[177] Kaufman, *Judicial Discretion*, 17 AM. L. REV. 567, 567 (1883).

guide the judge's decision. The question whether a decision is discretionary from the point of view of a trial court, therefore, depends upon the presence or absence of legal standards. It is fair to say, however, that such discretion is rare: as Justice Frankfurter once observed, "Discretion without a criterion for its exercise is authorization of arbitrariness."[178]

The concept of point of view thus illustrates the distinction between trial court discretion resulting from the absence of appellate review, and trial court discretion resulting from the absence of applicable legal standards. The two forms of discretion are related in a complicated manner: A trial court decision can be bound by legal rules and yet be immune from appellate supervision. But a decision that is truly unguided by legal standards will necessarily be discretionary from the point of view of an appellate court.[179]

The Court in *Rhinehart*, because of its implicit assumption that discretion was simply the power to choose, overlooked the distinction between these forms of discretion. The Court clearly held that the First Amendment does not prohibit appellate courts from viewing the decision to issue a restraining order as discretionary.[180] But the Court did not address the question whether such a decision is discretionary from the point of view of the trial court itself. Need the trial court consider constitutional standards when deciding whether to issue a restraining order, or are such standards irrelevant to its decision? The Supreme Court did not tell us. It did not even raise the issue.

The omission cannot be justified. Once the Court acknowledged that litigants retain some First Amendment interests in the dissemination of discovery information, it incurred a concomitant responsibility to articulate controlling constitutional principles for defining and protecting those interests. Since the requirements of the Constitution do not emanate solely from the commands of appellate courts, these principles would constrain trial court decisions even in the absence of appellate review.

It does not follow that such constitutional principles will necessarily convert trial courts into "instruments of the law" that are,

---

[178] Brown v. Allen, 344 U.S. 433, 496 (1953) (Opinion of Frankfurter, J.).

[179] See Friendly, *Indiscretion about Discretion*, 31 EMORY L.J. 747, 765 (1982).

[180] The Court approved an "abuse of discretion" standard of appellate review. 104 S.Ct. at 2209.

from their own perspective, without discretion. This is because the kind of trial court discretion that stems from applicable legal standards is a gradient which can exist in varying degrees. This can be seen if one imagines legal standards as arranged along a spectrum.[181] At one end are standards that give no guidance to a decision maker. An example would be a statute authorizing a policeman to regulate traffic "as he thinks fit."[182] Such a statute would deprive the policeman of any law to apply and would create a situation in which his decisions were, from his own point of view, discretionary. At the other end of the spectrum are standards that function as specific rules, mechanically requiring a decision maker to reach one result or the other. An example would be a statute authorizing a policeman to regulate an intersection by requiring traffic to move for two minutes in one direction, and three minutes in the other. Such a statute would leave virtually no room for the exercise of discretion. A policeman following its instructions would properly view himself as a mere "instrument of the law."

The vast majority of legal standards will fall in the middle range of the spectrum, and will neither completely cede nor completely withhold discretion. These standards will have an open texture requiring the exercise of independent judgment for their implementation. An example would be a statute authorizing a policeman to regulate traffic "to avoid undue congestion." When the Court in *Rhinehart* concluded that Rule 26(c) gave trial courts room for the exercise of "broad discretion," it meant this sense of discretion informed by legal standards. Ronald Dworkin calls this " 'discretion' in a weak sense," and observes that it exists whenever "for some reason the standards an official must apply cannot be applied mechanically but demand the use of judgment."[183]

"Weak" discretion exists in varying degrees. Different First Amendment standards will thus cede more or less weak discretion to trial courts in the issuance of restraining orders. A First Amendment standard could consist of specific and mechanical rules stating when restraining orders would constitutionally be deemed as neces-

---

[181] See Gifford, *Discretionary Decisionmaking in the Regulatory Agencies: A Conceptual Framework*, 57 S. CAL. L. REV. 101, 102 (1983).

[182] These examples are suggested by Jowell, *The Legal Control of Administrative Discretion*, 1973 PUB. LAW 178, 179–80.

[183] DWORKIN, note 1 *supra*, at 31.

sary for effective management of pretrial discovery. Or a First Amendment standard could consist of a more general statement of constitutional objectives, such as that restraining orders should not unnecessarily interfere with litigants' First Amendment rights. An important factor in the selection of an appropriate First Amendment standard should be the extent of weak discretion necessary to assure effective management of pretrial discovery.

B. DISCRETION AND APPELLATE CONTROL

It is often difficult to distinguish trial court discretion arising from the absence of appellate control from the kind of weak discretion entailed by the open texture of a legal standard. Commentators sometimes assume that as weak discretion increases, the possibility of effective appellate control correspondingly diminishes.[184] The assumption is inaccurate. The exercise of appellate control is independent of the specificity or generality of the law to be applied. Appellate courts can exercise strict control of trial court decision making even when applying general standards, and, conversely, there are situations (although rare) when appellate courts give only cursory review to judgments controlled by the most specific and mechanical of legal rules.[185]

Like weak discretion, trial court discretion arising from the absence of appellate review is a gradient that exists in varying degrees. The stricter the form of appellate review, the less discretion a trial court can be said to have. For our purposes, three forms of appellate control should be distinguished, which I shall call (1) independent review, (2) deference, and (3) delegation.

The "rule of independent review," which was strongly reaffirmed this Term, holds that it is the "constitutional responsibility" of an appellate court independently to examine the record in cases in which First Amendment rights are denied.[186] Appellate courts applying the rule essentially view trial court determinations of First Amendment rights as questions of law, to be independently redecided by the appellate court after full scrutiny of the record. The

---

[184] See, *e.g.*, Friendly, note 179 *supra*, at 760–61; Rosenberg, note 158 *supra*, at 663.

[185] For example, appellate courts commonly both accord the decisions of juries great deference and ask them to make those decisions pursuant to strict and rigorous rules of law.

[186] Bose Corp. v. Consumers Union, 104 S.Ct. 1949, 1959 (1984).

underlying assumption is that application of appropriate First Amendment standards will yield a single correct legal conclusion, which the trial court either did or did not reach. This is true even when applicable First Amendment standards are quite general and leave considerable room for the exercise of judgment on the part of the trial court.[187] In *Globe Newspaper Co. v. Superior Court*, for example, the Court held that First Amendment standards governing the closure of criminal trials entail a complex evaluation of numerous "factors," and that these standards require the exercise of "discretion" by the trial court.[188] Yet the Court independently reviews decisions to close criminal trials to determine if trial judges have in fact used their judgment to come to the "right" constitutional conclusion.[189] The rule of independent review thus gives appellate courts license to second guess the "weak discretion" that derives from the open-textured quality of certain constitutional standards.[190]

The rule of independent review prohibits appellate courts from viewing trial court decisions as discretionary. In *Rhinehart* the Court explicitly rejected independent review, stating that "[i]t is sufficient for purposes of our decision that the highest court in the state found no abuse of discretion in the trial court's decision to issue a protective order pursuant to a constitutional state law."[191] A fair interpretation of this passage would be that although the First Amendment does not require appellate courts to exercise the rule of independent review, it does require, at a minimum, that appellate courts reviewing decisions to issue restraining orders employ an "abuse-of-discretion" standard.

When an appellate court reviews a trial court decision for abuse of discretion, it usually begins with a ritual incantation: "The question, of course, is not whether this Court, or whether the Court of Appeals, would as an original matter have [done X]; it is whether

---

[187] See, *e.g.*, Connick v. Myers, 103 S.Ct. 1684, 1692 n.10 (1983); Nebraska Press Ass'n v. Stuart, 427 U.S. 539, 562 (1976).

[188] 457 U.S. 596, 608–09 (1982).

[189] See Press-Enterprise Co. v. Superior Court, 104 S.Ct. 819, 824 (1984); Richmond Newspapers Inc. v. Virginia, 448 U.S. 555 (1980).

[190] For a discussion of the intricate relationship between the rule of independent review and appellate court deference to trial court findings of fact, see Bose Corp. v. Consumers Union, 104 S.Ct. 1949, 1958–60 (1984).

[191] 104 S.Ct. at 2209.

the District Court abused its discretion in so doing."[192] The incantation is meant to signify that review for abuse of discretion, unlike the rule of independent review, is designed to insulate a trial court's exercise of judgment from second-guessing by an appellate court.[193] Appellate courts employ the abuse-of-discretion standard when they believe that the question before the trial court is susceptible of different satisfactory resolutions.

The abuse-of-discretion standard is commonly perceived to be incoherent. A noted commentator has suggested that "[t]he phrase 'abuse of discretion' does not communicate meaning. It is a form of ill-tempered appellate grunting and should be dispensed with."[194] One reason the standard is confused is that it encompasses two distinct situations that are almost never distinguished. In the first, which I shall call "deference," appellate courts retain control over the governing legal standard, but defer to trial court judgments in the implementation of that standard. In the second, which I shall call "delegation," appellate courts delegate to trial courts the power to determine the legal standards by which the correctness of their decisions will be judged.

If the standard of law to be applied has a sufficiently open texture, trial courts will have great latitude in choosing among alternative courses of action in situations of both deference and delegation.[195] For this reason those who view discretion as the power to choose often conflate the two situations. Consider, for example, the comments of Judge Henry Friendly, in the context of a case concerning a trial court's discretionary power to dismiss a complaint without prejudice pursuant to Fed. R. Civ. P. 41(a)(2):[196]

> [T]he fact that dismissal under Rule 41(a)(2) usually rests on the judge's discretion does not mean that this is always so. Several of the most important reasons for deferring to the trial judge's dis-

---

[192] Insurance Corp. v. Compagnie des Bauxites, 456 U.S. 694, 707 (1982).

[193] This concept is often expressed by the formulation that "A review of a trial court's action in the exercise of discretion does not depend upon whether we would have reached the same conclusion, but rather upon whether, as a matter of law, there was an abuse of discretion." Rogers v. Lyle Adjustment Co., 70 N.M. 209, 372 P.2d 797, 800 (1962). See McManus v. Larson, 122 Cal. App. 716, 10 P.2d 523, 525 (1923).

[194] Rosenberg, note 158 *supra*, at 659; see Friendly, note 179 *supra*, at 763–64.

[195] See, *e.g.*, Curtiss-Wright Corp. v. General Electric Co., 446 U.S. 1, 10–11 (1980); Arizona v. Washington, 434 U.S. 497, 510 & n.28 (1978).

[196] Noonan v. Cunard Steamship Co., 375 F.2d 69, 71 (2d Cir. 1967).

cretion—his observation of the witnesses, his superior opportunity to get 'the feel of the case,' . . . and the impracticability of framing a rule of decision where many disparate factors must be weighed— . . . are inapposite when a question arising in advance of trial can be stated in a form susceptible of a yes-or-no answer applicable to all cases.

Judge Friendly's underlying conception of discretion is that of choice. He speaks, for example, of "deferring to the trial judge's discretion." But this conception leads him to run together situations in which trial courts are given the power to choose because appellate courts cannot formulate "a rule of decision," with those situations in which trial courts are given the power to choose because of their superior access to pertinent facts such as "the feel of the case."[197] Judge Friendly overlooks the distinction between delegation and deference because each creates large areas free from the "surrounding belt of restriction," and he is primarily interested in the sweep, rather than the quality, of a trial court's freedom of choice.

Appellate court review in a situation of deference entails a tension between the articulation of a controlling legal standard and the preservation of a trial court's freedom of choice in the implementation of the standard. Appellate courts traditionally maintain this tension by enunciating a general legal "objective," such as the "interest in sound judicial administration," and then narrating the various factors that must be considered in attaining the objective.[198] Irrespective of the outcome of a particular decision, appellate courts can then exercise review to determine if a trial court has in fact considered all the appropriate factors,[199] or if it has considered certain inappropriate factors,[200] or if it has failed to give certain factors appropriate weight.[201] This kind of appellate control is precluded in

---

[197] Deference and delegation are similarly conflated in Friendly, note 179 *supra*, at 759–62, and in Rosenberg, note 158 *supra*, at 662–65.

[198] Curtiss-Wright Corp. v. General Electric Co., 446 U.S. 1, 10–11 (1980).

[199] See, *e.g.*, United States v. Lewis, 482 F.2d 632, 643–44 (D.C. Cir. 1973); Wiggins v. United States, 386 A.2d 1171, 1174 (D.C. 1978); In re Adoption of Driscoll, 269 Cal. App. 2d 735, 75 Cal. Rptr. 382, 384 (1969).

[200] See, *e.g.*, Arizona v. Washington, 434 U.S. 497, 510 n.28 (1978); United States v. Capriola, 537 F.2d 319, 320 (9th Cir. 1978); D.C. Federation of Civic Associations v. Volpe, 459 F.2d 1231, 1245–48 (D.C. Cir. 1971), *cert. denied*, 405 U.S. 1030 (1972); United States v. Shaughnessy, 180 F.2d 489, 490 (2d Cir. 1950).

[201] Moses H. Cone Memorial Hospital v. Mercury Construction Corp., 103 S.Ct. 927, 938–39 (1983); Piper Aircraft Co. v. Reyno, 454 U.S. 235 (1981).

situations of delegation, since trial courts are then authorized to determine which factors are legally pertinent for their decisions.[202] Trial court discretion vis-à-vis appellate review is at its maximum in situations of delegation.

Although the Court in *Rhinehart* strongly implied that appellate courts reviewing decisions to issue restraining orders are constitutionally obligated to use an abuse-of-discretion standard, it did not address the question whether such review should involve deference or delegation. As a matter of state law, the Supreme Court of Washington appeared to address the question as one involving deference:[203]

> Our understanding of the rule, contrary to that of the federal circuit courts in *In re Halkin* and *In re San Juan Star Co.*, is that 'good cause' is established if the moving party shows that any of the harms spoken of in the rule is threatened and can be avoided without impeding the discovery process. In determining whether a protective order is needed and appropriate, the court properly weighs the respective interests of the parties. The judge's major concern should be the facilitation of the discovery process and the protection of the integrity of that process, which necessarily involves consideration of the privacy interest of the parties and, in the ordinary case at least, does not require or condone publicity.

The passage is ambiguous, since it requires trial courts to weigh "the respective interests of the parties," and yet it never explains what should count as a cognizable interest of the party receiving the discovery information. Although this might be taken as ceding authority to trial courts to develop standards concerning the interests of parties receiving information, the overall thrust of the passage (and the opinion) is clearly that decisions to issue restraining orders should be guided by a "major concern" to facilitate the discovery process and to protect its integrity. Thus the Washington court seems to have conceptualized the situation as one of deference.

The Supreme Court, like the Washington court, understood discretion to be primarily a matter of trial court flexibility and choice, and thus did not distinguish among grades of appellate control. The Court did assert, however, that trial court "discretion"

---

[202] See, *e.g.*, INS v. Jong Ha Wange, 450 U.S. 139, 144–45 (1981).

[203] 654 P.2d at 690. The Court reviewed the issuance of the restraining order under an abuse of discretion standard.

is justified because the "trial court is in the best position to weigh fairly the competing needs and interests of parties affected by discovery,"[204] and the Court did not enunciate any factors to be weighed in that balance. Since the Court also concluded that litigants retain First Amendment interests in the dissemination of discovery information, it is fair to surmise that the Court considered these interests to be so vague or diffuse as to be articulable only through the case-by-case determinations of the trial court. It would seem, therefore, that a state appellate court reviewing the issuance of a restraining order pursuant to Rule 26(c) would treat issues of state law as a matter of deference, but issues of federal constitutional law as a matter of delegation. The Supreme Court did not explain why these two kinds of issues should be treated differently.

C. THE STRUCTURE OF DISCRETIONARY DECISIONS

Because the abuse-of-discretion standard is indiscriminately applied in situations of both deference and delegation, it is forced to serve somewhat inconsistent functions. In situations primarily involving delegation, the abuse-of-discretion standard is construed to permit review only on the basis of a dilute and generous principle of background rationality, assumed to apply to all decision makers in all circumstances.[205] In this modality, appellate courts characteristically say that "an abuse of discretion exists only when no reasonable person would take the position adopted by the trial court."[206] Appellate courts sometimes add to the criterion of rationality the requirement that trial court decisions not be "the result of partiality, prejudice, bias, or ill will."[207] Appellate courts also use

---

[204] 104 S.Ct. at 2209.

[205] See Texas Indemnity Ins. Co. v. Arant, 171 S.W.2d 915, 919 n.1 (Tex. Civ. App. 1943).

[206] Griggs v. Averbeck Realty, Inc., 92 Wash. 2d 576, 599 P.2d 1289, 1293 (1979). See, e.g., Lemons v. St. John's Hospital, 5 Kan. App. 2d 161, 613 P.2d 957, 960 (1980) ("If reasonable men could differ as to the propriety of the action taken by the trial court, then it cannot be said that the trial court abused its discretion"); Moser v. Wilhelm, 300 N.W.2d 840, 847 (N. Dak. 1981) ("An abuse of discretion is defined as an unreasonable, arbitrary, or unconscionable attitude on the part of the trial court").

[207] Mielcuszny v. Rosol, 317 Pa. 91, 176 A. 236, 237 (1934). See, e.g., Tobeluk v. Lind, 589 P.2d 873, 878 (Ala. 1979) ("We will not interfere with the trial court's determination unless it is shown that the court abused its discretion by issuing a decision which is arbitrary, capricious, manifestly unreasonable, or which stems from an improper motive").

the abuse-of-discretion standard to ensure that trial courts understand that they have the power to exercise discretion, since "[f]ailure to exercise choice in a situation calling for choice is an abuse of discretion."[208]

In situations primarily involving deference, the abuse of discretion standard is used by appellate courts to fulfill the very different function of enforcing applicable legal standards. Thus appellate courts will find an "abuse of discretion" if a trial court, in reaching its decision, entertained inappropriate considerations,[209] or if it failed to entertain certain appropriate considerations,[210] or if it did not appropriately weigh the factors it did consider.[211]

The abuse-of-discretion standard of review is thus used to preserve trial court flexibility and choice, and at the same time to screen trial court decisions for rationality, for improper motive or prejudice, and for compliance with pertinent legal principles. In order to perform these different functions, the abuse-of-discretion standard has been associated with a variety of devices designed to ensure that trial court decisions can be properly reviewed. These devices have been used in circumstances of both delegation and deference, although they appear to be more appropriately necessary in the latter situation.

Although an appellate court can review trial court decisions for abuse of discretion without requiring a record, findings, or any articulation of reasons, review in such circumstances can only be cursory.[212] If an appellate court wishes to assure itself that a trial court has exercised its discretion, or has made a reasonable decision, or has followed controlling principles of law, the appellate court can prescribe that discretionary decision making be accom-

---

[208] Johnson v. United States, 398 A.2d 354, 363 (D.C. 1979). See Seibert v. Minneapolis & St. Louis Ry. Co., 58 Minn. 58, 57 N.W. 1068, 1070 (1894); Grow v. Wolcott, 123 Vt. 490, 194 A.2d 403, 404 (1963); *cf.* Accardi v. Shaughnessy, 347 U.S. 260, 267–68 (1954).

[209] City of Elkhart v. Middleton, 265 Ind. 514, 356 N.E.2d 207, 211 (1976).

[210] Oppenheimer Fund, Inc. v. Sanders, 437 U.S. 340, 358–64 (1978).

[211] Piper Aircraft Co. v. Reyno, 454 U.S. 235 (1981). In situations of deference, appellate courts will characteristically defer to trial court judgments in the implementation of legal standards so long as these judgments are not "clearly unreasonable." Curtiss-Wright Corp. v. General Electric Co., 446 U.S. 1, 10 (1980).

[212] See Link v. Wabash Railroad Co., 370 U.S. 626 (1962); Woodruff v. Woodruff, 7 Ohio Misc. 87, 217 N.E.2d 264, 268 (1965).

panied by procedures to enhance reviewability. Appellate courts can require that there be a "rational basis in the evidence" to support a trial court's discretionary decision;[213] or they can compel a trial court to "disclose, by specific findings, the basis for its ultimate conclusion";[214] or they can mandate "that the exercise of discretion be accompanied by the trial court's articulation of the factors considered and the weight accorded to them."[215]

By combining these various devices, and by enforcing them, appellate courts can give teeth to the abuse-of-discretion standard of review. While such rigor is ordinarily associated with judicial review of administrative discretion,[216] it has also been applied to appellate review of judicial discretion in the pretrial management of a case. In *Gulf Oil Co. v. Bernard*,[217] for example, the Supreme Court used the abuse-of-discretion standard to review the issuance of a restraining order that essentially prohibited named plaintiffs and their counsel from communicating with any actual or potential plaintiff class members.[218] The Court did not reach the question of the order's constitutionality,[219] but instead held that the trial court had "abused its discretion" because it had issued the order without "a clear record and specific findings that reflect a weighing of the

---

[213] In re Coordinated Pretrial Proceedings in Petroleum Products Antitrust Litigation, 669 F.2d 620, 623 (10th Cir. 1982). See Curtiss-Wright Corp. v. General Electric Co., 446 U.S. 1, 10 (1980).

[214] Grow v. Wolcott, 123 Vt. 490, 194 A.2d 403, 407 (1963).

[215] United States v. Criden, 648 F.2d 814, 819 (3d Cir. 1981). See Hartung v. Hartung, 102 Wis. 2d 58, 306 N.W.2d 16, 21 (1981); City of Elkhart v. Middleton, 265 Ind. 514, 356 N.E.2d 207, 210 (1976). Judge Friendly has strongly argued that in situations of deference trial courts should be required to make explicit the grounds of their "discretionary" decisions: "Once it has been deemed appropriate to limit the range of discretion, whether through announcement of a principle of preference or the specification of factors, it becomes necessary that the trial court articulate the basis for its decision. Otherwise it will not be possible for an appellate court to determine whether the trial court's decision rest on an application of the proper rule or the mistaken assumption of some other rule." Friendly, note 179 *supra*, at 770.

[216] See, *e.g.*, Burlington Truck Lines, Inc. v. United States, 371 U.S. 156, 167–68 (1962); Motor Vehicle Mfrs. Ass'n v. State Farm Mut., 103 S.Ct. 2856, 2866–67 (1983).

[217] 452 U.S. 89 (1981).

[218] The restraining order was issued pursuant to Fed. R. Civ. P. 23(d), which authorizes judicial management of class actions.

[219] 452 U.S. at 101 n.15. The Court stated: "[A]lthough we do not decide what standards are mandated by the First Amendment in this kind of case, we do observe that the order involved serious restraints on expression. This fact, at minimum, counsels caution on the part of a district court in drafting such an order, and attention to whether the restraint is justified by a likelihood of serious abuses." *Id.* at 103–04.

need for limitation and the potential interference with the rights of the parties."[220]

The Court offered three reasons to justify the imposition of these requirements. First, the requirements would help create a "record useful for appellate review."[221] Second, they were necessary to "ensure that the court is furthering, rather than hindering, the policies embodied in the Federal Rules of Civil Procedure."[222] Third, and most interesting, the requirements would force the trial court to engage in a process of balancing in the course of which it would have explicitly to identify "the potential abuses being addressed."[223] In this manner the process of trial court choice could be structured so as to increase the likelihood that it would "result in a carefully drawn order that limits speech as little as possible, consistent with the rights of the parties under the circumstances."[224]

Bernard thus suggests that certain structural prerequisites can be imposed on discretionary decision making both to enhance the quality of decision making and to increase the chances of meaningful appellate review. I shall call these prerequisites "accountability requirements." Accountability requirements may have value even if trial court decisions entail the exercise of weak discretion and are discretionary from the point of view of appellate review.

The Court in *Rhinehart* did not explicitly address the issue of accountability requirements. It did not explain whether trial courts issuing restraining orders would be constitutionally required to compile a record, issue findings, or articulate "the need for a limitation and the potential interference with the rights of the parties."[225] It is thus open to question whether the First Amendment compels these accountability requirements to "ensure that the [trial] court is furthering, rather than hindering," its policies.

---

[220] *Id.* at 101.

[221] *Id.* at 102.

[222] *Ibid.*

[223] *Ibid.*

[224] *Id.* at 102. See Johnson v. United States, 398 A.2d 354, 364 (D.C. 1979): "In both the judicial and administrative spheres the requirement that the decision-maker compile a record makes certain that the facts of the case do not escape his attention and makes it more probable that the decision-maker will exercise his discretion in a proper manner." See also DAVIS, note 2 *supra*, at 97–141.

[225] The facts of *Rhinehart* are ambiguous. Although the trial judge made no specific findings, he did issue an opinion justifying entry of the restraining order. And the record in the case clearly provides a rational basis for the decision to issue the order.

V. The First Amendment, Discretion, and the Management of Pretrial Discovery

If restraining orders can appropriately be characterized as an internal management tool of the judicial system, they will be constitutional if necessary for achievement of the system's legitimate ends. This is true even though restraining orders constitute prior restraints and depend on the content of litigants' speech. The question remains, however, whether any particular restraining order is necessary for the supervision of pretrial discovery. The implicit position of Rule 26(c) is that effective administration of pretrial discovery requires that the answer to this question be committed to the discretion of trial judges. In *Rhinehart* the Supreme Court affirmed this position.

But this position is far too coarse to serve as a basis for constitutional analysis, both because it fails to distinguish among the various dimensions of discretion, and because it fails to appreciate that discretion is a matter of degree. More careful analysis would require an inquiry into the nature and extent of trial court discretion claimed to be necessary for effective pretrial administration.

A. RESTRAINING ORDERS AND "WEAK" DISCRETION

"Weak" discretion exists when a controlling legal standard is so open textured or general that its implementation requires the exercise of judgment. The First Amendment ordinarily limits weak discretion by requiring that legal standards authorizing the suppression of speech "set reasonably clear guidelines for law enforcement officials and triers of fact in order to prevent 'arbitrary and discriminatory' enforcement."[226] But some weak discretion is both unavoidable and constitutionally permissible. In *Feiner v. New York*, for example, the Court upheld the exercise of a "police officer's proper discretionary power" to suppress speech on the basis of a constitutional breach-of-the-peace statute.[227] At some

---

[226] Smith v. Goguen, 415 U.S. 566, 573 (1974).

[227] 340 U.S. 314, 319 (1951). Similarly, the Court has held that statutes governing decisions to issue parade or demonstration permits can be general enough to leave room for the "discretion" of a decision maker, so long as that discretion is limited to appropriate considerations of "time, place and manner." Cox v. New Hampshire, 312 U.S. 569, 575–76 (1941). See Cox v. Louisiana, 379 U.S. 536, 558 (1965).

point, however, controlling legal standards become so general as to leave "unfettered discretion"[228] in the hands of government officials, and this is constitutionally impermissible since speech might then be penalized on the basis of "personal predilections."[229]

There is no sharp line at which weak discretion passes into constitutionally forbidden license.[230] In the regulation of the speech of the general public, the Court's analysis of weak discretion can most kindly be described as confused. In the regulation of insubordinate speech, however, the distinction between permissible and impermissible weak discretion is tied to a functional analysis of the institutional authority in question. Weak discretion is constitutional when it is "necessary to the furtherance" of institutional goals.[231] As the Court said in a case challenging military regulation of speech as delegating excessive weak discretion: "For the reasons which differentiate military society from civilian society, we think Congress is permitted to legislate both with greater breadth and with greater flexibility when prescribing the rules by which the former shall be governed than it is when prescribing rules for the latter."[232]

Management situations characteristically involve weak discretion. This is because strict rules that leave no room for judgment in their implementation are unsuitable "where the action to be controlled is non-recurring" and in circumstances involving "personalized, individual application."[233] When rules are strictly applied in such situations, they can create an "unreasonableness"[234] that is fierce, unproductive, and "bureaupathic."[235] Morris Cohen long ago captured the dilemma "felt by every one who has to give orders to a human subordinate. You attempt to guard yourself

---

[228] Papachristou v. City of Jacksonville, 405 U.S. 156, 168 (1972).

[229] Kolender v. Lawson, 103 S.Ct. 1855, 1858–59 (1983).

[230] See Amsterdam, *The Void-for-Vagueness Doctrine in the Supreme Court*, 109 U. PA. L. REV. 67, 94–96 (1960). In part the placement of this line depends upon whether, "by the nature of the problems presented, legislatures simply cannot establish standards with great precision." Smith v. Goguen, 415 U.S. at 581.

[231] Procunier v. Martinez, 416 U.S. 396, 416–18 (1974).

[232] Parker v. Levy, 417 U.S. 733, 756 (1974).

[233] Jowell, note 182 *supra*, at 202. See PERROW, note 127 *supra*, at 162–63. Most management situations involve precisely such nonrecurring circumstances demanding the exercise of personal judgment. See KOTTER, THE GENERAL MANAGERS 122–24 (1982).

[234] BARDACH & KAGAN, GOING BY THE BOOK: THE PROBLEM OF REGULATORY UNREASONABLENESS 58–119 (1982).

[235] THOMPSON, MODERN ORGANIZATION 94 (1977).

against his mistakes or departures from your settled policy by laying down fixed rules. But when your subordinate rigorously follows these rules, you are vexed that he does so mechanically without using common sense or judgment."[236]

Most organizations want their managers to use their common sense and consequently prescribe fixed rules sparingly, tending instead to control their managers by setting general objectives or goals which the managers are expected to meet.[237] The more managerial performance is defined by its product or outcome, "the more discretion" is given the manager "to supply the means-ends connections."[238]

These considerations apply to judicial management of pretrial discovery. Pretrial discovery involves nonrecurring situations filled with "multifarious, fleeting, special, narrow facts that utterly resist generalization."[239] It involves the continual exercise of judgment,[240] the continual assessment of the intentions, goals, and good faith of litigants;[241] and it is for these reasons "not amenable to regulation by rule."[242] As a consequence both the Washington and the Federal rules of civil procedure do not prescribe detailed and mechanical rules to govern the management of pretrial discovery, and instead provide trial judges with the power and flexibility necessary to attain broadly stated institutional goals.[243]

To impose strict rules on the issuance of restraining orders would impose deep costs of unreasonableness and managerial inefficiency. The circumstances requiring issuance of such orders are simply too

---

[236] COHEN, LAW AND THE SOCIAL ORDER 262 (1982).

[237] See, *e.g.*, DRUCKER, MANAGEMENT: TASKS, RESPONSIBILITIES, PRACTICES 430–42 (1973); GALBRAITH, ORGANIZATION DESIGN 45–46 (1977); ODIORNE, MANAGEMENT DECISIONS BY OBJECTIVES (1969).

[238] MARCH & SIMON, note 128 *supra*, at 147.

[239] Rosenberg, note 158 *supra*, at 662.

[240] See text at notes 114–17 *supra*.

[241] See, *e.g.*, Resnik, note 111 *supra*, at 393.

[242] Rosenberg, note 158 *supra*, at 662. William Glaser, in his study of pretrial discovery, concluded: "Rules cannot anticipate every situation and supply detailed guidelines; the rules must have administrators who distinguish the legitimate from the illegitimate complaint and who can manage each situation." GLASER, note 116 *supra*, at 237.

[243] The Supreme Court of Washington stated that "the purpose of the discovery rule [is] to encourage full disclosure of all relevant facts so as to facilitate the administration of justice, acquaint the examiner with the testimony that will be given at trial, develop the truth, shorten and simplify the trial, eliminate elements of surprise, and permit the parties to prepare for trial." 654 P.2d at 678–79.

multifarious to be encompassed by any set of specific rules. The issue is not simply that a regime of strict, mechanical rules would impair the ability of trial courts to issue restraining orders when appropriate, but also that this impairment would adversely affect the capacity of trial judges to manage other aspects of pretrial discovery. Trial judges presently have broad discretion to control the exchange of discovery information so as to attain the general goals of pretrial discovery. But to the extent that strict rules are imposed on restraining orders, discretion to manage the exchange of information will also be constricted. Even if judges believe that pertinent discovery information should be produced, they may be unwilling to require its production if the presence of inflexible rules disables them from ensuring that such information will be properly used.

Even the *Halkin* opinion does not attempt to impose a regime of strict rules on the issuance of restraining orders, but rather proposes a series of general First Amendment principles meant to inform the judgment of trial judges.[244] The trial judge is instructed to consider factors like the nature of the First Amendment interests at stake and the extent of the harm to be averted.[245] It is perfectly proper to conceive First Amendment principles as ceding such weak discretion to trial judges. The Supreme Court has even held that with regard to the administrative decision to close a criminal trial, the First Amendment requires that trial judges exercise weak "discretion" so that their judgment may most accurately reflect the particular circumstances involved.[246]

Two consequences follow from this reasoning. First, the Court's conclusion in *Rhinehart* that the First Amendment does not prohibit Rule 26(c)'s delegation of "broad discretion" seems essentially correct. Although Rule 26(c) makes no effort to specify "narrow, objective and definite standards"[247] to govern the issuance of restraining orders, any attempt to do so would likely cripple trial courts' ability effectively to manage the pretrial exchange of discovery information. Second, the First Amendment standard governing

---

[244] See Brink v. DaLesio, 82 F.R.D. 664, 678 (D. Md. 1979).

[245] 598 F.2d at 191. The court stressed that these considerations must be evaluated in the context of "particular discovery material and a particular trial setting." *Id.* at 195.

[246] See Globe Newspaper Co. v. Superior Court, 457 U.S. 596, 608–10 (1982).

[247] Shuttlesworth v. Birmingham, 394 U.S. 147, 151 (1969).

the issuance of restraining orders should not itself contain specific standards. It would have been sufficient for the Court to have made clear that restraining orders seriously infringe litigants' First Amendment interests, and that this infringement should not take place unless necessary to attain the goals of pretrial discovery.

B. RESTRAINING ORDERS AND APPELLATE CONTROL

The issue that most sharply divides *Halkin* and *Rhinehart* is the degree of appellate control that should be exercised over decisions to issue restraining orders.[248] *Halkin* holds that appellate courts should apply the rule of independent review to such decisions; *Rhinehart* decides that appellate courts can view such decisions as involving a situation of delegation.

The Supreme Court's decision is plainly incorrect. Appellate courts normally treat trial court management of pretrial discovery as a question of deference, and indeed the Supreme Court of Washington has indicated that decisions to issue restraining orders under Rule 26(c) should be so viewed as a matter of state law.[249] Since there is an articulable First Amendment standard that should govern decisions to issue restraining orders, there is no justification for the Supreme Court's view that appellate courts treat such decisions as raising issues of delegation rather than of deference. The most that can reasonably be maintained is that appellate courts should retain control over the articulation of the applicable First Amendment standard, but should defer to trial courts in its implementation. The question is thus whether appellate courts should apply

---

[248] Thus one perceptive federal district court noted that the factors to be considered under *Halkin*'s First Amendment standard, and the factors to be considered under federal Rule 26(c)'s "good cause" standard, were virtually "identical." The real difference, the Court stated, "lies in the discretionary nature of the good cause standard. In determining whether there is good cause to enter a Rule 26(c) order, a court may, but does not have to, weigh these factors. Moreover, because a determination that good cause has been shown is reviewed under an abuse of discretion standard, it is less likely that the appellate court would substitute its judgment for that of the trial court even if, for example, it believed that more deference should have been given to the other party's First Amendment interests. Under . . . the [First Amendment standard], on the other hand, the court must find that definite criteria have been satisfied before issuing a protective order, and failure to do so will result in a reversal. To the extent that the discretion of the trial court is limited by [the First Amendment], therefore, [it] provide[s] more protection for a litigant's First Amendment rights." Koster v. Chase Manhattan Bank, 93 F.R.D. 471, 479–80 (S.D.N.Y. 1982).

[249] See text at note 203 *supra*.

the rule of independent review, or whether they should exercise deference.

Appellate courts normally view the management of pretrial discovery with considerable deference because trial courts are "in a far better position than a court of appeals to supervise and control discovery."[250] When First Amendment considerations are present, however, appellate courts ordinarily view trial court decisions as raising issues of law. In *Nebraska Press Ass'n v. Stuart*, for example, the Court applied the rule of independent review to a trial court decision to issue a gag order, even though the order was issued by a trial court that could be said to have had a more sensitive "feel for the case" than any appellate court. The Court, moreover, exercised independent review even though the First Amendment standard controlling the issuance of the gag order was extremely vague and involved the balancing of several factors.[251] Indeed, as the Court recently stressed, the rule of independent review is founded on the necessity of creating a check on the exercise of weak discretion arising from the generality of First Amendment standards:[252]

> Providing triers of fact with a general description of the type of communication whose content is unworthy of protection has not, in and of itself, served sufficiently to narrow the category, nor served to eliminate the danger that decisions by triers of fact may inhibit the expression of protected ideas. The principle of viewpoint neutrality that underlies the First Amendment itself . . . also imposes a special responsibility on judges whenever it is claimed that a particular communication is unprotected.

Thus whenever trial courts determine that speech is obscene, or uttered with actual malice, or constitutes fighting words, such determinations are reviewed by appellate courts as posing questions of law, and this enables appellate courts to determine if these questions have been rightly or wrongly decided.[253] The Court of Appeals in *Halkin* saw no reason to treat appellate review of restraining orders any differently. This position is attractive in the light of the extensive weak discretion characterizing decisions to issue restraining orders.

---

[250] ACF Industries, Inc. v. EEOC, 439 U.S. 1081, 1087 (1979) (Powell, J., dissenting from denial of certiorari).

[251] 427 U.S. 539, 562 (1976).

[252] Bose Corp. v. Consumers Union, 104 S.Ct. 1949, 1962 (1984).

[253] *Id.* at 1961–63.

The rule of independent review, however, is not invariably applied to the regulation of First Amendment rights. In *Glines*, for
example, the Court was willing to defer to military judgment concerning the censorship of speech.[254] This deference cannot simply
be interpreted as the respect owing to the "expertise" of those
charged with the administration of government institutions. In *Tinker* the Court refused to defer to the managerial authority of a state
school board. School officials are presumably as expert in the administration of their institution as military officials are in the management of theirs. The difference must therefore be attributed to
the Court's assessment of the need for deference in the achievement
of legitimate institutional goals.[255]

The issue presented in *Rhinehart* is therefore whether applying the
rule of independent review to the issuance of restraining orders
would impair the capacity of trial courts to manage pretrial discov-

---

[254] The Court reached a similar conclusion in Jones v. North Carolina Prisoners' Union,
433 U.S. 119 (1977), in which the Court upheld the authority of prison officials to suppress
First Amendment interests on the basis of "fears as to future disruptions" as long as such
fears were not "groundless." *Id.* at 127 n.5, 132–33. The Court concluded that such weak
discretion was necessary because of "the reasonable considerations of penal management"
and the "self-evident" interest in "preserving order and authority in prisons." *Id.* at 132, 136.
In reviewing the suppression of First Amendment rights, a "wide-ranging deference" was "to
be accorded the decisions of prison administrators." *Id.* at 126. "The necessary and correct
result of our deference to the informed discretion of prison administrators permits them, and
not the courts, to make the difficult judgments concerning institutional operations in situations such as this." *Id.* at 128. In Connick v. Myers, 103 S.Ct. 1684 (1983), on the other hand,
the Court was ambivalent about whether it should defer to decisions to regulate the speech of
government employees. The Court noted that if employee expression were only marginally
related to matters of public concern, and if such expression "interfered with working relationships" in a situation where "close working relationships are essential to fulfilling public
responsibilities," "a wide degree of deference to employer's judgment is appropriate. Furthermore, we do not see the necessity for an employer to allow events to unfold to the extent
that the disruption of the office and the destruction of working relationships is manifest
before taking action. We caution that a stronger showing may be necessary if the employee's
speech more substantially involved matters of public concern." *Id.* at 1692–93.

[255] In *Tinker* the Court's refusal to defer to the judgment of school officials did not necessarily extend to all school decisions regulating speech. Underlying the Court's opinion was the
notion that school authority over speech had definite limitations. The Court stated, for
example, that "[i]f a regulation were adopted by school officials forbidding discussion of the
Vietnam conflict, or the expression by any student of opposition to it anywhere on school
property except as part of a prescribed classroom exercise, it would be obvious that the
regulation would violate the constitutional rights of students, at least if it could not be
justified by a showing that the students' activities would materially and substantially disrupt
the work and discipline of the school." 393 U.S. at 513. The Court appears to have viewed
the ban on black armbands as just such a regulation. That the Court refused to defer to it
does not imply that it would also refuse to defer to different regulations that were within
what the Court was prepared to acknowledge as the legitimate authority of the school, as
for example those that occur in classroom settings.

ery. This issue can be analyzed by precisely defining the objectives served by the rule of independent review. Upon close inspection, the Court is notably vague as to the nature of these purposes. It says only that "[w]hen the standard governing the decision of a particular case is provided by the Constitution, this Court's role in marking out the limits of the standard through the process of case-by-case adjudication is of special importance."[256] But of what importance? There are two possibilities.

The importance of the rule of independent review might lie in the fact that the "process of case-by-case adjudication," through the classic alchemy of the common law, will eventuate in the enunciation of principles of law that are increasingly specific and strict, thus gradually reducing the weak discretion implicit in general First Amendment standards.[257] But to the extent that the rule serves this purpose, its function is ultimately to restrict the managerial flexibility of the trial judge in the supervision of pretrial discovery. If it is important to preserve such flexibility, then it would be better to forestall this process of "case-by-case" adjudication by imposing a rule of deference.

On the other hand, the "special importance" of the rule of independent review might refer not to its role in the development of more specific standards, but rather to its role in ensuring that justice is done in the individual case. If the general nature of First Amendment principles creates the danger that judgment to suppress speech might be exercised in a biased or improper manner, the function of the rule of independent review might be to oversee the exercise of judgment in each case so as to correct any such errors or bias. Independent review would thus undo the effects of improper suppression of speech.

If the rule of independent review is to serve this function, however, appellate review of restraining orders should be interlocutory in nature. This is because damage to First Amendment interests arises not merely from the outright suppression of speech, but also

---

[256] Bose Corp. v. Consumers Union, 104 S.Ct. at 1961.

[257] Thus Morris Cohen has observed: "Discretion, in general, represents more or less instinctive evaluation or appreciation of the diverse elements that enter into a complex; and such instinctive evaluation must precede conscious rulemaking. Rules are the limits that the continued exercise of discretion establishes." COHEN, note 236 *supra*, at 264. See Albermarle Paper Co. v. Moody, 422 U.S. 405, 413–21 (1975); CROSS, PRECEDENT IN ENGLISH LAW 214–16 (2d ed. 1968).

from government action which temporarily delays expression.[258]
An erroneous restraining order imposes additional damage for
every day that it remains in effect. For this reason the Court has
interpreted the First Amendment to require "immediate appellate
review" of judicial orders suppressing speech.[259] If the purpose of
the rule of independent review were to vindicate constitutional
rights, it too should be "immediate." *Halkin* clearly appreciated this
logic, for it held that restraining orders should be subject to immediate appellate review through the extraordinary writ of mandamus.[260]

To permit interlocutory appeals of restraining orders would
work a basic change in discovery practice. Under the law of most
jurisdictions, appeals are not allowed as a matter of right except
from final judgments.[261] Judicial orders regulating discovery, including restraining orders, are interlocutory and not appealable as a
matter of right until the ultimate disposition of a case.[262] The reasons for this policy were stated by the Court in *Cobbledick v. United
States*:[263]

> Congress from the very beginning has, by forbidding piecemeal
> disposition on appeal of what for practical purposes is a single
> controversy, set itself against enfeebling judicial administration.
> Thereby is avoided the obstruction to just claims that would
> come from permitting the harassment and cost of a succession of
> separate appeals from the various rulings to which a litigation
> may give rise, from its initiation to entry of judgment. To be
> effective, judicial administration must not be leadenfooted. Its
> momentum would be arrested by permitting separate reviews of
> the component elements in a unified cause.

[258] See, *e.g.*, Freedman v. Maryland, 380 U.S. 51 (1965); Carroll v. President and Commissioners of Princess Anne, 393 U.S. 175, 182 (1968); Nebraska Press Ass'n v. Stuart, 427
U.S. at 559.

[259] National Socialist Party of America v. Skokie, 432 U.S. 43, 44 (1977).

[260] 598 F.2d at 197–200.

[261] STERN, APPELLATE PRACTICE IN THE UNITED STATES 52–54 (1981); Glass v. Stahl
Specialty Co., 97 Wash. 2d 880, 883, 652 P.2d 948 (1982).

[262] See Bushman v. New Holland Div. of Sperry Rand Corp., 83 Wash. 2d 429, 518 P.2d
1078, 1079–80 (1974); Washington v. Superior Court, 193 P.2d 318, 319 (Wash. 1948);
HAYDOCK & HERR, DISCOVERY: THEORY, PRACTICE AND PROBLEMS 311–14 (1983). See,
Cutner, note 120 *supra*, at 947–48; Resnick, note 111 *supra*, at 411–14; International Products Corp. v. Koons, 325 F.2d 403, 406–07 (2d Cir. 1963). *Rhinehart* was heard on appeal
pursuant to a Washington rule permitting discretionary review of interlocutory decisions.
See R.A.P. 2.3.

[263] 309 U.S. 323, 325 (1940). See Coopers & Lybrand v. Livesay, 437 U.S. 463, 467 n.8
(1978); Firestone Tire and Rubber Co. v. Risjord, 449 U.S. 368, 373–74 (1981).

For these reasons, the ability of trial courts to manage pretrial discovery would be substantially impaired if restraining orders were to be routinely reviewable on interlocutory appeal.[264] Every time a trial court decided to condition discovery upon the issuance of a restraining order, the pretrial conduct of the case could potentially come to a halt during the months or perhaps years required for prosecution of an "immediate" appeal.[265] Trial courts would think twice about issuing restraining orders, and their usefulness as tools of pretrial management would be *pro tanto* diminished. The inner logic of the rule of independent review, therefore, when applied in the context of restraining orders, would tend toward conclusions that substantially impair the management flexibility of trial judges.

Despite this logic, it nevertheless can be contended that appellate courts should offer noninterlocutory independent review on the grounds that an ultimately correct disposition, however delayed, will be of importance to particular litigants. There are two considerations that weigh against this contention. The rule of independent review presupposes that appellate courts can scrutinize facts and law to determine the "correct" legal outcome. But each time an appellate court announces such an outcome, it establishes a precedent that will be binding on future trial court decisions. The accumulation of such precedents will in the end erode the weak discretion necessary to govern pretrial discovery. Appellate court deference, on the other hand, significantly diminishes both the number and force of such precedents.

It is not clear, moreover, that the question whether a restraining order should issue has any uniquely "correct" legal outcome. It is possible, for example, for a trial court to issue a restraining order

---

[264] The State of New York at present permits discovery orders to be appealed as a matter of right, and the general consensus is that this practice "is a prime source of delay and expense in litigation." Korn, *Civil Jurisdiction of the New York Court of Appeals and Appellate Divisions*, 16 BUF. L. REV. 307, 330, 332–33 (1966–67). See 7 WEINSTEIN, KORN, & MILLER, NEW YORK CIVIL PRACTICE § 5701.03 (1983). During the debate surrounding the enactment of 28 U.S.C. § 1292(b) (discretionary appeal), Charles E. Clark strongly "argued that 'upper-court policing of trial court activity is not a sound appellate function and, in view of its haphazard and freezing characteristics, can only be detrimental to effective court administration.' " Fish, note 120 *supra*, at 109. Clark viewed the availability of interlocutory appeals as creating the possibility of litigation strategies designed to erode an "adversary's powers of resistance." *Ibid.*

[265] A prime example is *Halkin* itself. The District of Columbia Circuit did not issue its decision until almost two years after the trial court had signed the restraining order.

because particular litigants are uncooperative and need to be kept on a short leash,[266] or because the bar practicing before it needs to be taught an object lesson.[267] These are classic managerial considerations, and they neither seem amenable to any uniquely correct legal solution, nor do they seem susceptible to appellate court determination. If such considerations are legitimate, it is not clear whether independent review can perform any useful function.

These objections are not dispositive, but when they are raised in a context in which the inner logic of independent review has been truncated, they provide support for the Court's conclusion that decisions to issue restraining orders constitutionally need only be reviewed under an abuse of discretion standard.

C. RESTRAINING ORDERS AND ACCOUNTABILITY REQUIREMENTS

The abuse-of-discretion standard is a mansion with many rooms. One such room, as *Gulf Oil Co. v. Bernard* makes clear, is the prescription that trial court decisions be made on the basis of "a clear record and specific findings that reflect a weighing of the need for a limitation and the potential interference with the rights of the parties." This prescription imposes three distinct accountability requirements on trial court decision making. Decisions must be supported by a record; they must be based upon specific findings; and there must be an articulation of the reasons for the decision. Imposing these requirements serves two purposes: it improves the quality of trial court decision making by forcing trial judges to reach decisions in a careful and self-conscious manner, and it provides a sufficient record for meaningful appellate review.

Decisions to issue restraining orders plainly can interfere with First Amendment rights. It would therefore appear to be constitutionally important to impose the *Bernard* requirements on such decisions if they would reduce the likelihood of improper restraining orders. The *Halkin* decision appears to have imposed some of these requirements, stating that trial courts must make "necessary findings" with respect to each element of the appropriate First Amendment standard.[268] The Court in *Rhinehart*, on the other hand, ap-

---

[266] See text at note 115 *supra.*

[267] See text at notes 113, 117 *supra.*

[268] 598 F.2d at 1892.

parently decided not to impose such requirements, stating in a cryptic footnote that "heightened First Amendment scrutiny of each request for a protective order" was inappropriate because it "would necessitate burdensome evidentiary findings."[269]

The Court's point is obscure. It might be that the *Bernard* requirements are so burdensome that they unduly restrict the flexibility necessary for pretrial management of a case. But why are these requirements compatible with effective pretrial management in *Bernard*, but not in *Rhinehart*? The Court's response is suggested by its citation[270] of *Zenith Radio Corp. v. Matsushita Elec. Indus. Co.*, a large antitrust case involving a restraining order covering "millions of pages of documents produced in discovery."[271] If the First Amendment were to require the trial court in *Zenith* to make findings, articulate reasons, and compile a record with respect to each of these pages of discovery information, the burden would clearly be overwhelming. That result calls to mind the blunt observation of a California district judge who refused to entertain a motion to vacate a restraining order covering "massive quantities of documents": "I might . . . require that defendants now justify the protective order as to each item which they believe should be protected. Some person would then be required to pass upon those justifications. I do not propose to be that person."[272]

The Court's concern for the special problems caused by large cases seem appropriate, but not insurmountable. It would be senseless to impose accountability requirements in a self-defeating fashion. In a case involving vast quantities of discovery information, it may be perfectly appropriate for a trial court to structure its decision to issue a restraining order on the basis of generic categories of documents, rather than on the basis of an item by item review. This is the present practice of those courts which interpret the "good cause" standard of Rule 26(c) to "require a particular and specific demonstration of fact."[273] Even *Halkin* conceded that in an appropriate case a trial court could issue "a blanket protective order

---

[269] 104 S.Ct. at 2209 n.23.

[270] *Ibid.*

[271] 529 F. Supp. 866, 874 (E.D. Pa. 1981).

[272] In re Coordinated Pretrial proceedings in W. Liquid Asphalt Cases, 18 F.R.Serv. 2d 1251, 1252 (N.D. Cal. 1974).

[273] See note 55 *supra* and the cases cited.

covering all documents in a large-scale exchange of files without prejudice to raising the merits of the protective order as applied to particular documents at a later time."[274] If accountability requirements are interpreted to apply in a reasonable fashion—which is to say, if they are interpreted not to impose an undue burden on trial courts—there does not appear to be any good reason to view them as inconsistent with effective trial court management of pretrial discovery.

One can ask, however, whether these accountability requirements contribute so significantly to the quality of trial court decision making as to justify their being imposed as a constitutional prerequisite. While there is no empirical evidence on this issue, it does seem plain that imposing special requirements on decisions affecting First Amendment interests invests these decisions with a gravity and importance commensurate with the constitutional issues at stake. Requiring decisions to issue restraining orders to meet the *Bernard* accountability requirements will distinguish these decisions from the "informal" atmosphere in which ordinary pretrial administrative decisions are made.[275] This is itself important, and it is also noteworthy that the Court has in other contexts required trial court decisions affecting First Amendment rights to be accompanied by specific findings and an articulation of reasons. Administrative decisions to close criminal trials are, for example, subject to such requirements.[276]

Even if these requirements only marginally improve the quality of trial court decision making, it would seem especially important to impose them on decisions to issue restraining orders, since such decisions are reviewed only for abuse of discretion and hence are unlikely to be reversed on appeal. Indeed, to the extent that the abuse-of-discretion standard is weak, it would also seem particularly appropriate that trial court decisions be accompanied by an articulation of reasons and specific findings, so that appellate courts will be more likely to detect erroneous interpretations of the controlling legal standard. This was the logic of *Bernard*, and it should

---

[274] 598 F.2d at 196 n.47.

[275] See Resnick, note 111 *supra*, at 407.

[276] See Press-Enterprise Co. v. Superior Court, 104 S.Ct. 819, 824 (1984); Globe Newspaper Co. v. Superior Court, 457 U.S. 596, 608 n.20 (1982).

have redoubled application in the constitutional context of restraining orders.

The facilitation of appellate court review can, however, have
adverse consequences. To the extent that accountability requirements further the creation of more and firmer appellate precedents,
they can also contribute to the erosion of weak trial court discretion. Appellate courts have also been known to use accountability
requirements as a bootstrap to increase the rigor of appellate review. These dynamics have in fact fueled much of American administrative law.[277] But accountability requirements are unlikely to
generate similar dynamics in the area of restraining orders. This is
because of the long and honored tradition of respecting trial court
discretion in the pretrial management of a case. The tradition is
stable because appellate courts trust trial judges in a way that they
have never trusted administrators. As a former judge of the Court
of Appeals for the Second Circuit put it: "I . . . begin with the
assumption that federal judges are men of high purpose who exercise authority in the best interests of justice as they see it. If this
were not so, the wide range of discretion that was left to district
judges by the Rules would not have been left to them."[278] A similar
assumption underlies the Court's opinion in *Rhinehart*, and it provides good reason to believe that appellate courts will not use accountability requirements to undermine necessary trial court discretion.

VI. CONCLUSION

This may suggest a conclusion that is, in the main, similar to
that intuitively attained by the Court in *Rhinehart*. That the Court
should have reached this conclusion is remarkable, for it flies in the
face of much received First Amendment wisdom. Restraining orders are prior restraints, they are based upon the content of speech,
and they are issued at the discretion of a state official. The Court's
disregard of these facts demonstrates the strength instinctively attributed to government interests in the internal management of

---

[277] See, *e.g.*, Sunstein, *Deregulation and the Hard-Look Doctrine*, 1983 SUPREME COURT
REVIEW 177, 181–84, 209–12.

[278] Waterman, *An Appellate Judge's Approach When Reviewing District Court Sanctions Imposed
for the Purpose of Insuring Compliance with Pretrial Orders*, 29 F.R.D. 420, 421 (1962).

speech. The very power of these interests, however, requires that they be carefully identified and analyzed, so that they may be confined to appropriate circumstances. This is impossible, however, without the development of a more adequate appreciation of the relationship of law to discretion. Discretion does not simply begin "where the law ends," and for that reason the Court in *Rhinehart* was deeply misguided in viewing trial court discretion to manage speech as a constitutional carte blanche.

DOUGLAS G. BAIRD

CHANGING TECHNOLOGY AND UNCHANGING DOCTRINE: SONY CORPORATION v. UNIVERSAL STUDIOS, INC.

In the mid-1970s, Sony Corporation began marketing a home video cassette recorder (VCR) called a Betamax. This machine contained a built-in color television tuner and an automatic timer. It could record over-the-air broadcasts and play them back on an ordinary television. In addition, the Betamax could play back tapes that were rented or purchased and, with a video camera, could record home movies. For either of these uses, however, the tuner and timer were unnecessary. As a practical matter, the machines Sony manufactured were designed to tape over-the-air television broadcasts. A consumer might want to tape a television broadcast for either of two reasons. He might buy a Betamax to build a permanent library of movies or television shows. Alternatively, he might want to use the machine's automatic timer to record a television program while he was doing something else (such as watching another program on a different channel). He could then watch the program several hours or several days later. This second use of the Betamax has become known as "time-shifting."

Last Term, the Supreme Court decided that Sony Corporation did not violate the rights of Walt Disney and Universal Studios when it made and sold the Betamax.[1] The Court relied heavily

Douglas G. Baird is Professor of Law, The University of Chicago.

AUTHOR'S NOTE: I thank Frank Easterbrook, Richard Epstein, Wendy Gordon, William Landes, Cass Sunstein, William Van Alstyne, and Paul Yanowitch for their help.

[1] Sony Corporation v. Universal City Studios, Inc., 104 S.Ct. 774 (1984).

upon fact-finding by the District Court, which tried the case in the late 1970s, and the Court did not squarely confront recent changes in video recorder technology. This case, like many others, shows the tension in common-law adjudication between binding parties to the record they create and establishing principles that will bind others in the future. The more important lesson to be drawn from *Betamax*, however, may be that copyright law itself has become too static and that, consequently, its basic doctrines may need to be reconsidered.

I

Betamax emphasizes how well-settled and well-understood basic principles of copyright law are. All the parties to the case agreed on the broad contours of the principles that should govern the dispute. The Constitution gives Congress the power to give authors and inventors the exclusive right to their writings and discoveries for a limited period of time in order to promote "Science and the useful Arts."[2] Unlike Continental intellectual property law, ours does not exist to reward artists and their work for their own sake.[3] Granting artists exclusive rights is a means of reaching a desired end. When artists have the right to control the dissemination of their work, they have a greater incentive to produce. As the Court itself noted over thirty years ago:[4]

> The economic philosophy behind the clause empowering Congress to grant patents and copyrights is the conviction that encouragement of individual effort by personal gain is the best way to advance public welfare through the talents of authors and inventors in "Science and useful Arts." Sacrificial days devoted to such creative activities deserve rewards commensurate with the services rendered.

The fundamental task confronting Congress in drafting copyright law and courts in construing it is to ensure that the exclusive rights that are created achieve their purpose and enhance our enjoyment of the arts.

---

[2] U.S. Const. art. I, § 8.

[3] For a discussion of French copyright law, which is founded on the idea that intellectual property laws should protect the "moral right" of authors, see Sarraute, *Current Theory on the Moral Right of Authors and Artists under French Law*, 16 AM. J. COMP. L. 465 (1968).

[4] Mazer v. Stein, 347 U.S. 201, 219 (1954).

The exclusive rights that authors enjoy can be either too generous or too meager. If the exclusive rights are too broad, the incentive given authors will be too costly. The public (and other authors) will find their access to books, film, music, and drama unnecessarily limited. If the author's rights are drawn too narrowly, however, the public will be deprived of works that greater rights (and their correspondingly greater economic rewards) would have induced. One must balance the need to ensure public access to whatever is produced against the need to give artists the incentive to create in the first instance. This balance permeates the Copyright Act and was at the heart of the dispute between Universal and Disney on the one hand and Sony on the other. The heart of Universal and Walt Disney's argument was that the public interest in television programs is best served in the long run if producers of copyrighted works can profit from videotaping done in the home. If they cannot, the quality and amount of their programming will suffer relative to what it would have been had they been able to control the taping. The heart of Sony's argument was that home video cassette recorders increased public access to the arts with little or no effect on the incentives of the producers.

Cases such as *Sony Corporation v. Universal Studios, Inc.* focus on the doctrines that have emerged over the past century as Congress and courts have tried to implement the balance between access and incentive. A holder of a copyright (such as Universal or Walt Disney) has the exclusive right to make "copies" of its work. Videotapes made at home are unambiguously "copies" because they are "material objects . . . in which a work is fixed by any method now known or later developed, and from which the work can be perceived, reproduced, or otherwise communicated, either directly or with the aid of a machine."[5] Unauthorized copying is excepted from the general rule when its use of the copyrighted work is "fair." The judicially developed concept of fair use has been codified in section 107 of the 1976 Copyright Act.[6]

---

[5] 17 U.S.C. § 101.

[6] 17 U.S.C. § 107 provides:

. . . [T]he fair use of a copyrighted work . . . for purposes such as criticism, comment, news reporting, teaching (including multiple copies for classroom use), scholarship, or research, is not an infringement of copyright. In determining whether the use made of a work in any particular case is a fair use the factors to be considered shall include—

The concept of fair use embraces some kinds of copying that were not at issue in *Betamax*. A critic, for example, may need to quote from a play in order to write a scathing review, and we do not want an author to be able to use his copyright as a means of stifling criticism. Similarly, we do not want to prevent someone who has a novel theory about a presidential assassination from presenting his theory because a copyright holder refuses to let him reproduce portions of a copyrighted film that the theory hinges on.[7] In *Betamax*, however, the *kind* of copying was not itself worth special protection. Section 107 does include consideration of whether the copying was of a "commercial nature" as a factor in deciding whether the use is fair. Home use of a VCR is not "commercial" in the sense that home users do not sell the tapes that they make and they enjoy no direct financial gain from the taping. But home users are not like scholars, reporters, or researchers who are engaged in some activity that Congress may have sought to protect.[8] Home users are garden-variety, passive consumers of copyrighted works. That they do not resell the tapes that they make suggests that they are less likely to impair a producer's incentive, not that what they are doing is worthy of protection for its own sake.

The strongest fair use argument that Sony made was squarely

---

(1) the purpose and character of the use, including whether such use is of a commercial nature or is for nonprofit educational purposes;

(2) the nature of the copyrighted work;

(3) the amount and substantiality of the portion used in relation to the copyrighted work as a whole; and

(4) the effect of the use upon the potential market for or value of the copyrighted work.

[7] These were the facts of Time, Inc. v. Bernard Geis Assocs, 293 F. Supp. 130 (S.D.N.Y. 1968). This aspect of the fair use defense has prevented the debate about the inherent conflict between the concept of copyright and the First Amendment from surfacing more often. Copyright's refusal to protect ideas (as opposed to a particular expression of those ideas) has also prevented such conflicts. One should note, however, that in cases such as *Bernard Geis*, the distinction between idea and expression is hard to draw, and it may be difficult to communicate an idea without taking advantage of someone else's expression.

[8] The importance of protecting researchers figured in an earlier case involving widescale photocopying by the National Institutes for Health and the National Library of Medicine. See Williams & Wilkins Co. v. United States, 487 F.2d 1345 (Ct. Cl. 1973), *aff'd by an equally divided Court*, 420 U.S. 376 (1975) (per curiam). One may question, however, whether it makes sense to treat scholars and researchers any differently from other users, commercial or otherwise. If it is important to provide access to ensure that an important issue of the day is addressed or that critical reviews are written, it should not matter whether the author's motives are commercial. Similarly, there is no reason why scholars or researchers should be able to acquire copyrighted works at bargain prices, when they have to pay the same price as the general public for everything else they need from pencils to microscopes.

focused on first principles. One of the purposes of the fair use doctrine is to ensure that copyright protection does not extend to instances in which the limitation on access is not offset by a correspondingly greater incentive to authors. An individual cannot make multiple copies of a book of poems and sell it. Such copying undercuts the market for the original work. Yet an individual should be able to copy a single poem and send it to a friend. Most authors would consent to such *de minimis* uses of their work, and we have no reason to protect those who would not consent. The copier would have no cost-effective way of bargaining for a license from the poet. Hence, if such copying were forbidden, access to the work would be unnecessarily limited: the friend would never see the poem, while the author would enjoy no additional royalty and his incentives to write would remain the same. Home videotaping is arguably "fair use" for this reason. A prohibition on home videotaping through a ban on the manufacture of the Betamax would make people worse off without giving Walt Disney or Universal any significant incentive to produce more or better work.[9]

The second major issue in *Betamax* arose because the principal defendant, Sony, was not itself a direct infringer: it did not record any of Disney or Universal's copyrighted works. Suing home users of the Betamax individually was impractical. Even if some or all home videotaping infringed their copyrights, Disney and Universal would be able to do little about it as long as Sony was free to sell the Betamax. Disney and Universal therefore sought to attack the problem at its source. They brought a lawsuit against William Griffiths, who had purchased a Betamax and used it to record some of their copyrighted works, and joined Sony as a defendant on the ground that by manufacturing and selling the machine, Sony was liable as a contributory infringer. They also charged Sony with contributing to the infringement of their copyrights by a man named Marc Wielage and several others who were not joined as defendants.[10]

---

[9] Gordon shows how this aspect of fair use poses the relevant inquiring for cases like *Betamax*. I return to this line of analysis later. See Gordon, *Fair Use as Market Failure: A Structural and Economic Analysis of the* Betamax *Case and Its Predecessors*, 82 COLUM. L. REV. 1600 (1982); text at notes 20–23 *infra*.

[10] See Universal City Studios, Inc. v. Sony Corp., 480 F. Supp. 429, 437–39 (C.D. Cal. 1979), *rev'd*, 659 F.2d 963 (9th Cir. 1981), *rev'd*, 104 S.Ct. 774 (1984).

Charges of contributory infringement arise most often in patent, not copyright, cases. A manufacturer will sell all the components for a patented machine along with instructions on how to assemble them. The manufacturer has not directly violated the inventor's patent rights because none of the individual components is patented and the manufacturer did not "make, use or sell" the patented device. Nevertheless, it acted in a way that made it easy for some-one else to violate the patent and hence is responsible for the in-fringement.[11] Similarly, a person who sets up a business that specializes in allowing customers to borrow copyrighted tapes and reproduce them with machines in the store contributes to the in-fringement of a composer's copyright.[12]

The doctrine of contributory infringement in either the patent or the copyright area comes upon a significant limitation. It is not enough that one sells something, such as an unpatented chemical, one use of which is patented (its use as a fertilizer, for example). Someone who is rewarded with a patent for discovering a new use of a previously known chemical should not be able through the doctrine of contributory infringement to gain exclusive rights to the chemical itself, which he did not discover. If he is allowed to cap-ture the value of all uses of the chemical, he will be rewarded for more than he created, and access to the chemical will be inappropri-ately limited. A holder of a patent or a copyright therefore should not be able to stop the sale of something that has substantial nonin-fringing uses, even if some who buy it will use it to infringe his rights. He should not be able to prevent the sale of something that is a "staple article of commerce."[13]

Contributory infringement always requires balancing. There may be significant savings in enforcement costs from being able to reach one person who enables many others to violate an intellectual property holder's rights. One must, however, weigh these savings against the costs of prohibiting the sale. A product will always have some noninfringing use. In some cases the balancing will be easier

---

[11] See Wallace v. Holmes, 29 F. Cas. 74 (No. 17,100) (C.C. Conn. 1871); Aro Mfg. Co. v. Convertible Top Co., 365 U.S. 336 (1961).

[12] See Elektra Records Co. v. Gem Electronics Distribs., Inc., 360 F. Supp. 821 (E.D.N.Y. 1973).

[13] See Dawson Chemical Co. v. Rohm & Haas Co., 448 U.S. 176 (1980).

than in others. Xerox Corporation, for example, should not be held a contributory infringer when it sells a photocopier, because many uses of the machine (such as copying letters, memoranda, and drafts of articles) do not infringe anyone's copyright. Many people, of course, use Xerox machines to infringe copyrights, but the cost of holding Xerox responsible for these violations is too large in the absence of a remedy that would limit recovery to damages from the copying of protected works. The authors should not be paid more than the amount the public values their work.

To prevail, Disney and Universal had to show both that home videotaping was not fair use and that Sony was liable as a contributory infringer. The second issue overlaps with the first: If enough uses are "fair," then substantial noninfringing uses of the machine exist and Sony cannot be held liable as a contributory infringer. In fact, in the litigation, little attention was paid or needed to be paid to the acts of either Griffiths or Wielage. As noted above, Wielage was not even named as a defendant, and Griffiths was a client of the lawyers of Disney and Universal. He was not represented at trial and Disney and Universal waived all claims for damages against him.[14]

Resolving the dispute in *Betamax* requires first an inquiry into what uses are typically made of a home video cassette recorder and then an analysis of whether such uses that involve copying of copyrighted works are "fair" within the meaning of the Copyright Act. A VCR with a built-in television tuner is a machine designed to record over-the-air broadcasts and nearly all that is broadcast is copyrighted. Those works that are uncopyrighted are typically either religious broadcasts or government-produced works, such as broadcasts of debates in the House of Representatives. This programming is only a small fraction of what is broadcast and one suspects that the number of people who record these programs for later or repeat viewing is trivial. Only a few films, such as *My Man Godfrey*, are in the public domain because of a failure to reregister the copyright. The number of films on which copyright has expired is very small and it is not likely to grow for several decades. Because of provisions in the 1976 Copyright Act that extended the term of existing copyrights, no sound film that is properly registered will

---

[14] See 480 F. Supp. at 437.

go into the public domain until the first decade of the next century.[15]

The alleged vice of the Betamax is that it is designed to infringe the rights of copyright holders generally, not just the rights of Disney and Universal. For this reason, the analogy to contributory patent infringement is imperfect. When one sells a chemical to farmers that has virtually no use other than use as a fertilizer, one infringes the rights of a particular individual, the person who holds a patent on using the chemical as a fertilizer, not the rights of patent holders generally. By contrast, a Betamax is objectionable only if copyright holders as a group object. If most do not, the machine has substantial noninfringing uses.

The District Court made a factual finding that holders of copyrights in sports, religious, and educational broadcasting would consent to some home videotaping. This finding, however, is relevant only if a significant number of these programs are in fact recorded and on this question little evidence was presented. It is hard to know whether a substantial number of copyright holders whose works are in fact copied would consent to home videotaping. Disney and Universal hold copyrights in 10 percent of network broadcasts during prime time (the hours during the evening between eight and eleven)[16] and the producers of another 80 percent of these broadcasts joined an amicus brief in their support before the Court.[17] Also joining the same brief were many of the copyright holders of programs aired on public television, ranging from *Masterpiece Theater* to *Sesame Street*. Even knowing that 90 percent of the copyright holders of network prime time broadcasts would not consent, however, is not dispositive. Much television broadcasting is not over one of the major networks and much is not shown

---

[15] Under the 1909 Act, a copyright that was properly renewed lasted for fifty-six years. Under the 1976 Act, all works published before 1977 had their copyright term extended an additional nineteen years. Because *The Jazz Singer*, the first feature-length sound film, was not made until 1927, no properly registered sound film will go into the public domain until 2002. See 17 U.S.C. § 304(a)–(b). But see 104 S.Ct. at 789 n.23 ("since copyright protection is not perpetual, the number of audiovisual works in the public domain necessarily increases each year").

[16] Prime viewing hours in the midwest are between seven and ten.

[17] See Brief of Amicus Curiae of Creators and Distributors of Programs, 104 S.Ct. 774 (1984). The Court rejected Universal and Walt Disney's argument that the support of these amici should be considered in weighing whether home videotaping was fair use. See 104 S.Ct. at 785 n.16.

during prime time. Moreover, the crucial issue is how many of those whose programs are copied would refuse to consent, not how many of those whose programs are telecast would refuse to consent. The most frequently copied programs are soap operas, and many of these do not appear in prime time.[18]

Nevertheless, many whose programs are copied would probably not consent. Outside of public television, copyright holders depend on advertisers who are willing to pay for the right to show commercials in conjunction with the broadcast of copyrighted works. Copyright holders such as Disney or Universal are largely motivated by profit, and hence they would refuse to consent if consent reduced the amount advertisers were willing to pay for having programs shown in conjunction with their commercials. The amount advertisers are willing to pay turns on how many and what sort of people watch their commercials. If home videotaping reduces the number of people who watch advertisers' commercials, it will reduce the amount of revenue producers such as Disney and Universal receive. Whether home videotaping reduces the royalties of copyright holders does not merely go to the question of whether copyright holders would consent to it; it is also the crucial component in the calculus of whether home taping is fair use. Under traditional doctrine, home taping should be allowed only if it substantially increases access to copyrighted works without significantly undercutting the producer's incentive.

Video cassette recorders may injure copyright holders in a number of ways. First, they may reduce the number of people who watch the same broadcast more than once. A serious user of a VCR will not watch a program when it is shown a second time with a different set of commercials. Instead, he will tape the show the first time it is aired and watch it again at his own convenience, not when the television station chooses to rebroadcast it. Sales of blank videotapes soared the first time *Gone With the Wind* was shown on network television. Conscientious parents videotape everything from one of the annual showings of *The Wizard of Oz* to weekly broadcasts of the *Smurfs*. As a result, the audience for the second

---

[18] See *The Video Revolution*, NEWSWEEK, August 6, 1984, at 53 (citing an A. C. Nielsen Co. study showing that the most commonly taped programs are *All My Children, General Hospital, Days of Our Lives, As the World Turns, Guiding Light, One Life to Live, Hill Street Blues, Dallas, The Young and the Restless, Dynasty, and Cheers*).

broadcast may become smaller than it would otherwise have been. If the audience is smaller, advertisers will pay less for having their commercials aired. Those who advertised on the first broadcast might pay more, because their commercials might be watched more than once. Nevertheless, the amount advertisers as a group collected might be less with the widespread use of VCRs: Even if those who taped the shows always watched the commercials, some commercials do not stand repeated viewing and many become quickly dated. A commercial announcing a Christmas sale does not have much value in July. As in the case of other empirical questions, the magnitude of this effect is hard to predict. Advertisers could make adjustments. They might run fewer advertisements that became dated. Moreover, the ability of viewers to time-shift might increase the number of people who watch the commercials, because more people would be able to watch the program the first time it is broadcast.

Viewers of videotapes do not usually watch commercials, however. It has always been easy to delete commercials while one is recording. Although the person doing the recording has to watch the commercials the first time, he does not have to watch them again. Moreover, everyone else in the same household (or neighborhood) can take advantage of the efforts of the viewer who does the recording.[19] Even if a program is recorded with commercials, all Betamax machines now come with a fast-forwarding device that allows viewers to scroll past commercials at thirteen times the normal speed without rising from their chairs.

The Court in *Betamax* relied on a factual finding by the District Court that viewers did not in fact fast-forward through commercials.[20] The District Court, however, only had before it information about the first home VCRs that were produced in the mid-1970s. To skip over a commercial with these early machines, viewers needed to leave their chairs, stop the machine, and press the fast-forward button. Moreover, they would have no way of knowing when to stop the tape because they could not see on the television what it was they were skipping. With this primitive technology, trying to avoid commercials was often more trouble than it

---

[19] I know a law professor (at a school other than Chicago) who paid his children to record his favorite television programs without the commercials.

[20] See 104 S.Ct. at 794 n.36.

was worth. The fast-forwarding device that Sony introduced after the trial phase of this litigation eliminated all these problems. The technology now exists to measure which viewers watch programs on videotape, but advertisers will simply not pay for those who watch the programs but not the commercials. If the advertisers pay less, copyright holders such as Walt Disney and Universal will make less.[21]

Some who use a VCR to record a program so that they can watch it later are not those who would have watched the show in the absence of the VCR. A lawyer will regularly record *The Days of Our Lives* by setting the automatic timer on his VCR. When he comes home in the evening, he will watch the program, but skip the commercials. Without the VCR, he would never be able to watch the show. One might argue that the copyright holder should not be able to complain about the additional access of the viewer, because without the VCR, he would not have been able to watch the program at all. In some cases, however, those who time-shift would, if they did not have a VCR, watch the program at the regular time with commercials.[22] Moreover, in asking whether a copyright holder is injured, one must make the appropriate comparison. One should not ask whether the copyright holder is worse off if home videotaping is permitted in a world with VCRs than he would be in a world without VCRs. Rather, the appropriate comparison is whether he would be better off with an exclusive right in a world with VCRs than he would be without such a right in that world.

Under traditional copyright doctrine, copyright holders enjoy the benefit of new technology, even if, in the absence of rights in the new technology, the rewards they enjoyed from preexisting technology would not diminish. A motion picture made from a novel does not diminish sales of the novel. In fact, it usually in-

---

[21] Nor should it be surprising if those whose works appear on public television, on which there are no or very few commercials, would refuse to consent to home videotaping. These producers ordinarily care about being compensated for their efforts and often they disseminate their works both on television and by other means. A movie that is shown on public television may also be available for purchase or rental. Consenting to home videotaping would undercut these markets. Public television, however, depends upon contributions from its viewers, and these might increase if copyright holders consented to some home videotaping. The increased revenues that might result from larger viewer contributions might offset the loss of revenue in other markets.

[22] At the margin, some who would have stayed home and watched *Dallas* with commercials will go to the opera, symphony, or Friday night poker instead because they have a VCR and the ability to watch it later (without commercials).

creases them. Nevertheless, part of the reward for those who write novels is the royalty they can collect from the movie based on the novel. One cannot argue that making a motion picture of a novel is "fair use" because it does not reduce sales of the book. Similarly, under existing doctrine, one should not be able to argue that home videotaping is "fair use" because it does not diminish the revenues of advertisers. The introduction of a new technology provides the artist with a new source of revenue and hence a new incentive to produce. In balancing the access of the public to art and the need to give artists incentives to produce, one cannot ignore the effect a new technology might have on the artist's willingness to produce. If authors can enjoy revenue by distributing another copy of his work, he has always been able to do it. It did not matter if the moviegoers did not read books. By similar logic, it should not matter that many soap opera addicts cannot watch television during the day.

Applying the fair use doctrine in cases such as *Betamax* would be justifiable only if copyright holder, as a general matter, were unable to reach an agreement with the copier. No corresponding reward (and the incentive that accompanies it) would offset the limit on access. The question that must be asked in *Betamax* and all similar cases is whether an agreement between the copyright holder and the copier (or someone who enables him to make the copy) is in fact possible. The experience of such organizations as ASCAP suggests that there are few kinds of copying where users cannot strike some kind of bargain with the copyright holders. By and large, those who set a positive price on viewing a copyrighted work should be able to enjoy access to it and provide a reward to the author at the same time. A number of devices, including most importantly blanket licenses, overcome the problems that would exist in negotiations between a single copyright holder and a single user.[23]

Compensating copyright holders for home videotaping in a world in which there are no substantial noninfringing uses of a

---

[23] See Gordon, note 9 *supra*. I once used the example of students in a classroom singing "Happy Birthday to You" or some other copyrighted song as an example of a *de minimis* use of a copyrighted work that fell within the scope of an artist's exclusive rights, but for which there was no means of collecting a royalty. (In this case, there is the public performance of a copyrighted work within the meaning of 17 U.S.C. § 106(4).) I stopped when a person in one class pointed out that the performance would be within the scope of a blanket license the university had negotiated with ASCAP.

VCR is possible. Holders of copyrights in television programming could form an ASCAP-like organization and condition Sony's sale of these machines on the payment of a flat fee, which Sony could then incorporate into the sale price. There is a holdout problem that might make this solution difficult to reach through private negotiations. Individual copyright holders would have an incentive not to join the organization and to threaten to bring individual actions against Sony. But the existence of the license would render the individual action ineffective. The argument that there were no substantial noninfringing uses would be unavailable if a number of copyright holders agreed to waive their rights in return for a fee.

The Court rejected Walt Disney and Universal's action against Sony because it thought time-shifting was fair use. It reached this conclusion in large part because Disney and Universal had not shown that time-shifting harmed them. The Court did not recognize that time-shifting probably reduces revenues for copyright holders, because most of those who time-shift do not watch commercials. Second, the Court did not squarely confront the nature of the copyright holder's damages, which included not merely lost advertising revenues, but the lost opportunity to exploit a new technology.

The failure of the Court to confront existing copyright doctrine and existing technology stems in large measure from the nature of litigation. An adversary process works effectively only as long as the process has an end as well as a beginning and all parties are bound by the record they create. The Court was bound by a record created in the mid-1970s, even though as a practical matter, it was reconciling both the technology and the law as they existed in 1984.

The Court also failed to evaluate the nature of Disney and Universal's damages, because it placed upon the plaintiffs the burden of showing injury and it found that they had not done so. Because the question of the damages Disney and Universal experienced arose in the context of Sony's argument that time-shifting was fair use, the Court probably placed the burden on the wrong party. The fair use doctrine is an exception to the usual rule that the copyright holder has the exclusive right to make copies. The burden of proving its elements, which include the lack of injury to the plaintiff, should rest on the defendant, the party claiming the exception. The more important point, however, goes not to the lawyer's issue of which party should bear the burden of proof, but to the way in which an adversary process is time-bound. Disney and Universal had to bring their action shortly after Sony introduced its machine, or the Betamax would have become so established that it would no longer be possible to obtain an effective remedy. Disney and Universal would be held to have slept on their rights. But at the time of the initial suit, when only a few hundred thousand machines had been sold, it was very difficult to gather information about how machines were used or what losses copyright holders would suffer.

II

Putting *Betamax* in perspective requires asking several additional questions. The first is the question what the stakes were, whether it made any difference how the Court decided the case. As to the first question, the stakes may have been smaller than many thought. Disney and Universal have many ways of disseminating a copyrighted work. They can show it in first-run movie theaters. They can sell copies to the general public. They can rent copies to the public. They can show their works on cable television. Copying may take place in some of these markets as well, but the dissemination of the work is to a more limited audience. Typically, producers will combine these various avenues of publication. Disney and Universal may not be that much worse off if they cannot control home use of the VCR. The rewards they capture may be only slightly smaller, and the largest effect may be not so much on what they produce, but rather on how they distribute it.[24]

In the world that exists after the Court's decision, movie producers may license fewer of their films for broadcast and those they do license may be released only after other markets (such as the home video rental market and the cable television market) have been exhausted. Ironically, those that suffer the most from the Court's decision may be neither Disney, Universal, nor consumers who have bought videotape machines, but television networks and consumers who have not bought them. Consumers who have VCRs

---

[24] One suspects that Walt Disney and Universal would not have litigated the case if they did not see that the benefits from succeeding (discounted by the probability of success) were greater than the costs of litigation. But the market (particularly the development of video rentals and cable television) has changed significantly since the litigation began. Moreover, the cost of the litigation (probably no more than several million dollars) is quite small relative to the revenue of the industry as a whole even in a single year. It may be worth litigating questions that will produce only small changes in the structure of the industry.

will be able to rent movies and Disney and Universal will enjoy revenues from these and other activities. In the process, however, television may have less attractive programming and fewer people may watch it. *Betamax*, if it has any substantial effect, may accelerate the decline of unscrambled over-the-air telecasts that new technologies are bound to bring about in any event.

But even this analysis may overstate the effects of the decision. Given existing notions of contributory infringement, the most that Walt Disney and Universal could have hoped for would have been an injunction against the manufacture of VCRs with built-in television tuners. It is only the existence of the tuner that makes possible the characterization that the Betamax is a machine whose only substantial use is the copying of copyrighted work. Because of the booming market in video rentals and because of the ready availability and increasing popularity of cheap, compact, and high quality video cameras, substantial noninfringing uses now exist for video recorders without tuners. Granting Walt Disney and Universal control over them would allow them to exploit the benefit consumers derived from all these other uses of the Betamax that do not come within the domain of the exclusive rights Congress gave them.

Yet an injunction against the manufacture of VCRs with tuners would change the world little. Those who wanted to build permanent libraries or simply time-shift would not be deterred. Instead of a VCR with a television tuner, one would need only a VCR without a tuner and a television with a video output jack. Most televisions now manufactured have one or easily could have one. The principal effect would be to prevent people who owned only one television from watching one program while recording another. The strategy of trying to prevent home video libraries or home time-shifting may have been doomed from the start.

In much of the debate over *Betamax*, little attention has been paid to whether the basic way in which the incentive-access principle is implemented is sound. Given television and videotape, it costs almost the same to show a film to a hundred people as to a million.[25]

---

[25] Motion pictures and other works of intellectual property come close to being public goods, although, unlike public goods such as national defense, exclusive ownership of them is possible. See Demsetz, *The Private Production of Public Goods*, 13 J.L. & ECON. 293 (1970). Of course, to say that motion pictures can be disseminated to additional people at little extra cost is not to say they can be distributed at no extra cost. See Stigler, *An Introduction to Privacy in Economics and Politics*, 9 J. LEGAL STUD. 623, 640–41 (1980).

The initial costs of creating a work may be staggeringly high, but the cost of providing it to an additional consumer is almost negligible. If the producer of a copyrighted work could price discriminate perfectly (and critical uses of the copyrighted work were not in issue), we could give that producer complete rights to the work and not concern ourselves with any of the problems of balancing the rights of the creators and consumers of copyrighted works. The producer would ensure that all who set a positive value on the work had access to it. But because perfect price discrimination is not possible, we draw limits upon the rights of the initial producer. A question we must ask is whether the limits that copyright law places upon the rights of the producer are appropriate.

Betamax turned crucially on the central importance copyright law attaches to the making of physical copies of works. It may no longer be appropriate to implement the balance between access and incentive in this way. Copyright law has traditionally given producers like Walt Disney the exclusive right to make copies except in those cases in which it lacked the ability to exploit this right, and hence the right reduced access without providing any offsetting incentive. Being true to this tradition might require a result opposite to the one we encountered in *Betamax*, but this argument may be incomplete. The traditional notion that an author should have the exclusive right to make copies is not inevitable. It does not necessarily fully implement the goals of the copyright clause of the Constitution when at issue is home videotaping or the copying of different kinds of computer software.[26]

One can make similar observations about other features of our copyright law, such as the first-sale doctrine.[27] Under traditional doctrine, a copyright holder can always prevent someone from making a copy, but once a copyright holder sells a copy he cannot prevent the purchaser from lending it to someone else. One might argue that despite traditional notions of copyright Walt Disney should not be able to prevent someone from videotaping *Snow White* when it broadcasts it on television. But one could challenge the first-sale doctrine equally well. Under current law, Disney will

---

[26] The scope of the protection for computer programs is not clear. See 17 U.S.C. § 117; Apple Computer, Inc. v. Franklin Computer Corp., 714 F.2d 1240 (3d Cir. 1983).

[27] See 17 U.S.C. § 109; Bobbs-Merrill Co. v. Straus, 210 U.S. 339 (1908). Congress limited the reach of the first-sale doctrine for phonograph records in 1984.

charge the same price to the home consumer who watches the cassette only once or twice a year as to the video store owner who rents it to a different customer every day, unless it has some way of identifying home users and some means of making sure they do not resell their copies to video stores. One can justify any rule of copyright either on the ground that it provides an incentive for authors or that it promotes access to copyrighted works. Such justifications are, however, somewhat ad hoc, and many copyright doctrine are as much a result of nineteenth-century formalisms as anything else. In the case of the first-sale doctrine, the formalism is that a covenant runneth not with a chattel.

In a world in which one wants to fine-tune the balance between access and incentive, it is far from given that it is better to forbid others from copying and forbid the copyright owner from retaining strings following sale than some other rule. Indeed, it is hard to tell, once one prohibits widescale commercial piracy, whether it makes much difference ultimately how the particular balance is struck. The only discernible effect may be on how works are disseminated, not what works are produced or who enjoys them.

In this last respect, *Betamax* may be both unlike most Supreme Court litigation and like most other kinds of litigation. The stakes when many cases are decided are quite small as far as the commonweal is concerned, not because parties fail to perceive their own interests, but because the principal effect of the law on our lives comes not from disputes at the margin, but from the most well-settled doctrine. At the edges, the stakes are often relatively small and the ability of parties to pilot their way around legal rules relatively large.

STEPHEN H. LEGOMSKY

IMMIGRATION LAW AND THE PRINCIPLE OF PLENARY CONGRESSIONAL POWER

Immigration law is a constitutional oddity. "Over no conceivable subject," the Supreme Court has repeatedly said, "is the legislative power of Congress more complete."[1] At the heart of that sentiment lies the "plenary power" doctrine, under which the Court has declined to review federal immigration statutes for compliance with substantive constitutional restraints. In an undeviating line of cases spanning almost one hundred years, the Court has declared itself powerless to review even those immigration provisions that explicitly classify on such disfavored bases as race, gender, and legitimacy.[2]

Why has all this happened? What is it about immigration that has engendered such radical judicial restraint? My view is that the explanation lies in the convergence of misconceived doctrinal theory with a range of external forces, and my conclusion is that the Court should abandon the special deference it has accorded Congress in the field of immigration.

Stephen H. Legomsky is Associate Professor of Law, Washington University School of Law.

AUTHOR'S NOTE.—The author gratefully acknowledges the thoughtful comments provided on previous drafts by Alex Aleinikoff, Patty Blum, Paul Craig, Jules Gerard, Bruce La Pierre, David Martin, Frank Miller, and Peter Mutharika.

[1] See Oceanic Steam Navigation Co. v. Stranahan, 214 U.S. 320, 339 (1909), quoted approvingly in Fiallo v. Bell, 430 U.S. 787, 792 (1977); Kleindienst v. Mandel, 408 U.S. 753, 766 (1972). Accord, Oloteo v. I.N.S., 643 F.2d 679, 680 (9th Cir. 1981).

[2] See, *e.g.*, Fiallo v. Bell, 430 U.S. 787 (1977) (gender and legitimacy); Fong Yue Ting v. United States, 149 U.S. 698 (1893) (race); Chae Chan Ping v. United States, 130 U.S. 581 (1889) (race).

For purposes of my argument, the term "immigration law" will be used to describe the body of law governing the admission and the expulsion of aliens. That is the sphere in which the plenary power doctrine has operated. It should be distinguished from the more general law of aliens' rights and obligations. Common issues encompassed by the latter include aliens' eligibility for social welfare programs, for selected occupations, and for government employment; limitations on aliens' rights to own land; aliens' tax liabilities; and aliens' military status.[3] In mild contrast with the plenary Congressional power over immigration, the Supreme Court has acknowledged that federal statutes in the aliens' rights area are reviewed for rationality when challenged as discriminatory, though admittedly that review has not been intensive in practice.[4] In addition, with one rapidly expanding exception,[5] state action classifying on the basis of alienage has been subjected to strict scrutiny.[6]

Even when the term "immigration" is defined in its strict sense, the plenary power doctrine has several dimensions that require explanation. It has, first, a territorial dimension. Immigration law distinguishes the exclusion of aliens who are outside the United States and seeking admission from the deportation of aliens who are within the United States seeking only to avoid expulsion.[7] The

---

[3] The leading work is MUTHARIKA, THE ALIEN UNDER AMERICAN LAW (1981) (2 vols.). See also CARLINER, THE RIGHTS OF ALIENS (1977); DAWSON & HEAD, INTERNATIONAL LAW, NATIONAL TRIBUNALS, AND THE RIGHTS OF ALIENS (1971); 1 GORDON & ROSENFIELD, IMMIGRATION LAW AND PROCEDURE §§ 1.30–1.46 (1984); KONVITZ, THE ALIEN AND THE ASIATIC IN AMERICAN LAW 148–218 (1946); cf. Weisman, *Restrictions on the Acquisition of Land by Aliens*, 28 AM. J. COMP. L. 39 (1980) (comparative study).

[4] Mathews v. Diaz, 426 U.S. 67, 82–83 (1976); Flemming v. Nestor, 363 U.S. 603, 611 (1960); cf. Hampton v. Mow Sun Wong, 426 U.S. 88, 103 (1976) (rational basis for Congressional action will be presumed to be actual basis).

[5] States may constitutionally disqualify aliens from participating in the political community, a term that has been defined with remarkable breadth. See, *e.g.*, County of Los Angeles v. Chavez-Salido, 436 U.S. 901 (1978); Foley v. Connelie, 435 U.S. 291 (1978); Skafte v. Rorex, 553 P.2d 830 (Col. 1976), *appeal dismissed*, 430 U.S. 961 (1977). But see Bernal v. Fainter, 104 S.Ct. 2312 (1984).

[6] See Bernal v. Fainter, 104 S.Ct. 2312 (1984); Nyquist v. Mauclet, 432 U.S. 1 (1977); Douglas v. Seacoast Products, Inc., 431 U.S. 265 (1977); Examining Bd. of Engineers, Architects, and Surveyors v. Flores de Otero, 426 U.S. 572 (1976); In re Griffiths, 413 U.S. 634 (1973); Sugarman v. Dougall, 413 U.S. 634 (1973); Graham v. Richardson, 403 U.S. 365 (1971); cf. Plyler v. Doe, 457 U.S. 202 (1982) (state denial of free public education to undocumented alien children violates equal protection).

[7] See generally GORDON & ROSENFIELD, note 3 *supra*, chs. 2, 4.

plenary power doctrine originated in the context of exclusion,[8] but it was soon extended to deportation[9] with certain qualifications noted below.[10]

The doctrine also has a temporal dimension. In the early years, the Court disavowed in absolute terms any judicial power to review the constitutionality of immigration legislation.[11] The more recent cases, in contrast, contain language that appears to leave the door slightly ajar.[12]

There is, moreover, what might be termed an organic dimension. In the typical case, the governmental organ whose power over immigration is held to be plenary is Congress.[13] Occasionally, however, the doctrine has effectively been extended to cover action of the Immigration and Naturalization Service (INS) as well.[14]

---

[8] Ekiu v. United States, 142 U.S. 651 (1892); Chae Chan Ping v. United States, 130 U.S. 581 (1889).

[9] Fong Yue Ting v. United States, 149 U.S. 698 (1893). Accord, Galvan v. Press, 347 U.S. 522 (1954); Harisiades v. Shaughnessy, 342 U.S. 580 (1952); United States ex rel. Turner v. Williams, 194 U.S. 279 (1904). But see the vigorous objections of Justice Brewer in *Fong Yue Ting*, 149 U.S. at 738. See also Hesse, *The Constitutional Status of the Lawfully Admitted Permanent Resident Alien: The Inherent Limits of the Power to Expel*, 69 YALE L.J. 262 (1959); Hesse, *The Constitutional Status of the Lawfully Admitted Permanent Resident Alien: The Pre-1917 Cases*, 68 YALE L.J. 1578 (1959).

[10] See notes 23–24 *infra* and accompanying text.

[11] *E.g.*, Lees v. United States, 150 U.S. 476, 480 (1893) (Congressional exclusion power is "absolute" and "not open to challenge in the courts"); Fong Yue Ting v. United States, 149 U.S. 698, 706 (1893) ("conclusive upon the Judiciary"); Ekiu v. United States, 142 U.S. 651, 659 (1892) (power "belongs to the political department"); Chae Chan Ping v. United States, 130 U.S. 581, 606 (1889) ("conclusive upon the Judiciary").

[12] *E.g.*, Fiallo v. Bell, 430 U.S. 787, 792 (1977) (power "*largely* immune" from judicial review) (emphasis added), 793 n.5 (accepting a "limited" judicial responsibility to review even those Congressional decisions concerning the exclusion of aliens); Harisiades v. Shaughnessy, 342 U.S. 580, 588–89 (1952) (Congressional decision "largely immune from judicial interference"); *cf.* Kleindienst v. Mandel, 408 U.S. 753, 769, 770 (1972) (executive action excluding alien withstands First Amendment challenge at least when "facially legitimate and bona fide" reason given). See especially the discussion of *Chadha*, notes 226–43 *infra* and accompanying text.

[13] See notes 7–12 *supra* and notes 15–26 *infra* and accompanying text.

[14] In Kleindienst v. Mandel, 408 U.S. 753 (1972), an alien was excluded under statutory provisions barring the admission of those who advocate, 8 U.S.C. § 1182(a)(28)(D), or write about, *id.* § 1182 (a)(28)(G)(v), world Communism. The statute allowed for discretionary waivers in the case of nonimmigrants. *Id.* § 1182(c)(3). The INS denied discretionary relief. The American university professors who had invited the alien to speak argued that, as applied by the INS, the statute violated their First Amendment rights. Although restrictions on political speech are ordinarily subjected to rigorous review, see note 21 *infra*, the Court relied on the plenary power doctrine, 408 U.S. at 765–67, in holding that the presence of a "facially legitimate and bona fide reason" would be enough to validate the executive action. When foreign affairs are implicated, some of the lower court decisions involving Iranian

Finally, the principle of plenary Congressional power over immigration has a rights dimension. Cutting across a wide spectrum of individual rights, the principle has been applied with greatest consistency to challenges based on constitutional provisions that protect substantive rights. As will be seen, its application to procedural due process is less certain.

Among the constitutional attacks on various immigration provisions have been those invoking substantive components of Fifth Amendment due process. Whether the claim is based directly on the infringement of a liberty interest or on discrimination between specified classes of aliens, the Supreme Court has effectively withheld review in those cases.[15]

The deference was especially noticeable in *Fiallo v. Bell*.[16] At issue was the constitutionality of an Immigration and Nationality Act provision discriminating against aliens who were illegitimate children and against the alien fathers of illegitimate American citizen children.[17] The classifications thus turned not only on alienage but also on such normally well scrutinized criteria as gender and legitimacy. The interest of which the plaintiffs were being deprived, though not one the Court has recognized as fundamental,[18] was an important one—family reunification. And, as the alien pointed out,[19] judicial review would in no way affect foreign affairs. Again, however, the Court declared the Congressional power "largely immune from judicial control" and declined to intervene.[20]

Similarly selective restraint is evident in those immigration cases raising First Amendment issues. During this century, the Court

---

students similarly suggest a plenary INS power. See notes 203–12 *infra* and accompanying text.

[15] *E.g.*, Fiallo v. Bell, 430 U.S. 787, 792 (1977) ("largely immune from judicial control"); Galvan v. Press, 347 U.S. 522, 530–31 (1954) ("formulation of these policies is entrusted exclusively to Congress"); Harisiades v. Shaughnessy, 342 U.S. 580, 588–89 (1952) ("largely immune from judicial interference"); Lees v. United States, 150 U.S. 476, 480 (1893) ("not open to challenge in the courts").

[16] 430 U.S. 787 (1977).

[17] 8 U.S.C. § 1101(b)(1)(D).

[18] Justice Marshall, dissenting, argued *inter alia* that the interest in family unity should be regarded as fundamental. 430 U.S. at 810.

[19] 430 U.S. at 796.

[20] *Id.* at 792. Compare *Fiallo* with Trimble v. Gordon, 430 U.S. 762 (1977). In *Trimble*, decided the same day as *Fiallo*, the Court struck down a state statute that prevented illegitimate children from inheriting by intestate succession from their fathers. But see *Fiallo*, 430 U.S. at 793 n.5 (accepting some limited judicial responsibility even in immigration cases).

has ordinarily reviewed speech restrictions by balancing the individual interest in free expression against the governmental interest asserted as a justification for restricting that freedom. Although the standards have varied, the Court has always required an unusually important governmental interest before upholding an infringement on political speech.[21] In the immigration cases, in contrast, the Court has relied on the plenary power doctrine to avoid performing *any* balancing of the relevant countervailing interests.[22]

The one partial exception to the absolute character of Congress's power over immigration concerns procedural due process. Despite a leading early decision to the contrary,[23] it is now accepted that aliens undergoing deportation proceedings are entitled to procedural due process.[24] The same principle seems to extend to those exclusion proceedings in which the aliens are returning residents, although again the cases are in conflict.[25] But when aliens are ex-

---

[21] To justify a deprivation of free political expression, the Supreme Court has required a "clear and present danger" of a sufficiently important evil, Dennis v. United States, 341 U.S. 494 (1951); Whitney v. California, 274 U.S. 357 (1927); Gitlow v. New York, 268 U.S. 652 (1925); Schenck v. United States, 249 U.S. 47 (1919); an actual incitement to violence, as distinguished from mere advocacy of an abstract doctrine, Yates v. United States, 354 U.S. 298 (1957); necessity to a compelling governmental interest, LaMont v. Postmaster General, 381 U.S. 301, 308 (1965); N.A.A.C.P. v. Button, 371 U.S. 415, 438 (1963); an intent to incite lawless action and a likelihood of doing so, Brandenburg v. Ohio, 395 U.S. 444 (1969); imminent danger of lawlessness, Hess v. Indiana, 414 U.S. 105 (1973). *Cf.* Shelton v. Tucker, 364 U.S. 479 (1960) (strict scrutiny of means used to achieve asserted governmental interest). For the history of the "clear and present danger" test, see KONVITZ, FIRST AMENDMENT FREEDOMS (1963); KONVITZ, FUNDAMENTAL LIBERTIES OF A FREE PEOPLE: RELIGION, SPEECH, PRESS, ASSEMBLY 280–341 (1957). See also EMERSON, THE SYSTEM OF FREEDOM OF EXPRESSION (1970); Emerson, *Toward a General Theory of the First Amendment*, 72 YALE L.J. 877 (1963); Fuchs, *Further Steps toward a General Theory of Freedom of Expression*, 18 WM. & MARY L. REV. 347 (1976).

[22] See, *e.g.*, Kleindienst v. Mandel, 408 U.S. 753, 769, 770 (1972); Harisiades v. Shaughnessy, 342 U.S. 580, 591–92 (1952); United States *ex rel.* Turner v. Williams, 194 U.S. 279, 294 (1904). Although the standard of review in the immigration cases has not matched that in other First Amendment cases, no view is expressed here as to the correctness of the ultimate results. But see Note, *First Amendment and the Alien Exclusion Power—What Standard of Review?* 4 CARDOZO L. REV. 457 (1983).

[23] Fong Yue Ting v. United States, 149 U.S. 698 (1893).

[24] Wong Yang Sun v. McGrath, 339 U.S. 33 (1950); Yamataya v. Fisher, 189 U.S. 86, 100 (1903) (dictum); *cf.* Ng Fung Ho v. White, 259 U.S. 276 (1922) (deportation of citizenship claimants). For subsequent qualifications of *Ng Fung Ho*, see Kessler v. Strecker, 307 U.S. 22, 34–35 (1939) (dictum); United States *ex rel.* Bilokumsky v. Tod, 263 U.S. 149 (1923). For the statutory response, see 8 U.S.C. §§ 1252(b) (general deportation procedure), 1105a(a)(5) (citizenship claimants).

[25] See Kwong Hai Chew v. Colding, 344 U.S. 590 (1953) (interpreting regulation as affording procedural protection to returning residents, so as to avoid constitutional doubts); *cf.* Kwock Jan Fat v. White, 253 U.S. 454 (1920) (returning resident who claims citizenship is

cluded as an initial matter, the law still appears to be as it was stated in *United States ex rel. Knauff v. Shaughnessy:* "Whatever the procedure authorized by Congress is, it is due process as far as an alien denied entry is concerned."[26]

I. THE THEORY

As the preceding discussion illustrates, immigration is an area in which the normal rules of constitutional law simply do not apply. What rationales might be invoked to support these judicial departures from established constitutional norms?

The theories criticized in this section are policy based. Apart from the weaknesses that they contain, the principle of special judicial abstinence in immigration cases cannot be justified even as a matter of precedent. A full historical treatment of the plenary power doctrine, from its origins to its current state, is beyond the scope of the present article. I do attempt such an analysis, however, in a separate paper now in progress. The argument will be that the Court's abdication of its ordinary constitutional functions evolved partly through an inadvertent fusion of federalism with individual rights. However, for present purposes, the Court's interpretations of its prior immigration decisions are assumed to be correct.

It will sometimes be necessary again to distinguish exclusion from deportation and procedure from substance. Surprisingly, most of the theories offered to support the plenary power doctrine and most of my criticisms of those theories will be seen to engulf both distinctions. When a particular argument is not equally applicable to all combinations, the differences will be pointed out.

With respect to procedural due process, a final qualification is necessary. As the Supreme Court observed in *Mathews v. Eldridge*,[27]

---

entitled to procedural due process). However, in Shaughnessy v. United States *ex rel.* Mezei, 345 U.S. 206 (1953), the Court rejected a procedural due process challenge by characterizing the regulation of aliens as "a fundamental sovereign attribute exercised by the Government's political departments largely immune from judicial control." *Id.* at 210. It distinguished *Chew* on such narrow grounds, see *id.* at 213–14, that the latter decision appeared to retain very limited vitality. But in Landon v. Plasencia, 103 S.Ct. 321, 329 (1982), the Court cited *Chew* approvingly. Explicitly holding that a returning resident alien is entitled to procedural due process, the Supreme Court left to the lower court the task of determining what process was due. See *Recent Development, Immigration Law: Process Due Resident Aliens upon Entering the United States,* 24 HARV. INT'L L.J. 198 (1983).

[26] 338 U.S. 537, 544 (1950). Accord, Landon v. Plasencia, 103 S.Ct. 321, 329 (1982) (dictum). For the statutory procedure, see 8 U.S.C. § 1226.

[27] 424 U.S. 319 (1976).

the scope of procedural protection afforded by the due process clause is a function of, *inter alia*, the magnitude of the individual interest at stake. One might assume that an alien seeking admission as an initial matter typically asserts a lesser individual interest than, say, a lawfully admitted permanent resident alien resisting deportation. Under that assumption, there is reason to provide less procedural protection in exclusion proceedings than in deportation proceedings. As others have shown, however, it does not follow that an excluded alien is constitutionally entitled to no procedural due process.[28] Important individual interests might well be at stake even in exclusion proceedings, and in any event it would be wrong to ignore crucial differences within the class of excluded aliens. The discussions in these writings amply address the argument that excluded aliens lack a sufficiently important personal interest to trigger procedural due process.

A. THE POLITICAL QUESTION THEORY: FOREIGN AFFAIRS[29]

Perhaps the most popular theory in support of the plenary power doctrine has been that the constitutionality of an immigration provision is a political question because foreign relations are implicated. Vague references to either foreign affairs or political questions have surfaced in some of the plenary power cases.[30] Judicial perceptions of foreign policy ingredients have prompted others to describe at least some of the plenary power cases as applications of the political question doctrine.[31] To the extent that the deference in immigration cases is based on the courts' general reluctance to interfere with the conduct of foreign relations, two assumptions are being made: that immigration decisions inherently affect foreign

---

[28] *E.g.*, Martin, *Due Process and Membership in the National Community: Political Asylum and Beyond*, 44 U. PITT. L. REV. 165 (1983); Aleinikoff, *Aliens, Due Process and "Community Ties": A Response to Martin*, 44 U. PITT. L. REV. 237 (1983).

[29] For general treatment of the political question doctrine, see NOWAK, ROTUNDA, & YOUNG, CONSTITUTIONAL LAW 109–20 (2d ed. 1983); TRIBE, AMERICAN CONSTITUTIONAL LAW 71–79 (1978); Weston, *Political Questions*, 38 HARV. L. REV. 296 (1925); Henkin, *Is There a "Political Question" Doctrine?* 85 YALE L.J. 597 (1976); Scharpf, *Judicial Review and the Political Question: A Functional Analysis*, 75 YALE L.J. 517 (1966).

[30] *E.g.*, Kleindienst v. Mandel, 408 U.S. 753, 766 n.6. (1972); Galvan v. Press, 347 U.S. 522, 530 (1954); Harisiades v. Shaughnessy, 342 U.S. 580, 588–91 (1952); United States *ex rel.* Knauff v. Shaughnessy, 338 U.S. 537, 542 (1950); Fong Yue Ting v. United States, 149 U.S. 698, 705–06 (1893).

[31] *E.g.*, KONVITZ, CIVIL RIGHTS IN IMMIGRATION 44 (1953); Scharpf, note 29 *supra*, at 579–81.

policy; and that decisions affecting foreign policy are political questions. Both assumptions require examination.

The connection between immigration and foreign policy derives ultimately from the fact that an immigration decision operates on the subject of a foreign state. Because a foreign state may intervene diplomatically on behalf of its nationals,[32] an adverse decision carries the potential for international tension. Moreover, even a decision favorable to the immigrant could undercut the bargaining power of the decision-making state in its negotiations with the state of which the immigrant is a national.[33]

For those reasons, there will certainly be times when a particular immigration provision, as applied to a particular fact situation, is so inextricably bound up with foreign policy that a court should not intrude. There might even be particular provisions that fit that description in all fact situations to which they could conceivably be applied. But it ignores reality to hold that every provision concerned with immigration, as applied to every fact situation it might encompass, is so intimately rooted in foreign policy that the usual scope of judicial review would hamper the effective conduct of foreign relations.[34] In *Fiallo*, for example, the Supreme Court assumed that no foreign affairs problem was present, but dismissed that fact as irrelevant, observing that in previous cases the scope of review had not depended on "the nature of the policy choice at issue."[35] Nor did the Second Circuit Court of Appeals precipitate a world crisis when it held in *Francis v. I.N.S.* that the availability of discretionary relief could not constitutionally be conditioned on the alien having left and returned to the United States.[36]

The Court's blanket technique of mechanically labeling immigration decisions as so ensconced in foreign policy that constitutional review is improper has precluded consideration of whether foreign

---

[32] See Sec. Ic *infra*.

[33] *E.g.*, Harisiades v. Shaughnessy, 342 U.S. 580, 591 (1952); *cf.* Hampton v. Mow Sun Wong, 426 U.S. 88, 104 (1976) (barring aliens from federal civil service permits President to bargain for reciprocal concessions).

[34] Even Congress seems to have discounted the foreign policy aspects of individual immigration decisions. It has vested principal control of immigration in the INS, which is part of the Justice Department; the State Department, whose responsibilities lie in the field of foreign affairs, has only a secondary role in administering the immigration laws. Compare 8 U.S.C. § 1103(a) with *id.* §§ 1104(a), 1201.

[35] 430 U.S. at 796.

[36] 532 F.2d 268 (2d Cir. 1976), discussed in notes 217–22 *infra* and accompanying text.

affairs were actually affected. A better approach would be to reserve the judicial deference for the special case in which the court concludes, after a realistic appraisal, that applying the normal standards of review would interfere with the conduct of foreign policy.

One might object that such an inquiry is too speculative. It might be argued that it would be worse to second-guess Congress on a matter as sensitive as immigration than it would be to sacrifice constitutional review in those cases that actually present no foreign policy problems.

Perhaps that is a valid argument for giving Congress the benefit of the doubt in close cases. But there is no need to throw out the baby with the bathwater. Several factors are available for a court to consider. Submissions by the government can be weighed. The legislative history of the particular statute can be consulted.[37] That a statutory provision deals only with immigrants of selected nationalities, and not with immigrants or aliens generally, is some evidence of a legislative focus on international relations. That evidence is not conclusive; the early plenary power cases discussed above, for example, dealt principally with statutory provisions that were limited to Asian immigrants and that can be explained far more convincingly by the domestic political forces discussed below. In other cases, however, statutory references to nationals of specified countries can be highly persuasive evidence that foreign affairs were considered. The Presidential Order and administrative regulations challenged in the Iranian cases are clear examples.[38] And statutes regulating alien enemies should certainly be assumed to reflect policy determinations that affect foreign affairs.[39]

Even when a particular immigration case is believed likely to present foreign policy considerations, it does not follow that the question is political. There has indeed been occasional judicial rhetoric suggesting that courts may never review the propriety of executive or Congressional acts in the field of foreign relations.[40] There have also, admittedly, been many cases in which the foreign

---

[37] *E.g.*, Silverman v. Rogers, 437 F.2d 102 (1st Cir. 1970).

[38] See notes 203–12 *supra* and accompanying text.

[39] See, *e.g.*, Johnson v. Eisentrager, 339 U.S. 763 (1950); Ludecke v. Watkins, 335 U.S. 160 (1948). But *cf.* Ex parte Kawato, 317 U.S. 69 (1942) (resident alien enemy has standing to sue in federal court).

[40] See, *e.g.*, Oetjen v. Central Leather Co., 246 U.S. 297, 302 (1918), acknowledged in Baker v. Carr, 369 U.S. 186, 211 n.31 (1962).

policy ramifications have in fact induced the courts to withhold review.[41]

At no time, however, have the courts gone to the extreme of refusing to review all decisions having possible effects on foreign policy. The courts have been adventurous in cases presenting such sensitive questions as human rights violations by foreign governments,[42] publication of the Pentagon papers,[43] certain passport issues,[44] certain military matters,[45] acquisition and loss of citizenship,[46] and even the legality of a Presidential Order seizing steel mills to avoid disruption of a war effort.[47] The constitutional text makes equally clear that the presence of foreign policy elements does not necessarily preclude review. It confers on the federal courts the jurisdiction to hear cases arising under treaties, cases affecting ambassadors, and disputes between an American state or

---

[41] *E.g.*, Goldwater v. Carter, 444 U.S. 996, 1003 (1979); Chicago & Southern Air Lines, Inc. v. Waterman Steamship Corp., 333 U.S. 103 (1948); Holtzman v. Schlesinger, 484 F.2d 1307 (2d Cir. 1973); Atlee v. Laird, 347 F. Supp. 689 (E.D. Pa. 1972). See also Baker v. Carr, 369 U.S. 186, 213–14 (1962) (summarizing cases refusing to review determinations of whether armed hostilities had ceased).

[42] Filartiga v. Pena-Irala, 630 F.2d 876 (2d Cir. 1980); Letelier v. Republic of Chile, 488 F. Supp. 665 and 502 F. Supp. 259 (D.D.C. 1980).

[43] New York Times Co. v. United States, 403 U.S. 713 (1971).

[44] *E.g.*, Aptheker v. United States, 378 U.S. 500 (1964); Kent v. Dulles, 357 U.S. 116 (1958).

[45] Kinsella v. United States *ex rel.* Singleton, 361 U.S. 234 (1960); Grisham v. Hagan, 361 U.S. 278 (1960); *cf.* Sterling v. Constantin, 287 U.S. 378 (1932) (state proclamation of marital law). But see Chappell v. Wallace, 103 S.Ct. 2362 (1983); Feres v. United States, 340 U.S. 135 (1950).

[46] In contrast with the uniform deference characterizing constitutional review of exclusion and deportation statutes have been the mixed results and the frequent assertiveness in the citizenship cases. On acquisition of citizenship, compare Rogers v. Bellei, 401 U.S. 815 (1971) (reasonableness test applied, though provision ultimately held reasonable); United States v. Wong Kim Ark, 169 U.S. 649 (1898) with Terrace v. Thompson, 263 U.S. 197, 220 (1923) (dictum); Elk v. Wilkins, 112 U.S. 94 (1884); Scott v. Sandford, 60 U.S. (19 How.) 393 (1856). For two extremes on the judicial role in reviewing challenges to naturalization requirements, compare In re Naturalization of 68 Filipino War Veterans, 406 F. Supp. 931 (N.D. Cal. 1975) (strict scrutiny) with Trujillo-Hernandez v. Farrell, 503 F.2d 954 (5th Cir. 1974) (nonjusticiable). See especially *Wong Kim Ark*, discussed in text accompanying notes 97–98 *infra*. The constitutional cases on loss of citizenship are similarly mixed. Compare Afoyim v. Rusk, 387 U.S. 253 (1967); Schneider v. Rusk, 377 U.S. 163 (1964); Kennedy v. Mendoza-Martinez, 372 U.S. 144 (1963); Trop v. Dulles, 356 U.S. 86 (1958); Perkins v. Elg, 307 U.S. 325 (1939) with Marks v. Esperdy, 377 U.S. 214 (1964); Perez v. Brownell, 356 U.S. 44 (1958), *overruled by Afroyim;* Savorgnan v. United States, 338 U.S. 491 (1950); Mackenzie v. Hare, 239 U.S. 299 (1915); Luria v. United States, 231 U.S. 9 (1913); Johannessen v. United States, 225 U.S. 227 (1912).

[47] Youngstown Sheet and Tube Co. v. Sawyer [The Steel Seizure Case], 343 U.S. 579 (1952).

its citizens and a foreign state or its citizens.[48] A federal statute provides specifically for suits against aliens, including alien diplomats.[49] Commentators, too, are in broad agreement that not all matters affecting foreign policy are beyond judicial cognizance.[50]

Thus, some questions affecting foreign policy have been reviewed and some have not. That indeed was a central message of *Baker v. Carr*, where the Supreme Court made clear that the classification of a particular decision as "political" requires a "discriminating inquiry into the precise facts and posture of the particular case, and the impossibility of resolution by any semantic cataloguing."[51] The plenary power doctrine, in contrast, assumes that immigration matters necessarily generate the kind of foreign policy problems that defy judicial resolution. To that extent, the cases have avoided the individualizing wisely prescribed, and have resorted to the "semantic cataloguing" soundly rejected, in *Baker*.

But if cataloging immigration cases is to be replaced by a more tailored approach, it becomes important to develop principles for determining whether an immigration case is too deeply rooted in foreign policy considerations to be subjected to normal judicial review. To formulate such principles, it is first necessary to identify those characteristics of foreign policy decisions that make judicial deference desirable. The principles can then be expressed in terms of the presence of those characteristics in the individual case.

Three such characteristics, all common features of political question cases, were cited in *Baker*: resolution of foreign policy issues often hinges on "standards that defy judicial application"; or requires exercise of a discretionary power demonstrably committed to a coordinate branch; or "uniquely demand[s] single-voiced statement[s] of the Government's views."[52] Standards defying judi-

---

[48] U.S. Const. art III, § 2.

[49] 28 U.S.C. § 1251.

[50] See generally HENKIN, FOREIGN AFFAIRS AND THE CONSTITUTION (1972); see also Scharpf, note 29 *supra*, at 585, 587.

[51] 369 U.S. 186, 217 (1962).

[52] *Id.* at 211. These three features are included in the Court's more general description of the patterns distilled from previous political question cases. *Id.* at 217. The first general group of political question cases listed by the Court consists of those reflecting a "textually demonstrable constitutional commitment of the issue to a coordinate political department." That approach is consistent even with the classical theory of constitutional review, under which the Court reviews congressional and executive acts because the Constitution requires the Court to do so. Even under so broad a conception of constitutional role, the Court will be excused from its duty if the Constitution exceptionally commits the particular question to one of the other two branches of government. See, *e.g.*, TRIBE, note 29 *supra*, at 71 n.1;

cial application might, in a given case, hinder the court's capacity to understand the reasons behind Congressional distinctions among aliens from various countries. Aliens have challenged the constitutionality of one statutory provision granting special immigration benefits to aliens from contiguous countries and one granting special benefits to Eastern Hemisphere aliens.[53] When reviewing the constitutionality of those types of provisions, which reflect conscious Congressional decisions to single out aliens from one particular country or group of countries, courts should consider whether there are foreign policy concerns that they lack the standards, as well as the information and expertise,[54] to evaluate. Similarly, if the facts of a particular immigration case raise an issue demonstrably committed to Congress, then the particular issue, though even then not necessarily the entire case, should be held nonjusticiable.

The last factor that *Baker* associates with foreign policy is a spe-

---

Wechsler, *Toward Neutral Principles of Constitutional Law*, 73 HARV. L. REV. 1, 7–9 (1957); Scharpf, note 29 *supra*, at 517–18. See also Luther v. Borden, 48 U.S. (7 How.) 1 (1849). The other prongs enumerated in Baker assume discretionary judicial powers to withhold constitutional review even when the Constitution does not commit the decision to a coordinate branch. Since proponents of the classical theory reject the notion that courts have such powers, see, *e.g.*, Wechsler, *supra;* Tigar, *Judicial Power, the "Political Question Doctrine," and Foreign Relations*, 17 U.C.L.A. L. REV. 1135 (1970); *cf.* Gunther, *The Subtle Vices of the "Passive Virtues"—a Comment on Principle and Expediency in Judicial Review*, 64 COLUM. L. REV. 1 (1964), they might stop at this point. For those theorists, the special deference in the immigration cases could not be justified by the remaining Baker factors because the courts lack the power to invoke those discretionary factors at all, and therefore to immigration cases in particular. Others, however, reject the classical theory. See, *e.g.*, BICKEL, THE LEAST DANGEROUS BRANCH (1962); Scharpf, note 29 *supra* (arguing that functional concerns explain the bulk of the political question cases). The Supreme Court's willingness in *Baker* to recognize political questions not predicated on constitutional compulsion implies a similar rejection. Consequently, the other two common features of foreign affairs cases cited in *Baker*—standards defying judicial application and the need for a single-voiced statement— require consideration. Finally, those categories that *Baker* includes in its general political question description but not in its foreign affairs discussion do not aid the analysis of the immigration cases. The reference to an initial policy determination requiring nonjudicial discretion begs the question of when the type of discretion a particular policy determination requires is nonjudicial. To the extent this strand focuses on the presence of a policy element, it would seem subsumed within the previous strand, since a wide policy component would make it more difficult for a court to resolve the question on the basis of principled standards. The prong resting on disrespect for a coordinate branch does add a new element. See, *e.g.*, *Baker*, 369 U.S. at 214, *citing* Field v. Clark, 143 U.S. 649, 672 (1892) (courts reluctant to scrutinize statute for compliance with formal prerequisites to enactment). That new element, however, suggests no apparent special applicability to immigration. Certainly the mere fact that a decision of a coordinate branch is being invalidated does not bring that prong into operation; otherwise constitutional review would never be appropriate. The last two prongs—an unusual need for adherence to an existing decision and the possibility of embarrassment from conflicting pronouncements—are considered in the text.

[53] See Alvarez v. District Director, 539 F.2d 1220 (9th Cir. 1976); Dunn v. I.N.S., 499 F.2d 856 (9th Cir. 1974).

[54] See Narenji v. Civiletti, 617 F.2d 745, 747–48 (D.C. Cir. 1980).

cial need for a single-voiced statement. Here it is necessary to distinguish between two ways in which governmental pronouncements can differ. One situation is that in which two or more equally authoritative bodies render conflicting decisions applicable during the same time period. That situation would arise, for example, if individual states were permitted to set their own immigration policies. As a result, relying on the need for uniformity, the early Supreme Court decisions held that the power to regulate immigration is exclusively[55] federal.[56]

A split of authority among courts of equal rank can also create the problem of conflicting decisions simultaneously in effect. Under the Immigration and Nationality Act, that problem can occur either at the district court level or at the court of appeals level.[57] The problem is no more likely to arise in immigration cases than in any other area of federal law,[58] however, and when it does, the most logical remedy is a conclusive decision from the Supreme Court. Nor does judicial reversal of either an executive decision or a Congressional decision create conflict. Once a decision is invalidated by a court, the ominous specter of "multifarious pronouncements" raised in *Baker*[59] does not come about.[60]

The second way in which official pronouncements can differ is that, although only one authoritative pronouncement is outstanding at a given point in time, the pronouncement is one that can change over the course of time. That problem is not one of conflict; it is one of finality and certainty. It results from the possibility that a given administrative or legislative decision will be overturned. The problem exists in the case of any reviewable decision, but it assumes special importance in matters affecting foreign affairs, where final decisions might be needed promptly.[61] Thus, if a par-

---

[55] Chy Lung v. Freeman, 92 U.S. (2 Otto.) 275 (1875); Henderson v. Wickham, 92 U.S. (2 Otto.) 259 (1875); The Passenger Cases, Smith v. Turner, *consolidated with* Norris v. City of Boston, 48 U.S. (7 How.) 283 (1849).

[56] Chinese Exclusion Case, 130 U.S. 581 (1889); The Head Money Cases, Edye v. Robertson, 112 U.S. 580 (1884).

[57] See 8 U.S.C. § 1105a(a, b).

[58] That point has been made by others. See, *e.g.*, Barker, *A Critique of the Establishment of a Specialized Immigration Court*, 18 SAN DIEGO L. REV. 25, 26–27 (1980); Wildes, *The Need for a Specialized Immigration Court: A Practical Response*, 18 SAN DIEGO L. REV. 53, 63 (1980).

[59] 369 U.S. at 217.

[60] See I.N.S. v. Chadha, 103 S.Ct. 2764, 2780 (1983).

[61] *E.g.*, Goldwater v. Carter, 444 U.S. 996 (1979).

ticular immigration case raises an issue that for some special reason requires a prompt final resolution, the Court should consider holding the issue nonjusticiable.

One last observation is that even a decision having a great impact on foreign affairs might be justiciable. In most of the cases cited earlier for the proposition that courts will review even those decisions containing strong foreign policy ingredients, violations of important individual rights were alleged.[62] In such cases, the courts should first isolate any policies that underlie the principle of deference in foreign policy matters and that apply to the particular cases. It should then balance those policies against the individual rights claimed to have been infringed. When performing the balancing, and in particular when evaluating the strength of the individual right, it would seem reasonable to consider not only the importance of the right the immigrant is asserting—in the present context a right of constitutional magnitude—but also the severity of the sanction resulting from the alleged deprivation of that right. Relevant to the latter would be the immigration status of the particular individual. Status might include whether the person was lawfully admitted and, if so, whether as a permanent resident or a temporary visitor.

In summary, the political question doctrine, whether or not invoked by name, accounts for some of the judicial restraint in the American immigration cases. Foreign relations concerns have been voiced, but as a justification for blanket deference in immigration cases they require two assumptions: that immigration inherently implicates foreign policy, and that foreign policy considerations call for judicial restraint.

Only in a few special instances do immigration cases realistically affect foreign policy. Accordingly, the court should ask, in each individual case, whether judicial review would interfere with foreign policy. To make that determination, a court might consider any submissions by the Government, the legislative history, and whether the provision in question distinguishes between immigrants of selected nationalities.

Even when foreign affairs will be affected, courts often review when the claimed violation of an individual right is important

---

[62] See notes 42–50 *supra* and accompanying text. See esp. Henkin, note 50 *supra*, ch. 10; Note, *Constitutional Limits on the Power to Exclude Aliens*, 82 COLUM. L. REV. 957, 973–74 (1982).

enough. In immigration cases, even when review might realistically be expected to affect foreign policy, the court should therefore balance the likely impact of its interference against the importance of the individual right allegedly violated. To gauge the impact on foreign affairs, the court should consider the factors that call for deference in cases involving foreign affairs: the lack of manageable standards, a demonstrable commitment to another branch, and any special need for the nation to speak with a single voice. To apply the last factor, the court should consider both uniformity and finality. In measuring the importance of the claimed deprivation, the court should take into account both the importance of the right and the severity of the resulting sanction.

B. THE GUEST THEORY

In many of the most deferential judicial opinions in the area of immigration, one common theme has been the depiction of the alien as a guest, to whom hospitality may be terminated at the pleasure of the host. The view seems to be that the alien aggrieved by governmental action has little cause for complaint because his or her very presence in the country is strictly a bonus.

That philosophy has emerged in various forms. Several cases have spoken of the aliens having "come at the Nation's invitation,"[63] or of the country's "hospitality" to aliens,[64] or of aliens' status as "guests."[65] In a leading British decision,[66] Lord Justice Widgery (as he then was) analogized immigration law to property law. He maintained that, just as a landlord need not explain a refusal to extend a lease, the Home Secretary need not explain a decision refusing to extend an alien's leave to remain in the United Kingdom.[67] Under that analogy, the nation's immigration laws represent the exercise by the "owners" of the national property of their collective right to use the property as they please.[68] Finally, the

---

[63] Carlson v. Landon, 342 U.S. 524, 534 (1952).

[64] Landon v. Plasencia, 103 S.Ct. 321, 325 (1982); Foley v. Connelie, 435 U.S. 291, 294 (1978); Fiallo v. Bell, 430 U.S. 787, 796 (1977); Harisiades v. Shaughnessy, 342 U.S. 580, 587 (1952).

[65] Mathews v. Diaz, 426 U.S. 67, 80 (1976).

[66] Schmidt v. Secretary of State for Home Affairs [1969] 2 Ch. 149 (C.A.).

[67] *Id.* at 173.

[68] Peter Schuck argues that the emergence of restrictive American immigration laws reflected in part the philosophy of individual autonomy to which the American legal system

Court has relied at least twice on the premise that the admission of an alien is not a "right"; it is a "privilege,"[69] "a matter of permission and tolerance."[70] The classification of an interest as a privilege is still another form of the guest theory.

The general, admittedly qualified,[71] demise of the right/privilege distinction has been chronicled elsewhere.[72] These sources contain powerful arguments against making the distinction conclusive as to whether procedural review is available. Repetition of those arguments would not be useful: it suffices here to note that, like the other forms of the guest theory, the right/privilege distinction in immigration law confuses the nation as a whole with its constituent parts. It can be granted *arguendo*[73] that a nation has unlimited power in international law to exclude and to expel aliens. It does not follow that the courts should refrain from determining whether the manner in which the national legislature exercises that power comports with the constitutional restrictions that the nation as a whole has elected to establish.

C. THE UNFAIR ADVANTAGE THEORY

One theory, advanced in *Harisiades v. Shaughnessy*, was that permanent resident aliens derive advantages from two sources of law:

---

was then committed. Under that philosophy, obligation was based principally on consent. Schuck draws an effective analogy between the landowner's right to exclude trespassers and the nation's right to exclude aliens. See Schuck, *The Transformation of Immigration Law*, 84 COLUM. L. REV. 1, 6–7 (1984). Note, however, that he offers his argument as a historical explanation for the adoption of a restrictive immigration policy. Widgery, L.J., in contrast, offered his analogy as a justification for judicial restraint.

[69] United States *ex rel.* Knauff v. Shaughnessy, 338 U.S. 537, 542 (1950).

[70] Harisiades v. Shaughnessy, 342 U.S. 580, 586–87 (1952). Accord, Landon v. Plasencia, 103 S.Ct. 321, 329 (1982) (dictum); *cf.* Jay v. Boyd, 351 U.S. 345, 354 (1956) (statutory interpretation affected by the fact that discretionary relief from deportation is matter of "grace," rather than "right"). See also GARIS, IMMIGRATION RESTRICTION 30 (1927) (right-privilege distinction invoked in Congressional debates over the Naturalization Act of 1798).

[71] See Smolla, *The Reemergence of the Right-Privilege Distinction in Constitutional Law: The Price of Protesting Too Much*, 35 STAN. L. REV. 69 (1982).

[72] See, *e.g.*, GORDON & ROSENFIELD, note 3 *supra*, § 15.3; French, *Unconstitutional Conditions: An Analysis*, 50 GEO. L.J. 234 (1961); Van Alstyne, *The Demise of the Right-Privilege Distinction in Constitutional Law*, 81 HARV. L. REV. 1439 (1968).

[73] This assumption is questioned in GOODWIN-GILL, INTERNATIONAL LAW AND THE MOVEMENT OF PERSONS BETWEEN STATES (1978); Nafziger, *A Commentary on American Legal Scholarship concerning the Admission of Migrants*, 17 U. MICH. J.L. REFORM 165 (1984); see also GOODWIN-GILL, THE REFUGEE IN INTERNATIONAL LAW (1984); R. PLENDER, INTERNATIONAL MIGRATION LAW (1972).

international law and the domestic law of the host country.[74] It noted that, in international law, aliens may request their nations to intervene diplomatically and may not be forced to participate in wars against their own nations.[75] The implication was that aliens should not expect to enjoy the same domestic rights as citizens, because aliens would then have two sets of rights and therefore be at an unfair advantage.

There are several answers. First, a court would not have to afford the alien the same domestic rights as a citizen in order to review for compliance with the particular constitutional provision the alien was invoking. There might indeed be a price that the Constitution expects the alien to pay for access to limited rights in international law, but it is not axiomatic that that price includes forfeiture of constitutional review.

Moreover, the same reasoning has not been applied to the question of legal disabilities attaching to alienage. The presence of those legal disabilities has not been thought to preclude imposing on aliens the additional disabilities borne by citizens.[76]

The practical significance of the alien's international law right to request diplomatic intervention might also be questioned. The alien's nation must be persuaded that there is a valid case and must be willing to raise the matter with the host country. The host nation must then be willing to accede to that request. Whether such a procedure adequately substitutes for constitutional protection seems dubious at best.

Finally, even if the alien's international law rights were of as much practical import as protection by the domestic law of the host

---

[74] 342 U.S. 580, 585–87 (1952); cf. R. v. Secretary of State for the Home Dept., ex parte Ayub [1983] 3 C.M.L.R. 140, 149 (Div. Ct.) (U.K. citizen might be barred from exercising EEC rights against the United Kingdom because doing so would create simultaneous EEC and international law rights) (dictum).

[75] 342 U.S. at 585–86. Accord, Foley v. Connelie, 419 F. Supp. 889, 897–98 (S.D.N.Y. 1976), aff'd, 435 U.S. 291 (1978). See also HARPER, IMMIGRATION LAWS OF THE UNITED STATES, pt. 7, § 1a, at 567 (3d ed. 1975); Convention Respecting the Laws and Customs of War on Land, Oct. 18, 1907, art. 23, reproduced in 36 Stat. 2277, 2302. See also LAWSON & BENTLEY, KIER & LAWSON'S CASES IN CONSTITUTIONAL LAW 69–74 (6th ed. 1979); STREET & BRAZIER, DE SMITH'S CONSTITUTIONAL AND ADMINISTRATIVE LAW 155 (4th ed. 1981).

[76] Even apart from vulnerability to exclusion or deportation, aliens are subject to a wide range of disabilities beyond those borne by citizens. See generally CARLINER, note 3 supra; 1 GORDON & ROSENFIELD, note 3 supra, §§ 1.30–1.46; MUTHARIKA, note 3 supra; Roh & Upham, The Status of Aliens under United States Draft Laws, 13 HARV. INT'L L.J. 501 (1972); Rosberg, Aliens and Equal Protection: Why Not the Right to Vote? 75 MICH. L. REV. 1092 (1977).

country, no basis is perceived for requiring the alien to make an election.[77] That the alien would have the opportunity to ask his or her country to ask the host nation to provide favorable treatment when international law has allegedly been violated does not show that the alien should not be able to invoke judicial protection when asserting a violation of domestic law.

D. THE ALLEGIANCE THEORY

Among the rationales offered by the Supreme Court in *Harisiades* to support its limited reading of an alien's constitutional protection was its statement that "[s]o long as the alien elects to continue the ambiguity of his allegiance, his domicile here is held by a precarious tenure."[78] As an argument for judicial deference, that position contains two components: that aliens lack clear allegiance to their resident countries, and that those who lack clear allegiance are not entitled to constitutional safeguards.

With respect to the first component, the Court's reference to aliens electing to continue their status implies that a decision not to become naturalized evidences a lack of allegiance. If the Court meant allegiance in the sense of loyalty, a number of observations should be made. In many cases aliens are statutorily ineligible for naturalization because of the duration of residence or the inability to meet some other prerequisite.[79] In those cases the continuation of alien status evidences nothing about the character of a person's loyalty. Even when an alien who is statutorily eligible elects not to apply for naturalization, a reluctance to renounce one's native citizenship does not necessarily reflect apathy toward the country of residence. Unless there is reason to expect that the interests of the two countries will directly clash, that decision cannot be taken as evidence of a lack of loyalty.[80] That the federal government drafts resident aliens into the military[81] illustrates beyond doubt its faith in their loyalty.

---

[77] *E.g.*, it has not been suggested that the two sets of rights possessed by dual citizens should result in forfeiture of their domestic rights.

[78] Harisiades v. Shaughnessy, 342 U.S. 580, 587 (1952).

[79] See 8 U.S.C. §§ 1421 *et seq.*

[80] See also Hesse, note 9 *supra*, 69 YALE L.J. at 277–78; Trop v. Dulles, 356 U.S. 86 (1958) (even desertion during wartime was held not to signify a dilution of allegiance for purposes of divestment of citizenship).

[81] See generally MUTHARIKA, note 3 *supra*, ch. 7; Roh & Upham, note 76 *supra*.

If the Court was referring to allegiance in its legal sense, a different analysis is necessary. Allegiance and protection have indeed been traditionally described as interdependent.[82] As has long been recognized, however, at least friendly aliens are deemed to bear at least temporary allegiance to the countries in which they reside.[83]

The second component is equally problematic. Even if it were true that a permanent resident alien lacked allegiance to the country of residence, it is questionable whether that factor should reduce the scope of judicial protection. Sensible policy-making might dictate that a person devoid of national allegiance not be given the responsibility for a task requiring loyalty. But it does not follow that a court should refuse to apply the normal standards of review when such a person is aggrieved by governmental action.

E. THE SOVEREIGNTY THEORY

One theory advanced in some of the plenary power cases,[84] with varying degrees of explicitness, is that the power either to exclude or to deport aliens is inherent in sovereignty, and that Congress's exercise of that power is therefore immune from substantive constitutional constraints. The argument thus relies both on the existence of an inherent, nonenumerated, Congressional power and on the idea that the plenary power doctrine follows from it.

---

[82] See STREET & BRAZIER, note 75 *supra*, at 155, 431–34; Cane, *Prerogative Acts, Acts of State and Justiciability*, 29 INT'L & COMP. L.Q. 680, 690–92 (1980); see generally Lauterpacht, *Allegiance, Diplomatic Protection and Criminal Jurisdiction over Aliens*, 9 CAMB. L.J. 330 (1947); Williams, *The Correlation of Allegiance and Protection*, 10 CAMB. L.J. 54 (1948). A variant of this argument is put forward by David Martin, who maintains that the level of procedural protection the country owes a particular class of aliens should depend in part on the strength of that class's commitment to the national community. See Martin, note 28 *supra*. But see Aleinikoff, note 28 *supra* (level of procedural protection should be based on strength of alien's ties to community).

[83] BORCHARD, DIPLOMATIC PROTECTION OF CITIZENS ABROAD 11 (1915). However their obligation is decribed as allegiance only in the limited sense that they have a duty to obey the nation's laws. *Id.* See also Fong Yue Ting v. United States, 149 U.S. 698, 735–37 (1893) (Brewer, J., dissenting), citing further sources. In addition, see Note, *Constitutional Limitations on the Naturalization Power*, 80 YALE L.J. 769, 778–79 (1971). Admittedly it is not clear to what extent that relationship continues when aliens are physically outside the country. See Cane, note 82 *supra*, at 690–92; STREET & BRAZIER, note 75 *supra*, at 155; Williams, note 82 *supra*.

[84] *E.g.*, Fiallo v. Bell, 430 U.S. 787, 792 (1977); Kleindienst v. Mandel, 408 U.S. 753, 766 (1972); Carlson v. Landon, 342 U.S. 524, 534 (1952); Shaughnessy v. United States *ex rel.* Mezei, 345 U.S. 206, 210 (1953); Harisiades v. Shaughnessy, 342 U.S. 580, 587–88 (1952); United States *ex rel.* Knauff v. Shaughnessy, 338 U.S. 537, 542 (1950). Accord, Palma v. Verdeyen, 676 F.2d 100, 103 (4th Cir. 1982).

The first element of that argument raises questions as to the source of the Congressional power over immigration. Several enumerated powers have been suggested.[85] They include the commerce power,[86] the naturalization power,[87] and the war power.[88] They include also a lesser known provision that denies Congress the power to prohibit, before 1808, the "Migration or Importation of such Persons as any of the States now existing shall think proper to admit";[89] this provision might be read as implying that Congress has the power to exclude such persons after 1808.[90]

But in the *Chinese Exclusion Case*, the Supreme Court sustained an immigration statute by locating a Congressional exclusion power within the concept of "sovereignty."[91] It was therefore unnecessary to tie the statute to one of the constitutionally enumerated powers. Other cases followed suit.[92]

Recognition of a sovereign nonenumerated Congressional power raises a battery of problems.[93] Nonetheless, it will be assumed *arguendo* that the Court has been right to view the Congressional exclusion power as an inherent incident of sovereignty. The point here is that, in any event, preclusion of judicial review for compliance with those constitutional limitations protecting individual rights is a non sequitur.[94] In *United States v. Curtiss-Wright Exporting Corp.*,[95] for example, the power to regulate foreign affairs was held to be inherent in sovereignty. Yet that holding did not prevent the

---

[85] See Toll v. Moreno, 458 U.S. 1, 10 (1983); The Passenger Cases, Smith v. Turner, *consolidated with* Norris v. City of Boston, 48 U.S. (7 How.) 283 (1849). For a good summary, see ALEINIKOFF & MARTIN, THE AMERICAN IMMIGRATION PROCESS, ch. 1 (to be published in 1985).

[86] U.S. Const. art. I, § 8, cl. 3.

[87] *Id.* art. I, § 8, cl. 4.

[88] *Id.* art. I, § 8, cl. 11.

[89] *Id.* art I., § 9, cl. 1.

[90] ALEINIKOFF & MARTIN, note 85 *supra*, ch. 1; Garis, note 70 *supra*, at 59–68; Berns, *The Constitution and the Migration of Slaves*, 78 YALE L.J. 198 (1968).

[91] Chae Chan Ping v. United States, 130 U.S. 581, 609 (1889).

[92] See note 84 *supra; cf.* United States v. Curtiss-Wright Exporting Corp., 299 U.S. 304 (1936) (foreign affairs power inherent in sovereignty).

[93] See ALEINIKOFF & MARTIN, note 85 *supra;* HENKIN, note 50 *supra*, at 15–28; Berger, *The Presidential Monopoly of Foreign Relations*, 71 MICH. L. REV. 1, 26–33 (1972); Levitan, *The Foreign Relations Power: An Analysis of Mr. Justice Sutherland's Theory*, 55 YALE L.J. 467 (1946).

[94] This point has been made by others. See HENKIN, note 50 *supra*, at 25; *Constitutional Limits*, note 62 *supra*, at 970–71.

[95] 299 U.S. 304 (1936).

Court in several subsequent cases from invalidating, as violative of individual rights limitations, federal action affecting foreign affairs.[96] And in *United States v. Wong Kim Ark*,[97] where the Court acknowledged the inherent power of every sovereign nation to decide who its citizens are,[98] it was nonetheless held that persons born in the United States to alien parents could not be denied citizenship. Indeed, if even the expressly enumerated powers are subject to constitutional limitations,[99] the case for limiting a merely implied power would seem to be even stronger.[100]

F. THE EXTRATERRITORIALITY THEORY

There is one important theory that applies only to the exclusion cases. The argument is that an alien cannot invoke the American Constitution in exclusion proceedings because the Constitution lacks extraterritorial effect.[101] At first glance, the response to this theory seems obvious. Since federal power derives from the Constitution, it is contradictory to uphold a statute having extraterritorial effect but to deny that its application is subject to constitutional limitations. If the Constitution is read to empower federal officials to act outside American territory, then it is not apparent why it should be interpreted as inapplicable for the purpose of limiting such action. In fact, the Supreme Court has on several occasions applied the Constitution to acts of American government officials outside United States territory.[102]

To meet this objection, one might observe, at least in the Supreme Court cases applying constitutional protections to governmental acts outside United States territory, that the aggrieved par-

---

[96] See notes 42–50 *supra* and accompanying text.

[97] 169 U.S. 649 (1898).

[98] *Id.* at 668.

[99] Monongahela Navigation Co. v. United States, 148 U.S. 312, 336 (1893).

[100] On this point, see Fong Yue Ting v. United States, 149 U.S. 698, 738 (1893) (Brewer, J., dissenting). *Cf.* Harisiades v. Shaughnessy, 342 U.S. 580, 599 (1952) (Douglas, J., dissenting) (implied power should be subject to express limitation).

[101] See, *e.g.*, Ng Fung Ho v. White, 259 U.S. 276, 282 (1922) (dictum); Lem Moon Sing v. United States, 158 U.S. 538, 547–48 (1895); Fong Yue Tue v. United States, 149 U.S. 698,738 (Brewer, J., dissenting). See also Schuck, note 68 *supra*, at 18–21 (classical view that aliens who are excluded lack constitutional protection), 62–65 (signs of change); see also *Constitutional Limitations*, note 62 *supra*, at 980–82.

[102] See, *e.g.*, the military court-martial cases cited in HENKIN, note 50 *supra*, at 327 n.42; see also United States v. Tiede, 86 F.R.D. 227 (U.S. Ct. for Berlin 1979).

ties were American citizens. Surely, the argument would run, the Constitution was never meant to confer rights on all people everywhere.

That argument has formidable intuitive appeal. But as a justification for the plenary power doctrine, it has its limits. Certainly the fact that a person is an alien does not, standing alone, render the Constitution inapplicable.[103] Similarly, the fact that a person is outside the United States does not eliminate constitutional protections, as illustrated by the extraterritorial cases discussed above. Even the combination of a person's being an alien and his being outside the country does not necessarily make the Constitution inapplicable. As mentioned earlier, returning resident aliens have been held entitled to procedural due process.[104] Finally, the Court has never suggested that residence in the United States is a prerequisite to constitutional protection. Although the issue does not appear to have arisen, it scarcely seems conceivable, for example, that a nonresident alien convicted of a crime in the United States would be held ineligible to complain of cruel and unusual punishment.

The analysis cannot, of course, stop at this point. If it did, it would be subject to the fair criticism that those three features— alienage, nonresidence, and absence from the United States— should not be viewed in isolation. While none of them taken individually precludes constitutional challenge, the combination of all three might be thought to have that effect.[105] That position is plau-

---

[103] The leading case is Yick Wo v. Hopkins, 118 U.S. 356 (1886). See also the cases holding state alienage classifications suspect, note 6 *supra*, and deportation cases presenting procedural due process challenges, notes 23–24 *supra* and accompanying text.

[104] See note 25 *supra* and accompanying text.

[105] There are cases consistent with that conclusion, but they reflect special considerations preventing their transfer to the exclusion context. In what have been termed the Insular Cases, for example, the Court held that certain constitutional provisions need not be observed by the governments of unincorporated American territories. See, *e.g.*, Balzac v. People of Porto Rico, 258 U.S. 298 (1922); Dorr v. United States, 195 U.S. 138 (1904); Hawaii v. Mankichi, 190 U.S. 197 (1903); *cf.* Downes v. Bidwell, 182 U.S. 244 (1901) (constitutional provision requiring uniform duties held inapplicable to unincorporated territories). In Reid v. Covert, 354 U.S. 1, 12–14 (1957), the Court limited the Insular Cases by observing that they involved recently acquired territories with "entirely different cultures and customs from those of this country," *id.* at 13, so that imposing American customs on them would be unwise. Other cases that might initially be thought to preclude suits by nonresident aliens abroad in fact reflect special principles limited to alien enemies in wartime. See, *e.g.*, Johnson v. Eisentrager, 339 U.S. 763 (1950); In re Yamashita, 327 U.S. 1 (1946); see also United States v. Caltex (Philippines), Inc., 344 U.S. 149 (1952).

sible, since a nonresident alien who is physically outside the United States might ordinarily be assumed to lack any connection with the United States, and therefore lack any standing to complain that our Constitution has been violated.

That last point can be conceded as a general proposition but challenged as a justification for the plenary power doctrine. Its defect is that it fails to explain some of the most significant Supreme Court decisions invoking the principle of plenary Congressional power to exlude aliens—most notably those in which the excluded alien had sought admission on the very basis of a close family relationship to an American citizen. In those cases, it is simply not true that the complainant lacked an American connection. There is something surreal about saying, for example, that the wife[106] or child[107] of an American citizen lacks significant ties to the United States.

G. THE POETIC JUSTICE THEORY

One final theory of limited application requires brief discussion. In *Harisiades v. Shaughnessy*,[108] the question was whether Congress could constitutionally deport permanent resident aliens on the basis of their past membership in the Communist party. The Court said that if American citizens can be sent to foreign countries "to stem the tide of Communism,"[109] it would be incongruous to spare alien Communists from the hardships of "Communist aggression."[110]

The Court did not distinguish Communist aggression from mere membership in the Communist party. If it had, it would have been forced to acknowledge that American citizens are perfectly free to join the Communist party. The, incongruity thus does not exist. Nor did the Court point out that permanent resident aliens, being liable to conscription,[111] can also be sent to foreign countries "to stem the tide of Communism." Although the Court's theory related only to those deportations based on one particular ground, the language evidences a political attitude that might well have in-

---

[106] United States *ex rel.* Knauff v. Shaughnessy, 338 U.S. 537 (1950).

[107] Fiallo v. Bell, 430 U.S. 787 (1977).

[108] 342 U.S. 580 (1952).

[109] *Id.* at 591.

[110] *Id.*

[111] See note 81 *supra*.

fluenced several of the Supreme Court decisions concerning alien Communists.[112]

II. THE EXTERNALITIES[113]

There can be little doubt today that a judge frequently has a practical choice between two or more dispositions of a particular case.[114] But that freedom, though broad, is not limitless. The flexibility inherent in the judicial process is constrained by the now familiar "steadying factors" that Karl Llewellyn assembled as a response to what he perceived as the excesses of legal realism.[115] Probably the most significant of those constraints is the professional office occupied by the judge.[116]

One who seeks to explain the courts' refusals to interfere with Congress in the immigration sphere must consider both judicial freedom and its limitations. The plenary power decisions were accompanied by reasoned opinions. The most immediate explanation for any individual decision, therefore, is the specific legal doctrine articulated in the opinion. If the recognition of Karl Llewellyn's steadying factors is not to be a mere platitude, this explanation must be taken seriously.

But legal doctrine is not the only influence on judicial decision making. One can apply to the immigration cases the increasingly well accepted view that various factors not typically acknowledged

---

[112] See notes 181–89 *infra* and accompanying text.

[113] Commentary on the external factors affecting American judges has become more abundant in recent years, particularly with respect to such variables as personal backgrounds and attitudes. But most of the writing on external factors in general, and especially that on the specific factors of judicial role perception and contemporary political forces, has focused on British judges. It will therefore be necessary to refer frequently to the latter studies, which will be cited only for propositions that can reasonably be extrapolated to the American judiciary.

[114] See, *e.g.*, BLOM-COOPER & DREWRY, FINAL APPEAL 152 (1972); HART, THE CONCEPT OF LAW 12–13 (1961); PATERSON, THE LAW LORDS 194–95 (1982) (Law Lords regard themselves as having choices); Palley, *Decision Making in the Area of Public Order by English Courts*, OPEN UNIVERSITY, D203, block 2, pt. 3, at 41, 79–87 (1976). One writer distinguishes between "trouble" cases, where courts have choices, and "clear" cases, where they do not. Seidman, *The Judicial Process Reconsidered in the Light of Role Theory*, 32 MOD. L. REV. 516, 521 (1969). For elaboration of the specific mechanisms affording this freedom of choice, see Palley, *supra*, at 75–83; see also GRIFFITH, THE POLITICS OF THE JUDICIARY 1–2, 185 (1977).

[115] LLEWELLYN, THE COMMON LAW TRADITION—DECIDING APPEALS 19–61 (1960). See also Palley, note 114 *supra*, at 87–88; *cf.* JAFFE, ENGLISH AND AMERICAN JUDGES AS LAW-MAKERS 44 (1969) (rational standards can be available even for policy choices).

[116] LLEWELLYN, note 115 *supra*, at 45–46.

in courts' opinions contribute heavily to the results. Those factors will be described here as "external."[117] Among them are several that deserve consideration in the immigration context: the personal backgrounds and political attitudes of the judges; the judges' own perceptions of their roles in the legal system; and the political forces—"political" here being used in its broadest sense to encompass social and economic forces as well—prevailing in society at the time cases are decided.[118]

A. SOCIAL BACKGROUNDS AND ATTITUDES

Two kinds of variables will be considered together in this subsection. There are the background variables of the individual judge. These include social class, family, religion, ethnicity, previous experience, education, professional training, ethos and traditions, vulnerability to professional opinion, involvement in party politics, age, sex, and level of legal distinction attained.[119] Second, there are the attitudinal variables, a term used here to encompass the judge's values, general ideological orientation, and views on specific policy questions.[120]

The hypothesis that the backgrounds and attitudes of the federal[121] judges have contributed to the plenary power doctrine rests on three suppositions: that a judge's background and attitudes influence his or her decisions; that in the federal judiciary conservative backgrounds and conservative political views predominate; and

---

[117] The term "external" is one of convenience. At least one of the listed variables, role perception, is often explicitly included in the court's opinion and thus not neatly severable from doctrine, as discussed below. Although rarer, even the other major influences discussed in this section—attitudinal variables and prevailing political forces—can be revealed by the opinion. See notes 175–80 *infra* and accompanying text.

[118] These factors have been culled from a more comprehensive list of variables compiled by Claire Palley, note 114 *supra*, § 4. Palley groups these variables into two categories. Those internal to the judge include personal background, attitudes concerning specified values and policies, interaction with others, and perception of judicial role. Those external to the judge include the way in which the cases are set in motion and the relationship between courts and several other bodies—*e.g.*, the legislature, the executive, the press, the general public, pressure groups, and judges of other courts.

[119] All but the last two are taken from Palley, note 114 *supra*, § 4.1. Pre-judicial experience, however, has been expanded to include all previous experience, including judicial experience on a lower court, see *e.g.*, MARVELL, APPELLATE COURTS AND LAWYERING 180 (1978) (effect of previous trial court experience), and judicial experience accumulated by a judge on the same court.

[120] See generally Palley, note 114 *supra*, § 4.2.

[121] Immigration cases are litigated in federal court. See 8 U.S.C. §§ 1105a, 1329.

that politically conservative views tend generally to translate into relatively narrow definitions of immigrants' rights.

At first glance, all the pieces of this hypothesis might seem plausible. As to the first piece, numerous recent studies now show empirically[122] what many writers had sensed intuitively[123]—that a judge's background and attitudes often profoundly affect his or her decisions. Many judges freely acknowledge such influences.[124]

The second piece might also be thought present. Judges are "conditioned by the conservative impact of legal training and professional legal attitudes and associations."[125] The vast majority of federal judges have amassed considerable financial net worth by the time they are appointed.[126] Ethnic minorities are extremely underrepresented in relation to the general population.[127] Prosecutorial experience and corporate connections are very common among federal judges.[128] These and other background similarities[129] coalesce to produce a certain degree of homogeneity on the federal bench.

---

[122] For an extensive bibliography, listing primarily American empirical studies, see Tate, *Paths to the Bench in Britain: A Quasi-experimental Study of the Recruitment of a Judicial Elite*, 28 WESTERN POL. Q. 108, 109 n.2 (1975). See esp. Martin, *Women on the Federal Bench: A Comparative Profile*, 65 JUDICATURE 306, 307 & n.3 (1982); Nagel, *Multiple Correlation of Judicial Backgrounds and Decisions*, 2 FLA. ST. U.L. Rev. 258, 266–67 (table 1), 268–69 n.37 (bibliography) (1974). But *cf.* Cann, *Social Backgrounds and Dissenting Behavior on the North Dakota Supreme Court 1965–71*, 50 N. DAK. L. REV. 773 (1974) (results inconclusive).

[123] *E.g.*, ABEL-SMITH & STEVENS, IN SEARCH OF JUSTICE 171 (1968); CARDOZO, THE NATURE OF THE JUDICIAL PROCESS 167–79 (1921); DWORKIN, TAKING RIGHTS SERIOUSLY 4, 6 (1977); Palley, note 114 *supra*, §§ 4.1, 4.2; LORD RADCLIFFE, NOT IN FEATHER BEDS 212–16 (1968); *cf.* FARMER, TRIBUNALS AND GOVERNMENT 170 (1974); MACDONALD, IMMIGRATION LAW AND PRACTICE 4 (1983). But see Lord Devlin, *Judges, Government, and Politics*, 41 MOD. L. REV. 501, 506 (1978) (acknowledging homogeneity of judicial attitudes but questioning whether such attitudes influence judicial decision making).

[124] MARVELL, note 119 *supra*, at 180–81.

[125] SCHMIDHAUSER, JUDGES AND JUSTICES—THE FEDERAL APPELLATE MACHINERY 99 (1979). Many have made analogous observations about the British judiciary. The leading work is GRIFFITH, note 114 *supra*. See also Lord Evershed, M.R., *The Judicial Process in Twentieth Century England*, 61 COL. L. REV. 761, 773–74 (1961); Lord Devlin, note 123 *supra*, at 505 (1978); Lord Devlin, *Judges and Lawmakers*, 39 MOD. L. REV. 1, 8 (1976).

[126] See the statistics compiled by Goldman, *Reagan's Judicial Appointments at Mid-Term: Shaping the Bench in His Own Image*, 66 JUDICATURE 334, 346 (1983) (as of March 1983); see also Goldman, *Carter's Judicial Appointments: A Lasting Legacy*, 64 JUDICATURE 344 (1981).

[127] SCHMIDHAUSER, note 125 *supra*, at 59–61; Glick, *Federal Judges in the United States: Party, Ideology, and Merit Nomination*, 12 LOYOLA L.A. L. REV. 767, 800–801, 805, 806 (1979); see also JACKSON, JUDGES 254 (1974).

[128] JACKSON, note 127 *supra*, at 252–55.

[129] All but a handful of federal judges are male. Glick, note 127 *supra*, at 801, 805, 806; JACKSON, note 127 *supra*, at 248, 253; Martin, note 122 *supra*, at 307 (1982); SCHMIDHAUSER,

Finally, although one whose views are generally regarded as politically conservative will not necessarily be less predisposed to take a pro-immigrant position on substantive immigration policy than one who is generally regarded as politically liberal,[130] there has historically been at least a positive correlation between general political liberalism and sympathy toward immigrants.[131] Such a correlation is not surprising. Substantive immigration policy questions frequently implicate values to which political conservatives and political liberals attach differing weights. These values include stability,[132] the interests of the State in preference to certain interests of the individual, effective law enforcement,[133] property rights,[134] views on race relations,[135] nationalism,[136] the balance between national security and civil rights,[137] and the distribution of

---

note 125 *supra*, at 59. Supreme Court Justices, and to a lesser extent lower federal judges, tend generally to come from families enjoying a relatively high social status. Glick, note 127 *supra*, at 800; JACKSON, note 127 *supra*, at 252–53, 328; SCHMIDHAUSER, note 125 *supra*, at 52, 96 (Supreme Court Justices), 55, 97 (circuit judges).

[130] Even apart from the frequent difficulty of labeling a particular viewpoint as "liberal" or "conservative," it is of course possible for a person to hold clearly liberal views on some issues and clearly conservative views on others. Moreover, self-interest can conflict with a person's usual ideological propensities; for example, an immigrant with generally conservative views, or an employer with those same views, might favor a liberal immigration policy. Finally, even a person with consistently liberal views might favor a restrictive immigration policy out of a belief that its net effect would be to further liberal values. For example, a political liberal might believe that restricting immigration would improve racial harmony, although that particular argument is ordinarily invoked by conservatives. See, *e.g.*, the discussions provided by GRANT & MARTIN, IMMIGRATION LAW AND PRACTICE 356 (1982); MACDONALD, note 123 *supra*, at 16–17; MOORE & WALLACE, SLAMMING THE DOOR—THE ADMINISTRATION OF IMMIGRATION CONTROL 2–4 (1975). Alternatively, a political liberal might favor restrictions in the hope of improving the wages or working conditions of poorly paid domestic workers. See, *e.g.*, DeCanas v. Bica, 424 U.S. 351 (1976), where a legal services organization represented migrant farmworkers in their action challenging the hiring of illegal aliens.

[131] See, *e.g.*, the problems discussed by GARRARD, THE ENGLISH AND IMMIGRATION, 1880–1910, at 10, 132–33, 203–09 (1971).

[132] Several of the patterns identified by GAINER, THE ALIEN INVASION 212 (1972), can be seen to rest ultimately on the public perception of a threat to either cultural or economic stability. See also Sec. IIC *infra;* MOORE & WALLACE, note 130 *supra*, at 26.

[133] One who places a high value on effective law enforcement would be especially likely to take a conservative view on issues involving illegal entrants, immigrants who overstay their leave, and immigrants who commit non-immigration-related crimes.

[134] See the discussion of the guest theory, analogizing immigration law and landlord-tenant law, Sec. IB *supra*.

[135] See note 132 *supra*.

[136] *E.g.*, the deportation of Iranian nationals during the American hostage crisis. See notes 203–12 *infra* and accompanying text.

[137] *E.g.*, El-Werfalli v. Smith, 547 F. Supp. 152 (S.D.N.Y. 1982). See also R. v. Secretary of State for Home Affairs, ex parte Hosenball [1977] 1 W.L.R. 700 (C.A.).

wealth.[138] Occasionally, even people's feelings about the ideological creeds of the immigrants themselves can influence attitudes toward immigration.[139]

Yet, taken as a whole, the hypothesis that a conservative set of judicial attitudes has contributed to the plenary power doctrine does not seem convincing. Its greatest weakness is that it does not account for the selective nature of the judicial decisions. As I have argued, constitutional liberties that have been meticulously protected in other areas have received no protection in the immigration cases.

Perhaps the difficulty stems from placing undue weight on the homogeneously conservative influences I have identified. Those influences certainly exist, but they are tempered by factors that tend to promote ideological diversity. The American judicial appointment process has been described by leading writers as one that emphasizes political affiliation over legal distinction, at least as compared with the British process for appointing judges.[140] The American emphasis on political considerations, whatever its deficiencies, does favor ideological diversity. Some of that diversity results from the direct consideration of political ideology in the selection process,[141] particularly at the Supreme Court level.[142]

---

[138] See, *e.g.*, Fogel, *Illegal Aliens: Economic Aspects and Public Policy Alternatives*, 15 SAN DIEGO L. REV. 63, 76 (1977); Hofstetter, *Economic Underdevelopment and the Population Explosion: Implications for the U.S. Immigration Policy*, 45 LAW & CONTEMP. PROB. (No. 2) 55 (1983); Manulkin & Maghame, *A Proposed Solution to the Problem of the Undocumented Mexican Alien Worker*, 13 SAN DIEGO L. REV. 42, 45 (1975); SELECT COMM'N ON IMMIGRATION AND REFUGEE POLICY, FINAL REPORT, U.S. IMMIGRATION POLICY AND THE NATIONAL INTEREST 37 (1981) (hereinafter SCIRP); Hon. W. Smith, *Introduction* [to symposium], 45 LAW & CONTEMP. PROB. (No. 2) 3, 3–4 (1983).

[139] Some of the early colonial leaders, for example, feared a large influx of immigrants holding monarchist views. See DAVIE, WORLD IMMIGRATION 38–39 (1936); GARIS, note 70 *supra*, at 25–26; JONES, AMERICAN IMMIGRATION 80 (1960); PROPER, COLONIAL IMMIGRATION LAWS 90–91 (1967). See also notes 181–89 *infra* and accompanying text (alien Communist decisions of early 1950s).

[140] See JAFFE, note 115 *supra*, at 62–63, 67; TRIBE, note 29 *supra*, at 49–50. For general descriptions of the politics of federal judicial appointments, see CHASE, FEDERAL JUDGES— THE APPOINTING PROCESS (1972); Glick, note 127 *supra*, at 772–92; JACKSON, note 127 *supra*, at 247–76. At the district and circuit judge levels, senatorial politics can be more important than Presidential politics. *Id.* at 249, 310.

[141] Lord Devlin, note 125 *supra*, 39 MOD. L. REV. at 6; Glick, note 127 *supra*, at 772; Goldman, note 126 *supra*, 66 JUDICATURE at 337 n.2; JACKSON, note 127 *supra*, at 270–73; JAFFE, note 115 *supra*, at 61; SCHMIDHAUSER, note 125 *supra*, at 66, 86, 90.

[142] Glick note 127 *supra*, at 773. Ideology is less important in choosing district and circuit judges. *Id.* at 779.

Ideological diversity can also result indirectly. The overwhelming majority of federal judges belong to the political party of the President who appointed them,[143] and positive correlations have been observed between membership in one of the two major political parties and ideological views on several subject areas likely to come before the courts.[144] Thus a change in the Presidency—especially when the new President is of a different political party—can be followed by an infusion of new ideologies and values into the federal courts.

For these reasons, personal attitude does not convincingly explain the peculiar deference the Court has displayed toward Congress in immigration cases. Other "external" factors show greater promise.

B. PERCEPTION OF ROLE

One study of judicial behavior defines role as "the cluster of normative expectations which exist at any given time as to the behavior and attributes required of a person who holds a particular status or position."[145] That definition usefully emphasizes both that role comprises expectations and that those expectations are normative rather than descriptive. Another formulation defines role as "functions, duties, and powers."[146] The latter definition has the advantage of providing greater specificity with respect to the objects of the normative expectations—the sorts of behavior and attributes about which the expectations are held. Here I will combine the two definitions and use the term "role of a court" to mean the normative expectations concerning the functions, duties, and powers of a court.[147]

That combined definition permits distinctions based on the holder of the expectations.[148] Several writers, through differing

---

[143] From 1952 to 1979, the figure was over 90 percent. *Id.* at 801, 805, 806.

[144] See Nagel, note 122 *supra*, at 266–68. For a bibliography of empirical studies linking party membership to judicial decision making, see *id.* at 268–69 n.37.

[145] PATERSON, note 114 *supra*, at 3, 202 (1982).

[146] Palley, note 114 *supra*, at 41.

[147] See also Seidman, note 114 *supra*, at 517 (1969) (role is complex of obligations that make up a social position).

[148] PATERSON, note 114 *supra*, at 3, 202–03, uses the term "reference groups" to describe the holders of the expectations.

methodologies, have argued convincingly that a judge's own perception of role is one of the central factors influencing judicial decision making,[149] a view I accept.

Although role perception is treated here as merely one of several discrete determinants of judicial behavior, it cannot be divorced entirely from the other two major contributors examined in this section. The previous discussion was framed as a consideration of the effect that background and attitudinal variables have on judicial decision making. It can as easily be viewed, however, as reinforcement for the position that John Griffith articulates in role language: that judges perceive their role as the protection of the public interest in a stable society,[150] and that that role perception is in fact what is important.[151] Further, the more broadly judges perceive their roles, the more important the social and political attitudes of the judges become.

Similarly, the following discussion will consider the effect of contemporary political forces on judicial decision making. That discussion could be characterized equally well as a vindication of Justice Cardozo's prescriptive view that, when making law, a judge's role is to be guided by the values prevailing in society, rather than by his or her own values.[152]

What is the relationship between judicial role perception and the plenary power doctrine? American judges are not ordinarily thought of as passive observers, at least in comparison with their British counterparts.[153] More deeply influenced by the legal realists, American judges have been more prone to acknowledge the choice element present in many judicial decisions.[154] Judicial activ-

---

[149] See GRIFFITH, note 114 *supra*, at 189–90; Palley, note 114 *supra*, § 4.4; see also PATERSON, note 114 *supra*; Seidman, note 114 *supra*. The further question which groups are most influential in causing judges to perceive their roles the way they do is examined in an empirical study of the Appellate Committee of the House of Lords. See PATERSON, esp. at 33–34, 119–21 (most important reference group for most Law Lords is their fellow Law Lords).

[150] GRIFFITH, note 114 *supra*, at 212–13.

[151] *Id.* at 189–90.

[152] CARDOZO, note 123 *supra*, at 105–07 (but ascribing relatively little practical significance to that distinction, *id.* at 105–06, 108–11).

[153] See, *e.g.*, JAFFE, note 115 *supra*, at 2–5; Palley, note 114 *supra*, at 55.

[154] See 1 DAVIS, ADMINISTRATIVE LAW TREATISE §§ 2.17, 2.18 (2d ed. 1978); JAFFE, note 115 *supra*, at 2; ZANDER, THE LAW-MAKING PROCESS 230 (1980).

ism[155] in the United States is typically regarded as being especially evident in constitutional matters.[156]

Yet, in the immigration arena, the plenary power doctrine reflects precisely the opposite bent. The question presented is why such a deferential view of judicial role has been adopted in the plenary power cases. I suggest two answers.

The first can be found in the previous section. Role perception is ordinarily thought of as an "external" factor. But an explicit statement of the court's perception of its role can appear in a judicial opinion. When it does, it becomes part of the legal doctrine. In the constitutional cases concerned with immigration legislation, the fusion of doctrine and role perception is especially visible. The prominent doctrinal issue in those cases is the appropriate standard of review. The Court views its role narrowly, and it says so. Accordingly, the doctrinal justifications offered in the opinions and discussed in Section I simultaneously explain the results of the cases and the Court's perception of its role. In particular, as discussed above in Section IA, the Court perceives the judicial role as especially narrow when, as the Court assumes to be the case with immigration, foreign affairs are affected.

Second, part of the judicial role is observance of *stare decisis*. The more support the plenary power doctrine accumulated, the more entrenched it became. In *Galvan v. Press*, Justice Frankfurter provided an explanation on which subsequent plenary power cases[157] would rely:[158]

> [M]uch could be said for the view, were we writing on a clean slate, that the Due Process Clause qualifies the scope of political discretion heretofore recognized as belonging to Congress in regulating the entry and deportation of aliens. . . .

---

[155] The term "activism" has been used to convey several distinct meanings. It can refer to decision making that is wider than necessary to decide the case, decision making that extends the scope of existing rules, or decision making that reflects the "social, political and economic consequences." Palley, note 114 *supra*, at 55 n.1. Those meanings focus, respectively, on the scope of the holding in relation to the facts, the degree to which the holding changes existing law, and the factors it is permissible for a court to consider in reaching a decision. Palley points out that the term "activism" logically could be, but ordinarily is not, used to denote a restrictive application of law. Other definitions could also be used.

[156] JAFFE, note 115 *supra*, at 2–5.

[157] *E.g.*, Fiallo v. Bell, 430 U.S. 787, 792 n.4 (1977); Kleindienst v. Mandel, 408 U.S. 753, 766–67 (1972).

[158] 347 U.S. 522, 530–31 (1954).

> But the slate is not clean. . . . [T]hat the formulation of these policies is entrusted exclusively to Congress has become about as firmly embedded in the legislative and judicial tissues of our body politic as any aspect of our government.

Even an activist judge with liberal political views might hesitate before voting to dislodge a line of authority so long and so unyielding.

C. CONTEMPORARY SOCIAL AND POLITICAL FORCES[159]

A court's decision can also be affected by the contemporary political forces operating in society.[160] To the extent that this influence exists because a judge personally shares the prevailing public opinion, this factor is simply a specific application of the attitudinal variables discussed earlier. One of the background variables shaping the attitudes is the current tide of public opinion, to which the judge, being human, is susceptible. But to the extent that political forces affect the decision because the judge is hesitant to defy public opinion, regardless of whether he or she personally shares that opinion, these influences are distinct from the attitudinal variables and require separate treatment.

Some general observations about public attitudes toward immigrants are thus in order. First, immigrants have perennially been unpopular. Whether for cultural, economic, political, or environmental reasons, various immigrant waves have typically received at least mixed, and more commonly hostile, public reactions.[161]

---

[159] For a thoughtful description of the philosophical forces historically affecting the totality of immigration law (not just the case law), see Schuck, note 68 *supra*.

[160] See generally GRIFFITH, note 114 *supra*, at 55–171 (author provides numerous examples of judicial decisions influenced by, *inter alia*, prevailing social and political forces); see also Palley, note 114 *supra*, at 57 (courts aware judgments might be scrutinized by press, general public, and pressure groups), 58 (judges might retreat from sensitive issues if particular decision would be unacceptable or would create stress in society); *cf.* CARDOZO, note 123 *supra*, at 106–11 (judicial lawmaking should reflect moral notions prevailing in society); Lord Devlin, note 125 *supra*, 39 MOD. L. REV. at 2–6 (arguing that British judges should not make law without a consensus); Prosser, *Politics and Judicial Review: The Atkinson Case and Its Aftermath*, 1979 PUBL. L. 59, 83.

[161] That was true even in colonial days. DAVIE, note 139 *supra*, at 35–56 (1936); GARIS, note 70 *supra*, at x, 17–18; see also Gleason, *The Melting Pot: Symbol of Fusion or Confusion?* 16 AMER. Q. 20 (1964). The pages that follow discuss public reactions to specific immigrant waves. See also the accounts given in Purdy & Fitzpatrick v. State, 71 Cal. 2d 566, 580, 456 P.2d 645, 654, 79 Cal. Rptr. 77, 86 (1969); Sei Fujii v. State, 38 Cal. 2d 718, 740–52, 242 P.2d 617, 632–39 (1952) (Carter, J., concurring); *cf.* Faruki v. Rogers, 349 F. Supp. 723, 729 (D.D.C. 1972) (noting frequent oppression of immigrants). The common reasons for this

Equally important for present purposes, a sharp increase in the volume of immigration has historically been followed by an increase in the level of anti-immigrant sentiment.[162]

That latter phenomenon is significant here. Not surprisingly, periods in which the courts are deciding large numbers of immigration cases are typically those of high-volume immigration, as the discussion below will show.[163] This is true in part because a higher level of immigration would naturally be expected to result in greater absolute numbers of disputes and therefore more litigation. It is true also because high-volume immigration has tended to culminate in restrictive legislation,[164] which in turn produces higher numbers of excluded or deported immigrants.[165]

Thus, unhappily for immigrants, the periods in which their large numbers make their presence all the more unpopular tend to be the very periods in which they are most frequently before the courts.

---

general antipathy are summarized in BENTLEY, AMERICAN IMMIGRATION TODAY 14–16 (1981); GAINER, note 132 *supra*, at 212; GARRARD, note 131 *supra*, at 3–5; see generally CURRAN, XENOPHOBIA AND IMMIGRATION, 1820–1930 (1975); Rostow, *The Japanese American Cases—a Disaster*, 54 YALE L.J. 489 (1945); TRIBE, note 29 *supra*, at 1053–54.

[162] See notes 166–202 *infra* and accompanying text. This phenomenon is not peculiarly American. For example, English public reaction to Irish immigrants in the nineteenth century has been tied to the public perception of increased volume. GAINER, note 132 *supra*, at 212; see generally Gilley, *English Attitudes to the Irish in England, 1780–1900*, in HOLMES (ed.), IMMIGRANTS AND MINORITIES IN BRITISH SOCIETY 81 *et seq.* (1978); see also May, *The Chinese in Britain, 1860–1914*, *id.* at 111 *et seq.* Similar animosity toward Jewish immigrants arriving in England around the turn of the century is recounted in FOOT, IMMIGRATION AND RACE IN BRITISH POLITICS 103–06 (1965); GARRARD, note 131 *supra*, at 23–47, 56–65; Holmes, *J. A. Hobson and the Jews*, in HOLMES, *supra*, at 148–52; JONES, IMMIGRATION AND SOCIAL POLICY IN BRITAIN 72–88 (1977); Thornberry, *Law, Opinion, and the Immigrant*, 25 MOD. L. REV. 654, 656–57 (1962). Various complaints were lodged against the new immigrants. See GAINER, *supra*, at 15–35 (depressing wages and working conditions), 36–59 (aggravating housing shortage), 99–107 (involved in anarchist movement), 107–28 (threat to racial purity); GARTNER, THE JEWISH IMMIGRANT IN ENGLAND, 1870–1914, at 276 (1960) ("sweating" practice in industry), 278 (racial objections); Kiernan, *Britons Old and New*, in HOLMES, *supra*, at 53 (lowering wages and taking up needed housing). Some of the animosity was undoubtedly tempered either by genuine sympathy, GARTNER, *supra*, at 274, or by embarrassment at being perceived as racially prejudiced or as uncharitable to people fleeing violent persecution, GARRARD, note 131 *supra*, at 5–10, 203–09; JONES, *supra*, at 72. Finally, as to the effect of large-scale black and Asian immigration to Britain, see EVANS, IMMIGRATION LAW 2 (2d ed. 1983); FOOT, *supra*, at 25–79; GAINER, *supra*, at 212; MOORE & WALLACE, note 130 *supra*, at 2–4, 26; Wood, in GRIFFITH (ed.), COLOURED IMMIGRANTS IN BRITAIN, at 3, 219–25 (1960).

[163] The correlation is not perfect, since political factors other than high volume can spur litigation. See, *e.g.*, the McCarthy era cases, notes 181–89 *infra* and accompanying text, and the Iranian cases, notes 203–12 *infra* and accompanying text.

[164] See notes 166–73 *infra* and accompanying text.

[165] See, *e.g.*, VAN VLECK, THE ADMINISTRATIVE CONTROL OF ALIENS 19 (1932).

Further, the precedents established in those cases constrain the courts even during future periods of relative quiet.

These factors may help to explain both the creation and the preservation of the plenary power doctrine. Chinese immigrants began arriving in California in earnest around 1850, when labor was in short supply. By 1869, however, the labor market had become glutted and the presence of the Chinese unwelcome.[166] The migration continued, and anti-Chinese prejudice intensified.[167] In 1882, responding to nativist sentiment, Congress passed the Chinese Exclusion Act, the first statute restricting entry on racial grounds.[168]

During the 1880s, a new wave of immigrants started coming to California from Japan.[169] The Japanese immigrants became the main target of anti-Asian prejudice,[170] and were sometimes lumped together with the Chinese in propaganda that warned of the "Yellow Peril."[171] Much of that hostility found expression in the anti-Japanese resolutions of several state legislatures, the debates on which contained some of the most vicious anti-Japanese rhetoric of the period.[172] In 1924, Congress reacted by prohibiting the entry of all Japanese immigrants.[173]

---

[166] See CHUMAN, THE BAMBOO PEOPLE: THE LAW AND JAPANESE-AMERICANS 3–4 (1976). The completion of the transcontinental railroad in 1869 enabled more American workers to come to California at a time when the post–Civil War depression had already reduced the need for labor. *Id.*

[167] *Id.* at 4, 7–9; CURRAN, note 161 *supra*, at 78–90; Ferguson, *The California Alien Land Law and the Fourteenth Amendment*, 35 CAL. L. REV. 61, 62–63 (1947); HANDLIN, IMMIGRATION AS A FACTOR IN AMERICAN HISTORY 167 (1959); 1 KONVITZ, note 3 *supra*, at 11–12; Seller, *Historical Perspectives on American Immigration Policy: Case Studies and Current Implications*, 45 LAW & CONTEMP. PROB. (No. 2) 137, 153 (1982); TUNG, THE CHINESE IN AMERICA 1820–1973, at 1–2, 8 *et seq.* (1974). For a contemporary account of the anti-Chinese feeling, see COOLIDGE, CHINESE IMMIGRATION (1909).

[168] Act of Aug. 3, 1882, 22 Stat. 214. See CHUMAN, note 166 *supra*, at 7–8; Abrams, *American Immigration Policy: How Strait the Gate?* 45 LAW & CONTEMP. PROB. (No. 2) 107, 108 (1983).

[169] CHUMAN, note 166 *supra*, at 11.

[170] *Id.* at 11, 15–19; CURRAN, note 161 *supra*, at 91–92; Ferguson, note 167 *supra*, at 63–73; HANDLIN, note 167 *supra*, at 167; HERMAN, THE JAPANESE IN AMERICA 1843–1973, at 6 *et seq.* (1974); Huizinga, *Alien Land Laws: Constitutional Limitations on State Power to Regulate*, 32 HASTINGS L.J. 251, 252–53 (1980); KONVITZ, note 3 *supra*, at 22, 157–58; McGovney, *The Anti-Japanese Land Laws of California and Ten Other States*, 35 CAL. L. REV. 7, 13–14 (1947).

[171] CHUMAN, note 166 *supra*, at 73–77.

[172] *Id.* at 19, 42.

[173] The Act of May 26, 1924, 43 Stat. 153, § 13(c), excluded all aliens "ineligible to citizenship." The Supreme Court had held in Ozawa v. United States, 260 U.S. 178 (1922), that the Japanese were ineligible for citizenship.

It was during this era of public hostility to Asians that the Supreme Court adopted and solidified the plenary power doctrine.[174] In many cases, the Asian ancestry of the particular aliens prompted judicial tirades about their negative influences. Justice Field, a presidential hopeful who had been instrumental in persuading Congress to restrict Chinese immigration,[175] was one of the central figures in this drama. In *Chew Heong v. United States*,[176] he dissented from a statutory interpretation that he considered too liberal. In an opinion that can fully be appreciated only when read in its entirety, Justice Field launched a vitriolic attack on the Chinese as a race and delivered an explicit appeal to the will of the people. Five years later, it was Justice Field who authored the majority opinion in the *Chinese Exclusion Case*, where the Court first recognized an inherent, nonenumerated, Congressional power to exclude aliens.[177]

But Justice Field was not alone in his denunciations of the Chinese. Justice Bradley wrote in 1884 that "Chinese of the lower classes have little respect for the solemnity of an oath."[178] Even Justice Brewer, who dissented when the Supreme Court extended the plenary power doctrine from exclusion to deportation, conceded that the challenged statute had been "directed only at the obnoxious Chinese," who were a "distasteful class."[179] His fear was that the precedent would affect other ethnic groups in the future.[180]

The Supreme Court decisions of the early 1950s breathed new vigor into the plenary power doctrine. This was the period in which the national preoccupation with Communism was at its peak.[181] The aliens in most of those cases had been charged with

---

[174] The principal building blocks were Chae Chan Ping v. United States [The Chinese Exclusion Case], 130 U.S. 581 (1889); Ekiu v. United States, 142 U.S. 651 (1892); and Fong Yue Ting v. United States, 149 U.S. 698 (1893). See also Lee Lung v. Patterson, 186 U.S. 168 (1902); Chin Ying v. United States, 186 U.S. 202 (1902); Chin Bak Kan v. United States, 186 U.S. 193 (1902); Li Sing v. United States, 180 U.S. 486 (1901); Fok Yong Yo v. United States, 185 U.S. 296 (1902); Lem Moon Sing v. United States, 158 U.S. 538 (1895).

[175] KONVITZ, note 3 *supra*, at 10–11 n.29.

[176] 112 U.S. 536, 560–78 (1884).

[177] 130 U.S. 581 (1889). See notes 91–92 *supra* and accompanying text.

[178] Chew Heong v. United States, 112 U.S. 536, 579 (1884) (Bradley, J., dissenting).

[179] Fong Yue Ting v. United States, 149 U.S. 698, 743 (1893). In fairness to Justice Field, it should be noted that he, too, balked at extending the plenary power doctrine from exclusion to deportation. *Id.* at 744–61.

[180] *Id.* at 743.

[181] See generally KONVITZ, EXPANDING LIBERTIES 120–21 (1966). For a summary of the anti-Communist legislation enacted during that period, see *id.* at 134–42. Konvitz also

possessing various ties to the Communist party, and the results, not surprisingly, were extreme.[182]

Apart from the anti-Communist political forces relevant to those cases specifically involving alien Communists, there prevailed during that period a more general public hostility toward aliens.[183] This hostility became apparent after the Second World War,[184] and might simply have been part of the traditional anti-alien backlash accompanying a major war.[185] The hostility might have flowed also from a publicly perceived association of aliens with subversive causes, and from the traditional public refusal to tolerate in aliens the same degree of political radicalism tolerated in the native born.[186] And some part of the anti-alien atmosphere might have been due to racial fears, as evidenced by the statements offered to support the national origins quota system embodied in the Immigration and Nationality Act of 1952.[187]

The combined effect of these anti-Communist and anti-alien forces was to create an atmosphere conducive to the retention of strict Congressional and Presidential control over aliens, and thus the preservation of the plenary power doctrine. The anti-Communist instincts expressed in *Harisiades* have already been quoted.[188] It was probably to be expected that in *Galvan v. Press*,[189] decided in 1954, the Court would at the very least decline to overrule a principle as deeply entrenched as the plenary power doctrine by then had become, even if the Court had otherwise been inclined to intervene.

---

argues, *id.* at 122, that political forces affected the Supreme Court's decision in Dennis v. United States, 341 U.S. 494 (1951).

[182] *E.g.*, Galvan v. Press, 347 U.S. 522 (1954); Harisiades v. Shaughnessy, 342 U.S. 580 (1952); United States *ex rel.* Knauff v. Shaughnessy, 338 U.S. 537 (1950); *cf.* Shaughnessy v. United States *ex rel.* Mezei, 345 U.S. 206 (1953) (alien excluded as security risk, plenary power doctrine bars review); Jay v Boyd, 351 U.S. 345 (1956) (deportation of alien Communist, but plenary power doctrine not at issue).

[183] KONVITZ, note 31 *supra*, at 123–26 (1953).

[184] *Id.* at 123.

[185] See HIGHAM, STRANGERS IN THE LAND 194–233 (2d ed. 1963); Seller, note 167 *supra*, at 150–51.

[186] KONVITZ, note 31 *supra*, at 122; see also Reimers, *Recent Immigration Policy: An Analysis*, in CHISWICK (ed.), THE GATEWAY: U.S. IMMIGRATION ISSUES AND POLICIES 28 (1982).

[187] Act of June 27, 1952, Pub. L. 82–414, 66 Stat. 163. See Reimers, note 186 *supra*, at 25–27.

[188] See notes 108–12 *supra* and accompanying text.

[189] 347 U.S. 522 (1954). See notes 157–58 *supra* and accompanying text.

From the 1960s on, the Supreme Court has only infrequently addressed constitutional challenges to immigration legislation, probably because the plenary power doctrine has left little room in which to litigate such issues. But on those few occasions when the Supreme Court did discuss the previous plenary power doctrine cases, the Court consistently reaffirmed it.[190] This judicial conservatism in this subarea of immigration law cannot be attributed to a general conservatism in society. During much of that period—specifically the early to mid-1960s—political liberalism flourished on many important issues. There evolved a new appreciation both for civil rights in general and for equal economic opportunities in particular. The Civil Rights Act became law in 1964.[191] The contrast invites an inquiry into why the plenary power doctrine has been allowed to survive.

Part of the explanation lies undoubtedly in the enormous force, illustrated by *Galvan v. Press*, of almost a century of precedent. As discussed earlier, the Court's perception of its role includes great emphasis on the desirability of following such well established precedent. As also noted earlier, the Court has perceived a general connection between immigration and foreign policy, and that has narrowed its role perception further. In addition, for those judges whose substantive attitudes toward immigration are conservative already, attitude reinforces role perception in this context. Finally, in at least two of the modern cases, special considerations might have influenced the outcome.[192] One possible explanation, therefore, is simply that these factors have prevailed over the general liberalism dominating some of this time period.

It is submitted, however, that other important forces have interacted with those factors. Chief among them is that, as the previous discussion has shown, immigrants have been consistently unpopular, at least during this century. That is not to say that the

---

[190] *E.g.*, Fiallo v. Bell, 430 U.S. 787 (1977); Kleindienst v. Mandel, 408 U.S. 753 (1972); Boutilier v. INS, 387 U.S. 118 (1967). But *cf.* I.N.S. v. Chadha, 103 S. Ct. 2764 (1983), discussed in notes 226–43 *infra* and accompanying text.

[191] Civil Rights Act of 1964, Pub. L. 88-352, 78 Stat. 241.

[192] In Boutilier v. INS, 387 U.S. 118 (1967), the charge against the alien was homosexual conduct, which, despite the liberalism of the 1960s, had still not attained public acceptance. In Kleindienst v. Mandel, 408 U.S. 753 (1972), the exclusion order was based on the alien's radical political views; the case might be, in part, an example of society's unwillingness to accept in aliens the same level of political unorthodoxy it will accept in citizens. See note 186 *supra* and accompanying text.

general public has always favored restricting the prevailing immigration policy, for there have certainly been periods in which immigration has been encouraged as economically beneficial.[193] But the immigrants themselves, although tolerated during such periods, have never been popular as a group, as the history of prejudice toward one wave of immigrants after another, discussed earlier, reveals.[194] The liberalism of the 1960s had its limits. When challenges to Congressional or Presidential control over immigration arose, it was inevitable that those limits would be tested.

During this time period, the general unpopularity of immigrants has been exacerbated by public reaction to Mexican immigrants in particular. As early as the 1930s, although the numbers of Mexican immigrants to the United States remained low,[195] prejudice and discrimination were common.[196] Today, now that Mexico is by far the single largest source of annual immigration,[197] prejudice toward both Mexican aliens and even American citizens of Mexican ancestry has become rampant.[198]

---

[193] *E.g.*, the American colonists encouraged immigration. BENTLEY, note 161 *supra*, at 14; CHUMAN, note 166 *supra*, at 53; CURRAN, note 161 *supra*, at 11; KONVITZ, note 3 *supra*, at 1; PROPER, note 139 *supra*, ch. 2; VAN VLECK, note 165 *supra*, at 3; Seller, note 167 *supra*, at 140–41; Hoyt, *Naturalization under the American Colonies: Signs of a New Community*, 67 POL. SCI. Q. 248, 262 (1952); Risch, *Encouragement of Immigration as Revealed in Colonial Legislation*, 45 VA. MAGAZINE 1, 9 (1937); see also The Passenger Cases, 48 U.S. (7 How.) 283, 401 (1849) (McLean, J.). In the 1850s, Chinese immigrants were needed in California to work in the orchards, on farms, in mines, in transportation, and in manufacturing. CHUMAN, note 166 *supra*, at 3–4. During the Second World War, Mexican braceros were imported to build railroads and to work in the fields. BENTLEY, note 161 *supra*, at 37.

[194] The 1965 amendments that finally abolished the national origins quota systems were consistent with the public desire to eliminate racial discrimination. Even at that time, however, the public opinion polls showed that the majority did not want more immigrants. See Reimers, note 186 *supra*, at 33.

[195] MORRIS & MAYIO, CURBING ILLEGAL IMMIGRATION 6 (1982).

[196] See CORTES (ed.), THE MEXICAN AMERICAN AND THE LAW (1974). For a detailed account of one major governmental effort to apprehend and deport illegal aliens from Mexico, see GARCIA, OPERATION WETBACK: THE MASS DEPORTATION OF MEXICAN UNDOCUMENTED WORKERS IN 1954 (1980), esp. at 143–44 (public associated "wetbacks" with crime, poverty, and disease).

[197] See BENTLEY, note 161 *supra*, at 38.

[198] *Id.* at 40–42 (in Southwest); Bronfenbrenner, *Hyphenated Americans—Economic Aspects*, 45 LAW & CONTEMP. PROB. (No. 2) 9, 25 (1983); Martin & Houstoun, *European and American Immigration Policies*, 45 LAW & CONTEMP. PROB. (No. 2) 29, 44 (1983); Nafziger, *An Immigration Policy of Helping Bring People to the Resources*, 8 DENVER J. INT'L L. & POLICY 607 (1979); SAMORA, LOS MOJADOS: THE WETBACK STORY 98–105 (1971) (exploitation of illegal Mexican entrants); Smith, note 138 *supra*, at 3; see also Study, *Consular Discretion in the Immigrant Visa-issuing Process*, 16 SAN DIEGO L. REV. 87, 142 & n.366 (1978).

Further tarnishing the public image of aliens is the dramatic scale of illegal immigration. Accurate estimates of the illegal alien population have not yet been obtained, but there is no doubt that the figure is in the millions.[199] About two-thirds of the illegal entrants are believed to be Mexicans.[200] For various reasons, illegal alien workers can be and often are employed at substandard pay and under substandard conditions.[201] This phenomenon breeds resentment in American workers, who perceive, rightly or wrongly, that illegal aliens are thereby aggravating the unemployment rate and depressing the wages and working conditions of American laborers.[202] Moreover, even apart from economic concerns, these mass violations of federal law evoke law enforcement values the breach of which further damages the public image of aliens.

Although the recent batch of plenary power doctrine cases decided by the Supreme Court has not involved Mexican litigants, there are ways in which the public reaction to Mexican immigration might have contributed indirectly to those results. First, a large influx of aliens from any one country can create a general climate unfavorable to immigrants, as can be seen from the earlier discussion. This climate can induce judicial conservatism either because a judge's personal attitude might itself be shaped by public opinion or because a judge might perceive his or her role as requiring the consultation of public opinion before making law. Moreover, to the extent that either attitude or contemporary political forces are considered, the emphasis at the Supreme Court level on precedential

---

[199] Abrams, note 168 *supra*, at 112–13; Chapman, *A Look at Illegal Immigration: Causes and Impact on the United States*, 13 SAN DIEGO L. REV. 34, 34–35 (1975); Corwin, *The Numbers Game: Estimates of Illegal Aliens in the United States 1970–1981*, 45 LAW & CONTEMP. PROB. (No. 2) 223 (1983); Fogel, note 138 *supra*, at 72; HALSELL, THE ILLEGALS 4 (1978); Manulkin & Maghame, note 138 *supra*, at 43–45; MORRIS & MAYIO, note 195 *supra*, at 1; Salinas & Torres, *The Undocumented Mexican Alien: A Legal, Social, and Economic Analysis*, 13 HOUSTON L. REV. 863, 866 (1976); Schuck, note 68 *supra*, at 41–42; SCIRP, note 138 *supra*, at 37; Smith, note 138 *supra*, at 3. Studies of the total numbers of illegal aliens and the numbers of Mexican illegal aliens have been criticized as sloppy. Bustamante, *Immigrant from Mexico: The Silent Invasion Issue*, in BRYCE-LAPORTE (ed.), SOURCEBOOK ON THE NEW IMMIGRATION 139–44 (1980).

[200] MORRIS & MAYIO, note 195 *supra*, at 4.

[201] See, *e.g.*, BENTLEY, note 161 *supra*, at 152–55; Fogel, note 138 *supra*, at 66; SAMORA, note 198 *supra*, at 98–105.

[202] *Bentley*, note 161 *supra*, at 152–55; Salinas & Torres, note 199 *supra*, at 864; see also Nafziger, *A Policy Framework for Regulating the Flow of Undocumented Mexican Aliens into the United States*, 56 ORE. L. REV. 63, 69–72 (1977) (arguing that undocumented Mexican aliens cause only minimal displacement of American workers).

effect vis-à-vis consequences to the individual parties would be expected to render insignificant the nationality of the particular alien litigant.

In some cases, however, the nationality of the particular alien has legal relevance. The most striking examples are the lower court decisions involving Iranian students. Those decisions reflect a strong and unwavering progovernment tilt.[203] Especially instructive is *Yassini v. Crosland*.[204] During the Iranian hostage crisis, President Carter ordered the Attorney General to summon all Iranian students to INS offices for inspection, and to identify and deport any Iranian students who were violating the immigration laws.[205] The INS,[206] purporting to implément the Presidential Order, issued a directive revoking the permission previously granted to all Iranian nationals to remain in the United States until a specified date.[207] One of the alien's arguments in *Yassini* was based on *Hampton v. Mow Sun Wong*, where the Supreme Court had laid down an important principle:[208]

> When the Federal Government asserts an overriding national interest as justification for a discriminatory rule which would violate the Equal Protection Clause if adopted by a State, due process requires that there be a legitimate basis for presuming that the rule was actually intended to serve that interest. If the agency which promulgates the rule has direct responsibility for fostering or protecting that interest, . . . [or] if the rule were *expressly mandated* by the Congress or the President, we might presume that any interest which might rationally be served by the rule did in fact give rise to its adoption.

Since the INS and the Justice Department have no direct responsibility for making foreign policy, the question would seem to be

---

[203] In addition to the cases cited in notes 204, 211 *infra*, see Shoaee v. I.N.S., 704 F.2d 1079 (9th Cir. 1983); Torabpour v. I.N.S., 694 F.2d 1119 (8th Cir. 1982); Ghorbani v. I.N.S., 686 F.2d 784 (9th Cir. 1982); Shoja v. I.N.S., 679 F.2d 447 (5th Cir. 1982); Akhbari v. U.S.I.N.S., 678 F.2d 575 (5th Cir. 1982); Ghajar v. I.N.S., 652 F.2d 1347 (9th Cir. 1981). But *cf.* Mashi v. I.N.S., 585 F.2d 1309 (5th Cir. 1978) (before seizure of hostages).

[204] 618 F.2d 1356 (9th Cir. 1980).

[205] 15 WEEKLY COMPILATION OF PRESIDENTIAL DOCUMENTS 2107 (1979).

[206] The Attorney General's powers to implement the immigration laws, including the power to issue regulations, have been delegated to the Commissioner of the INS. See 8 C.F.R. § 2.1 (1984).

[207] See *Yassini*, 618 F.2d at 1359.

[208] 426 U.S. 88, 103 (1976). See Comment, *Federal Civil Service Employment: Resident Aliens Need Not Apply*, 15 SAN DIEGO L. REV. 171 (1977).

whether the INS directive was expressly mandated by either the Immigration and Nationality Act or the Presidential Order. Rather than address that question, the Court in *Yassini* disposed of the due process argument by concluding that the INS directive was "within the scope" of the Presidential Order.[209] But there is a vast difference between an agency action that is "expressly mandated" by Presidential order and one that is merely "within the scope" of it. If a rational agency action is expressly mandated by the President, then, as *Mow Sun Wong* concedes, the action is valid.[210] To uphold a directive assertedly justified only by an interest that the agency has no responsibility for fostering, however, runs precisely counter to the philosophy and the result of *Mow Sun Wong*. Nothing in the Presidential Order expressly, or for that matter even implicitly, mandated the termination of permission previously granted Iranian nationals to remain in the United States. The directive simply reflected the judgment of the INS that this sanction would help to resolve the Iranian crisis. Thus the practical effect of the Court's holding is to expand the plenary power doctrine, extreme already when used to insulate Congressional action from meaningful constitutional review, to cover INS action in particular. Other circuits have had similarly little difficulty in sustaining the constitutionality of INS regulations selectively disadvantaging Iranian nationals in ways not mandated by Congress or the President.[211]

When it is considered that contrary dispositions were available in those cases, that in *Yassini* a contrary conclusion on the constitutional issue seemed dictated by *Mow Sun Wong*, and that the panel in *Yassini* was composed of three judges ordinarily regarded as quite liberal,[212] the results might seem surprising. The surprise disappears when the depth of the public outcry against Iran following the seizure and continued detention of the American hostages is recalled. The courts might well have believed it unthinkable to flout so intense a public mood by striking down a retaliatory action of the executive branch.

---

[209] 618 F.2d at 1362.

[210] That was the case in Narenji v. Civiletti, 617 F.2d 745 (D.C. Cir. 1980), where the INS had simply executed a foreign policy decision of the President.

[211] *E.g.*, Nademi v. I.N.S., 679 F.2d 811, 814 (10th Cir. 1982); Malek-Marzban v. I.N.S., 653 F.2d 113, 116 (4th Cir. 1981).

[212] The panel in *Yassini* consisted of Judges Tuttle, Tang, and Hug.

III. THE PRACTICE

The lower court opinions frequently reflect a tone consistent with that of the Supreme Court's plenary power decisions. Even apart from the Iranian cases discussed earlier,[213] numerous lower courts have virtually declined to review Congressional immigration Acts for compliance with substantive constitutional constraints.[214]

At the same time, however, a number of courts are beginning to show signs of extreme disquiet. Faced with constitutional challenges to harsh legislation, courts uneasy over the concept of plenary Congressional power have begun doing what courts typically do when hemmed in by unacceptable doctrine. They strain to find means of escape. When the only exits seem blocked by logical barriers, the movement can be slowed. But eventually, if the doctrine is intolerable, even artificial detours prevail over the alternative of submission.

On the question of plenary Congressional power over immigration, the beginnings of that process are now visible. At first, the phenomenon was largely confined to rhetoric. Some courts assumed the power to invalidate federal immigration statutes that draw irrational distinctions, only to find the particular legislation rational.[215] But recently the results have begun to match the rhetoric. Two district court decisions have held deportation provisions unconstitutional as applied to the particular facts, though both were ultimately reversed on appeal.[216] Other decisions, discussed below, still stand. They reveal at least three distinct devices by which courts anxious to palliate the rigors of the plenary power doctrine have occasionally succeeded.

---

[213] See notes 203–12 *supra* and accompanying text.

[214] *E.g.*, Palma v. Verdeyen, 676 F.2d 100, 103 (4th Cir. 1982); Pierre v. INS, 547 F.2d 1281, 1289–90 (5th Cir. 1977); Buckley v. Gibney, 332 F. Supp. 790 (S.D.N.Y.), *aff'd*, 449 F.2d 1305 (2d Cir. 1971); *cf.* Knoetze v. United States, 634 F.2d 207, 211–12 (5th Cir. 1981) (alien has no due process rights when visa revoked, even if after entry). For an especially extreme decision, see Jean v. Nelson, 727 F.2d 957, 963 (11th Cir. 1984) (*en banc*) (Attorney General may discriminate on basis of national origin when detaining excluded aliens), *cert. granted*, 105 S.Ct. 563.

[215] *E.g.*, United States v. Barajas-Guillen, 632 F.2d 749, 752–54 (9th Cir. 1980); Menezes v. INS, 601 F.2d 1028, 1034 (9th Cir. 1979); Castillo-Felix v. INS, 601 F.2d 459, 467 (9th Cir. 1979); Alvarez v. District Director, 539 F.2d 1220, 1224 (9th Cir. 1976); Noel v. Chapman, 508 F.2d 1023, 1028–29 (2d Cir. 1975).

[216] Acosta v. Gaffney, 413 F. Supp. 827 (D.N.J. 1976), *rev'd* 558 F.2d 1153 (3d Cir. 1977); Lieggi v. USINS, 389 F. Supp. 12 (N.D. Ill. 1975), *rev'd in unrep'd decision*, see 529 F.2d 530 (7th Cir. 1976). The Third Circuit decision in *Acosta* accords with Gonzalez-Cuevas v. INS, 515 F.2d 1222 (5th Cir. 1975); Aalund v. Marshall, 461 F.2d 710 (5th Cir. 1972).

One technique has been to draw distinctions between distinctions. A classic illustration is provided by the Second Circuit decision in *Francis v. I.N.S.*[217] A deportable alien applied for discretionary relief. The applicable provision had been interpreted to require, *inter alia*, that the alien has departed from and returned to the United States.[218] The alien, who had remained in the United States, argued that it would be irrational, and thus violative of equal protection, to treat him less favorably than an alien who had left and returned but who was otherwise similarly situated.

The court acknowledged the Congressional power "to create different standards of admission and deportation *for different groups* of aliens."[219] It then said: "However, once those choices are made, individuals *within a particular group* may not be subjected to disparate treatment on criteria wholly unrelated to any legitimate governmental interest."[220] Finding no rational basis for the challenged distinction, the court held the provision unconstitutional as applied. Variants of this reasoning have been employed in other modern opinions.[221]

The technique adopted in *Francis* has one fatal flaw: it proves too much. Any classification contained in an immigration statute could be characterized either as a distinction between groups or as a

---

[217] 532 F.2d 268 (2d Cir. 1976).

[218] Immigration and Nationality Act § 212(c), 8 U.S.C. § 1182(c). The alien became deportable upon being convicted of possession of marijuana. *Id.* § 241(a)(11), 8 U.S.C. § 1251 (a)(11).

[219] 532 F.2d at 273 (emphasis added). It added a footnote conceding that "the validity of distinctions drawn by Congress with respect to deportability is not a proper subject for judicial concern." *Id.* at 273 n.8, quoting Oliver v. INS, 517 F.2d 426, 428 (2d Cir. 1975); Bronsztejn v. INS, 526 F.2d 1290, 1291 (2d Cir. 1975).

[220] 532 F.2d at 273 (emphasis added).

[221] In Tapia-Acuna v. INS, 640 F.2d 223 (9th Cir. 1981), the Ninth Circuit followed *Francis*. Explaining its selection of the standard of review, the court said: "Like the Second Circuit, this court applies the rational basis test to federal immigration statutes distinguishing *among groups of aliens.*" *Id.* at 225 (emphasis added). The court's emphasis on distinctions among groups was precisely the opposite of the *Francis* court's emphasis on distinctions between individuals within a group. In Alvarez v. District Director, 539 F.2d 1220 (9th Cir. 1976), the court distinguished between governmental action treating aliens "as a class" and governmental action drawing classifications "among aliens." *Id.* at 1224 n.3. It suggested in dictum that the former triggered strict scrutiny; in support, the court erroneously cited cases applying strict scrutiny to state statutes discriminating against aliens. *Id.* For classifications among aliens, the court assumed that the rational basis test applied. The court did not consider the applicability of the plenary power doctrine to either type of classification. *Cf.* Menezes v. INS, 601 F.2d 1028, 1034 (9th Cir. 1979) ("discrimination *within* the class of aliens—allowing benefits to some aliens but not to others" requires rational basis), quoting partly from Mathews v. Diaz, 426 U.S. 67, 80, 81–83 (1976).

distinction within a group, as the court sees fit. Everything turns on how the particular group is defined. In *Francis*, for example, the court implicitly treated those aliens who satisfied all the statutory criteria other than the leave-and-return requirement as a single group. It was therefore able to read the statute as distinguishing, within that group, between the individual who has left and returned and the individual who has remained in the country. If anything, however, it would seem at least as intuitive to define the group as consisting of those people who meet all the statutory requirements, including the leave-and-return element. If the group were so defined, the statute would be one that provides different standards for different groups—discretionary relief for those who satisfy all the statutory elements and no discretionary relief for those who do not. So characterized, the statute would not be reviewable for rationality under the court's formulation.[222]

To carry this analysis one step further, the reasoning adopted in *Francis* is fundamentally inconsistent with the actual results of the Supreme Court's plenary power decisions. In *Fiallo*, for example, analogous reasoning would have enabled the Court to say that Congress validly provided special benefits to children of American citizens, but that, having chosen to do so, Congress could not then distinguish between legitimate and illegitimate children within that group unless the distinction was rationally related to a permissible Congressional objective. Similar reasoning could have been applied to any other plenary power decision upholding a statutory classification. The distinction between distinctions would either swallow the plenary power doctrine entirely or give the courts an unfettered discretion whether to invoke it. Distinctions between groups and systematic distinctions between individuals within a group are in fact one and the same.

A second device for avoiding the harshness of the plenary power doctrine is to create an exception, thus far limited to aliens facing deportation, and possibly to returning resident aliens facing exclusion, for procedural due process.[223] This technique, too, has its share of problems. As others have shown, it is an exception that the Supreme Court has displayed little consistency in recognizing.[224]

---

[222] See note 219 *supra*.

[223] See notes 23–26 *supra*.

[224] See, *e.g.*, Hart, *The Power of Congress to Limit the Jurisdiction of Federal Courts: An Exercise in Dialectic*, 66 HARV. L. REV. 1362, 1387–96 (1953); Scharpf, note 29 *supra*, at 578–81

Apart from the problem of inconsistency, why should such fundamental constitutional liberties as the First Amendment freedoms and equal protection receive less judicial supervision than procedural due process? The logic of the opinions suggests that Congress could constitutionally enact legislation deporting all black aliens, but only if each alien is given a predeportation hearing at which there is an opportunity to prove he or she is in fact white.[225] This is not the place for an exegesis on the function of process in relation to either justice or the appearance of justice. It is enough to observe that the important individual interests that are frequently at stake in immigration cases, and that have induced the Supreme Court at least sporadically to recognize procedural due process, are present also in those cases where substantive constitutional defects are alleged. The substantive/procedural dichotomy is thus objectionable not only because of the inconsistency with which it has been applied, but also because the limitation to procedural due process leaves too wide an area unguarded.

A third technique for avoiding the principle of judicial noninterference with immigration statutes is to acknowledge the plenary nature of the Congressional power, but to proceed as if the word "plenary" were meaningless. This strategy was adopted by the Supreme Court in *I.N.S. v. Chadha*,[226] a decision that requires close examination.

---

n.218. Several lower courts have been assertive in addressing procedural due process challenges, particularly in the asylum context. See generally Martin, note 28 *supra*, at 168–71; Note, *Filling the Immigration Void: Rodriguez-Fernandez v. Wilkinson—an Excludable Alien's Right to be Free from Indeterminate Detention*, 31 CATH. L. REV. 335 (1982); Note, *United States Asylum Procedures: Current Status and Proposals for Reform*, 14 CORNELL INT'L L.J. 405 (1981); Note, *The Constitutional Rights of Excluded Aliens: Proposed Limitations on the Indefinite Detention of the Cuban Refugees*, 70 GEO. L.J. 1303 (1982); see also Augustin v. Sava, 735 F.2d 32 (2d Cir. 1984). Outside the specific context of asylum, see generally Appleman, *Right to Counsel in Deportation Proceedings*, 14 SAN DIEGO L. REV. 130 (1976); Aleinikoff, note 28 *supra*; Schuck, note 68 *supra*, at 66–68; *cf.* Gardner, *Due Process and Deportation: A Critical Examination of the Plenary Power and the Fundamental Fairness Doctrine*, 8 HASTINGS CONST. L.Q. 397 (1981) (advocating safeguards applicable in criminal proceedings).

[225] I do not suggest that Congress would contemplate such a statute today. Rather, this extreme example is offered to illustrate the arbitrariness of allowing review for procedural due process while denying review for compliance with substantive constitutional guarantees. It might be objected that the Supreme Court would surely find some way to strike down such a statute in the unlikely event it were ever enacted, but the older cases used the plenary power doctrine to uphold statutes explicitly discriminating on the basis of race, and the modern Supreme Court decisions continue to cite those cases approvingly. See, *e.g.*, Fiallo v. Bell, 430 U.S. 787, 792 (1977); Kleindienst v. Mandel, 408 U.S. 753, 765–66, 766 n.6 (1972). The Court might indeed fashion an escape route from the plenary power doctrine if a statute as extreme as the one hypothesized were ever enacted, but to do so would spell the end of the plenary power doctrine as we know it.

[226] 103 S.Ct. 2764 (1983).

The Immigration and Nationality Act gives the Attorney General the discretion to suspend the deportation of an otherwise deportable alien who meets several statutory prerequisites.[227] The statute further provides, however, that either house of Congress may nullify the suspension by passing a resolution to that effect.[228] An alien whose grant of suspension had been disapproved by the House of Representatives argued that the "legislative veto"[229] was unconstitutional. The Court ultimately agreed. It reasoned that the power the statute purported to confer on the House was "legislative" in character, and that, under the constitutional scheme for preserving separation of powers, a legislative power may be exercised only upon a vote of both houses of Congress, followed by either a Presidential signature or a Congressional override of a Presidential veto.[230]

But how could the Court reach the merits at all? The House action was valid unless the immigration statute that expressly purported to authorize it was unconstitutional. In the light of the "plenary" Congressional power to regulate immigration, how was it that the constitutionality of the statute could even be reviewed? The House of Representatives argued that the case presented a nonjusticiable political question because the statutory provision was an exercise of the Congressional power to "establish an uniform Rule of Naturalization."[231] The Court responded: "The plenary authority of Congress over aliens under [the naturalization clause] is not open to question, but what is challenged here is whether Congress has chosen a constitutionally permissible means of implementing that power."[232] It then reviewed the various prongs of the political question doctrine collected in *Baker v. Carr*[233] and, concluding that none applied to the present case, found the constitutional question justiciable. Although the same reasoning could as easily have been invoked in the plenary power cases,[234] the Court

---

[227] See Immigration & Nationality Act § 244(a), 8 U.S.C. § 1254(a).

[228] *Id.* § 244(c), 8 U.S.C. § 1254(c).

[229] See 103 S.Ct. at 2771 n.2.

[230] 103 S.Ct. at 2780–88, relying on U.S. Const. art. I, §§ 1, 7.

[231] U.S. Const. art. I, § 8, cl. 4. See 103 S.Ct. at 2778–79.

[232] 103 S.Ct. at 2779.

[233] 369 U.S. 186 (1962).

[234] See Sec. IA *supra*.

made no attempt to reconcile its decision with those cases, not one of which was cited in the opinion.

One writer cautions against reading undue significance into *Chadha*. He points out that the Court was preoccupied with the broad constitutional questions concerning legislative vetoes and, further, that in any case the Court reaffirmed the "plenary authority of Congress over aliens."[235]

As to the first point, it is undoubtedly true that the Court's overriding concern was with the validity of legislative vetoes in general, not with this particular provision of the Immigration and Nationality Act. In the past fifty years, 295 legislative veto provisions, cutting across numerous boundaries,[236] have been enacted by Congress.[237] All are potentially endangered by the decision in *Chadha*.[238] Under these circumstances, it would indeed be shortsighted to think that the Court's primary concern in *Chadha* was with immigration law.

At the same time, the Court's avoidance of the plenary power doctrine could not have been inadvertent. In one of its briefs, the House of Representatives spent twelve pages arguing that the Court should invoke the doctrine in this case.[239] During the course of that discussion, the House brief cited practically every major plenary power decision. Particular attention was focused on the distinction between inherent sovereign powers, which the brief faulted the lower court for failing to consider, and enumerated powers, such as the commerce clause and the naturalization clause, on which the lower court had assumed the statute rested.[240] The distinction is important because, as discussed earlier, the Supreme Court has frequently cited the sovereignty theory to support its limited view of the judicial role. Yet, as revealed in the excerpt quoted above, the Supreme Court disregarded the House argument

---

[235] Schuck, note 68 *supra*, at 59 n.319.

[236] Objections to the broad sweep of the Court's holding are voiced in Strauss, *Was There a Baby in the Bathwater? A Comment on the Supreme Court's Legislative Veto Decision*, 1983 DUKE L.J. 789.

[237] Abourezk, *The Congressional Veto: A Contemporary Response to Executive Encroachment on Legislative Prerogatives*, 52 IND. L. REV. 323, 324 (1977).

[238] Justice Powell would have avoided that result by limiting the holding to the case in which the decision being vetoed was "judicial" in character. See 103 S.Ct. at 2788–92.

[239] See No. 80–1832, Second Supplemental Brief of House of Representatives, at 10–22.

[240] *Id.* at 13–16.

and assumed that the statute rested solely on an enumerated power, the naturalization clause. In doing so, it omitted reference to any of the plenary power cases cited in the brief.

Consequently, it seems clear that the Court made a conscious decision not to apply the plenary power doctrine. Given the enormity of its impact across a broad spectrum of governmental activity, the decision might still be dismissed as one in which the Court simply subordinated its continued belief in the wisdom of the plenary power doctrine to its belief that legislative veto provisions are invalid. Under that scenario, the *Chadha* decision is not compelling evidence of an emerging new Supreme Court philosophy on constitutional review in immigration cases. But it does establish one more obstacle to the perpetuation of the plenary power doctrine. It will no longer be possible for the Court, without ignoring *Chadha*, to dismiss an alien's constitutional attack simply by labeling the Congressional power "plenary." It will have to distinguish *Chadha*, though, as will be seen, distinctions are possible.

As to the second point—that the Court did reaffirm the plenary nature of the Congressional authority over immigration—the response is more direct. In the same sentence in which the Court described the power as "plenary," it framed the issue as whether Congress's exercise of that power conforms with the Constitution. Further, the Court ultimately invalidated the exercise of this admittedly plenary power. In the light of the Court's actions, it is not clear what, if anything, the word "plenary" actually adds.[241]

The above discussion suggests that *Chadha* will speed the demise of the plenary power doctrine because the device by which the Court escaped the doctrine could logically be invoked in *any* case addressing the constitutionality of immigration legislation. It is further possible, though for the reasons given earlier unlikely, that *Chadha* is more than simply a precedent that will make continuation of the plenary power doctrine more difficult. It might additionally reflect the Court's independent desire to soften the principle of plenary Congressional power over immigration. Support for that possibility can be found in the patterns of the Court's previous

---

[241] Even before *Chadha*, courts had frequently described particular powers as "plenary," only to hold that the exercise of those plenary powers may nonetheless be reviewed for compliance with affirmative constitutional guarantees. In addition to the cases cited in *Chadha*, 103 S.Ct. at 2779, see Delaware Tribal Business Comm. v. Weeks, 430 U.S. 73, 83–84 (1977); Liddick v. City of Council Bluffs, 232 Iowa 197, 5 N.W.2d 361, 382 (1942).

rhetoric. As observed earlier, the language in which the plenary power doctrine is couched has become progressively less absolute.[242] Whatever meaning the Court in *Chadha* implicitly assigned to the word "plenary" is necessarily in keeping with that trend.

At the risk of jeopardizing the continued demise of the plenary power doctrine, I hasten to add that there will be ways of reconciling *Chadha* with the other plenary power cases if future courts are sufficiently determined to preserve the latter. One possibility is simply to distinguish *Chadha* as a procedural case. The argument would be that the Court's only constitutional objection was to the procedure Congress had provided for disapproving a grant of suspension; Congress could constitutionally disapprove such a grant only pursuant to the legislative procedure prescribed by the Constitution. Once characterized as procedural, the decision could be analogized to the procedural due process cases. As discussed above,[243] those cases arguably suggest an exception to the principle of plenary Congressional power.

Alternatively, the *Chadha* holding that a political question was not presented might in the future be limited to constitutional challenges based on separation of powers. The plenary power doctrine is itself a principle by which the Court refrains from interfering with what it perceives to be the province of Congress. Thus, *Chadha* might be rationalized as a case in which the Court could have avoided such interference only at the cost of permitting Congress to invade the territory of the Executive. If so characterized, the *Chadha* rationale would be inapplicable to constitutional attacks based on individual rights.

IV. THE FUTURE

We have entered a new phase in the life of the plenary power doctrine. This stage is characterized by a judicial willingness, so far episodic, to cut away at the notion of plenary Congressional power over immigration. The assaults have come from several directions.

At the Supreme Court level, the most noticeable change has been in rhetoric. The progression from absolute statements of noninter-

---

[242] See notes 11, 12 *supra*.

[243] See notes 23–26, 223–25 *supra* and accompanying text.

ference to hazier statements of relative deference has been steady.[244] In *Chadha*, despite its concession that Congress's power to regulate immigration is "plenary," the Court struck down a provision of the Immigration and Nationality Act without acknowledging the plenary power cases cited in the briefs.

But the most impressive inroads into the concept of plenary Congressional power have been made by the lower courts. Although it is too early to describe their activities as a full-scale rebellion, it is fair to say that discontent is spreading rapidly. Several circuits have translated the plenary power doctrine into a rational basis test.[245] Two of the most influential circuits in immigration matters—the Second and the Ninth[246]—have ultimately held immigration legislation unconstitutional, as applied to the facts of the cases.[247] Fictional distinctions have been drawn between statutes that distinguish within a group and those that distinguish between groups.[248] And much judicial activism has been reflected in those immigration cases raising issues of procedural due process.[249]

It is often difficult to separate prediction from prescription. But a number of conditions do seem to favor the continued expansion of these judicial devices for addressing constitutional claims on their merits. As Peter Schuck has shown, the past few years have witnessed a more general trend of bringing immigration closer to the mainstream of public law.[250] The liberalizations in constitutional review are an important part of this renaissance. Further, as shown in the first section of this article, the doctrinal theories advanced from time to time in support of plenary Congressional power over immigration are becoming increasingly difficult to defend. Finally, those lower courts that are persuaded by the policy arguments in

---

[244] See notes 11, 12 *supra* and accompanying text.

[245] See, *e.g.*, Newton v. I.N.S., 736 F.2d 336, 339–43 (6th Cir. 1984); Tapia-Acuna v. I.N.S., 640 F.2d 223, 225 (9th Cir. 1981); Narenji v. Civiletti, 617 F.2d 745, 747 (D.C. Cir. 1980); Francis v. I.N.S., 532 F.2d 268 (2d Cir. 1976).

[246] During the twelve-month period ending June 30, 1983, more than 60 percent of the immigration cases filed in the federal courts of appeals were filed in the Ninth Circuit. ANN. RPT. OF THE DIRECTOR OF THE ADMINISTRATIVE OFFICE OF THE UNITED STATES COURTS 101 (1983). The Second Circuit was next busiest. *Id.*

[247] See the discussions of *Francis* and *Tapia-Acuna*, notes 217–22 *supra* and accompanying text.

[248] See notes 217–22 *supra* and accompanying text.

[249] See notes 223–25 *supra* and accompanying text.

[250] Schuck, note 68 *supra*.

favor of constitutional review now have a Supreme Court decision on which they can rightly rely. The *Chadha* decision, whatever might have motivated it, not only reviewed on the merits but ultimately invalidated a federal statutory provision regulating the deportation of aliens.[251]

From the cases discussed in this article, the beginnings of familiar historical patterns can now be discerned. Courts faced with doctrine they consider unworkable create exceptions, some more artificial than others. The exceptions build until they threaten to swallow the rule. When the writing is on the wall, the courts take the final step of candidly overruling the original principle. The opinions typically describe the historical evolution of the rule, identify the exceptions, expose the analytical inadequacies of the exceptions, observe the inevitable direction of the tide, and conclude that the time has come to lay the general principle to rest.[252]

When that last point is reached in the present context, the plenary power doctrine will be frankly disavowed. Constitutional review of immigration legislation will enter another, perhaps final, stage. This next stage will be marked by a return to general principles of constitutional law. It will be unnecessary for courts to distinguish immigration statutes from other federal statutes.

Even then, critical questions will remain. Immigration cases, like any others, are certainly capable of raising political questions. As suggested earlier, general political question principles will have to be applied to individual fact situations as they arise. The application of those principles can be aided by considering certain factors of particular significance in immigration law.[253] And when an immigration case does present a justiciable constitutional issue, there will arise the question precisely what standard of review the general principles actually dictate—not an easy question in this context.[254]

---

[251] Judges who reject the policy arguments for constitutional review of immigration legislation have arguable means of distinguishing *Chadha*. See note 243 *supra* and accompanying text.

[252] A classic illustration of this process is the doctrine that occupiers of property owe a lesser duty to licensees than they do to invitees. The opinions in several of the cases that have abolished the licensee/invitee distinction noted the historical origins of the traditional principle, the growing body of artificial exceptions, and the clear direction of the case law. See, *e.g.*, Kermarec v. Compagnie Générale Transatlantique, 358 U.S. 625, 629–32 (1959); Rowland v. Christian, 69 Cal. 2d 108, 443 P.2d 561, 70 Cal. Rptr. 97 (1968).

[253] See notes 37–39, 52–62 *supra* and accompanying text.

[254] Aliens are a politically powerless group in several respects. They cannot vote. See Hampton v. Mow Sun Wong, 426 U.S. 88, 102 (1976) (all states deny aliens the vote); ELY,

But constitutional review there will finally be. A finding that the subject matter concerns immigration will no longer end the inquiry.

V. CONCLUSION

For almost a century, the Supreme Court has treated immigration law as sui generis. It has bestowed upon Congress the untrammeled authority to make decisions concerning the admission and expulsion of aliens. So great has been the power of the word "immigration" that its mere mention has been enough to propel the Court into a cataleptic trance.

In the past, one of the greatest obstacles to reexamining the plenary power doctrine has been the "clean slate" philosophy articulated by Justice Frankfurter.[255] The precedent has simply become too deeply embedded. My aim has been to clean the slate.

Today there are indications of change. The trend has been to nudge immigration closer to the central currents of American constitutional law. The courts are becoming anxious to confine the application of the plenary power doctrine within some broadly defined boundaries. To accomplish this, courts dissatisfied with the

---

DEMOCRACY AND DISTRUST 161 (1980). Aliens tend generally to be unpopular. At least certain subgroups of aliens are typically poorer than the general population. See Manulkin & Maghame, note 138 supra, at 45; Roberts, The Board of Immigration Appeals: A Critical Appraisal, 15 SAN DIEGO L. REV. 29, 32–33 (1977). And other avenues of political input are blocked by aliens' relative lack of familiarity with such important national institutions as the legal system, language, and customs. See, e.g., Hampton v. Mow Sun Wong, 426 U.S. 88, 102 (1976); Wong Yang Sun v. McGrath, 339 U.S. 33, 46 (1950); Roberts, supra, at 33. This peculiar vulnerability underlies the Supreme Court decisions holding alienage to be a suspect classification for purposes of state equal protection claims. See the cases cited in note 6 supra. These considerations could be made the starting point for an argument that federal immigration statutes should be subjected to strict scrutiny. Aliens have no more political protection against federal action than they have against state action. Perhaps they have even less. See Schuck, note 68 supra, at 22–23. Further, such factors as immutability of status and history of discrimination also serve as indicia of suspectness, see, e.g., Frontiero v. Richardson, 411 U.S. 677, 684–86 (1973); see also San Antonio Ind. School Dist. v. Rodriguez, 411 U.S. 1, 104–05 (1973) (Marshall, J., dissenting), and they seem no less applicable to federal action than to state action. The counterargument would be that, in the light of the federal powers to exclude and deport aliens, a federal immigration provision should not initially be presumed to have been directed at impermissible ends. The burden on one arguing for strict scrutiny of federal immigration statutes would be to demonstrate that on balance there is still sufficient reason to be suspicious of the federal motives. For an excellent discussion of this problem, see Rosberg, The Protection of Aliens from Discriminatory Treatment by the National Government, 1977 SUPREME COURT REVIEW 275.

[255] See notes 157–58 supra and accompanying text.

governing principles have recently crafted a variety of techniques for circumventing them.

These ameliorative devices, while presenting some imposing logical difficulties, are likely to continue to proliferate. Eventually, the plenary power doctrine will become unable to support their weight. When the inevitable breaking point is reached, the Supreme Court will candidly admit that neither precedent nor policy warrants retaining this remarkable departure from the fundamental principle of constitutional review.

ALBERT W. ALSCHULER

"CLOSE ENOUGH FOR GOVERNMENT WORK": THE EXCLUSIONARY RULE AFTER LEON

I. INTRODUCTION

In *United States v. Leon*,[1] the Supreme Court further modified the Fourth Amendment exclusionary rule of *Weeks v. United States*[2] and *Mapp v. Ohio*.[3] It held that unlawfully obtained evidence could be introduced in the prosecution's case-in-chief so long as law enforcement officers had seized the evidence "in objectively reasonable reliance on a subsequently invalidated search warrant."[4] Although the Court's holding was limited to situations in which police officers had obtained judicial warrants in advance of their actions, the Court's reasoning extended beyond these situations and appeared to foreshadow a general restriction of the exclusionary rule.[5] Unsurprisingly, both the dissenting opinions in *Leon* and the

---

Albert W. Alschuler is Professor of Law, The University of Chicago.

AUTHOR'S NOTE: I am grateful for the extraordinarily helpful suggestions of Stephen J. Schulhofer.

[1] 104 S.Ct. 3405 (1984).

[2] 232 U.S. 383 (1914).

[3] 367 U.S. 643 (1961).

[4] 104 S.Ct. at 3421.

[5] The Supreme Court said that the exclusionary rule "cannot be expected, and should not be applied, to deter objectively reasonable law enforcement activity." *Id.* at 3419. It added, "[W]here the officer's conduct is objectively reasonable, 'excluding the evidence will not further the ends of the exclusionary rule in any appreciable way. . . .'" *Id.* at 3420. After thus saying without qualification that the exclusionary rule should not reach the products of

earlier academic commentary on the issues that the case presented focused primarily on the propriety of withdrawing the exclusionary remedy when police officers had entertained an objectively reasonable belief in the propriety of their actions.[6]

Although *Leon* substantially restricted the scope of the exclusionary rule as a device for reviewing the actions of law enforcement officers, it restricted use of the rule to review the actions of judges and magistrates still more. The Court refused to apply even a "reasonable good faith" standard to a decision by a judge or magistrate to issue a search or arrest warrant. Insisting that the goal of the exclusionary rule was to deter unconstitutional actions by police officers rather than by judges, the Court limited effective review of the issuance of a warrant to cases in which the warrant's illegality was so apparent that any police officer should have recognized it. Under *Leon*, negligent, grossly negligent, reckless, and even deliberate violations of the Fourth Amendment by judges will not lead to the exclusion of unlawfully obtained evidence unless a police officer would have had "no reasonable grounds for believing that the warrant was properly issued."[7] This article explores the asserted basis of this aspect of the *Leon* ruling and its ramifications, discussing only secondarily the effect that a law enforcement officer's "reasonable good faith" should have on the review of his own conduct.

"objectively reasonable" law enforcement activity, the Court observed: "This is particularly true, we believe, when an officer acting with objective good faith has obtained a search warrant from a judge or magistrate and acted within its scope." *Ibid.* Any reading of *Leon* that would withdraw the exclusionary remedy only when police officers had obtained search warrants would be unprincipled. The Court treated "with warrant" searches merely as an illustration of a broader category of "objectively reasonable" law enforcement conduct, and the rationale of *Leon* seems to entitle the state to an opportunity to establish "objective reasonableness" in every case. Moreover, although the class of searches regarded as "objectively reasonable" might be narrowly confined, it could not sensibly be confined to searches authorized by warrants. At a minimum, the class must include cases in which law enforcement officers have relied reasonably on legal pronouncements contained in authoritative sources other than subsequently invalidated warrants—for example, subsequently overruled Supreme Court decisions and subsequently invalidated statutes. But see *Leon*, 104 S.Ct. at 3415 n.8.

[6] See, *e.g.*, Mertens & Wasserstrom, *The Good Faith Exception to the Exclusionary Rule: Deregulating the Police and Derailing the Law*, 70 GEO. L.J. 365 (1981); Ashdown, *Good Faith, the Exclusionary Remedy, and Rule-oriented Adjudication in the Criminal Process*, 24 WM. & MARY L. REV. 335 (1983); Kamisar, *Gates, "Probable Cause," "Good Faith," and Beyond*, 69 IOWA L. REV. 551 (1984).

[7] 104 S.Ct. at 3421.

II. The Issuance and Review of Search and Arrest Warrants until 1984

At the outset, some familiar facts merit review. Search and arrest warrants commonly are issued by judges whose formal qualifications are substantially less rigorous than those of other judges. In many states these justices of the peace, magistrates, and municipal and county court judges need not be lawyers, and they often are not lawyers in fact.[8] In urban areas, these lower court judges frequently have high caseloads.[9] Because the trial of a civil or criminal case before one of these judges is likely to be informal, many states afford a litigant dissatisfied with the trial's outcome the right to a trial de novo in a higher court more sharply circumscribed by substantive and procedural safeguards.[10]

Proceedings for the issuance of a search or arrest warrant before one of these judges are invariably ex parte: one cannot give the target of a contemplated search or arrest the opportunity to oppose the issuance of a warrant and retain much confidence that the object or person sought will be found if the warrant issues. The judge or magistrate therefore hears only one side—the side that seeks a warrant. If the judge accepts the arguments presented by this side, no losing litigant can seek direct review of this ruling in a higher court. When a judge or magistrate refuses to issue a warrant, however, his ruling may not end the matter. Another judge or magistrate may issue a warrant on the basis of the same evidence that the first judge found insufficient.[11] A police officer disappointed by a judge's refusal to authorize a search or arrest sometimes can try another judge.[12]

---

[8] See Silberman, Non-Attorney Justice in the United States: An Empirical Study (1979). In Shadwick v. City of Tampa, 407 U.S. 345 (1972), the Supreme Court upheld a warrant issued by a court clerk, an official who was neither a lawyer nor a judge.

[9] See, *e.g.*, Barrett, *Criminal Justice: The Problem of Mass Production*, in The American Assembly, the Court, the Public and the Law Explosion 85, 117–18 (Jones ed. 1965) ("The Los Angeles Municipal Court . . . finds itself so pressed that in large areas of its caseload it averages but a minute per case in receiving pleas and imposing sentence").

[10] *E.g.*, Mass. Gen. Laws Ann., ch. 218 § 27A (West 1974); 42 Pa. Con. Stat. Ann § 1123 (Purdon 1981); see Colten v. Kentucky, 407 U.S. 104, 112 n.4 (1971).

[11] One federal district court has, however, disapproved the practice. United States v. Davis, 346 F. Supp. 435 (S.D. Ill. 1972).

[12] See Tiffany, McIntyre, & Rotenberg, Detection of Crime 120 (1967).

Like other judicial officers, magistrates and justices of the peace enjoy "absolute immunity" from civil lawsuits seeking redress for unlawful official actions.[13] However malicious or deliberate a judge's wrongful authorization of a search or arrest, no civil remedy for his misconduct is available. Magistrates and justices of the peace commonly can be removed from office by the same authority that hired them—sometimes by other judges and more frequently by the electorate through defeat at the next scheduled election or through recall. Nevertheless, no one aggrieved by a judicially authorized search or arrest, however improper, has a right to any administrative or electoral remedy.

Until *Leon*, despite the unavailability of appellate, civil, and administrative remedies, judicial decisions to issue search and arrest warrants were frequently reviewed by higher courts. The Fourth Amendment exclusionary rule supplied the mechanism for this review. When a search or arrest warrant had led to the discovery of incriminating evidence, a criminal defendant whose privacy had been invaded could seek suppression of the evidence at trial. At the ensuing suppression hearing, the existence of probable cause for issuance of the warrant would be subjected to adversary testing for the first time. Precedents and arguments would be marshaled, and witnesses sometimes would be heard. A defendant who failed to secure the suppression of challenged evidence and who then was convicted at trial could obtain appellate review of the denial of his motion to suppress. Moreover, the granting of a defendant's motion to suppress often was subject to appellate review at the behest of the state. Through the review mechanism established by the exclusionary rule, courts had developed a variety of familiar rules to guide the determination of probable cause—rules, for example, concerning the significance of an informant's admission against penal interest,[14] the presumed reliability of a "citizen informant,"[15] the need to confirm the statements of an anonymous informant through independent investigation before issuing a warrant or con-

---

[13] Ammons v. Baldwin, 705 F.2d 1445, 1447 (5th Cir. 1983); O'Neil v. City of Lake Oswego, 642 F.2d 367, 368 n.2 (9th Cir. 1981); Cato v. Mayes, 270 Ind. 653, 388 N.E.2d 530 (1979); see Stump v. Sparkman, 435 U.S. 349, 355 (1978).

[14] See United States v. Harris, 403, 573, 583 (1971).

[15] *E.g.*, People v. Kurland, 28 Cal. 3d 376, 392, 618 P.2d 213, 223, 168 Cal. Rptr. 667, 677 (1980), *cert. denied*, 451 U.S. 987 (1981); People v. Saar, 196 Colo. 294, 299, 584 P.2d 622, 626 (1978).

ducting a search,[16] the propriety of considering hearsay evidence in deciding whether to issue a search or arrest warrant,[17] and the inadequacy of an affidavit that fails to specify the underlying circumstances in sufficient detail to enable a magistrate to make an independent determination of probable cause.[18]

When one court reviews a ruling by another, it sometimes asks only whether the court that made the ruling under review exceeded the limits of its discretion. In *Leon*, the Supreme Court observed that its prior decisions had never mandated a de novo review of judicial decisions to issue search and arrest warrants. The Court described the pre-*Leon* approach to the review of warrants in the following terms:[19]

> [W]e have expressed a strong preference for warrants and declared that "in a doubtful or marginal case a search under warrant may be sustainable where without one it would fail." . . . Reasonable minds frequently may differ on the question whether a particular affidavit establishes probable cause, and we have thus concluded that the preference for warrants is most appropriately effectuated by according "great deference" to a magistrate's determination. . . .
>
> Deference to the magistrate, however, is not boundless. It is clear, first, that the deference accorded to a magistrate's finding of a probable cause does not preclude inquiry into the knowing or reckless falsity of the affidavit on which that determination was based. . . . Second, courts must also insist that the magistrate purport to "perform his 'neutral and detached' function and not serve merely as a rubber stamp for the police." . . .
>
> Third, reviewing courts will not defer to a warrant based on an affidavit that does not "provide the magistrate with a substantial basis for determining the existence of probable cause."

III. THE COURT'S NEW APPROACH TO THE REVIEW OF SEARCH AND ARREST WARRANTS: A MOUSE OR A MONSTER?

A. LEON'S MILD COUNTENANCE

⸌The Fourth Amendment proscribes unreasonable searches and seizures, and the pre-*Leon* approach to the review of warrants that

---

[16] See Illinois v. Gates, 103 S.Ct. 2317, 2326 (1983).

[17] See Draper v. United States, 358 U.S. 307, 311–13 (1959).

[18] See Aguilar v. Texas, 378 U.S. 108 (1964); Illinois v. Gates, 103 S.Ct. 2317 (1983).

[19] 104 S.Ct. at 3417.

the Supreme Court described had been grounded in concepts of reasonableness. As a matter of substantive Fourth Amendment law, a reviewing court would defer "in a doubtful or marginal case" to the ruling of the judge or magistrate who had issued a warrant but would limit its deference in the ways that *Leon* specified.

The Supreme Court was plainly dissatisfied with its pre-1984 mode of reviewing the issuance of search and arrest warrants. In the Court's view, this mode depended on an unreflective application of the exclusionary rule. *Leon* maintained that "only in the first of [the] three situations [in which the Court had noted that deference to the magistrate is not boundless] has the Court set forth a rationale for suppressing evidence obtained pursuant to a search warrant; in the other areas, it has simply excluded such evidence without considering whether Fourth Amendment interests will be advanced."[20]

The Court then suggested three reasons for concluding that the continued exclusion of all evidence obtained through searches pursuant to invalid warrants would not significantly advance Fourth Amendment interests:[21]

> First, the exclusionary rule is designed to deter police misconduct rather than to punish the errors of judges and magistrates. Second, there exists no evidence suggesting that judges and magistrates are inclined to ignore or subvert the Fourth Amendment or that lawlessness among these actors requires application of the extreme sanction of exclusion. . . . Third, and most important, we discern no basis, and are offered none, for believing that exclusion of evidence seized pursuant to a warrant will have a significant deterrent effect on the issuing judge or magistrate.

This analysis led the Court to its conclusion that application of the exclusionary rule should be restricted to situations in which a police officer who had obtained or executed a warrant had "no reasonable grounds for believing that the warrant was properly issued."[22]

The Court explained how its new recognition that the exclusionary rule was intended to influence the behavior of law enforcement

---

[20] *Id.* at 3418.

[21] *Ibid.*

[22] *Id.* at 3421.

officers rather than judges would alter its earlier approach to the review of search and arrest warrants:[23]

> Suppression . . . remains an appropriate remedy if the magistrate or judge in issuing a warrant was misled by information in an affidavit that the affiant knew was false or would have known was false except for his reckless disregard of the truth. . . . The exception we recognize today will also not apply in cases where the issuing magistrate wholly abandoned his judicial role . . . ;[[24]] in such circumstances, no reasonably well-trained officer should rely on the warrant. Nor would an officer manifest objective good faith in relying on a warrant based on an affidavit "so lacking in indicia of probable cause as to render official belief in its existence entirely unreasonable." . . . Finally, depending on the circumstances of the particular case, a warrant may be so facially deficient—*i.e.*, in failing to particularize the place to be searched or the things to be seized—that the executing officers cannot reasonably presume it to be valid. . . . In so limiting the suppression remedy, we leave untouched the probable-cause standard and the various requirements for a valid warrant.

Reading this language, one inevitably notices the verbal similarity of the pre-*Leon* approach to the review of warrants and the post-*Leon* approach, and one might wonder whether the Supreme Court had labored mightily to give birth to a mouse. Although *Leon* altered the conceptual basis for the judicial review of an improperly issued warrant—focusing on the reasonableness of the police officers who had obtained and executed this warrant rather than directly on the existence of probable cause—the Court might not have altered the "bottom line" substantially. Prior to *Leon*, reviewing courts were to defer to magistrates in all except three situations.[25] In the first of these situations, the Supreme Court's new approach would effect no change: a police officer who had intentionally or recklessly deceived a magistrate could not rely reasonably on the warrant that he had fraudulently procured. In the second and third situations, moreover, the Court apparently did no more than add the adjectives "wholly" and "entirely" to its prior standards. At most, the

---

[23] 104 S.Ct. at 3421–22.

[24] The entire phrase was "where the issuing magistrate wholly abandoned his judicial role in the manner condemned in Lo-Ji Sales, Inc. v. New York, 442 U.S. 319 (1979)." For a discussion of the Court's use of *Lo-Ji Sales*, see text at note 42 *infra*.

[25] See text at note 19 *supra*.

Court might have shifted the review of search and arrest warrants from an "abuse of discretion" standard to a "gross abuse of discretion" standard.

B. THE BEAST WITHIN

1. *A hand faster than the eye.* On several occasions during the past fifteen years, the Supreme Court has substituted new standards for old without clearly mandating a significant change in outcomes. For example, in *McMann v. Richardson*,[26] the Court announced that it would no longer ask directly whether a defendant's plea of guilty had reflected a "knowing and intelligent" waiver of his constitutional rights. The Court would ask instead whether the legal advice that the defendant's attorney had given him was "within the range of competence demanded of attorneys in criminal cases."[27] The Court explained, "In our view, a defendant's plea of guilty based on reasonably competent advice is an intelligent plea. . . . "[28]

The effect of this doctrinal substitution was not immediately clear. When a defendant has been fully advised by his attorney, his guilty plea will indeed reflect a knowing abandonment of his rights. A knowing waiver can be equated with a competently counseled waiver so long as one adheres to a sufficiently demanding concept of competence.

Nevertheless, the Court's shift in standards required a reviewing court to make an unseemly, ad hominem judgment about a member of the bar before setting a guilty plea aside; and at least at the time of the *McMann* decision, legal standards for evaluating the competency of counsel were extraordinarily ungenerous.[29] The dissenting Justices in *McMann* protested that "what is essentially involved . . . is nothing less than the determination of the Court to preserve the sanctity of virtually all judgments obtained by means of guilty pleas."[30] At the time of the *McMann* decision, this judgment might

---

[26] 397 U.S. 759 (1970).

[27] *Id.* at 770–71.

[28] *Id.* at 770.

[29] See, *e.g.*, Krutchen v. Eyman, 406 F.2d 304, 312 (9th Cir. 1969) ("conduct so incompetent as to make a farce or mockery of justice"); Lunce v. Overlade, 244 F.2d 108 (7th Cir. 1957) ("the equivalent of no representation at all"). Compare Strickland v. Washington, 104 S.Ct. 2052, 2064 (1984) ("whether counsel's conduct so undermined the proper functioning of the adversarial process that the trial cannot be relied on as having produced a just result").

[30] 397 U.S. at 786 (Brennan, J., dissenting).

have seemed alarmist; but despite some ebbs and flows, subsequent developments have tended to confirm its accuracy.[31]

Similarly, the Supreme Court once insisted that a state-court defendant who had not been informed of his federal constitutional rights and who therefore had failed to assert a constitutional claim at trial could later assert this claim in federal habeas corpus proceedings.[32] A federal court would deny relief, however, if the state court's asserted deprivation of federal rights had been "harmless."[33] In *Wainwright v. Sykes*,[34] the Supreme Court revised the scope of habeas corpus review by altering the "deliberate bypass" and "harmless error" standards. It held that before a petitioner who had failed to assert a right at trial could obtain habeas corpus relief, he would be required to show both "cause" for his nonassertion of the right and "actual prejudice" as a result of its denial.

Again the significance of the Court's change in categories seemed unclear. If a denial of rights had not been "harmless," it might have appeared to a person less sophisticated than a Supreme Court Justice that "actual prejudice" had occurred.[35] Similarly, if a petitioner had not been advised of his rights and had not had any realistic opportunity to assert them, "cause" for his default might have seemed apparent. When the Supreme Court announced its "cause and prejudice" standard, it said that it would leave development of the standard to later cases; for the moment, the Court thought it sufficient to observe that the new standard was different from the old.[36] Again, however, later decisions revealed that the Court had not been playing idle word games. The Court's new standard soon substantially limited the scope of federal habeas corpus review.[37]

---

[31] See, *e.g.*, Tollett v. Henderson, 411 U.S. 258 (1973); Bordenkircher v. Hayes, 434 U.S. 357 (1978); Corbitt v. New Jersey, 439 U.S. 212 (1978); Haring v. Prosise, 103 S.Ct. 2368 (1983) (inability to challenge guilty plea despite antecedent violation of constitutional rights "does not rest on any notion of waiver").

[32] Fay v. Noia, 372 U.S. 391 (1963).

[33] See, *e.g.*, Milton v. Wainwright, 407 U.S. 371, 372 (1972).

[34] 433 U.S. 72 (1977).

[35] The Court's new standard plainly indicated that a habeas corpus petitioner would bear the burden of demonstrating prejudice. Whether this standard was intended to have a substantive effect as well remained a mystery until United States v. Frady, 456 U.S. 152, 170–72 (1982) (suggesting that only the likelihood of "a fundamental miscarriage of justice" would be treated as "actual prejudice").

[36] Wainwright v. Sykes, 433 U.S. 72, 75 (1977).

[37] See Engle v. Isaac, 456 U.S. 107 (1982); United States v. Frady, 46 U.S. 152 (1982). For an instance in which the Court declared expressly that "the inquiry under [its new

In *Leon*, although the Supreme Court altered the conceptual foundation and the legal standard for the review of searches authorized by magistrates, it implied that higher-court review would lead to the continued exclusion of evidence in several categories of cases. A closer look at the types of cases in which the exclusion of evidence will remain appropriate under *Leon* suggests, however, that the Court has foreclosed virtually all judicial review of magisterial decisions to authorize searches, seizures and arrests.

First. The Court said, "Suppression . . . remains an appropriate remedy if the magistrate or judge in issuing a warrant was misled by information in an affidavit that the affiant knew was false or would have known was false except for his reckless disregard of the truth."[38] In a case of the sort that the Court described, use of the exclusionary remedy would not correct a judicial error, for the only error alleged is a police officer's fraudulent procurement of a warrant. Although pre-*Leon* standards of review will survive *Leon* in this sort of case, these earlier standards had all but precluded judicial relief for this sort of deliberate police dishonesty.

In support of its statement that suppression would remain an appropriate remedy for the deliberate or reckless falsification of affidavits in support of warrants, the Court cited its decision in *Franks v. Delaware*, but *Franks* had held that a defendant could not secure a hearing on the truthfulness of a police officer's affidavit until he had made "a substantial preliminary showing that a false statement knowingly and intentionally, or with reckless disregard for the truth, was included by the affiant in the warrant affidavit. . . ."[39] Justice Rehnquist's dissenting opinion in *Franks* predicted that "ingenious lawyers" would subvert the requirement of a substantial preliminary showing,[40] but the ingenious lawyers whom I know wish that Justice Rehnquist would tell them how. Far from subverting the requirement, these lawyers would be content if they merely know how to satisfy it.

---

formulation was] the same" as under the old and then used the new formulation to change the inquiry substantially, compare Rakas v. Illinois, 439 U.S. 128, 139 (1978), with Rawlings v. Kentucky, 448 U.S. 98, 105–06 (1980). See Alschuler, *Interpersonal Privacy and the Fourth Amendment*, 4 No. ILL. L. REV. 1, 15–16 (1983).

[38] 104 S.Ct. at 3421.

[39] 438 U.S. 154, 155–56 (1978).

[40] *Id.* at 187 (Rehnquist, J., dissenting).

In filing affidavits for warrants (as in testifying at later judicial proceedings), police officers need not reveal the identity of the people whose information they allege has established probable cause for a search.[41] When a defense attorney can question neither the police officer who filed an affidavit nor the unnamed informant described in the affidavit, he usually has no way to determine whether the informant made the statements attributed to him or even whether the informant existed. Unless perjurious police officers lie in artless, obvious ways or attend religious meetings, repent their misconduct, and confess their dishonesty to defense attorneys, *Franks*'s requirement of a substantial preliminary showing becomes an insurmountable "Catch 22": A defense attorney cannot develop the facts until he secures a hearing, and he cannot secure a hearing until he develops the facts. The first group of cases in which the Supreme Court suggested that use of the exclusionary remedy would persist was essentially an empty shell before *Leon*.

Second. The Court said, "The exception we recognize today will also not apply in cases where the issuing magistrate wholly abandoned his judicial role in the manner condemned in *Lo-Ji Sales, Inc. v. New York*;[42] in such circumstances, no reasonably well-trained officer should rely on the warrant."[43] As in *McMann*, this formulation required a reviewing court to make a distasteful, ad hominem judgment before affording relief. The court could suppress challenged evidence only after accusing a judicial officer of a total abdication of his responsibilities. Nevertheless, the Court's citation of *Lo-Ji Sales* indicated that this second shell was not empty. The Court had discovered one of its prior cases in which, despite the fact that police officers had obtained a warrant authorizing their search, the post-*Leon* exclusionary rule would lead to the suppression of unlawfully obtained evidence.

In *Lo-Ji Sales*, a police officer who had purchased two films at an "adult" bookstore took them to a town justice, who viewed them and concluded that they were obscene. The officer alleged in his affidavit that he had observed "similar" films and printed matter on display at the store. On the basis of his representation, the town justice issued a warrant authorizing a search of the bookstore and a

---

[41] McCray v. Illinois, 386 U.S. 300 (1967).

[42] 442 U.S. 319 (1979).

[43] *Leon*, 104 S.Ct. at 3422.

seizure of additional copies of the two films. Moreover, the town justice approved another request included in the officer's application for a warrant—a request that the justice accompany police officers during their execution of the warrant to determine which items were subject to seizure. The warrant was left blank after language authorizing officers to seize "[t]he following items that the Court independently [on examination] has determined to be possessed in violation of Article 235 of the Penal Law. . . ."

After a group of eleven officials (including the town justice) entered the bookstore, the justice viewed various films and magazines and, on determining that many of these materials were obscene, authorized their seizure. A police officer recorded the titles of these items. After the seizure had been completed, these titles—several hundred of them—were added to the warrant. The Supreme Court, noting that "the Fourth Amendment [does not] countenance open-ended warrants, to be completed while a search is being conducted . . . or after the seizure has been carried out,"[44] unanimously reversed the defendant's conviction of obscenity in the second degree.

Cases in which magistrates "wholly abandon their judicial role" by conducting searches and seizures are undoubtedly rare, and the Supreme Court did not leave the door to continued judicial review of magisterial decisions very widely open by preserving the exclusionary remedy for these exiguous cases. Nevertheless, the Court's apparent conclusion that any reasonably well-trained officer would have recognized the illegality of the seizure in *Lo-Ji Sales* seemed strained, and the difficulty of finding even one Supreme Court decision in favor of suppression that would survive *Leon* may suggest how substantial a change this decision is likely to yield in cases of judicial or magisterial error.

In *Lo-Ji Sales*, a magistrate's determination of probable cause had preceded every seizure. Moreover, to make his determination of probable cause, the magistrate had merely inspected material that the bookstore had offered for sale to the public. Although the warrant procedures employed in *Lo-Ji Sales* were not the procedures contemplated by the Fourth Amendment, a police officer might have concluded that the process of bringing the magistrate to a

---

[44] *Lo-Ji Sales, Inc.*, 442 U.S. at 325.

mountain of books rather than a mountain of books to the magistrate was the "functional equivalent" of constitutionally dictated warrant procedures. The Supreme Court ultimately concluded that there were persuasive reasons for rejecting this claim of functional equivalency, but not everyone with a law school education and years of experience in the legal profession would have recognized them. For example, the trial judge who denied the defendant's motion to suppress did not recognize them, nor did the Appellate Division of the New York Supreme Court that affirmed the defendant's conviction.[45] Perhaps any reasonably well-trained police officer would have known more law than the justices of the New York Appellate Division, but it seemed indelicate of the United States Supreme Court to say so.[46]

Third. The Court observed that a police officer would not "manifest objective good faith in relying on a warrant based on an affidavit 'so lacking in indicia of probable cause as to render belief in its existence entirely unreasonable.' "[47] To afford relief under this formulation, a reviewing court would not be required to accuse a judicial officer of perversity. It would be enough to accuse him of incompetence. If a pellet is to be discovered under any of the surviving shells of protection against erroneous rulings by magistrates, this one holds the greatest promise. Nevertheless, a court cannot consider a magistrate's competence directly even under this formulation. As with the other categories in which the exclusion of evidence remains appropriate, the court cannot view the magistrate's action with its own eyes but must look through the eyes of a

---

[45] *Id.* at 324–25.

[46] Perhaps the Court's argument was only that after its decision in *Lo-Ji Sales*, a reasonably well-trained police officer would recognize the illegality of the procedures employed in that case. Nevertheless, a conscientious police officer who read all 1,635 pages of the leading law school casebook on criminal procedure would find only one reference to *Lo-Ji Sales*. He would discover this reference in the fine print at the end of footnote (b) on page 194, and the reference would not tell him what the case had held. It merely asks, "Is the magistrate sufficiently detached . . . [i]f he assists the police in execution of the warrant? See Lo-Ji Sales, Inc. v. New York. . . ." KAMISAR, LA FAVE, & ISRAEL, MODERN CRIMINAL PROCEDURE: CASES, COMMENTS AND QUESTIONS 294 n.b (5th ed. 1980).

[47] *Leon*, 104 S.Ct. at 3421–22. The Court noted a fourth category as well: "Finally, depending on the circumstances of the particular case, a warrant may be so facially deficient—*i.e.*, in failing to particularize the place to be searched or the things to be seized—that the executing officers cannot reasonably presume it to be valid." *Id.* at 3422. The Court indicated the emptiness of this category in a companion case to *Leon*. See Massachusetts v. Sheppard, 104 S.Ct. 3424 (1984); text at notes 104–12 *infra*.

hypothetical police officer, one suitably deferential to higher authority. The court must ask, not merely whether the magistrate was incompetent, but whether his incompetence was so apparent that a reasonable police officer should have refused to seek or execute the warrant that the magistrate issued. Situations in which a police officer can fairly be expected to know more law than a judge and to act on the basis of this perception are undoubtedly rare.

In short, *Leon* makes America's least qualified judicial officers almost the only judicial officers whose rulings are not subject to significant review by higher courts. This irony is compounded by the fact that lower court judges issue their search and arrest warrants on the basis of *ex parte* presentations and commonly must act in haste. The issuance of warrants without probable cause was one of the grievances of the American Revolution, and it was an evil that the framers of the Constitution condemned unmistakably. Under *Leon*, however, virtually the only check on the issuance of a warrant without probable cause is the conscience of a single magistrate. *Leon* makes the decision to issue a warrant without probable cause less subject to correction than almost any other erroneous judicial decision.[48]

2. *The double confusion of a double standard.* Although *Leon* all but immunized judicial decisions to issue search and arrest warrants from higher court review, this development marked only a short step beyond a ruling that the Supreme Court had made a year earlier. In *Illinois v. Gates*,[49] the Supreme Court had broadened substantially the discretion to err that it had afforded magistrates. Under *Gates*, a reviewing court could hold unconstitutional a search that a magistrate had authorized only if the magistrate lacked "a substantial basis for determining the existence of probable cause."[50]

---

[48] Of course courts ordinarily do not review lower-court decisions that have become moot. The Supreme Court takes the view that, once a search has occurred, a mistaken decision to authorize it cannot be corrected and has no continuing consequences to which a person whose privacy has been invaded is entitled to object. See *Leon*, 104 S.Ct. at 3412. Whatever the merits of this view, the effects of entirely exempting the decisions of magistrates from judicial review are no less unfortunate.

[49] 103 S.Ct. 2317 (1983).

[50] *Id.* at 2332. The Court developed this standard through characteristic (although possibly inadvertent) prestidigitation. In Jones v. United States, 362 U.S. 257 (1960), the Supreme Court upheld the constitutionality of a challenged search and remarked, "[T]here was a substantial basis for [the magistrate] to conclude that narcotics were probably present in the apartment, and that is sufficient." *Id.* at 271. In *Gates*, the Supreme Court first cited the

Had the Supreme Court concluded in 1984 that the standards it had articulated in 1983 were unsatisfactory, of course it could have modified these standards.[51] For example, the Court might have replaced an "abuse of discretion" standard with a "conscience-shocking abuse of discretion" standard. In *Leon*, however, the Court did not modify the substantive standards of *Gates*. At least nominally, it addressed only the question of remedy, asking which violations of substantive Fourth Amendment standards ought to require the exclusion of unlawfully seized evidence.

The *Leon* majority suggested that this two-tiered approach to Fourth Amendment litigation possessed virtue that a simple modification of substantive Fourth Amendment standards would have lacked. Despite its restriction of the exclusionary rule, the Court noted that reviewing courts could guide the conduct of magistrates and police officers by ruling on substantive Fourth Amendment issues before considering the appropriateness of the exclusionary remedy.[52] It may be instructive to consider how a reviewing court would conduct this two-stage analysis in a case in which a search had been authorized by a warrant.

The court first would apply the standards of *Gates* to weigh the validity of the warrant. Only if it concluded that the magistrate had

---

language of *Jones* to support the following proposition: "[T]he traditional standard for review of an issuing magistrate's probable cause determination has been that so long as the magistrate had a 'substantial basis for . . . conclud[ing]' that a search would uncover evidence of wrongdoing, the Fourth Amendment requires no more." *Gates*, 103 S.Ct. at 2331 (citing *Jones*). Shortly thereafter, the Court quoted the "substantial basis" language of *Jones* once again: "[T]he duty of a reviewing court is simply to ensure that the magistrate had a 'substantial basis for . . . conclud[ing]' that probable cause existed." *Id.* at 2332 (citing *Jones*). That the Court elevated a ruling in one case into "the traditional standard" was not particularly distressing, but that the Court almost immediately transformed this "traditional standard" in the process of restating it was troublesome. A "substantial basis for concluding that a search would uncover evidence of wrong-doing" might qualify as a rough definition of probable cause. This formulation would not suggest that a search warrant should be upheld despite the absence of probable cause for issuing it. Nevertheless, a "substantial basis for concluding that probable cause existed" apparently refers to a substantial basis for finding this substantial basis. This second formulation does suggest that a decision to issue a search warrant may be upheld despite the absence of probable cause—so long as a magistrate had a "substantial basis" for the erroneous judgment that probable cause existed. It was the second and more tolerant formulation that the Supreme Court quoted in *Leon*. 104 S.Ct. at 3417. The standard of *Gates*—whether a magistrate had a substantial basis for finding a substantial basis—seemed to involve "a form of double billing," but *Leon* took *Gates* one step further—to a form of triple billing. See text at note 103 *infra*.

[51] See, *e.g.*, United States v. Ross, 46 U.S. 798 (1982) (overruling Robbins v. California, 453 U.S. 420 (1981)).

[52] *Leon*, 104 S.Ct. at 3422.

lacked a "substantial basis" for issuing the warrant would it turn to the question of remedy. Under *Leon*, it would exclude the challenged evidence if the warrant had been "based on an affidavit 'so lacking in indicia of probable cause as to render official belief in its existence entirely unreasonable.' "[53]

The legal mind is a wonderful instrument, reputedly capable of thinking about a thing that is attached to something else without thinking about the thing to which it is attached.[54] Even the legal mind, however, might balk at attempting to distinguish between an affidavit "so lacking in indicia of probable cause as to render belief in its existence entirely unreasonable" and an affidavit affording no "substantial basis for determining the existence of probable cause." It would be difficult for a reviewing court to take the Supreme Court's new, two-stage approach to the review of warrants literally. In the great majority of cases, a court confronted with an allegedly invalid warrant would be likely to accept the Supreme Court's invitation to forgo the first step and leap to the "bottom line."[55]

The *Leon* decision reflected a misuse of remedial doctrine to effectuate substantive concerns. Justice Stevens appropriately began his *Leon* dissent by pointing to the language and structure of the Fourth Amendment.[56] The first clause of the Amendment proscribes unreasonable searches, and the second adds meaning to the first in three situations. It reveals that searches conducted pursuant to warrants must be condemned as unreasonable unless these warrants have been supported by oath or affirmation, unless they particularly describe the place to be searched and the persons or things to be seized, and unless they have been issued upon probable cause. Of the three constitutional requisites of a valid warrant, the requirement of probable cause has been by far the most important in the historical development of the Amendment, and the Supreme Court has extended this requirement to searches conducted without warrants as well as to those that have been authorized by judicial officers.[57]

---

[53] *Ibid.*

[54] See Arnold, *Criminal Attempts—the Rise and Fall of an Abstraction*, 40 YALE L.J. 53, 58 (1930) (quoting an unpublished manuscript by T. R. Powell).

[55] See *Leon*, 104 S.Ct. at 3422.

[56] *Id.* at 3446 (Stevens, J., dissenting).

[57] See, *e.g.*, Whiteley v. Warden, 401 U.S. 560, 566 (1971).

The term "probable cause" is itself extraordinarily flexible and adds relatively little to the central term "reasonable." The Supreme Court's definitions of "probable cause" invariably have been cast in terms of the perceptions of a "reasonable" or "prudent" officer;[58] and when focusing on the evidentiary justification for a search, the Court occasionally has treated the terms "reasonable search" and "search with probable cause" as interchangeable.[59]

This equation may be somewhat misleading. The framers of the Fourth Amendment used the term "probable cause" to denote what Justice Stevens called "particularized evidence of wrongdoing,"[60] and arguments that dragnet seizures or invasions of privacy in the course of a criminal investigation can be reasonable despite the lack of particularized evidence defy the constitutional judgment.[61] The Fourth Amendment, however, does not specify the exact amount of evidence necessary to justify any intrusion upon property, liberty, or privacy. Once the threshold of unsupported or broadly generalized suspicion is passed, the framers of the Amendment left the question of justification to be resolved by the courts. Moreover, the Supreme Court's past attempts to treat probable cause as "a single, familiar standard"[62] and to divide the concept of probable cause into distinct analytic components[63] have foundered before the variety of searches, seizures, and arrests that the Fourth Amendment was designed to control.[64] *Gates* not only broadened the deference to be afforded magistrates, but also, and more important, it emphasized that probable cause is a flexible requirement of case-by-case justification, thus restoring the concept to its original role. Putting aside the Supreme Court's ruling concerning when searches without warrants are permissible (rulings that are immate-

---

[58] *E.g.*, Stacey v. Emery, 97 U.S. 642, 645 (1878); Brinegar v. United States, 338 U.S. 160, 175–76 (1949); Henry v. United States, 361 U.S. 98, 102 (1959); Beck v. Ohio, 379 U.S. 89, 91 (1964).

[59] See Camera v. Municipal Court, 387 U.S. 523, 538 (1967).

[60] *Leon*, 104 S.Ct. at 3453 (Stevens, J., dissenting).

[61] But *cf.* United States v. Martinez-Fuerte, 428 U.S. 543 (1976); United States v. Dionisio, 410 U.S. 1 (1973); Immigration & Naturalization Serv. v. Delgado, 104 S.Ct. 1758 (1984).

[62] See Dunaway v. New York, 442 U.S. 200, 213 (1979).

[63] See, *e.g.*, Spinelli v. United States, 393 U.S. 410 (1969). See also Moylan, *Hearsay and Probable Cause: An Aguilar and Spinelli Primer*, 25 MERCER L. REV. 741 (1974).

[64] See Alschuler, *Bright Line Fever and the Fourth Amendment*, 45 U. PITT. L. REV. 227, 243–56 (1984).

rial when a warrant has in fact been obtained), the Fourth Amendment's central rule of reason remains in large measure an open-ended concept to be filled with meaning by the courts.

Justice Stevens's dissent in *Leon* emphasized the Supreme Court's ability to avoid its troubling division of right and remedy and its confusing two-stage analysis by addressing issues of "reasonable reliance" within the substantive rubric of the Fourth Amendment.[65] Justice Brennan's dissenting opinion, joined by Justice Marshall, noted that the concept of "objectively reasonable reliance upon an objectively unreasonable warrant" is "mind-boggling."[66] The majority, however, declined to devote so much as a line of its opinion to an explanation of why its year-old resurrection of a more flexible and accommodating Fourth Amendment in *Gates* was inadequate to satisfy its concerns. In this respect as well as others,[67] the majority seemed to manifest its view of the exclusionary rule by restricting the rule gratuitously.

In explaining why unlawfully obtained evidence sometimes should be admitted at trial, the *Leon* majority quoted language from a dissenting opinion in which Justice White, who wrote the majority opinion, earlier had advocated a similar modification of the exclusionary rule:[68]

> In short, where the officer's conduct is objectively reasonable,
> . . . "excluding the evidence will not further the ends of the
> exclusionary rule in any appreciable way; for it is painfully ap-

---

[65] 104 S.Ct. at 3446–47 (Stevens, J., dissenting).

[66] *Id.* at 3446 (Brennan, J., dissenting).

[67] Most notably, the Court refused to consider whether under the recently announced standards of Illinois v. Gates, 103 S.Ct. 2317 (1983), the search in *Leon* was supported by probable cause. See 104 S.Ct. at 3412. Governmental officers are not often "objectively reasonable" when they conduct "objectively unreasonable" searches, and some Supreme Court Justices may have doubted that the issue that they wished to decide would come before them in the ordinary course of litigation. If these Justices were determined to endorse a "reasonable belief in reasonableness" standard, they may have thought it necessary to decide the issue in a case in which, in all probability, they would not have found a Fourth Amendment violation at all. When a court decides an issue on the basis of an artificially truncated record, it may rule in a way that would have been difficult to justify had all issues in a case been developed and their relationships explored. The Supreme Court's refusal to consider the probable cause issue in *Leon* illustrates the danger of deciding part of a case in isolation from the whole. The Court did indeed think about a thing that was attached to something else without thinking about the thing to which it was attached. *Cf.* text at note 54 *supra.*

[68] *Leon,* 104 S.Ct. at 3420 (quoting Stone v. Powell, 428 U.S. 465, 539–40 (White, J., dissenting).

> parent that . . . the officer is acting as a reasonable officer would
> and should act under the circumstances. Excluding the evidence
> can in no way affect his future conduct unless it is to make him
> less willing to do his duty."

Surely it distorts the English language to contend that an officer
who had conducted an unreasonable search has acted "as a reasonable officer would and should act under the circumstances," and
the claim that in conducting a search in violation of the Fourth
Amendment an officer may merely have done his duty is astonishing.

The conceptual confusion of a "reasonable belief in reasonableness" standard was underscored by the Court's repeated insistence
that the relevant standard was one of "objective" reasonableness
and that " '[s]ending state and federal courts into the minds of
police officers would produce a grave and fruitless misallocation of
resources.' "[69] Arguing that the only purpose of the exclusionary
rule was the deterrence of official misconduct, proponents of restricting the rule once maintained that this purpose could not be
achieved when the officials responsible for a search had acted in a
"good faith" belief that their conduct was lawful.[70] Confronted
with the response that this standard would encourage ignorance of
existing legal standards, these advocates generally conceded that
the test should not be entirely subjective but should focus on a
government official's "reasonable" good faith.[71] In *Leon*, however,
the subjective component of the modification disappeared.[72] The

---

[69] *Id.* at 3421 n.23.

[70] *E.g.*, Wright, *Must the Criminal Go Free if the Constable Blunders?* 50 TEX. L. REV. 736 (1972).

[71] *E.g.*, Bernardi, *The Exclusionary Rule: Is a Good Faith Standard Needed to Preserve a Liberal Interpretation of the Fourth Amendment?* 30 DE PAUL L. REV. 51 (1982).

[72] In declaring that its standard was "objective" rather than "subjective," the Supreme Court said very little. An "objective" test becomes nearly indistinguishable from a "subjec-tive" test when a wide enough range of case-specific circumstances and personal characteris-tics are considered in judging "reasonableness." An "objective" standard does invariably differ from a "subjective" standard in its treatment of direct evidence of an actor's state of mind—evidence which always must proceed from the actor himself. Unlike a "subjective" standard, an "objective" standard declares both admissions of subjective bad faith and protes-tations of subjective good faith immaterial. Nevertheless, an objective standard may differ from a subjective standard only in this one respect. When a person's state of mind must be inferred from surrounding circumstances, every circumstance that could lead a factfinder to infer "subjective" bad faith also may bear on whether the actor's conduct was "objectively reasonable." The issue is simply whether this circumstance is one that a standard of "objec-tive reasonableness" takes into account when it asks whether conduct was "reasonable under

Court reinvented the concept of objective reasonableness that had been the touchstone of Fourth Amendment jurisprudence all along.[73] While continuing to insist that the only significant function

---

the circumstances." The Supreme Court's treatment of this basic issue seemed muddled. Immediately after declaring that " '[s]ending state and federal courts into the minds of police officers would produce a grave and fruitless misallocation of judicial resources,' " the Court declared: "Accordingly, our good faith inquiry is confined to the objectively ascertainable question whether a reasonable well-trained officer would have known that the search was illegal despite the magistrate's authorization. In making this determination, all of the circumstances—including whether the warrant application had previously been rejected by a different magistrate—may be considered." 104 S.Ct. at 3421 n.23. In suggesting that the *Leon* test looks only to the viewpoint of a hypothetical "reasonably well-trained officer," the Court implied that the extent of any individual officer's knowledge should be disregarded. Attempting to discover whether an officer had learned of a particular judicial ruling, for example, apparently would be the kind of subjective inquiry that would lead to a grave and fruitless misallocation of resources. Nevertheless, the rejection of a warrant application by a magistrate is significant only because it conveys special knowledge to an officer, advising him of one judge's conclusion that a proposed search would be illegal. Although the Supreme Court intimated that the same special knowledge might be disregarded if it came from another source—an instructor at the police academy, for example—no reason for distinguishing among the possible sources of special knowledge seems apparent. One can imagine a dialogue between two police officers, one a seasoned veteran and the other a recruit just beginning her first assignment:

> ROOKIE: I realize that I don't know the ropes, but is it legal to search an apartment on the basis of the flimsy evidence that we have in this case?
> VET: No, it's probably illegal. Certainly if I were a "neutral and detached magistrate," I would not approve a search on the basis of this ridiculous evidence. Nevertheless, you and I are "officers engaged in the often competitive enterprise of ferreting out crime," and I believe that we can slip our warrant application past old Magistrate Dodder, whom we keep in the basement of the courthouse for these purposes.

One can imagine further that, unbeknown to these two officers, an officer assigned to the police internal affairs division has tape-recorded their conversation. Moreover, this officer has given the resulting tape recording to a defense attorney who is challenging the search that the two officers later conducted pursuant to Magistrate Dodder's authorization. The defense attorney offers the tape recording in evidence. The tape recording is plainly inadmissible to show the veteran officer's lack of "objectively reasonable reliance" on the warrant that Magistrate Dodder issued. The repeated declaration that the *Leon* standard is "objective" must mean at least that an officer's statement concerning his subjective state of mind is immaterial. Nevertheless, the recording might be admissible to show the rookie officer's lack of "objectively reasonable reliance." As to this officer, the veteran's statement could be regarded as an "external circumstance." This statement would have conveyed to the rookie the same information that she might have received in more ambiguous form had Magistrate Sharp rejected the warrant application prior to its presentation to Magistrate Dodder; and the Supreme Court said in *Leon*, "In making this determination, all of the circumstances—including whether the warrant application had previously been rejected by a different magistrate—may be considered."

[73] Nevertheless, the Fourth Amendment's standard of "objective reasonableness" looks primarily to evolving cultural norms of reasonableness. The *Leon* majority sometimes framed its standard in a different way, asking whether a "reasonably well-trained officer would have known that the search was *illegal*" (emphasis added). 104 S.Ct. at 3421 n.23. This formulation intimated that the Supreme Court might treat a search as "objectively unreasonable" only when law enforcement officers had violated established legal norms. On this view, so

of the exclusionary rule was to deter official misconduct, the Court apparently made the rule inapplicable to some cases of deliberate violation of law by the police.

Although the Supreme Court announced its restriction of the exclusionary rule in 1984, doomsday prophesies of unfettered surveillance by Big Brother undoubtedly would be unwarranted.[74] It might be less unfair, however, to suggest that *Leon* fulfilled the different Orwellian prophesy of governmental newspeak: The Supreme Court did not declare in *Leon* that war is peace or that hate is love, but it did proclaim that a law enforcement officer could believe reasonably in the reasonableness of an unreasonable action.

3. *Two perspectives on reasonableness.* Almost buried in *Leon*'s discussion of remedial issues was a substantive Fourth Amendment issue of considerable difficulty:[75] Should the reasonableness of governmental actions be judged under the Fourth Amendment from an *ex post* or an *ex ante* perspective? Should a search or seizure be declared unreasonable if, with the benefit of reflection, hindsight, and legal research, one concludes that the search or seizure was inappropriate (the *ex post* perspective)? Or should one take account of the specific circumstances in which law enforcement officers and other officials found themselves, recognize that these officials may have been required to make hasty decisions without benefit of law clerks, and ask whether, in the light of both general standards of decency and whatever legal guidance may have been available, these officials did as well as could have been expected in determining whether to search, seize, or arrest (the *ex ante* perspective)? To

---

long as existing legal standards either supported a search or remained unsettled, a court could not condemn the search as "unreasonable." A police officer's conduct sometimes may be "objectively unreasonable," however, simply because he should have known that he was conducting a search that courts were very likely to hold unconstitutional. *Cf.* United States v. Johnson, 456 U.S. 537, 561 (1982). Moreover, legal standards may be unsettled only because a Fourth Amendment issue has yet to come before the courts. In this situation, cultural norms concerning privacy (rather than legal norms) may render a search "objectively unreasonable." Certainly the "objective reasonableness" standard of tort law has not depended on whether an alleged tortfeasor would have known that his conduct was contrary to established legal norms. Although positive law is an important consideration in assessing "reasonableness," it should not be the only thing that a reviewing court considers.

[74] Despite Justice Brennan's proclamation that "[i]t now appears that the Court's victory over the Fourth Amendment is complete," *Leon*, 104 S.Ct. at 3430 (Brennan, J., dissenting), *Leon* has not made the United States into Iran.

[75] The issue is so difficult, in fact, that the views expressed here are not the same as those that I expressed in my initial examination of the problem. See Alschuler, note 64 *supra*, at 232–34.

what extent is the reasonableness of a search indistinguishable from the reasonableness of the officials who conducted and authorized the search, and to what extent can the two issues appropriately be separated?

Proponents of a "reasonable good faith exception" to the exclusionary rule have protested that judges commonly have subjected police officers to *ex post* demands for perfection in their rulings on Fourth Amendment issues.[76] As these critics have described the process, judges with the advantage of years of legal training and experience, the use of extensive law libraries, the benefit of collegial deliberation, and the assistance of capable law clerks, have reviewed at their leisure the propriety of a police officer's actions. The judges commonly have divided upon the issue. Then these judges have written opinions analyzing a multiplicity of factual and legal concerns at length and in detail. The officer whose actions prompted this activity may have had only a moment to analyze the factual and legal issues presented in a tense and fast-breaking situation. Nevertheless, his actions may have been held unconstitutional simply because he took a position ultimately adopted by four appellate judges rather than five.[77] The call for a "reasonable good faith exception" to the exclusionary rule can be seen as a denunciation of this sort of Monday-morning quarterbacking by the judiciary. It can be seen as a demand for judicial evaluation of the conduct of law enforcement officers from an *ex ante* rather than an *ex post* perspective. It can also be seen as a plea for judicial recognition that a search may have been "excusable" even when, on reflection, it does not seem "justified."

Nevertheless, the claim that judges have evaluated the conduct of police officers from an *ex post* perspective has rested largely on undemonstrated assumptions. A court's close division on the propriety of a police officer's conduct does not itself establish that any member of the court ignored the difficulty of the officer's situation or that any member judged this conduct with the benefit of hindsight. Courts can divide on questions of excuse just as they can on

---

[76] See, *e.g.*, United States v. Ross, 655 F.2d 1159, 1204 (D.C. Cir. 1981) (Wilkey, J., dissenting); United States v. Williams, 622 F.2d 830, 842 (5th Cir. 1980), *cert. denied*, 449 U.S. 1127 (1981); Schroeder, *Deterring Fourth Amendment Violations: Alternatives to the Exclusionary Rule*, 69 GEO. L.J. 1361, 1380–81, 1419 (1981).

[77] Some of the language of this paragraph has been derived with minor modification from Alschuler, note 64 *supra* at 232.

questions of justification. Moreover, judges may recognize the need for speedy, unreflective action in the field although their own opinions offer more than instinctive, one-sentence responses to the totality of the circumstances. To the extent that judges already have taken an *ex ante* perspective in making their judgments of Fourth Amendment reasonableness, modifications of the exclusionary rule to ensure this *ex ante* perspective are unnecessary. Indeed, by forcing a court to ask again the question that it already has answered, these modifications may yield unmanageable conceptual confusion.

Although judges undoubtedly have taken an unfair *ex post* perspective on some occasions, proponents of modifying the exclusionary rule generally have failed to consider whether the correction of this error ought to be achieved by mandating the appropriate *ex ante* vantage point as a matter of substantive Fourth Amendment law rather than by leaving the substantive law intact and altering the law of remedies.

Initially, the following analysis treats the choice between *ex post* and *ex ante* perspectives simply as a question of substantive Fourth Amendment interpretation. When the Fourth Amendment condemns "unreasonable searches," does it refer to searches that with the benefit of reflection now seem unreasonable? Or does the Amendment refer to searches that officials should have recognized as inappropriate at the time that they occurred? The analysis then considers whether the treatment of this issue has been advanced by transforming it into a remedial issue; it focuses in greater detail on the Supreme Court's decision to withhold the exclusionary remedy when a search could have "seemed like a good idea at the time" to officers who secured a warrant.

A judge who reviews a search is likely to hold it unconstitutional only if he concludes that some official responsible for the search engaged in deliberate misconduct or else made a mistake of fact, a mistake of law, or a mistake in judgment. To some extent, judges appear to have treated these different types of mistakes differently in choosing between *ex post* and *ex ante* perspectives.

Under the Fourth Amendment, the reasonableness of judgments of fact is to be judged *ex ante*. No one whose privacy has been invaded by a search can secure a remedy of any sort for an official's mistake of fact so long as this mistake was "reasonable." The mid-thirteenth-century treatise of Henri de Bracton addressed what then might have been regarded as a difficult question: If a person who had been declared an outlaw proved to be innocent, was the declaration of outlawry to be regarded as unlawful? Bracton's response was that the mistaken declaration of outlawry remained lawful so long as it had been supported by "presumptive cause."[78]

Since Bracton's time, the choice of perspective has not usually seemed difficult in judging governmental mistakes of fact.[79] When police officers arrest the innocent Miller in the reasonable belief that he is the guilty Hill, their arrest is supported by probable cause and is lawful.[80] When they search an apartment without a reasonable belief that stolen property is to be found and nevertheless find stolen property, their search is unsupported by probable cause and is unlawful. The constitutional concept of probable cause thus mandates a consistent *ex ante* perspective in the examination of factual mistakes.[81] For this reason, efforts to extend "modifications" of the exclusionary rule to cases of reasonable factual mistake have been particularly feckless.[82] The exclusionary rule does not reach cases of reasonable factual mistake, for in these situations, the Fourth Amendment has not been violated.

---

[78] 2 Bracton, De Legibus et Consuetudinibus Angliae 356–57 (Thorne trans. 1968).

[79] At least it has not seemed difficult when a search or seizure appeared justified *ex ante* but later turned out to rest upon a misapprehension of critical factual circumstances. In some contexts—for example, admiralty actions seeking recovery for the improper seizure of a vessel—courts have shifted from the *ex ante* to the *ex post* perspective when, despite an apparent lack of *ex ante* reasonableness, the vessel or other thing seized in fact had been subject to seizure. See, *e.g.*, Slocum v. Mayberry, 15 U.S. 1, 9–10, 2 Wheat. 1, 5 (1817); The Charming Betsy, 6 U.S. 64, 120–22, 2 Cranch 34, 68–70 (1804). *Cf.* California v. Minjares, 443 U.S. 916, 921 (1979) (Rehnquist, J., dissenting from denial of stay).

[80] California v. Hill, 401 U.S. 797 (1971).

[81] Byars v. United States, 273 U.S. 28, 29 (1927); Pierson v. Ray, 386 U.S. 547, 555 (1967). Although courts invariably have taken an *ex ante* perspective when the relevant standard is "probable cause," a few courts have failed to adhere to this perspective when the relevant standard is "consent." These courts have held that a reasonable *ex ante* perception of effective consent cannot validate a search when, from an *ex post* perspective, effective consent was lacking. See, *e.g.*, United States v. Elrod, 441 F.2d 353, 356 (5th Cir. 1971). Nevertheless, courts have failed to apply an *ex ante* perspective to factual mistakes by law enforcement officers only in the context of "consent searches," and even in this context, departures from the *ex ante* perspective appear unusual. Most courts have held that a search based on a reasonable misapprehension of effective consent cannot violate the Constitution's proscription of "unreasonable" searches. *E.g.*, People v. Henderson, 33 Ill. 2d 225, 229–30, 210 N.E.2d 483, 485 (1965); People v. Tremayne, 20 Cal. App. 3d 1006, 1015 98 Cal. Rptr. 193, 198 (1971).

[82] See, *e.g.*, Ball, *Good Faith and the Fourth Amendment: The "Reasonable" Exception to the Exclusionary Rule*, 69 J. Crim. L. & Criminology 635 (1978); Ariz. Rev. Stat. Ann. § 13-3925 (1982); Colo. Rev. Stat. § 16-3-308 (1983).

Although all courts have recognized that factual circumstances must be judged *ex ante*, some courts may not have applied an *ex ante* perspective to perceptions of law or to the exercise of judgment. They may have asked what an ideal response to the apparent factual circumstances would have been, not simply whether all governmental officials responsible for a search or seizure acted reasonably. If pressed to justify this *ex post* approach, a judge might emphasize that the decision to admit or exclude evidence is different from the decision to grant or withhold a remedy against a police officer or other public official. If the issue truly were one of "judging" the official responsible for a search, an *ex ante* approach would be appropriate.[83] Nevertheless, the exclusion of evidence does not punish this official, disparage his integrity or competence, or cost him money.[84] Perhaps this official was required to make a hasty, unreflective decision; but the judge is not. When the benefit of hindsight is in fact available, it seems artificial to forgo it. The decision to admit or exclude evidence can be made on a better basis than the initial decision to search, and the question of admissibility is therefore distinct from the question whether any individual acted improperly in authorizing or conducting a search.

This argument for an *ex post* perspective can rest on either of two propositions. The first and probably less attractive is that the admission of evidence at trial can violate the Constitution although the search that uncovered the evidence did not. This proposition truly separates the propriety of a seizure from the propriety of admitting the resulting evidence, and it could be regarded, not as viewing an officer's seizure from an *ex post* perspective, but as making an independent, *ex ante* judgment concerning the admission of evidence. If one views every disclosure of personal information as a distinct invasion of privacy, severing the decision to admit evidence from the decision to seize it may not be as farfetched as it seems.[85]

---

[83] See Pierson v. Ray, 386 U.S. 547, 555 (1967) (officers not liable in damages under federal civil rights statute "if the jury found that [they] reasonably believed in good faith that the arrest was constitutional"); but see United States v. Ehrlichman, 546 F.2d 910 (D.C. Cir. 1976) (official properly convicted of crime whether or not he reasonably believed that a search was constitutional).

[84] Of course this view is inconsistent with the claim that the exclusionary rule seeks to reduce unconstitutional conduct by "punishing" it (rather than by withdrawing one affirmative incentive to engage in it). See note 131 *infra*.

[85] Current concepts of the Fourth Amendment emphasize its protection of privacy rather than its protection of property. See Katz v. United States, 389 U.S. 347 (1967); accord, Boyd

Nevertheless, it obviously rests on a more expansive view of the exclusionary rule than the rule's most fervent proponents have asserted. Few would argue for an *ex post* perspective on the ground that the admission of previously seized evidence can be a constitutional wrong so independent of the seizure that the exclusionary rule should reach the products of lawful searches.

The second proposition unmistakably views the seizure itself from an *ex post* perspective. It contends that a search could have violated the Fourth Amendment although a reasonable person in the situation of those who authorized and conducted the search could not have been expected to know it at the time. This proposition advances another expansive concept of Fourth Amendment rights. It declares that the Fourth Amendment may have entitled a person to more protection than governmental officials could reasonably have been expected to give him. It proclaims that a person may have been wronged by his failure to receive the benefit of hindsight in a situation in which he could not have received the benefit of hindsight. It assigns all of the burdens of unavoidable haste and justifiable imperfection to the government and none of these inescapable burdens to the rest of us. Under this concept of Fourth Amendment rights, a judge might make a retrospective judgment that it would have been better to obtain the challenged evidence in another way, recognize that ordinary mortals could not reasonably have been expected to obtain the evidence in that way, and then remedy the retrospectively perceived "wrong" by forever depriving the government of the challenged evidence.

If this concept of substantive Fourth Amendment rights were

---

v. United States, 116 U.S. 616 (1886). The essence of a Fourth Amendment violation is often that a police officer acquires personal information that he is not entitled to have. When the officer discloses this information in court, he aggravates his wrong; with disclosure, not only does the officer know things that he is not entitled to know, but others—the judge, jurors, and spectators—know these things as well. See Mertens & Wasserstrom, note 6 *supra*, at 377–78. The distance between the proposition that disclosure can aggravate an initial wrong and the proposition that disclosure can be a distinct wrong is short. When a search occurred under the pressure of a difficult situation that demanded a hasty response, the resulting invasion of privacy may appear "excusable" but not "justified." Nevertheless, the "excuse" disappears once the pressures of the difficult situation are absent. If, on leisurely reflection from an *ex post* perspective, it appears that the search was "something that one would rather had not happened," a court can prevent further injury by excluding whatever evidence this search uncovered. On this view, the admission of evidence can be wrongful although the search that uncovered it was not.

accepted, it might be only a short step to the evaluation of factual circumstances from an *ex post* perspective. When a defendant challenges the admissibility of evidence obtained by a search, one of the things that a judge is likely to know with the benefit of hindsight is that the search uncovered evidence of a crime. From an Olympian perspective that takes account of after-acquired knowledge and insight, the search, although wrongful *ex ante*, may not be wrongful *ex post* because the officers guessed correctly. When one has the benefit of hindsight, perhaps it is foolish not to use it. If extended to its limit, however, this principle would be more likely to work to the disadvantage of defendants than to their advantage. Searches that appeared improper *ex ante* might be validated much more often than searches that seemed proper *ex ante* would be condemned.

When police officers have arrested an innocent person on the basis of probable cause to believe him guilty, they have not acted wrongfully; it is likely to seem a corollary of this proposition that the innocent person, although injured, has not been wronged. Perhaps, with the benefit of hindsight, it could be claimed that the officers did indeed wrong the victim of their mistaken identification, but for most of the history of the common law, this view has been rejected. Because it is fair and appropriate for officers to act on the basis of reasonable appearances, the hapless victims of mistaken identification have been required to endure the consequences of official actions that appeared justified *ex ante* but that later seemed mistaken. Similarly, when officers have done as well as they could have been expected to do, it may be appropriate for the rest of us to endure the consequences of some of their mistakes of law and errors of judgment. Any other view might mark an extravagant construction of a constitutional provision that proscribes unreasonable but not imperfect searches.

At the same time, a rigorously *ex ante* view of Fourth Amendment reasonableness—a view that asks only whether individual police officers and other officials acted reasonably—sometimes would lead to troublesome results. It would in fact produce some of the same incongruous results as a withdrawal of the exclusionary remedy whenever law enforcement officers had entertained a "reasonable good faith belief" in the lawfulness of their actions.

Whether cast in substantive or in remedial form, an *ex ante* perspective might have altered the outcome of most of the cases in which the Supreme Court discovered violations of the Fourth Amendment during the twenty-three years between *Mapp v. Ohio*[86] and *United States v. Leon*. Surely, for example, the officers in *Katz v. United States*[87] acted in "reasonable good faith" when they attached electronic surveillance equipment to the outside of a telephone booth that they expected the defendant to use; the Supreme Court had not yet departed from its ruling in *Olmsted v. United States*[88] that wiretapping accomplished without any trespass upon an individual's property could not violate this person's Fourth Amendment rights. Similarly, in the light of prior judicial rulings, the officers in *Chimel v. California*[89] apparently acted in "reasonable good faith" when, as an incident of a lawful arrest, they searched the entire house of the person whom they had arrested. Moreover, the officers in *Payton v. New York*[90] apparently acted in "reasonable good faith" when they entered a private residence without a warrant to effect a felony arrest.[91]

Of course, in proscribing unreasonable searches, the Fourth Amendment limits not only the conduct of the police but also the conduct of all governmental officers.[92] Accordingly, at least so long as one focuses on the substantive concept of reasonableness rather than on the appropriateness of the exclusionary remedy, an *ex ante* approach cannot be confined to the actions of the individual officers who have conducted a search—or even to the conduct of "the law enforcement profession as a whole."[93] An individual police officer is likely to have acted reasonably in conducting a search that apparently had been authorized or approved by a higher or more knowledgeable authority—a higher-ranking police officer, for example, or a magistrate, or a state legislature, or the Supreme Court. When, however, the higher authority had acted unreasonably in authorizing or approving the search, the search must be condemned as unconstitutional even when viewed from an *ex ante* vantage point.

---

[86] 367 U.S. 643.

[87] 389 U.S. 347 (1967).

[88] 277 U.S. 438 (1928).

[89] 395 U.S. 752 (1969).

[90] 445 U.S. 573 (1980).

[91] For a persuasive analysis of this issue, see Kamisar, note 6 *supra*, at 597–608.

[92] Indeed, professional police forces were unknown at the time the Fourth Amendment was enacted. See, *e.g.*, LANE, POLICING THE CITY—BOSTON 1822–1885, at 1 (1967).

[93] Compare Dunaway v. New York, 442 U.S. 200, 221 (1979) (Stevens, J., concurring).

For example, a police officer who executes a warrant usually acts reasonably in relying on the magistrate's determination of probable cause; but if the magistrate's determination of probable cause was unreasonable, the search remains unlawful. Similarly, a police officer who, immediately prior to *Chimel*, thoroughly searched a room in which he had made a lawful arrest apparently would have acted reasonably under the Supreme Court's ruling in *United States v. Rabinowitz*.[94] Nevertheless, if the Court's approval of such a wide-ranging search incident to arrest had been unreasonable, the search would have violated the Fourth Amendment.

Recognition that an *ex ante* concept of reasonableness must extend to all governmental agencies and officers tends to limit the incongruity of this *ex ante* approach. The fact that the conduct of the law enforcement officers in *Chimel* was reasonable *ex ante* becomes immaterial, for example, once one concludes that the Supreme Court's authorization of this conduct was unreasonable from an *ex ante* perspective. Nevertheless, the *ex ante* perspective remains somewhat troublesome even when extended to all officials responsible for a search. When the Supreme Court held in *Olmsted* that the Fourth Amendment did not restrict nontrespassory wiretapping, it probably did not act "unreasonably." Indeed, if one credits the view that the framers of the Amendment intended their general language to leave room for judicial development in the light of evolving experience, one might conclude that this ruling was correct in 1928, but that by 1967 it could be seen to have authorized actions that later courts could properly condemn as unconstitutional. On an evolutionary view of the Fourth Amendment, a search or seizure can be unreasonable although no one within the government acted unreasonably in authorizing or conducting it. Moreover, apart from the fact that an officer may rely reasonably on outdated standards, a series of reasonable decisions by successive actors may build on each other and may lead to action that, in the aggregate, becomes unjustified.[95]

---

[94] 339 U.S. 56 (1950).

[95] For example, a court may reasonably articulate a general rule that officers may dispense with arrest warrants in exigent circumstances. Nevertheless, in formulating this rule, the court may not focus directly on situations in which evidence would be lost unless officers entered a home without a warrant to make an arrest for a very minor crime. A group of officers subsequently may interpret the rule to permit them to make warrantless home arrests in minor cases so long as delay would lead to a loss of critical evidence. The officers' action,

An appropriate concept of Fourth Amendment reasonableness therefore cannot rest entirely upon an *ex ante* view of challenged conduct. Equally, an appropriate concept of reasonableness cannot rest entirely on an *ex post* view. A sound theory of the Fourth Amendment should accommodate some understandable errors of judgment without treating the past as the invariable baseline for measuring reasonableness and without precluding the development of Fourth Amendment law. Fourth Amendment standards should take account of the difficulty of the circumstances that may have confronted individual officers and should ask whether they did as well as could have been expected, but, at least in some circumstances, it should not regard the answer to this query as the end of the quest.

In seeking an appropriate blend of *ex ante* and *ex post* perspectives, a court might focus initially on the reasonableness of the conduct of the officers responsible for a search and seizure. Then, if the court concluded that the officers had acted reasonably, it might ask whether there was some reason why this determination of *ex ante* reasonableness should not resolve the case at hand. The court might qualify its *ex ante* approach by adopting a "societal" or *ex post* perspective in cases of reliance on standards that have become outdated or incomplete, and in cases of cumulative error.

A better and simpler way of combining the two antithetical viewpoints might be to return to the language of the Fourth Amendment. This language implicitly invites the use of an amalgamated *ex ante* and *ex post* perspective. The issue is not whether, on reflection, the search was "something that one would rather had not happened," nor is it merely whether the search was "excusable." A line should be drawn somewhere between "excuse" and "justification," and this line probably cannot be expressed in language more precise than that of the Amendment itself. A court should ask whether, in the light of the inevitable imperfections of human enterprise, the person challenging a search or seizure truly was treated in a way that the court regards as unfair or unreasonable and not merely as

---

like the court's, may be reasonable, but the two reasonable judgments together may lead to a serious intrusion on privacy for the sake of a minor gain to law enforcement. When the justification for this intrusion is faced directly, the intrusion may seem unreasonable although no individual acted unreasonably from an *ex ante* perspective. See Welsh v. Wisconsin, 104 S.Ct. 2091 (1984) (plainly applying an *ex post* perspective to an arrest under circumstances like those described above—but not in a case arising under the exclusionary rule).

imperfect. In the end, the phrase "unreasonable searches and sei-zures" probably cannot be reduced much farther.

In *Leon*, the Supreme Court apparently took a significant step toward a different combination of the *ex ante* and *ex post* perspec-tives. Ever since the Court held in *Linkletter v. Walker*[96] that its decision in *Mapp v. Ohio* should be applied only prospectively, the Court has endorsed the view that a rule appropriate for guiding the future may be inappropriate for judging the past. Similarly, the Court in *Leon* may have envisioned a regime in which courts would use one viewpoint to evaluate the past and a different viewpoint to govern the future.

After *Leon*, a court must take an *ex ante* view of a challenged search or seizure in every case, for whether individual law enforce-ment officers acted reasonably under all the circumstances will be ultimately the determinative issue. If the officers acted unreason-ably, the court must exclude the evidence that they obtained. If they acted reasonably from an *ex ante* perspective, the court cannot properly exclude the evidence that they seized.

Nevertheless, *Leon* requires a court to view a challenged search from an *ex ante* perspective only in deciding whether to afford relief to the defendant before it. The court also may view the challenged search from an *ex post* perspective and may ask what other officers ought to do if the same situation were to recur. Upon concluding that the conduct of the officers in the case at hand should not be repeated tomorrow, the court may rule that yesterday's search vio-lated the Fourth Amendment. This substantive ruling would not alter the outcome of the case before the court, but it would provide a warning that the court might measure the reasonableness of fu-ture searches from a different baseline. Under *Leon*, in other words, a court must employ an *ex ante* perspective in deciding whether the defendant in the case before it is entitled to a remedy, but it may employ an *ex post* perspective in deciding whether this defendant's rights have been violated.

If this strange regime of bifurcated adjudication had been in place prior to 1984, the victorious defendants in cases like *Katz*, *Chimel*, and *Payton* would have been denied relief. Even as these defendants were imprisoned, however, the Supreme Court's deci-sions in their cases might have worked significant changes in gov-

---

[96] 381 U.S. 618 (1965).

erning constitutional standards. Americans might have come to remember these cases not for their landmark rulings but for their stirring landmark dicta. *Leon*'s separation of right and remedy often would deny relief to the litigants in whose cases new constitutional standards were announced,[97] and it would depart from the Supreme Court's earlier approach to questions of prospectivity in other significant ways as well.[98] Moreover, although the Court maintained that federal courts would not violate article III of the Constitution by ruling on Fourth Amendment issues that could not alter the resolution of the cases before them,[99] this practice has a number of the vices of the advisory opinions that article III long has been held to preclude.[100]

No rational nonindigent defendant in a case like *Katz* would seek a major revision of Fourth Amendment doctrine that, in the light of the unmistakable reasonableness of official reliance on prior doctrine, plainly could not benefit him. Some commentators have maintained that civil liberties organizations and public defender

---

[97] *Cf.* Stoval v. Denno, 388 U.S. 293, 301 (1967).

[98] Most notably, the practical effect of *Leon* is likely to be the application of all law-changing Fourth Amendment decisions only prospectively. See note 73 *supra*. The Supreme Court had clearly rejected this approach two years before *Leon*. United States v. Johnson, 457 U.S. 537 (1982). In addition, Professor Kamisar has observed, "Over the years the Court has employed an 'extraordinary diversity of rules' for locating the 'cut-off point' for application of law-changing decision." Kamisar, note 6 *supra*, at 601–02. Nevertheless, the Court always has articulated some "cut-off point." At the very least, a search conducted the day after a law-changing decision was announced would be governed by the rules articulated by the decision. Under *Leon*, however, courts will apparently be required to determine on a case-by-case basis whether the conduct of a police officer who had pursued a search in ignorance of a law-altering decision one day, one week, or one month after the decision had been rendered was "objectively unreasonable." Surely instantaneous knowledge of judicial decisions cannot fairly be demanded. Courts also will be required to consider whether a law enforcement officer can remain "objectively reasonable" although he never learns of some judicial decisions at all.

[99] 104 S.Ct. at 3422.

[100] See Muskrat v. United States, 219 U.S. 346 (1911). When rulings have no immediate consequences, one concern is that they are likely to be of poor quality. A court encouraged to announce significant Fourth Amendment rulings in dicta could easily fall into an undue activism or an unrealistic perfectionism. To be sure, the current Supreme Court is unlikely to succumb to this temptation, but a successor Court might. Indeed, one commentator has urged the adoption of a "reasonable good faith exception" to the exclusionary rule primarily on the ground that the exclusionary rule of *Weeks* and *Mapp* has inhibited broad readings of Fourth Amendment requirements. Bernardi, *The Exclusionary Rule: Is a Good Faith Standard Needed to Preserve a Liberal Interpretation of the Fourth Amendment?* 30 DE PAUL L. REV. 51 (1980). Expansive interpretations of the Fourth Amendment in dicta coupled with the enforcement of these interpretations through the exclusion of evidence in subsequent cases might ultimately become the Burger Court's ironic legacy.

agencies seeking the welfare of future, unknown clients would continue to afford the courts adequate opportunities (or perhaps excessive opportunities) to alter existing Fourth Amendment law.[101] Other commentators have been less confident that institutional law offices would assume the role that individual litigants to some extent had abandoned.[102] If institutional law offices did assume this role, however, significant Fourth Amendment litigation might become little more than an institutional office's advocacy of some part of its agenda before a court that might have a corresponding agenda for the future of its own. When courts view litigants merely as trimmings for their rulings and cases merely as occasions for advancing general visions of the future, the sense of individual worth and individual entitlement that differentiates our culture from some others is likely to diminish.

The choice between *ex post* and *ex ante* perspectives may have been the "real issue" in *Leon* (and the "real difficult" issue as well). Ultimately, however, despite its apparently unequivocal endorsement of an *ex ante* perspective in determining Fourth Amendment cases, the Supreme Court did not address this issue in a coherent way. In the years before *Leon*, although the Supreme Court had left the basic choice of perspective unresolved in many Fourth Amendment contexts, it had not done so in the context of reviewing searches that judicial officers had authorized by issuing warrants in advance. The Court had insisted that these searches were not to be subjected to *ex post* demands for perfection. It had held that a magistrate's decision to issue a warrant was entitled to "great deference," and it recently had emphasized the strength of the presumption in favor of the validity of warrants by requiring reviewing courts to defer to a magistrate's decision so long as the magistrate had a "substantial basis" for his determination of probable cause. In *Leon*, the Court expressly limited its holding to situations in which search or arrest warrants had been issued, situations in which the Court already had mandated the use of an *ex ante* vantage point.

---

[101] See Beytagh, *Ten Years of Non-Retroactivity: A Critique and a Proposal*, 61 VA. L. REV. 1557, 1613–14 (1975). *Cf. Leon*, 104 S.Ct. 3422 n.25.

[102] See Mertens & Wasserstrom, note 6 *supra*, at 451 n.494; Kamisar, note 6 *supra*, at 603–04; Schaefer, *Prospective Rulings: Two Perspectives*, 1982 SUPREME COURT REVIEW 1, 22; Mishkin, *Foreword: The High Court, The Great Writ, and the Due Process of Time and Law*, 79 HARV. L. REV. 56, 61 (1965).

Leon therefore did not involve any shift from an *ex post* to an *ex ante* perspective. It involved what Wayne R. LaFave has called "a form of double billing."[103] Under *Leon*, after viewing a challenged search from an *ex ante* perspective and asking whether a magistrate had acted reasonably in approving it, a court must view the search from an *ex ante* perspective once again. It must ask whether the police officer who obtained and executed the warrant could have believed reasonably that the magistrate had believed reasonably that the search was supported by probable cause (that is, by circumstances that would have led a person to believe reasonably that evidence of a crime would be uncovered). This strange query—not whether a search was reasonable from an *ex ante* perspective but whether a police officer had believed reasonably that it was reasonable—invites slippage. *Leon*'s qualification of the exclusionary rule encourages reviewing courts to declare, "The search was improper. It was in fact improper from any perspective that we might adopt. Nevertheless, it was close enough for government work."

IV. Magistrates and Police Officers: Judging Stereotypes and Judging People

A. BEHOLD, A SIMPLE DETECTIVE'S GOOD FAITH HEALETH THE GREAT BEFUDDLEMENT OF A MIGHTY JUDGE: MASSACHUSETTS V. SHEPPARD

Leon not only created a two-tiered standard for judging rights and rationing remedies: it also created a double standard for reviewing the actions of police officers and judges. When the Supreme Court considered a companion case to *Leon*, its refusal to apply to magistrates even the reduced standards of review that it applied to police officers determined the Court's decision.

In *Massachusetts v. Sheppard*,[104] careful police investigation had established probable cause to believe that Osborne Sheppard had murdered Sandra Boulware and that a search of Sheppard's residence would reveal evidence of the crime. A police detective prepared an affidavit to support his request for a search warrant and described the items that he expected to find. He showed this

---

[103] Address by Wayne R. LaFave to the Workshop on Teaching Criminal Justice of the Association of American Law Schools, in Chicago (Oct. 15, 1983).

[104] 104 S.Ct. 3424 (1984).

affidavit to the district attorney and to the district attorney's first assistant. They, as well as a police sergeant who reviewed the affidavit, agreed that it established probable cause. Because the courts were closed on Sunday, the detective had difficulty finding an appropriate search warrant form. He ultimately located one headed, "Search Warrant—Controlled Substance." After making some alterations in this form, he brought it to the home of a judge who had agreed to consider his application for a warrant.

When the judge examined the application and said that he would authorize the search, the police detective informed him that, despite the detective's minor alterations, the form remained inappropriate. After looking unsuccessfully for a different form, the judge advised the detective that he would make the necessary changes. Although the judge did make some changes in the form, he did not alter the critical part. The warrant as issued still authorized a search for controlled substances rather than for the bloody clothing, wire, and other grisly evidence of a homicide that the police in fact sought. Nevertheless, the officers who executed the warrant searched for the evidentiary items listed in the detective's application, and they discovered a substantial amount of incriminating material.

The Fourth Amendment declares that warrants must particularly describe the persons or things to be seized, and the defendant contended that the search warrant's misspecification of the things to be seized had made the search invalid. Under the circumstances of the case, this contention was not one that a court was likely to embrace for its powerful equitable appeal; the argument rested on the asserted compulsion of specific constitutional language. Indeed, the state's brief might colorably have described the issue presented in *Sheppard* as, "Shall a mindless technicality allow a murderer to go free?"[105]

Although the defendant's contention derived some support from the language of the Fourth Amendment, it was not obviously correct. When a police officer's affidavit in support of a search warrant has been attached to the warrant, courts have held that the affidavit's specificity can remedy what otherwise would be a fatal defect

---

[105] Although the police had established clear probable cause for a search of Sheppard's residence, the evidence that they had discovered would have been unlikely to yield a finding of guilt beyond a reasonable doubt. I have borrowed my phrasing of the question presented in *Sheppard* from a remark by Frank H. Easterbrook.

in the body of the warrant.[106] The Supreme Court could have endorsed these rulings and could have extended them by holding inconsequential the presence or absence of a staple or paperclip.

The Court also might have held that, even if the warrant in *Sheppard* had violated the Fourth Amendment, the error was harmless. The principal vice of general warrants is that they authorize general searches,[107] yet the police had not conducted a general search. The warrant's lack of specificity had not dimmed the quality of the defendant's life, and the warrant's alleged defect was therefore harmless in the sense that it did "not affect substantial rights" of the defendant.[108]

Courts have been reluctant to apply the harmless error doctrine to Fourth Amendment violations—and often for good reason. This doctrine, if applied to unlawful searches in the same manner as to other constitutional violations, could remove a principal incentive for law enforcement officers to obtain judicial warrants before conducting searches. Whenever a search without a warrant was supported by probable cause, a court might hold the lack of a warrant harmless, for had the police sought a warrant, a competent magistrate would have issued it. The defendant's property and privacy therefore would have been invaded to the same extent whether or not the constitutional violation had occurred. In retrospect, it could be seen that the failure to obtain a warrant had not affected substantial rights of the defendant.

If a court were to approve a "rights" rather than an "incentives" theory of the exclusionary rule (if, in other words, the court were to focus only on the individual defendant who had challenged a warrantless search and were to view the exclusionary rule as resting on what Kamisar has called a "principled basis" rather than an "empir-

---

[106] See United States v. Johnson, 690 F.2d 60, 64 (3d Cir. 1982), *cert. denied*, 459 U.S. 1214 (1983); United States v. Wuagneux, 683 F.2d 1343, 1351 n.6 (11th Cir. 1982), *cert. denied*, 104 S.Ct. 69 (1983); see also United States v. Johnson, 541 F.2d 1311, 1315 (8th Cir. 1976).

[107] An additional vice of general warrants may be that they fail to afford adequate notice of the limits of the power to search. Nevertheless, because the defendant in *Sheppard* was not at home when the police conducted their search, the "notice" function that the warrant might have served seemed immaterial. See 104 S.Ct. at 3449 (Stevens, J., concurring in the judgment in *Sheppard* and dissenting in *Leon*).

[108] See Fed. R. Crim. P. 52. The harmless error doctrine is ordinarily applied during the appellate review of asserted trial errors, but that is not its only application. See United States v. Ravich, 421 F.2d 1196, 1201–02 (2d Cir. 1970) (improper execution of search warrant at night constituted harmless error because premises were unoccupied, *per* Friendly, J.); WRIGHT, FED. PRAC. & PROC.: CRIM. 2d § 852 (1982).

ical proposition"[109]), this application of the harmless error doctrine to all warrantless searches supported by probable cause would seem plausible.[110] The harmless error doctrine becomes unattractive only when one endorses an "incentives" theory of the rule, for this application of the doctrine would remove a significant incentive to obey the Fourth Amendment. The claim that the exclusionary rule sometimes can influence the conduct of law enforcement officers may, in fact, have its greatest plausibility when the choice between searching with and searching without warrants is at issue.[111]

The impulse to invoke the exclusionary rule to lessen affirmative incentives for deliberate misconduct is far stronger than the impulse to use the rule to discourage negligent error. For example, the prospect of exclusion seems very unlikely to reduce the chance that an official would carelessly overlook the critical language of a warrant when he sought to alter it. In *Sheppard*, unlike a situation in which a police officer had conducted a search without a warrant, neither a "rights" nor an "incentives" theory of the exclusionary rule argued against a conventional application of the harmless error doctrine. By invoking the doctrine, the Supreme Court could have signaled its willingness to enforce the right to specificity, but only when it mattered.

In *Sheppard*, the Supreme Court assumed that the warrant's erroneous description of the things to be seized had violated the Fourth Amendment and that this error was prejudicial. The Court nevertheless withheld the exclusionary remedy. Applying the standards of *Leon*, it concluded that the police detective had relied reasonably on the judge's assurance that he would make appropriate alterations in the search warrant form, and it therefore refused to suppress the evidence that the search had uncovered. The Court wrote:[112]

> An error of constitutional dimensions may have been committed with respect to the issuance of the warrant, but it was the judge,

---

[109] See Kamisar, *Does (Did) (Should) the Exclusionary Rule Rest on a "Principles Basis" rather than an "Empirical Proposition?"* 16 CREIGHTON L. REV. 565 (1983).

[110] Nevertheless, this application of the harmless error doctrine would not be inevitable under a "rights" theory of the exclusionary rule. A search warrant can assure the occupants of the premises to be searched that the police have appropriate authorization and will act within appropriate limits. See Camara v. Municipal Court, 387 U.S. 523, 532 (1967). The lack of a warrant that can perform this "notice" or "credentials" functions may be harmful despite the existence of probable cause.

[111] See Alschuler, *The Prosecutor's Role in Plea Bargaining*, 36 U. CHI. L. REV. 50, 82–83 (1968).

[112] 104 S.Ct. at 3429.

not the police officers, who made the critical mistake. "[T]he exclusionary rule was adopted to deter unlawful searches by police, not to punish the errors of magistrates and judges."

Had the Court reviewed the judge's actions in the same way that it reviewed the detective's, it could not have reached the same result. The detective's conduct may have been "objectively reasonable," but the judge's was not. On the assumption that a prejudicial constitutional error had occurred, a "reasonable" good faith exception would not have prevented application of the exclusionary rule to the products of the search that this official had authorized. Instead, an "unreasonable," "mindless," or "blithering" good faith exception would have been necessary.

The appropriateness of the Supreme Court's double standard for the members of two occupational groups, one apparently regarded as substantially more trustworthy than the other, is the principal focus of the final section of this article. Nevertheless, the Supreme Court's approach to this issue reflected a style of thought that has come to dominate the approach of many lawyers and social scientists to legal problems. Justice Brennan's dissent in *Leon* embraced the same mode of analysis in its discussion of what has become a favorite issue of social scientists in the exclusionary rule debate.

B. THE BOTTOM-LINE COLLECTIVIST-EMPIRICAL MENTALITY (WITH A COMMENT ON A LEON DISSENT ANALYSIS OF THE "COSTS" OF THE EXCLUSIONARY RULE)

The pragmatism that has dominated twentieth-century American thought has had what I will call a "collectivist" bent. I use the word "collectivist," not in the way that my dictionary uses it (to mean "socialist"), but rather to describe the process of viewing a collectivity of things or people all at once—the process of studying the forest while disregarding every tree. At least until recently, there has been a growing tendency on the part of lawyers and social scientists to judge every action in terms of one criterion: How much has this action altered the entire world for good or ill? From a pragmatic, utilitarian, empiricist perspective, nothing that happens seems to matter very much unless it is "typical" or "widespread," or at least "statistically significant." Both the majority and dissenting opinions in *Leon* illustrated the extent to which this collectivist mode of thought has become characteristic of the times.

When confronted with a claim of injustice in particular cases, social scientists commonly treat the claim as an empirical proposition concerning a universe of cases. They apparently assume that this claim of injustice would be irrelevant to the formulation of policy unless it implicitly carried with it an empirical assertion concerning the frequency of the injustice alleged. Indeed, empiricists may believe that they are merely giving moralists the benefit of the doubt by reading empirical propositions into their arguments. Nevertheless, after misconstruing an argument based on principle, the social scientists typically challenge the implied empirical proposition.

Justice Brennan's dissenting opinion in *Leon* exemplified this error. The opinion declared:[113]

> At the outset, the Court suggests that society has been asked to pay a high price—in terms either of setting guilty persons free or of impeding the proper functioning of trials—as a result of excluding relevant physical evidence in cases where the police, in conducting searches and seizing evidence, have made only an "objectively reasonable" mistake concerning the constitutionality of their actions. . . . But what evidence is there to support such a claim? Significantly, the Court points to none, and indeed, as the Court acknowledges . . . , recent studies have demonstrated that the "costs" of the exclusionary rule—calculated in terms of dropped prosecutions and lost convictions—are quite low.

Justice Brennan then cited studies indicating that federal courts had excluded unlawfully seized evidence in only 1.3 percent of all criminal cases filed by federal prosecutors and that suppression motions had been successful in only 0.7 percent of all criminal cases in a large, nine-county, state-court sample. Moreover, federal prosecutors had refused to prosecute only 0.2 percent of the cases in which felony arrests had been made on the ground that they anticipated the exclusion of seized evidence; and in California, "only 0.8 percent of all arrests were rejected for prosecution because of illegally seized evidence."[114]

Justice Brennan faulted the majority for its failure to offer "evidence" of the excessive costs of the exclusionary rule, and he strongly implied that, in the absence of empirical proof concerning a collectivity of cases, claims of excessive costs should be rejected. Without any analysis of case disposition patterns, however, an op-

---

[113] 104 S.Ct. at 3441 (Brennan, J., dissenting).

[114] *Id.* at 3441.

ponent of the exclusionary rule could note that application of the rule might mandate the release of next year's Son of Sam despite the fact that the guilt of this mass murderer had been established beyond a doubt. The rule could require the killer's release simply because the police had uncovered critical evidence against him by looking in the glove compartment of his automobile when they should not have done so. An opponent of the rule might contend that a sane society does not release a proven murderer, and that it certainly does not do so because of a police wrong that pales beside the murderer's own.[115] When confronted with the empirical response voiced by Justice Brennan—that this sort of case does not happen very often—this advocate might regard the empiricist with incredulity. The response would have no bearing on the normative claim of injustice that the advocate had advanced.

Even were the exclusionary rule to be evaluated from a global perspective, the figures cited by Justice Brennan would be immaterial. Neither the costs nor the benefits of the exclusionary rule are at stake in the vast majority of criminal cases. No seizure of tangible evidence is likely to occur, for example, in simple assault or embezzlement cases. Analyses of the proportion of all cases in which the exclusionary rule is invoked, however, effectively draw large numbers of these irrelevant cases into the picture and treat them as relevant.[116]

In a jurisdiction with a great many simple assault cases and other cases in which no seizure of tangible evidence is at issue, the proportion of cases in which the exclusionary rule is invoked is likely to

---

[115] The opponent of the exclusionary rule might reasonably make this argument despite the fact that strict observance of the Fourth Amendment by the police itself would have left the murderer undetected. Only a bottom-line empiricist (and an incautious one at that) would regard the release of a proven murderer as indistinguishable from the initial failure to detect a murderer. A person might be willing to pay the "price" of allowing a killer to go free when the odds were only one in 100 that a search would reveal his identity and yet be unwilling to pay the same price when the search with only one chance in 100 had succeeded. To escape the *ex post* perspective altogether, one must have the legal mind. But *cf.* Stewart, *The Road to Mapp v. Ohio and Beyond: The Origins, Development and Future of the Exclusionary Rule in Search-and-Seizure Cases*, 83 COLUM L. REV. 1365, 1392–93 (1983); *Leon*, 104 S.Ct. at 3436–37 (Brennan, J., dissenting). I do not suggest that the "proportionality" argument advanced by my hypothesized opponent of the exclusionary rule would support *Leon*'s modification of the rule or that the *Leon* majority itself relied on this argument. My purpose in this discussion is to explore in general terms how an analysis of the "costs" and "benefits" of the exclusionary rule ought to proceed.

[116] The definitive review of the empirical literature is Davies, *A Hard Look at What We Know (and Still Need to Learn) about the "Costs" of the Exclusionary Rule: The NIJ Study and Other Studies of "Lost" Arrests*, 1983 A.B.F. RES. J. 611.

be small. In a jurisdiction with fewer of these cases, the proportion is likely to be higher. The presence or absence of simple assault cases, however, has no bearing on the "costs" of the exclusionary rule. If any number mattered, it might be the absolute number of cases in which the exclusionary rule had yielded "lost convictions" rather than the proportion of cases in which convictions had been lost. Social scientists with graduate training in statistics have faulted each others' methodologies without recognizing that every effort to "measure" the costs of the exclusionary rule has used denominators that may or may not have made their numerators look small but that consistently have obfuscated the issue.

Criteria and standards for determining whether a quantity of criminals released as a result of the exclusionary rule is "large" or "small" are not apparent. If one were to conclude that the exclusionary rule had yielded "few" lost convictions, however, one might wonder why. The rule might have induced police officers to observe Fourth Amendment requirements and might therefore have produced substantial "benefits" but very few "costs." Or the rule might have induced police officers, not to refrain from unlawful searches, but to lie about them; and defense attorneys might have been unable to combat the police officers' frequent perjury.[117] On this hypothesis, the exclusionary rule might have increased the amount of police lawlessness and in that sense yielded significant "costs," but it might have yielded few "benefits."

Another possibility is that evidence has been rarely suppressed because judges and prosecutors have winked at Fourth Amendment violations. Still another is that defense attorneys have failed to investigate their cases adequately or have been reluctant to undertake the work of filing and litigating suppression motions and have urged their clients to plead guilty. The exclusionary rule might have yielded few "costs" either because it has been effectual or because it has been ineffectual. Without knowing more, one cannot determine whether the infrequency of "lost convictions" says something good or something bad about the rule.

---

[117] See, *e.g.*, Garbus, *Police Perjury: An Interview with Martin Garbus*, 8 CRIM. L. BULL. 363, 365 (1972) (defense attorney who had appeared in approximately 150 drug cases over the course of thirteen years had no doubt that the police had "shaped" their testimony in every case); Sevilla, *The Exclusionary Rule and Police Perjury*, 11 SAN DIEGO L. REV. 839 (1974); Grano, *A Dilemma for Defense Counsel: Spinelli-Harris Search Warrants and the Possibility of Police Perjury*, 1971 U. ILL. L.F. 405, 408–09.

The figures laboriously gathered by the social scientists and cited by Justice Brennan therefore do not significantly advance efforts to evaluate the exclusionary rule from a global perspective. More important, nothing is gained by yielding to the empiricist impulse to "collectivize" the decision. Although widespread injustice is more to be deplored than isolated injustice, this fact offers no justification for isolated injustice that courts have the power to prevent. The critical issue in evaluating the exclusionary rule is whether the results that it yields in individual cases are appropriate.[118]

In an individual case, the "costs" of applying the exclusionary rule are likely to be apparent. The "benefits" of applying the rule may extend to other cases and may be more difficult to measure. Nevertheless, if the worth of the exclusionary rule depends on any sort of cost-benefit analysis, the costs and benefits of applying the rule in individual cases mark the appropriate judicial inquiry.

A defender of the exclusionary rule might protest that an effort to weigh tangible costs in one case against speculative benefits in other cases tilts the inquiry and sets the stage for the certain triumph of those who contend that costs outweigh benefits. Opponents of the exclusionary rule have indeed claimed victory only because the utilitarian claims of proponents of the rule have not been susceptible to clear empirical proof. Dissenting in *Bivens v. Six Unknown Named Agents*, Chief Justice Burger illustrated this common approach to cost-benefit analysis as well as the tendency to "collective" decisions when he wrote, "Some clear demonstration of the benefits and effectiveness of the exclusionary rule is required to justify it in view of the high price that it exacts from society—the release of countless guilty criminals."[119]

The sense of protagonists on both sides that certain costs must triumph over uncertain benefits reveals two other characteristic

---

[118] This article's advocacy of a case-specific focus does not deny that the need to develop general and easily administered rules may be an appropriate part of cost-benefit analysis. A demonstration that the toleration of injustice in one case would produce a "greater good" in other cases often may be an appropriate response to a claim of unfairness; the rejection of such a claim merely on the ground that the alleged injustice happens infrequently, by contrast, is indecent. A global perspective that shunts aside individual cases for no better reason than their statistical insignificance may contribute to a sense that individuals and their problems do not matter. Moreover, because people may not care very much about the community when the community does not care very much about them, a collectivist viewpoint may contribute to individual alienation or self-absorption. In the end, individual worth and community worth may be reciprocal rather than opposing values; and ironic though it may seem, a collectivist perspective that discounts the worth of the individual and of case-specific claims may diminish the sense of general community welfare that it seeks to advance.

[119] 403 U.S. 388; 416 (Burger, C.J., dissenting) (1971).

errors of our times. They are the tendency to demand empirical proof in areas in which it is unavailable and the further tendency to demand evidence of a particular sort—quantitative evidence strong enough to exclude with a high degree of certainty all hypotheses but the one proposed.

In most of life, people exercise judgment and reach conclusions in the absence of mathematically rigorous "proof." One who abandons artificial social science conventions and assesses the benefits of the exclusionary rule on the basis of reasonable inferences from nonquantitative evidence is likely to conclude that, in the generation since *Mapp v. Ohio*,[120] the exclusionary rule has influenced the conduct of American police officers substantially and for the better.[121]

Even were the encouraging experience of the past generation unavailable, however, and even were courts required to speculate about the benefits of the exclusionary rule, they should speculate. The fact that costs are concrete and benefits speculative does not demonstrate that the costs "outweigh" the benefits. In view of the high, tangible, and measurable costs of such governmental programs as maintaining armaments, imprisoning criminals, educating students and exploring space, a demand for clear empirical proof that costs are matched by benefits—a demand of the sort often made by opponents of the exclusionary rule—would go a long way toward reducing governmental budgets to zero. As Justice Brennan's dissenting opinion in *Leon* revealed, bottom-line collectivist-empiricism is an unfortunate way of talking about cases. More significantly, the majority opinion in *Leon* revealed that it is an unfortunate way of talking about people.[122]

C. ARE POLICE OFFICERS AND JUDGES APPROPRIATELY REGARDED AS MEMBERS OF DIFFERENT SPECIES?

In 1948, in his opinion for the Court in *Johnson v. United States*,[123] Justice Jackson spoke in a single sentence of a "neutral and detached

---

[120] 367 U.S. 643 (1961).

[121] See, *e.g.*, Mertens & Wasserstrom, note 6 *supra*, at 395 n.138, 389 n.157, 399–401; Alschuler, *Implementing the Criminal Defendant's Right to Trial: Alternatives to the Plea Bargaining Systems*, 50 U. CHI. L. REV. 931, 968–69 (1983); Segura v. United States, 104 S.Ct. 3380, 3404 (1984) (Stevens, J., dissenting).

[122] Compare White, *The Fourth Amendment as a Way of Talking about People: A Study of Robinson and Matlock*, 1974 SUPREME COURT REVIEW 165 (1974).

[123] 333 U.S. 10 (1948).

magistrate" and a police "officer engaged in the often competitive enterprise of ferreting out crime."[124] In the years since Justice Jackson wrote these phrases, Supreme Court opinions have referred to "neutral and detached" magistrates in forty-five cases and to police officers "engaged in the often competitive enterprise of ferreting out crime" in forty.[125] The Court often has seemed incapable of discussing magistrates and police officers without invoking Justice Jackson's memorable modifiers. In *Leon*, for example, the majority described magistrates as "neutral" or as "neutral and detached" nine times.

Just who competes with whom in the often competitive enterprise of ferreting out crime may not be entirely apparent, and when one discovers that fewer than 10 percent of all police officers make more than half of all arrests,[126] one may wish that the law enforcement enterprise were more competitive than it is. Nevertheless, Justice Jackson's imagery obviously was not meant to be taken literally. It has provided a way for the Supreme Court to say delicately what tact would not permit the Court to say forthrightly: that although magistrates typically are high-minded judicial officers with a suitable regard for constitutional principles, police officers are typically zealots whose "gangbusters" mentality leads them to disregard individual rights.

In analyzing proposed modifications of the exclusionary rule, commentators sometimes have challenged the Supreme Court's occupational stereotypes, but only by offering crude stereotypes of their own. These commentators have not disputed the Supreme Court's view that police officers typically are "bad guys." They merely have argued that magistrates are bad guys, too. Their contention is that magistrates belong to a subspecies of scoundrel called "rubber stamps" and that these officials routinely approve requests for search and arrest warrants without exercising the independent judgment that the warrant process is designed to secure.[127] The

---

[124] *Id.* at 14.

[125] LEXIS searches conducted by Andrew Kandel, a second-year student at the University of Pennsylvania Law School, and Brian Gaffney, a second-year student at the University of Chicago Law School, Genfed Library, Sup. file, Oct. 1984.

[126] See FORST, LUCIANOVIC, & COX, WHAT HAPPENS AFTER ARREST, ch. 4 (1977); SILBERMAN, CRIMINAL VIOLENCE, CRIMINAL JUSTICE 276 (1978).

[127] See, *e.g.*, 2 LAFAVE, SEARCH AND SEIZURE § 4.1 (1978); Kamisar, note 111 *supra*, at 569–70; LaFave & Remington, *Controlling the Police: The Judge's Role in Making and Reviewing Law Enforcement Decisions*, 63 MICH. L. REV. 987, 994–95 (1965).

Leon majority responded to this empirical contention only briefly: "Although there are assertions that some magistrates become rubber stamps for police and others may be unable effectively to screen police conduct, . . . we are not convinced that this is a problem of major proportions."[128] None of the protagonists appear to have suggested that the "proportions" of the problem and the effort to characterize occupational groups as good guys or bad guys were irrelevant to the issue presented in *Leon*.

As an empirical matter, magistrates as a group probably are more "neutral and detached" than police officers as a group. The warrant process may indeed rest in part on the perception that the occupational norms of magistrates and judges are likely to lead them to approach the decision whether to invade privacy from a different perspective from that of the officers whose requests for warrants they review.[129] The *Leon* majority nonetheless went substantially beyond this sound (although, in this context, irrelevant) generalization and advanced a number of more dubious empirical propositions—propositions about the ways in which police officers and magistrates respond to the exclusion of unlawfully seized evidence. The majority opinion declared:[130]

> To the extent that proponents of exclusion rely on its behavioral effects on judges and magistrates in these areas, their reliance is misplaced. . . . [W]e discern no basis, and are offered none, for believing that exclusion of evidence seized pursuant to a warrant will have a significant deterrent effect on the issuing judge or magistrate. Many of the factors that indicate that the exclusionary rule cannot provide an effective "special" or "general" deterrent for individual offending law enforcement officers apply as well to judges or magistrates. And, to the extent that the rule is thought to operate as a "systemic" deterrent on a wider audience, it clearly can have no such effect on individuals empowered to issue search warrants. Judges and magistrates are not adjuncts to the law enforcement team; as neutral judicial officers, they have no stake in the outcome of particular criminal prosecutions. The threat of exclusion thus cannot be expected significantly to deter them.

---

[128] 104 S.Ct. at 3418.

[129] The warrant process also may rest in part on the virtues of obtaining "a second opinion" from a person who has not been involved in the investigation of a particular case and, to a lesser extent, on the virtues of making a formal record of the justification for a search before it occurs. The perception that judges and police officers have different occupational norms may not be the only reason for the search warrant requirement. *Cf.* note 8 *supra*.

[130] 104 S.Ct. at 3418.

This statement revealed, among other things, an odd view of the motivations of police officers. The exclusionary rule does not depend for its effectiveness on the proposition that police officers have a special "stake" in punishing criminals not shared by magistrates and other members of the public—the people whom "good" police officers seek to serve. One goal of the exclusionary rule may be to influence conduct, but the rule does not "punish" police officers by fining them, by imprisoning them, by disciplining them, or even by frustrating their distinctive lust for punishment.[131] Indeed, the principal mechanism by which the exclusionary rule reduces official misconduct may be almost the opposite of the one envisioned by the Supreme Court. The rule provides opportunities for courts to adjudicate Fourth Amendment questions—the only significant opportunities that they have. It thereby permits courts to give legal guidance to officers willing to receive it—those "good guy" officers who seek to comply with constitutional norms and who do not fit the Supreme Court's "gangbusters" stereotype.[132]

In suggesting that the behavior of magistrates is unaffected by the invalidation of their decisions through rulings on motions to suppress, the majority's analysis also revealed a strange view of the motivations of judges. This view is likely to be of special interest to the judges of the United States Court of Appeals for the Ninth Circuit. The invalidation of a lower-court decision through a ruling on a motion to suppress seems unlikely to have a different behavioral effect than the invalidation of this decision through some other review mechanism. During its October 1983 Term, the Supreme

---

[131] The rule declares that courts will not provide a market for things that law enforcement officers have taken without justification—that is, for things that these officers have misappropriated. In some respects, the arguments for the rule are analogous to the arguments against providing a private market for privately misappropriated property. The primary argument in both situations—one that the Supreme Court has shunted aside in recent years—is moralistic: Even were it shown that a person's refusal to receive stolen property would not reduce the incidence of theft, this person should refuse to receive stolen property. A secondary argument, however, is pragmatic: A person's refusal to receive stolen property removes one incentive for theft and may thereby reduce the incidence of this misconduct. It may do so, moreover, although other incentives for theft remain. Still, a refusal to receive stolen property does not itself "punish" the thief or "deter" his wrongful appropriation of property; it threatens no "sanction" for this misconduct. See Amsterdam, *Perspectives on the Fourth Amendment*, 58 MINN. L. REV. 349, 431–32 (1974). The reduction of affirmative incentives for wrongdoing is one means by which the exclusionary rule may affect police behavior; another and more important mechanism is described in the text following this footnote.

[132] See Alschuler, note 121 *supra*, at 968–69.

Court reversed thirty-one Ninth Circuit decisions (including that court's decision in *Leon*).[133] Over the course of the Term, the Supreme Court affirmed only one Ninth Circuit ruling.[134] The judges of the Ninth Circuit may be pleased to learn that when a higher court sets aside a lower court's ruling, the process is not intended to affect future behavior or to "deter" judicial error.

The Supreme Court's attempt to differentiate police officers from magistrates on the ground that the exclusionary sanction is "ill-fitted to the job-created motivations of judges"[135] seemed not only misguided but backward. Critics of the exclusionary rule have maintained that law enforcement officers "count" arrests rather than convictions in measuring productivity; that they are indifferent to the ultimate outcome of most criminal prosecutions; that they respond to norms of "police culture" rather than to legal norms; that their distinctive culture does not disapprove all unlawful searches; that they may not discover that their misconduct has led to the exclusion of evidence (especially when the exclusion is ordered by an appellate court); and that even when they know that their searches have been held illegal, they may be frustrated, baffled, and insufficiently informed of the basis for judicial rulings to be able to correct their errors.[136]

Judges, however, can presumably understand judicial rulings if anyone can, and they seem more likely than police officers to read advance sheets. Moreover, judicial officers need not respond to the demands and expectations of a nonjudicial hierarchy. They seem much more likely than police officers to value the approval of other judges. Unlike professional reputations within police departments that are reported to measure productivity only by counting arrests, the professional reputations of judges seem likely to depend as much on the quality as on the quantity of their work. Most important, critics of the exclusionary rule have yet to suggest that "judi-

---

[133] LEXIS search conducted by Andrew Kandel, a second-year student at the University of Pennsylvania Law School, Genfed Library, Cir. file, Oct. 1984. The thirty-one cases include two in which the Supreme Court affirmed in part and reversed in part.

[134] *Ibid.*

[135] 104 S.Ct. at 3418 n.15 (quoting with approval Commonwealth v. Sheppard, 387 Mass. 488, 506, 441 N.E.2d 725, 735 (1982)).

[136] See, *e.g.*, Bivens v. Six Unknown Named Agents, 403 U.S. 388, 416–17 (1971) (Burger, C.J., dissenting); Oaks, *Studying the Exclusionary Rule in Search and Seizure*, 37 U. CHI. L. REV. 665, 724–32 (1970).

cial culture" is seriously in conflict with legal norms. Contrary to the Supreme Court's assertions, the exclusionary remedy is likely to influence the behavior of magistrates at least as much as it influences the behavior of police officers.

Apart from its strained assertions about the differing job motivations of judges and police officers, the Supreme Court offered only one reason for its refusal to apply to magistrates the same standard of reasonableness that it applied to the police:[137] "[T]here exists no evidence suggesting that judges and magistrates are inclined to ignore or subvert the Fourth Amendment or that lawlessness among these actors requires application of the extreme sanction of exclusion."[138] Although left to implication, the second half of the Court's comparison was apparent: unlike magistrates, police officers are inclined to ignore or subvert Fourth Amendment rights, and lawlessness among these officers does require application of the extreme sanction of exclusion.

Like the proportion of cases in which the exclusionary rule has led to lost convictions, the relative frequency of constitutional violations by police officers and magistrates had no bearing on the issue in *Leon*. Although the Supreme Court's stereotyping reflected a style of thought that is now commonplace, the stereotyping was insulting and irrelevant. If magistrates are less inclined "to ignore or subvert the Fourth Amendment" than police officers, the application of the exclusionary rule to their conduct simply would result in the exclusion of evidence less often. One need not judge the prevalence of misconduct by the members of various groups to conclude that the same deterrent and remedial principles should apply to the same misconduct.

The Supreme Court may have been correct that the "rubber-stamping" of police requests by magistrates is not "a problem of major proportions," but this judgment supplied no reason for failing to remedy the problem in the "minor" proportion of cases in which it occurs. Whatever the frequency or infrequency of these cases, the justification for excluding evidence in an individual case

---

[137] The Court in fact advanced three propositions in support of its statement that "[t]o the extent that proponents of exclusion rely on its behavioral effects on judges and magistrates in these areas, their reliance is misplaced." 104 S.Ct. at 3418. One of these propositions, however, was merely conclusory. "First," the Court said, "the exclusionary rule is designed to deter police misconduct rather than to punish the errors of judges and magistrates." *Id.*

[138] 104 S.Ct. at 3418.

of magisterial error stands on the same footing as the justification for excluding such evidence in a case of police error. Like Justice Brennan's analysis of the "costs" of the exclusionary rule, the double standard that the *Leon* majority articulated for police officers and magistrates reflected the perverse modern tendency to transform every search for normative principles into the factual assessment of empirical propositions.

Occupational differences may be relevant to legal issues. For example, the special responsibilities of the President of the United States may justify affording him an immunity from suit that courts would not afford to governmental clerks.[139] In *Leon*, however, the Supreme Court did not suggest that a difference in function warranted its double standard. In fact, when deciding whether to conduct or authorize a search, police officers and magistrates perform essentially the same task. To justify its double standard, the Court relied primarily on the assumption that the decisions of magistrates are to be trusted and the decisions of police officers are not. The same sort of collectivist judgment might justify application of the exclusionary rule to unlawful searches by some law enforcement agencies and not others, depending on the general reputations of these agencies for professionalism and adherence to constitutional standards.

Although law enforcement officers may cheer *Leon* and the Supreme Court's willingness to apply reduced standards to the review of their conduct, the Court in fact insulted them. *Leon* portrayed police officers, not as public servants entitled to the presumption of respect that the Court afforded to other governmental officers, but as the objects of justifiable suspicion and concern. The Court exempted every magistrate, however lawless, from direct judicial review but no police officer, however decent. Moreover, the Court did so on the basis of sweeping judgments about the occupational groups to which these officials belonged. Any suggestion that *Leon*'s modification of the exclusionary rule reflected the Supreme Court's sympathy for America's beleaguered police officers therefore would be ironic. This suggestion would reflect a single-minded focus on the "bottom line" of the *Leon* decision and a total disregard of the way in which the Supreme Court got there.

---

[139] See, *e.g.*, Doe v. McMillan, 412 U.S. 306, 319 (1973).

V. Conclusion

This article has not been primarily about the merits or de-merits of the Fourth Amendment exclusionary rule but about the need for principled line drawing in determining the scope of this rule. Whether the rule should be retained involves difficult matters of judgment and is a subject of legitimate debate. People of good will, sensitivity, intelligence, and judgment can favor application of the rule to all products of unlawful seizure, oppose the rule alto-gether, or favor a variety of intermediate solutions.[140] Nevertheless, an approach that asks whether a police officer could have believed reasonably that a magistrate could have believed reasonably that a person could have believed reasonably that a search would uncover evidence of a crime is not a coherent intermediate solution. Before laying a series of reasonableness standards on top of one another in bewildering overkill, the Supreme Court might have considered whether a single reasonableness standard—the one written by the framers of the Fourth Amendment—would have been enough.

Moreover, any remedial principle that is considered appropriate for police officers (be it the traditional exclusionary rule or some new version) ought to apply equally to other public officials who may authorize searches and seizures. By exempting judicial officers from review merely on the basis of statistical judgments about the occupational group to which they belong, *Leon* subordinated the search for general principles of justice to a widely shared—but unfortunate and irrelevant—empiricism.

---

[140] See, *e.g.*, Kaplan, *The Limits of the Exclusionary Rule*, 26 STAN. L. REV. 1027 (1974).

STEPHEN A. CONRAD

POLITE FOUNDATION: CITIZENSHIP AND COMMON SENSE IN JAMES WILSON'S REPUBLICAN THEORY

I. INTRODUCTION: JAMES WILSON AND THE CONCEPT OF POLITENESS

During the last two decades there have been many attempts by historians and political scientists to elucidate the visions of the Republic that were conceived in late eighteenth century America. Several of these scholars have aimed at summarizing early American republican theory in general; more have focused on the ideas of one or another individual theorist.[1] I seek to shed light on an important but largely neglected element in early American republican culture—the "polite" element. And in pursuing this aim I shall focus on yet another Founder, James Wilson, variously known in

Stephen A. Conrad is Assistant Professor of Law, Indiana University (Bloomington).

AUTHOR'S NOTE: I thank Michael Ansaldi, Stanley Katz, Judith Shklar, and Rogers Smith for their helpful comments on an earlier version of this essay, and I gratefully acknowledge my debt to Robert W. Jevon, Jr., for his assistance in research.

[1] Important reviews of the burgeoning literature on early American republicanism are to be found in Shalhope, *Toward a Republican Synthesis: The Emergence of an Understanding of Republicanism in American Historiography*, 29 WM. & MARY Q. 49 (3d ser. 1972); Ross, *The Liberal Tradition Revisited and the Republican Tradition Addressed*, in HIGHAM & CONKIN (eds.), NEW DIRECTIONS IN AMERICAN INTELLECTUAL HISTORY 116–31 (1979); Pocock, *The Machiavellian Moment Revisited: A Study in History and Ideology*, 53 J. MOD. HIST. 49 (1981); Shalhope, *Republicanism and Early American Historiography*, 39 WM. & MARY Q. 334 (3d ser. 1982). For a contrasting viewpoint, see Kramnick, *Republican Revisionism Revisited*, 87 AM. HIST. REV. 629 (1982); DIGGINS, THE LOST SOUL OF AMERICAN POLITICS: VIRTUE, SELF-INTEREST, AND THE FOUNDATION OF MODERN LIBERALISM (1984); and the work of Appleby cited in note 31 *infra*.

his day as a successful lawyer, a framer of constitutions, an apologist for Federalism, an Associate Justice of the first United States Supreme Court, and an exponent of contemporary philosophy.

Wilson's eminence in most of his public capacities has seldom been questioned. Yet despite the general acknowledgment of his renown, the significance of his public career and published ideas has remained shadowy. He came to be viewed by even his most insightful colleagues in public life as an anomaly. And of the few studies that examine Wilson's career or ideas in depth, none goes very far toward resolving the paradox of his reputation as a Founder who approximated Madison in importance and ability, but who, in certain aspects of his character and thought, appears to have been curiously out of harmony with both the "original understanding" and most later understandings of what the American Republic could and should be.[2]

The greatest progress toward explaining Wilson's paradoxical reputation has come in the scholarship of Robert McCloskey, the modern editor of Wilson's collected works and the author of interpretative essays on his constitutional thought. It was McCloskey who distinguished two features of Wilson's republican vision that not only rendered it in some ways ahead of its time but seem even now to place Wilson's vision beyond the accrued constitutional tradition of the last two hundred years. McCloskey noted both the distinctive penchant for "synthesis" in Wilson's constitutional

---

[2] See, e.g., the estimation of Wilson by John Adams in 1 BURNETT (ed.), LETTERS OF MEMBERS OF THE CONTINENTAL CONGRESS 175 (1921), and that by Washington in 29 FITZPATRICK (ed.), THE WRITINGS OF GEORGE WASHINGTON, FROM THE ORIGINAL MANUSCRIPT SOURCES, 1745–1799, at 290 (1939). A collection of twentieth-century estimations of Wilson's prominence in many of his public roles can be found in 55 AM. L. REG. (o.s. 1907) [46 n.s.]. For the purposes of the present essay, the most significant works on Wilson are ADAMS, POLITICAL IDEAS OF THE AMERICAN REVOLUTION (1922); ADAMS, SELECTED POLITICAL ESSAYS OF JAMES WILSON (1930); SMITH, JAMES WILSON, FOUNDING FATHER, 1742–1798 (1956); SEED, JAMES WILSON (1978); WHITE, THE PHILOSOPHY OF THE AMERICAN REVOLUTION (1978). Most important of all are the essays cited in note 3 infra. For extensive bibliographies listing other works on Wilson, see SEED, supra, at 217–21; Young, The Services of James Wilson in the Continental Congress (Ph. D. dissertation, Lehigh Univ. 1954) 335–53. Among the notable comparisons of Wilson's importance with that of Madison are FARRAND, THE FRAMING OF THE CONSTITUTION OF THE UNITED STATES 197–98 (1913); DICTIONARY OF AMERICAN BIOGRAPHY, s.v. Wilson, James (Sept. 14, 1742– Aug. 21, 1798) 329; MAIER, THE OLD REVOLUTIONARIES: POLITICAL LIVES IN THE AGE OF SAMUEL ADAMS 290 (1980). For a telling illustration of the scholarly orthodoxy that dismisses Wilson from the ranks of preeminent founders, see MORRIS, SEVEN WHO SHAPED OUR DESTINY: THE FOUNDING FATHERS AS REVOLUTIONARIES 2 (1973).

theory and the unusual "optimism" that colored Wilson's republican vision as a whole.[3]

Building on the work of McCloskey and others, I contend that in order to understand Wilson's contributions and reputation, it is necessary to consider both his penchant for synthesis and his optimism in relation to his concept of politeness. This perspective should be interesting if only because it tells us something thus far overlooked about the early development of Wilson's social thought, several years before he emerged as a political pamphleteer and a framer of constitutions. The greatest advantage of this perspective is, however, that it brings into focus Wilson's mature reflections about the "polite" foundation that he came to believe so important in sustaining the republican culture of the new nation.

In fact, Wilson's first published works appeared six years before his first political pamphlet was printed in 1774. These were a series of "Addisonian essays"[4] written by Wilson, together with his friend William White,[5] and published in a Philadelphia newspaper, the *Pennsylvania Chronicle*, in 1768, only three years after Wilson's emigration from Scotland. Eager for a diversion from their respective studies in law and divinity, Wilson and White penned their essays under the signature "The Visitant" and from what at least one contemporary reader took to be the point of view of "a very polite sort of gentleman."[6] Indeed, the first of the sixteen essays was devoted wholly to the subject of politeness, which the Visitant there defined as *"the natural and graceful expression of the social virtues."*[7] If carefully read and analyzed in the context of all the essays in the series, throughout which "politeness" remained a prominent topic, this deceptively simple definition suggests a great deal about

---

[3] 1 McCloskey (ed.), The Works of James Wilson 1–48, esp. 24–25, 41 (1967); McCloskey, *James Wilson*, in 1 Friedman & Israel (eds.), The Justices of the United States Supreme Court, 1789–1969: Their Lives and Major Opinions 79 (1969), and see esp. 81, 85, 88, 91, 96.

[4] Dictionary of American Biography, note 2 *supra*, at 327; *cf.* Smith, note 2 *supra*, at 35.

[5] Dictionary of American Biography, note 2 *supra*. *Cf.* Smith, note 2 *supra*, at 28, 32, 224; Bird Wilson [James Wilson's son], Memoir of the Life of the Right Reverend William White, D.D., Bishop of the Protestant Episcopal Church in the State of Pennsylvania (1839).

[6] *The Visitant [No. 11]*, Pennsylvania Chronicle, and Universal Advertiser (Philadelphia), April 4–April 11, 1768.

[7] *The Visitant [No. 4]*, Pennsylvania Chronicle, Feb. 15–Feb. 22, 1768.

what the young Wilson considered to be the meaning and importance of politeness in the social culture around him.

For example, even in this pithy definition there is a clear allusion to Wilson and White's argument, developed throughout the essays, that one key to the meaning of politeness lay in the observable fact that politeness is "expressed" most completely in a certain ideal yet attainable model of "conversation."[8] As for the practical importance of politeness, they saw it chiefly in the remarkable capabilities of politeness for "improving" individuals and their relations in nearly every sphere of social life.[9]

The distinctive model of conversation Wilson and White envisioned—and claimed to find often adopted among the citizens of Philadelphia—was a model then widely thought to be exemplified in Wilson's native Scotland, especially by the current rage there for "discussion" clubs and "philosophical" societies.[10] In these clubs and societies what was deemed to make the conversation quintessentially "polite" was that it was, in the words of the Visitant, at the same time both "useful and entertaining."[11] Indeed, the young Benjamin Rush, another Philadelphian destined for eminence, sent back to America in the 1760s reports of his student sojourn in Edinburgh that pointed to the relish of "useful and pleasing" conversation as the characterizing social phenomenon of enlightened culture in Scotland.[12] Moreover, Rush, much like the Visitant, began to observe as early as 1766 that this enlightened routine of pleasing but useful conversation was coming to be more and more commonplace in his own Philadelphia.[13]

---

[8] *Ibid.*

[9] *Ibid. Cf. The Visitant [No. 2],* PENNSYLVANIA CHRONICLE, Feb. 1–Feb. 8, 1768; *The Visitant [No. 5],* PENNSYLVANIA CHRONICLE, Feb. 22–Feb. 29, 1768.

[10] Among the many works on the eighteenth-century Scottish Enlightenment, none better highlights what it was deemed to owe to the dynamic of polite conversation than the contemporary classic by JOHN RAMSAY, Esq., of Ochtertyre, SCOTLAND AND SCOTSMEN IN THE EIGHTEENTH CENTURY (ALLARDYCE ed. 1888). *Cf.* MCELROY, SCOTLAND'S AGE OF IMPROVEMENT: A SURVEY OF EIGHTEENTH-CENTURY LITERARY CLUBS AND SOCIETIES (1969); KEMPT, CONVIVIAL CALEDONIA (1893); HONT & IGNATIEFF (eds.), WEALTH AND VIRTUE: THE SHAPING OF POLITICAL ECONOMY IN THE SCOTTISH ENLIGHTENMENT (1983).

[11] *The Visitant [No. 6],* PENNSYLVANIA CHRONICLE, Feb. 29–March 7, 1768.

[12] CORNER (ed.), THE AUTOBIOGRAPHY OF BENJAMIN RUSH 43–44 and *passim* (1948).

[13] 1 BUTTERFIELD (ed.), LETTERS OF BENJAMIN RUSH 29 (1951), but contrast 2 *id.* at 1038; *cf.* 1 *id.* at 31n., 51, 52n., 507.

Leaving aside the question whether this optimism of the Visitant and Benjamin Rush was justified by the realities of Philadelphia social life, it is nevertheless clear that their synthetic ideal of polite conversation did rest on more than fond hopes or an unexplained regard for the mode of the day. In fact, the theoretical underpinnings of this ideal were quite elaborate. For example, they included a wholesale invocation of neoclassical aesthetics, as the Visitant suggested in specifying that the manner in which politeness is expressed is both "natural and graceful."[14] Some earlier commentators on politeness, having less confidence in the possibility of this happy synthesis, confessed their suspicions that no little hypocrisy is entailed by politeness, concerned as it is with "appearances" and "the opinion of others" and therefore aiming as it does to reconcile what is natural with what is graceful.[15] The Visitant, however, disavowed any such doubts. To the contrary, as grounds for his confidence in the moral capabilities of politeness he appealed to the current precepts of neo-Ciceronianism that tended so much to identify "virtue" with "decency."[16] On the authority of this identification, he then assured his readers that in its essence true politeness, though patently "deliberate," is not at all "artificial" and, though always concerned with "complaisance," is never "hypocritical."[17]

To the Visitant there were, however, grounds still more compelling for his optimism about the theoretical coherence of the concept of politeness and about the prospects for the general practice of polite conversation throughout society. These reassurances he found principally in the contemporary theories of human nature to which his definition of politeness alludes in referring to "the social

---

[14] See, e.g., POCOCK, BOILEAU AND THE NATURE OF NEO-CLASSICISM 8–12 (1980). For the neoclassical aesthetics of the Visitant generally, see The Visitant [No. 10], PENNSYLVANIA CHRONICLE, March 28–April 4, 1768.

[15] For example, [Abel Boyer?], THE ENGLISH THEOPHRASTUS, OR THE MANNERS OF THE AGE 101–10 (Conversation, Society, Civility, Politeness) (1702), esp. 108. On Boyer as the English Theophrastus, see GREENOUGH, A BIBLIOGRAPHY OF THE THEOPHRASTAN CHARACTER IN ENGLISH 151 (1947); DICTIONARY OF NATIONAL BIOGRAPHY, S.V. Boyer, Abel. Cf. Wagstaff [Jonathan Swift], A Complete Collection of Genteel and Ingenious Conversation, according to the Most Polite Mode, in PARTRIDGE (ed.), SWIFT'S POLITE CONVERSATION 13 [editor's introduction], 31–32 (1963). Cf. [Joseph Addison], The Spectator, No. 119, July 17, 1711, in 1 BOND (ed.), THE SPECTATOR 486–89 (1965).

[16] The Visitant [No. 4], PENNSYLVANIA CHRONICLE, Feb. 15–Feb. 22, 1768.

[17] Ibid.; The Visitant [No. 1], PENNSYLVANIA CHRONICLE, Jan. 25–Feb. 1, 1768.

virtues." For, within the cultural context in which the Visitant was writing, the virtues deemed social in origin and effect held primacy of place, not only in the hierarchy of the moral canon, but also as a matter of "fact." Such was the import of many of the best known contemporary "scientific" investigations into human nature, not least among them those undertaken by the "Scottish school" of philosophers and sociologists.[18] Indeed, the Scottish school was characterized by its tendency to portray as an empirically verifiable proposition the roseate view that man is by nature predominantly sociable and that this fact governs much of everyday life and historical development.[19]

"Sociability" was thus thought to be a dependable and salutary wellspring in human nature, from which countless social virtues emerged, "decency" and "complaisance" certainly to be counted among them.[20] But the polite social virtue that the Visitant considered to be most important of all was something rather different. This was the social virtue he called "sense" or "good" sense or "plain" sense,[21] and for him, it epitomized the moral capabilities of politeness.

The Visitant went so far as to indicate that in order to be genuinely polite, conversation must be informed and constrained by this good or plain sense.[22] His clearest explanation of what he meant by "sense" came in an essay in which he contrasted the precarious sequence of mental acts involved in "reasoning" with the simpler, more immediate, and more trustworthy operations of "sense."[23] He also made clear that he was using this pregnant term "sense" to denote not merely the operations of the physical senses but also, by analogy, something more. He insisted that "sensible conversation" offers its unique opportunities for moral improvement primarily because "the most important moral truths are dis-

---

[18] Swingewood, *Origins of Sociology: The Case of the Scottish Enlightenment*, 21 BRIT. J. SOC. 164 (1970).

[19] BRYSON, MAN AND SOCIETY: THE SCOTTISH INQUIRY OF THE EIGHTEENTH CENTURY (1945), esp. 148–72; CHITNIS, THE SCOTTISH ENLIGHTENMENT: A SOCIAL HISTORY 6, 93–94 (1976).

[20] *The Visitant [No. 4]*, PENNSYLVANIA CHRONICLE, Feb. 15–Feb. 22, 1768.

[21] *The Visitant [No. 1]*, PENNSYLVANIA CHRONICLE, Jan. 25–Feb. 1, 1768; *The Visitant [No. 3]*, PENNSYLVANIA CHRONICLE, Feb. 8–Feb. 15, 1768.

[22] *The Visitant [No. 2]*, PENNSYLVANIA CHRONICLE, Feb. 1–Feb. 8, 1768.

[23] *The Visitant [No. 13]*, PENNSYLVANIA CHRONICLE, April 18–April 25, 1768.

covered not by reasoning, but by that act of the mind" fittingly known as "perception by the moral sense."[24]

This moral sense the Visitant assumed to be a common, if not quite universal, attribute of mankind.[25] And, indeed, the idea of commonality lay at the heart of what "sense" signified to him. "Sensible conversation," according to his conception, arises from matters of common "observation" and addresses matters of "general importance."[26] Moreover, he added, such conversation imposes a duty to recur to that part of one's "character," or personality, common to the members of one's society. In fact, it was on account of his view of the importance of this duty that he considered women generally more "polite" and "sensible" than men, the typical man tending to "appear" in "society" too much in his individual "character," for example, as "the Lawyer," "the Merchant," or "the Politician," rather than as the plain "man of sense."[27] Far from fearing that a general recourse to the common fund of good sense might impede the social dynamics of improvement through exchange of diverse "sentiments," the Visitant maintained that such recourse was absolutely necessary in order both to redeem the socializing promise of politeness and to profit to the fullest from its enlightening and didactic capabilities.[28]

Given the Visitant's elaborate and optimistic appreciation of the capabilities of politeness for promoting improvements in knowledge, virtue, and the cohesion of society, we might expect that he would have had something in particular to say, as well, about the political significance of politeness. Some earlier commentators had touched briefly on this theme.[29] But in the essays of the Visitant, Wilson and White wrote nothing about it. Some twenty years later, however, James Wilson, speaking and writing alone, at a time when political experience had added a great deal to his own education and that of America, found that he did have something to say about the significance of politeness for politics in the new Republic.

---

[24] *Ibid.*

[25] *Ibid.*

[26] *The Visitant [No. 2]*, PENNSYLVANIA CHRONICLE, Feb. 1–Feb. 8, 1768.

[27] *Ibid.*

[28] *Ibid.*

[29] *E.g.*, ENGLISH THEOPHRASTUS, note 15 *supra*, at 104; PARTRIDGE, note 15 *supra*, at 39 [Swift's introduction].

II. The Ideological Significance of Politeness in the New Republic

Much of the recent scholarship treating the politics of the new Republic from the drafting of the Constitution in 1787 to the election of 1800 has emphasized the so-called ideological tensions manifest in that early period of constitutional settlement. With the War for Independence won and much of the machinery of government set in place, these years were a time when reflective citizens pondered questions about what the new nation really meant and how government could best implement the principles for which America had fought. Although this period was an opportunity for relatively peaceful reflection on these questions, it also clarified the difference between groups or parties that answered such questions from what sometimes appeared to be opposing points of view. Whether the political contest happened to be between Federalists and Antifederalists, Federalists and Republicans, "political realists" and "political idealists," or any two groups of consciously antagonistic partisans, such contests seem often to have implicated two fundamentally differing views of human nature. And these two antithetical views sometimes took on the features of distinct and potent ideologies.[30]

In the terms recently used by Joyce Appleby to characterize this pervasive antithesis, one of these ideologies derived from "the ornate concept of constitutional balances and civic virtue of classical republicanism," while the other derived from "the simple—simplistic even—affirmation about human nature . . . [that envisioned a modern republic] of benignly striving individuals . . . [living in] an undifferentiated society of private negotiators."[31] This

---

[30] See, e.g., KENYON (ed.), THE ANTIFEDERALISTS at lxiii (1966); Howe, *Republican Thought and the Political Violence of the 1790's*, 19 AM. Q. 147 (1967); WOOD, THE CREATION OF THE AMERICAN REPUBLIC, 1776–1787, at 471–518, 567–615 (1969); KERBER, FEDERALISTS IN DISSENT: IMAGERY AND IDEOLOGY IN JEFFERSONIAN AMERICA (1970), esp. 173–215; BANNER, TO THE HARTFORD CONVENTION: THE FEDERALISTS AND THE ORIGINS OF PARTY POLITICS IN MASSACHUSETTS, 1789–1815, at 22–52 (1970); Banning, *Republican Ideology and the Triumph of the Constitution, 1789 to 1793*, 31 WM. & MARY Q. 167 (3d ser. 1974); ZVESPER, POLITICAL PHILOSOPHY AND RHETORIC: A STUDY OF THE ORIGINS OF AMERICAN PARTY POLITICS (1977); Cohen, *Explaining the Revolution: Ideology and Ethics in Mercy Otis Warren's Historical Theory*, 37 WM. & MARY Q. 200 (3d ser. 1980). *Cf.* BUEL, SECURING THE REVOLUTION: IDEOLOGY IN AMERICAN POLITICS, 1789–1815, esp. ix–xii, 1–7, 91–92, 113 (1972).

[31] Appleby. *The Social Origins of American Revolutionary Ideology*, 64 J. AM. HIST. 935 (1978), esp. 955, 956, 958. *Cf.* APPLEBY, CAPITALISM AND A NEW SOCIAL ORDER: THE

ideological antithesis between the republicanism of "virtue" and the republicanism of "commerce" has, indeed, become a dominant motif not only in Appleby's scholarship on the early Republic, but also in the recent work of many other historians and political theorists who are interested in this period and in the general problem of constitutional republicanism.[32]

This same ideological antithesis, present in America throughout much of the eighteenth century but especially evident by the 1790s, lent particular significance to James Wilson's bent toward synthesis and to his earnest optimism. Predisposed to synthesize current ideas, and drawing on contemporary philosophy, Wilson was inclined to "reconcile" this antithesis, in order to put the Founding itself on a more secure foundation, by solving, to the satisfaction of both ideological camps, what he took to be the central problem in the operative theory of constitutional republicanism.

This problem was one familiar both to classical and modern political theory, but by the late eighteenth century Montesquieu had addressed it most provocatively by formulating it as an apparent contradiction. In *The Spirit of the Laws* he inquired how the citizens in a republic could possibly become "better than their circumstances" so as to maintain the life of their regime and forestall the otherwise inevitable decay of their liberty. Montesquieu was quite prudent in avoiding any claim that his extended consideration of this problem afforded a definite solution to it. But, according to some of his most perceptive modern readers, in book 5, chapter 6, of *The Spirit of the Laws* he did hint at a theoretically possible solution, which entailed an amalgamation of the ethics of "civic virtue" with the urges of "possessive individualism" in order to create a fund of "bourgeois virtues" that might prove capable of preserving a modern republic.[33]

REPUBLICAN VISION OF THE 1790's (1984); Appleby, *Liberalism and the American Revolution*, 49 NEW ENG. Q. 3 (1976); Appleby, *Commercial Farming and the "Agrarian Myth" in the Early Republic*, 68 J. AM. HIST. 833 (1982).

[32] Pocock, *Virtue and Commerce in the Eighteenth Century*, 3 J. INTERDIS. HIST. 119 (1972); POCOCK, THE MACHIAVELLIAN MOMENT: FLORENTINE POLITICAL THOUGHT AND THE ATLANTIC REPUBLICAN TRADITION (1975); Lerner, *Commerce and Character: The Anglo-American as New-Model Man*, 36 WM. & MARY Q. 3 (3d ser. 1979); Lerner, *The Supreme Court as Republican Schoolmaster*, 1967 SUPREME COURT REVIEW 127. And see generally Shalhope, *Republicanism and Early American Historiography*, 39 WM. & MARY Q. 334 (3d ser. 1982).

[33] MONTESQUIEU, THE SPIRIT OF THE LAWS 45–46 (Nugent trans.; Neuman ed. 1949). *Cf.* MONTESQUIEU, THE PERSIAN LETTERS 62–66, 284–85 (LOY ed. and trans. 1961). This interpretation of Montesquieu I owe to POCOCK, MACHIAVELLIAN MOMENT, note 32 *supra*,

By 1790, however, it appeared that the political experience of the
American Revolution and the remorseless theorizing of acute eighteenth-century "economic observers"[34] made it impossible for most
thoughtful Americans to sustain anything like a delicately balanced, Montesquieuian dualism as an answer to the ideological
tensions between the republicanism of virtue and the republicanism
of commerce. If, as Appleby and others have implied, the general
political consciousness of the American Republic by 1790 was such
that this central problem in republican theory was beyond a principled resolution, it is remarkable that James Wilson was not at all
resigned to this state of affairs. As a political realist, Wilson acknowledged the problem and the apparent contradiction it presented, but as a political idealist, he remained undaunted. He announced, "I wish to reconcile what is seemingly contradictory,"[35]
and he undertook to justify this motto chiefly by expounding a
"comprehensive" theory of the civic culture of American republicanism that would not only incorporate the true meaning of the
American Revolution, but would also resolve the ideological tensions of the early national period. What is striking in Wilson's
enterprise is that, for his inspiration and for much of the content of
his theory, he drew so heavily on the concept of politeness.

An ideal opportunity for Wilson to elaborate his theory of American republicanism came in 1790, when he was offered the first
professorship of law in the College of Philadelphia and was called
upon to give a series of lectures there. Wilson accepted the appointment and subsequently delivered an undetermined number of his
Lectures on Law, which extend to over 650 pages in McCloskey's
edition. Never revised for publication, however, they are, in the
words of the modern editor, "prolix and uneven." In fact, Wilson
never finished writing the full series that he originally contemplated. Moreover, although addressed primarily to law students,

---

esp. at 485, and to Martin Diamond, *Ethics and Politics: The American Way*, in HORWITZ (ed.),
THE MORAL FOUNDATIONS OF THE AMERICAN REPUBLIC 39–72, esp. 64–65 (1977). *Cf.*
Lerner, *Commerce and Character*, note 32 *supra*; MCCOY, THE ELUSIVE REPUBLIC: POLITICAL
ECONOMY IN JEFFERSONIAN AMERICA (1980), esp. 78n., 236–37. An interesting quantitative
study of Montesquieu's "influence" on the founding generations is Lutz, *The Relative Influence
of European Writers on Late Eighteenth-Century American Political Thought*, 77 AM. POL. SCI.
REV. 189 (1984). See also MACPHERSON, THE POLITICAL THEORY OF POSSESSIVE INDIVID-
UALISM: HOBBES TO LOCKE (1962)

[34] Appleby, *Social Origins of American Revolutionary Ideology*, note 31 *supra*, at 955.

[35] 1 MCCLOSKEY, note 3 *supra*, at 185.

the lectures provide surprisingly little commentary on the substance of American law. Instead, they range over diverse topics that Wilson encountered in his public career and private studies. They testify throughout to his accumulated civic experience, most notably that as a framer of both the federal Constitution of 1787 and the Pennsylvania Constitution of 1790. Indeed, the lectures amount to a comprehensive exposition of Wilson's published and unpublished thoughts on politics, law, government, and society. According to McCloskey, they constituted Wilson's "pretension to challenge the renown of the *Federalist Papers*, but extending to a far wider terrain."[36]

McCloskey's conjecture about Wilson's grand hopes for the *Lectures* is quite persuasive; and, as with other scholars who have carefully read Wilson's *Lectures*, McCloskey's recognition of their topical scope is apt. But when it comes to specifying what McCloskey called the "central theme" of these lectures, he might be said to have fallen short of fully appreciating the scope of Wilson's vision and the ideological significance of what was, in fact, Wilson's "central theme." McCloskey concluded that the theme of the lectures is Wilson's anticipation of "a central truth about the American legal system: that it would grow by the accretion of custom and acceptance rather than by the fiat of legislators; that popular government and the rule of law would be more complementary than antithetical."[37]

Wilson did indeed anticipate the creative vitality and democratic authority of "customary," or common, law in America. And in his day he had a virtually unmatched faith in the compatibility of popular rule with the rule of law. But Wilson's vision encompassed more than legal foresight and democratic faith. The immediate significance of his synthetic arguments extended beyond "reconciling" those two republican ideals so often supposed to be at odds with one another: popular democracy and stable government. If

---

[36] McCloskey, in 1 FRIEDMAN & ISRAEL, note 3 *supra*, at 90–91; SMITH, note 2 *supra*, at 308, 309, 314; SEED, note 2 *supra*, at 150; Preface by Bird Wilson, in 1 McCLOSKEY, note 3 *supra*, at 59–65. The original edition of the lectures is that in BIRD WILSON (ed.), THE WORKS OF THE HONOURABLE JAMES WILSON, L.L.D.: LATE ONE OF THE ASSOCIATE JUSTICES OF THE SUPREME COURT OF THE UNITED STATES, AND PROFESSOR OF LAW IN THE COLLEGE OF PHILADELPHIA (1804). See also ANDREWS (ed.), THE WORKS OF JAMES WILSON, 1742–1798 (1896).

[37] McCloskey, in 1 FRIEDMAN & ISRAEL, note 3 *supra*, at 92.

Wilson can fairly be said to have articulated any central theme in his *Lectures*, that theme lies in their profoundest argument: that the American republic had been established on novel principles; that these principles had generated constitutions and other legal institutions of unprecedented promise; but that this promise would be fulfilled only through fidelity to those principles; and that the task at hand, therefore, was nothing less than to formulate and put into practice what Wilson called a "comprehensive" theory of the new Republic as a new-model society. Much of the immediate significance of Wilson's response to the task he saw at hand, it might be argued, lay in his attempt to synthesize the dissonant theories of human nature and society that were current in the inchoate republican culture of America in 1790.

There was nothing especially novel in America about Wilson's interest in the social foundation of politics and government. As historians like Bernard Bailyn, Gordon Wood, James Hutson, and J. G. A. Pocock have contended, the belief that politics and government should provide a sphere in which American society could realize its capacity for "civic virtue" was a motivating force, if not, indeed, the idée fixe, behind the successful ideology of the War for Independence and of much of the constitution making and constitutional politics that followed, from the break with Britain until the early nineteenth century. This force was the "Country" ideology, first expounded in its fullest terms by Bolingbroke and soon transplanted to America. In fact, this ideology became a source from which many Americans, from the first advocates of Independence to the last diehard Antifederalists and beyond, drew their inspiration. Wilson's own political sociology and civic psychology, however, are not reducible to the Country ideology of his day. Throughout his *Lectures on Law*, in continually referring to "human nature," he was referring to something that in his view more accurately reflected the everyday tendencies of human behavior than did the nostalgic idealism of the Country ideology.[38]

---

[38] BAILYN, THE ORIGINS OF AMERICAN POLITICS (1968), esp. 3–58; BAILYN, THE IDEOLOGICAL ORIGINS OF THE AMERICAN REVOLUTION (1967), esp. 34–54; WOOD, note 30 *supra*, at 65–70; Hutson, *Country, Court, and Constitution: Antifederalism and the Historians*, 38 WM. & MARY Q. 351 (3d ser. 1981); POCOCK, MACHIAVELLIAN MOMENT, note 32 *supra*, at 529; ROBBINS, THE EIGHTEENTH-CENTURY COMMONWEALTHMAN (1959); KRAMNICK, BOLINGBROKE AND HIS CIRCLE: THE POLITICS OF NOSTALGIA IN THE AGE OF WALPOLE (1968). *Cf.* BANNING, THE JEFFERSONIAN PERSUASION: EVOLUTION OF A PARTY IDEOLOGY (1978), esp. 42–69, 124–25, 130–40, 273–74.

On the other hand, when Wilson insisted on the "fundamental" significance of human nature, he did not mean merely that all inquiry into politics and government must be guided by the data of psychology. He did endorse this principle, as did a great many other political thinkers in the second half of the eighteenth century. Rather, in looking on questions about human personality as fundamental questions for American society and government, Wilson endorsed something both more and less than the elementary methodological principle that prescribed "scientific" inquiry into the facts of human nature.

By 1790 this principle, in its most general formulation, had come to be identified above all with David Hume, who, in his *Treatise of Human Nature,* had first announced it as a credo and followed its implications to the most astonishing and notoriously skeptical conclusions.[39] In Wilson's view, however, a republican science of human nature should no more give itself over to the modish objectivity of philosophical skepticism than it should succumb to the nostalgia of the Country ideology. What mattered most to Wilson, neither the complete ideologue nor the complete philosopher, were practical conceptions that would faithfully embody republican principles.[40] Thus, in his characteristic appeal to the "first principles" of human nature, he had recourse to a specific and almost palpable conception of polite personality that he had observed as a social reality, but in which he saw unappreciated implications. It was, in his estimation, no shortcoming, but rather the great strength of his own "scientific" conclusions about the facts and capabilities of polite personality in America, that these conclusions were not only less heroic than Bolingbroke's neoclassical idea of a politics of virtue, but also less "demonstrable" than Hume's acute propositions about man's psychological nature. If anything, the disinterested logic of "demonstration" had even less place in Wilson's republican science than did a reliance on the extraordinary virtue of civic heroism.

At the same time, however, Wilson did not wish to underestimate the importance of civic virtue in the Republic. Nor did he wish to underestimate the political importance of the "knowledge"

---

[39] GRAVE, THE SCOTTISH PHILOSOPHY OF COMMON SENSE (1960).

[40] *Cf.* DICTIONARY OF AMERICAN BIOGRAPHY, note 2 *supra,* at 329–30; DELAHANTY, THE INTEGRALIST PHILOSOPHY OF JAMES WILSON 1–2 (1969).

made available by recent advances in natural and social philosophy. In fact, it was his assumption about a general concurrence between progress in knowledge and progress in virtue that was at the heart of his polite approach to a comprehensive theory of the American Republic.[41]

One indication that this polite approach was, in America, not altogether unique to Wilson can be glimpsed in the most celebrated passage from the pen of that fellow Philadelphian whose own personal experience and Federalist politics so often coincided with Wilson's—Benjamin Rush. In 1786 Rush wrote to Richard Price:[42]

> Most of the *distresses* of our country, and of the *mistakes* which Europeans have formed of us, have arisen from the belief that the American Revolution is *over*. This is so far from being the case that we have only finished the first act of the great drama. We have changed our forms of government, but it remains yet to effect a revolution in our principles, opinions, and manners so as to accommodate them to the forms of government we have adopted. This is the most difficult part of the business of the patriots and legislators of our country. . . . I wish to see this idea inculcated by your pen. Call upon the rulers of our country to lay the foundation of their empire in *knowledge* as well as virtue.

Rush himself promoted this "Second American Revolution" by devoting his pen and his time, particularly during the 1780s, to a number of efforts at social reform: in education, in the antislavery movement, on behalf of temperance, and even against the death penalty.[43] But in his letter to Price, Rush seemed to call not merely for particular reform campaigns but also for a new general conception of republican society itself. And it was of the utmost importance to Rush that while this reconception should accord with republican ideals, it must be securely based not on ideals but on the solid foundation of "knowledge." Moreover, the context of this famous passage from Rush's letter makes clear that he thought it necessary that this foundation include knowledge about more than the *res publicae* of law and politics: This knowledge must extend to "everything else" directly or indirectly "connected with the ad-

---

[41] 1 McCLOSKEY, note 3 *supra*, at 147.

[42] 1 BUTTERFIELD, note 13 *supra*, at 388.

[43] *Ibid*. See, *e.g.*, *id*. at 76–79, 81–82, 388, 475–76, 479–80, 491–95; CORNER, note 12 *supra*, at 82. *Cf*. HAWKE, BENJAMIN RUSH: REVOLUTIONARY GADFLY 358–80 (1971).

vancement of republican . . . principles," including the "opinions" and "manners"—the personality—of the citizens at large.

Notwithstanding this celebrated call by Rush for a comprehensive theory of republican society, neither he, nor the versatile Price, nor many of their respective compatriots ever went very far toward answering it. Except for James Wilson, none of the American political leaders of the Founding generations, least of all Madison, seems ever to have attempted to set forth a systematic statement of his own view of politics, law, and government in relation to a general theory of human nature. This is true even of Jefferson, whose interest in such relationships is well known. The point is, however, not that the Founders were uninterested in this subject, but rather that they tended to find it intractable. Madison, writing as Publius in *The Federalist No. 37*, exemplified this attitude of curiosity combined with skeptical resignation when he remarked, "The faculties of the mind itself have never yet been distinguished and defined, with satisfactory precision, by all the efforts of the most acute and metaphysical philosophers. Sense, perception, judgment, desire, volition, memory, imagination, are found to be separated by such delicate shades, and minute graduations, that their boundaries have eluded the most subtle investigations, and remain a pregnant source of ingenious disquisition and controversy."[44]

Having decided that determinate knowledge about the human personality was unavailable, Madison, both at the Convention of 1787 and in *The Federalist*, focused on institutional political science, to which he looked for answers to the immediate questions about how best to contrive "the interior structure of government" in America. And though Madison's political science was expressly predicated on certain underlying, prudent assumptions about human nature, these assumptions were never so fully crystallized that they constrained him from moving, over the course of his public career, from the camp of the Federalists to that of the Republicans.

---

[44] See PRICE'S OBSERVATIONS ON THE IMPORTANCE OF THE AMERICAN REVOLUTION AND THE MEANS OF MAKING IT A BENEFIT TO THE WORLD (1784); the 1785 edition is reprinted in PEACH (ed.), RICHARD PRICE AND THE ETHICAL FOUNDATIONS OF THE AMERICAN REVOLUTION 177–214 (1979). On Madison's view of human nature, see MEYERS (ed.), THE MIND OF THE FOUNDER: SOURCES OF THE POLITICAL THOUGHT OF JAMES MADISON, at xxi–xxii (2d ed. rev. 1981). See also the article by Ketcham cited in note 45 *infra*. But for a viewpoint contrasting with that expressed here, see Wright, *The Federalist on the Nature of Political Man*, 59 ETHICS 1 (1949); *cf.* THE FEDERALIST 26–41 (WRIGHT ed. 1961). *The Federalist [No. 37]* is here quoted from THE FEDERALIST 235 (COOKE ed. 1961).

One implication of this intriguing flexibility in Madison's political alignments is that his life-long, judicious inconclusiveness on questions about human nature opened the way for him to come to pragmatic accommodations with the alternative republican ideologies that pervaded the early national period.[45]

It is in just this respect that Wilson presents such a contrast to Madison—and to all the other prominent Founders. For, by devising a comprehensive theory of individual personality, social culture, and political citizenship on which to base his own vision of republican law and government, Wilson sought neither to align himself with one or the other ideology of the day nor to reach accommodations with them, but to effect a thoroughgoing "reconciliation," or synthesis, of these ideologies on the basis of the superseding authority of "scientific" knowledge.

III. The Phenomena of Polite Personality and the Prospects for Polite Citizenship

Wilson's inaugural law lecture, delivered on December 15, 1790, was more than a ceremonial academic event; it was also something of a state occasion. A newspaper of the day records that those in attendance included "[t]he President of the United States, with his lady—also the Vice-President, and both houses of Congress [t]he President and both houses of the Legislature of Pennsylvania, together with a great number of ladies and gentlemen . . . the whole comprising a most brilliant and respectable audience."[46] Wilson himself remarked on the presence of the many dignitaries, but in so doing he took the opportunity to address his audience in general and, at the same time, to introduce an argument that would overarch his entire series of lectures. "[A]ddress[ing] a fair audience so brilliant as this," he said "[t]here is one encouraging reflection, however, which greatly supports me. The whole of my respectable

---

[45] *The Federalist [No. 51]*, from THE FEDERALIST 347 (COOKE ed. 1961). Ketcham, *James Madison and the Nature of Man*, 19 J. HIST. IDEAS 62 (1958). MEYERS, note 44 *supra*, at xxxiii–xlvii; *cf.* Zvesper, *The Madisonian Systems*, 37 W. POL. Q. 236 (1984). For an interpretation that seeks to emphasize Madison's "republican faith," see Riemer, *The Republicanism of James Madison*, 69 POL. SCI. Q. 45 (1954).

[46] PENNSYLVANIA PACKET, and DAILY ADVERTISER (Philadelphia), Dec. 25, 1790.

audience is as much distinguished by its politeness, as part of it is distinguished by its brilliancy."[47]

From this suggestion that the Philadelphia public at large was distinguished by its politeness, Wilson, in subsequent lectures, would develop an argument implying that politeness is an essential element of the social foundation of republican citizenship. In Wilson's estimation, it was in large part the politeness of American society that had made a constitutional republic possible and would, if cultivated, thenceforth keep the Republic sound. It was, in other words, the politeness of the general citizenry, and not the "brilliancy" (the exceptional talent, virtue, or knowledge) of public leaders, that would be the social *materia* of the democratic republic that Wilson envisioned.

Wilson's theory about the polite foundation of republican law and government was not, he took pains to make clear, the product of idle speculation on his part. Shortly after his ceremonial first lecture he turned to the task of presenting his students with an empirical justification for this polite theory. But even before he undertook his elaborate statement of this justification, he began to make his case for the political significance of politeness by setting out a master analogy, to which he would continually refer throughout the lectures. This was an analogy between what Wilson saw as the two principal threats to the fortunes of republicanism. One of these threats came from the orthodox legal theory predicated on the "despotick" conception of law as "a command from superiour to inferiour"; the other came from the fashionable "metaphysicks" of the day that seemed to indicate a skeptical denial of the possibility of knowledge itself. Wilson focused on that consummate "antirepublican lawyer," William Blackstone, as the leading advocate of this "despotick" theory of law, and therefore as the chief enemy of the legitimate "science of government." In the forum of "metaphysicks," on the other hand, Wilson singled out the clever skeptic David Hume as the most extreme modern proponent of Pyrrhonism, and therefore as the most insidious enemy of "all . . . sound philosophy." It is interesting that Wilson looked on Blackstone and Hume as a pair. But what is more interesting is that Wilson ulti-

---

[47] 1 McCLOSKEY, note 3 *supra*, at 69.

mately considered Hume the more pernicious of the two, because the errors of "absolute skepticism" seemed to him even more profoundly subversive of "all true liberty" than did the errors of the "despotick" theory of law and government. For this reason, it was one of Wilson's guiding purposes in his lectures to show his students how "necessary" for the preservation of the Republic it was "to lay the foundation of knowledge deep and solid."[48]

As Wilson acknowledged, he was chiefly indebted for his understanding of Hume's ingenious epistemology to Hume's fellow Scottish philosopher Thomas Reid. In fact, among the many anxious contemporary critics of Hume, it was Reid who was by 1790 generally considered the foremost. Reid had launched his rebuttal to Hume in 1764, with the publication of his short but dense *Inquiry on Human Nature*, and had thereafter widened the scope of his arguments in two longer, derivative works published in the 1780s.[49] Like nearly all the luminaries of the Scottish Enlightenment, Reid had first broached his ideas in the congenial setting of a discussion club. But, whereas most of the great books of the Scottish Enlightenment were, at bottom, unmistakably the products of individual genius, notwithstanding the encouragements the authors often received from comrades in their respective clubs and societies, both Reid's *Inquiry* and his Common Sense school emerged as genuinely collective products. They grew out of the give and take among the members of his unusually small, serious, and long-lived club of philosophers. This was the Aberdeen Philosophical Society, which Reid originated in 1758, but which soon came to include other Common Sense thinkers—notably George Campbell, James Beattie, and Alexander Gerard—who made important early contributions to the school in their own right.[50]

It is this distinctive institutional background of Reid's Common Sense school—namely, its origins in the convivial but earnest con-

---

[48] *Id.* at 79, 103–05, 214, 216, 221–22.

[49] *Id.* at 216–17. *Cf.* Leavelle, *James Wilson and the Relation of the Scottish Metaphysics to American Political Thought*, 57 POL. SCI. Q. 394 (1942). On Reid's rebuttal to Hume, see generally Davie, *Hume and the Origins of the Common Sense School*, 6 REV. INT'LE PHIL. 213 (1952); GRAVE, note 39 *supra*, at 1–6. For Reid's *Inquiry* and his later books, see his collected works in HAMILTON (ed.), THE WORKS OF THOMAS REID (6th ed. 1863).

[50] Conrad, Citizenship and Common Sense: The Problem of Authority in the Social Background and Social Philosophy of the Wise Club of Aberdeen (Ph. D. dissertation, Harvard Univ. 1980).

versations of a club of provincial philosophers—that, to some extent, explains the polite character of the tenets of the school.[51] These polite tenets of Common Sense were not without ideological significance in their native setting. For example, recent interpretations have tended to portray the imperative affirmations of eighteenth-century Common Sense as part of a conservative intellectual reaction in Scotland to modernizing ideas, especially the ideas of "determinism" and "materialism."[52]

Although James Wilson, lecturing in republican Philadelphia in 1790, warmly "embraced" this Scottish philosophy of Common Sense and extolled Reid above all other modern philosophers, the ideological significance of the polite tenets of Common Sense was for Wilson, understandably, quite different from what it was for Reid. Writing in a nation whose politics and government had been effectively "engrossed" by England in the Union of 1707, Reid and his Scottish colleagues chose expressly to set aside from their principal concerns the question what their Common Sense philosophy might contribute to "the sound principles of a lawyer or statesman." Wilson, however, looked to philosophy, especially Common Sense philosophy, to answer just such practical civic purposes. As he apologized in his *Lectures*, he had labored over his studies in epistemology and psychology not with any intention to devise a complete philosophical system, but merely to ascertain "just conceptions of man in two most important characters, as an author, and as a subject of law." By 1790 Wilson felt his studies had supplied what he sought. Guided by Reid and others, he felt he had come to understand the phenomena of human personality, at least insofar as their civic significance.[53]

It was extremely important to Wilson that his conceptions of man be "just," that is, empirically valid. Few serious thinkers in Wilson's own political culture would have disagreed with this emphasis. But Wilson pursued a distinctive line of argument when he insisted, following Reid, that in any properly scientific inquiry into

---

[51] *Id.* at 158–285 (chs. iv–v).

[52] Phillipson, *Towards a Definition of the Scottish Enlightenment*, in FRITZ & WILLIAMS (eds.), CITY AND SOCIETY IN THE EIGHTEENTH CENTURY 125–47 (1973); DAVIE, THE SOCIAL SIGNIFICANCE OF THE SCOTTISH PHILOSOPHY OF COMMON SENSE (1973); GRAVE, note 39 *supra.*

[53] 1 MCCLOSKEY, note 3 *supra*, at 199, 212, 216, 217, 222.

human nature and man's capacity for knowledge, the method of investigation and proof must be strictly descriptive and phenomenological[54] rather than metaphysical and logical. Indeed, said Wilson, it was precisely Hume's artful accomplishments in "metaphysicks" and "logic" that had served Hume so well in "demonstrating," with such brilliant internal consistency, his presumptuous and ultimately "absurd" conclusions about human nature.[55]

Wilson meant to horrify his law students by quoting in the *Lectures* the most notorious of Hume's logically demonstrated absurdities: that the human mind is nothing but "a bundle or collection of different perceptions, which succeed each other with an inconceivable rapidity, and are in a perpetual flux and movement. . . . There is properly no simplicity in the mind at one time; nor identity in it at different times; whatever natural propensity . . . we have to imagine that simplicity and identity: they are successive perceptions only, that constitute the mind."[56] For Wilson, and for Reid, such a conclusion seemed to deny the possibility of any human knowledge whatsoever and to "annihilate" the human personality completely. Adverting to the crux of the matter, Wilson invited consideration particularly of the civic implications of Hume's reduction of personality to "a bundle of impressions and ideas." Wilson asked what such a conception of human nature implied about man's capacity for that cardinal republican virtue, probity, and about the feasibility of "consent" and "convenant" within a republican system of law: "If one set of ideas make a convenant; if another successive set—for be it remembered they are all in succession—break this covenant; and if a third set are punished for breaking it; how can we discover justice to form any part of this system?"[57]

If, as Wilson's question implied, Hume's skeptical conclusions

---

[54] The term "phenomenological" is used here in the same sense in which it was used by William Hamilton, a nineteenth-century proponent of Common Sense, that is, in contradistinction to the term ontological. See 1 MANSEL & VEITCH, HAMILTON'S LECTURES ON METAPHYSICS AND LOGIC 121 (1859): "If we consider the mind merely with the view of observing and generalising the various phaenomena it reveals . . . we have . . . one department of mental science; and this we call the PHAENOMENOLOGY OF THE MIND." *Cf.* Reid's *Inquiry* in 1 HAMILTON, note 49 *supra*, at 140, 157, 163.

[55] 1 McCLOSKEY, note 3 *supra*, at 197, 202, 210–11, 395–96. *Cf.* 1 HAMILTON, note 49 *supra*, at 129, 182; GRAVE, note 39 *supra*, at 87–91; Conrad, note 50 *supra*, at 247, 262–67.

[56] 1 McCLOSKEY, note 3 *supra*, at 214; *cf. id.* at 210.

[57] *Id.* at 215; *cf. id.* at 202.

posed a challenge to all thoughtful citizens' belief in the integrity of the human personality as the basis of individual responsibility, and if Hume's "logic" suggested, therefore, that the possibility of justice was precluded by the facts of human nature itself, how then should a devoted republican meet the challenge and rebut Hume's logic? Wilson's answer, for which he turned primarily to Reid and his school, was that the true theory of human personality and republican citizenship must appeal to an authority more fundamental than the conclusions of nicely reasoned logic. Such an appeal, Wilson argued, must turn to the imperative principles of unimpeachable "common sense," principles that are to be accorded precedence over the fallible propositions of logic precisely because these principles rest on authority more "scientific," that is, more empirically evident, than the authority of fragile human reason, on which any chain of logical propositions entirely depends.[58]

Reid, in his consolidation of eighteenth-century Common Sense philosophy, taught that the sources of the authority for such reassuring Common Sense principles are many, but of paramount importance to him and his school was the authority of the physical senses themselves. Reid's own rigorous analysis of the operations of the senses was the most cogent since Berkeley's studies of "vision." But Reid also went beyond examination of the physical senses, and, by means of analogy to the operations of these senses, sought to restore to certain "intuitions" a degree of epistemological authority that had been discounted ever since the publication of Locke's profoundly anti-intuitionist and immensely influential *Essay concerning Human Understanding*. Specifically, said Reid, these authoritative intuitions are those that are of such compelling persuasive force that it is "absurd," that is, meaningless, to deny them or their truth. Like the reliable knowledge of the physical world that is given to men by their physical senses operating in regular, if sometimes imperfect, corroboration of one another, these undeniable intuitions about unseen, unheard, unfelt reality are common to all men of "sound constitution" and self-evidently true to all men who are capable of a minimum degree of reflection—thus Reid's shibboleth "common sense" to denote these intuitions. And not only is the knowledge supplied by common sense "dictated" by internal reflection and reinforced by the common experiences of mankind,

---

[58] *Id.* at 210, 212–13, 223.

it is further justified by evidence extrinsic to these intuitions but nonetheless representative of their contents. For example, language amply provides such extrinsic evidence of this important intuitive knowledge. In fact, various members of the late eighteenth-century Scottish Common Sense school looked particularly to the common elements of language as a source of trustworthy "discursive" knowledge in much the same way that the Visitant, in his polite essays, looked to "sensible conversation" as the best commonly available source of moral education and intellectual improvement.[59]

As I have suggested, in his *Lectures* Wilson rehearsed in considerable detail the arguments of the Common Sense philosophers. One of his chief purposes in so doing was to give his law students an appreciation particularly for these philosophers' phenomenological methodology. Reflecting themes he had introduced years before in the essays of the Visitant, Wilson pointed out that this was a "polite" methodology, in that it emphasized a process of careful reflection upon the data of common observation. And it put a premium on accurate description of phenomena, whether internal or external, rather than on speculative explanation of these phenomena. It was also, in its direct if not simple address of natural phenomena, a naive methodology—but all the more "scientific" for that, because, by looking exclusively at the commonly experienced, indeed, "undeniable" facts of human nature and the external world, Common Sense phenomenology seemed to epitomize the inductive rigor so dear to the British scientific tradition of the age.[60]

While the methodology of the Common Sense thinkers thus appropriated to itself the prestige of contemporary British science, Common Sense philosophy also reflected the pioneering sociological perspective that typified the Scottish Enlightenment. This perspective was especially evident in the Common Sense approach to

---

[59] *Id.* at 130–35, 137, 143, 198, 210–13, 394. 1 HAMILTON, note 49 *supra*, at 117–19, 184, 193–94, 195, 205, 208–09. See JONES, EMPIRICISM AND INTUITIONISM IN REID'S COMMON SENSE PHILOSOPHY (1927); DANIELS, THOMAS REID'S INQUIRY: THE GEOMETRY OF VISIBLES AND THE CASE FOR REALISM (1974), esp. 24–60. On Berkeley's studies of vision, see STACK, BERKELEY'S ANALYSIS OF PERCEPTION (1970). See also CAMPBELL, THE PHILOSOPHY OF RHETORIC 46 (BITZER ed. 1963) (1st ed. 1776); BEATTIE, AN ESSAY ON THE NATURE AND IMMUTABILITY OF TRUTH 306 (5th ed. corrected 1774) (1st ed. 1770).

[60] *Cf.* Laudan, *Thomas Reid and the Newtonian Turn of British Methodological Thought*, in BUTTS & DAVIS (eds.), THE METHODOLOGICAL HERITAGE OF NEWTON 103–31 (1970); ELLOS, THOMAS REID'S NEWTONIAN REALISM (1981).

"faculty psychology," a topic much discussed by English-speaking students of human nature throughout the eighteenth century. Reid displayed this affinity for the sociologist's point of view by arguing that many of the "faculties" and "operations" of the individual psyche can properly be understood only if they are considered as social faculties and social operations of the mind. And even though not every faculty of the psyche operates with reference principally to society, the most important of them clearly do. Reid's chief example was the mental faculty that the Common Sense forebears Shaftesbury and Francis Hutcheson had called the "moral sense."[61]

Convinced of the real existence of this moral sense by the painstaking empirical inquiries of Reid and his school, Wilson explained at length in his *Lectures* how Common Sense philosophy had verified beyond doubt the great sway that moral perceptions "regularly" exert over human conduct, in much the same way that men's physical perceptions direct their physical actions. And it was, to Wilson, the automatic, "active," indeed, routinely irresistible character of the operations of the moral sense that afforded the best evidence with which to rebut the antisocial, antirepublican implications of Hume's theory of human nature. For, in answer to Hume, the Common Sense school had "proved," whereas earlier moralists had (as the Visitant's essays reflect) merely asserted, not only that human nature is well designed for social life, but that human nature inclines men routinely, if not always, to act in accord with the dictates of this moral sense. On the basis of scientific evaluation of the capabilities of the moral sense, then, men could prudently be expected to display those "qualities" of conduct that are prerequisites for republican citizenship. In Wilson's view, such qualities included not only the fundamental civic virtue of probity, but also, for example, "respect" for the "safety and security" of "persons" and their "property."[62]

The most interesting aspect of Wilson's endorsement of the Common Sense rehabilitation of moral sense theory lay, however, in his appreciation that the Common Sense philosophers pointed the way to an extraordinary theoretical reconciliation between the two "faculties of the mind" that have the greatest civic importance

---

[61] 1 MCCLOSKEY, note 3 *supra*, at 230–36. *Cf.* RAPHAEL, THE MORAL SENSE (1947), esp. 146–92 (ch. 5, "Thomas Reid").

[62] 1 MCCLOSKEY, note 3 *supra*, at 143, 203, 232–33.

of all, "the will" and "the understanding." "No division has been more common, and, perhaps, less exceptional," said Wilson in reference to orthodox faculty psychology, "than that of the powers of the mind into those of the understanding and those of the will. And yet even this division, I am afraid, has led to a mistake."[63] Turning then to what was his single most important contention about human nature, Wilson said:[64]

> The mistake I believe to be this; it has been supposed, that in the operations ascribed to the will there was no employment of the understanding; and that in those ascribed to the understanding, there was no exertion of the will. But this is not the case. It is probable, that there is no operation of the understanding, in which . . . the will has not some share. On the other hand, there can be no energy of the will, which is not accompanied with some act of the understanding. In the operations of the mind, both faculties generally, if not always, concur. . . .

This contention about the general concurrence of the will and the understanding was, for Wilson, fraught with moral and civic implications. And he was not unfair in claiming that his attention to this matter was somewhat unusual. In fact, Hannah Arendt, in her critique of the civic culture of the early American Republic, pointed out that the Founders generally seem not to have paid much attention to the significance of either "the faculty of the will—the trickiest and most dangerous of modern concepts and misconceptions" or "opinion and judgment, . . . [the] two politically most important, rational faculties."[65] But Wilson's study of the Common Sense "justification" of moral sense theory led him to the keenest interest in the political significance of "willing" and "judging," the latter being, in his view, the crucial step in, the process of "understanding." And, having learned from Reid that certain fundamental moral perceptions "act" in the mind not only to command man's belief in their "truth," but also to inform man's judgment, enforce his assent, and regulate his conduct,[66] Wilson arrived, through a succession of arguments, at the conclusion that the moral sense regularly operates to coordinate the impulses of the

---

[63] *Id.* at 199.

[64] *Ibid.*

[65] ARENDT, ON REVOLUTION 225, 229 (2d ed. rev. 1965).

[66] 1 McCLOSKEY, note 3 *supra*, at 143, 203, 208–09, 225, 232–33, 392–96. *Cf.* RAPHAEL, note 61 *supra*, at 152–58.

will with the knowledge supplied by the process of understanding, especially by the decisive phase in that process, the ultimate act of judgment.[67]

If Wilson was "justified" in his belief in the ability of the moral sense to reconcile the operations of man's will with those of his understanding, and especially with man's ultimate judgments on common matters of fundamental importance, then there was a bright prospect for the institution of a new model of citizenship in the American Republic. For, if the moral sense was amenable to refinement through the routines of polite culture, then even the most vexed contradictions in the theory of republican citizenship could be "reconciled."[68]

Among these contradictions, the one that most concerned Wilson was the one that posed the definitive conceptual problem for a liberal theory of republican government: How, in a republican regime, is the supremacy of the private, self-regarding sphere in the life of each citizen to be reconciled with the obligation of the People at large to perform the public-regarding duties of citizenship? It is interesting that Wilson did not propose to solve this problem by blinking at the magnitude of the apparent dilemma. More vividly even than Locke himself, Wilson stated his liberal creed that "domestick society," that is, the private social life of each individual, must be deemed intrinsically superior in dignity to all public matters, including law and government. At the same time, unlike Madison and all those who projected for America a civic routine of benign self-interest, Wilson, notwithstanding his liberal creed, plainly envisioned a conscientious regard for the public welfare as essential to everyday civic life in the Republic. Rather than depreciate either the self-regarding element or the public-regarding element in what Wilson acknowledged to be his "apparently contradictory" conception of republican citizenship, and rather than discount either of the prevailing ideologies, each of which exalted one of these two elements as the mainspring of republican citizenship, Wilson appealed to his fundamental theory of human nature in order to harmonize the two elements, reconcile the two ideologies, and thereby resolve the contradiction at its core.[69]

---

[67] 1 McCLOSKEY, note 3 *supra*, at 143, 394.

[68] *Id.* at 143, 198, 203, 396.

[69] 1 *id.* at 77, 86–87, 109, 305; 2 *id.* at 579.

In Wilson's *Lectures* the most concise description of this harmonization, reconciliation, and resolution is to be found in a passage in which Wilson considers the significance of the popular right of suffrage. Indeed, this passage captures the essence of the central argument of Wilson's polite theory of republicanism. In his view, while the establishment of a republican "superstructure" of law and government does afford the essential opportunities for true republicanism in America, these opportunities can be realized only in the fundamental sphere of the social life of the People "out of doors":[70]

> The man, who enjoys the right of suffrage, on the extensive scale which is marked by our constitutions, will *naturally* turn his thoughts to the contemplation of publick men and publick measures. . . . I am far from insinuating, that every citizen should be an enthusiast in politicks, or that the interests of himself, his family, and those who depend on him . . . should be absorbed in Quixote speculations about the management or the reformation of the state. But there is surely a golden mean in things; and there can be no real incompatibility between the discharge of one's publick, and that of his private duty. Let private industry receive the warmest encouragement; for it is the basis of publick happiness. But . . . [a]t no moment shall a little relaxation be allowed? That relaxation, if properly directed, may prove to be *instructive as well as agreeable*. It may consist in reading a newspaper, or in conversing with a fellow citizen. . . . Under our constitutions, a number of important appointments must be made at every election. To make them is, indeed, the business only of a day. But it ought to be the business of much more than a day, to be prepared for making them well. . . . A habit of *conversing and reflecting* on these subjects, and of governing his actions by the result of his deliberations, would produce, in the mind of the citizen, a uniform, a strong, and a lively sensibility to the interests of his country. . . . By these means . . . pure and genuine patriotism . . . which consists in liberal investigation and disinterested conduct, is produced . . . and strengthened in the mind. . . .

Here, in the emphasis on a routine of social conversation and personal reflection at once "instructive" and "agreeable," is a vivid but naive conception of republican citizenship predicated on the very same notion of politeness that the Visitant commended to his readers in 1768. Here too is the same naive optimism that led the

---

[70] 1 *id*. at 404–05 (emphasis added); *cf*. 2 *id*. at 787–88 (Wilson's speech of Dec. 31, 1789, to the Pennsylvania state constitutional convention).

Visitant to envision a happy synthesis reconciling, and harnessing in tandem, inclinations and duties apparently at odds with one another. Moreover, according to Wilson's view of the matter by the time he composed his *Lectures* in 1790 and 1791, the naïveté of his vision of the civic capability of politeness was not a shortcoming of his conception of polite citizenship. On the contrary, the empirical "justification" of his conception lay precisely in its naïveté, because the naïveté, the naturalness, signified how faithful his conception was to the scientific truths of human nature itself.

In so justifying his conception of polite citizenship, Wilson relied above all on the Common Sense principle that indicated a natural and regular concurrence between the operations of man's understanding and those of his will. On the basis of this concurrence, Wilson saw a prospect for the eventual discovery of a certain "unanimity concerning [the] first principles" of knowledge in moral and civic science that would attain a degree of authority comparable to that of the recent Newtonian discoveries of certain universal "first principles" of knowledge in "mathematicks and natural philosophy."[71] This prospect, in turn, led Wilson to the conclusion that, in any well-contrived republic where the citizens cultivated the enlightening and socializing routines of politeness, there would be good reason to expect the development of both a genuine community of "uniform interests" and a sound community of "deliberate" wills, with both based on a fundamental community of "discursive knowledge."

IV. CONCLUSION

In many respects James Wilson's polite republican theory, especially in its conception of polite citizenship, presents a striking contrast to the conventional reconstruction of James Madison's prudent, disenchanted republicanism. And it is, after all, the republican vision ascribed to Madison, writing as Publius, that has tended to dominate the American constitutional tradition. But the contrast between Wilson's and Madison's respective visions should not be overestimated. Indeed, such Madison scholars as Douglass Adair and Marvin Meyers have not allowed the polite element in Madi-

---

[71] 1 *id.* at 226, 394. *Cf.* Norton, *George Turnbull and the Furniture of the Mind*, 36 J. HIST. IDEAS 701 (1975).

son's own thought to go entirely unnoticed. It would also be a mistake to try to reduce all of Wilson's wide-ranging ideas about society, politics, law, and government entirely to the polite "first principles" of his popular sociology and Common Sense philosophy. In any case, it is apparent that on occasion Wilson was inclined, like Madison, to view a question about the "interior structure of government" as absolutely crucial in itself. For example, at the 1787 Convention Wilson argued for a Council of Revision even more stubbornly than did Madison, and not, it would seem, from any conviction that polite society at large or Common Sense judgments could in any way inform deliberations on the "nice" policy questions that such a council would face.[72]

Wilson's polite orientation was, however, essential to his fundamental conception of citizenship. Upon further consideration, it may even become evident that such matters as his familiar theory of federalism and his less familiar thoughts on common law jurisprudence also derived from this polite orientation.[73] Indeed, in all its manifestations, Wilson's polite approach to the problems of republicanism promises to be instructive as an authentic complement to Madisonian theory.

Moreover, appreciation of this polite orientation makes it easier to see why Wilson has remained a relatively obscure Founder despite his many contributions to the Founding. Most conventional explanations of Wilson's quick and lasting decline into obscurity point to particular facts of his later career—especially the disgrace following on his financial scandals and the "charmlessness" of his ambition.[74] But, going beyond the personal accidents of Wilson's career, attention to the essentially polite orientation of many of his ideas uncovers another, deeper explanation. Wilson's polite tendency to bridge the ideological gap of the day and otherwise to "reconcile what is seemingly contradictory" proved an important

---

[72] Adair (ed.), *James Madison's Autobiography*, 2 WM. & MARY Q. 191, esp. 195, 197 (3d ser. 1945); MEYERS, note 44 *supra*, at xx (1st ed. 1973). On the Federalist authors generally, see EPSTEIN, THE POLITICAL THEORY OF THE FEDERALIST (1984); FURTWANGLER, THE AUTHORITY OF PUBLIUS: A READING OF THE FEDERALIST PAPERS (1984); Diggins, *The Oyster and the Pearl: The Problem of Contextualism in Intellectual History*, 23 HIST. & THEORY 159, 160–61 (1984). See also 2 FARRAND (ed.), THE RECORDS OF THE FEDERAL CONVENTION OF 1787 73 (2d ed. rev. 1937); 1 McCLOSKEY, note 3 *supra*, at 137.

[73] I plan to give further consideration to these matters in two forthcoming articles.

[74] 1 FRIEDMAN & ISRAEL, note 3 *supra*, at 80, 81, 86, 92, 94–95; SMITH, note 2 *supra*, at 376–88.

part of his undoing. In striving to be "comprehensive," Wilson at times appeared to behave hypocritically—championing popular democracy while cultivating conservative political alliances, and defending the rights of "persons" over those of "property" while scheming obsessively to increase his own sizable fortune. Moreover, many of Wilson's ideas must have rendered his republicanism sometimes platitudinous, sometimes tainted with opportunism.[75]

Although Wilson paid a personal price for his mismanagement of his later career, his distinctively articulated republican vision deserves something better than the neglect he brought on himself. Because his vision greatly impressed and guided many of his contemporaries, his peculiarly comprehensive republicanism has, at the least, a symptomatic historical importance. For, if there was in Wilson's republicanism an aspect of hypocrisy (or delusion), then there is ample reason to acknowledge an important place for such problematic hypocrisy in the "rhetoric of legitimation"[76] that was occasioned by the Founding.

In this essay I have emphasized the significance of Wilson's aspiration to serve as a comprehensive theorist, anxiously concerned with "first principles" and determined to formulate a republican theory that would "comprehend" not just the salient ideologies of the ratification era, but also what Wilson took to have been the very animus of the American Revolution—the principle that consent is the sole basis of all legal and political obligation. Faithful to these aims, Wilson developed a conception of citizenship that indicates the rich variety of early American republicanism, both in that Wilson's conception derived not at all from what Morton Horwitz has called the orthodox eighteenth-century "will theory of law" and in that it incorporated, but was not limited to, the inchoate notions of "volitional citizenship" that James Kettner has documented in the early law of the Republic.[77] It is significant, as well, that Wilson sought to expound a consent theory of liberal republicanism that

---

[75] 1 FRIEDMAN & ISRAEL, note 3 *supra*, at 85–90; SMITH, note 2 *supra*, at 159–68, 235, 243, 262–80; 1 FARRAND, note 72 *supra*, at 605–06. *Cf.* WHITE, note 2 *supra*, at 132–36, 227–28.

[76] SHKLAR, ORDINARY VICES 75 (1984), and ch. 2 generally; *cf. id.* at ch. 6 ("Bad Characters for Good Liberals").

[77] HORWITZ, THE TRANSFORMATION OF AMERICAN LAW, 1780–1860 19 (1977). Kettner, *The Development of American Citizenship in the Revolutionary Era: The Idea of Volitional Allegiance*, 18 AM. J. LEGAL HIST. 208 (1974); *cf.* KETTNER, THE DEVELOPMENT OF AMERICAN CITIZENSHIP, 1608–1870, at 247 (1978).

was in no way tied to the profound but constraining myth of a social contract, or to any legal or quasi-legal form whatsoever. Indeed, nothing about Wilson's republican vision is more significant than the irony that one of the preeminent lawyers of the Founding generations sought to locate the Founding not in the events that erected a "superstructure" of republican law and government but rather in the evidence of and prospects for a "polite" foundation.

FRANK H. EASTERBROOK

AGREEMENT AMONG THE JUSTICES: AN EMPIRICAL NOTE

People complain that the Supreme Court is becoming increasingly fractured. Both the popular and the scholarly commentary repeats the theme that there are more and more, longer and longer, separate opinions. Some say this is attributable to a failure of the Justices to consult and compromise. Others say it is caused by a failure of leadership. Still others maintain that the Court has embarked on a course of deciding political and ethical rather than legal issues, and that because there are no right answers to these questions, the Justices are doomed to endless bickering. The critics are united on only two propositions: that the amount of disagreement is increasing, and that this reflects poorly on the Court.

The critics are wrong on both counts. Disagreement is not necessarily a bad thing. It may be healthy or even necessary if the Court is to fulfill its assigned function. And it turns out that disagreement has not burgeoned. I present in this article a measure of agreement that attempts to capture what is important about separate and dissenting opinions—whether the Justices who do not join the majority disagree with the Court's rationale. Measured by this standard, rather than by cruder measures of the number of separate opinions, the level of disagreement has been remarkably stable for the last forty years.

No doubt the number and length of separate and dissenting

Frank H. Easterbrook is Lee and Brena Freeman Professor of Law, The University of Chicago.

AUTHOR'S NOTE: I thank Richard A. Epstein, Geoffrey Miller, Richard A. Posner, Geoffrey R. Stone, and Cass R. Sunstein for helpful comments on an earlier draft.

opinions continue to increase.[1] This is not necessarily bad. Fracturing is inevitable. The Court selects hard cases for decision, and cases are hard because existing precedents and the temper of the times allow more than one outcome. The ratio between the number of cases heard by the Court and those decided by lower courts and potentially reviewable has fallen. If a given portion of all cases in the lower courts is "hard," and the Court takes the most difficult of those, its docket will become more and more difficult over time. The process by which the Court decides cases ensures that it will accumulate inconsistent precedents, and these give rise to further disagreements.[2] Presidents sometimes appoint as Justices people known to disagree with existing cases. These forces and more ensure that unanimity is the exception. More dissent may show nothing but more difficult cases. Indeed, an increase in the number of dissenting opinions does not even show an increase in dissent.

I need not defend an increase in dissent unless there has been one. People who say that the Court is more fractured today than ever before usually point to the total number of separate opinions or votes. They count as dissents all votes that depart from the Court's disposition in any particular. These measures are unsatisfactory, though, because they do not reflect the reasons for the disagreement.

The Court's main function is to settle disputes about legal principles. The pertinent measure of disagreement on such a court is disagreement about the nature of these principles. We would like to know whether today's dissent shows a separate rationale (and thus augurs differences in future cases) or stems from circumstances peculiar to the case. Often a Justice will dissent for procedural reasons, even though he agrees with the Court's articulation of the rules. For example, the Justice may think that the Court should remand the case to permit the lower court to apply the rule in the first instance. A Justice may characterize evidence in the record

---

[1] Data demonstrating this appear in CASPER & POSNER, THE WORKLOAD OF THE SUPREME COURT (1976); Casper & Posner, *The Caseload of the Supreme Court: 1975 and 1976 Terms*, 1977 SUPREME COURT REVIEW 87; Hellman, *The Business of the Supreme Court under the Judiciary Act of 1925: The Plenary Docket in the 1970's*, 91 HARV. L. REV. 1709 (1978); and the summary tables in each November's HARVARD LAW REVIEW. See also FRANKFURTER & LANDIS, THE BUSINESS OF THE SUPREME COURT: A STUDY IN THE FEDERAL JUDICIAL SYSTEM (1928), for data on earlier years.

[2] See Easterbrook, *Ways of Criticizing the Court*, 95 HARV. L. REV. 802 (1982).

differently from his colleagues. A Justice may believe that a sentence or two is best left unsaid, even though he does not challenge its substance. These differences lead to opinions styled "dissents," but they do not reflect real disagreement about the law. On the other hand, opinions styled concurrences may demonstrate an irreconcilable schism within the Court. Both the nondissenting dissent and the dissenting concurrence occur with some frequency.

Summary statistics about dissent also may disguise areas of substantial agreement among the Justices. They may, for example, frequently reach the same conclusions in construing statutes even though they are at loggerheads on constitutional issues. Greater disagreement on constitutional issues might reflect the greater difficulty of these issues in light of the vague clauses the Justices must interpret, but perhaps it might reflect the greater play of philosophical differences.

I have attempted to determine the extent of *real* disagreement among the Justices and how it has changed. It is not possible to do so by using mechanical counts of dissenting or concurring opinions. Instead I read all of the cases from nine Terms: 1983, 1982, 1981, 1978, 1973, 1963, 1953, 1943, and 1933. I placed each case in one of three categories—statutory, constitutional, or common law—that best represented its principal issues. The Justices have more discretion in constitutional than in statutory cases because of the age and vagueness of the text. They have still more in common-law cases, in which no text at all controls, and they are free to rewrite their own decisions.

Then I determined the extent to which separate, concurring, and dissenting opinions reflected disagreement with either the legal rules announced by the majority or the principal arguments offered in support of those rules. I counted any significant disagreement on reasoning or the rule of decision as a "dissent." I treated Justices who declined to address the principal question, or who concurred or dissented without opinion, as if they had not participated. (These Justices expressed no view on the rationale or rule of decision, so I could not tell the extent to which there was real disagreement.) I counted most other expressions of opinion as concurrences. An Appendix explains the criteria in more detail.

There is a substantial element of subjectivity in these classifications. The task could not be delegated to a research assistant. Another reader of these cases might disagree with the treatment of some opinions. Nonetheless, disagreements of this sort are likely to even out over large numbers of cases. In any event, my criteria were constant from Term to Term, so that the numbers reported below should be reasonably accurate measures of *changes* in the extent of real agreement among the Justices on legal issues.

The estimates of dissent that arise from this survey are substantially below the estimates that appear in more mechanical counts. It is well to remember that even these estimates overstate the extent of disagreement. Often the dissent will say something like: "I agree with the Court on steps A, B, C, and D of the argument, but I part company at step E." I count this as a dissent, even though the dissenter agrees with most of the Court's reasoning. Similarly, when a case has multiple issues a Justice may agree with both the reasoning behind and the disposition of several issues, yet disagree with reasons or result on some other subject. I usually count this as a dissent, although in some cases the issues are so disparate that I have treated the case as if the issues had been raised in separate cases and counted dissents accordingly.

One more thing requires explanation. A count of dissenting votes per case or per Term may be misleading. Three dissenting votes are more significant when seven or eight Justices vote than when nine do. In some Terms Justices were ill during part of the Term, and in every Term I have treated some Justices as not voting in some cases on grounds explained above. Thus I present a figure called "Percent Dissenting" to reflect the portion of Justices present and giving reasons who disagreed with the Court's rationale or rule of decision. If nine Justices voted and two dissented, the percentage of dissent is 22 percent, if seven voted and two dissented the percent dissent is 29 percent, and so on.

One thing stands out clearly. The rate of real disagreement hovers around 20 percent and has not risen in forty years (see table 1).

There are some regularities in addition to the overall rate of disagreement. Constitutional cases produce significantly more disagreement than statutory cases. Common-law cases—those in which the Court is guided only by its earlier decisions—produce less disagreement, even though the Justices have the greatest leeway to impress their views on the law. The total rate of disagreement is a product of both the rate of disagreement by category of cases (table 1) and the percentage of cases in each category (table 2). This has changed over the years.

TABLE 1

DISAGREEMENT BY CATEGORY OF CASE

Term	Statutory (%)	Constitutional (%)	Common Law (%)	Total (%)
1933	5.58	7.87	3.49	5.63
1943	15.88	26.10	12.08	17.33
1953	16.83	20.51	25.97	20.31
1963	13.40	25.18	16.26	18.23
1973	20.53	20.04	14.89	21.26
1978	17.08	25.61	18.26	21.53
1981	19.34	25.54	23.13	22.65
1982	17.76	25.44	14.13	20.26
1983	18.72	21.41	13.21	19.10

A substantial increase in the proportion of constitutional cases on the docket, together with the traditionally higher rate of dissent in these cases, accounts for the increase in the overall rate of disagreement through the 1970s. A decrease in the proportion of constitutional cases brought the overall rate of disagreement down again in the 1980s—though there was also a decrease in the rate of disagreement across the board.

Most of the total dissenting votes occur in the 5–4 and 6–3 divisions. The bulk of the cases, statutory and constitutional alike, thus have two dissents or fewer. Table 3 shows what percentage of the total cases have no dissent, no or one dissent, and two or fewer dissents.

TABLE 2

PERCENTAGE OF CASES IN EACH CATEGORY

Term	Statutory (%)	Constitutional (%)	Common Law (%)
1933	43.04	28.48	28.48
1943	56.06	22.73	21.21
1953	47.37	23.68	28.95
1963	42.42	34.85	22.73
1973	33.53	43.71	22.75
1978	34.21	49.34	16.45
1981	38.24	41.18	20.59
1982	48.48	38.79	12.73
1983	41.47	43.98	14.16

TABLE 3
FREQUENCY OF DISSENT BY TYPE OF CASE

TERM	No Dissent				One Dissent or None				Two Dissents or Fewer			
	Statutory	Constitutional	Common Law	Total	Statutory	Constitutional	Common Law	Total	Statutory	Constitutional	Common Law	Total
1933	80.88	80.00	84.44	81.65	83.82	80.00	93.33	85.44	88.24	82.22	95.56	88.61
1943	47.30	23.33	57.14	43.94	56.76	33.33	64.29	53.03	74.32	50.00	82.14	70.45
1953	44.44	33.33	22.73	35.53	55.56	38.89	31.82	44.74	69.44	66.67	59.09	65.79
1963	42.86	26.09	50.00	38.64	67.86	28.26	60.00	52.27	82.14	52.17	66.67	68.18
1973	32.14	24.66	52.63	33.53	51.79	34.25	68.42	47.90	58.93	46.58	71.05	56.29
1978	51.92	22.67	32.00	34.21	57.69	36.00	52.00	46.05	67.31	49.33	72.00	59.21
1981	40.00	25.71	25.71	31.18	46.15	34.29	42.86	40.59	63.08	50.00	48.57	54.71
1982	41.25	23.44	47.62	35.15	55.00	34.38	61.90	47.88	67.50	46.88	71.43	60.00
1983	44.93	27.40	45.83	37.35	53.62	41.00	66.67	50.00	60.87	61.64	83.33	64.46

TABLE 4
PERCENTAGE OF CASES WITH FOUR DISSENTS

Term	Statutory (%)	Constitutional (%)	Common Law (%)
1933	2.99	11.11	4.44
	(1.10)	(1.41)	(.55)
1943	12.16	16.67	7.14
	(1.52)	(1.51)	(1.35)
1953	2.78	16.67	18.18
	(1.53)	(1.47)	(1.52)
1963	5.36	19.57	13.33
	(1.32)	(1.60)	(1.75)
1973	21.43	17.81	21.05
	(1.58)	(1.59)	(1.64)
1978	17.31	22.67	16.00
	(1.73)	(1.63)	(1.44)
1981	20.00	28.57	20.00
	(1.62)	(1.59)	(1.52)
1982	22.50	28.13	4.76
	(1.62)	(1.54)	(1.38)
1983	24.64	17.81	12.50
	(1.70)	(1.46)	(1.37)

The larger percentage of statutory and common-law cases decided with two or fewer dissents does not reflect indifference by the Justices to these cases. To the contrary, statutory cases appear to elicit great disagreements, as table 4 shows. A dissent by four Justices establishes not only that the Court found the case hard but also that the Justices took the subject seriously. Table 4 reports the percentage of cases (by category) decided with four dissents (5–4 or 4–4). It also shows the standard deviation of the number of dissenting votes in parentheses.

The percentage of statutory cases decided with four dissents has been rising. The standard deviation of the number of dissents in statutory cases also is high, in many years higher than that of constitutional cases. (The standard deviation rises with the dispersion of the number of dissents. A Term characterized by 9–0 and 5–4 cases has a much higher standard deviation than one in which 7–2 and 6–3 dispositions predominate.) I infer that statutory cases increasingly fall into two categories. One comprises cases that the Court takes to resolve a conflict or to settle some issue with greater importance in practice than in principle; it decides many of these cases 9–0 or 8–1. The other comprises cases that raise recurring questions of principle, such as how broadly to read criminal statutes.[3] These statutory questions frequently divide the Court 5–4.

The data on the rate of real disagreement among the Justices suggest, though they do not prove, that the recent cries of alarm and dismay about the expression of separate views are not well founded. The traditional restraints on the expression of separate views lapsed when Chief Justice Hughes resigned. Since Harlan Stone became Chief Justice in 1941, the Justices have stated their individual views frequently. The rate of real disagreement has remained almost constant since then. A small increase in the 1970s has been followed by a small reduction in the 1980s. Perhaps the rate of real disagreement was close to 20 percent in earlier years, too, although the Justices refrained from expressing this disagreement.

The stability in the rate of disagreement may be attributable to case selection. Instead of taking the hardest, most divisive cases available to them, the Justices might take some easier ones. The lower rate of disagreement in statutory cases may stem from this. The Court takes many statutory cases because of the practical importance of the subject rather than the difficulty of the principles at stake. Perhaps, too, there is some natural rate of dissent toward which the institution tends; when the Justices become more contentious, they modify their case selection rules. I do not have any other plausible explanation of the constant rate of disagreement.[4]

Even if there were a good explanation of the constant rate of real disagreement, it would be necessary to understand why the rate of disagreement depends on the subject of the case. Why would not the Justices continue taking statutory cases until, at the margin, they provoked as much disagreement as constitutional cases? It is possible that this happens now. Maybe the differences in the aggregate rates of disagreement come from a body of inframarginal cases that the Court takes, in the expectation of reaching a lopsided decision, because of the importance of the dispute. It is possible,

[3] Chief Justice Burger and Justices White, Marshall, Blackmun, and Powell frequently read criminal statutes broadly, while Justices Brennan, Rehnquist, Stevens, and O'Connor are likely to take a narrow view. *E.g.*, United States v. Yermian, 104 S.Ct. 2936 (1984); Dixon v. United States, 104 S.Ct. 1172 (1984).

[4] I conjectured in 1982 that the rate of disagreement was bound to increase as the Justices heard a smaller and smaller portion of the disputes within their jurisdiction. Easterbrook, note 2 *supra*, at 807. It looks as if I was wrong.

too, that some Justices withhold expressions of disagreement in statutory and common-law cases. These cases may settle the interpretation of a statute or resolve some important dispute but have little general importance. Stare decisis is apt to prevent the Court from revisiting the topic. One or two Justices who disagree with the majority may keep the disagreement to themselves, even though they would express an equivalent disagreement in a constitutional case. (The higher standard deviation of dissents in statutory cases suggests that something reduces the number of such cases with one or two dissents.)

Although the rate of real disagreement has been roughly constant, the rate of total disagreement has been rising. Why are Justices filing more "spurious" dissents—objections to dicta, unnecessary excursions into topics the majority does not reach, and the like—than ever before? The existence of these spurious dissents shows that the Court can tolerate more disharmony than that reflected in the rate of real dissents. Some blame the rise of spurious dissent on an increase in the number of law clerks, but the Justices are free to spurn the advice and the drafts of their clerks. For now we must count as a mystery the increase in the number of spurious dissents.

The data also shed some light on the contention that the Justices are dominated by political and ideological, rather than legal, concerns. Such concerns should produce a great deal of real disagreement. The Court's cases are the most hotly contested of the day, those in which sophisticated lawyers can make plausible arguments for a number of different dispositions. The Justices have an especially free hand in constitutional and common-law cases. That the Court decides so many cases by lopsided votes shows that the Justices frequently find the disputes governed by some identifiable rule. The Justices either agree on many fundamental premises or are constrained by doctrine, political forces, public opinion, and scholarly criticism to behave as if they do.

APPENDIX

In counting expressions of disagreement, I tried to choose a method that would emphasize disagreements about principle rather than the outcome of a particular case. When the disagreement in one case portends disagreement about the result in future cases or the application of other principles, it was treated as a dissent. Otherwise it was treated as a concurrence or a nonvote. Thus opinions agreeing with the majority's rationale but disagreeing with the disposition of the case (perhaps because of the choice between reversal and remand) usually were counted as concurrences. I counted opinions objecting to dictum as concurrences—provided that the objecting Justice did not complain about the substance of the dictum, in which case the opinion was a dissent. If a Justice filed a separate opinion expressing views additional to, but not in conflict with, the majority, I treated this, too, as a concurrence.[5]

Sometimes cases present recurring disagreements. For example, Justices Brennan and Marshall believe that capital punishment is unconstitutional and will vote to reverse any sentence of death. Counting this expression of opinion as a dissent in every case would overstate the real extent of disagreement on the Court, however, because these Justices also frequently express views on the issues the Court took the case to resolve. In cases of standing disagreements I searched for discussions of the principal issues under consideration. If, say, Justices Brennan and Marshall agreed with the Court's reasoning on an evidentiary issue (the one the Court took the case to hear) before going on to dissent, I treated their position as concurring. If they simply dissented on account of their view of capital punishment without expressing a view on the merits, I treated the position as dissenting.

---

[5] Some examples from the 1983 Term show how this worked. Jefferson Parish Hospital District No. 2 v. Hyde, 104 S.Ct. 1551 (1984), a 9–0 reversal of an antitrust judgment, is treated as a 5–4 case because four Justices argued for abolition of the per se rule against certain tie-ins, while five Justices kept but modified the per se rule. EEOC v. Shell Oil Co., 104 S.Ct. 1621 (1984), a 9–0 reversal of an order dismissing the EEOC's complaint, also is treated as a 5–4 case. Although the Justices agreed that a charge by a Commissioner of the EEOC need not detail the evidence, they used different rationales that might produce different results in future cases. In Justices of Boston Municipal Court v. Lydon, 104 S.Ct. 1805 (1984), all nine Justices agreed that an order granting habeas corpus had to be reversed, but it also was treated as 5–4. Two Justices concluded that the lower court lacked jurisdiction, and two more believed that the majority had used an inappropriate rationale on the merits (though it reached the right result). Another two justices stated that, as an original matter, they would have found an absence of jurisdiction but followed precedent nonetheless. I counted these (and similar expressions elsewhere) as concurrences. In contrast, I treated United States v. Doe, 104 S.Ct. 1237 (1984), as a 9–0 case even though there were dissents and concurrences. The dissent agreed with most of the majority's reasoning but maintained that the correct disposition was affirmance rather than remand; the dissent believed that part of the majority's opinion was dicta. Two concurring opinions also offered different interpretations of the majority's position and expressed divergent views about the appropriate treatment of some kinds of future disputes. I counted this (and similar cases) as 9–0 because there was no dispute about the result or rationale of the *category* of cases represented by *Doe*, even though the opinions indicated that variations on the theme would produce disagreements. Similarly, I treated Tower v. Glover, 104 S.Ct. 2820 (1984), as a 9–0 case even though four Justices refused to join one paragraph of the opinion. These Justices believed the paragraph to be gratuitous, but they did not disagree with any aspect of the majority's reasoning that was necessary to resolve the dispute, and the concurrence did not establish any substantive disagreements that would be important in future cases.

Because I was searching for disagreements on principles, I disregarded some cases and some votes entirely. Cases dismissed as improvidently granted were ignored, even if the Justices gave reasons for the dismissals. Cases decided without opinion also were ignored. If a Justice concurred or dissented without opinion, I treated that Justice as not sitting. It was impossible to tell why the Justice did not join the prevailing opinion. A case-specific reason would have been treated as a concurrence, a principled reason as a disagreement. The only available course was to disregard the vote. This increases the measure of agreement. It also biases my method toward finding an increase in disagreement. In earlier years Justices dissented or concurred without opinion more frequently than they do now, so that the exclusion of these votes had its principal effects in the earlier years. (There were never very many unexplained votes, so the effect is slight.) I used the same method of exclusion when a Justice objected to a summary disposition by refusing to vote on the merits.[6]

Because the Court's practices about handling related cases have changed over the years, I disregarded some cases from the early years of the study. The current practice is to consolidate related cases for a single opinion and to deny review or vacate others summarily after holding them in abeyance. In earlier years the Court was more likely to hear related cases in tandem and dispose of them in short separate opinions. In order to maintain uniformity, I removed earlier cases from the count when they would have been dealt with today by consolidation or remand without opinion.

In most cases I recorded a disagreement whenever a Justice parted ways with his colleagues on any issue of precedential importance. Sometimes, though, a case contained issues so disparate that such a method would have overstated the extent of disagreement. This might occur, for example, when some Justices refused to vote on the merits because they thought the Court had no jurisdiction. I treated some such cases as if there had been separate submissions of the separable issues.[7] I did this most

---

[6] So, for example, I treated Massachusetts v. Upton, 104 S.Ct. 2085 (1984), as a case in which only seven Justices participated, because of the following notation (*id*. at 2091): "Justice Brennan and Justice Marshall dissent from the summary disposition of this case and would deny the petition for certiorari." On the other hand, Florida v. Meyers, 104 S.Ct. 1852 (1984), was treated as 9–0. Three Justices dissented because they objected to the grant of review, but they also agreed with the majority that the lower court had committed legal error.

[7] One example from the 1983 Term: South Carolina v. Regan, 104 S.Ct. 1107 (1984). Five Justices agreed that the Court had jurisdiction of the case despite the Anti-Injunction Act, and these five also agreed on the reasons. Two groups of Justices expressed separate views on the jurisdictional issue and concurred in the judgment. But one of the five Justices in the majority on jurisdiction would have dismissed the case because, in his view, the plaintiff was so sure to fail on the merits that it was inappropriate to entertain the case at all. The other Justices thought the case should be heard. I treated this as two cases. One, decided 5–4, covered the jurisdictional issue; the other, decided 8–1, addressed the propriety of entertaining the complaint.

frequently when cases had no majority opinion, which accounts for the fact that the tables show very few cases with five or six dissents. (But when, for example, there was a single issue and three groups of three Justices apiece used three different rationales, I recorded the case as having six dissents.)

The case counts given in the text thus reflect some subtractions and some additions from the usual count of "all cases decided with opinion." Note, too, that I counted summary dispositions (cases decided without oral argument) in the same way I counted plenary dispositions. Because I was looking for disagreements on principles, every case decided with a substantial explanation was the same as any other. The following tables show that summary dispositions have a little less disagreement than plenary dispositions, but not so much less that inclusion of summary dispositions is inappropriate. Opinions issued without oral argument have the same precedential effect as other opinions, and they are one response to the Court's increasing caseload. Often the Court chooses summary disposition when the majority is especially strong about its views, and it is appropriate to include such displays of agreement in the count.

Finally, a few words about the categories. A case is a "statutory" matter when the Court indicates that the principal dispute is about the construction of a federal statute. Thus cases arising out of claims that federal laws preempt state laws are statutory rather than constitutional. So too are cases involving administrative procedure and the implication of private rights of action.

A case is "common law" when its disposition turns on federal or state decisional law rather than statutory or constitutional text. Original jurisdiction cases, admiralty, torts, contracts, Indian law, the law of evidence (before the Federal Rules of Evidence), and most questions of judicial procedure go into this category.

A question about original or appellate jurisdiction could be placed in any of the three categories, depending on the Court's approach. A claim that the plaintiff lacked "standing" was a constitutional issue if the Court addressed the minimum requirements of Article III, but it was a common-law issue if the Court invoked extraconstitutional "prudential" considerations, and a statutory question if the Court held that the plaintiff's claim did not fall within the "zone of interests" established by a statute. Other questions were apportioned among the three categories in similar ways.

1933 Term

Vote	Statutory			Constitutional			Common Law			All Cases		
	Argued	Summary	Total	Argued	Summary	Total	Argued	Summary	Total	Argued	Summary	Total
9–0	52	1	53	30	0	30	33	2	35	115	3	118
8–0	1	0	1	4	0	4	3	0	3	8	0	8
7–0	1	0	1	0	0	0	0	0	0	1	0	1
6–0	0	0	0	2	0	2	0	0	0	2	0	2
All X–0	54	1	55	36	0	36	36	2	38	126	3	129
X–0 (%)	80.60	100.00	80.88	80.00	0	80.00	83.72	100.00	84.44	81.29	100.00	81.65
8–1	2	0	2	0	0	0	4	0	4	6	0	6
7–1	0	0	0	0	0	0	0	0	0	0	0	0
6–1	0	0	0	0	0	0	0	0	0	0	0	0
5–1	0	0	0	0	0	0	0	0	0	0	0	0
All X–1	2	0	2	0	0	0	4	0	4	6	0	6
X–1 or better	56	1	57	36	0	36	40	2	42	132	3	135
X–1 or better (%)	83.58	100.00	83.82	80.00	0	80.00	93.02	100.00	93.33	85.16	100.00	85.44
7–2	3	0	3	1	0	1	0	0	0	4	0	4
6–2	0	0	0	0	0	0	1	0	1	1	0	1
5–2	0	0	0	0	0	0	0	0	0	0	0	0
4–2	0	0	0	0	0	0	0	0	0	0	0	0
All X–2	3	0	3	1	0	1	1	0	1	5	0	5
X–2 or better	59	1	60	37	0	37	41	2	43	137	3	140
X–2 or better (%)	88.06	100.00	88.24	82.22	0	82.22	95.35	100.00	95.56	88.39	100.00	88.61
6–3	6	0	6	2	0	2	0	0	0	8	0	8
5–3	0	0	0	1	0	1	0	0	0	1	0	1
4–3	0	0	0	0	0	0	0	0	0	0	0	0
All X–3	6	0	6	3	0	3	0	0	0	9	0	9
X–3 or better	65	1	66	40	0	40	41	2	43	146	3	149
X–3 (%)	8.96	0.00	8.82	6.67	0	6.67	0.00	0.00	0.00	5.81	0.00	5.70
5–4	2	0	2	5	0	5	2	0	2	9	0	9
4–4	2	0	2	5	0	5	2	0	2	0	0	0
All X–4	2	0	2	5	0	5	2	0	2	9	0	9
X–4 (%)	2.99	0.00	2.94	11.11	0	11.11	4.65	0.00	4.44	5.81	0.00	5.70
5 dissents	0	0	0	0	0	0	0	0	0	0	0	0
6 dissents	0	0	0	0	0	0	0	0	0	0	0	0
Total cases	67	1	68	45	0	45	43	2	45	155	3	158
Percentage of all cases	42.41	.63	43.04	28.48	0.00	28.48	27.22	1.27	28.48	98.10	1.90	
Total dissents	34	0	34	31	0	31	14	0	14	79	0	79
Dissent/case	.507	0	.5	.689	0	.689	.326	0	.311	.51	0	.5
Percentage dissenting	5.67	0.00	5.58	7.87	0	7.87	3.66	0.00	3.49	5.74	0.00	5.63

1943 Term

Vote	Statutory			Constitutional			Common Law			All Cases		
	Argued	Summary	Total	Argued	Summary	Total	Argued	Summary	Total	Argued	Summary	Total
9–0	23	0	23	4	0	4	9	3	12	36	3	39
8–0	7	1	8	0	0	0	2	0	2	9	1	10
7–0	3	1	4	2	0	2	0	0	0	5	1	6
6–0	0	0	0	1	0	1	2	0	2	3	0	3
All X–0	33	2	35	7	0	7	13	3	16	53	5	58
X–0 (%)	45.83	100.0	47.30	23.33	0	23.33	52.00	100.0	57.14	41.73	100.0	43.94
8–1	6	0	6	0	0	0	1	0	1	7	0	7
7–1	1	0	1	2	0	2	0	0	0	3	0	3
6–1	0	0	0	1	0	1	0	0	0	1	0	1
5–1	0	0	0	0	0	0	1	0	1	1	0	1
All X–1	7	0	7	3	0	3	2	0	2	12	0	12
X–1 or better	40	2	42	10	0	10	15	3	18	65	5	70
X–1 or better (%)	55.56	100.0	56.76	33.33	0	33.33	60.00	100.0	64.29	51.18	100.0	53.03
7–2	5	0	5	3	0	3	5	0	5	13	0	13
6–2	6	0	6	0	0	0	0	0	0	6	0	6
5–2	2	0	2	2	0	2	0	0	0	4	0	4
4–2	0	0	0	0	0	0	0	0	0	0	0	0
All X–2	13	0	13	5	0	5	5	0	5	23	0	23
X–2 or better	53	2	55	15	0	15	20	3	23	88	5	93
X–2 or better (%)	73.61	100.0	74.32	50.00	0	50.00	80.00	100.0	82.14	69.29	100.0	70.45
6–3	7	0	7	5	0	5	2	0	2	14	0	14
5–3	1	0	1	2	0	2	1	0	1	4	0	4
4–3	1	0	1	2	0	2	0	0	0	3	0	3
All X–3	9	0	9	9	0	9	3	0	3	21	0	21
X–3 or better	62	2	64	24	0	24	23	3	26	109	5	114
X–3 (%)	12.50	0.00	12.16	30.00	0	30.00	12.00	0.00	10.71	16.54	0.00	15.91
5–4	9	0	9	5	0	5	2	0	2	16	0	16
4–4	0	0	0	0	0	0	0	0	0	0	0	0
All X–4	9	0	9	5	0	5	2	0	2	16	0	16
X–4 (%)	12.50	0.00	12.16	16.67	0	16.67	8.00	0.00	7.14	12.60	0.00	12.12
5 dissents	1	0	1	1	0	1	0	0	0	2	0	2
6 dissents	0	0	0	0	0	0	0	0	0	0	0	0
Total cases	72	2	74	30	0	30	25	3	28	127	5	132
Percentage of all cases	54.55	1.52	56.06	22.73	0.00	22.73	18.94	2.27	21.21	96.21	3.79	
Total dissents	101	0	101	65	0	65	29	0	29	195	0	195
Dissent/case	1.403	0	1.365	2.167	0	2.167	1.16	0	1.036	1.535	0	1.477
Percentage dissenting	16.26	0.00	15.88	26.10	0	26.10	13.62	0.00	12.08	18.01	0.00	17.33

1953 Term

Vote	Statutory			Constitutional			Common Law			All Cases		
	Argued	Summary	Total	Argued	Summary	Total	Argued	Summary	Total	Argued	Summary	Total
9–0	8	0	8	5	0	5	2	0	2	15	0	15
8–0	5	0	5	0	0	0	1	1	2	6	1	7
7–0	3	0	3	1	0	1	1	0	1	5	0	5
6–0	0	0	0	0	0	0	0	0	0	0	0	0
All X–0	16	0	16	6	0	6	4	1	5	26	1	27
X–0 (%)	44.44	0.00	44.44	33.33	0	33.33	19.05	100.0	22.73	34.67	100.0	35.53
8–1	2	0	2	0	0	0	0	0	0	2	0	2
7–1	2	0	2	1	0	1	0	0	0	3	0	3
6–1	0	0	0	0	0	0	2	0	2	2	0	2
5–1	0	0	0	0	0	0	0	0	0	0	0	0
All X–1	4	0	4	1	0	1	2	0	2	7	0	7
X–1 or better	20	0	20	7	0	7	6	1	7	33	1	34
X–1 or better (%)	55.56	0	55.56	38.89	0	38.89	28.57	100.0	31.82	44.00	100.0	44.74
7–2	4	0	4	4	0	4	1	0	1	9	0	9
6–2	1	0	1	1	0	1	4	0	4	6	0	6
5–2	0	0	0	0	0	0	1	0	1	1	0	1
4–2	0	0	0	0	0	0	0	0	0	0	0	0
All X–2	5	0	5	5	0	5	6	0	6	16	0	16
X–2 or better	25	0	25	12	0	12	12	1	13	49	1	50
X–2 or better (%)	69.44	0	69.44	66.67	0	66.67	57.14	100.0	59.09	65.33	100.0	65.79
6–3	4	0	4	1	0	1	1	0	1	6	0	6
5–3	3	0	3	2	0	2	3	0	3	8	0	8
4–3	2	0	2	0	0	0	0	0	0	2	0	2
All X–3	9	0	9	3	0	3	4	0	4	16	0	16
X–3 or better	34	0	34	15	0	15	16	1	17	65	1	66
X–3 or better (%)	25.00	0	25.00	16.67	0	16.67	19.05	0.00	18.18	21.33	0.00	21.05
5–4	1	0	1	3	0	3	4	0	4	8	0	8
4–4	0	0	0	0	0	0	0	0	0	0	0	0
All X–4	1	0	1	3	0	3	4	0	4	8	0	8
X–4 (%)	2.78	0	2.78	16.67	0	16.67	19.05	0.00	18.18	10.67	0.00	10.53
5 dissents	0	0	0	0	0	0	1	0	1	1	0	1
6 dissents	1	0	1	0	0	0	0	0	0	1	0	1
Total cases	36	0	36	18	0	18	21	1	22	75	1	76
Percentage of all cases	47.37	0.00	47.37	23.68	0.00	23.68	27.63	1.32	28.95	98.68	1.32	100.0
Total dissents	51	0	51	32	0	32	47	0	47	130	0	130
Dissent/case	1.417	0	1.417	1.778	0	1.778	2.238	0	2.136	1.733	0	1.711
Percentage dissenting	16.83	0	16.83	20.51	0	20.51	27.17	0.00	25.97	20.57	0.00	20.31

1963 Term

Vote	Statutory			Constitutional			Common Law			All Cases		
	Argued	Summary	Total	Argued	Summary	Total	Argued	Summary	Total	Argued	Summary	Total
9–0	18	1	19	10	2	12	12	2	14	40	5	45
8–0	3	0	3	0	0	0	1	0	1	4	0	4
7–0	2	0	2	0	0	0	0	0	0	2	0	2
6–0	0	0	0	0	0	0	0	0	0	0	0	0
All X–0	23	1	24	10	2	12	13	2	15	46	5	51
X–0 (%)	44.23	25.00	42.86	22.73	100.0	26.09	48.15	66.67	50.00	37.40	55.56	38.64
8–1	8	1	9	1	0	1	3	0	3	12	1	13
7–1	3	1	4	0	0	0	0	0	0	3	1	4
6–1	0	0	0	0	0	0	0	0	0	0	0	0
5–1	1	0	1	0	0	0	0	0	0	1	0	1
All X–1	12	2	14	1	0	1	3	0	3	16	2	18
X–1 or better	35	3	38	11	2	13	16	2	18	62	7	69
X–1 or better (%)	67.31	75.00	67.86	25.00	100.0	28.26	59.26	66.67	60.00	50.41	77.78	52.27
7–2	5	1	6	8	0	8	2	0	2	15	1	16
6–2	2	0	2	3	0	3	0	0	0	5	0	5
5–2	0	0	0	0	0	0	0	0	0	0	0	0
4–2	0	0	0	0	0	0	0	0	0	0	0	0
All X–2	7	1	8	11	0	11	2	0	2	20	1	21
X–2 or better	42	4	46	22	2	24	18	2	20	82	8	90
X–2 or better (%)	80.77	100.0	82.14	50.00	100.0	52.17	66.67	66.67	66.67	66.67	88.89	68.18
6–3	4	0	4	9	0	9	4	1	5	17	1	18
5–3	2	0	2	2	0	2	0	0	0	4	0	4
4–3	0	0	0	0	0	0	0	0	0	0	0	0
All X–3	6	0	6	11	0	11	4	1	5	21	1	22
X–3 or better	48	4	52	33	2	35	22	3	25	103	9	112
X–3 (%)	11.54	0.00	10.71	25.00	0.00	23.91	14.81	33.33	16.67	17.07	11.11	16.67
5–4	2	0	2	9	0	9	4	0	4	15	0	15
4–4	1	0	1	0	0	0	0	0	0	1	0	1
All X–4	3	0	3	9	0	9	4	0	4	16	0	16
X–4 (%)	5.77	0.00	5.36	20.45	0.00	19.57	14.81	0.00	13.33	13.01	0.00	12.12
5 dissents	1	0	1	1	0	1	0	0	0	2	0	2
6 dissents	0	0	0	1	0	1	1	0	1	2	0	2
Total cases	52	4	56	44	2	46	27	3	30	123	9	132
Percentage of all cases	39.39	3.03	42.42	33.33	1.52	34.85	20.45	2.27	22.73	93.18	6.82	
Total dissents	61	4	65	103	0	103	41	3	44	205	7	212
Dissent/case	1.173		1.161	2.341		2.239	1.519		1.467	1.667	.778	1.606
Percentage dissenting	13.56	11.43	13.40	26.34	0.00	25.18	16.94	11.11	16.36	18.93	8.75	18.23

1973 Term

Vote	Statutory			Constitutional			Common Law			All Cases		
	Argued	Summary	Total	Argued	Summary	Total	Argued	Summary	Total	Argued	Summary	Total
9–0	10	1	11	11	5	16	11	3	14	32	9	41
8–0	5	0	5	2	0	2	1	2	3	8	2	10
7–0	2	0	2	0	0	0	1	0	1	3	0	3
6–0	0	0	0	0	0	0	0	2	2	0	2	2
All X–0	17	1	18	13	5	18	13	7	20	43	13	56
X–0 (%)	31.48	50.00	32.14	20.97	45.45	24.66	43.33	87.50	52.63	29.45	61.90	33.53
8–1	8	0	8	6	0	6	3	1	4	17	1	18
7–1	2	1	3	1	0	1	2	0	2	5	1	6
6–1	0	0	0	0	0	0	0	0	0	0	0	0
5–1	0	0	0	0	0	0	0	0	0	0	0	0
All X–1	10	1	11	7	0	7	5	1	6	22	2	24
X–1 or better	27	2	29	20	5	25	18	8	26	65	15	80
X–1 or better (%)	50.00	100.0	51.79	32.26	45.45	34.25	60.00	100.0	68.42	44.52	71.43	47.90
7–2	2	0	2	7	0	7	1	0	1	10	0	10
6–2	1	0	1	1	0	1	0	0	0	2	0	2
5–2	1	0	1	1	0	1	0	0	0	2	0	2
4–2	0	0	0	0	0	0	1	0	0	0	0	0
All X–2	4	0	4	9	0	9	19	0	1	14	0	14
X–2 or better	31	2	33	29	5	34	19	8	27	79	15	94
X–2 or better (%)	57.41	100.0	58.93	46.77	45.45	46.58	63.33	100.0	71.05	54.11	71.43	56.29
6–3	9	0	9	14	5	19	3	0	3	26	5	31
5–3	2	0	2	4	0	4	0	0	0	6	0	6
4–3	0	0	0	0	0	0	0	0	0	0	0	0
All X–3	11	0	11	18	5	23	3	0	3	32	5	37
X–3 or better	42	2	44	47	10	57	22	8	30	111	20	131
X–3 (%)	20.37	0.00	19.64	29.03	45.45	31.51	10.00	0.00	7.89	21.92	23.81	22.16
5–4	12	0	12	12	1	13	8	0	8	32	1	33
4–4	0	0	0	0	0	0	0	0	0	0	0	0
All X–4	12	0	12	12	1	13	8	0	8	32	1	33
X–4 (%)	22.22	0.00	21.43	19.35	9.09	17.81	26.67	0.00	21.05	21.92	4.76	19.76
5 dissents	0	0	0	2	0	2	0	0	0	2	0	2
6 dissents	0	0	0	1	0	1	0	0	0	1	0	1
Total cases	54	2	56	62	11	73	30	8	38	146	21	167
Percentage of all cases	32.34	1.20	33.53	37.13	6.59	43.71	17.96	4.79	22.75	87.43	12.57	
Total dissents	99	1	100	143	19	162	48	1	49	290	21	311
Dissent/case	1.833	.5	1.786	2.306	1.727	2.219	1.6	.125	1.289	1.986	1	1.862
Percentage dissenting	21.06	5.88	20.53	26.09	19.19	25.04	18.11	1.56	14.89	22.60	11.67	21.26

1978 Term

Vote	Statutory			Constitutional			Common Law			All Cases		
	Argued	Summary	Total	Argued	Summary	Total	Argued	Summary	Total	Argued	Summary	Total
9–0	12	2	14	10	3	13	5	0	5	27	5	32
8–0	10	0	10	3	1	4	2	1	3	15	2	17
7–0	3	0	3	0	0	0	0	0	0	3	0	3
6–0	0	0	0	0	0	0	0	0	0	0	0	0
All X–0	25	2	27	13	4	17	7	1	8	45	7	52
X–0 (%)	52.08	50.00	51.92	19.40	50.00	22.67	33.33	25.00	32.00	33.09	43.75	34.21
8–1	2	0	2	7	1	8	3	0	3	12	1	13
7–1	1	0	1	1	1	2	1	1	2	3	2	5
6–1	0	0	0	0	0	0	0	0	0	0	0	0
5–1	0	0	0	0	0	0	0	0	0	0	0	0
All X–1	3	0	3	8	2	10	4	1	5	15	3	18
X–1 or better	28	2	30	21	6	27	11	2	13	60	10	70
X–1 or better (%)	58.33	50.00	57.69	31.34	75.00	36.00	52.38	50.00	52.00	44.12	62.50	46.05
7–2	3	0	3	8	0	8	3	1	4	14	1	15
6–2	1	0	1	2	0	2	0	1	1	3	1	4
5–2	1	0	1	0	0	0	0	0	0	1	0	1
4–2	0	0	0	0	0	0	0	0	0	0	0	0
All X–2	5	0	5	10	0	10	3	2	5	18	2	20
X–2 or better	33	2	35	31	6	37	14	4	18	78	12	90
X–2 or better (%)	68.75	50.00	67.31	46.27	75.00	49.33	66.67	100.0	72.00	57.35	75.00	59.21
6–3	4	1	5	11	1	12	3	0	3	18	2	20
5–3	2	0	2	5	1	6	0	0	0	7	1	8
4–3	0	0	0	0	0	0	0	0	0	0	0	0
All X–3	6	1	7	16	2	18	3	0	3	25	3	28
X–3 or better	39	3	42	47	8	55	17	4	21	103	15	118
X–3 (%)	12.50	25.00	13.46	23.88	25.00	24.00	14.29	0.00	12.00	18.38	18.75	18.42
5–4	7	1	8	16	0	16	4	0	4	27	1	28
4–4	1	0	1	1	0	1	0	0	0	2	0	2
All X–4	8	1	9	17	0	17	4	0	4	29	1	30
X–4 (%)	16.67	25.00	17.31	25.37	0.00	22.67	19.05	0.00	16.00	21.32	6.25	19.74
5 dissents	0	0	0	1	0	1	0	0	0	1	0	1
6 dissents	1	0	1	2	0	2	0	0	0	3	0	3
Total cases	48	4	52	67	8	75	21	4	25	136	16	152
Percentage of all cases	31.58	2.63	34.21	44.08	5.26	49.34	13.82	2.63	16.45	89.47	10.53	
Total dissents	69	7	76	161	8	169	35	5	40	265	20	285
Dissent/case	1.438	1.75	1.462	2.403	1	2.253	1.667	1.25	1.6	1.949	1.25	1.875
Percentage dissenting	16.87	19.44	17.08	27.24	11.59	25.61	18.82	15.15	18.26	22.34	14.49	21.53

1981 Term

Vote	Statutory Argued	Statutory Summary	Statutory Total	Constitutional Argued	Constitutional Summary	Constitutional Total	Common Law Argued	Common Law Summary	Common Law Total	All Cases Argued	All Cases Summary	All Cases Total
9–0	21	2	23	11	0	11	5	1	6	37	3	40
8–0	3	0	3	1	2	3	2	0	2	6	2	8
7–0	0	0	0	1	2	3	1	0	1	2	2	4
6–0	0	0	0	0	1	1	0	0	0	0	1	1
All X–0	24	2	26	13	5	18	8	1	9	45	8	53
X–0 (%)	40.68	33.33	40.00	21.31	55.56	25.71	27.59	16.67	25.71	30.20	38.10	31.18
8–1	4	0	4	4	0	4	4	0	4	12	0	12
7–1	0	0	0	1	1	2	1	1	2	2	2	4
6–1	0	0	0	0	0	0	0	0	0	0	0	0
5–1	0	0	0	0	0	0	0	0	0	0	0	0
All X–1	4	0	4	5	1	6	5	1	6	14	2	16
X–1 or better	28	2	30	18	6	24	13	2	15	59	10	69
X–1 or better (%)	47.46	33.33	46.15	29.51	66.67	34.29	44.83	33.33	42.86	39.60	47.62	40.59
7–2	6	2	8	7	0	7	1	0	1	14	2	16
6–2	2	1	3	1	1	2	0	0	0	3	2	5
5–2	0	0	0	2	0	2	0	1	1	2	1	3
4–2	0	0	0	0	0	0	0	0	0	0	0	0
All X–2	8	3	11	10	1	11	1	1	2	19	5	24
X–2 or better	36	5	41	28	7	35	14	3	17	78	15	93
X–2 or better (%)	61.02	83.33	63.08	45.90	77.78	50.00	48.28	50.00	48.57	52.35	71.43	54.71
6–3	7	1	8	11	1	12	8	3	11	26	5	31
5–3	2	0	2	2	0	2	0	0	0	4	0	4
4–3	1	0	1	0	0	0	0	0	0	1	0	1
All X–3	10	1	11	13	1	14	8	3	11	31	5	36
X–3 or better	46	6	52	41	8	49	22	6	28	109	20	129
X–3 (%)	16.95	16.67	16.92	21.31	11.11	20.00	27.59	50.00	31.43	20.81	23.81	21.18
5–4	12	0	12	18	1	19	7	0	7	37	1	38
4–4	1	0	1	1	0	1	0	0	0	2	0	2
All X–4	13	0	13	19	1	20	7	0	7	39	1	40
X–4 (%)	22.03	0.00	20.00	31.15	11.11	28.57	24.14	0.00	20.00	26.17	4.76	23.53
5 dissents	0	0	0	1	0	1	0	0	0	1	0	1
6 dissents	0	0	0	0	0	0	0	0	0	0	0	0
Total cases	59	6	65	61	9	70	29	6	35	149	21	170
Percentage of all cases	34.71	3.53	38.24	35.88	5.29	41.18	17.06	3.53	20.59	87.65	12.35	
Total dissents	102	9	111	145	10	155	59	12	71	306	31	337
Dissent/case	1.729	1.5	1.708	2.377	1.111	2.214	2.034	2	2.029	2.054	1.476	1.982
Percentage dissenting	19.58	16.98	19.34	27.00	14.29	25.54	23.05	23.53	23.13	23.29	17.82	22.65

1982 Term

Vote	Statutory			Constitutional			Common Law			All Cases		
	Argued	Summary	Total	Argued	Summary	Total	Argued	Summary	Total	Argued	Summary	Total
9–0	30	0	30	11	0	11	8	1	9	49	1	50
8–0	3	0	3	0	0	0	0	1	1	3	1	4
7–0	0	0	0	1	1	2	0	0	0	1	1	2
6–0	0	0	0	0	2	2	0	0	0	0	2	2
All X–0	33	0	33	12	3	15	8	2	10	53	5	58
X–0 (%)	42.86	0.00	41.25	20.00	75.00	23.44	42.11	100.0	47.62	33.97	55.56	35.15
8–1	10	1	11	6	1	7	2	0	2	18	2	20
7–1	0	0	0	0	0	0	0	0	0	0	0	0
6–1	0	0	0	0	0	0	0	0	0	0	0	0
5–1	0	0	0	0	0	0	1	0	1	1	0	1
All X–1	10	1	11	6	1	7	3	0	3	19	2	21
X–1 or better	43	1	44	18	4	22	11	2	13	72	7	79
X–1 or better (%)	55.84	33.33	55.00	30.00	100.0	34.38	57.89	100.0	61.90	46.15	77.78	47.88
7–2	9	0	9	7	0	7	2	0	2	18	0	18
6–2	1	0	1	1	0	1	0	0	0	2	0	2
5–2	0	0	0	0	0	0	0	0	0	0	0	0
4–2	0	0	0	0	0	0	0	0	0	0	0	0
All X–2	10	0	10	8	0	8	2	0	2	20	0	20
X–2 or better	53	1	54	26	4	30	13	2	15	92	7	99
X–2 or better (%)	68.83	33.33	67.50	43.33	100.0	46.88	68.42	100.0	71.43	58.97	77.78	60.00
6–3	6	1	7	14	0	14	4	0	4	24	1	25
5–3	1	0	1	2	0	2	1	0	1	4	0	4
4–3	0	0	0	0	0	0	0	0	0	0	0	0
All X–3	7	1	8	16	0	16	5	0	5	28	1	29
X–3 or better	60	2	62	42	4	46	18	2	20	120	8	128
X–3 (%)	9.09	33.33	10.00	26.67	0.00	25.00	26.32	0.00	23.81	17.95	11.11	17.58
5–4	17	1	18	17	0	17	1	0	1	35	1	36
4–4	0	0	0	1	0	1	0	0	0	1	0	1
All X–4	17	1	18	18	0	18	1	0	1	36	1	37
X–4 (%)	22.08	33.33	22.50	30.00	0.00	28.13	5.26	0.00	4.76	23.08	11.11	22.42
5 dissents	0	0	0	0	0	0	0	0	0	0	0	0
6 dissents	0	0	0	0	0	0	0	0	0	0	0	0
Total cases	77	3	80	60	4	64	19	2	21	156	9	165
Percentage of all cases	46.67	1.82	48.48	36.36	2.42	38.79	11.52	1.21	12.73	94.55	5.45	
Total dissents	119	8	127	142	1	143	26	0	26	287	9	296
Dissent/case	1.545	2.667	1.588	2.367	.25	2.234	1.368	0	1.238	1.84	1	1.794
Percentage dissenting	17.30	29.63	17.76	26.59	3.57	25.44	15.57	0.00	14.13	20.66	12.50	20.26

1983 TERM

	Statutory			Constitutional			Common Law			All Cases		
Vote	Argued	Summary	Total	Argued	Summary	Total	Argued	Summary	Total	Argued	Summary	Total
9–0	26	0	26	16	2	18	9	0	9	51	2	53
8–0	3	1	4	1	0	1	2	0	2	6	1	7
7–0	0	0	0	0	1	1	0	0	0	0	1	1
6–0	1	0	1	0	0	0	0	0	0	1	0	1
All X–0	30	1	31	17	3	20	11	0	11	58	4	62
X–0 (%)	44.12	100.0	44.93	24.64	75.00	27.40	52.38	0.00	45.83	36.71	50.00	37.35
8–1	6	0	6	7	0	7	5	0	5	18	0	18
7–1	0	0	0	2	0	2	0	0	0	2	0	2
6–1	0	0	0	0	0	0	0	0	0	0	0	0
5–1	0	0	0	1	0	1	0	0	0	1	0	1
All X–1	6	0	6	10	0	10	5	0	5	21	0	21
X–1 or better	36	1	37	27	3	30	16	0	16	79	4	83
X–1 or better (%)	52.94	100.0	53.62	39.13	75.00	41.10	76.19	0.00	66.67	50.00	50.00	50.00
7–2	5	0	5	9	0	9	3	0	3	17	0	17
6–2	0	0	0	5	1	6	0	0	0	5	1	6
5–2	0	0	0	0	0	0	0	1	1	0	1	1
4–2	0	0	0	0	0	0	0	0	0	0	0	0
All X–2	5	0	5	14	1	15	3	1	4	22	2	24
X–2 or better	41	1	42	41	4	45	19	1	20	101	6	107
X–2 or better (%)	60.29	100.0	60.87	59.42	100.0	61.64	90.48	33.33	83.33	63.92	75.00	64.46
6–3	7	0	7	14	0	14	0	1	1	21	1	22
5–3	1	0	1	1	0	1	0	0	0	2	0	2
4–3	2	0	2	0	0	0	0	0	0	2	0	2
All X–3	10	0	10	15	0	15	0	1	1	25	1	26
X–3 or better	51	1	52	56	4	60	19	2	21	126	7	133
X–3 (%)	14.71	0.00	14.49	21.74	0.00	20.55	0.00	33.33	4.17	15.82	12.50	15.66
5–4	17	0	17	11	0	11	2	1	3	30	1	31
4–4	0	0	0	2	0	2	0	0	0	2	0	2
All X–4	17	0	17	13	0	13	2	1	3	32	1	33
X–4 (%)	25.00	0.00	24.64	18.84	0.00	17.81	9.52	33.33	12.50	20.25	12.50	19.88
5 dissents	0	0	0	0	0	0	0	0	0	0	0	0
6 dissents	0	0	0	0	0	0	0	0	0	0	0	0
Total cases	68	1	69	69	4	73	21	3	24	158	8	166
Percentage of all cases	40.96	.60	41.57	41.57	2.41	43.98	12.65	1.81	14.46	95.18	4.82	
Total dissents	114	0	114	135	2	137	19	9	28	268	11	279
Dissent/case	1.676	0.00	1.652	1.957	.5	1.877	.905	3.000	1.167	1.696	1.375	1.681
Percentage dissenting	18.97	0.00	18.72	22.24	6.06	21.41	10.16	36.00	13.21	19.21	16.67	19.10